Professional Java Tools for Extreme Programming
Ant, XDoclet, JUnit, Cactus, and Maven

Professional Java Tools for Extreme Programming
Ant, XDoclet, JUnit, Cactus, and Maven

Richard Hightower
Warner Onstine
Paul Visan
Damon Payne
Joseph D. Gradecki
Kate Rhodes
Robert Watkins
Erik Meade

WILEY

Wiley Publishing, Inc.

Professional Java Tools for Extreme Programming

Published by
Wiley Publishing, Inc.
10475 Crosspoint Boulevard
Indianapolis, IN 46256
www.wiley.com

Copyright © 2004 by Wiley Publishing, Inc., Indianapolis, Indiana

Published by Wiley Publishing, Inc., Indianapolis, Indiana

Published simultaneously in Canada

For general information on our other products and services or to obtain technical support, please contact our Customer Care Department within the U.S. at (800) 762-2974, outside the U.S. at (317) 572-3993 or fax (317) 572-4002.

Wiley also publishes its books in a variety of electronic formats. Some content that appears in print may not be available in electronic books.

Library of Congress Card Number:

ISBN: 0-7645-5617-7

Manufactured in the United States of America

10 9 8 7 6 5 4 3 2 1

Credits

Authors
Richard Hightower
Warner Onstine
Paul Visan
Damon Payne
Joseph D. Gradecki
Kate Rhodes
Robert Watkins
Erik Meade

Executive Editor
Robert Elliott

Book Producer
Ryan Publishing Group, Inc.

Copy Editors
Liz Welch
Linda Recktenwald

Compositor
Gina Rexrode

Vice President & Executive Group Publisher
Richard Swadley

Vice President & Executive Publisher
Robert Ipsen

Vice President and Publisher
Joseph B. Wikert

Executive Editorial Director
Mary Bednarek

Editorial Manager
Kathryn A. Malm

About the Authors

Richard Hightower

Richard Hightower is Chief Mentor/Consultant for ArcMind, a full-service software development company. Rick is a software engineer by training who specializes in software development tools and processes, and developing enterprise applications using J2EE, XML, UML, JDBC, SQL, and open source technologies. Formerly he was the Senior Software Engineer for Java Architecture at Intel's Enterprise Architecture Lab. Rick is the co-author of *Professional Jakarta Struts*, and he contributed two chapters to the book *Mastering Tomcat*.

Rick has spoken at a variety of industry conferences and events, including JavaOne, TheServerSide.com Software Symposium JDJEdge, WebServicesEdge, and the Complete Programmer Network software symposiums.

Warner Onstine

Warner Onstine is a founder and CTO of Interface Guru, a leading Web Usability firm where he consults on back-end technology issues with specific emphasis on how technology and usability work together to present the user with an easy-to-use interface. Warner also runs his own custom development shop, Sandcast Software, which focuses on community and team-oriented software.

Warner got his first computer, a TI-99 4/A, when he was 9 and almost immediately attempted to program a game in Basic on it, which did not work. He stubbornly refuses to get rid of that machine though, along with his trusty NeXT Turbo MonoStation, upon which he got his first taste of Objective-C. This eventually led to Java, skipping right over C++.

His strong community background soon led him to open source, where he has had the chance to meet and interact with several incredible individuals from Jakarta and other open source communities. This also has helped him to keep an open eye on the trends that will soon shape the new landscape—one of his specialties.

Another skill he has is in assisting companies with making the right choices at the right time, utilizing XP, in-depth knowledge of their subject area, and the currently available tools germane to their problem. Warner is also a co-founder and President of the Tucson Java Users Group, which he helped form in 2001, which keeps him rather busy at times. Previously, Warner worked at eBlox, Inc. (a Web development company), Intalio, Inc. (a bay-area Business Process Management Server company), and the University of Arizona Main Library on the Digital Library Team.

Paul Visan

Paul Visan is an expert J2EE developer. He serves as a Principal Software Engineer for eBlox, Inc, where he finds that open source tools are invaluable to his work. Paul is a proud Romanian native, now living in the heart of Tucson Arizona. He is a regular contributor to IBM's developerWorks, for which he has written a series of tutorials on Java Web Services. Paul would like to thank Andrew Barton, Nicholas Lesiecki, Tim Ryan, and Victoria McSherry for helping with this book.

Damon Payne

Damon Payne currently works as the Microsoft Business Group manager for Centare Group, Ltd. in Milwaukee, WI. Damon is very passionate about open source technology in the Java and Microsoft .NET worlds. His other professional interests include Mobile development, data persistence patterns, and product development. When not programming or speaking Damon enjoys raising his wonderful daughter, Brooke, home theater, and music.

Joseph D. Gradecki

Joseph D. Gradecki is a software engineer at Comprehensive Software Solutions, where he works on their SABIL product, a enterprise-level securities processing system. He has built numerous dynamic, enterprise applications using Java, AspectJ, servlets, JSPs, Resin, MySQL, BroadVision, XML, and more. He is the author of Mastering JXTA and the coauthor of MySQL and Java Developer's Guide (with Mark Matthews and Jim Cole). Joeholds Bachelors and Masters degrees in Computer Science and is currently pursuing a Ph.D.

Kate Rhodes

Kate Rhodes is a self-taught programmer, serial entrepreneur, and occasional musician with a Japanese nickname and an unstoppable urge to learn new things, solve new problems, and write open source apps. She's got too many pets, too many projects, and too little time. If she could afford an army of programming minions she'd have one.

She's ranked better than most and worse than some. She's worked in impressive places you've possibly heard of and unimpressive places you've never heard of. She's done some stuff she's very proud of and some she isn't. And so long as life keeps offering up interesting new challenges for her to learn from, she's happy. If you're overcome with curiosity you can always see what Kate and her wife are up to at www.masukomi.org.

Robert Watkins

Robert Watkins is a Brisbane, Australia-based software developer of nine years' experience. He's been called a programmer, a software engineer, an architect, and a few other things (many unprintable), but mostly ignores the titles and does what he has to do. These days he is mostly working in J2EE and related technologies, and is a passionate advocate of agile development techniques. When not working, he spends most of his time with his wife and twin children, and when he gets a chance, he takes time out to read Terry Pratchett novels. Robert is also one of the developers on the CruiseControl project.

Erik Meade

Erik Meade is an employee of Wells Fargo, who attended XPImmersionTwo, interviewed at XPImmersionThree, coached at XPImmersionFour, and hung out on the evenings of XPImmersionFive. He is the edior of junit.org and an evangelist of JUnit, Ant, CruiseControl, HttpUnit, Tomcat, and open source in general. He is also a contributor to JUnitPerf.

Contents

Contents

Part II: Automated Building and Continuous Integration

Chapter 4: Ant Primer 37

Chapter 5: Building Java Applications with Ant 67

Contents

Contents

Contents

Contents

Contents

Contents

Contents

Contents

Contents

Contents

Contents

Introduction

This book describes techniques for implementing the Extreme Programming practices of automated testing and continuous integration using open source tools.

Let's unpack that statement. Automated testing and continuous integration are two of the twelve core practices of the Extreme Programming (XP) software development methodology. Extreme Programming is a lightweight software development process that focuses on feedback, communication, simplicity, and courage. The full XP process is summarized in Chapter 1; suffice it to say for now that it consists of common-sense development practices practiced religiously and in concert.

Two of these common-sense practices are testing and frequent integration. Almost no software development shop would consider leaving these steps out of its process entirely—after all, a system has to be integrated to ship, and it must be tested to ensure that the customers accept the shipment. Thanks to the dot-com shakeout, most of the shops that did skip these practices are now out of business. Still, many software companies either struggle with implementing these processes, or acknowledge that they should be done but claim that "things are just too busy right now" to do them. This book explains and demonstrates the use of software tools to help put these valuable practices into place.

Why Spend So Much Time on the Tools?

We focus on tools, ironically enough, because XP is a human-centric development philosophy. It recognizes that the key challenges of writing software are human challenges—such as getting people to work together, helping programmers learn, and managing emotions. Its four core values (communication, feedback, simplicity, and courage) are human values. Most books published on XP so far have focused on the human issues: outlining the philosophy, spreading the ideology (*Extreme Programming Explained* was described by Kent Beck as a manifesto), and talking about the *feeling* of writing software. By doing so, Kent Beck and the originators of XP have followed their own philosophy: Solve the most pressing problems first. However, the current books do not cover the technical details of implementing some of their practices. That's where books like this one come in.

We will explain how to set up continuous integration and automated testing in a Java environment (specifically J2EE, although most of the tools apply generally). Technical detail will be addressed, and we will offer loads of examples to show the tools in action. Specifically, we will cover how to use Abbot, Ant, AntHill, Bugzilla, Cactus, CruiseControl, CVS, Eclipse, HttpUnit, Jemmy, jfcUnit, JMeter, JUnit, Maven, and other tools to write automated tests and achieve continuous integration.

Who Should Read this Book

Although this book speaks from an XP perspective, you need not practice XP to benefit from it. Anyone who needs help automating testing and integration can benefit from the tools and practices outlined herein. If you know nothing about Extreme Programming, you should probably read the rest of this Introduction, along with Chapter 1 to get a sense of the practices covered in this book, both alone and in their XP context. In particular the Introduction touches on the value of automated testing and continuous integration for all developers.

This book assumes you are at least a moderately experienced Java developer. Because it covers the application of testing and integration tools to the J2EE platform, this book also expects familiarity with J2EE technologies and development practices. Those who are not interested in J2EE applications will still find plenty of worthwhile material, because most of these tools can be applied to almost any Java (or, in the case of JMeter and HttpUnit, even non-Java) software project. Developers who aren't familiar with J2EE but who want to apply these tools and techniques to a J2EE application may also want to pick up a comprehensive J2EE book like *Expert One-on-One: J2EE Design and Development* by Rod Johnson.

Why Open Source?

It is hard to miss the growing prominence of open source development in software engineering. Open source development tools offer compelling advantages over traditional tools—especially for XP development. The advantages fall into two categories. First, open source tools are practical. Second, the open source philosophy is closely aligned with XP.

Open source tool offer several practical advantages:

>**The price is right.** Open source software can almost always be obtained for free; all the tools we cover in this book can be downloaded at no cost from the Internet. Free software means no immediate overhead for yourself or your company, which is always a benefit, but in this case not the major one. The major benefit in the case of these tools is that their adoption will not be hampered by corporate red tape or management worried about buying into the latest fad. Once you have downloaded JUnit, for example, and you've fallen in love with it and spread it to your team—speeding development and improving quality— no one will want to throw roadblocks in your way. Starting the adoption of XP by asking for $7,500 worth of whiz-bang deployment tools might invite skepticism.

>**The tools are high quality.** Programmers use open source development tools every day. Because improving the tool means improving their immediate situation, open source development tools often receive many contributions and bug fixes. Improvement and features come fast and furious.

>**The tools are the standard.** Especially in the case of JUnit and Ant, the tools covered in this book are the standards in their field. Countless open source projects use Ant, and JUnit (upon which several of the tools are based) was written by Kent Beck (the godfather of XP) and Erich Gamma (co-author of the OO classic *Design Patterns: Elements of Reusable Object-Oriented Software*).

Synergy Between XP and Open Source

Extreme Programming and open source development are closely aligned ideologically. Both foster an open, giving style of collaborative development—they share a certain *vibe*, if you will. Both philosophies acknowledge human weakness—no code is perfect, and the assistance of others in finding and fixing problems is gratefully acknowledged. All open source code is commonly owned (as XP would have it). Many open source projects use and benefit from automated testing, which is especially important when code from a wide variety of sources must be integrated. Both systems demand small, incremental releases. Of course, both philosophies also focus heavily on the code— open source is founded on the premise that reading code is enjoyable, educational, and helpful.

The list could continue for quite a while. By using open source tools (and by giving back to the open source community in the form of feedback, assistance, and code) you practice some of the values and processes that make XP great.

Read the Source

If you are looking for more information than this book provides on any of the tools, the best place to start is the source code. In addition to containing the Javadoc (another handy reference), the source code is the definitive authority on the tool's behavior. Open-source software exists because (in addition to liking free stuff) programmers value the ability to dig into the work of fellow coders. By reading the source carefully, you can gain insight into how the program works, insight into the domain, and, if you are lucky, insight into the arcane art of programming itself. If you are unlucky enough to encounter a bug while using the tool, having the source handy can help you determine where the bug lies.

Automated Testing: A Summary

XP regards testing as central to the activity of software development. To quote Dan Rawsthorne from the afterword of *Extreme Programming Installed*, "XP works because it is validation-centric rather than product-centric." Testing software continuously validates that the software works and that it meets the customer's requirements. Automating the tests ensures that testing will in fact be continuous. Without testing, a team is just guessing that its software meets those requirements. XP cannot be done without automated testing, nor can *development* be done successfully without it. All software projects need to satisfy the intended customer and to be free of defects.

Tests and Refactoring

Another core XP practice is refactoring (changing existing code for simplicity, clarity, and/or feature addition). Refactoring cannot be accomplished without tests. If you don't practice XP, you may not be refactoring religiously. Even the most stable or difficult-to-change projects require occasional modification. To do it right, programmers will have to change the existing design. That's where automated testing comes in.

Object-oriented programming (and, to a lesser extent, other programming styles) separates interface from implementation. In theory, this means you can change the underlying logic behind a class or method, and dependent code will handle the change seamlessly. Entire books have been written about this powerful abstraction. However, if in practice the programmers are scared to change the underlying logic for fear of disturbing code that interacts with the interface, then this separation might as well not exist. Comprehensive tests (run frequently) verify how the system should work and allow the underlying behavior to change freely. Any problems introduced during a change are caught by the tests. If Design A and Design B produce equivalent results when tested, the code can be migrated from one to the other freely. With testing in place, programmers refactor with confidence, the code works, and the tests prove it.

Types of Automated Tests

Unit tests are the most talked-about test in XP; however, they are only a part of the testing picture. Unit tests cooperate with integration tests, functional tests, and auxiliary tests (performance tests, regression tests, and so on) to ensure that the system works totally.

Unit Tests: JUnit

Unit tests are the first (and perhaps the most critical) line of tests in the XP repertoire. Writing a unit test involves taking a unit of code and testing everything that could possibly break. A unit test usually exercises all the methods in the public interface of a class. Good unit tests do not necessarily test every possible permutation of class behavior, nor do they test ultra-simple methods (simple accessors come to mind); rather, they provide a common-sense verification that the code unit behaves as expected. With this verification, the public interface gains meaning. This approach makes changing unit behavior easier, and also provides a convenient (and verifiable) guide to the behavior of the unit. Developers can consult a test to discover the intended use of a class or method.

In XP, unit tests become part of the cycle of everyday coding. Ideally, programmers write tests *before* the code, and use the test as a guide to assist in implementation. The authors both work in this mode, and we find ourselves unable to live without the guidance and corrective influence of unit tests. After a unit is complete, the team adds the test to the project's test suite. This suite of unit tests runs multiple times per day, and all the tests always pass. This sounds extreme; however, a 100 percent pass rate on unit tests is far more sane than the alternative: a piece of vital production code that *does not work*. (If the code isn't vital, why is it in the project?)

Verifying each class builds a higher-quality system because it ensures that the building blocks work. Unit tests also lead the way toward clean architecture. If a developer writes a test three times for the same code in different locations, laziness and irritation will compel her to move the code to a separate location.

JUnit is a lightweight testing framework written by Erich Gamma and Kent Beck (one of the chief proponents of XP). The authors based its design on SUnit, a successful and popular unit-testing framework written by Beck for Smalltalk. The simplicity of the framework lends itself to rapid adoption and extension. All the testing tools covered in this book (with the exception of JMeter, a GUI tool) interact with or extend the JUnit frame.

Integration/In-Container Tests: Cactus

Unit testing covers Object X, but what about related Objects Y and Z, which together make up subsystem A? Unit tests are deliberately supposed to be isolated. A good unit test verifies that no matter what chaos reigns in the system, at least *this* class functions as expected. Several papers have been written (many can be found at http://www.junit.org) about strategies to avoid dependencies in unit tests (the core idea is to provide mock implementations of objects upon which the tested class depends). By all means, the unit tests should be made as independent as possible.

In their book *Extreme Programming Installed*, Jeffries et al. have an interesting observation about errors that show up only in collaborations between classes; they say, "Our own experience is that we get very few of these errors. We're guessing here, that somehow our focus on testing up front is preventing them." They go on to admit, "When they do show up, such problems are difficult to find." Good unit testing should indeed catch most errors, and the behavior of the *entire* system falls under the category of *acceptance testing* (also known as *functional testing*); however, a good test suite should verify subsystem behavior as well. *Integration testing* occupies the gray area between unit and acceptance testing, providing sanity-check testing that all the code cooperates and that subtle differences between expectation and reality are precisely localized. Integration tests may not always run at 100 percent (a dependency class may not be completed yet, for instance); however, their numbers should be quite high (in the 80 to 90 percent range).

An important variety of integration tests is the *in-container test*. The J2EE development model dictates *components* residing in a *container*. Components rely on *services* provided by the container. Interaction with those services needs to be verified. Although some interactions can be successfully mocked-up, creating mocked implementations for all the services provided by a J2EE container would consume time and verify behavior imperfectly. Some services, such as behaviors specified by deployment descriptors, could be very difficult to test, because container implementations differ.

The Cactus framework provides access to J2EE Web containers (which in turn usually provide access to other types of containers, such as EJB containers). By allowing tests to exercise code in the container, Cactus spares developers the chore of providing extensive or difficult mock-ups (they can use the real services, instead). This approach also provides an extra measure of feedback, because the code runs in an environment that is one step closer to its production habitat. In the case of single objects that just interact with container services, in-container tests serve as quick-and-dirty unit tests.

Acceptance/Functional Tests: HttpUnit

Functional testing ensures that the whole system behaves as expected. These tests are also called *acceptance tests* because they verify for the customer that the system is complete. (In other words, a Web site is not done until it can log in users, display products, and allow on-line ordering.) Functional tests are daunting in some ways (they are not an immediate productivity aid like unit tests), but they are crucial to measuring progress and catching any defects that slipped past the other tests or result from unimplemented/incomplete features. Acceptance tests are written by the customer (the programmers may implement them) because they are for the customer. Unit testing verifies for the programming team that the Foo class works correctly. Acceptance tests verify for the customer (who may not know a Foo from a Bar) that their whole system works correctly.

Acceptance tests are less dependent upon specific implementation: For example, during an aggressive refactoring, the team may decide they no longer need a SubCategory object. If so, the

SubCategoryTest goes to execute in the Big Container in the Sky. The team modifies the integration tests (if necessary) to account for the new system structure. However, the functional tests remain unchanged, validating that the user's experience of the catalog navigation system remains unchanged.

Functional tests do not need to *always* run at 100 percent, but they should do so before the software is released. Functional tests often verify specific *stories* (an XP representation of a customer-requested feature). As such, they can track progress through a development cycle. Each test that runs represents a finished feature.

Unfortunately but understandably, no one has written a universal acceptance-testing tool. JUnit can work on just about any Java class, but an acceptance-testing tool must be tailored to the needs of a specific application. For a number-crunching program, acceptance testing could be as easy as verifying inputs versus outputs. For a data-entry application, a GUI recording and playback tool might be necessary.

We chose to cover HttpUnit, a testing API that allows programmatic calls to Web resources and inspection of the responses. The framework cooperates with JUnit and exposes the underlying structure of an HTML page to allow easy verification of structural elements. (The response to show_product.jsp returns a table with product prices.) It seemed a natural fit for the focus of this book, because J2EE is heavily concerned with Web components. Acceptance testing the deeper components of J2EE might not even require a special framework because of the low level of presentation logic involved.

Performance Tests: JUnitPerf and JMeter

Several types of testing exist besides basic verification of function parallel tests (verifies that a new system exactly like an old system), performance tests, validation tests (the system responds well to invalid input), and so on. Of these, performance testing is perhaps the most widely applicable. After all, the most functional system in the world won't be worth a dime if end users give up on the software in disgust. Client-side applications that perform poorly are trouble; server-side applications that drag are emergencies. J2EE applications are usually hosted on servers handling anywhere from hundreds to thousands (and up!) of transactions per minute, so a small section of inefficient code can bring a system to its knees. In this sort of environment, performance ranks with functional (or even unit) testing in its priority.

We will not be covering performance profiling tools (critical to solving performance issues); rather, we'll discuss the testing tools used to uncover these problems early. JUnitPerf does unit performance testing—it *decorates* existing JUnit tests so that fail if their running times exceed expectations. Such tests support refactoring by verifying that performance-critical code remains within expected boundaries. JMeter provides functional performance testing—measuring and graphing response times to requests sent to a remote server (Web, EJB, database, and so on). With JMeter, customers can write acceptance tests like, "The Web server will maintain a three second or better response time to requests with a 150 user simultaneous load."

Continuous Integration: A Summary

Continuous integration is another XP practice that benefits from the use of good software tools. In essence, continuous integration means building a complete copy of the system so far (and running its full test suite) several times per day. By doing this, you can be sure the system is ready to walk out the door (at least as ready as it could possibly be) at any moment. This process must be relatively automatic (a single command, perhaps on a timer, builds and tests the whole system), or no one would ever do it. There are several reasons for spending the set-up time and energy to achieve continuous integration: The customer and team can see progress on the system, integration bugs are reduced, and the tests are run frequently.

Visible Progress

Continuous integration includes something subtle that goes beyond its practical benefits. It affirms the unity of the team development effort. The built and tested system acts as a center of gravity toward which all development is pulled. As a developer, you know that as soon as you check code into the repository, it will be pulled into the main development stream. You're less likely storm off in your own direction if you know that later that day your code will be playing with the entire system. Anyone can see the state of the working system at any time; and as more acceptance tests pass and new features show up in the built system, coders sense the progress towards the goal and gain confidence in its eventual attainment. (If the built system languishes and acceptance test scores don't rise, this signals serious trouble that might have lain dormant far longer in an un-integrated system.)

Reduced Integration Pain

If class X doesn't jibe with class Y, it makes sense to know about the problem as soon as possible. The longer the X and Y go before meeting, the fuzzier the authors' memories will be on the subject when the time comes to discover the show-stopping X vs. Y bug. Continuous integration makes sure the incompatible dance partners meet within hours or minutes. Not only does it solve the immediate problem (the defect introduced by incompatible changes), but it forces the developers concerned to examine why the defect might have occurred in the first place: "Ah, I see, Sandra already refactored the CapriciousDictator class, so there's no reason for me to have added the extraEnforcement method to OppressiveRegime." A cleaner (and working!) system results.

Restart!

The first big software project I worked on was a mess...but it had continuous integration. Why? The team, who were a bunch of inexperienced Java developers, couldn't get a reliable build running on anyone's machine. Too many dependencies and libraries had to be linked in for anyone to get them straightened out with the mounting pressure of an impossible deadline. Finally, we had someone cobble together a shell-based build script that compiled all the code that currently resided on the integration server. Because no one could compile individual files locally, in order to see something work, it had to be uploaded to the integration server.

With five or six developers working simultaneously, the script was run (and the Web server restarted) about once every five minutes. The developer hoping to integrate had to shout for permission before actually restarting the server: "Anybody mind a restart?!" The result was chaos—but if anyone's changes clashed, we knew about it within seconds.

Tests Run Frequently

Unit testing is an integral part of a continuously integrated system. The build is not complete until the unit tests have all passed at 100 percent and the functional and integration tests have run. The result is not only a system that runs but also one that is proven to run correctly. Tests lose value if they aren't run frequently. If they are run as often as the build, and the build is frequent, they provide a constant update on how the system performs.

Continuous Integration and J2EE

Under the J2EE development model, applications undergo significant customization during assembly and deployment. Wrapping and packaging a full J2EE application requires in-depth knowledge of different archive formats (JARs, WARs, and EARs), deployment descriptors, and methods of deploying applications and components into existing containers. Given the complexity of a J2EE build, an automated build tool is required.

Unlike many of the other practices of XP, achieving continuous integration is mainly a technical feat. Once an automated process is in place, using it should be easy (and beneficial) enough that developers barely have to breathe on it to keep the monster rolling. All a shop needs to begin continuous integration is a tool set to help automate and put together a repeatable build. This book will cover Ant, the emerging standard for build automation in Java.

Ant allows developers to write tests in an XML build script that calls on Java classes to do its work. The tool is cross-platform (a critical criteria for any Java-based tool) and easy to extend and modify. Ant performs all the basic tasks of a build tool: compilation, archive creation, classpath management, and so on. It also supports test and report automation as well as a variety of miscellaneous useful tasks, such as source control interaction, FTP, and property file editing. This arsenal of predefined build tasks allows developers to automate complicated build processes with ease. After some work with Ant, a Java application can be retrieved from source control, built, customized to its intended environment (production versus integration for instance), tested, and deployed to a remote server with a single command.

Ant is still the industry-standard tool for continuous integration, but several other tools are now available which offer an alternative approach to continuous integration. First among these tools is Maven. Maven offers a well-defined project layout, built-in unit testing through Maven's JUnit plug-in, built-in code visualization and reporting that includes a number of ready-to-run reports to help your team focus on the project, and integration with other agile technologies: Maven includes plug-ins for code coverage, CVS check-in, code formatting, code style violations, and bug tracking.

Another interesting continuous integration tool is CruiseControl. Like Ant, CruiseControl was designed to be extended. All of the components it uses are built around a plug-in architecture (inspired by a similar mechanism in Ant), and writing your own plug-in to support your own environment is easy. CruiseControl supports a number of types of version control repositories are supported, including CVS (which is also covered in this book). Although CruiseControl was built to use Ant build scripts, it also comes with support for Maven.

We also cover AntHill in this book; it is available in both open source and commercial versions (we only discuss the open source version in this book). AntHill offers a controlled build process, the ability to track and reproduce builds, the ability to signal a build status (through e-mail, CM labels, etc.), and a fully automated build process that can run tests and generate metrics.

How This Book Is Organized

This book is divided into eight parts:

Part I: Key Concepts: This part begins with an overview of the Extreme Programming methodology—a short course for beginners and a review for practitioners. The overview allows you to see where the practices covered in this book (automated testing and continuous integration) fit into the larger picture of XP. Chapter 2 explains the J2EE build and deployment model, highlighting the need for an automated build tool to assist in the process.

Part II: Automated Building and Continuous Integration: In this part we discuss tow powerful tools that will be used throughout many chapters of the book: Ant and XDoclet. Chapters 4 through 6 cover the core function of Ant needed to achieve continuous integration with Ant, and Chapter 7 covers the core functions of XDoclet. The remainder of this part show you how to modify these two tools and use them together to build a variety of applications, including EJBs and Struts. Part IV of this book discusses alternative solutions to Ant.

Part III: Automated Java Testing: In this part we focus on JUnit, JUnitPerf, and Bugzilla—tools that enable us to automate testing. Our focus here is on Java applications; chapters later in the book discuss automated testing for J2EE applications.

Part IV: Automated J2EE Testing: One of the largest parts of the book, it focuses on tools that enable us to automate a variety of tests for J2EE applications. We use Cactus for in-container testing of servlets and EJBs, Cactus and JspTestCases in tandem to test custom tags, JMeter to run performance testing, HttpUnit for functional testing, and code coverage with jcoverage.

Part V: Automated Swing Testing: In our experience, many developers fail to adequately test their Swing components. Often it seems that developers simply aren't aware of that there are tools available to help. We attempt to remedy that problem in this part of the book by addressing three tools that take very different approaches to the task: Jemmy, jfcUnit, and Abbot.

Part VI: Continuous Integration, Project Management, and IDEs: This part of the book discusses tools that build on, or entirely replace, Ant. First among these tools is Maven. We also discuss CruiseControl and AntHill. Each of these tools offers a unique approach to combining continuous integration, project management, and support for IDEs.

Part VII: API and Tag Reference: Here we supply additional resources that developers need to make full use of some of the tools covered in this book: Ant, Cactus, HttpUnit, JUnit, and JUnitPerf. We cover these tools in standard Javadoc style and include extensive code samples illustrating their use in context.

Part VIII: Appendix: Appendix A of the book provides a detailed discussion of the sample applications and the case studies that we build, test, and refactor multiple times during the course of the book. Full code listings for these applications are included here.

What's on the Web Site

All the configuration scripts, build scripts, applications, and other source code in this book are available online at www.wrox.com. Posted along with the sample code and installation instructions are errata (especially necessary for fast-moving open source APIs) and other follow-up information. Information about other books in this series is available at www.wrox.com.

1

Introduction to Extreme Programming

This chapter is a brief overview of the Extreme Programming (XP) methodology as it applies to developing enterprise-level software in Java. The tools described elsewhere in this book will help you realize many of the goals of XP, but you do not have to adopt the entire XP methodology to get value out of this book and chapter. Automated testing, for example, can help you refactor code regardless of whether you are doing pair programming. Continuous integration can help you detect and fix problems early in the lifecycle of the system regardless of whether your customer is on site. However, because this book discusses XP throughout, it is useful to have a short overview of the entire methodology. If you are already familiar with XP, you may want to turn directly to Chapter 2, "J2EE Deployment Concepts."

XP Overview

XP is a lightweight methodology that focuses on coding as the main task. With XP, the code-centric activities are in every stage of the software development lifecycle. Some practitioners of more traditional methodologies (most seem to be CASE tool vendors) have criticized XP, claiming that it involves reckless coding and is not a real process.

On the contrary, XP is an extremely disciplined methodology that centers on constant code review; frequent testing; customer involvement and rapid feedback; incessant refactoring and refining the architecture; continuous integration to discover problems early in the development process; ongoing design and redesign; and constant planning. The following sections of this chapter discuss the core values, principles, and practices of XP.

Four Values of XP

Kent Beck, originator of the XP methodology, defined four key values of XP:

❑ Communication

❑ Simplicity

❑ Feedback

❑ Courage

Communication is facilitated through pair programming, task estimation, iteration planning, and more. The goal of communication is to provide a place where people can freely discuss the project without fear of reprisal.

Simplicity may seem counterintuitive because it is common in our industry to overly complicate our development projects. The aim of a project is not for the alpha developer to show his technical prowess, but to deliver value to the customer. Don't over-design algorithms. Don't create an artificial intelligence system when all you need is a few if statements. Don't use EJB or XSLT just because doing so will look nice on your résumé. Choose the simplest design, technology, algorithms, and techniques that will satisfy the customer's needs for the current iteration of the project.

Feedback is crucial and is obtained through code testing, customers' stories, small iterations/frequent deliveries, pair programming/constant code reviews, and other methods. For example, if you are unit-level testing all the code you write several times a day, you are constantly getting feedback about the quality and production worthiness of the system. If something is wrong, you will know right away, instead of being unpleasantly surprised the night before product launch.

Courage is all about being brave enough to do what is right. Have you ever worked on a project where people were afraid to throw away code? I have. The code was horrible and convoluted, and it systematically broke every style, rule, and convention. Yet management and quite a few developers were afraid to throw away the code because they weren't sure how discarding it would affect the system. If you follow the tenets of XP, you will not have this problem. Unit regression testing builds an intense sense of courage. When you know the changes you make will not break the system in some unforeseen way, then you have the confidence to refactor and re-architect code. Testing is key to courage.

If, after several iteration of a project, you find a cleaner, less expensive, more performant way of developing a system, you will have the courage to implement it. I have, and it is a blast.

If the Code Smells, Refactor It

In his landmark book *Refactoring: Improving the Design of Existing Code*, Martin Fowler describes code that needs to be refactored as having a certain objectionable smell.

We have to have the courage to throw away code. Coding, like writing, gets better with revisions.

Five Principles of XP

Building on the four values of XP, Beck created five overriding principles for XP development:

- ❑ Provide rapid feedback
- ❑ Assume simplicity
- ❑ Make incremental changes
- ❑ Embrace change
- ❑ Do quality work

The idea behind rapid feedback is that the faster you get feedback, the more quickly you can respond to it and the more it guides the process of designing, coding, and delivering the system. This feedback does not simply focus on automated testing and continuous integration to spot problems early, but also encompasses short iterations that are given to the customer to ensure that the system they need is ultimately delivered. This constant steering and learning helps keep the cost of change low and enables the developer to assume simplicity.

Assuming simplicity means treating every problem as a simple problem until proven otherwise. This approach works well, because most problems are easy to solve. However, it is counterintuitive to common thought on reuse and software design. Assuming simplicity does not mean skipping the design step, nor does it mean simply slinging code at a problem. Assuming simplicity requires that you design *only* for the current iteration. Because you are getting rapid feedback from the customer as requirements change, you will not waste time redoing code that was designed to be thermonuclear-resistant when all that was needed was a little waterproofing. The fact is, the customer's requirements always change during the development process, so why not embrace the alterations? My feeling has always been that the true test of every design is when the rubber meets the road—that is, when you are coding.

Incremental change fits nicely with simplicity. Don't over-design a system. It is always better to do a little at a time. Let's say you have decided to redo a Web application that currently uses XSLT (a technology for transforming XML data) so that it instead uses JavaServer Pages (JSP; a technology that is commonly used to create dynamically generate Web pages), to improve performance of the system.

Instead of attacking the whole system, why not just incrementally change the pages that get the most traffic first, thus getting the biggest bang for the buck while minimizing risk? As more and more of the system is done, you may decide to leave some parts using XSLT; or, after partially finishing the JSP version, you may decide to do something else. By testing and deploying on a small scale, you can make decisions based on live feedback that you otherwise could not make. This is the rubber hitting the road. (By the way, I am making no design judgments on XSL or JSP. This is just an example for illustration.)

It has been said that a picture is worth a thousand words. Well, a working model deployed to production is worth a thousand pictures. This is the synergy among rapid feedback, incremental change, and keeping it simple. XP goes further than incrementally changing the system. XP relishes change; it embraces change.

Have you ever heard a developer or a project manager declare that once the requirements were set, the customer should not change them? I have. This requirement seemed logical, but wait—isn't the system being built for the customer?

Conversely, XP developers relish and embrace change. Change is expected, because you are delivering business value incrementally to the customer. The customer has plenty of time to give rapid feedback and request needed changes. This process improves the quality of the system by ensuring that the system being built is the one the customer really needs. Customer are happy because they can steer the next revision before the project gets too far off track from their current business needs.

One of the things that drove me to XP was the principle of quality work. I feel better about myself when I deliver quality work. Early in my career, my team was required to certify that every line of code was tested: 100 percent "go code" and 85 percent exception-handling code. At first I was shocked.

I soon realized that certifying the testing of every line of code caused us to write some extremely clean code. No one had the same three lines of code in three different places, because if they did, they would have to certify nine lines of code instead of three. This discipline led to less code to maintain and made it easier to make changes because we made the change in only one place.

From that point on, I loved testing. I liked knowing that the code I wrote worked and that I had a test to prove it. This attitude is extremely important, because we are constantly bombarded with new technology and things to learn. As I said, quality work drove me to XP. Previously I wrote my own tests using JPython, a scripting language for the JVM, which I still use for prototyping. Then, I heard about JUnit, and from JUnit I learned about XP.

Of course, the quality work principle applies to more than making you happy. You would much rather write quality code and deliver a quality solution to the customer than write sloppy code and deliver a shoddy solution that does not meet the customer's need. Customers would much rather receive quality code than something that just does not work. It has been said that customers will sometimes forget that software was delivered late, but they will never forget poor quality.

When I was initially learning about XP, it seemed to be about 90 percent common sense, 8 percent "Aha!", and 2 percent revolution. So far, we have been covering the common sense and "Aha!" The next section covers these as well as the revolution.

Twelve Practices of XP

In his landmark book on XP, Beck iterated four basic practices: coding, testing, listening, and designing. These practices are expressed further in 12 major areas of practice, as follows:

- ❑ Planning game
- ❑ Small releases
- ❑ Simple design
- ❑ Testing
- ❑ Continuous integration
- ❑ Refactoring
- ❑ Pair programming
- ❑ Collective ownership

❑   40-hour week

❑   On-site customer

❑   Metaphor

❑   Coding standard

Planning Game

The purpose of the planning game is to determine the scope of the current iteration. This step is centered on determining the tasks that are most important to the customer and accomplishing these tasks first. The planning game encompasses the customer's determining the scope of the project, priority of features, composition of the various releases, and delivery dates. The developers assist the customer with technical feedback by estimating task duration, considering consequences and risks, organizing the team, and performing technical risk management by working on the riskiest parts of the project first. The developers and the customers act as a team.

Time is recorded against stories to further refine your estimates of future stories, making project estimation more accurate as time goes on. Customer stories are recorded on index cards. These stories explain the features of the system. The developers work with the customer to decided which stories will be implemented for that iteration.

Small Releases

The philosophy behind the small releases practice is to provide the most business value with the least amount of coding effort. The features have to be somewhat atomic. A feature must implement enough functionality for it to have business value. This step may be counterintuitive, but the idea is to get the project into production as soon as possible. Small releases get feedback from the customer and reduce risk by making sure the software is what the customer wants. In essence, this step uses the Paredo rule: 80 percent of the business value can be completed with 20 percent of the effort. Small releases go hand in hand with the planning game to decide what features will give the biggest bang for the buck, and they also work with the practice of keeping designs simple.

Simple Design

The idea behind simple design is keep the code simple. The simplest design possible does not try to solve future problems by guessing future needs. The simplest design passes the customer's acceptance test for that release of the software.

The simplest design passes all the tests, has no duplicate logic code, and is not convoluted but expresses every developer's purpose. This step goes hand in hand with small releases. If your architecture is not expressed well and is built to anticipate future needs, you will not be able to deliver it as quickly. We are developers, not fortunetellers. We don't have a crystal ball, so the best way to anticipate customers' future needs is to give them a working system and get feedback from them. Most customers don't know exactly what they need until you deliver something tangible that they can react to. Remember, a picture is worth a thousand words, and a working model is worth a thousand pictures.

Testing

The practice of testing is key to XP. How will you know if a feature works if you do not test? How will you know if a feature still works after you refactor, unless you retest? If you admit that you don't know everything, and that the code will change and evolve, then you'll realize the need for a way to test the code when you change it.

The tests should be automated so you can have the confidence and courage to change the code and refactor it without breaking the system! This approach is the opposite of waterfall development.

Code is in a liquid state, so it can be re-architected, refactored, or thrown out and completely redone. Later, the tests can show that the system still works. Testing keeps the code fluid. Because tests typically check the public interface of classes and components, the implementation of the system can change drastically while the automated tests validate that the system still fulfills the contract of the interfaces. A feature does not exist unless a test validates that it functions. Everything that can potentially break must have a test. JUnit and friends will help you automate your testing.

Continuous Integration

Continuous integration is a crucial concept. Why wait until the end of a project to see if all the pieces of the system will work? Every few hours (at least once every day) the system should be fully built and tested, including all the latest changes. By doing this often, you will know what changes broke the system, and you can make adjustments accordingly instead of waiting until modifications pile up and you forget the details of the changes.

In order to facilitate continuous integration, you need to automate the build, distribution, and deploy processes. Doing so can be quite complicated in a J2EE environment. Ant can help you integrate with source control, Java compilation, creating deployment files, and automating testing. It can even send emails to the group letting them know what files broke the build or what tests did not pass.

Using Ant to perform continuous integration changes the whole development blueprint of your project. With a little discipline and setup time, continuous integration reduces problems linked with team development—particularly time spent fixing integration bugs. Integration bugs are the most difficult to uncover because often they lie unexposed until the system is integrated and two subsystems intermingle for the first time. Suddenly the system breaks in peculiar, unpredictable ways. The longer integration bugs survive, the harder they are to exterminate. Using Ant and JUnit to implement continuous integration often makes such a bug apparent within hours after it has been introduced into the system. Furthermore, the code responsible for this bug is fresh in the mind of the developer; thus, it is easier to eradicate. As Fowler and Foemmel state, continuous integration can "slash the amount of time spent in integration hell" (see their article at www.martinfowler.com/articles/continuousIntegration.html).

Ant can be used to automate the following tasks:

❑   Obtaining the source from configuration management system (CVS, Perforce, VSS, or StarTeam, and so on)

❑   Compiling the Java code

❑   Creating binary deployment files (JAR, WARs, ZIP)

❑   Automating testing (when used in conjunction with tools like JUnit)

Developers often talk about automated building and testing but seldom implement them. Ant makes automated building and testing possible and plausible. Ant and JUnit combine well to allow teams to build and test their software several times a day. Such an automated process is worth the investment of time and effort. Automated builds and tests need the following, as stated by Fowler and Foemmel:

- ❏ A single place for all the source code where developers can get the most current sources—typically, a configuration management system

- ❏ A single command to build the system from all the sources (in our case, an Ant buildfile)

- ❏ A single command to run an entire suite of tests for the system (in our case, an Ant buildfile that integrates with JUnit)

- ❏ A good set of binaries that ensures developers have the latest working components (such as JAR files that contain classes)

Refactoring

The act of refactoring enables developers to add features while keeping the code simple, thus keeping the code simple while still being able to run all the tests. The idea is to not duplicate code nor write ugly, smelly code. The act of refactoring centers on testing to validate that the code still functions. Testing and refactoring go hand in hand. Automated unit-level tests will give you the courage to refactor and keep the code simple and expressive.

Refactoring is not limited to when you need to add a feature—refactoring is different than adding a feature. However, the catalyst for refactoring is often the need to add features while keeping the code simple. XP says not to guess what future features your customer wants. You cannot design in a vacuum. As you receive feedback, you will need to add features that will cause you to bend the code in new directions. Many software project management books say that once a project matures, adding two new features will cause one existing feature to break. The books make this statement as if such an occurrence is normal and acceptable. However, this is not the nature of software development; this is the nature of using a methodology and development environment in which adding new features and refactoring are not coupled with testing. Testing makes refactoring possible.

You will know when you need to refactor, because you will hear a little voice in the back of your head nagging you: Don't take a shortcut, make it simple, make it expressive. If the code stinks, you will fix it. If you don't hear that little voice or you aren't listening, then your pair-programming partner is there to guide you in the right direction.

Pair Programming

Pair programming is probably the most revolutionary practice of XP—and it is usually the one managers have the hardest time swallowing. On the surface, their reaction is easy to understand: If our projects are behind, then how will having two programmers work on the same task help speed things up? Why have two developers with one keyboard and one monitor?

If you think it is expensive to have two developers work together, how expensive will it be when you have to replace the whole system because it is impossible to maintain and every change causes massive ripple effects? You have undoubtedly seen it happen, and it is not a pretty picture.

I know from experience that pair programming works. For one thing, it improves communication among team members. A large part of what we do depends on the work of other developers. The developer you team with one day is not necessarily the developer you will team with the next day. In fact, the developer you team with in the morning may not be the developer you will team with in the afternoon. This process breeds better communication and cross-pollination of ideas. How often does your team reinvent a piece of code that another developer worked on?

Also, if one person knows much about a particular technical subject matter (such as EJB or Oracle) or business domain (such as accounting, semiconductor equipment, or aerospace), what better way for other developers to learn than to pair-program with that person?

What about quality? Pair programming provides constant feedback and ensures that the person who is coding is refactoring, testing, and following the coding standard. As Solomon stated, "By iron, iron itself is sharpened. So one man sharpens the face of another."

And, while one developer is focusing on the coding, the other developer can be thinking about the bigger picture: how this code will fit in with the other system. Typically, the developer who is not coding at the time is taking notes so that nothing falls through the cracks.

A few careless programmers can ruin a project team. Just like one rotten apple can spoil the whole bunch, sloppy code breeds more sloppy code. Pretty soon the team is addicted to the quick fix. In addition, because more and more of the code reeks, no one wants to own it. Pair programming is in lockstep with the practice of collective ownership.

Collective Ownership

The XP practice of collective ownership states that anyone can make a change to the system. You don't have to wait. No one owns a class. Everyone contributes, and if you need to make a change or refactor something to get it to work with a new feature, you can. Besides, you have the tests to make sure your changes did not break the system, and the old version is still in source control if anyone needs to refer to it, which is rare.

In addition, because many classes have corresponding automated test code, anyone can see how the code and API of classes were suppose to work. So, collective programming goes hand in hand with automated testing. Testing is part of what makes collective ownership possible.

Some developers will know some sections better than other developers, but all take ownership and responsibility for a system. If no one knows a particular part, the unit tests exercise the API and check that you did not break the system with your changes. Thus, you do not have to wait for another team member (let's call him Jon) to fix something. If Jon is busy helping Doug, you will fix the system with Nick, your pair-programming partner. If Jon is sick, the knowledge of a particular subsystem is not lost. Because Jon was pair programming with Andy, Andy knows about the system—and, in fact, so does Paul.

In addition, if you did not practice collective ownership and you had some critical parts of the system, then everyone would need to wait until you were done. Or, you would have to work a very long week to accomplish the task so you wouldn't hold up Paul, Doug, Andy, and Nick. Your family would like you to spend more time with them, and you want to work a 40-hour week.

40-Hour Week

The 40-hour week practice states that if you cannot do your work in a 40-hour week, then something is wrong with the project. Let's face it, burned-out developers make lots of mistakes. No one is saying that you should never put in a 90-, 80-, 70-, or 60-hour week, but such a schedule should not be the norm. An unstated reality to this practice is to make your time count by working hard and getting the most out of your time. Long meetings should be rare, as should unnecessary red tape. Any activity that gets in the way of providing the most business value into the next release of your current projects should be avoided like the plague. Make the most of your time, and 40-hour weeks will be enough most of the time. In addition, keeping normal office hours will give you more opportunity to talk about features with your 9-to-5 customers.

On-Site Customer

The on-site customer practice states that if at all possible, the customer should be available when the developers need to ask questions. And, if at all possible, the customer should be physically located with the developers.

The customer must be available to clarify feature stories. The customer is also involved in the planning game, and this process is easier if the customer is not remote. The developers work with the customer to decided which stories are implemented for that iteration. The customer also helps write and refine the stories—which typically involves ad hoc and planned discussions with the developers. The stories, which are recorded on index cards, are written in a simple dialect that both the developers and customer understand, using a common metaphor.

Metaphor

A *metaphor* is a common language and set of terms used to envision the functionality of a project. These terms can equate to objects in the physical world, such as accounts or objects. Other times, metaphors can be more abstract, like windows or cells. The idea is for the customer and developers to have the same vision of the system and be able to speak about the system in a common dialect.

Coding Standard

XPers should follow the practice of using a coding standard. You must be able to understand one another's code. Luckily for us Java developers, we have the coding standard set by Sun; you should be able to make some light adjustments and make this coding standard your coding standard.

Your coding standard should state the proper use of threads, language constructs, exception use, no duplicate code logic, and so on. The coding standard should be more than just a guide on where to put your curly brace; it should denote style and common practices and conventions that your team will follow. Java developers have tons of reference material for coding style and standards. Like many things, developers will follow the standard if they voluntarily create it and buy into it.

Adopting XP?

As we've stated before, you do not have to adopt XP to get value out of this book. For example, automated testing can help you refactor code regardless of whether you are doing pair programming.

Here's another example: If you use Unified Modeling Language (UML) use cases with a case tool instead of stories written on index cards, continuous integration and small release cycles will still be beneficial for getting rapid feedback. The point is, you may decide to do things in addition to the process. Or, your corporate culture may have an adverse reaction to things like pair programming.

> **UML and CASE tools**
>
> Some XP advocates swear by never using CASE tools. They say that the only UML should be written with a pencil on an index card. I don't agree. As long as the CASE tool can continually keep the model in sync with the code, then the tool can be very beneficial. In addition, some CASE tools can speed development by generating the necessary boilerplate code for design patterns.
>
> Beck notes that whether you draw diagrams that generate code or write out code, it is still code.

One of the first areas to focus on when adopting XP is automated testing. Begin by writing tests for code that you are about to add functionality to, refactor, or fix. The key is to add automated tests slowly to code written before you adopted XP, and always employ automated testing with newly developed code. Do not write tests for code you are not working on. Later, when you begin doing integration tests, you will want to automate the build, test, and integration cycle.

My company has adopted XP. We adhere to the 12 XP practices. However, I am not a purist. I believe that other software processes can benefit from automated testing, simple designs, continuous integration, incremental releases, and constant refactoring.

Beck states that XP's 12 practices will not fit every project. XP also will not fit every organization's culture. Regardless, J2EE development can benefit from automated testing, simple designs, continuous integration, incremental releases, and constant refactoring. This book focuses on tools to perform automated testing and continuous integration for J2EE to enable refactoring and incremental releases.

Summary

XP is a lightweight methodology that focuses on coding as the main task. XP is based on four values: communication, simplicity, feedback, and courage. Communication is facilitated through pair programming, task estimation, iteration planning, and more. Simplicity means avoiding making things overly complicated and insisting that the basics be addressed first and foremost. Feedback is given by way of testing, customer stories, small iterations/frequent deliveries, pair programming/constant code reviews, and so on. Courage means the courage to do what is right whether you have to refactor a working system, throw code away, cancel a project, or insist on quality.

XP is based on five principles: rapid feedback, assuming simplicity, making incremental changes, embracing change, and doing quality work. In his landmark book on XP, Beck iterated four basic practices: coding, testing, listening, and designing. These practices are expressed further in 12 major areas of practice: the planning game, small releases, simple design, (automated) testing, continuous integration, refactoring, pair programming, collective ownership, a 40-hour week, an on-site customer, metaphor, and adherence to a coding standard. This book focus on two practices of XP: automated testing and continuous integration.

J2EE Deployment Concepts

This chapter is an overview of several key concepts for assembling and deploying J2EE applications. In Chapter 6, "Building J2EE Applications with Ant," we use Ant to create Java ARchive (JAR) files, Web ARchive (WAR) files, and Enterprise JavaBean (EJB) JARs, so you will need to have a background in the various deployment descriptors for these modules. If you already have considerable experience with J2EE applications, you may want to skip to Chapter 3, "Storing and Managing Code with CVS."

The J2EE platform provides component models for assembling applications. J2EE lets you "divide and conquer" an application by buying and building components and wiring them together into an application. Java and J2EE support the following components:

❑ **Client Components**

    ❑ JavaBeans

    ❑ Applets

❑ **Web Application Components**

    ❑ Servlets

    ❑ JSPs

    ❑ TagLibs

❑ **Enterprise JavaBeans**

    ❑ Session beans

    ❑ Stateless session beans

    ❑ Entity beans

Each component executes in a container. To interoperate with various containers, these components require deployment descriptor files, configuration files, property files, and/or metadata files, and other configuration files. All these files describe the components and how they will interact with other components and their container environment.

Deployment can be a complex matter. A typical deployment might involve creating an Enterprise ARchive (EAR) file that can contain JAR and WAR files. The JAR files can in turn contain enterprise beans. The WAR file can in turn contain Web components (servlets, TagLibs, JavaBeans, and JSP), HTML pages, images, Java class files, and other JAR files that contain application components (JavaBeans, client-side remote references to enterprise beans and applets). The deployment descriptor for a Web application (which we will cover later) may contain env-entry elements that are mapped to the Java Naming and Directory Interface (JNDI) names java:comp/env (the context), ejb-ref (describes enterprise beans), and resources-ref (maps Java Messaging Service, Java Database Connectivity, and mail resources so that the Web application can use them).

The next two figures show the block diagrams of the two J2EE applications that we build, test, and deploy throughout this book (see Appendix A, "Example Applications Used in This Book" for details on these applications). The first figure shows our HelloWorld application, and the second shows the pet store application. As you can see, several different types of components need to be deployed to multiple servers and containers.

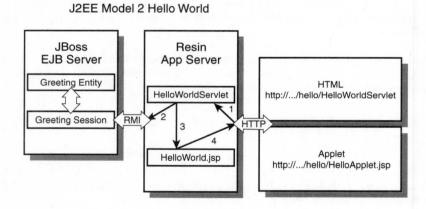

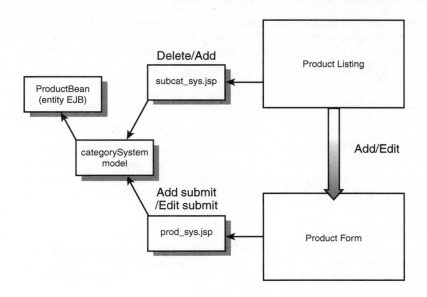

To say that configuration management of a typical J2EE enterprise application is complex is an understatement. In chapters 5 and 6 we will use Ant to help facilitate this process. Otherwise, continuous integration would be pretty tough with the complexities of the J2EE deployment environment.

The remainder of this chapter describes the basic J2EE components and how they are deployed. We also explain the JAR file format, because many components and sets of components are packaged in either a JAR file or some variation of a JAR file.

The JAR File

JAR stands for Java ARchive, although it seems to be an obvious pun on the fact that Java components are called beans ("a jar of beans"). A JAR file is a collection of other files. JAR files use the ZIP file format, which supports compression.

Many components, subsystems, and modules are deployed in JAR files or some variation of a JAR file. There are JAR files for JavaBeans and applets. Other JAR files contain libraries of Java code. There are JAR files that contain Enterprise JavaBeans. Then there are variations of JAR files that contain other JAR files and JavaServer Pages (JSPs) like the WAR files. The king of all JAR files, the EAR file, can contain other JAR files, EJB JAR files, and WAR files.

Each JAR file contains a manifest file called MANIFEST.MF, which is located in the JAR file's META-INF directory. The manifest file is a text file that consists of entries that describe the contents of the JAR file. The main section of the manifest file contains configuration information and specifies the application or extension the JAR file is associated with.

JAR files were originally developed to package Java applets and their requisite components (.class files, images, and sounds). The boon to applet development was that the applet could be downloaded to a browser in a single file, so the browser didn't have to download many files—a major boost to efficiency and speed.

JAR Files and Applets

For applets, JAR files are specified in the HTML applet tag's "archive" parameter. This parameter causes the browser to load the JAR file, which contains the applet code. For example:

```
<applet
      code= "xptoolkit.applet.HelloWorldApplet"
      archive="helloapplet.jar"
      width=200 height=200>
</applet>
```

Applet delivery has complex problems and solutions. It's supposed to be easy to request a browser to open a JAR file. The problem is that one major Web browser vendor decided not to support Java any longer. The vendor froze its version of Java at version JDK 1.1.5. Thus, you can use the applet tag we just described if you do not use any features of Java newer than JDK 1.1.5.

Another major vendor of Web browsers supported the later versions of Java, but at the time its browser support of Java was not very robust. Thus, Sun had two choices: It could wait for the browser to catch up or write its own Java plug-in for the major browsers. The good folks at Sun decided to write their own plug-in for Java. A tag that supports both Netscape and Microsoft may look like this:

```
<object classid="clsid:8AD9C840-044E-11D1-B3E9-00805F499D93"
     codebase="http://java.sun.com/products/plugin/1.2.2/jinstall-1_2_2-
win.cab#Version=1,2,2,0"
            height="200" width="200" align="center">
            <param name="java_code"
                      value="xptoolkit.applet.HelloWorldApplet">
            <param name="java_archive" value="helloapplet.jar">
            <param name="type" value="application/x-java-applet">

            <comment>
                <embed type="application/x-java-applet"
                      codebase="http://java.sun.com/products/plugin/"
                      height="200"
                      width="200"
                      align="center"
                 java_code="xptoolkit.applet.HelloWorldApplet"
                 java_archive="helloapplet.jar">
            <noembed>
            </comment>
              <p> Java is cool. Get a browser that supports the plugin.
                 </ br>
              </p>
            </noembed>
            </embed>
            </object>
```

The embed tag is for Netscape Navigator, and the "java_archive" parameter specifies the JAR file that contains the applet code. The object tag works with Microsoft Internet Explorer, and it uses the "java_archive" parameter to specify the JAR file.

JSP has a plug-in tag that helps simplify this issue for you. The plug-in tag specifies the JAR file that the applet needs in its "archive" parameter. It is demonstrated as follows:

```
<jsp:plugin type="applet"
            code="xptoolkit.applet.HelloWorldApplet"
            archive="helloapplet.jar"
            height="200"
            width="200"
            align="center">
    <jsp:fallback>
<!-- This fallback message will display if the plugin does not work. /-->
        <p> Java is cool. Get a browser that supports the plugin. </ br>
            Or we will hunt you down and melt your computer!
        </p>
    </jsp:fallback>
</jsp:plugin>
```

An example of using this technique to launch applets appears in chapter 6.

Executable JAR Files

In addition to supporting applets, Java supports JAR files so that double-clicking a JAR file (or the equivalent gesture on your OS) will automatically run the application in the JAR file. In order to do this, you must specify the name of the application's startup class in the JAR manifest file. The startup class is called the *main class*.

You can run a JAR file that specifies a main class as follows:

```
C:\tmp\app\lib> java -jar greetapp.jar
```

To specify a main class for a JAR file, you specify the "Main-Class" attribute in the JAR manifest file:

```
Main-Class :  xptoolkit.HelloWorld
```

An example of how to create an executable JAR file with Ant appears in chapter 5.

This was just a brief introduction to JAR files. Later chapters contain plenty of examples that show you how to use Ant to build the various distribution files based on the JAR format you need and use.

Web Applications and the WAR File

Web applications consist of the following components: JSPs, TagLibs, and servlets. You describe these components and their relationship with a metadata deployment filed named web.xml. The web.xml file is a deployment descriptor defined by the Servlet Specification. The deployment descriptor is stored in the root of the WEB-INF directory. The Web application deployment descriptor holds the following information for the Web application container:

❑   ServletContext init parameters

❑   Session configuration

❑   Servlet/JSP definitions

❑   Servlet/JSP URI mappings

❑   Mime type mappings

❑   Error pages

❑   Security

❑   JNDI environment

❑   Referenced EJBs

❑   Maps resources, such as JDBC connections, URL factory, JMS resources, and mail resources

The Web application is usually contained in a WAR file. A WAR file is a single archive file with the .war file extension. Like a JAR file, a WAR file uses the ZIP file format. Unlike a JAR file, a WAR file cannot be placed on the classpath. The WAR file contains all the components of a Web application, including support libraries and HTML files. The WAR file holds the HTML and JSP files in the root of the WAR file, and it holds the servlets and related classes in the WEB-INF/classes directory. Any supporting libraries (JAR files) the JSP or servlets need are held in the WEB-INF/lib directory. A WAR file can hold all the files a Web application needs for deployment.

A directory structure for a Web application may look something like this:

```
Web Application Archive file Root
 |
 |    index.html
 |    HelloWorld.jsp
 |
 \---WEB-INF
      |    web.xml
      |
      +---classes
      |    \---xptoolkit
      |        |
      |        \---web
      |            HelloWorldServlet.class
      |
      \---lib
            greetmodel.jar
```

This example has index.html and HelloWorld.jsp in the root directory. It also has the servlet xptoolkit.web.HelloWorldServlet in the /WEB-INF/classes directory. In addition, the support library greetmodel.jar is in the /WEB-INF/lib directory. The greetmodel.jar file has JavaBeans and classes that are needed by HelloWorld.jsp and xptoolkit.web.HelloWorldServlet. Note that this example is based on a sample we will use in chapters 5 and 6.

As we stated earlier, the web.xml file sets environment settings for the Web application. An example deployment descriptor for a Web application from previous WAR file may look like this:

```
<web-app>
    <error-page>
        <error-code>404</error-code>
        <location>/HelloWorldServlet</location>
    </error-page>

    <servlet>
        <servlet-name>HelloWorldServlet</servlet-name>
        <servlet-class>xptoolkit.web.HelloWorldServlet</servlet-class>
        <init-param>
          <param-name>Greeting.class</param-name>
          <param-value>xptoolkit.model.HelloWorldBean</param-value>
        </init-param>
    </servlet>

    <servlet>
        <servlet-name>HelloWorldJSP</servlet-name>
        <jsp-file>HelloWorld.jsp</jsp-file>
    </servlet>

    <servlet-mapping>
        <servlet-name>HelloWorldServlet</servlet-name>
        <url-pattern>/HelloWorldServlet</url-pattern>
    </servlet-mapping>

    <servlet-mapping>
        <servlet-name>HelloWorldJSP</servlet-name>
        <url-pattern>/HelloWorldJSP</url-pattern>
    </servlet-mapping>

</web-app>
```

This deployment descriptor creates two servlet definitions: one for HelloWorld.jsp (a JSP compiles to a servlet before use) and one for xptoolkit.web.HelloWorldServlet. The deployment descriptor then maps a few URI mappings for the servlets that were defined. A servlet mapping maps a servlet to a URI.

This was just an introduction to the Web application and WAR files. For a detailed description, refer to the Java Servlet Specification (http://java.sun.com/j2ee/). The parts of the deployment descriptor that we used here are explained as we build the sample applications deployed in Chapter 6, "Building J2EE Applications with Ant."

Enterprise Beans and the EJB JAR File

Enterprise JavaBeans use the JAR file format to package enterprise beans. The EJB JAR file is used to package un-assembled enterprise beans and to package assembled beans. *Un-assembled enterprise beans* have only generic information created by the bean developer. *Assembled enterprise beans* have information for a particular environment stored in the deployment descriptor by the application assembler. Basically, there are different roles for building and deploying enterprise beans. In this book, we are both the bean provider and the application assembler (in addition to the deployer and the administrator). However, the techniques we present can be adapted to situations in which assembling and deploying are performed by separate organizations.

Like the Web application WAR file, the EJB JAR file has a deployment descriptor. It is stored in the META-INF directory in a file called ejb-jar.xml. This deployment descriptor contains the following information:

- **Structural information for an Enterprise Bean:**
    - Name
    - Class type
    - Home interface
    - Remote interface
    - Bean type (session or entity)
    - Reentrancy indication
    - State management information (stateful session)
    - Persistence management information (container managed persistence [CMP] entity)
    - Primary key class (entity)
    - Container managed fields (CMP entity)
    - Environment entries (accessible via JNDI)
    - Resource manager connection factory references
    - References to other EJBs
    - Security role references

- **Application assembly information:**
    - Binding of Enterprise bean references
    - Security roles
    - Method permissions
    - Linking of security roles
    - Transaction attributes for beans and methods

The following listing is an example of an EJB deployment descriptor; it's based on an example in chapter 6.

```
<ejb-jar>

<description>
This ejb-jar file contains the Enterprise beans for the
Model 2 Hello World application.
```

```xml
    </description>

    <ejb-client-jar>client-greet-ejbs.jar</ejb-client-jar>

    <enterprise-beans>

        <entity>
            <description>
                The GreetingEntityBean is a do nothing bean to demonstrate
                how to deploy an Enterprise bean with Ant.
            </description>
            <ejb-name>GreetingEntityBean</ejb-name>
            <home>xptoolkit.ejbs.GreetingEntityHome</home>
            <remote>xptoolkit.ejbs.GreetingEntityRemote</remote>
            <ejb-class>xptoolkit.ejbs.GreetingEntityBean</ejb-class>
            <transaction-type>Container</transaction-type>
            <reentrant>True</reentrant>
            <prim-key-class>java.lang.Integer</prim-key-class>
            <persistence-type>Bean</persistence-type>
        </entity>

        <session>
            <description>
                The GreetingSessionBean is a do nothing bean to demonstrate
                how to deploy an Enterprise bean with Ant.
            </description>
            <ejb-name>GreetingSessionBean</ejb-name>
            <home>xptoolkit.ejbs.GreetingSessionHome</home>
            <remote>xptoolkit.ejbs.GreetingSessionRemote</remote>
            <ejb-class>xptoolkit.ejbs.GreetingSessionBean</ejb-class>
            <session-type>Stateful</session-type>
            <transaction-type>Container</transaction-type>

            <ejb-ref>
                <description>
                    This sets up a references from the Entity bean to the
session bean.
                    Thus, the session bean can look up the Entity bean in
                    its environment space.
                </description>
                <ejb-ref-name>ejb/GreetingEntityBean</ejb-ref-name>
                <ejb-ref-type>Entity</ejb-ref-type>
                <home>xptoolkit.ejbs.GreetingEntityHome</home>
                <remote>xptoolkit.ejbs.GreetingEntityRemote</remote>
                <ejb-link>GreetingEntityBean</ejb-link>
            </ejb-ref>

        </session>

    </enterprise-beans>

    <assembly-descriptor>
        <container-transaction>
            <method>
```

```
            <ejb-name>GreetingSessionBean</ejb-name>
            <method-name>*</method-name>
        </method>
        <trans-attribute>Supports</trans-attribute>
    </container-transaction>

    <container-transaction>
        <method>
            <ejb-name>GreetingEntityBean</ejb-name>
            <method-name>*</method-name>
        </method>
        <trans-attribute>Supports</trans-attribute>
    </container-transaction>

</assembly-descriptor>
</ejb-jar>
```

This listing defines two enterprise beans: GreetingSessionBean and GreetingEntityBean. The session bean has a reference to the entity bean. We'll explain this example in more detail in chapter 6. Notice that the enterprise-bean element defines entity and session sub-elements. The entity and session elements contain references to the remote, home, and bean classes. These classes are defined in the root of the bean class just like classes of a regular JAR file. For example, the directory structure of the EJB file described in the previous listing may look like this:

```
EJB Jar File root
|
|    client-greet-ejbs.jar
|
+---META-INF
|        MANIFEST.MF
|        ejb-jar.xml
|
\---xptoolkit
     |
     \---ejbs
             GreetingEntityBean.class
             GreetingEntityHome.class
             GreetingEntityRemote.class
             GreetingSessionBean.class
             GreetingSessionRemote.class
             GreetingSessionHome.class
```

This example is based on one presented in chapter 6. For more information about EJB JAR files and EJB deployment descriptors, refer to the official EJB specifications online at http://java.sun.com/products/ejb/.

Enterprise Applications and the EAR File

Once you create all your components, you may want to deploy them as a single logical unit called an *enterprise application*. Doing so will ease the deployment and help ensure that the environment of the staging server is the same or at least as close as possible to the one on the production server.

An enterprise application can be contained in single JAR file with the extension .ear, called an enterprise archive (EAR) file. The EAR file contains many JAR files, EJB JAR files, and WAR files called *modules*. Following is an example of a deployment descriptor for an EAR file:

```
<application>
  <display-name>Hello World Application</display-name>
  <description>Hello World Application.</description>
  <module>
    <web>
      <web-uri>hello.war</web-uri>
      <context-root>helloworld</context-root>
    </web>
  </module>
  <module>
    <ejb>greet-ejbs.jar</ejb>
  </module>
</application>
```

This deployment descriptor would correspond to the following directory structure of an EAR file:

```
Enterprise Archive file root
|    greet-ejbs.jar
|    hello.war
|
\---META-INF
        application.xml
```

This is based on a real example that is presented in chapter 6. To find out more about EAR files and EAR deployment descriptors, refer to the J2EE Specification chapters "Application Assembly" and "Deployment."

Conclusion

This chapter covered the basic J2EE components and how they are deployed, and the various archive files in which J2EE components are deployed (WAR, EAR, EJB JAR, and JAR).

We talked about the many types of J2EE-supported components: JavaBeans, applets, servlets, JSP, TagLibs, session beans, stateless session beans, and entity bean. We also discussed how to create deployments that interoperate with various containers using deployment descriptor files and archive files. Deployment files make deployment easier because they describe the components, how the components interact with other components, and how the components interact with their container environment.

Storing and Managing Code with CVS

One of the most important things you can do, as a developer, is version source code and other project files. What does it mean to "version" a file? According to Merriam Webster, a version is a *variant or type of an original*, and that's exactly what we mean in professional software development. In an iterative development process (and is it ever exactly right the first time?) files undergo numerous changes before and after a software package is released. In this chapter, we will discuss the benefits of versioning and examine a freely-available open source tool for storing and managing code: CVS.

Where to Get Concurrent Versions System (CVS)

CVS is an open source tool of inestimable value to the software development community. The most recent version is 1.11.13 and can be downloaded at: http://ccvs.cvshome.org/servlets/ProjectDownloadList.

The Benefits of Versioning

Performing versioning on project files has a multitude of benefits. Consider the following very common real world situations:

❑ Some functionality may cease to work when new requirements are introduced or refactoring occurs in some classes. Rather than try to remember how something used to work, a version control system can show exactly what code was changed, making it easier to fix bugs.

❑ Often there will be a quality assurance or testing team for projects. These teams usually wish to test the project at recreatable milestones. In order to accurately document the results of their testing and recreate issues a versioning system that can somehow label a project release milestone is very helpful.

❑ The version control system provides a central place to disseminate project files to all development staff on a team.

❑ A good version control system can allow developers to work in the same modules of a system at the same time by assisting with module merging and allowing files to be locked to prevent concurrent modification.

❑ A good version control system allows or requires developers to make notes of changes to modules; in this way other developers can quickly assess the nature of the changes made and plan their own module integration accordingly.

Let us introduce the idea of a *code repository*, then, to assist with the versioning process. We will define a code repository as some piece of software whose job is to keep track of our files, and all the different versions or *revisions* of our files as well as any milestones we define and comment history we enter. In order to be most useful, a source code repository should be

❑ Accessible through a well-published protocol so that disparate clients will have easy access to it

❑ Support multiple users accessing the repository and ideally keep a history of which users have made changes to files

About CVS

CVS, the Concurrent Versions System, is an open source versioning software system that supports many if not all of the requirements of an ideal version control system as defined in the previous section. CVS originated as UNIX shell scripts and was eventually re-written as CVS in the late 1980s. CVS shines the most when used to keep track of text files. It does a good job of displaying deltas, merging text differences, and in some cases even adding version information to source files automatically.

CVS is originally a command line tool, but many other tools such as WinCVS and NetBeans provide GUI's to access CVS repositories.

CVS is in widespread use as a means of disseminating open source projects on the Internet. The Apache family of projects, JBoss, and many others offer anonymous CVS access for nightly source drops.

CVS Foundations

The CVS examples in this chapter are ran against CVS version 1.11.13, running on a standard LINUX server. While it is possible to run CVS on the Windows platform, you are most likely to encounter it running on a UNIX or LINUX system when working on open source projects.

The CVS Local Server

In order to acquaint you with the process of using CVS, a test cvs repository is needed. Rather than incur the cost of setting up a complete remote repository, we will create a CVS local repository and use that for the client-side examples. A complete step-by-step for creating a remote CVS repository is covered in the latter half of this chapter.

From this point forward, let us make the assumption that we are a user "wrox" with a home directory on a Linux server called "linuxserver". To most closely follow the examples, create a user called wrox on your Linux server. To create the local repository, log in to linuxserver. For the first examples, we'll tell CVS to create a repository right here in wrox's home directory, and then connect to it.

A CVS local repository is one that cannot be connected to via a network connection from machines other than the one CVS is running on. In our case, we don't need to share the repository either, so we'll create it in our /home/wrox directory.

1.   Create a directory cvsroot in the wrox home directory. The complete path should be /home/wrox/cvsroot.

2.   Now, to simplify future operations, add an environment variable called CVSROOT. Capitalization matters, as always. This variable will point to the CVS directory created in Step 1.

3.   Create the variable by editing /home/wrox/.bash_profile and adding the following lines of code:

```
CVSROOT=/home/wrox/cvsroot
export CVSROOT
```

To make the changes take effect, type the following:

```
. .bash_profile on the command line.
```

This environment variable is very significant. In the absence of command line arguments specifying the CVS repository location to use, CVS will pull this value from the environment. Now, we are ready to tell CVS to create a new repository. In act of creating a repository CVS creates administrative files necessary to use the directory as a repository. Installation is simple; type the following at the command line.

```
[wrox@linuxserver wrox]$ cvs init
```

Now, cd to /home/wrox/cvsroot and type ls CVSROOT. You should see something very similar to the following output.

```
[wrox@linuxserver cvsroot]$ ls CVSROOT/
checkoutlist     config.v        Emptydir     modules.v    taginfo
checkoutlist.v   cvswrappers     history      notify       taginfo.v
commitinfo       cvswrappers.v   loginfo      notify.v     val-tags
commitinfo.v     editinfo        loginfo.v    rcsinfo      verifymsg
config           editinfo.v      modules      rcsinfo.v    verifymag.v
[wrox@linuxserver cvsroot]$
```

The next step is to create a directory within our $CVSROOT to contain files for the examples, rather than keep them in root. Make a directory called /home/wrox/cvsroot/client for testing CVS client commands. We are now ready to begin versioning source code.

CVS Commands

CVS commands share a generally common command structure that might seem a bit odd at first. The first part is always "cvs", directly following by any arguments to cvs itself, followed by the cvs command you wish to execute and finally any arguments to that cvs command. Thus, we can say cvs commands have the following form:

```
cvs -"cvs arguments here" "cvs command name" "arguments to the command"
```

We will see this form for the login command below.

Note, the CVS log in step can be skipped for the local repository we've created. Keep remote logins in mind, but skip to the section entitled "Checking Out Code" below.

CVS commands, by default, use recursive behavior. So, if you are at the top of a large development tree and issue a cvs commit or update command, the entire tree from that point down will be affected. This may sometimes be what you want, but it can be a headache when committing large numbers of files at once unintentionally. You can cancel a CVS commit operation by exiting the text editor without saving changes, and choosing the abort option.

Connecting to a CVS Server

The first step to accessing a CVS repository is determining the CVS connection information and logging in. You must have valid user credentials on the remote server. Many open source projects have set up an "anoncvs" user with read-only access to the repository; if you are part of a development team the sysadmin will probably give you this information. The CVS client must know what login protocol will be used, what user credentials to send, where the server is, and the path to the repository on that server.

The general form for a cvs login statement, is:

```
:method:[[user][:password]@]hostname[:[port]]/path/to/repository
```

The "pserver" method, short for password server, is the most common authentication method, and the only one we will focus on in this chapter. For the rest of the chapter, assume the following cvs login information:

```
cvs -d :pserver:wrox@localhost:/usr/local/cvsroot login
```

What are the pieces of this login command? As stated above, the first part is always cvs, followed by any arguments to the cvs command. The –d argument tells cvs what CVS ROOT to use for the operations. If this argument is missing, the cvs command searches your environment for a CVSROOT value. This is then used without the need to include in on the command line. Often this is the most convenient way to use cvs, so it is wise to add an export CVSROOT=your cvs root here in whatever login scripts are appropriate to your shell. In the standard bash shell, this is accomplished by adding the information above to the .bash_profile file in the user home directory. Note that we have not specified the password, cvs will ask for the user password. Typing the login string shown above should produce output similar to the following:

```
[wrox@linuxserver wrox]$ cvs -d :pserver:wrox@localhost:/usr/local/cvsroot
login
Logging in to :pserver:wrox@localhost:2401/usr/local/cvsroot
```

```
CVS password:
[wrox@linuxserver wrox]$
```

Typing ls –a at the command prompt, you will see that there is now a file called .cvspass found in your home directory. This file stores your password, but not in plain text. This, combined with the $CVS-ROOT environment setting, will allow us to work without specifying login information or the location of the server until such time as we log out. Should you need to connect to different cvs servers, use the cvs logout command and log in with new information.

Checking Out Code

Now logged in, we are ready to begin using the repository. The command to get a local copy of the files in the repository for the first time is cvs co (check out). The command form is

```
cvs co {checkout options} {modules to check out}
```

There are many arguments to the checkout command, but we need only concern ourselves with the basics here.

❑   By default, checkout recursively gets all directories beneath the module specified.

❑   The –r {revision/tag name} will allow a specific version of a file or files to be retrieved, instead of the most current which is the default. Creating tags will be discussed in more detail later.

❑   The –P option helps clean up the local source tree. It is hard to entirely remove a directory from the cvs repository, but you can remove all the files in a directory; this command "prunes" empty directories.

There are no files in the repository yet so of course checkout won't produce any source files. The cvs co command will tell CVS to initialize our working directory with the CVS specific files it needs, similary to cvs init creating the repository. Therefore, cvs co is the first command we issue. From /home/wrox, type the following:

```
[wrox@linuxserver wrox]$ cvs co client
cvs checkout: Updating client
? client/Test.java
[wrox@linuxserver wrox]$
```

The cvs client will report the status of the operations you ask it to perform, unless you suppress these messages. After issuing the checkout command, you will notice that there is a directory called CVS created underneath client. These files should not be edited by hand—they are administrative files created by cvs to store data about the status of files. A CVS directory will be created in every directory you add to the repository.

Adding Files

Now, we will add a Java file into the repository. Create the following simple Java file in the /home/wrox/client/ directory.

```
package com.wrox.projosdev.client;
/**
 * A class to test the cvs client commands
```

```
   *
   */
public class Test {
  public static void main(String[] args) {
    System.out.println("CVS is the best!");
    Test.printArgs(args);
    Test test = new Test();
    test.doSomething(test.new InnerPeace());
  }
  public void doSomething(Object object) {
    System.out.println("You gave me " + object.getClass().getName() );
  }
  private static void printArgs(String[] args) {
    for (int i = 0; i < args.length; ++i) {
      System.out.println("Arg[" + i + "] " + args[i]);
    }
  }
  private class InnerClash {
  }
  private class InnerPeace {
  }
}
```

Assume for now that this file performs some business purpose. On any project the structure of the source directory should of course match the Java package structure, which is skipped here for expediency.

Now its time to add Test.java to the repository. The command to add files to the repository is

```
cvs add {options} {files}
```

The relevant options to cvs add will be discussed below. For now, type

```
cvs add Test.java
```

You should see output similar to the following:

```
[wrox@linuxserver client]$ cvs add Test.java
cvs add: scheduling file 'Test.java' for addition
cvs add: use 'cvs commit' to add this file permanently
[wrox@linuxserver client]$
```

Adding to CVS is a two-stage process then, with part one being add and part two being commit. The semantics of cvs commit will be discussed in detail below in the "Updating Modules" section. For now, trust that typing

```
command cvs commit Test.java
```

is the next step. Upon hitting enter, you are greeted with a change log message screen.

```
Type your change message here: Version 1.0 of Test program
CVS: ----------------------------------------------------------------------
CVS: Enter Log. Lines beginning with 'CVS:' are removed automatically
```

```
CVS:
CVS: Added Files:
CVS:    Test.java
CVS: ------------------------------------------------------------------
```

For the default "wrox" user created, the editor is the venerable *vi*. This is configurable within the shell environment. Save the log message, and you should see output indicating the file is in the repository.

```
RCS file: /home/wrox/cvsroot/client/Test.java,v
done
Checking in Test.java;
/home/wrox/cvsroot/client/Test.java,v  <--  Test.java
initial revision: 1.1
done
[wrox@linuxserver client]$
```

Now the file is in the repository! Take note of the line stating "initial revision: 1.1". This will be important later. This is our first *revision* of a file; we can use the revision number to get back to this state at any time.

CVS uses the notion of "sticky tags" and "sticky options" to store information about files, such as a tag the file is part of. The sticky tag most likely to be used on a Java project is the binary keyword substitution. Remember that the core functionality of CVS is versioning text files, so we must tell it to treat binary files specially. Suppose there is a certain version of the Tomcat servlet engine needed to compile a project, distributed as servlet.jar.

On most projects, jar files are kept in their own directory. This is a good time to introduce another concept: adding directories. To add a directory in CVS, create the local directory, lib in this case, and issue the cvs add command. You should see:

```
[wrox@linuxserver client]$ cvs add lib
Directory /home/wrox/cvsroot/client/lib added to the repository
```

> **Some versions of CVS have difficulty removing directories; make sure you want to add a directory before committing it to the repository.**

Now that the lib directory is part of the repository, we can copy the servlet.jar file into it. To add the file to the repository, issue the "cvs add" command again but this time with extra arguments.

```
cvs add —kb servlet.jar
```

With these options, CVS will treat the file as binary and not mangle it with text-processing routines.

At this point we introduce another cvs command we can use to see what information CVS might be keeping about files. To check on the status of the JAR file we just added, we will use the cvs status command:

```
cvs status {files}
```

The output should look like this:

```
[wrox@linuxserver lib]$ cvs status servlet.jar
====================================================================
File: servlet.jar       Status: Up-to-date
    Working revision:    1.1      Fri Dec 26 02:31:32 2002
    Repository revision: 1.1      /home/wrox/cvsroot/client/lib/servlet.jar,v
    Sticky Tag:          (none)
    Sticky Date:         (none)
    Sticky Options:      -kb
[wrox@linuxserver lib]$
```

The cvs status command delivers several useful pieces of information. Most prominent are the Status and, in this case, the Sticky Options data. Status can tell you the status of your local file related to the file in the repository. Status messages you will most commonly see are listed below. In the Sticky Options section, you can see that CVS recognized the -kb options.

Following are several useful status messages that CVS produces:

❑ **Up-to-date:** The local file match the file in the repository.

❑ **Locally Modified:** The local file has been changed, but you have not committed the changes yet. See the "Updating Modules" section to learn how to commit changes.

❑ **Needs Checkout:** Another developer has made changes to the file. See the "Updating Modules" section to learn how to get repository changes.

❑ **Needs Merge:** Both you, and another developer, have made changes to the same file. This is common, but cvs can automatically handle merging most small changes. For larger differences, see the section on "Resolving Merge Conflicts."

Updating Modules

Updating modules in CVS is a two way street. A developer must store changes in the repository and also be sure to stay in sync with the changes being made by other developers. This process may take place several times per week, or several times per day depending on the pace of your project.

When working on a development team, many people are likely to be changing the same files, sometimes at the same time. It is a CVS best practice to always perform a CVS Sanity Check (shown below) before checking in new code.

The CVS update command format, used to bring working directories in sync with the repository.

```
cvs update {options} {files}
```

The most common options to the cvs update command are as follows:

❑ **cvs update –d** This should most likely be included every time an update is performed. Remember that CVS uses the files within the CVS directories to determine how to go about updating a source tree. However, other developers could add directories not present in your local tree. The -d option tells CVS to check for new directories.

❑ **cvs update –C {file or files}** Sometimes while working on a file you make irreparable damages and just need to get back to what exists in the repository without merging. Using the -C option will give you a "Clean" copy of the file.

❑ **cvs update –P** "Prune" empty directories, removes clutter from the working tree even though the directories technically still exist in CVS.

❑ **cvs update –r {tag or revision}** Get a specific version or tag of a file. This option, and its counterpart the –A option, will be discussed in more detail in the section on creating a tag.

The next step in updating modules we have already seen. The cvs commit command is used to send changes to the server. The "CVS Sanity Check" was mentioned earlier. This is a sequence of steps that should be taken in this order for the smoothest operation of a project using CVS for version control.

Performing a CVS Sanity Check:

1. Update project files. The importance of this cannot be overstated. You must bring your source tree in sync with the repository.

2. Resolve any merge conflicts that arise. It is best to confer with other developers if possible.

3. Make sure the project still compiles. This is quick and painless with Ant.

4. If your project uses an automated Unit Testing strategy, make sure the unit test suite(s) for the project still completes successfully. Unit testing with JUnit is a great way to ensure the project is always in a running state.

5. You have now taken the extra time to be a responsible developer. Your colleagues and project manager will thank you. Go ahead and commit your changes.

Retrieving the changes made by other developers is accomplished using the cvs update command. Storing changes in the repository is accomplished using the cvs commit command.

Locking Files

Several other version control systems use a "check out and lock" model, whereby the client tool sets file permissions on your local copy to keep you from changing the file unless you ask the server to give you exclusive write access to that file. CVS does not attempt to do this sort of policing, code is checked out writeable on the local filesystem. Anyone who sees fit can edit any file at any time and, if they have write access to the repository, commit their changes.

Creating a Branch in CVS

Often it may be useful to mark the current state of the repository with a tag, such that the development or testing team can always guarantee the ability to role a project back to the state it is in at a specific moment in time. Branching and tags can be one of the most confusing topics within CVS; this need not be the case.

Suppose the two files we have so far added to the local repository have undergone several iterations, and are ready to go through user testing of some sort. According to the project milestones, this milestone shall be called Release Candidate 1, or RC1 for short. The development team needs to keep working on the source tree, adding bug fixes and new features slated for Version 2 of the system. By creating a branch, development can continue on the new version, but Release Candidate 1 can be recreated at any time as well.

What is the difference between a branch and a revision? A revision is a specific version of a file. The first revision of the Test.java file was 1.1, the second 1.2, and so on. Since a branch captures a certain state of the source tree, consider a branch "a collection of certain revisions."

The cvs command for creating a branch is

```
cvs tag -b {branch name}
```

Let's create a branch in the local repository called RC1. Remember that CVS commands use a recursive behavior by default, so change directory to /home/wrox/client, the top of our working directory. Type cvs tag –b RC1. You should see the following output:

```
[wrox@linuxserver client]$ cvs tag -b RC1
cvs tag: Tagging .
T Test.java
cvs tag: Tagging lib
T lib/servlet.jar
[wrox@linuxserver client]$
```

The tag has now been created *in the repository*. This means the state of the system at the time the RC1 tag was created has been saved. However, type

```
cvs status Test.java"
```

and you will see there are no sticky tags on the file. This means the working directory is still pointing to the main development trunk. Depending on your situation, there are two ways to proceed.

If, for the foreseeable future, you need to keep working on Release Candidate 1, the cvs update command can be used to bring the RC1 tag into the working directory.

Often, developers will find themselves in the position of being simultaneously in two roles. On one hand they must make bug fixes to a stable branch, RC1 in our case, and also begin implementing new features in the main development trunk. In this scenario, it is easiest to keep two working directories, one of which has the RC1 stick tag. Consider the following list of commands to accomplish this task, using the same local example:

1. Create a directory to contain the RC1 branch.

2. Issue a cvs checkout command, with the -r RC1 option to get all files from the RC1 branch.

3. Use cvs status to obtain a visual confirmation that the checkout command worked:

```
===================================================================
File: Test.java          Status: Up-to-date

    Working revision:    1.5      Sat Feb 27 01:05:58 2004
    Repository version:  1.5      /home/wrox/cvsroot/client/Test.java.v
    Sticky Tag:          RC1 (branch: 1.5.2)
    Sticky Date:         (none)
    Sticky Options:      (none)

[wrox@linuxserver client]$
```

Notice that now that we have specified the RC1 branch, all files in the source tree will have the RC1 sticky tag. Changes can be made to these files without affecting the main development trunk, and changes in the main trunk will not be reflected in the RC1 branch.

Removing Files from CVS

Now that we have done many examples with Test.java, the time has come to remove it from the repository, as it is no longer needed on the project and is just in the way.

```
[wrox@linuxserver client]$ cvs remove Test.java
cvs remove: file `Test.java' still in working directory
cvs remove: 1 file exists; remove it first
[wrox@linuxserver client]$
```

So, working files must be deleted from the file system first. Delete the file with the command rm. Now issue the cvs remove command again.

```
Removing Test.java;
/home/wrox/cvsroot/client/Test.java,v  <--  Test.java
new revision: delete; previous revision: 1.2
done
[wrox@linuxserver client]$
```

Now the file has been removed from the repository.

Setting Up CVS on the Server

Now that you know the basics of using CVS, the server administration can be discussed.

Assuming you are running a newer 2.4.x Linux kernel, your system used xinetd instead of inetd for configuring network services. Make sure you already have the CVS client program installed and in your PATH. There should be a directory which stores all xinetd configuration files, /etc/xinetd.d by default.

```
cd /etc/xinetd.d
```

Touch a file called cvspserver, and use a command line editor, such as *vi* to edit the file.

Now, insert the following text into the cvspserver file:

```
service cvspserver
{
    port        = 2401
    socket_type = stream
    protocol    = tcp
    wait        = no
    user        = root
    passenv     = PATH
    server      = /usr/ bin/cvs
    server_args = -f --allow-root=/usr/local/cvsroot pserver
}
```

Make sure the server attribute corresponds to the location of the cvs executable on your server. If you don't know this value, type which cvs to discover the binary executable.

Once this configuration file has been created, xinetd needs to be told to reload its configuration files. This is usually done by asking xinetd to restart. Issue the following command:

```
/etc/init.d/xinetd restart
```

You should see the process stop and start. You are now ready to use the cvs server. CVS must be told to init the new server repository. Choose the location where you would like to keep the CVS repository, and issue the following command as root. Make sure this matches the allow-root part of the server_args line in your cvspserver file. Its once again easiest to set CVSROOT in the environment.

```
cvs init
```

The cvs command has now set up a repository. Change directory to $CVSROOT and create a directory called "projosdev", users can now access this module on the cvs server. It is important that users accessing the repository have write access to this directory. Create a group called cvsusers, and give that group write access to the $CVSROOT directory.

Unlike other services that use daemons, there is no cvsd; rather, the cvs client program actually acts as the server. Therefore no entries to the startup scripts are needed.

CVS Pitfalls and Solutions

CVS can be cryptic to understand at times. Here are some common stumbling blocks, along with solutions

Up-to-Date Check Failed for "file"

You will most likely see this during your CVS career. It is a highly recommended practice to *always* call cvs update before attempting to commit files into the repository. CVS will give this message when you attempt to commit a file that has been modified in the repository since the last time you updated. Update your working copy, resolve any merge conflicts, and call commit again.

Recovering a File Deleted with "cvs remove"

When a file is in the way and no longer needed, you remove it from the repository with cvs remove. However, you may later decide the file is needed once again. There are several bad ways to fix this problem; we will use a safe way. Assuming you would like to recover the most recent version of the file before it was removed, you can trick CVS into giving you the file back. At the end of the CVS Foundations section, we removed Test.java from the local repository. To recover the file:

```
[wrox@linuxserver client]$ cvs update -j1.2 -j1.1 Test.java
cvs update: warning: Test.java was lost
U Test.java
RCS file: /home/wrox/cvsroot/client/Attic/Test.java,v
retrieving revision 1.2
```

```
retrieving revision 1.1
Merging differences between 1.2 and 1.1 into Test.java
```

Now you can commit the file and keep on working.

CVS Files in Source Drops

Often, as part of a source drop or an automated build and deployment solution, a snapshot needs to be taken of the repository. In such cases the CVS specific directories aren't needed and in fact just clutter up the distribution. To get a clean snapshot of the repository, use cvs export instead.

Using CVS on the Windows Platform

A Win32 port of CVS is freely available on the Internet. However, there are a couple of common issues to be aware of:

❑ On a Windows based CVS server, the CVSROOT may look like c:/files/cvsroot/modulename. Some CVS clients take issue with this in the remote CVS root string, since the ":" character is used to separate other parts of the login.

❑ To CVS, the files Foo.java and foo.java are different files. To windows filesystems, however, they are the same file. This can create a headache when developers try to fix the problem by checking in a new file with a capitalized first letter and CVS keeps saving it with a lowercase letter. Removing and re-adding the file usually fixes this.

Resolving Merge Conflicts

When more than one devloper works on the same file at the same time, one of them will commit it first. The other developer, not as quick on the draw or perhaps with larger changes, is then stuck resolving merge conflicts.

CVS will warn you when there are merge conflicts. If you don't see these messages, don't worry, the compiler will catch them for you when attempting to build the project. A CVS merge conflict message will look something like this:

```
Merging differences between 1.1 and 1.2 into Test.java
rcsmerge warning: overlaps during merge
cvs update: conflicts found in Test.java
```

Now, you must find the merge conflicts in the file. Using your editor, open the file and search for <<<, the string CVS uses to mark the beginning of a merge conflict. The conflict area will look something like this:

```
<<<<<<< Test.java
        test.doSomething(test.new InnerPeace());
=======
        test.doSomething(test.new InnerConflict());
>>>>>>> 1.2
```

The first part, the less than signs, shows the offending area in your local copy. All of your code will be between this marker and the line of equals signs inserted by CVS. After the equals signs is the code that was in the most recent version in the repository, up to the line of greater than signs. After the greater than signs the file is fine (unless there are more merge conflicts; these will be marked in the same fashion). Determine what should be kept, and commit the file.

Using CVS from NetBeans/Forte

Updating source files from within the IDE is a great feature available in many of the popular Java editors today. NetBeans has an excellent CVS client implementation; to use it, follow these steps:

1. Create a new project that will contain the files you intend to get from CVS.

2. Right click on filesystems; CVS is mounted just like a local directory or JAR file.

3. Now we can set up the CVSROOT connect string similar to how it was done on the command line.

4. Click next and login into the CVS remote server, with the credentials we created earlier in the chapter.

5. At the last step, we need to choose a module to check out. Remember that we created a module called projosdev during the CVS server setup. Type projosdev in the Checkout text area, and select OK.

NetBeans will do an initial checkout of the files in the projosdev module. Notice that NetBeans displays the current CVS status of all files mounted in filesystems beneath the working directory you chose. This is fairly helpful especially when other developers may modify files, and the [Ncheckout] status message appears.

When you right click on the files located beneath the CVS mount, a CVS menu appears now. This menu contains all the CVS commands needed to do all the versioning described in this chapter through NetBeans.

> **To add arguments to CVS commands in the right click menu, hold down the CTRL key.**

Other Software

If you are performing development on the Windows platform and using CVS for source code management, you may find WinCVS useful. The tool is written in C++ and distributed freely under the standard GPL. Download from http://www.wincvs.org/.

Many developers find it a boon to be able to store snippets of code, or entire projects, on a central server so they can look up solutions to problems wherever they go. HTTP is still the most firewall-friendly way to access data from work. There are many tools facilitating the administration of repositories and browsing of source trees over HTTP. One of the originals is WebCVS, which can be found at http://stud.fh-heilbronn.de/~zeller/cgi/cvsweb.cgi/.

CVS Home (http://www.cvshome.org) contains browsable CVS manuals in HTML form, as well as a wealth of FAQ and How-To resources and links to other CVS pages.

Ant Primer

This chapter is an introduction to the fundamental concepts and techniques involved in using Ant to achieve continuous integration on your projects. *Ant* is a build tool that enables you to automate the build process. In that respect, Ant is similar to the make tool; but unlike make, Ant was designed specifically for Java development. Ant is written in Java, so it works across platforms and does not rely on shell-specific commands that vary greatly in function and usage from operating system to operating system. Instead, Ant relies on the Java platform to perform file access, compilation, and other tasks you need to build your Java projects.

Where To Get Ant

Ant was developed by The Apache Software Foundation as part of their Jakarta project. Ant 1.6.1 is distributed with The Apache Software License, Version 2.0 and can be downloaded at:

http://ant.apache.org/bindownload.cgi

A major advantage of Ant is its extensibility. Ant is easily extensible using cross-platform Java classes. You can also extend Ant by writing custom Java tasks and using the scripting task, which works with JavaScript (Rhino), Python, NetRexx, and others. In addition, if you must, you can call out to shell scripts, OS executables, and OS commands with the Ant exec task. Then, later, you can write a cross-platform version of the task in Java or with the Ant scripting task, which uses XML for its syntax.

The build-and-deploy cycle should be automated so you don't incorporate operator error. Writing a build script also documents the build process. Documentation becomes critical when a developer leaves your company. By using Ant, your company retains the knowledge needed to deploy the system, because the build-and-deploy process is automated by an Ant script (called a buildfile) and not locked away in the departed developer's IDE (which was set up for his local development environment). Another benefit of using Ant is that the script that automates the build-and-deploy process in effect also documents that process; unlike most IDEs' binary project configuration files, an Ant buildfile is written in human-readable text.

What Is Your Favorite IDE?

Ant complements Integrated Development Environments (IDEs); Ant does not replace IDEs, nor do IDEs replace Ant. IDEs can greatly simplify Java development, but they are not good for automating the build-and-deploy process of a complex project. Every software process needs a repeatable build system, and IDEs do not provide such a system.

Developers become attached to the IDE they use. At our company, we use several different IDEs, including Eclipse, Borland JBuilder, NetBeans, Forte CE, Visual Age for Java, JDE (Java development environment for Emacs), and Ultra Edit. Ant reduces the potential havoc by providing a standard on which to base our build-and-deploy process.

You can use Ant for the organization of deployment and for automated builds. Ant supports the concept of *continuous integration*, as described in the next section. Using Ant to perform continuous integration changes the whole development blueprint of your project. With a little discipline and setup time, continuous integration reduces problems linked with team development.

Developers often talk about automated building and testing but seldom implement it. Ant makes automated building and testing possible and plausible. Ant and JUnit combine well to allow teams to build and test their software several times a day. Such an automated process is worth the sweat. You will find out who broke what sooner—before you forget who did what. You will find integration bugs before they become strange and unpredictable.

Alternatives to Ant exist. However, Ant has become the de facto standard for automating Java builds. For example, Sun's pet store J2EE blueprint application uses Ant. The other day, we went to the Orion application server site to look at some examples, and all of them had corresponding Ant buildfiles. Of course, many of the projects at Apache's Jakarta have Ant buildfiles. Ant is popular because it is easy to learn and extend. In addition, several IDEs and development tools support Ant—for example, the NetBeans IDE and Together Control Center.

The next section will cover the mechanics of using Ant to create buildfiles.

Basics of Using Ant

This section is a quick tutorial covering the basics of Ant. You will learn about projects, targets, properties, tasks, filesets, pathelements, and other key concepts. Upon completion of this chapter, you should understand Ant well enough to write your own Ant buildfiles.

Projects, Targets, and Tasks

Ant's build scripts, called *buildfiles,* are written in XML. Every buildfile contains one *project* element. A *project* element contains *target* elements. Each *target* consists of a set of *task* elements.

A task performs a function such as copying a file, compiling a project, or creating a JAR file.

A target is a collection of tasks and properties. A target can depend on other targets, meaning that a target does not execute until the targets it depends on are executed (for example, you would normally want to compile classes before you put them in a JAR). To indicate that a target depends on another target, you use the *depends* attribute. Thus, you may have something like the set of targets in the following listing (we left out the tasks associated with the targets; we'll cover them later).

The project is a group of related targets. Although you can define any target you like, a set of standard naming conventions exists, as we discuss in the section "Standard Targets."

```
<project name="myproject" default="all" basedir=".">

    <target name="all" depends="clean,fetch,build,test,docs,deploy">
        ...
    </target>

    <target name="clean" >
        ...
    </target>

    <target name="fetch" >
        ...
    </target>

    <target name="build" depends="clean" >
        ...
    </target>

    <target name="test" depends="build" >
        ...
    </target>


    <target name="docs" depends="clean" >
        ...
    </target>


    <target name="deploy" depends="build, test" >
        ...
    </target>

    <target name="publish" depends="deploy" >
        ...
    </target>

</project>
```

This listing contains a build target that could, for example, compile the source and create JAR and WAR files. Notice that the build target depends on the execution of the tasks associated with the clean target (the tasks are not shown). The test target in turn depends on the build target. The order of the dependencies expressed with the target's "depend" attribute in this example is quite logical. For example, you can't test the code if it does not build—after the code is built, it's tested.

You can give targets any name that you like. However, people generally use common Ant names to create buildfiles, as discussed in the next section.

Standard Targets

Steve Loughran wrote an Ant guide called *Ant In Anger*. This guide explains many pitfalls and recommends ways to use Ant. Two very useful suggestions are a list of names for targets and how to divide buildfiles.

The following are some of Steve's recommended names for Ant top-level targets:

- ❏ **test:** Run the junit tests.
- ❏ **clean:** Clean out the output directories.
- ❏ **deploy:** Ship the JARs, WARs, and so on to the execution system.
- ❏ **publish:** Output the source and binaries to any distribution site.
- ❏ **fetch:** Get the latest source from the CVS tree.
- ❏ **docs/javadocs:** Outputs the documentation.
- ❏ **all:** Perform clean, fetch, build, test, docs, and deploy.
- ❏ **main:** The default build process (usually build or build and test).

The following are some recommended names for Ant internal targets:

- ❏ **init:** Initialize properties and perform other intialization tasks; read in per-user property files.
- ❏ **init-debug:** Initialize debug properties.
- ❏ **init-release:** Initialize release properties.
- ❏ **compile:** Perform the actual compilation.
- ❏ **link/jar:** Make the JARs or equivalent.
- ❏ **staging:** Carry out any pre-deployment process in which the output is dropped off and then tested before being moved to the production site.

We'll discuss some of the thoughts from *Ant in Anger* in this chapter and the next; however, we strongly suggest that you read this guide, because it contains excellent guidelines for using Ant. The guide is included with the Ant binary distribution under the docs directory.

Before we go any further, let's look at a simple example to cement some of the concepts of Ant. The next section presents a straightforward buildfile.

Simple Example

Let's start with a very small, straight-forward example of using Ant. We will begin with the now-infamous "hello world" example. It will create an output directory and then compile a Java source file called HelloWorld.java to the output directory.

The Java source file HelloWorld.java is stored in ./src/xptoolkit as follows:

```
package xptoolkit;
public class HelloWorld{
    public static void main(String []args){
        System.out.println("Hello World!");
    }
}
```

The following ant buildfile, build.xml, compiles the source file:

```
<project name="hello" default="compile">

  <target name="prepare">
    <mkdir dir="/tmp/classes" />
  </target>

  <target name="compile" depends="prepare">
    <javac srcdir="./src" destdir="/tmp/classes" />
  </target>


</project>
```

When you run Ant from the command line, it looks for a buildfile called build.xml in the current working directory. To specify a buildfile with a different name, you must specify the buildfile name using the –buildfile command-line argument (discussed in detail later).

Notice that the hello project has targets called compile and prepare. The hello project specifies the compile target as the default target. The compile target has a task called javac, which compiles the location specified by srcdir to the directory specified by the "destdir" attribute. The built-in task javac compiles Java source. Because the default directory location for a project is the current working directory, the javac task will look for a directory called src (srcdir="./src") under the current working directory and compile the contents of the src directory to the /tmp/classes directory.

Notice that the compile target's "depends" attribute points to the prepare target (depends="prepare"). As a result, all the tasks associated with the prepare target will be executed before the tasks associated with the compile target. This is a good thing--otherwise, the javac task might try to compile the source code to a directory that did not exist.

As you can see, you can use the targets and their dependencies to logically build, deploy, and test a complex system. The next section shows you how to set up your Ant buildfiles.

Setting Up Your Environment

If you are running Unix, install Ant in ~/tools/ant; if you are running Windows, install Ant in c:\tools\ant. You can set up the environment variables in Windows by using the Control Panel. However, for your convenience, we created a Unix shell script (setenv.sh) and a Windows batch file (setenv.bat) to set up the needed environment variables.

Your UNIX setenv.sh should look something like this:

```
#
# Setup build environment variables using Bourne shell
#
export USR_ROOT=~
export JAVA_HOME=${USR_ROOT}/jdk1.5
export ANT_HOME=${USR_ROOT}/tools/ant
export PATH=${PATH}:${ANT_HOME}/bin
```

Your Windows setenv.bat should look something like this:

```
:
: Setup build environment variables using DOS Batch
:
set USR_ROOT=c:
set JAVA_HOME=%USR_ROOT%\jdk1.5set
CLASSPATH=%USR_ROOT%\jdk1.5\lib\tools.jar;%CLASSPATH%
set ANT_HOME=%USR_ROOT%\tools\Ant
PATH=%PATH%;%ANT_HOME%\bin
```

Both of these setup files begin by setting JAVA_HOME to specify the location where you installed the JDK. This setting should reflect your local development environment—make adjustments accordingly. Then, the files set up environment variable ANT_HOME, the location where you installed Ant. The examples in this book assume that you have installed Ant in c:\tools\ant on Windows and in ~/tools/ant on Unix; make adjustments if necessary. There are sample setup scripts as well the sample code at this book's Web site (www.wrox.com).

Running Ant for the First Time

To run the sample Ant buildfile, go to the directory that contains the project files. On our computer, they are stored under /CVS/XPToolKit/examples/chap4. The directory structure and files looks like this:

```
/CVS/XPToolKit/examples/chap4
    setenv.bat
    setenv.sh
    build.xml
        ./src/xptoolkit
            HelloWorld.java
```

To run Ant, navigate to the examples/chap4 directory and type ant. As stated earlier, Ant will find build.xml, which is the default name for the buildfile. For example, here is the command-line output you should expect:

```
$ ant
Buildfile: build.xml

prepare:
    [mkdir] Created dir: /tmp/classes

compile:
    [javac] Compiling 1 source file to /tmp/classes

BUILD SUCCESSFUL

Total time: 3 seconds
```

Notice that the targets and their associated tasks are displayed. That's it! We wrote our first Ant buildfile. In the next section, we describe how to use Ant properties.

Working with Properties

You'll often find it helpful to define properties. The properties in Ant are similar to the properties in java.lang.System.getProperites(). The properties can be set by the property task; so, the properties can also be set outside Ant. You can use properties for task attributes by placing the property name between "${" and "}", similar to the way environment variables are set in the Bourne shell. For example, if an "outputdir" property is set with the value "/tmp", then the "outputdir" property could accessed in an attribute of a task: ${outputdir}/classes would be a resolved to /tmp/classes.

Thus we could change the Ant buildfile to use properties as follows:

```
<project name="hello" default="compile">

  <property name="outputdir" value="/tmp"/>

  <target name="prepare">
    <mkdir dir="${outputdir}/classes" />
  </target>

  <target name="compile" depends="prepare">
    <javac srcdir="./src" destdir="${outputdir}/classes" />
  </target>

</project>
```

This Ant buildfile defines the "outputdir" property. Then, the buildfile uses the property in the "dir" attribute of the mkdir task of the prepare target and the "destdir" attribute of the javac task of the compile target. The property is used in many attributes; then, if it has to change, you only change it once. For example, if you change the location of the output directory using properties, you only have to make the change once, in one—not two—attribute assignments. Using properties this way can make your buildfiles flexible.

43

Paths, Filesets, Patternsets, and Selectors

Of course, your Java source files are unlikely to be as simple as the "hello world" example. You may need to use external libraries. For example, you may need to use one or more external libraries (JAR or ZIP files) with Java binaries to compile the source code of your project.

Ant can make it simple to set up the classpath for your project. You can use the path element tag, which can contain pathelement tags and filesets. There are two types of pathelements: path and location.

A location pathelement sets a single JAR or directory, and a path pathelement sets a colon- or semicolon-separated list of locations (directories and JARs) similar to the CLASSPATH environment variable. The fileset can define a group of files from one directory. This is convenient, for example, when all your library files (JAR files) are in one directory and you don't want to specify them by name. These concepts are much harder to explain than to show; so, look at the next example.

The following is a simple example that uses the Apache Log4J library file (log4j.jar) as if the HelloWorld.java source code needed it. The example shows several ways to set up the path:

```
<project name="hello" default="compile">

  <property name="lib" value="../lib"/>
  <property name="outputdir" value="/tmp"/>

  <path id="1">
    <pathelement location="." />
    <pathelement location="${lib}/log4j.jar"/>
  </path>

  <path id="2">
    <pathelement path=".;${lib}/log4j.jar"/>
  </path>

  <path id="3">
    <pathelement location="." />
    <fileset dir="${lib}">
        <include name="**/*.jar"/>
    </fileset>
  </path>

  <target name="compile">

    <javac srcdir="./src" destdir="${outputdir}/classes" >
        <classpath refid="1"/>
    </javac>

    <javac srcdir="./src" destdir="${outputdir}/classes" >
        <classpath refid="2"/>
    </javac>

    <javac srcdir="./src" destdir="${outputdir}/classes" >
        <classpath refid="3"/>
    </javac>
```

```
        <javac srcdir="./src" destdir="${outputdir}/classes" >
            <classpath id="1">
                <pathelement location="." />
                <pathelement location="${lib}/log4j.jar"/>
            </classpath>
        </javac>

    </target>
</project>
```

Notice that the three path tags define almost the same classpath, with the exception that the classpath with the id of 3 includes all JAR files that exist in ${lib}. Here the tags are repeated without the rest of the buildfile for clarity:

```
<path id="1">
  <pathelement location="." />
  <pathelement location="${lib}/log4j.jar"/>
</path>

<path id="2">
  <pathelement path=".;${lib}/log4j.jar"/>
</path>

<path id="3">
  <pathelement location="." />
  <fileset dir="${lib}">
      <include name="**/*.jar"/>
  </fileset>
</path>
```

Also notice that to use these three path tags with the javac task, you need only set the reference of the classpath element to the reference id of the paths defined previously. Here they are, referenced respective to the last example:

```
<javac srcdir="./src" destdir="${outputdir}/classes" >
    <classpath refid="1"/>
</javac>

<javac srcdir="./src" destdir="${outputdir}/classes" >
    <classpath refid="2"/>
</javac>

<javac srcdir="./src" destdir="${outputdir}/classes" >
    <classpath refid="3"/>
</javac>
```

It's important to note that the javac task with <classpath refid="1"/> would set the classpath to the path set defined by <path id="1">. This is called referring to a classpath *by reference*. In addition, you can refer to a path in-line using the classpath subtag in the javac task, demonstrated as follows:

```
<javac srcdir="./src" destdir="${outputdir}/classes" >
    <classpath id="1">
        <pathelement location="." />
```

```
            <pathelement location="${lib}/log4j.jar"/>
        </classpath>
    </javac>
```

There will be times when you need to build a fileset that includes some files and excludes others. For example:

```
<fileset dir="./src" casesensitive="yes">
  <include name="**/*.java"/>
  <exclude name="**/*BAD*"/>
</fileset>
```

This fileset is designed to pull all of the files within the ./src directory based on a case sensitive search and include all files with a .java extension in them. At the same time, the system needs to exclude any files with the text BAD embedded anywhere in the filename. You will also notice that through these examples, we've hardcoded the srcdir to be "./src". In most cases you will use a property name for the source files as well. For example, we would use:

```
<fileset dir="${src.dir}">
  <include name="**/*.java"/>
</fileset>
```

In this code example, we've set the source directory for the fileset to be ${src.dir}. We will of course need to set this property in the build file at some point.

Selectors

Now we've built our filesets using the criteria of the filename—the file has an extension of .java, appears in a directory trees, etc.—but what if we wanted to use other criteria? Ant allows additional criteria for file selection like these core selectors:

❑ **<contains>**: Select files based on whether or not they contain a specific text string. Its attributes are:

  ❑ test="value" where value is the text to test against.

  ❑ casesensitive="value" where value is true/false.

  ❑ ignorewhitespace="value" where value is true/false.

```
    <fileset dir="${src.dir}"
             includes="**/*.java"
     >
      <contains test"fullCode"/>
    </fileset>
```

❑ **<date>**: Select files based on their modification date.

  ❑ datetime="value" where value is the time to test against MM/DD/YY HH:MM AM or PM.

  ❑ millis="value" where value is the number of milliseconds since 1970 to test against.

  ❑ when="value" where value is before, after, equal.

```
<fileset dir="${src.dir}">
  <date
   datetime="2/2/2004 12:00 AM"
   when="after"
 />
</fileset>
```

❑ **<depend>:** Select files based on whether their modification date is recent when compared to other files.

  ❑ targetdir="value" where value is the directory to compare against.

  ❑ granularity="value" where value is the number of milliseconds to compare with.

```
<fileset dir="${src.dir}">
  <depend targetdir="dir"
          granularity="1000"
  />
</fileset>
```

❑ **<depth>:** Select files at a particular directory depth.

  ❑ min="value" where value is the minimum number of level below the base.

  ❑ max="value" where value is the maximum number of level below the base to be selected.

```
<fileset dir="${src.dir}"
        includes="**/*.java"
 >
  <depth min="1" max="4" />
</fileset>
```

❑ **<different>:** Select files that are different from other files.

  ❑ targetdir="value" where value equals the directory to compare files with.

  ❑ ignoreFileTimes="value" where value is true/false to determine if file times are ignored; default is true.

  ❑ granularity="value" where value is number of milliseconds used to determine if a file is different.

```
<fileset dir="${src.dir}">
  <different targetdir="dir"
             granularity="100"
  />
</fileset>
```

❑ **<filename>:** Select files based on filename, such as <include> and <exclude>.

  ❑ name="value" where value is the name of the file to include.

  ❑ casesensitive="value" where value is true/false.

  ❑ negate="value" where value is either true/false. A true value turns this selector into an exclude.

```
<fileset dir="${src.dir}">
  <filename name="FileF.java"/>
</fileset>
```

❑ **<present>:** Select files based on whether they exist or not in a specific location.

  ❑ targetdir="value" where value is the directory to compare against.

  ❑ present="value" where value is srconly and both. srconly means they only appear in the src directory and not the targetdir; both means the files are selected if they appear in both directories.

```
<fileset dir="${src.dir}">
  <present targetdir="deploy"/>
</fileset>
```

❑ **<containsregexp>:** Select files based on a regular expression.

  ❑ expression="value" where value is the regular expression.

```
<fileset dir="${src.dir}">
  <containsregexp expression="a[1..9]b"/>
</fileset>
```

❑ **<size>:** Select files based on their size.

  ❑ value="value" where value = filesize.

  ❑ units="value" where value = k, M, G or IEC standard. Not required.

  ❑ where="value" where value = less, more, equal.

```
<fileset dir="${src.dir}">
  <size value="5" units="Ki" when="more"/>
</fileset>
```

❑ **<type>:** Select files based on whether they are files or directories.

  ❑ type="value" where value = dir or file.

```
<fileset dir="${src.dir}">
  <type type="dir"/>
</fileset>
```

For an example of how to use the selectors, consider the following code that will only pull files with a size greater than 5 kb:

```
<fileset dir="${src.dir}">
  <size value="5" units="Ki" when="more"/>
</fileset>
```

In this fileset we are pulling all files that are more than 5 kb within the ${src.dir}. The units can be changed to be any of k, M, or G; if the units attribute is not included in the element, then the default is bytes.

If just one selector doesn't fit the needs of your <fileset>, you can use a Selector Container. The Selector Containers allow the various selectors to be combined with each other in a Boolean fashion. The current containers are:

❑ **<and>:** Select a file if it matches all contained selectors.

❑ **<majority>:** Select a file if it. matches a majority of the contained selectors.

❑ **<none>:** Select a file only it matches none of the contained selectors.

❑ **<not>:** Reverses the result of a single selector.

❑ **<or>:** Selects a file if it matches one contained selectors.

To see how the selector containers work, let's consider the <and>. For example:

```
<fileset dir="${src.dist}" includes="**/*.java">
    <and>
        <contains test="CoreCode" />
        <date datetime="12/31/2003 12:00 AM" when="after"/>
    </and>
</fileset>
```

In this fileset, we want to match all of the files with a .java extension that contain the text CoreCode and have a current modified date after 12/31/2003. If a file matches both of the selectors, contains and date, then it will match the <and> selector container. Clearly the use of the selectors and the containers provides for a quite complex and comprehensive way to choose files.

Patternsets

If you want to match a set of files but you aren't interested in the granularity of the selector but you still want to be able to reuse the matches, the patternset might be the answer. For example, we might have a set of files that match on the following filename criteria:

```
<include name="core/**/*.java"/>
<include name="extended/**/*.java" if="extended"/>
<exclude name="**/*BAD*"/>
```

These criteria will match all java files in the core directory structure as well as the files in the extended directory structure, but only if the extended property is set. In addition, the BAD files will be excluded. If this is a common fileset in your code, you can build a patternset. For example:

```
<patternset id="coreandextended">
  <include name="core/**/*.java"/>
  <include name="extended/**/*.java" if="extended"/>
  <exclude name="**/*BAD*"/>
</patternset>
```

This specific pattern of include and exclude elements can be referenced in fileset elements or a task that includes an implicit fileset just by using the id. For example:

```
<fileset>
  <patternset refid="coreandextended"/>
</fileset>
```

In addition to the <include> and <exclude> elements, the patternset supports the includes, includesfile, excludes, excludesfile attributes. The patternset id can be used within any Ant construct that allows the <patternset> element. For example, we could have a <patternset> like the following:

```
<patternset id="jarpath">
  <include name="prodjars/**/*.jar" unless="extended"/>
  <include name="devjars/**/*.jar" if="extended"/>
  <exclude name="**/*BAD*"/>
</patternset>
```

This patternset will include all jars in one of two paths, prodjars or devjars, based on the value of the extended property. This patternset could be used if you have specific jars used during production that don't include specific optimizations or logging found in the devevelopment jars. When we build a <target> for compiling our project, we will include a <path> element that uses the patternset. For example:

```
<path id="base.path">
  <pathelement path="${classpath}"/>
    <fileset>
        <patternset refid="jarpath"/>
    </fileset>
  <pathelement location="classes"/>
</path>
```

Finally, we would build a <target> using the path id which uses our patternset id:

```
<target>

  <javac>

 <classpath refid="base.path">

  </javac>

</target>
```

Conditional Targets

You don't always have to execute a target. You can write targets that are executed only when a certain property is set or when a certain property is not set. For example, let's say we need to run a buildfile in the Windows XP (no pun intended) development environment and the Solaris production environment. Our development environment does not have the same directory structure as our production environment; thus, we may write a script that looks like this:

```
<project name="hello" default="run">

  <target name="setupProduction" if="production">

      <property name="lib" value="/usr/home/production/lib"/>
      <property name="outputdir" value="/usr/home/production/classes"/>

  </target>
```

```
    <target name="setupDevelopment" unless="production">

        <property name="lib" value="c:/hello/lib"/>
        <property name="outputdir" value="c:/hello/classes"/>

    </target>

    <target name="setup" depends="setupProduction,setupDevelopment"/>

    <target name="run" depends="setup">
      <echo message="${lib} ${outputdir}" />
    </target>


</project>
```

Notice that the setupDevelopment target uses unless="production". This means the target should be executed unless the production property is set. Also notice that the setupProduction target uses if="production". This means to execute this target only if the production property is set. Now we need to set the property (or not set it) to control the behavior of the tasks.

To set a property when you execute Ant, you need to pass the property to Ant. This technique is similar to the way you would pass a system property to the Java interpreter. When you execute Ant, you pass the argument –Dproduction=true (it does not have to equal true, it just has to be set). Following is an example of running the buildfile (build2.xml) in production mode:

```
C:\...\chap2>ant -buildfile build2.xml -Dproduction=true
Buildfile: build2.xml

setupProduction:

setupDevelopment:

setup:

run:
      [echo] /usr/home/production/lib /usr/home/production/classes

BUILD SUCCESSFUL

Total time: 0 seconds
```

From this output, we can see that run was the default target for the project. The run target depended on setup, which depended on our two conditional targets (depends="setupProduction,setupDevelopment"). Thus, because we set the production property on the command line (-Dproduction=true) the setupProduction target was executed rather than setupDevelopment. Running setupProduction sets the "outputdir" and "lib" properties to their Unix environment values. We can see this by looking at the output of the run target's echo task (<echo message="${lib} ${outputdir}" />), which displays the following:

```
run:
      [echo] /usr/home/production/lib /usr/home/production/classes
```

What happens when you have deployment descriptor files that differ between the two environments? You use filters, as discussed in the next section.

Using Filters

Filters can be used to replace tokens in a file with their proper values for that particular environment. One scenario that comes to mind follows the example in the previous section. Let's say we have a production database and a development database. When deploying to production or development, we want the values in our deployment descriptor or properties file that refer to the JDBC URL of the needed database to refer to the correct database:

```
<project name="hello" default="run">

  <target name="setupProduction" if="production">

<filter token="jdbc_url" value="jdbc::production"/>

  </target>

  <target name="setupDevelopment" unless="production">

<filter token="jdbc_url" value="jdbc::development"/>

  </target>

  <target name="setup" depends="setupProduction,setupDevelopment"/>

  <target name="run" depends="setup">

    <copy todir="/usr/home/production/properties" filtering="true">
      <fileset dir="/cvs/src/properties"/>
    </copy>

  </target>

</project>
```

Again, setupProudction and setupDevelopment are executed conditionally based on the production property. But this time, instead of setting properties, they set filters as follows:

```
  <target name="setupProduction" if="production">

<filter token="jdbc_url" value="jdbc::production"/>

  </target>

  <target name="setupDevelopment" unless="production">

<filter token="jdbc_url" value="jdbc::development"/>

  </target>
```

The filter in the setupProduction target sets jdbc_url to jdbc::production. The filter in the setup-Development target sets jdbc_url to jdbc::development. The copy task in the run target turns on filtering, which applies the filter to all in the fileset. Thus, the copy task will copy recursively all the files from the /cvs/src/properties directory into the /usr/home/production/properties directory, replacing all the occurrences of the string "@jdbc_url@" with "jdbc::production" if the "production" property is set or jdbc::development if the "production" property is not set.

Of particular warning here is the fact that any file in the given fileset will be searched for the @filter@ string and this includes binary files. There is a good chance a binary file will become corrupt during the 'filter' process therefore, only text files should be in the copied from directory.

Filtersets

As you might expect, we can have more than one filter in our target that needs to be replaced. Building on our previous example, in addition to the jdbc_url, there is also a specific table within the database that we need to access. The code has been written such that the table name is used through the many SQL statements. Thus, we will have another filter like

```
    <target name="setupProduction" if="production">

  <filter token="jdbc_url" value="jdbc::production"/>
  <filter token="table" value="accounts"/>

    </target>

    <target name="setupDevelopment" unless="production">

  <filter token="jdbc_url" value="jdbc::development"/>
  <filter token="table " value="tempacc"/>

    </target>
```

When the –D command-line option is provided, both of the <filter> elements will be executed by the <copy> command. Of course, this isn't going to work for us because the <copy> element is pulling the properties file and not the source code. So let's look at another option for filtering that uses the concept of a filterset. Filtersets are designed to:

❏   Group like filters.

❏   Assign a reference ID to the filterset.

❏   Choose the begintoken and endtoken.

For example, we might build a filterset containing several filters that will be used to change our source code as well as the jdbc_url:

```
    <project name="hello" default="run">

  <target name="setupProduction" if="production">

  <filter token="jdbc_url" value="jdbc::production"/>
```

```
            <filterset id="myFilterSet" begintoken="(*)" endtoken="(*)">
              <filter token="TABLE" value="accounts"/>
              <filter token="USERNAME" value="fullprod"/>
            </filterset>


      </target>

      <target name="setupDevelopment" unless="production">

    <filter token="jdbc_url" value="jdbc::development"/>

            <filterset id="myFilterSet" begintoken="(*)" endtoken="(*)">
              <filter token="TABLE" value="tempacc"/>
              <filter token="USERNAME" value="readtemp"/>
            </filterset>


      </target>

      <target name="setup" depends="setupProduction,setupDevelopment">

        <copy toDir="${build.dir}">
          <filterset refid="myFilterSet"/>
          <fileset dir="${cvssrc.dir}"/>
        </copy>

      </target>

      <target name="run" depends="setup">

        <copy todir="/usr/home/production/properties" filtering="true">
          <fileset dir="/cvs/src/properties"/>
        </copy>

      </target>

   </project>
```

In this example, we've added two filtersets to the production and development targets. There are a few new attributes to discuss within the filtersets. The first is the id used to assign a value to the filterset which can be used with a refid elsewhere throughout the build file. The second is the use of the begintoken and endtoken attributes. Typically, the filtering will check to find the replacement text using the matching text of @value@ but using a filterset allows us to change those values. In our example, we've changed them to (*)value(*).

We've also added another <copy> element to the build script within the setup target. Here we will be pulling the source code from a directory where the source code was pulled from CVS and placing the new files in a build directory. During the copy, the system will filter the code and replace our TABLE and USERNAME values depending on the production property. Notice we've used the refid attribute to specify the filterset to use in our example.

FilterChains and FilterReaders

If you have been a Unix developer, you have probably come to take the redirection abilities of the shell for granted. It is not uncommon to do things like this:

```
ps —ef  | grep myprocess | more
```

This command sequence says to first obtain a listing of the currently executing processes, store the results in a temporary buffer, pass the buffer to the application called grep which will return any lines in the buffer with the text myprocess in it and finally control the output of the text to the screen using the more command. The | symbol which is called a pipe allows the chaining together of the various Unix shell commands.

As you might expect, this capability was one of the common requests of the Ant team and it has been delivered in the form of FilterChains and FilterReaders. A FilterChain is basically a grouping of FilterReaders which are either user defined or built-in generic filters. Let's look at an example before getting into specifics. Here is a filterchain that will pull all of the lines in the source code that contains one of two strings "Today's Date Is" or "date is". Those strings which contain the strings will be further passed to the <replacetokens> filter which will update the @DATE @ strings with today's date. The FilterChain allows for the piping of various FilterReaders.

```
<copy toDir="${src.dir}" tofile="${dest.file}">
  <filterchain>
  <linecontains>
          <contains value="Today's Date Is">
          <contains value="date is">
  </linecontains>
  <replacetokens>
        <token key="DATE" value="${TODAY}"/>
  </replacetokens>
   </filterchain>

  <fileset dir="${cvssrc.dir}"/>
</copy>
```

FilterChains can be used in several tasks including concat, copy, loadfile, loadproperties, and move. The built-in FilterReaders are defined here:

❑   **ClassConstants:** This is a built-in filter that will pull all of the constants defined in a specific Java class and output those constants as Ant property values. For example:

```
<loadproperties srcfile="FileFReader.class">
  <filterchain>
    <classconstants/>
  </filterchain>
</loadproperties>
```

In this example, the constants found in the class FileFReader will be extracted in the format of name=value.

❑ **ConcatFilter:** This is a built-in filter that will either prepend or append a specific file to all of the files pulled as part of the filter or copy. For example:

```
<copy toDir="${src.dir}" tofile="${dest.file}">
  <filterchain>
  <concatfilter prepend="source2.txt">
  </filterchain>
  <fileset dir="${cvssrc.dir}"/>
</copy>
```

❑ **DeleteCharacters:** This is built-in filter that will remove specific characters from the supplied data. You can use backslashes in the specific removal string. For example:

```
<loadfile srcfile="myfile.txt" property="${filehead}">
  <filterchain>
    <deletecharacters chars="bad"/>
  </filterchain>
</loadfile>
```

❑ **EscapeUnicode:** This is a built-in filter that will convert all non-ASCII characters to their escaped equivalent. For example:

```
<filterchain>
  <escapeunicode/>
</filterchain>
```

❑ **ExpandProperties:** This is a built-in filter that will search through the supplied data and substitute a value for all Ant properties of the form ${ name }. For example, if we have a file called header.txt with an Ant style variable of ${url}, then the following filter will replace it with www.company.com.

```
<property name="url" value="www.company.com" />
<loadfile property="myfile" srcFile="header.txt">
  <filterchain>
    <expandproperties/>
  </filterchain>
</loadfile>
```

❑ **FilterReader:** The FilterReader filter is a base filter used to allow a developer the ability to create their own filters.

❑ **HeadFilter:** This is a built-in filter that reads x lines from a file and optionally skips y number of lines and places the lines in a specific property For example:

```
<loadfile srcfile="myfile.txt" property="${filehead}">
  <filterchain>
    <headfilter lines="25"/>
  </filterchain>
</loadfile>
```

If you need to skips some lines first before capturing then use the skip attribute. For example:

```
<loadfile srcfile="myfile.txt" property="${filehead}">
  <filterchain>
    <headfilter lines="25" skip="5"/>
  </filterchain>
</loadfile>
```

❑ **LineContains:** This is a built-in filter that pulls lines which contain a specific text string. For example, this filter will read the myfile.txt file, look for a couple string and place the results in the myfile property.

```
<loadfile srcfile="myfile.txt" property="myfile">
  <filterchain>
    <linecontains>
      <contains value="DATE">
      <contains value="New Name">
    </linecontains>
  </filterchain>
</loadfile>
```

❑ **LineContainsRegExp:** This is a built-in filter that works in the same manner can LineContains but instead we have the ability to be a regular expression. For example:

```
<loadfile srcfile="myfile.txt" property="myfile">
  <filterchain>
    <linecontainsregexp>
      <regexp pattern="date*">
    </linecontainsregexp>
  </filterchain>
</loadfile>
```

❑ **PrefixLines:** This is a built-in filter that will append a specific text string to all lines. For example:

```
<loadfile srcfile="myfile.txt" property="myfile">
  <filterchain>

    <prefixlines prefix="DONE" />
  </filterchain>
</loadfile>
```

❑ **ReplaceTokens:** This is a built-in filter that works in the same manner as the <filter> element by replacing specific tokens within the data. There is also the option of changing the begin and end tokens. For example:

```
<loadfile srcfile="myfile.txt" property="myfile">
  <filterchain>
    <replacetokens>
      <token key="DATE" value="${today}">
      <tokenchar begintoken="(*)"
                 endtoken="**" />
    </replacetokens>
  </filterchain>
</loadfile>
```

❑ **StripJavaComments:** This is a built-in filter that strips all comments from the data. For example:

```
<loadfile srcfile="myfile.java" property="myfile">
  <filterchain>

    <stringjavacomments />
  </filterchain>
</loadfile>
```

❑ **StripLineBreaks:** This is a built-in filter that strips all linebreaks from the data. The default line-break is '\r\n\ but can be changed with the linebreaks param. For example:

```
<loadfile srcfile="myfile.java" property="myfile">
  <filterchain>
    <striplinebreaks />
  </filterchain>
</loadfile>
```

To change the linebreak characters, use the following example:

```
<loadfile srcfile="myfile.java" property="myfile">
  <filterchain>
    <striplinebreaks>
   <linebreaks="[]"/>
    </striplinebreaks>
  </filterchain>
</loadfile>
```

❑ **StripLineComments:** This is a built-in filter that will remove all lines that begin with specific comment characters. For example:

```
<loadfile srcfile="myfile.java" property="myfile">
  <filterchain>
<striplinecomments>
 <comment value="//"/>
</striplinecomments>
  </filterchain>
</loadfile>
```

❑ **TabsToSpaces:** This is a built-in filter that will convert all tabs into a specific number of spaces. The default number of spaces is 8. For example:

```
<loadfile srcfile="myfile.java" property="myfile">
  <filterchain>

    <striplinebreaks />
  </filterchain>
</loadfile>
```

To change the number of spaces:

```
<loadfile srcfile="myfile.java" property="myfile">
  <filterchain>

    <striplinebreaks>
      <lines="5"/>
    </striplinebreaks>
  </filterchain>
</loadfile>
```

❏ **TailFilter:** This is a built-in filter that reads the tail of the supplied data in the opposite fashion as the HeadFilter. For example:

```
<loadfile srcfile="myfile.txt" property="myFile">
  <filterchain>
    <tailfilter lines="25"/>
  </filterchain>
</loadfile>
```

Nested Builds

Each project (library module, Web application, set of Enterprise JavaBeans, applet, and so on) should have its own directory with its own buildfile. A large project can depend on lots of other projects. Ant allows one Ant buildfile to call another. Thus, you may have an Ant file that calls a hierarchy of other Ant buildfiles. You can nest buildfiles using this method to build many projects and their dependent projects.

The ant task runs a specified buildfile. The ant task can be used to build subprojects and related projects. You have the option of specifying the buildfile name or just the directory (the file build.xml in the directory specified by the "dir" attribute is used). You also have the option of specifying a particular target to execute. If you do not specify a target to execute, the default target is used. Any properties that you set in the called project are available to the nested buildfile.

The following are some examples of calling another Ant buildfile from your Ant buildfile. We can call a buildfile from the current buildfile and pass a property as follows:

```
<ant antfile="./hello/build.xml">
    <property name="production" value="true"/>
</ant>
We can call a buildfile from the current buildfile. When you call the ant
task, if you don't specify an antfile attribute, then it will use
./hello/build.xml) as follows:<ant dir="./hello"/>
```

Notice above that we only specified the directory. The default buildfile is build.xml; if you only specify the directory, then build.xml is assumed.

We can call a buildfile from the current buildfile and specify that the run target should execute (if the run target was not the default target, it would execute anyway) as follows:

```
<ant antfile="./hello/build.xml"  target="run"/>
```

Listeners and Loggers

Keeping track of what Ant is doing during a build is important for the Configuration Management team as well as the developers. Ant provides two different mechanisms to handle the tracking including listeners and loggers. A listener is triggered based on seven events:

❑ Build started

❑ Build finished

❑ Target started

❑ Target finished

❑ Task started

❑ Task finished

❑ Message logged

The Ant supplied loggers are used within the Ant command-line process. For example:

```
ant —logger <loggerclassname>
```

The loggers are:

❑ **DefaultLogger:** This is the standard output produced by Ant when no –logger command-line class is provided. As an example, using a version simple build.xml script, the command line

```
ant —logger org.apache.tools.ant.DefaultLogger
```

produces the following output:

```
Buildfile: build.xml

all:

clean:

build:
    [mkdir] Created dir: /home/node2/hello/classes
    [javac] Compiling 1 source file to /home/node2/hello/classes

build:

jar:
    [mkdir] Created dir: /home/node2/hello/dist/lib
     [jar] Building jar:
/home/node2/hello/dist/lib/HelloWorld.jar

BUILD SUCCESSFUL
Total time: 1 minute 15 seconds
```

❑ **NoBannerLogger:** This logger will eliminate the empty targets from the output. Using the same build script as above, the command line

```
ant —logger org.apache.tools.ant.nobannerLogger
```

produces the following output:

```
Buildfile: build.xml

build:
    [mkdir] Created dir: /home/node2/hello/classes
    [javac] Compiling 1 source file to /home/node2/hello/classes

jar:
    [mkdir] Created dir: /home/node2/hello/dist/lib
      [jar] Building jar:
/home/node2/hello/dist/lib/HelloWorld.jar

BUILD SUCCESSFUL
Total time: 27 seconds
```

Notice how the empty targets are not displayed.

❑ **MailLogger:** If you would like to send emails to users based on the output from the Ant build, you can use the MailLogger. There are numerous property to be set with MailLogger. The specific ones are:

  ❑ **MailLogger.mailhost:** The host for the mailer.

  ❑ **MailLogger.user:** The user to use if authorization is required on your mailer.

  ❑ **MailLogger.password:** The password to use if authorization is required on your mailer.

  ❑ **MailLogger.from:** The from address for the mailer.

  ❑ **MailLogger.replyto:** The replyto address for the mailer.

  ❑ **MailLogger.failure.to:** A comma-separated list of email addresses.

  ❑ **MailLogger.success.to:** A comma-separated list of email addresses.

To use the MailLogger, set the above property in the build script and execute Ant with the following command-line:

```
ant -logger org.apache.tools.ant.listener.MailLogger
```

After the build has executed, the specified users in the failure.to or success.to properties will be sent the test from the DefaultLogger.

The Ant loggers works with the listeners to provide output to standard print streams as well as specific a logging level.

❑ **XmlLogger:** This logger will produce an XML file called log.xml with the Ant output. The command line is:

```
ant -listener org.apache.tools.ant.XmlLogger
```

The resulting output is quite extensive and provides many different outputs from the build.

Common Tasks

Ant includes quite a few common tasks already implemented, several of which we've discussed already (the javac and copy elements, for instance). In this section we will explore some of the other common tasks that will be useful in your quest of automating java builds. The following tasks aren't the only ones available, so you should consult the Ant documentation for a complete list.

BuildNumber

If you would like to have Ant keep track of a build number for you, then the BuildNumber task can be used. This task will attempt to read a number from a specific file, increment the number and then write the number back to the file. If a file is not specified, the task will try to open a file called build.number. The format of the task is:

```
<buildnumber/>
<buildnumber file="version"/>
```

Chmod

If you are working under a Unix-based file system, you can use the chmod task to change the permissions on a file or set of files. For example:

```
<chmod perm="w+w">
  <fileset dir="dist">
    <include name="**/deploy/**"/>
  </fileset>
</chmod>
```

This chmod common task will set all files within the deploy path to world writable.

CVS

If you use the CVS version-control software package, you will want to take advantage of Ant's common task called cvs that enables you to pull code from the repository. Here's an example task:

```
<cvs cvsRoot=":pserver:node2@localhost:/home/node2/repository"
     package="HelloWorld"
     dest="${cvs.dir}"
  />
```

This task will log into a CVS server on the local machine, extract the project called HelloWorld and place the resulting files in the cvs.dir directory. There are many options to the cvs common task, so consult the Ant manual. See also chapter 3 of this book for more information about CVS.

Parallel

There may be times when you need to execute numerous Ant tasks at the same time or without waiting for one task to complete before starting another one. A good example is creating a task for starting up a project once it has been built. If you need to start more than one VM, you will need to use the parallel task. For example:

```
<project>

 <target name="start">

        <parallel>
                <java... VM 1 here>
                <java... VM 2 here>
        </parallel>

 </target>

</project>
```

In this example, specifying a target of start will cause two Java Virtual Machines to be started without one VM having to execute before the second one starts.

Jar

In most cases the result of an Ant build will or should be a JAR file. The JAR task can be used for this purpose. Here's an example of the task:

```
<jar destfile="${deploy}/lib/app.jar"
        basedir="${build}/classes"
 />
```

This task will take all of the class files found in the ${build} directory and place them in a JAR file called app, which it then places in the ${deploy}/lib directory.

Mappers

When we create a target that pulls specific files such as the compile sequence, we know that the .java files will be converted to .class files. For the most part, we only specify the source files but not the target files. It just so happens that Ant handles all of the details for us using a mapper class; the specific mapper is called FileNameMapper. If you need to change the way the mapping is performed from source to target files, a <mapper> element should be used. The basic format of the <mapper> element is:

```
<mapper
 type="mapper type"
 classname="the classname of the mapper if not built-in"
 classpath="the classpath to find the class specified in classname"
 classpathref="a reference to use for the classpath"
 from="depends on the mapper"
 to="depends on the mapper"
 />
```

Ant includes a number of built-in mappers:

❑   **Identity:** This mapper will use the source name as the target name. For example:

```
<depend targetdir="build/classes">
```

```
        <mapper type="identity"/>
    </depend>
```

If the source filename is FileFReader.java then the target will be FileFReader.java.

❑ **Flatten:** This mapper will strip all path information from the source file name and set the target to just the filename itself. For example:

```
    <depend targetdir="build/classes">
        <mapper type="flatten"/>
    </depend>
```

If the source filename is /usr/local/FileReader, then the target will be FileReader.

❑ **Merge:** This mapper will ignore the source filename and output a specific target value. For example:

```
    <depend targetdir="build/classes">
        <mapper type="merge" to="outputName.txt"/>
    </depend>
```

If the source filename is File.txt, then the output will be outputName.txt.

❑ **Glob:** This mapper will match files based on the 'to' expression which needs to contain a single * wildcard, and it produce a target file using the matched text and the pattern in the 'from' expression. For example:

```
    <depend targetdir="build/classes">
        <mapper type="glob" from="*.java" to="*.java.txt"/>
    </depend>
```

❑ **Regexp:** This mapper works in a similar manner as glob, but instead both the 'to' and 'from' expressions are allowed to be regular expressions. The values of \0-\9 are used as references to the specific matches from the 'from' expression. For example:

```
    <depend targetdir="build/classes">
        <mapper type="regexp" from="*a[1..9]" to="\0java.txt"/>
    </depend>
```

For this example, we would match on anya3 and the results would be anyjava.txt.

❑ **Package:** This mapper will convert from a / delimited filepath to one with periods. For example:

```
    <depend targetdir="build/classes">
        <mapper type="package" from="*.java" to="New-*"/>
    </depend>
```

For this example, the filename /usr/local/file would become New-usr.local.file.

❑ **Unpackage:** This mapper will convert from a period based filepath to one with / characters.

Conclusion

This chapter covered the basics of using Ant and the concepts of buildfiles, projects, targets, conditional targets, tasks, filesets, filters, nested buildfiles, and properties. Our discussion included the basics styles and naming conventions for Ant buildfiles.

The chapter also explained the importance of Ant in its relationship to continuous integration. Chapter 4 uses these basics to build sample Java applications, and chapter 5 uses this information to build J2EE applications. By the end of Chapter 11, you should be able to build and deploy the following: Enterprise JavaBeans, Web components (servlets and JSPs), applets, and Java applications. You should also be able to combine these elements into projects and subprojects that can be easily managed and deployed on both a production and development environment.

Building Java Applications with Ant

This chapter explains the techniques involved in using Ant to build and deploy Java applications in an orchestrated fashion. Once you understand these fundamental techniques, you will be ready for the complexities of Chapter 6, "Building J2EE Applications with Ant," in which we build a Model 2 application complete with EJBs, servlets, and JSPs.

During the course of this chapter, we will build a "Hello World" example. Because the emphasis is on how to *build* components with Ant—and not the mechanics of implementing these various components—the example is meant to be as simple as possible. We will package the application and the common JAR, construct a buildfile that creates an applet, and construct a master buildfile that coordinates the entire build.

The source code for the Hello World example is divided into several directories. Each directory has its own Ant buildfile, which contains instructions to compile the components and package the binaries. Each directory also includes the requisite configuration files (such as manifest files). The master Ant buildfile, located in the root directory, calls the other buildfiles and coordinates the entire build.

This divide-and-conquer technique for organizing components into separate directories is quite common with Ant. It may seem like overkill on a simple project like this one, but consider building a system with 50 components. Each component has its own set of deployment descriptors and configuration files, and each component is deployed in different containers. The divide-and-conquer technique becomes necessary to mange the complexity—it also makes it easier to reuse components.

Following is the directory structure for the Hello World project. We will use this same structure for the more complex example in Chapter 6:

```
Model 2 Hello World root
+---Model
+---Application
+---Applet
+---WebApplication
+---EJBeans
```

The Model directory holds the common code (in this simple project, only the application will access the common code). The Application directory holds the Java application code, including the manifest file that marks the deployment JAR as executable. The Applet directory holds the applet code. The WebApplication and EJBeans directories are discussed in Chapter 6.

Hello World Model Project

In Chapter 4 we used a Hello World example that was contained in one file. The Hello World example in this chapter is more complex because it uses several classes.

This section explains the basic structure for all the buildfiles and directories you use in this example and the rest of the book. We introduce the three Java class files: a GreetingBean class, a GreetingFactory class, and a Greeting interface. Then, we discuss how to build these files with Ant and break down the Ant buildfiles' target execution step by step. We also explain how to use the Ant command-line utility to build the files with Ant.

Overview of Model Classes

The GreetingFactory knows how to create a Greeting object. Here is the listing for the GreetingFactory:

```
package xptoolkit.model;

public class GreetingFactory {
    private GreetingFactory(){}

    public Greeting getGreeting()throws Exception {
     String clazz = System.getProperty("Greeting.class",
                             "xptoolkit.model.GreetingBean");
        return (Greeting)Class.forName(clazz).newInstance();
    }

    public static GreetingFactory getGreetingFactory(){
        return new GreetingFactory();
    }

}
```

Next we have a Greeting interface that defines the contract of a Greeting object—that is, what type of behavior it supports. The Greeting interface is as follows:

```
package xptoolkit.model;

public interface Greeting extends java.io.Serializable{
    public String getGreeting();
}
```

Finally, the GreetingBean class implements the Greeting Interface. GreetingBean is defined as follows:

```
package xptoolkit.model;

public class GreetingBean implements Greeting{

    public GreetingBean(){}

    public String getGreeting(){
      return "Hello World!";
    }
}
```

The GreetingBean returns the message "Hello World!" just like the message in the Chapter 4 application. To create a Greeting instance, you use the GreetingFactory. The default implementation of the GreetingFactory gets the implementation class from a property and instantiates an instance of that class with the Class.forName().newInstance() method. It casts the created instance to the Greeting interface.

These two lines of code create the Greeting instance from the GreetingFactory's getGreeting() method:

```
String clazz = System.getProperty("Greeting.class",
                    "xptoolkit.model.GreetingBean");
return (Greeting)Class.forName(clazz).newInstance();
```

Thus any class that implements the Greeting interface can be substituted as the Greeting.class system property. Then, when the class is instantiated with the factory's getGreeting() method, the application uses the new implementation of the Greeting interface.

We use this technique in Chapter 6 to add support for EJBs to the Web application seamlessly. We create an Ant script that can deploy the same Web application to use either enterprise beans or another bean implementation just by setting an Ant property. Later, we also map the Greeting interface with the use bean action of a JSP when we implement the Model 2 using servlets and JSP.

Creating a Project Directory Structure for Model

This part of the sample application uses the smallest buildfile. Basically, we just need to create a JAR file that acts as a common library. We don't need any special manifest file or deployment files. This is the most basic buildfile and directory structure you will see in this example. Here is the directory structure for the Model directory:

```
Root of Model
|    build.xml
|
+---src
    +---xptoolkit
        \---model
                GreetingFactory.java
                Greeting.java
                GreetingBean.java
```

Notice that there are only four files in the Model directory and subdirectories. Also notice that the name of the Ant file is build.xml. Remember from Chapter 4 that build.xml is the default buildfile; if Ant is run in this directory, it automatically finds build.xml without you having to specify it on the command line. Let's dig into the model buildfile.

Creating a Buildfile for a Shared Library

The model buildfile has six targets: setProps, init, clean, delete, prepare, compile, package, and all. The buildfiles in this example have similar targets:

❏ **setProps:** Sets up the output directory ("outputdir") property if it is not already set. This behavior is important so we can easily set a different output directory from the command line or from another buildfile that invokes this buildfile, and yet have a reasonable default.

❏ **init:** Initializes all the other properties relative to the "outputdir" property defined in the setProps target; init depends on setProps.

❏ **clean:** Cleans up the output directories and the output JAR file.

❏ **prepare:** Creates the output directories if they do not already exist.

❏ **compile:** Compiles the Java source files for the model into the build directory defined in the init target.

❏ **package:** Packages the compiled Java source into a JAR file.

❏ **all:** Runs all the tags. It is the default target of this build project.

Analysis of the Model Project Buildfile

The following listing shows the entire buildfile for the model project. In this section we provide a step by step analysis of how this buildfile executes. All the buildfiles in the Hello World example are structured in a similar fashion, so understanding the model project's buildfile is essential to understanding the others. A quick note on naming conventions: As you see from the first line of code in the next listing, the project name for this buildfile is model. Thus we refer to this buildfile as the *model project buildfile*. This naming convention becomes essential once we begin dealing with the five other buildfiles in this project.

```
<project name="model" default="all" >


    <target name="setProps" unless="setProps"
                        description="setup the properties.">
        <property name="outdir" value="/tmp/app/" />
```

```
    </target>

    <target name="init" depends="setProps"
                        description="initialize the properties.">
        <tstamp/>
        <property name="local_outdir" value="${outdir}/model" />
        <property name="build" value="${local_outdir}/classes" />
        <property name="lib" value="${outdir}/lib" />
        <property name="model_jar" value="${lib}/greetmodel.jar" />
    </target>

    <target name="clean" depends="init"
                    description="clean up the output directories and jar.">
        <delete dir="${local_outdir}" />
        <delete file="${model_jar}" />
    </target>

    <target name="prepare" depends="init"
                        description="prepare the output directory.">
        <mkdir dir="${build}" />
        <mkdir dir="${lib}" />
    </target>

    <target name="compile" depends="prepare"
                        description="compile the Java source.">
        <javac srcdir="./src" destdir="${build}" />
    </target>

    <target name="package" depends="compile"
                    description="package the Java classes into a jar.">
        <jar jarfile="${model_jar}"
            basedir="${build}" />
    </target>

    <target name="all" depends="clean,package"
                    description="perform all targets."/>

</project>
```

Let's go over the model project buildfile and each of its targets in the order they execute. First, the model project sets the all target as the default target, as follows:

```
<project name="model" default="all" >
```

The all target is executed by default, unless we specify another target as a command-line argument of Ant. The all target depends on the clean and package targets. The clean target depends on the init target. The init target depends on the setProps target, and thus the setProps target is executed first.

Following is the setProps target defined in build.xml:

```
<target name="setProps" unless="setProps"
                        description="setup the properties.">
    <property name="outdir" value="/tmp/app/" />
</target>
```

The setProps target executes only if the "setProps" property is not set (unless="setProps"). Thus, if a parent buildfile calls this buildfile, it can set the "setProps" property and override the value of outdir so that the setProps target of this file does not execute (we give an example of this later). If the setProps target executes, it sets the value of outdir to /tmp/app.

Next, the init target is executed. Following is the init target defined in build.xml:

```
<target name="init" depends="setProps"
                    description="initialize the properties.">
    <tstamp/>

    <property name="local_outdir" value="${outdir}/model" />
    <property name="build" value="${local_outdir}/classes" />
    <property name="lib" value="${outdir}/lib" />
    <property name="model_jar" value="${lib}/greetmodel.jar" />
</target>
```

The init target uses the tstamp task to get the current time, which is used by the javac task to see if a source file is out of data and needs to be compiled. The init target defines several properties that refer to directories and files needed to compile and deploy the model project. We will discuss the meaning of these properties because all the other buildfiles for this example use the same or similar properties. The init target defines the following properties:

❑ The "local_outdir" property defines the output directory of all the model project's intermediate files (Java class files).

❑ The "build" property defines the output directory of the Java class files.

❑ The "lib" property defines the directory that holds the common code libraries (JAR files) used for the whole Model 2 Hello World example application.

❑ The "model_jar" property defines the output JAR file for this project.

> **As a general rule, if you use the same literal twice, you should go ahead and define it in the init target. You don't know how many times we've shot ourselves in the foot by not following this rule. This buildfile is fairly simple, but the later ones are more complex. Please learn from our mistakes (and missing toes).**

Now that all the clean target's dependencies have executed, the clean target can execute. The clean target deletes the intermediate files created by the compile and the output common JAR file, which is the output of this project. Here is the code for the clean target:

```
<target name="clean" depends="init"
        description="clean up the output directories and jar.">

  <delete dir="${local_outdir}" />
  <delete file="${model_jar}" />

</target>
```

Remember that the all target depends on the clean and package targets. The clean branch and all its dependencies have now executed, so it is time to execute the package target branch (a *branch* is a target and all its dependencies). The package target depends on the compile target, the compile target depends on the prepare target, and the prepare target depends on the init target, which has already been executed.

Thus, the next target that executes is prepare, because all its dependencies have already executed. The prepare target creates the build output directory, which ensures that the lib directory is created. The prepare target is defined as follows:

```
<target name="prepare" depends="init"
                description="prepare the output directory.">

    <mkdir dir="${build}" />
    <mkdir dir="${lib}" />
</target>
```

The next target in the package target branch that executes is the compile target—another dependency of the package target. The compile target compiles the code in the src directory to the build directory, which was defined by the "build" property in the init target. The compile target is defined as follows:

```
<target name="compile" depends="prepare"
                description="compile the Java source.">

    <javac srcdir="./src" destdir="${build}"/>
</target>
```

Now that all the target dependencies of the package target have been executed, we can run the package target. Whew! The package target packages the Java classes created in the compile target into a JAR file that is created in the common lib directory. The package target is defined as follows:

```
<target name="package" depends="compile"
                description="package the Java classes into a jar.">

    <jar jarfile="${model_jar}"
        basedir="${build}" />
</target>
```

Running an Ant Buildfile

In this section, we discuss how to run the Hello World model project buildfile. There are three steps to running the Ant buildfile:

1. Set up the environment.

2. Go to the directory that contains the build.xml file for the model.

3. Run Ant.

Successfully running the buildscript gives us the following output:

```
Buildfile: build.xml

setProps:
```

```
init:

clean:

prepare:
    [mkdir] Created dir: C:\tmp\app\model\classes

compile:
    [javac] Compiling 3 source files to C:\tmp\app\model\classes

package:
      [jar] Building jar: C:\tmp\app\lib\greetmodel.jar

all:

BUILD SUCCESSFUL

Total time: 3 seconds
```

If you do not get this output, check that the properties defined in the init target make sense for your environment. If you are on a Unix platform and the buildfile is not working, make sure that the /tmp directory exists and that you have the rights to access it. Alternatively, you could run the previous script by doing the following on the command line:

```
$ ant -DsetProps=true -Doutdir=/usr/rick/tmp/app
```

Basically, you want to output to a directory that you have access to, just in case you are not the administrator of your own box. If from some reason Ant still does not run, make sure you set up the Ant environment variables (refer to Chapter 4 for details).

After successfully running Ant, the output directory for the model project will look like this:

```
Root of output directory
\---app
    +---lib
    |         greetmodel.jar
    |
    \---model
        \---classes
            \---xptoolkit
                \---model
                        GreetingFactory.class
                        Greeting.class
                        GreetingBean.class
```

Notice that all the intermediate files to build the JAR file are in the model subdirectory. The output from this project is the greetmodel.jar file, which is in ${outdir}/app/lib. The next project, the application project, needs this JAR file in order to compile. In the next section, we discuss how to build a standalone Java application with Ant that uses the JAR file (greetmodel.jar) from the model project.

Hello World Application Project

The goal of the Hello World application project is to create a standalone Java application that uses greetmodel.jar to get the greeting message. The application project buildfile is nearly identical to the model project buildfile, so we focus our discussion on the differences between the two buildfiles. We also explain how to make a JAR file an executable JAR file.

Overview of Application Java Classes

The Java source code for this application is as simple as it gets for the Hello World Model 2 examples. Here is the Java application:

```
package xptoolkit;

import xptoolkit.model.GreetingFactory;
import xptoolkit.model.Greeting;

public class HelloWorld{

    public static void main(String []args)throws Exception{
        Greeting greet = (Greeting)
          GreetingFactory.getGreetingFactory().getGreeting();

        System.out.println(greet.getGreeting());

    }
}
```

As you can see, this application imports the GreetingFactory class and the Greeting interface from the model project. It uses the GreetingFactory to get an instance of the Greeting interface, and then uses the instance of the Greeting interface to print the greeting to the console.

Creating a Project Directory Structure for the Application

The directory structure of the Hello World Java application is as follows:

```
Hello World Application root
|    build.xml
|
+---src
|    |
|    +---xptoolkit
|            HelloWorld.java
|
\---META-INF
        MANIFEST.MF
```

Notice the addition of the META-INF directory, which holds the name of the manifest file we will use to make the application's JAR file executable. The only other file that this project needs is not shown; the file is greetmodel.jar, which is created by the model project (the reason for this will become obvious in the following sections).

Creating a Manifest File for a Standalone Application

The goal of this application is for it to work as a standalone JAR file. To do this, we need to modify the manifest file that the application JAR file uses to include the main class and the dependency on greetmodel.jar. The manifest entries that this application needs look something like this:

```
Manifest-Version: 1.0
Created-By: Rick Hightower
Main-Class: xptoolkit.HelloWorld
Class-Path: greetmodel.jar
```

The Class-Path manifest entry specifies the JAR files that the JAR file that holds the Hello World Java application needs to run (in our case, greetmodel.jar). The Main-Class manifest entry specifies the main class of the JAR file—that is, the class with the main method that is run when the executable JAR file executes.

Creating an Ant Buildfile for a Standalone Application

The following listing shows the application project buildfile; you'll notice that it is very similar to the model project buildfile. It is divided into the same targets as the model project buildfile: setProps, init, clean, delete, prepare, mkdir, compile, package, and all. The application project buildfile defines the properties differently, but even the property names are almost identical (compare with the model project buildfile earlier in this chapter).

```
<project name="application" default="all" >


    <target name="setProps" unless="setProps"
                        description="setup the properties.">
<property name="outdir" value="/tmp/app" />
    </target>

    <target name="init" depends="setProps"
                        description="initialize the properties.">
      <tstamp/>
      <property name="local_outdir" value="${outdir}/java_app" />
      <property name="build" value="${local_outdir}/classes" />
      <property name="lib" value="${outdir}/lib" />
      <property name="app_jar" value="${lib}/greetapp.jar" />
    </target>

    <target name="clean" depends="init"
                        description="clean up the output directories.">
        <delete dir="${build}" />
        <delete file="${app_jar}" />
    </target>

    <target name="prepare" depends="init"
                        description="prepare the output directory.">
        <mkdir dir="${build}" />
        <mkdir dir="${lib}" />
    </target>
```

```
    <target name="compile" depends="prepare"
                        description="compile the Java source.">

        <javac srcdir="./src" destdir="${build}">
            <classpath >

                <fileset dir="${lib}">
                    <include name="**/*.jar"/>
                </fileset>

            </classpath>

        </javac>

    </target>

    <target name="package" depends="compile"
                    description="package the Java classes into a jar.">
        <jar jarfile="${app_jar}"
            manifest="./META-INF/MANIFEST.MF"
            basedir="${build}" />
    </target>

    <target name="all" depends="clean,package"
                        description="perform all targets."/>

</project>
```

One of the differences in the application project buildfile is the way that it compiles the Java source:

```
    <target name="compile" depends="prepare"
                        description="compile the Java source.">

        <javac srcdir="./src" destdir="${build}">
            <classpath >

                <fileset dir="${lib}">
                    <include name="**/*.jar"/>
                </fileset>

            </classpath>

        </javac>

    </target>
```

Notice that the compile target specifies all the JAR files in the common lib directory (<include name="**/*.jar"/>). The greetmodel.jar file is in the common lib directory, so it is included when the javac task compiles the source. Another difference is the way the application project's buildfile packages the Ant source as follows:

```
<target name="package" depends="compile"
            description="package the Java classes into a jar.">
    <jar jarfile="${app_jar}"
        manifest="./META-INF/MANIFEST.MF"
      basedir="${build}" />
</target>
```

Notice that the package target uses the jar task as before, but the jar task's manifest is set to the manifest file described earlier. This is unlike the model project buildfile, which did not specify a manifest file; the model used the default manifest file. The application project buildfile's manifest file has the entries that allow us to execute the JAR file from the command line.

In order to run the Hello World Java application, after we run the application project's buildfile, we go to the output common lib directory (tmp/app/lib) and run Java from the command line with the -jar command-line argument, as follows:

```
$ java -jar greetapp.jar
Hello World!
```

You may wonder how it loaded the Greeting interface and GreetingFactory class. This is possible because the manifest entry Class-Path causes the JVM to search for any directory or JAR file that is specified (refer to the JAR file specification included with the Java Platform documentation for more detail). The list of items (directory or JAR files) specified on the Class-Path manifest entry is a relative URI list. Because the greetmodel.jar file is in the same directory (such as /tmp/app/lib) and it is specified on the Class-Path manifest, the JVM finds the classes in greetmodel.jar.

One issue with the application project is its dependence on the model project. The model project must be executed before the application project. How can we manage this? The next section proposes one way to manage the situation with an Ant buildfile.

Hello World Main Project

The Hello World Java application depends on the existence of the Hello World model common library file. If we try to compile the application before the model, we get an error. The application requires the model, so we need a way to call the model project buildfile and the application project buildfile in the right order.

Creating a Master Buildfile

We can control the execution of two buildfiles by using a master buildfile. The master buildfile shown in the following listing and is located in the root directory of the Model 2 Hello World Example of the main project. This buildfile treats the model and application buildfile as subprojects (the model and application projects are the first of many subprojects that we want to fit into a larger project).

```
<project name="main" default="build" >


    <target name="setProps" unless="setProps"
```

```xml
                                  description="setup the properties.">
            <property name="outdir" value="/tmp/app" />
            <property name="setProps" value="true" />
    </target>


    <target name="init" depends="setProps"
                        description="initialize the properties.">
        <property name="lib" value="${outdir}/lib" />
    </target>

    <target name="clean" depends="init"
                        description="clean up the output directories.">
        <ant dir="./Model" target="clean">
            <property name="outdir" value="${outdir}" />
            <property name="setProps" value="true" />

        </ant>

        <ant dir="./Application" target="clean">
            <property name="outdir" value="${outdir}" />
            <property name="setProps" value="true" />
        </ant>

        <delete dir="${outdir}" />

    </target>


    <target name="prepare" depends="init"
                        description="prepare the output directory.">
        <mkdir dir="${build}" />
        <mkdir dir="${lib}" />
    </target>


    <target name="build" depends="prepare"
            description="build the model and application modules.">

        <ant dir="./model" target="package">
            <property name="outdir" value="${outdir}" />
            <property name="setProps" value="true" />
        </ant>

        <ant dir="./application" target="package">
            <property name="outdir" value="${outdir}" />
            <property name="setProps" value="true" />
        </ant>
    </target>

</project>
```

Analysis of the Master Buildfile

Notice that the main project buildfile simply delegates to the application and model subproject and ensures that the subprojects' buildfiles are called in the correct order. For example, when the clean target is executed, the main project's buildfile uses the ant task to call the model project's clean target. Then, the main project calls the application project's clean target using the ant task again. Both are demonstrated as follows:

```
<target name="clean" depends="init"
                    description="clean up the output directories.">
    <ant dir="./Model" target="clean">
        <property name="outdir" value="${outdir}" />
        <property name="setProps" value="true" />
    </ant>

    <ant dir="./Application" target="clean">
        <property name="outdir" value="${outdir}" />
        <property name="setProps" value="true" />
    </ant>

    <delete dir="${outdir}" />

</target>
```

A similar strategy is used with the main project's build target. The build target calls the package target on both the model and application subprojects, as follows:

```
<target name="build" depends="prepare"
        description="build the model and application modules.">

    <ant dir="./model" target="package">
        <property name="outdir" value="${outdir}" />
        <property name="setProps" value="true" />
    </ant>

    <ant dir="./application" target="package">
        <property name="outdir" value="${outdir}" />
        <property name="setProps" value="true" />
    </ant>

</target>
```

Thus, we can build both the application and model projects by running the main project. This may not seem like a big deal, but imagine a project with hundreds of subprojects that build thousands of components. Without a buildfile, such a project could become unmanageable. In fact, a project with just 10 to 20 components can benefit greatly from using nested buildfiles. We will use this same technique as we create the Web application in Chapter 6, the applet, and the EJB of this project. The master buildfile orchestrates the correct running order for all the subprojects. We could revisit this main project after we finish each additional subproject and update it. In the next section, we will discuss the applet buildfile.

The Applet Project

The applet project is a simple applet that reads the output of the HelloWorldServlet (defined in Chapter 6) and shows it in a JLabel. The dependency on the Web application is at run time; there are no compile-time dependencies to the Web application. We'll discuss the applet here and the Web application in the next chapter.

Overview of the Applet Class

The meat of the applet implementation is in the init() method, as follows:

```
public void init(){
    URL uGreeting;
    String sGreeting="Bye Bye";

    getAppletContext()
.showStatus("Getting hello message from server.");

    try{
        uGreeting = new URL(
                getDocumentBase(),
                "HelloWorldServlet");

        sGreeting = getGreeting(uGreeting);
    }
    catch(Exception e){
        getAppletContext()
.showStatus("Unable to communicate with server.");
        e.printStackTrace();
    }
    text.setText(sGreeting);

}
```

The init() method gets the document base (the URL from which the applet's page was loaded) URL from the applet context. Then, the init() method uses the document base and the URI identifying the HelloWordServlet to create a URL that has the output of the HelloWorldServlet:

```
uGreeting = new URL( getDocumentBase(), "HelloWorldServlet");
```

It uses a helper method called getGreeting() to parse the output of the HelloWorldServlet, and then displays the greeting in the Applet's JLabel (text.setText(sGreeting);). The helper method is as follows:

```
private String getGreeting(URL uGreeting)throws Exception{
    String line;
    int endTagIndex;
    BufferedReader reader=null;
    . . .

reader = new BufferedReader(
                new InputStreamReader (
                        uGreeting.openStream()));
```

```
        while((line=reader.readLine())!=null){
            System.out.println(line);

            if (line.startsWith("<h1>")){
                getAppletContext().showStatus("Parsing message.");
                endTagIndex=line.indexOf("</h1>");
                line=line.substring(4,endTagIndex);
                break;
            }
        }
        ...
    return line;
}
```

Basically, the method gets the output stream from the URL (uGreeting.openStream()) and goes through the stream line by line looking for a line that begins with <h1>. Then, it pulls the text out of the <h1> tag.

The output of the HelloServlet looks like this:

```
<html>
<head>
<title>Hello World</title>
</head>
<body>
<h1>Hello World!</h1>
</body>
```

The code that the helper method retrieves appears in bold. The following listing shows the complete code for HelloWorldApplet.

```
package xptoolkit.applet;
import javax.swing.JApplet;
import javax.swing.JLabel;
import java.awt.Font;
import java.awt.BorderLayout;
import java.applet.AppletContext;
import java.net.URL;
import java.io.InputStreamReader;
import java.io.BufferedReader;

public class HelloWorldApplet extends javax.swing.JApplet {

    JLabel text;


    public HelloWorldApplet() {
        this.getContentPane().setLayout(new BorderLayout());
        text = new JLabel("Bye Bye");
        text.setAlignmentX(JLabel.CENTER_ALIGNMENT);
        text.setAlignmentY(JLabel.CENTER_ALIGNMENT);
        Font f = new Font("Arial", Font.BOLD, 20);
        text.setFont(f);
        getContentPane().add(text,BorderLayout.CENTER);
```

```
    }

    public void init(){
        URL uGreeting;
        String sGreeting="Bye Bye";

        this.doLayout();
        getAppletContext()
.showStatus("Getting hello message from server.");

        try{
            uGreeting = new URL(
                    this.getDocumentBase(),
                    "HelloWorldServlet");

            sGreeting = getGreeting(uGreeting);
        }
        catch(Exception e){
            getAppletContext()
.showStatus("Unable to communicate with server.");
            e.printStackTrace();
        }
        text.setText(sGreeting);

    }

    private String getGreeting(URL uGreeting)throws Exception{
        String line;
        int endTagIndex;
        BufferedReader reader=null;


        try{
            reader = new BufferedReader(
                    new InputStreamReader (
                            uGreeting.openStream()));
            while((line=reader.readLine())!=null){
                System.out.println(line);
                if (line.startsWith("<h1>")){
                    getAppletContext().showStatus("Parsing message.");
                    endTagIndex=line.indexOf("</h1>");
                    line=line.substring(4,endTagIndex);
                    break;
                }
            }
        }
        finally{
            if (reader!=null)reader.close();
        }
        return line;
    }

}
```

Creating a Buildfile for the Applet

The applet project buildfile is quite simple, as shown in the following listing; it is structured much like the application project buildfile.

```
<project name="applet" default="all" >


    <target name="setProps" unless="setProps"
                        description="setup the properties.">
        <property name="outdir" value="/tmp/app" />
    </target>


    <target name="init" depends="setProps"
                        description="initialize the properties.">
        <tstamp/>

        <property name="local_outdir" value="${outdir}/applet" />
        <property name="build" value="${local_outdir}/classes" />
        <property name="lib" value="${outdir}/lib" />
        <property name="jar" value="${lib}/helloapplet.jar" />
    </target>

    <target name="clean" depends="init"
                        description="clean up the output directories.">
        <delete dir="${build}" />
        <delete dir="${jar}" />
    </target>


    <target name="prepare" depends="init"
                        description="prepare the output directory.">
        <mkdir dir="${build}" />
        <mkdir dir="${lib}" />
    </target>

    <target name="compile" depends="prepare"
                        description="compile the Java source.">
        <javac srcdir="./src" destdir="${build}" />
    </target>

    <target name="package" depends="compile"
            description="package the Java classes into a jar.">
        <jar jarfile="${jar} "
            basedir="${build}" />
    </target>

    <target name="all" depends="clean,package"
                        description="perform all targets."/>

</project>
```

Building the Applet with Ant

To build the applet, we need to navigate to the Applet directory, set up the environment, and then run Ant at the command line. To clean the output from the build, we run "ant clean" at the command line. Both building and cleaning the applet are demonstrated as follows.

First we build the applet:

```
C:\CVS\...\MVCHelloWorld\Applet>ant
Buildfile: build.xml

setProps:

init:

clean:
   [delete] Deleting directory C:\tmp\app\lib

prepare:
    [mkdir] Created dir: C:\tmp\app\applet\classes
    [mkdir] Created dir: C:\tmp\app\lib

compile:
    [javac] Compiling 1 source file to C:\tmp\app\applet\classes

package:
      [jar] Building jar: C:\tmp\app\lib\helloapplet.jar

all:

BUILD SUCCESSFUL

Total time: 4 seconds
```

Now we clean the applet:

```
C:\CVS\...\MVCHelloWorld\Applet>ant clean
Buildfile: build.xml

setProps:

init:

clean:
   [delete] Deleting directory C:\tmp\app\applet\classes
   [delete] Deleting directory C:\tmp\app\lib

BUILD SUCCESSFUL

Total time: 0 seconds
```

Hello World Recap

It's important to recap what we have done. We created a common Java library called model.jar. This model.jar file is used by a Web application and a standalone executable Java application in an executable JAR file. We created an applet that can communicate with the Web application we will create in Chapter 6. Once the applet loads into the browser, the applet communicates over HTTP to the Web application's HelloWorldServlet, which is covered in depth in Chapter 6.

In Chapter 4 we set up the GreetingFactory so that it talks to an enterprise session bean that in turn talks to an enterprise entity bean. The Web application buildfile is set up so that with the addition of a property file, it can talk to either the enterprise beans or to the local implementation in the model library.

Conclusion

Also in Chapter 6, we took a very complex project with a few components and subsystems, albeit a simple implementation, and built it in an orchestrated fashion. We showed how to create a Java application in an executable JAR and a Java applet in a JAR. We also demonstrated how to package a set of classes that is shared by more than one application in a JAR.

Building J2EE Applications with Ant

This chapter explains techniques for using Ant to build and deploy J2EE applications. The first example we use is a continuation of the Hello World application from Chapter 5. The Hello World example in this chapter includes an applet, a Web application, an application, enterprise beans, support libraries, and other components. This may be the only Hello World example that has an applet, servlet, session bean, entity bean, and JSP and attempts to be Model 2.

You're probably thinking, "Why should I implement the most complex Hello World application in the world?" This example, although a bit of overkill to say "Hello World," is as simple as possible while demonstrating how to build and deploy a J2EE application and its components with Ant. By working through this example, you will understand how to use Ant to build these different types of components and applications, and how to combine them by nesting buildfiles. In the last section of this chapter, we use these techniques to begin implementing a more realistic application: the sample pet store introduced in Chapter 5. We will build on the pet store application and refactor it at the end of every subsequent chapter in this section of the book. The remaining chapters in this part of the book will build on the pet store case study (see Appendix A for a full description and the complete code listing).

Hello World

The Model 2 HelloWorld example for this chapter is the simplest example of Model 2 architecture—also known as Model-View-Controller (MVC)—for JSP servlets. In this example, the applet and JSP are the view; the servlet and enterprise session bean are the controller; and the object model is a Java class and later an entity bean.

The GreetingFactory from Chapter 5 is set up so it talks to an enterprise session bean that in turn talks to an enterprise entity bean. The Web application buildfile is set up so that if we add one property file, it can talk to either the enterprise beans or to the local implementation in the original model library (common code) defined in Chapter 5.

The source code for the Model 2 Hello World example is divided into several directories for each component, and each directory has its own Ant buildfile. A master Ant buildfile in the root directory calls the other buildfiles. The directory structure is as follows:

```
Model 2 Hello World root
+---Model
+---EJBeans
+---Application
+---Applet
+---WebApplication
```

The Model directory holds the common code. The EJBeans directory holds the enterprise beans code and the deployment descriptor files. The Application directory holds the Java application code including the manifest file that marks the deployment JAR as executable. The Applet directory holds the applet code. The WebApplication directory holds HTML files, deployment descriptors, JSP files, and servlet Java source.

Because each component has its own set of deployment descriptors and configuration files, it makes sense to separate components into their own directories; this practice also makes it easier to reuse the components in other projects and applications. Each directory has its own Ant buildfile, which knows how to compile the components, package the binaries, and include the requisite configuration files (deployment descriptors and manifest files).

In the next section, we cover the Web application buildfile—the heart of this example.

Web Application Project

The Web application is another subproject of the Model 2 Hello World application; it consists of a servlet, two JSPs, an HTML file, and a deployment descriptor. This section describes how to build a WAR file with a deployment descriptor. We also explain how to map servlets and JSPs to servlet elements in the deployment descriptor and how to map the servlet elements to URLs. In addition, this section breaks down the webapplication project buildfile step by step, and shows how to use the buildfile to build and deploy the Web application.

Web Application Project Directory Structure

The following are the files that we build into a Web application:

```
Web application root directory
|    build.xml
|
+---JSP
```

```
|          HelloWorld.jsp
|          HelloApplet.jsp
|
+---src
|    \---xptoolkit
|         \---web
|                HelloWorldServlet.java
|
+---HTML
|          index.html
|
\---meta-data
          web.xml
```

Notice that the webapplication project includes only six files. There are four subdirectories: JSP, src, HTML, and meta-data, and the root directory holds the build.xml file. The JSP directory contains two JSPs: HelloWorld.jsp and HelloApplet.jsp. Under the src directory is the Java source for the servlet xptoolkit.web.HelloWorldServlet.java. The web.xml file under the meta-data directory holds the deployment file for this Web application.

HelloWorldServlet.java

The servlet is contained in the class xptoolkit.web.HelloWorldServlet (see the next listing). Like the Java application, it uses the Greeting interface and the GreetingFactory class that are packaged in greet-model.jar, the output of the model project.

```java
package xptoolkit.web;
import javax.servlet.http.HttpServlet;
import javax.servlet.http.HttpServletRequest;
import javax.servlet.http.HttpServletResponse;
import javax.servlet.http.HttpSession;
import javax.servlet.ServletException;
import javax.servlet.ServletConfig;
import javax.servlet.ServletContext;
import javax.servlet.RequestDispatcher;

/* import the classes to create a greeting object or type greeting */
import xptoolkit.model.GreetingFactory;
import xptoolkit.model.Greeting;


public class HelloWorldServlet extends  HttpServlet{

    public void init(ServletConfig config) throws ServletException{
        super.init(config);
            /* Read in the greeting type that the factory should create */
        String clazz = config.getInitParameter("Greeting.class") ;
        if(clazz!=null)System.setProperty("Greeting.class",clazz);

    }
```

```
public void doGet(HttpServletRequest request,
                              HttpServletResponse response)
                                      throws ServletException{
  RequestDispatcher dispatch;
  ServletContext context;
/*Get the session, create a greeting bean, map the greeting
   bean in the session, and redirect to the Hello World JSP.
 */
  try {


        /* Create the greeting bean and map it to the session. */
    HttpSession session = request.getSession(true);
    Greeting greet = (Greeting)
        GreetingFactory.getGreetingFactory().getGreeting();
    session.setAttribute("greeting", greet);


        /* Redirect to the HelloWorld.jsp */
    context = getServletContext();
    dispatch = context.getRequestDispatcher("/HelloWorldJSP");
    dispatch.forward(request, response);
  }catch(Exception e){
     throw new ServletException(e);
  }
}

 /* Just call the doGet method */
 public void doPost(HttpServletRequest request,
                              HttpServletResponse response)
                                      throws ServletException{
   doGet(request, response);
 }

}
```

Analyzing HelloWorldServlet

HelloWorldServlet is a simple servlet; it reads in the servlet initialization parameters in the init() method, as follows:

```
String clazz = config.getInitParameter("Greeting.class") ;
```

It uses the value of the initialization parameter "Greeting.class" to set the System property "Greeting.class", as follows:

```
System.setProperty("Greeting.class",clazz);
```

You will recall from Chapter 5 that the GreetingFactory uses the system property "Greeting.class" to decide which implementation of the Greeting interface to load. Now let's get to the real action: the doGet() and doPost() methods.

When the doGet() or doPost() method of the HelloWorldServlet is called, the servlet uses the GreetingFactory to create a greeting as follows:

```
Greeting greet = (Greeting)
        GreetingFactory.getGreetingFactory().getGreeting();
```

The HelloWorldServlet then maps the greeting object into the current session (javax.servlet.http .HttpSession) under the name "greeting", as follows:

```
session.setAttribute("greeting", greet);
```

Finally, the HelloWorldServlet forwards processing of this request to the JSP file HelloWorld.jsp by getting the request dispatcher for the HelloWorldServlet from the servlet's context, as follows:

```
/* Redirect to the HelloWorld.jsp */
context = getServletContext();
dispatch = context.getRequestDispatcher("/HelloWorldJSP");
dispatch.forward(request, response);
```

You may notice that the context.getRequestDispatcher call looks a little weird. This is the case because HelloWorld.jsp is mapped to /HelloWorldJSP in the deployment descriptor for the servlet. (We will discuss the deployment descriptor later.) Next, let's examine HelloWorld.jsp.

HelloWorld.jsp

HelloWorld.jsp exists to show the world the message it gets from the Greeting reference that the HelloWorldServlet mapped into session. The HelloWorld.jsp code is as follows:

```
<jsp:useBean id="greeting" type="xptoolkit.model.Greeting"
                                        scope="session"/>
<html>
<head>
<title>Hello World</title>
</head>
<body>
<h1><%=greeting.getGreeting()%></h1>
</body>
```

If you are a Web designer at heart, we understand if you are shocked and horrified by this HTML code. But for a moment, let's focus on the following two lines of code from the JSP:

```
<jsp:useBean id="greeting" type="xptoolkit.model.Greeting"
                                        scope="session"/>

<h1><%=greeting.getGreeting()%></h1>
```

Notice that the jsp:useBean action grabs the greeting reference that we put into the session with the HelloWorldServlet. Then, we print out the greeting with the JSP scriptlet expression <%=greeting.getGreeting()%>.

This sums up what the Model 2 Hello World Web application does. We will discuss the other JSP, HelloApplet.jsp, after we examine the applet subproject. For now, the next section explains why the servlet could forward HelloWorldJSP to the JSP HelloWorld.jsp.

Deployment Descriptor for the HelloWorld Web Application

In order to configure the JSPs and servlets, we need a deployment descriptor. The following code defines a simple deployment descriptor that assigns names and mappings to the JSPs and servlet. Please note that the deployment descriptor goes in the web.xml file:

```xml
<?xml version="1.0" encoding="ISO-8859-1"?>

<!DOCTYPE web-app
  PUBLIC "-//Sun Microsystems, Inc.//DTD Web Application 2.2//EN"
  "http://java.sun.com/j2ee/dtds/web-app_2_2.dtd">

<web-app>
    <error-page>
        <error-code>404</error-code>
        <location>/HelloWorldServlet</location>
    </error-page>

    <servlet>
        <servlet-name>HelloWorldServlet</servlet-name>
        <servlet-class>xptoolkit.web.HelloWorldServlet</servlet-class>
        <init-param>
          <param-name>Greeting.class</param-name>
          <param-value>@Greeting.class@</param-value>
        </init-param>
    </servlet>

    <servlet>
        <servlet-name>HelloWorldJSP</servlet-name>
        <jsp-file>HelloWorld.jsp</jsp-file>
    </servlet>

    <servlet-mapping>
        <servlet-name>HelloWorldServlet</servlet-name>
        <url-pattern>/HelloWorldServlet</url-pattern>
    </servlet-mapping>

    <servlet-mapping>
        <servlet-name>HelloWorldJSP</servlet-name>
        <url-pattern>/HelloWorldJSP</url-pattern>
    </servlet-mapping>

</web-app>
```

The deployment descriptor defines two servlet elements, one for the HelloWorldServlet and one for the HelloWorldJSP. If you are wondering why there is a servlet element for the HelloWorldJSP, remember that HelloWorld.jsp is compiled to a servlet before it is used for the first time. The HelloWorldServlet

servlet element maps to the servlet (<servlet-class>xptoolkit.web.HelloWorldServlet</servlet-class>). The HelloWorldJSP element maps to the JSP file HelloWorld.jsp (<jsp-file>HelloWorld.jsp</jsp-file>). Then, the servlet mapping elements map the servlet element to specific URL patterns.

Thus HelloWorldServlet maps to /HelloWorldServlet (<url-pattern>/HelloWorldServlet</url-pattern>); this is relative to the Web application location from the root of the server. And, the HelloWorldJSP servlet element is mapped to the /HelloWorldJSP URL pattern (<url-pattern>/HelloWorldJSP</url-pattern>).

The buildfile must deploy the descriptor to a place where the application server can find it. It does this by packaging the HTML files, JSP files, Java servlet, and deployment descriptor in a WAR file. The next section describes the buildfile for this project.

Buildfile for the HelloWorld Web Application

This project has many more components than the other subprojects. As you would expect, the webapplication project buildfile (see the next listing) is much more complex, but it builds on the foundation set by the model project—that is, the webapplication project buildfile has the same base targets with the same meanings: setProps, init, clean, delete, prepare, mkdir, compile, package, and all.

To the base targets, the webapplication project's buildfile adds the prepare_metadata and deploy targets. The prepare_metadata target sets up the Ant filtering for the deployment descriptor (we talk about this in detail towards the end of this section). The deploy target adds the ability to deploy to both Resin and Tomcat Web application servers. The remaining details of this buildfile are covered in the applet and the enterprise beans sections later in this chapter.

```
<project name="webapplication" default="all" >

    <target name="setProps" unless="setProps"
                        description="setup the properites.">
        <property name="outdir" value="/tmp/app" />

    </target>


    <target name="init" depends="setProps"
                        description="initialize the properties.">
      <tstamp/>
      <property name="local_outdir" value="${outdir}/webapps" />
      <property name="lib" value="${outdir}/lib" />
      <property name="dist" value="${outdir}/dist" />

      <property name="build" value="${local_outdir}/webclasses" />
      <property name="meta" value="${local_outdir}/meta" />

      <property name="deploy_resin" value="/resin/webapps" />
      <property name="deploy_tomcat" value="/tomcat/webapps" />

      <property name="build_lib" value="./../lib" />
      <property name="jsdk_lib" value="/resin/lib" />
    </target>
```

```
<target name="clean_deploy" >

    <delete file="${deploy_resin}/hello.war" />
    <delete dir="${deploy_resin}/hello" />
    <delete file="${deploy_tomcat}/hello.war" />
    <delete dir="${deploy_tomcat}/hello" />
</target>

<target name="clean" depends="init,clean_deploy"
                    description="clean up the output directories.">
    <delete dir="${local_outdir}" />
    <delete file="${dist}/hello.war" />
</target>


<target name="prepare" depends="init"
                    description="prepare the output directory.">
    <mkdir dir="${build}" />
    <mkdir dir="${dist}" />
    <mkdir dir="${build_lib}" />
</target>



<target name="compile" depends="prepare"
                    description="compile the Java source.">
    <javac srcdir="./src" destdir="${build}">
        <classpath >

            <fileset dir="${lib}">
                <include name="**/*.jar"/>
            </fileset>

            <fileset dir="${jsdk_lib}">
                <include name="**/*.jar"/>
            </fileset>

            <fileset dir="${build_lib}">
                <include name="**/*.jar"/>
            </fileset>

        </classpath>
    </javac>

</target>

<target name="prepare_meta_ejb" if="ejb">
    <filter token="Greeting.class"
            value="xptoolkit.model.GreetingShadow"/>
</target>

<target name="prepare_meta_noejb" unless="ejb">
    <filter token="Greeting.class"
```

```
                            value="xptoolkit.model.GreetingBean"/>
      </target>

      <target name="prepare_meta"
              depends="prepare_meta_ejb, prepare_meta_noejb">
          <copy todir="${meta}" filtering="true">
              <fileset dir="./meta-data"/>
          </copy>
      </target>

      <target name="package" depends="compile">

          <mkdir dir="${meta}" />

          <antcall target="prepare_meta" />

          <war warfile="${dist}/hello.war" webxml="${meta}/web.xml">
              <!--
                  Include the html and jsp files.
                  Put the classes from the build into the classes directory
                  of the war.
              /-->
          <fileset dir="./HTML" />
          <fileset dir="./JSP" />
            <classes dir="${build}" />

              <!-- Include the applet. /-->
            <fileset dir="${lib}" includes="helloapplet.jar" />

        <!-- Include all of the jar files except the ejbeans and applet.
             The other build files that create jars have to be run in the
             correct order. This is covered later.
      /-->
          <lib dir="${lib}" >
              <exclude name="greet-ejbs.jar"/>
              <exclude name="helloapplet.jar"/>
            </lib>
          </war>

    </target>

    <target name="deploy" depends="package">
        <copy file="${dist}/hello.war" todir="${deploy_resin}" />

        <copy file="${dist}/hello.war" todir="${deploy_tomcat}" />


    </target>

    <target name="all" depends="clean,package"
                        description="perform all targets."/>

  </project>
```

The final output of the Web application project is a single WAR file. The WAR file is built (not surprisingly) by the package target. Here is the listing for the package target:

```
<target name="package" depends="compile">

    <mkdir dir="${meta}" />
    <antcall target="prepare_meta" />

    <war warfile="${dist}/hello.war" webxml="${meta}/web.xml">
      <!--
          Include the html and jsp files.
          Put the classes from the build into the classes directory
          of the war.
      /-->
      <fileset dir="./HTML" />
      <fileset dir="./JSP" />
      <classes dir="${build}" />

      <!-- Include the applet. /-->
      <fileset dir="${lib}" includes="helloapplet.jar" />

      <!-- Include all of the jar files except the ejbeans
and applet.
  /-->
      <lib dir="${lib}" />
    </war>

</target>
```

As you can see, this package target is much larger than the other two we've discussed (model and application). For now we'll defer a detailed discussion of the second and third lines of code:

```
    <mkdir dir="${meta}" />
    <antcall target="prepare_meta" />
```

These lines do some processing on the web.xml deployment descriptor file and put the file in the directory defined by ${meta} directory (note that the "meta" property is set in the init target). We explain the processing done to the deployment descriptor in the section "Enterprise JavaBeans" found later in this chapter. Next, the package target calls the war task, which is as follows:

```
    <war warfile="${dist}/hello.war" webxml="${meta}/web.xml">
        <fileset dir="./HTML" />
        <fileset dir="./JSP" />
        <classes dir="${build}" />
        <fileset dir="${lib}" includes="helloapplet.jar" />
        <lib dir="${lib}" />
    </war>
```

The WAR file hello.war is put in the distribution directory (dist), which is specified by the war task's "warfile" attribute (warfile="${dist}/hello.war"). The dist directory is another common directory that is used by the main project's buildfile later to build an enterprise archive (EAR) file; the "dist" property is defined in the init target. The "webxml" attribute of the war task defines the deployment descriptor to use; it's the one we processed at the beginning of the package target. The web.xml file is put in the WAR file's WEB-INF/ directory.

In addition, the war task body specifies three file sets. One file set includes the helloapplet.jar file (which we discuss in the section "HelloWorld.jsp Applet Delivery" later in this chapter) and all the files in the HTML and JSP directories. The war task body also specifies where to locate the classes using <classes dir="${build}" />. This command puts the classes in the WEB-INF/classes directory.

The webapplication project's buildfile defines a slightly more complex compile target, as follows:

```
<target name="compile" depends="prepare"
                       description="compile the Java source.">
    <javac srcdir="./src" destdir="${build}">
        <classpath >

            <fileset dir="${lib}">
                <include name="**/*.jar"/>
            </fileset>

            <fileset dir="${build_lib}">
                <include name="**/*.jar"/>
            </fileset>

        </classpath>
    </javac>

</target>
```

Notice that this compile target defines two file sets. One file set (<fileset dir="${build_lib}">) is used to include the classes needed for servlets (such as import javax.servlet.*). The other file set (<fileset dir="${lib}">) is used to include the Greeting interfaces and the GreetingFactory class. The only real difference from the application compile target is the inclusion of the JAR file for servlets. The "build_lib" property is defined in the webapplication project's init target, as follows:

```
<property name="build_lib" value="./../lib" />
```

The good thing about this approach is that if we need additional JAR files, we can put them in the build_lib. The second file set (<fileset dir="${build_lib}">) grabs all the JAR files in the ./../lib directory.

The webapplication project's buildfile adds a few convenience targets geared toward Web applications. The deploy target copies the WAR file that this buildfile generates to the webapps directory of Tomcat and Resin. (Tomcat is the reference implementation servlet engine of the Java specification. Resin is an easy-to-use Java application server that supports JSPs, EJBs, J2EE container specification, XSL, and so on.) Without further ado, here is the deploy target:

```
<target name="deploy" depends="package">
        <copy file="${dist}/hello.war" todir="${deploy_resin}" />
        <copy file="${dist}/hello.war" todir="${deploy_tomcat}" />
</target>
```

Both Tomcat and Resin pick up the WAR files automatically, in the interest of doing no harm and cleaning up after ourselves. The webapplication project's buildfile also adds an extra clean_deploy target that deletes the WAR file it deployed and cleans up the generated directory, as follows:

```
<target name="clean_deploy" >
    <delete file="${deploy_resin}/hello.war" />
    <delete dir="${deploy_resin}/hello" />
    <delete file="${deploy_tomcat}/hello.war" />
    <delete dir="${deploy_tomcat}/hello" />
</target>
```

"Great," you say. "But what if the application server I am deploying to is on another server that is half way around the world?" No problem; use the following FTP task:

```
<ftp server="ftp.texas.austin.building7.eblox.org"
        remotedir="/deploy/resin/webapps"
        userid="kingJon"
        password="killMyLandLord"
        depends="yes"
        binary="yes"
>


    <fileset dir="${dist}">
      <include name="**/*.war"/>
    </fileset>

</ftp>
```

Building and Deploying the Web Application

This section explains how to build and deploy the Web application. The buildfile assumes that you have Resin and Tomcat installed in the root of your drive. You may need to make adjustments to the buildfile if you installed Resin or Tomcat in another directory or if you are using another J2EE-compliant Web application server.

To build the Web application, follow these steps:

1. Navigate to the WebApplication directory, set up the environment, and then do the following at the command line:

```
C:\CVS\...\MVCHelloWorld\WebApplication>ant
```

You will get the following output:

```
Buildfile: build.xml

setProps:
```

```
init:

clean_deploy:

    [delete] Could not find file C:\resin\webapps\hello.war to
delete.
    [delete] Could not find file C:\tomcat\webapps\hello.war to
delete

clean:

    [delete] Could not find file C:\tmp\app\dist\hello.war to
delete.

prepare:

    [mkdir] Created dir: C:\tmp\app\webapps\webclasses
    [mkdir] Created dir: C:\tmp\app\dist

compile:

    [javac] Compiling 1 source file to
C:\tmp\app\webapps\webclasses

package:

    [mkdir] Created dir: C:\tmp\app\webapps\meta

prepare_meta_ejb:

prepare_meta_noejb:

prepare_meta:

    [copy] Copying 1 file to C:\tmp\app\webapps\meta
    [war] Building war: C:\tmp\app\dist\hello.war

all:

BUILD SUCCESSFUL
```

Chapter 6

2. Deploy the WAR files to the application server. If you install Resin or Tomcat off the root directory, then you can run the deploy target. Otherwise, modify the appropriate deploy properties defined in the init target. To deploy the application with Ant, do the following:

```
C:\CVS\?.\MVCHelloWorld\WebApplication>ant deploy

Buildfile: build.xml


...

...


deploy:
        [copy] Copying 1 file to C:\resin\webapps
        [copy] Copying 1 file to C:\tomcat\webapps


BUILD SUCCESSFUL


Total time: 0 seconds
```

3. After we run the application, we start Resin or Tomcat, and then hit the site with our browser. (More on this subject later.) We can also clean out the directories when we are ready to deploy a new version, as follows:

```
C:\CVS\...\MVCHelloWorld\WebApplication>ant clean
```

The output looks like the following:

```
Buildfile: build.xml


setProps:


init:


clean_deploy:
    [delete] Deleting: C:\resin\webapps\hello.war
    [delete] Deleting: C:\tomcat\webapps\hello.war


clean:
    [delete] Deleting directory C:\tmp\app\webapps
    [delete] Deleting: C:\tmp\app\dist\hello.war


BUILD SUCCESSFUL


Total time: 0 seconds
```

Notice that we delete the WAR files and the deployment directories. This is just good house-cleaning for when we do a build and deploy. In the next section, we will run the webapplication project.

Running the Web Application

Now that we've built and deployed the webapplication project, let's run it. We start our servlet engine and then open the site in our browser—for example, http://localhost/hello/HelloWorldServlet. (Resin's default setup is port 8080, so you may have to adjust the URL.) Here is what the Web application looks like when it's running:

You may notice a couple of things. The application URL is defined in a directory called hello (http://localhost/hello/HelloWorldServlet). By default, Tomcat and Resin unjar our WAR file in a directory called *<War file File Name>*. Later, we will use the EAR file to override this default behavior in a neutral application server way.

The HelloWorldServlet part of the application's URL is defined by a mapping in the deployment descriptor as follows:

```
<servlet>
    <servlet-name>HelloWorldServlet</servlet-name>
    <servlet-class>xptoolkit.web.HelloWorldServlet</servlet-class>
    <init-param>
      <param-name>Greeting.class</param-name>
      <param-value>@Greeting.class@</param-value>
    </init-param>
</servlet>
```

```
<servlet-mapping>
    <servlet-name>HelloWorldServlet</servlet-name>
    <url-pattern>/HelloWorldServlet</url-pattern>
</servlet-mapping>
```

The servlet tag declares the servlet and gives it a name. The servlet mapping assigns the HelloWorldServlet the URL pattern /HelloWorldServlet. We could change the URL pattern to /PeanutButter, and the URL http://localhost/hello/PeanutButter would work:

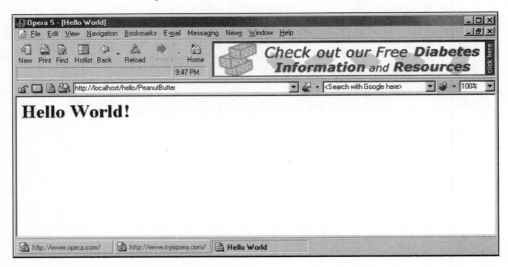

Actually, we mapped the 404 error to HelloWorldServlet as well, so the server sends any URL it does not recognize to HelloWorldServlet to process (for the benefit of people with fumble fingers).

The next section describes a simple applet project that integrates with the webapplication project. Then, we will discuss Enterprise JavaBean deployment and enterprise archive files.

HelloWorld.jsp Applet Delivery

Now the applets JAR we built in Chapter 5 becomes part of the Web application. It is put in the Web application where the browser can find it. The Web application has a JSP page, HelloApplet.jsp, which has a jsp:plugin tag that delivers the applet to the browser. The HelloApplet.jsp with the jsp:plugin action is listed as follows:

```
<html>
<head><title>Hello World Applet</title></head>
<body>
<jsp:plugin type="applet"
            code="xptoolkit.applet.HelloWorldApplet"
            archive="helloapplet.jar"
            height="200"
```

```
            width="200"
            align="center">
    <jsp:fallback>
    <!-- This fallback message will display if the plugin does not work. /-->
        <p> Java is cool. Get a browser that supports the plugin. </ br>
            Or we will hunt you down and melt your computer!
        </p>
    </jsp:fallback>
</jsp:plugin>

</body>
</html>
```

This shows how the applet is delivered to the browser. How is the applet included in the Web application's WAR file in the first place? We explain in the next section.

Including an Applet in a WAR File

If you look at the webapplication project buildfile, you will note that the war task in the package target does the following:

```
<war warfile="${dist}/hello.war" webxml="${meta}/web.xml">
        <fileset dir="./HTML" />
        <fileset dir="./JSP" />
        <classes dir="${build}" />
        <fileset dir="${lib}" includes="helloapplet.jar" />
        <lib dir="${lib}" />
</war>
```

The fileset directive

```
<fileset dir="${lib}" includes="helloapplet.jar" />
```

tells the war task to include only the helloapplet.jar file from the lib directory. Because this file set is not a classes- or lib-type file set, helloapplet.jar goes to the root of the WAR file. In contrast, the special lib and classes file sets put their files in WEB-INF/lib and WEB-INF/classes, respectively. The end effect is that the browser is able to get the applet.

After we build the applet, we go back and rebuild the Web application and then deploy it. We run Ant in the root of both the projects' home directories (if you get a compile error, be sure you have built the model, because the Web application depends on it). After everything compiles and the appropriate JAR and WAR files are built, we deploy the webapplication project by using the deploy target of the webapplication buildfile. Then we run the applet, as demonstrated in the following figure.

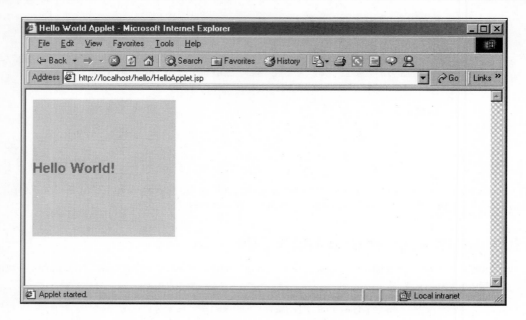

It's important to recap what we have done. We created a common Java library called model.jar. This model.jar is used by a Web application and a regular Java application that is a standalone executable Java application in an executable JAR file. We create an applet that is loaded with a JSP page that has the jsp:plugin action. Once the applet loads into the browser, the applet communicates over HTTP to the Web application's HelloWorldServlet. HelloWorldServlet calls the getGreeting() method on the GreetingFactory, which is contained in the model.jar file.

In the next section, we set up the GreetingFactory so that it talks to an enterprise session bean that in turn talks to an enterprise entity bean. The Web application buildfile is set up so that after we add one property file, it can talk to either the enterprise beans or to the local implementation in the model library.

Enterprise JavaBeans

In this section, we create two simple enterprise beans and demonstrate how to build an EJB JAR file. We also create a local proxy class—the shadow bean—that knows how to speak to the enterprise beans. The shadow bean implements the Greeting interface and can be plugged-in in place of the GreetingBean from the model library. The session bean communicates with the entity bean, so its deployment descriptor entry must reference the entity bean. Let's start by examining the files in this project.

Directory Structure of the Enterprise Beans Project

This project has more files than any other project in this example:

```
Root directory of the Enterprise beans
|    build.xml
|
+---src
```

```
    |   \---xptoolkit
    |   |
    |   |
    |   +---ejbs
    |   |       GreetingEntityBean.java
    |   |       GreetingEntityHome.java
    |   |       GreetingEntityRemote.java
    |   |       GreetingSessionBean.java
    |   |       GreetingSessionRemote.java
    |   |       GreetingSessionHome.java
    |   |
    |   |
    |   \---model
    |           GreetingShadow.java
    |
+---META-DATA
|       ejb.xml
|
|
+---jboss_clientlib
|       jnp-client.jar
|       jbosssx-client.jar
|       jboss-client.jar
|       ejb.jar
|
\---jboss_props
        jndi.properties
```

We used JBoss, an open-source implementation of Enterprise JavaBeans. For JBoss, four JAR files and one properties file are used for the client-side deployment. If you decide to use JBoss, then you have the same or similar JAR files for packaging your client (depending on the version of JBoss you're using).

There are six Java source files, which we'll discuss in depth. These six files define two Enterprise JavaBeans. In addition, one deployment descriptor describes the two Enterprise JavaBeans to the EJB container. There is nothing specific about the deployment descriptor or the Enterprise JavaBeans to JBoss; they should work on any J2EE-compliant EJB application server. Of course, build.xml is the Ant buildfile that takes all this raw material and forms it into a client-side JAR file and an EJB JAR file that can be deployed in any J2EE EJB application server. In the following parts of this section, we describe each of these files. Let's start with the entity bean.

The HelloWorld Entity Bean

Like most classes in this example, the entity bean is a simple object that returns a greeting. In fact, because the entity is generally used to represent a view of rows in a database, we had to cheat a little and define a static variable to simulate a primary key. The entity bean consists of three classes: the GreetingEntityHome interface; the GreetingEntityRemote interface; and the implementation, the GreetingEntityBean class. The Home and Remote interfaces are part of the beans contract with the EJB container. The following listing shows the source code for the Hello World entity bean, GreetingEntityBean.

```
package xptoolkit.ejbs;
import javax.ejb.EntityBean;
import javax.ejb.EntityContext;
import javax.ejb.EJBException;
import javax.ejb.CreateException;
import javax.ejb.FinderException;

public class GreetingEntityBean implements EntityBean{

    static int pkid;

    public Integer ejbCreate(){
       return new Integer(++pkid);

    }
    public void ejbPostCreate()throws CreateException{
    }

    public Integer ejbFindByPrimaryKey(Integer i)throws FinderException{
        return new Integer(1);
    }
    public void ejbActivate(){}
    public void ejbLoad(){}
    public void ejbPassivate(){}
    public void ejbRemove(){}
    public void ejbStore(){}
    public void setEntityContext(EntityContext cotext){}
    public void unsetEntityContext(){}

    public String getGreeting(){
      return "Hello World!";
    }

}
```

The next listing shows the GreetingEntityHome interface.

```
package xptoolkit.ejbs;

import javax.ejb.EJBHome;
import javax.ejb.CreateException;
import javax.ejb.FinderException;
import java.rmi.RemoteException;

public interface GreetingEntityHome extends EJBHome{

    GreetingEntityRemote create() throws RemoteException, CreateException;
    GreetingEntityRemote findByPrimaryKey(Integer i)throws RemoteException,
FinderException;
}
```

The next listing shows the GreetingEntityRemote interface.

```
package xptoolkit.ejbs;
import javax.ejb.EJBObject;
import java.rmi.RemoteException;

public interface GreetingEntityRemote extends EJBObject {

    public String getGreeting()throws RemoteException;
}
```

As you can probably see by looking at the implementation of GreetingEntityBean, it does not do much. Most of the methods are to fulfill the contract with the container. A few of the methods fake a primary key id semantic, but that is beyond the scope of this book. Instead, focus on the following method of the entity bean implementation:

```
public String getGreeting(){
   return "Hello World!";
}
```

This method returns the now-infamous greeting. The session bean connects with the entity bean and calls this method. In order to do this, the deployment descriptor must be configured properly.

The Session Bean

This session bean's sole purpose in life is to connect to the entity bean and call the entity bean's getGreeting() method. Like the entity bean, the HelloWorld session defines three source files: one for the implementation bean class, one for the remote interface, and one for the home interface. The three classes are the GreetingSessionBean class, the GreetingSessionRemote interface, and the GreetingSessionHome interface, respectively.

The next three listings provide the full source code for the remote, home, and implementation. Here is the source for the GreetingSessionBean class:

```
package xptoolkit.ejbs;

import javax.rmi.PortableRemoteObject;
import javax.naming.InitialContext;

import javax.ejb.SessionBean;
import javax.ejb.SessionContext;
import javax.ejb.EJBException;
import javax.ejb.CreateException;

public class GreetingSessionBean implements SessionBean{

    public void setSessionContext(SessionContext context)
                                        throws EJBException{
    }

    public void ejbCreate() throws  CreateException{
    }
```

```
    public void ejbRemove() throws EJBException{
    }

    public void ejbActivate() throws EJBException{
    }

    public void ejbPassivate() throws EJBException{
    }

    public String getGreeting(){
        GreetingEntityHome home;
        GreetingEntityRemote remote;
        InitialContext jndiContext;
        Object ref;
        String greeting="bye bye";

        try {
         jndiContext = new InitialContext();
         ref  = jndiContext.lookup
                  ("java:comp/env/ejb/GreetingEntityBean");

         home = (GreetingEntityHome)
                PortableRemoteObject.narrow (ref,
                                  GreetingEntityHome.class);
         remote = home.create();
         greeting = remote.getGreeting();
         System.out.println("Greeting: " + greeting);
        }
        catch (Exception e){
            throw new EJBException(e);
        }
        return greeting;
    }

}
```

Following is the source for the GreetingSessionHome interface.

```
    package xptoolkit.ejbs;

    import javax.ejb.EJBHome;
    import javax.ejb.CreateException;
    import java.rmi.RemoteException;

    public interface GreetingSessionHome extends EJBHome{
        public GreetingSessionRemote create()
                                 throws CreateException, RemoteException;

    }
```

And finally, here is the source for the GreetingSessionRemote interface.

```
    package xptoolkit.ejbs;
```

```
import javax.ejb.EJBObject;
import java.rmi.RemoteException;

public interface GreetingSessionRemote extends EJBObject{
        public String getGreeting()throws RemoteException;
}
```

Like the entity bean, the session bean's main focus is the getGreeting() method. The getGreeting() method of the session bean calls the entity bean's getGreeting() method. But first it has to look it up. Let's break down the getGreeting() method down step by step, because it is important when we discuss the deployment descriptor in the next part of this section.

First the method defines five variables, as follows:

```
GreetingEntityHome home;
GreetingEntityRemote remote;
InitialContext jndiContext;
Object ref;
String greeting="bye bye";
```

The home variable creates an instance of GreetingEntityBean (a reference to its remote). The remote variable holds a reference to the remote proxy of GreetingEntityBean. The session bean never calls GreetingEntityBean directly; instead, it talks to the remote interface (a detailed discussion is beyond the scope of this book). The jndiContext looks up the GreetingEntityBean's home interface in the naming service provided by the EJB container that uses the JNDI API interface. The ref object holds a reference to the home object before it is narrowed into the home interface. (The narrow concept is similar to casting, but it could involve a CORBA narrow, which is beyond the scope of this book—please view it as a cast.) Finally, the greeting variable holds the greeting message returned from the entity bean. Now, let's look at the rest of the method step by step.

First we get the JNDI initial context. The entity beans environment is defined in the deployment descriptor, and the EJB container provides this context (environment) to the enterprise bean at runtime (more on this in the deployment descriptor part of this section) as follows:

```
jndiContext = new InitialContext();
```

Next we get the home reference from the jndiContext. Note that the home is mapped to this location by the deployment descriptor as follows:

```
ref  = jndiContext.lookup
          ("java:comp/env/ejb/GreetingEntityBean");
```

Now that we have the home interface reference, we can narrow it down to a real home interface (the PortableRemoteObject.narrow is needed for compatibility with CORBA IIOP—that is, RMI over IIOP) as follows:

```
home = (GreetingEntityHome)
        PortableRemoteObject.narrow (ref,
                    GreetingEntityHome.class);
```

Now we have a real home object proxy; thus, we can use the home to create the remote object reference to the entity bean as follows:

```
remote = home.create();
```

Once we have the remote interface, we can begin using it to call the entity bean. The first and only method we call is getGreeting(), as follows:

```
greeting = remote.getGreeting();
```

Just to prove to ourselves that we were able to call the session bean, we print out the message, which shows up in the stdout for the EJB server we are using for this book:

```
System.out.println("Greeting: " + greeting);
```

As you can see, the method for session bean just delegates the call to the entity bean. The nice thing is that the entity bean is looked up with JNDI. This approach demonstrates one enterprise bean talking to another enterprise bean. In the next section, we create a proxy bean that takes care of all the complexities of dealing with JNDI on the client side.

The Shadow Proxy Bean

The shadow bean is a proxy and an adapter for the client side. It is a proxy in that it has the same methods as the remote interface and all calls to it are delegated to the remote interface. The shadow handles all access to the JNDI interface, the home reference to create the session bean's remote interface. The shadow even handles non-compliant J2EE servlet engines, by allowing the JNDI properties to be loaded as a class resource. Note that a servlet engine can be servlet specification–compliant without being J2EE container-compliant. It is an adapter in that it adapts the remote interface of the session bean to the xptoolkit.model.Greeting interface. The code for the proxy is shown next.

```
package xptoolkit.model;

import java.util.Properties;
import javax.rmi.PortableRemoteObject;
import javax.naming.InitialContext;

import xptoolkit.ejbs.GreetingSessionRemote;
import xptoolkit.ejbs.GreetingSessionHome;
import xptoolkit.ejbs.GreetingEntityRemote;
import xptoolkit.ejbs.GreetingEntityHome;

import java.io.InputStream;


public class GreetingShadow implements Greeting{
    GreetingSessionRemote remote;
    static Properties env = new Properties();
    static {
        InputStream is;
        try{
            is=
            GreetingShadow.class.getResourceAsStream("/jndi.properties");
```

```
                env.load(is);
            }
        catch(Exception e){
            System.out.println(""+e);
            System.out.println();
            e.printStackTrace();
        }
    }

    public GreetingShadow() {
        GreetingSessionHome home;
        InitialContext jndiContext;
        Object ref;

        try{
            jndiContext = new InitialContext(env);
            ref  = jndiContext.lookup("GreetingSessionBean");
            home = (GreetingSessionHome)
             PortableRemoteObject.narrow (ref, GreetingSessionHome.class);
            remote = home.create();
        }
        catch(Exception e){
            System.out.println(e.getMessage());
            System.out.println();System.out.println();
            e.printStackTrace();
        }
    }

    public String getGreeting() {
        String greeting="bye bye";
        try{
            greeting=remote.getGreeting();
        }
        catch(Exception e){}
        return greeting;
    }

}
```

The bean tries to load the properties needed to run the JNDI naming service (that is, to create the initial context):

```
    static {
        InputStream is;
        try{
            is=
            GreetingShadow.class.getResourceAsStream("/jndi.properties");
            env.load(is);
        }
        catch(Exception e){
            System.out.println(""+e);
            System.out.println();
            e.printStackTrace();
        }
    }
```

As you can see, this code is not very robust. However, if you are expecting the properties for JNDI to be loaded elsewhere, the code won't complain. For example, some Web application servers allow you to set up the JNDI environment in the configuration file for the server. If you decide to use these features of the Web application server, then this code works regardless—and because it is in the static initializer block, it runs only once.

The constructor of the GreetingShadow class tries to load the initial context based on the properties loaded in the static initializer block. If those properties are not set, JNDI uses the initial context that is configured for this environment; if nothing is set or the wrong JNDI initial context is mapped, then you will not be able to look up the home object of GreetingSessionBean. Otherwise, the following code is a lot like the code for the session to talk to the entity, except now it is the shadow (client side proxy) talking to the session. Look at the following code and compare it to the session code talking to the entity code:

```
public GreetingShadow() {
   GreetingSessionHome home;
   InitialContext jndiContext;
   Object ref;

   try{
       jndiContext = new InitialContext(env);
       ref  = jndiContext.lookup("GreetingSessionBean");
       home = (GreetingSessionHome)
       PortableRemoteObject.narrow (ref, GreetingSessionHome.class);
       remote = home.create();
   }
   catch(Exception e){
       System.out.println(e.getMessage());
       System.out.println();System.out.println();
       e.printStackTrace();
   }
}
```

Next, all methods (such as getGreeting()) are delegated to the remote interface that was create in the constructor. This is demonstrated as follows:

```
public String getGreeting() {
    String greeting="bye bye";
    try{
        greeting=remote.getGreeting();
    }
    catch(Exception e){}
    return greeting;
}
```

The important thing to note is that because the GreetingShadow implements the Greeting interface, it can be swapped out for GreetingBean. All we have to do is set the system property "Greeting.class" to "GreetingShadow", and the GreetingFactory will instantiate it on a call to getGreeting() instead of GreetingBean. If you recall, HelloServlet reads a "Greeting.class" servlet parameter and uses it to set the system property "Greeting.class". Thus, if we change the "Greeting.class" servlet parameter in the Web application deployment descriptor, we can swap the local GreetingBean with the remote proxy GreetingShadow. We accomplish this trick with the buildfile for the Web application at the end of this section. First, let's look at the deployment descriptor for the Enterprise JavaBeans. (Note that the jndi.properties file may need to be changed for your environment; refer to the EJB documentation of your EJ application server.)

The Enterprise JavaBeans Deployment Descriptor

As we discussed in Chapter 2, "J2EE Deployment Concepts," the Enterprise JavaBean deployment descriptor sets up the environment for the Enterprise JavaBeans that we are going to deploy. The next listing shows the Enterprise JavaBean deployment descriptor (ejb-jar.xml) for our Hello World application.

```
<ejb-jar>

<description>
This ejb-jar files contains the Enterprise beans for the
model 2 Hello World application.
</description>
<enterprise-beans>
    <entity>
        <description>
            The GreetingEntityBean is a do nothing bean to demonstrate
            how to deploy an Enterprise bean with Ant.
        </description>
        <ejb-name>GreetingEntityBean</ejb-name>
        <home>xptoolkit.ejbs.GreetingEntityHome</home>
        <remote>xptoolkit.ejbs.GreetingEntityRemote</remote>
        <ejb-class>xptoolkit.ejbs.GreetingEntityBean</ejb-class>
        <transaction-type>Container</transaction-type>
        <reentrant>True</reentrant>
        <prim-key-class>java.lang.Integer</prim-key-class>
        <persistence-type>Bean</persistence-type>
    </entity>
    <session>
        <description>
            The GreetingSessionBean is a do nothing bean to demonstrate
            how to deploy an Enterprise bean with Ant.
        </description>
        <ejb-name>GreetingSessionBean</ejb-name>
        <home>xptoolkit.ejbs.GreetingSessionHome</home>
        <remote>xptoolkit.ejbs.GreetingSessionRemote</remote>
        <ejb-class>xptoolkit.ejbs.GreetingSessionBean</ejb-class>
        <session-type>Stateful</session-type>
        <transaction-type>Container</transaction-type>

        <ejb-ref>
            <description>
                This sets up a references from the Entity bean to the
                    session bean.
                Thus, the session bean can look up the Entity bean in
                    its environment space.
            </description>
            <ejb-ref-name>ejb/GreetingEntityBean</ejb-ref-name>
            <ejb-ref-type>Entity</ejb-ref-type>
```

```
            <home>xptoolkit.ejbs.GreetingEntityHome</home>
            <remote>xptoolkit.ejbs.GreetingEntityRemote</remote>
            <ejb-link>GreetingEntityBean</ejb-link>
        </ejb-ref>
    </session>


</enterprise-beans>
<assembly-descriptor>
    <container-transaction>
        <method>
            <ejb-name>GreetingSessionBean</ejb-name>
            <method-name>*</method-name>
        </method>
        <trans-attribute>Supports</trans-attribute>
    </container-transaction>

    <container-transaction>
        <method>
            <ejb-name>GreetingEntityBean</ejb-name>
            <method-name>*</method-name>
        </method>
        <trans-attribute>Supports</trans-attribute>
    </container-transaction>

</assembly-descriptor>
</ejb-jar>
```

This deployment descriptor is fairly standard. We'll point out some areas of interest. Inside the session bean's descriptor element is a sub-element to define a reference to the entity bean, as follows:

```
<ejb-ref>
    <description>
        This sets up a references from the Entity bean to the
            session bean.
        Thus, the session bean can look up the Entity bean in
            its environment space.
    </description>
    <ejb-ref-name>ejb/GreetingEntityBean</ejb-ref-name>
    <ejb-ref-type>Entity</ejb-ref-type>
    <home>xptoolkit.ejbs.GreetingEntityHome</home>
    <remote>xptoolkit.ejbs.GreetingEntityRemote</remote>
    <ejb-link>GreetingEntityBean</ejb-link>
</ejb-ref>
```

This is how the session bean can find the entity bean. The container takes care of the setting for the initial context (unlike the shadow, where we loaded the properties from jndi.properties). In addition, the container reads the ejb-ref element and maps GreetingEntityBean's home into the GreetingSessionBean's environment context. Cool!

As you can see, we have a lot of files to manage. We have JAR files and a JNDI property file that must be locatable by the client-side shadow's class loader. We also have a set of classes (remote and home) that must be packaged in the client-side shadow's JAR file. On the flip side, we have a deployment descriptor and six Java files that need to be packaged in the server-side JAR file for two the Enterprise JavaBeans.

The Ant buildfile, which is described in the next section, takes care of all these complexities. It documents the process and ensures the build is repeatable.

The Enterprise Bean Buildfile

As we stated, the output of the buildfiles is two JAR files. One JAR file is for the EJB's container; and the other file is for the server. Also, unlike the war command, there is no special command to build EJB JAR files. Frankly, you don't need a special command because EJB JAR files are very similar to regular JAR files. The following listing contains the complete buildfile for the enterprise beans.

```
<project name="enterprise_beans" default="all" >

    <target name="setProps" unless="setProps"
                            description="setup the properites.">
        <property name="outdir" value="/tmp/app" />
        <property name="jboss" value="/jboss/jboss/deploy" />
    </target>

    <target name="init" depends="setProps"
                            description="initialize the properties.">
        <tstamp/>
        <property name="ejbout" value="${outdir}/ejbs" />
        <property name="build" value="${ejbout}/ejb-jar" />
        <property name="client" value="${ejbout}/ejb-jar-client" />
        <property name="dist" value="${outdir}/dist" />
        <property name="lib" value="${outdir}/lib" />
        <property name="meta-data" value="${build}/META-INF" />
        <property name="build_lib" value="./../lib" />
        <property name="ejb_lib" value="/JBoss/jboss/lib/ext" />
    </target>

    <target name="clean_jboss" if="jboss">
        <delete file="${jboss}/greetbeans.jar" />
    </target>

    <target name="clean" depends="init,clean_jboss"
                            description="clean up the output directories.">
        <delete dir="${build}" />
        <delete dir="${meta-data}" />
        <delete dir="${client}" />
        <delete dir="${dist}/greet-ejbs.jar" />
    </target>


    <target name="prepare" depends="init"
                            description="prepare the output directory.">
        <mkdir dir="${build}" />
        <mkdir dir="${lib}" />
        <mkdir dir="${meta-data}" />
        <mkdir dir="${client}" />
```

```
        <mkdir dir="${dist}" />
</target>

<target name="compile" depends="prepare"
                        description="compile the Java source.">
    <javac srcdir="./src" destdir="${build}" >
        <classpath >
            <pathelement location="." />

            <fileset dir="${build_lib}">
                <include name="**/*.jar"/>
            </fileset>

            <fileset dir="${lib}">
                <include name="**/*.jar"/>
            </fileset>

            <fileset dir="${ejb_lib}">
                <include name="**/*.jar"/>
            </fileset>
        </classpath>
    </javac>
</target>

<target name="config_jboss_jndi" if="jboss">
    <copy todir="${client}" >
        <fileset dir="./jboss_props" />
    </copy>
</target>

<target name="config_jndi" depends="config_jboss_jndi" />


<target name="package" depends="compile,config_jndi"
            description="package the Java classes into a jar.">

 <copy todir="${client}" >

     <fileset dir="${build}" excludes="**/*Bean*"
                            includes="**/*.class*" />

 </copy>

 <copy file="./META-DATA/ejb.xml" tofile="${meta-data}/ejb-jar.xml" />

 <jar jarfile="${dist}/greet-ejbs.jar"
        basedir="${build}" />

 <jar jarfile="${lib}/client-greet-ejbs.jar"
        basedir="${client}" />
</target>

<target name="deploy_jboss" depends="package" if="jboss">
    <copy file="${dist}/greet-ejbs.jar" todir="${jboss}" />
```

```
        <copy todir="${lib}"  >
            <fileset dir="./jboss_clientlib" />
        </copy>
    </target>

    <target name="deploy" depends="package,deploy_jboss"
                    description="deploys the jar file to the ejb server.">
    </target>


    <target name="all" depends="clean,deploy"
                    description="perform all targets."/>

</project>
```

Analyzing the Buildfile for Enterprise Beans

This buildfile is structured like the other buildfiles. It has similar targets that do similar things. One key difference is that the package target for this buildfile outputs two JAR files instead of one, as follows:

```
<target name="package" depends="compile,config_jndi"
                description="package the Java classes into a jar.">

  <copy todir="${client}" >

        <fileset dir="${build}" excludes="**/*Bean*"
                                    includes="**/*.class*" />

  </copy>

  <copy file="./META-DATA/ejb.xml" tofile="${meta-data}/ejb-jar.xml" />

  <jar jarfile="${dist}/greet-ejbs.jar"
        basedir="${build}" />

  <jar jarfile="${lib}/client-greet-ejbs.jar"
        basedir="${client}" />
</target>
```

Because the client JAR file (client-greet-ejbs.jar) does not need the implementation classes (GreetingEntityBean and GreetingSessionBean), the output classes are copied to a temporary directory and a file set is defined that excludes all files with the substring *Bean* in them. This is demonstrated as follows:

```
<copy todir="${client}" >

        <fileset dir="${build}" excludes="**/*Bean*"
                                    includes="**/*.class*" />

</copy>
```

After we copy the buildfiles to the ${client} output directory, we jar them into the client file as follows:

```
<jar jarfile="${lib}/client-greet-ejbs.jar"
     basedir="${client}" />
```

The astute reader may wonder about the jndi.properties file that the shadow needs to create the initial context. Notice that the package target depended on compile and config_jndi targets. The config_jndi depends on the config_jboss_jndi target, which in turn copies the jndi.properties file located in ./jboss_props to the client directory that is jarred, as follows:

```
<target name="config_jndi" depends="config_jboss_jndi" />

<target name="config_jboss_jndi" if="jboss">
    <copy todir="${client}" >
        <fileset dir="./jboss_props" />
    </copy>

</target>
```

Notice that the config_jboss_jndi target is executed only if the jboss environment variable is set. Thus you can easily turn it off by not setting this environment variable. If you wanted to set up a similar mechanism for, for example, Orion (another J2EE application server environment that supports EJB), you could add a config_orion_jndi dependency to the config_jndi target, and then define a config_orion_jndi target that copies the jndi.properties file from the ./orion directory. Note that it is not necessary to use either if the servlet engine you are using is also a J2EE-compliant container.

That takes care of the client-side bean. What about the sever-side bean—the EJB bean for the EJB container, which needs the deployment descriptor? Remember, we said that Ant does not have a special task as it does for the WAR file. Thus, we need to build an exact replica of the directory structure needed by the EJB JAR file and then jar the directory. The prepare target prepares the output directory for the server side. Then, the package target copies the deployment descriptor to the correct location and jars the location as follows.

First we copy the deployment descriptor to the right location:

```
<copy file="./META-DATA/ejb.xml"
                    tofile="${meta-data}/ejb-jar.xml" />
```

Next we jar the location:

```
<jar jarfile="${dist}/greet-ejbs.jar"
     basedir="${build}" />
```

You may want to examine the metadata and build property settings, demonstrated as follows:

```
<target name="init" depends="setProps"
                    description="initialize the properties.">
    <tstamp/>
    <property name="ejbout" value="${outdir}/ejbs" />
    <property name="build" value="${ejbout}/ejb-jar" />
    <property name="client" value="${ejbout}/ejb-jar-client" />
    <property name="dist" value="${outdir}/dist" />
```

```
        <property name="lib" value="${outdir}/lib" />
        <property name="meta-data" value="${build}/META-INF" />
        <property name="build_lib" value="./../lib" />
    </target>
```

Another difference between this buildfile and the webapplication project buildfile is that the deploy target works with JBoss instead of Resin and Tomcat like the Web application. The deploy target is set up in a similar fashion to the way the config_jndi is set up, in that it can easily be modified to support more types of application server—even remote servers using the ftp task, as we mentioned earlier in this chapter. Here is the deploy target:

```
    <target name="deploy_jboss" depends="package" if="jboss">
        <copy file="${dist}/greet-ejbs.jar" todir="${jboss}" />
        <copy todir="${lib}"  >
            <fileset dir="./jboss_clientlib" />
        </copy>
    </target>

    <target name="deploy" depends="package,deploy_jboss"
                description="deploys the jar file to the ejb server.">
    </target>
```

Notice that it copies the server-side JAR (greet-ejbs.jar) to the JBoss deployment directory, and it copies all the support libraries that the client-side JAR needs to the common directory (<copy todir="${lib}"... <fileset dir="./jboss_clientlib" ...).

The next part of this section covers a little magic that we do to the webapplication buildfile to use either the enterprise beans or the local version of the greeting bean.

Defining the ejb Property in the Web Application Buildfile

All the buildfile snippets in this part of the section are for the webapplication project. By defining the "ejb" property, the webapplication project has the option of deploying/configuring whether the Web application that is deployed uses enterprise beans. Notice that the prepare_meta target, which is a dependency of the prepare target, has two dependencies prepare_meta_ejb and prepare_meta_noejb, demonstrated as follows:

```
    <target name="prepare_meta"
            depends="prepare_meta_ejb, prepare_meta_noejb">
        <copy todir="${meta}" filtering="true">
            <fileset dir="./meta-data"/>
        </copy>
    </target>
```

The prepare_meta_ejb target is executed only if the "ejb" property is set as follows:

```
    <target name="prepare_meta_ejb" if="ejb">
        <filter token="Greeting.class"
                value="xptoolkit.model.GreetingShadow"/>
    </target>
```

If the "ejb" property is set, then the target creates a filter token called Greeting.class. Here, we set the value of Greeting.class to GreetingShadow. Conversely, the prepare_meta_ejb target is executed only if the "ejb" property is not set, as follows:

```
<target name="prepare_meta_noejb" unless="ejb">
    <filter token="Greeting.class"
            value="xptoolkit.model.GreetingBean"/>
</target>
```

Here, we set GreetingBean as "Greeting.class". But how is this used by the application? You may recall that HelloWorldServlet uses the servlet parameter "Greeting.class" to set the system property "Greeting.class" that is used by the GreetingFactory to create an instance of Greeting. We put an Ant filter key in the webapplication project deployment descriptor, as follows:

```
<servlet>
    <servlet-name>HelloWorldServlet</servlet-name>
    <servlet-class>xptoolkit.web.HelloWorldServlet</servlet-class>
    <init-param>
      <param-name>Greeting.class</param-name>
      <param-value>@Greeting.class@</param-value>
    </init-param>
</servlet>
```

If we copy this file using the filter command after the filter token Greeting.class has been set, then *@Greeting.class@* is replaced with the value of our token Greeting.class, which is set to xptoolkit.model .GreetingShadow in the prepare_meta_ejb target and to xptoolkit.model.GreetingBean in the prepare_meta_noejb target. Notice that the prepare_meta target copies the deployment descriptor with filtering turned on, as follows:

```
<copy todir="${meta}" filtering="true">
    <fileset dir="./meta-data"/>
</copy>
```

Running the Buildfiles

In order to get the webapplication project to run with the enterprise beans, we do the following.

1. Navigate to the EJBeans directory and build the EJB buildfile, as follows:

    ```
    C:\CVS\...\MVCHelloWorld\EJBeans>ant
    ```

    For the EJB file, the deploy target is part of the all-target dependency, so it is deployed just by running it.

2. Build the webapplication project with the "ejb" property set so that the correct Greeting.class is set in the webapplication project deployment descriptor, as follows:

    ```
    C:\CVS\...\MVCHelloWorld\WebApplication>ant -Dejb=true deploy
    ```

    Note that you may want to run both of these buildfiles with the clean option before you attempt to deploy.

3. Now that we have the application deployed, we start the EJB server (we used JBoss installed in /jboss) and the Web application server (we used Resin installed in /resin) and try the application as before. If we set up everything correctly, we get something like the following message in the stdout of our EJB container. The following is from JBoss:

```
[GreetingSessionBean] Greeting: Hello World!
```

You should have a buildfile for each major subsystem or component in your application. A medium-size application could have 50 to 100 subsystems and components with separate buildfiles. The small example that we presented in this chapter now has five buildfiles that must be executed in the correct order. Having 5 buildfiles and expecting a deployer, system admin, or fellow developer to execute them in the right order is loony; expecting a fellow developer, system admin, or deployer to build 50 buildfiles in the correct order is suicide.

Besides, human intervention defeats the purpose of automating the buildfile process (having a repeatable build). What we need is a master buildfile that manages all the complexities of this simple Hello World application. In the next section, we create such a buildfile to manage the complexities of building these five projects and perform some special deployment magic.

EAR Enterprise Application

In addition to having a master buildfile called main (we discussed the master buildfile in Chapter 4), we want to deploy all our applications into an application server that can accept them. The main buildfile serves two purposes:

- ❑ It ensures that all the subprojects are created in the correct order.
- ❑ It builds an enterprise archive (EAR) file so that the EJBs and Web applications can be easily deployed to a single application server.

The HelloWorld Main Project Buildfile

The main project's buildfile is structured (not surprisingly, we hope) very much like the other buildfiles. There are setProps, init, prepare, clean, build, and package targets. One of the key differences is that the main buildfile delegates the clean and build targets to the subproject while ensuring that they execute in the correct order. Also, the package section creates an EAR file. Refer to the following listing to see the final main buildfile.

```
<project name="main" default="package" >


    <target name="setProps" unless="setProps"
                        description="setup the properites.">
        <property name="outdir" value="/tmp/app" />
        <property name="setProps" value="true" />
    </target>


    <target name="init" depends="setProps"
```

```
                                    description="initialize the properties.">
        <tstamp/>
        <property name="dist" value="${outdir}/dist" />
        <property name="deploy" value="${outdir}/deploy" />

        <property name="build" value="${outdir}/classes" />
        <property name="lib" value="${outdir}/lib" />
    </target>

    <target name="clean" depends="init"
                        description="clean up the output directories.">

        <ant dir="./Model" target="clean">
            <property name="outdir" value="${outdir}" />
            <property name="setProps" value="true" />

        </ant>

        <ant dir="./EJBeans" target="clean">
            <property name="outdir" value="${outdir}" />

            <property name="setProps" value="true" />
            <property name="jboss" value="/tools/jboss/jboss/deploy" />

        </ant>

        <ant dir="./WebApplication" target="clean">
            <property name="outdir" value="${outdir}" />

            <property name="setProps" value="true" />
            <property name="ejb" value="true" />
        </ant>

        <ant dir="./Application" target="clean">
            <property name="outdir" value="${outdir}" />

            <property name="setProps" value="true" />
        </ant>

        <delete dir="${outdir}" />
    </target>

    <target name="prepare" depends="init"
                        description="prepare the output directory.">
        <mkdir dir="${build}" />
        <mkdir dir="${lib}" />
        <mkdir dir="${dist}" />
        <mkdir dir="${deploy}" />
        <mkdir dir="${dist}/META-INF" />
    </target>

    <target name="build" depends="prepare"
            description="build the model and application modules.">

        <ant dir="./Model" target="package">
```

```
                <property name="outdir" value="${outdir}" />
                <property name="setProps" value="true" />
        </ant>

        <ant dir="./EJBeans" target="deploy">
                <property name="outdir" value="${outdir}" />
                <property name="setProps" value="true" />
                <property name="jboss" value="/tools/jboss/jboss/deploy" />
        </ant>

        <ant dir="./Applet" target="package">
                <property name="outdir" value="${outdir}" />
                <property name="setProps" value="true" />
        </ant>

        <ant dir="./WebApplication" target="deploy">
                <property name="outdir" value="${outdir}" />
                <property name="setProps" value="true" />
                <property name="ejb" value="true" />
        </ant>

        <ant dir="./Application" target="package">
                <property name="outdir" value="${outdir}" />
                <property name="setProps" value="true" />
        </ant>
    </target>

    <target name="package" depends="build">
        <copy file="./META-INF/application.xml"
                                todir="${dist}/META-INF" />

        <jar jarfile="${deploy}/hello.ear"
                                basedir="${dist}" />
    </target>

</project>
```

Analyzing the Buildfile for the Enterprise Application

The build target uses the ant task (<ant...>) to call the other Ant buildfiles. The build target is as follows:

```
<target name="build" depends="prepare"
        description="build the model and application modules.">

    <ant dir="./Model" target="package">
            <property name="outdir" value="${outdir}" />
            <property name="setProps" value="true" />
    </ant>

    <ant dir="./EJBeans" target="deploy">
            <property name="outdir" value="${outdir}" />
            <property name="setProps" value="true" />
            <property name="jboss" value="/tools/jboss/jboss/deploy" />
    </ant>
```

```
<ant dir="./Applet" target="package">
    <property name="outdir" value="${outdir}" />
    <property name="setProps" value="true" />
</ant>

<ant dir="./WebApplication" target="deploy">
    <property name="outdir" value="${outdir}" />
    <property name="setProps" value="true" />
    <property name="ejb" value="true" />
</ant>

<ant dir="./Application" target="package">
    <property name="outdir" value="${outdir}" />
    <property name="setProps" value="true" />
</ant>
</target>
```

Notice that each call to invoke another buildfile sets the relative directory of the subproject's buildfile (<ant dir="./Model" target="package">) and the target of the buildfile. Because we named each buildfile of each subproject build.xml, we only need to specify the directory. In addition to specifying the target that we want to execute, the ant task passes two properties to each subproject, as follows:

```
<property name="outdir" value="${outdir}" />
<property name="setProps" value="true" />
```

The second property ensures that the subproject's setProps target is not executed, by setting the property "setProps". Remember, the "setProps" property for each project is not executed if the setProps property is set (<target name="setProps" unless="setProps">). The first property ensures that the value of the outdir of the main project is passed to the subproject. When we combine these two properties, it's easy to set a new directory for all the output of the main project and all its subprojects at the command line, demonstrated (using bash) as follows:

```
rick@CANIS_MAJOR /usr/rick/cvs/XPToolKit/examples/chap5/MVCHelloWorld

$ ant -DsetProps=no -Doutdir=/usr/rick/output
```

These lines could be used to redirect the output to a directory to which you have access, if you are developing on a Unix box.

The clean target follows many of the same concepts as the build target, so we will not discuss it in detail. The next major piece of the main project is the package target, as follows:

```
<target name="package" depends="build">
    <copy file="./META-INF/application.xml"
                            todir="${dist}/META-INF" />

    <jar jarfile="${deploy}/hello.ear"
                            basedir="${dist}" />
</target>
```

This code copies the application.xml metadata from the ./META-INF directory to the distribution directory. The distribution directory is also where the webapplication project buildfile's package target and the enterprise beans project buildfile's package target put their WAR and EJB JAR file, respectively.

The next task is for the main's package target to jar the WAR, EJ JAR, and application.xml files into a JAR file format. It does this with the jar task, as follows:

```
<jar jarfile="${deploy}/hello.ear"
              basedir="${dist}" />
```

The output of the file is hello.ear, which is put into the deployment directory. The deployment directory is defined in the init target (for example, /tmp/deploy). The application.xml file is the deployment descriptor for the EAR file.

Enterprise Application Deployment Descriptor

If our intention is to deploy the Web application and the enterprise beans as a single logical unit, it may be useful to create an EAR file as we did. In order for the J2EE container to understand what we are deploying, we have to tell it with the deployment descriptor in the following listing.

```
<application>
  <display-name>Hello World Application</display-name>
  <description>Hello World Application.</description>

  <module>
    <web>
      <web-uri>hello.war</web-uri>
      <context-root>helloworld</context-root>
    </web>
  </module>

  <module>
    <ejb>greet-ejbs.jar</ejb>
  </module>

</application>
```

Looking at this code, you may wonder why we don't list the model library, the applet JAR, the enterprise bean client JAR, and so on. Remember, they were included with the WAR file. Instead, the deployment descriptor describes two modules: our Hello World Web application and our Hello World enterprise beans. First the Web application:

```
<module>
  <web>
    <web-uri>hello.war</web-uri>
    <context-root>helloworld</context-root>
  </web>
</module>
```

Notice that the URI for the Web application is set to helloworld; thus, when we deploy it, it runs under the helloworld directory (http://localhost/helloworld). Next, we defined the Enterprise JavaBean module as follows:

```
<web>
  <web-uri>hello.war</web-uri>
  <context-root>helloworld</context-root>
</web>
```

We can use it to deploy in one simple step to any J2EE container that supports both Web applications and enterprise beans.

The Pet Store Case Study

The Web application for the pet store baseline is much like the one in the Hello World application. For simplicity and ease of development, most of the presentation tier is implemented in JSP. We added a nonsensical servlet just for demonstration purposes. Note that in the real world, we use Struts, a framework from Apache, and we have many Java classes to deploy—we use Struts in several examples later in this book.

You may recall from the last case study that the main project buildfile for its build and clean target calls the webapplication subproject buildfile's clean and deploy targets respectively. The webapplication subproject buildfile's deploy target is defined as follows:

```
<target name="deploy" depends="package">
    <copy file="${dist}/${pet_war}" todir="${deploy_resin}" />
    <copy file="${dist}/${pet_war}" todir="${deploy_tomcat}" />
</target>
```

The deploy target copies the WAR file specified by ${pet_war} to both the Resin and Tomcat deployment directories. (Resin and Tomcat are both J2EE Web application servers.) The deploy target depends on the package target. The package target creates the WAR file that is deployed to Resin and Tomcat, which is defined as follows:

```
<target name="package" depends="compile">
    <mkdir dir="${meta}" />
    <war warfile="${dist}/${pet_war}" webxml="${meta}/web.xml">
        <!--
            Include the html and jsp files.
            Put the classes from the build into the classes directory
            of the war. Exclude web.xml file and WEB-INF directory.
        /-->
    <fileset dir="./public-html" >
        <exclude name="WEB-INF" />
        <exclude name="web.xml"/>
      </fileset>
      <classes dir="${build}" />
    <lib dir="${lib}"  />
    </war>
</target>
```

As you will notice, the package target is much like the one in the Hello World Web application sample. The package target uses the war task to create a WAR file. The WAR file includes all the libraries in the lib (${lib})—namely, the petmodel.jar file created in the model subproject. It also includes the web.xml Web application deployment descriptor using the "webxml" attribute. The following listing contains the complete Web application.

```xml
<project name="webapplication" default="all" >
    <target name="setProps" unless="setProps"
                        description="setup the properites.">
        <property name="outdir" value="/tmp/petstore" />
    </target>

    <target name="init" depends="setProps"
                        description="initialize the properties.">
     <tstamp/>
     <property name="local_outdir" value="${outdir}/webapps" />
     <property name="lib" value="${outdir}/lib" />
     <property name="dist" value="${outdir}/dist" />
     <property name="build" value="${local_outdir}/webclasses" />
     <property name="meta" value="public-html/WEB-INF" />
     <property name="deploy_resin" value="/resin/webapps" />
     <property name="deploy_tomcat" value="/tomcat/webapps" />
     <property name="appstub" value="pet" />

     <property name="pet_war" value="${appstub}.war" />
     <property name="build_lib" value="./../lib" />
    </target>

    <target name="clean_deploy" >

        <delete file="${deploy_resin}/${pet_war}" />
        <delete dir="${deploy_resin}/${appstub}" />
        <delete file="${deploy_tomcat}/${pet_war}" />
        <delete dir="${deploy_tomcat}/${appstub}" />
    </target>

    <target name="clean" depends="init,clean_deploy"
                        description="clean up the output directories.">
        <delete dir="${local_outdir}" />
        <delete file="${dist}/${pet_war}" />
    </target>

    <target name="prepare" depends="init"
                        description="prepare the output directory.">
        <mkdir dir="${build}" />
      <mkdir dir="${dist}" />
    </target>

    <target name="compile" depends="prepare"
                        description="compile the Java source.">
        <javac srcdir="./java" destdir="${build}">
            <classpath >
                <fileset dir="${lib}">
                    <include name="**/*.jar"/>
```

```
                    </fileset>

                    <fileset dir="${build_lib}">
                        <include name="**/*.jar"/>
                    </fileset>
                </classpath>
            </javac>
        </target>

        <target name="package" depends="compile">
            <mkdir dir="${meta}" />
            <war warfile="${dist}/${pet_war}" webxml="${meta}/web.xml">
                <!--
                    Include the html and jsp files.
                    Put the classes from the build into the classes directory
                    of the war. Exclude web.xml file and WEB-INF directory.
                /-->
                <fileset dir="./public-html" >
                    <exclude name="WEB-INF" />
                    <exclude name="web.xml"/>
                </fileset>
                  <classes dir="${build}" />
                <lib dir="${lib}"   />
                </war>
        </target>

        <target name="deploy" depends="package">
            <copy file="${dist}/${pet_war}" todir="${deploy_resin}" />
            <copy file="${dist}/${pet_war}" todir="${deploy_tomcat}" />
        </target>

        <target name="all" depends="clean,deploy"
                            description="perform all targets."/>

    </project>
```

As you can see, the standard targets are present in this buildfile as they are in the Hello World example, the model subproject, and the rest of the buildfiles in this book. This makes it easy to tell what the buildfiles are doing at a glance. You also may notice that the optional "description" attribute is set for each target. This also helps to document your targets and can be shown when running Ant.

The next case study will include the Test subproject buildfile using junit and the junitreport tasks. Then, it will add EJBeans support with a new subproject, and rerun the tests to ensure that the refactored CategorySystem still functions.

Summary

In this chapter, we took a very complex project with many components and subsystems (albeit a simple implementation) and deployed it to an enterprise application server and servlet engine, and to both at the same time with the EAR file. We demonstrated the use of three types of deployment descriptors for Web applications, enterprise bean modules, and enterprise applications. We also demonstrated how to use a similar set of tags to create consistent sets of related buildfiles. Finally, we showed how to assemble all these buildfiles into a single project using a master buildfile to coordinate the building and deploying of the application. The last part of the chapter presented a case study showing a more realistic version of an enterprise application.

7

XDoclet Primer

How many times have you sat down at your computer ready to begin working on your next EJB, Struts, or SOAP project only to realize you have a mountain of benign coding ahead of you. Constructs such as home interfaces, configuration files, XML, and others begin to flood your mind, and you wonder why you have to write all of this support code just to set the foundation for your new application. Why can't some code generator just write all of this "basic" code for you?

Your mind travels back to the days when Byte magazine arrived in the mailbox at over one-inch thick. Embedded in the pages was an article or advertisement about a new code generation application that was going to end coding as we knew it. Depending on your point of view, that situation never quite developed because the code generation applications were just too rigid. Looking at the clock you see that 20 minutes have passed and you aren't any closer to getting your project started.

Today, we do have an option available that helps with the development of much of the support code needed in current technologies. XDoclet is the answer, and this code generation tool will bring a new edge to your software development practices and save you both time and money in the process. In this chapter, we are tasked with understanding what XDoclet is, its capabilities, the things it cannot do, and how to use it.

What Is XDoclet?

When teaching new computer science students, one of the most important issues in software development I try to get across is the need to document the code. There must be some defect in the documentation gene when software engineers are created, because no matter how hard this topic is pounded, nobody seems to get it right. In an attempt to help with the defective gene, Java architects chose to provide the technology of self-documenting code within the language itself and provide the tools for building much of the needed documentation. This technology is called *Javadoc*, and we need to explore it before looking at XDoclet. Of course, no code is self-documenting without the software engineer providing the necessary tags within the code, but that's another story.

Javadoc is a technology in which defined attributes are placed in comment blocks of the code in order to provide a processor application with information about the code itself. Consider this example:

```
/**
 * The JavaHelpMe class has been documented
 * using multiple lines of comments
 */

public class JavaHelpMe {
}
```

Here we have a simple class with a comment block used to describe the class. All of the text between the beginning /* and the closing / symbols will be ignored by the Java compiler and left for the reader of the code or Javadoc. The comment blocks can be found on many of the language constructs, as we see here:

```
/**
 * The JavaHelpMe class has been documented
 * using multiple lines of comments
 */
public class JavaHelpMe {

  /** a method comment */
  public int returnHelpO {
  }
}
```

Of course, these comments blocks aren't anything new because we used the same type of construct when we wrote our C code; at least we were suppose to comment that code. The Javadoc technology adds to the comment blocks using tags and tag descriptions. For example:

```
/**
 * The JavaHelpMe class has been documented
 * using multiple lines of comments
 * @see com.my.class
 */
public class JavaHelpMe {

  /** a method comment
   *  @return int value
   */
  public int returnHelpO {
  }
}
```

In this example, we've added two Javadoc tags, @see and @return. Each of these tags will be processed by Javadoc and specific actions taken when encountered. In the case of the @see, additional output will be added to the description of the class like this:

```
See Also: class
```

where class is a link to another Javadoc page.

There are countless more Javadoc tags that can be found at http://java.sun.com/j2se/javadoc/. By using the Javadoc tags, the code can basically self-document as long as the developer uses the tags and provides comment blocks. So, getting to our point of this section, XDoclet is a technology that uses tags in the same manner as Javadoc, but instead of producing help files, the XDoclet system produces code.

Code Generation Templating

XDoclet is a tool that requires input files in order to process them and produce some type of output. During the processing of the input files, XDoclet will discover known tags and process the tags using a series of templates. The templates determine what kind of code is produced by specific tags. Obviously, the richer the template, the more code will be generated. The following figure shows an example of the processing taking place with XDoclet.

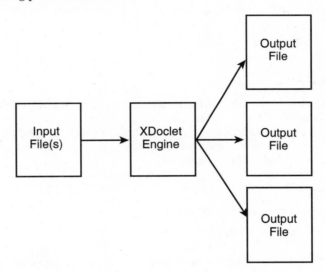

Of course, XDoclet will need a way to obtain the input files, as we see in the previous figure. Instead of reinventing another preprocessor for XDoclet, the XDoclet team chose to use the power of Ant to trigger the XDoclet process. Through a series of tasks and subtasks, discussed in more detail later, an Ant build script will trigger XDoclet to process specific source files and subsequently generate new code in the form of Java, configuration files, and others. Therefore, all a developer needs to do is provide an Ant task for XDoclet, define specific XDoclet tags within their source code, and sit back as the code is automatically generated.

XDoclet has found support in a variety of different technologies including:

❏   Eclipse

❏   EJB

❏   Hibernate

- ❑ JBoss
- ❑ JDO
- ❑ JMX
- ❑ MockObjects
- ❑ SOAP
- ❑ Servlets
- ❑ Struts
- ❑ WebLogic

Many of the these technologies will be covered later in this book as they pertain directly to XDoclet. Our goal in the remainder of this chapter is to guide you through the basics of using XDoclet so you are ready to apply it.

Installing XDoclet

As mentioned earlier, XDoclet requires Ant in order to do its required work and, of course, Java. For this reason, the first step in installing XDoclet is to install Ant. Once Ant is in place and has been verified to be working correctly, you can fire up your browser and surf to http://xdoclet.sourceforge.net. On this page, you can click the link Download And Install, on the left navigation bar. This link will bring you to a page where you can download XDoclet. The options include:

- ❑ **xdoclet-lib-1.x:** Includes libs
- ❑ **xdoclet-bin-1.x:** Includes libs, samples, and docs
- ❑ **xdoclet-src-1.x:** Includes all source code

For most developers, just download the binary and uncompress it on your system. Within the uncompressed files, you will find a directory called /lib. You will need to keep track of this directory and set the appropriate variable within your Ant build script.

Configure Ant

The Ant build tool is designed to work with targets, tasks, and subtasks. In order for Ant to know about a task, it has be defined within a <taskdef> tag. For example, if we wanted to use the ejbdoclet task in our project, we would have the following <taskdef>:

```
<taskdef name="ejbdoclet"
  classname="xdoclet. modules. ejb.EjbDocletTask"
  classpathref="xdoclet. lib. path"
/>
```

This <taskdef> begins with the name of the task defined as ejbdoclet. This is a standard naming convention but it can be changed as needed. The name of the task is followed by the classname defining the exact class that will execute the task, and classpathref defines where the class can be found. Since XDoclet is a tool that can generate a varied number of outputs, there can be more than one <taskdef> tag in an Ant build.xml file. For example, we might need to generate code for both EJBs as well as WEB constructs, so our build.xml file would include the following code:

```
<taskdef name="ejbdoclet"
  classname="xdoclet.modules.ejb.EjbDocletTask"
  classpathref="xdoclet.lib.path"
/>
<taskdef name="webdoclet"
  classname="xdoclet.modules.web.WebDocletTask"
  classpathref="xdoclet. lib.path"
/>
```

As you begin to use Ant, it becomes clear that some task definitions need to be part of a single target in order to handle dependencies between tasks. In this case, we might wrap our tasks, like this:

```
<target name="xdoclet">
  <taskdef name="ejbdoclet"
    classname="xdoclet.modules.ejb.EjbDocletTask"
    classpathref="xdoclet. lib.path"
  />
  <taskdef name="webdoclet"
    classname="xdoclet.modules.web.WebDocletTask"
    classpathref="xdoclet.lib.path"
  />
</target>
```

If you don't want to create a specific <target> element for the task definitions, they can be placed in the <init> target found in most Ant build scripts. With our defined tasks and target, we can look at building a specific <target> element for the code we need to process with XDoclet.

For this example, let's assume we have a directory called \ejbsrc, which currently contains some source input files, and a destination directory called \ejbcode. We will be using XDoclet to handle some ejb tags within the input files. Our Ant <target> element would look like the following:

```
<target name="generateEJB" depends="xdoclet">
<ejbdoclet destdir="ejbcode">
<fileset dir="ejbsrc">
<include name="* */*Bean.java"/>
</fileset>

<deploymentdescriptor destdir="deployment"/>

<homeinterface />
<localinterface />
<localhomeinterface />
</ejbdoclet>
</target>
```

As you can see from this target, we define the destination directory for our resulting source code as well as the location of the fileset to process. A specific deployment descriptor directory is also defined. Finally, the EJB subtasks are listed to process our implementation file.

A Simple Example

By far the crowning jewel in the XDoclet arena involves ejbdoclet and the ability to produce all of the files necessary to support EJBs. For this reason it is fitting to use the ejbdoclet task as the foundation for a simple example before moving to the remaining chapters, where we will provide much more information on using XDoclet with various technologies, including EJBs. In this example, we will build an entity bean for the following table:

```
CREATE TABLE comments (
  ID int not null auto-increment primary key,
  storyID int,
  comment varchar(255),
  ts timestamp
);
```

This simple table can be used to store comments about a story as you might find in a portal-type application. For our environment, we will assume the existence of Java, Ant, and XDoclet on the development system. For our entity bean, we will need to produce four different files:

❑ Deployment descriptor

❑ Local interface

❑ Local home interface

❑ Implementation file

Using XDoclet, we need only to write a single file, the implementation file, and include the appropriate XDoclet files. Here's an example of the implementation file we produced using XDoclet tags:

```
package com.company.database;

/**
 * @ejb.bean        type="CMP"
 *          cmp-version="2.x"
 *          name="CommentBean"
 *          jndi.name="cmr/User"
 *          view-type="local"
 *          primkey-field="ID"
 *
 * @ejb.pk         class="java.lang.Integer"
 *
 * @ejb:findersignature="java.util.Collection findAll()"
 *          unchecked="true"
 *          query="SELECT OBJECT(s) FROM comment AS s"
 *
 * @ejb.home       generate="local"
```

```
 *            local -class="database.CommentHome"
 *
 * @ejb.interface      generate="local"
 *           local-class="database.Comment"
 *
 * @ejb-persistence      table-name="comments"
 */

public abstract class CommentBean extends EntityBean {

  private EntityContext ctx;
  private String ID;
  private String StorylD;
  private String Comment;
  private String ts;

/**
 *   @ejb.pk-field
 *   @ejb.interface-method      view-type="local"
 *   @ejb.persistent-field
 */
public abstract String getID() {
}

/**
 *   @ejb.interface-method      view-type="local"
 *   @ejb.persistent-field
 */
public abstract String getStoryID() {
}

/**
 *   @ejb.interface-method      view-type="local"
 *   @ejb.persistent-field
 */
public abstract String getComment() {
}

/**
 *   @ejb.interface-method      view-type="local"
 *   @ejb.persistent-field
 */
public abstract String getTs() {
}

/**
 *   @ejb.interface-method      view-type="local"
 */
public abstract void setStoryID(String id) {
}

/**
 *   @ejb.interface-method      view-type="local"
 */
```

```
public abstract void setComment(String comment) {
}

/**
*   @ejb.interface-method      view-type="local"
*/
public abstract void setTs(String ts) {
}

public Integer ejbCreate(String c, String s, String t) throws CreateException
{
  setStorylD(s);
  setComment(c);
  setTs(t);
}

public void ejbPostCreate(String c, String s, Stringt) {
}
public void ejbRemove() throws RemoveException {
}

public void ejbStore() {
}

public void ejbLoad() {
}

public void ejbActivate() {
}

public void ejbPassivate() {

public void setEntityContext(EntityContext ctx) {
  this.ctx = ctx;
}

public void unsetEntityContext() {
  this.ctx = null;
}
```

As you can clearly see, the implementation file for our entity bean consists primarily of tags and just a few actual Java statements. Before we look at an Ant build script to process our implementation file, let's take a moment and discuss what each of the tags is telling the XDoclet processor to generate. All of the XDoclet tags have a common format:

```
@namespace.tag-name attribute-name="attribute value"
```

The @namespace part of the tag relates to the tasks defined for XDoclet. We will touch on tasks later in the chapter, but tasks include ejb, hibernate, and others. A tag can be zero or more attributes, depending on how they are defined. Each attribute will have a value associated with it to help with the code generation. A full description of all tags available in XDoclet can be found at http://xdoclet.sourceforce.net.

Looking back at our code, the first comment block is used to control the code generation for the entire bean class. The tag, @ejb.bean, sets the tone for the entire code generation in that it indicates to the generator that we are going to be building an EJB bean. As you can see, our XDoclet tags aren't restricted to just a description as in the case of Javadoc tags, but instead we have some number of attributes for the tag. In our example, the @ejb.bean tag is using six different attributes:

```
type="CMP" cmp-version="2.x"
name="CommentBean"
jndi.name="cmr/User"
view-type="local"
primkey-field="ID"
```

The type="CMP" attribute, or parameter, indicates the bean we are building will be container managed.

The cmp-version="2.x" attribute indicates the CMP version begin used.

The name="CommentBean" attribute tells the code generator the name of the bean being created. The bean name is the same as the class name defined within the implementation file, as our example shows.

The jndi.name="cmr.user" attribute indicates the value to use for the jndi component.

The view-type="local" attribute indicates the access type of this bean. The options here include local, remote, and both.

The primkey-field="ID" attribute indicates which column within our table relating to the bean is used as the primary key field. Looking back at our schema for the database table, we can see that the ID field has the clause of primary key associated with it, so that field is used as the value for this attribute.

Now that the code generator knows we are building an EJB, we have to add a few additional tags at the class level to provide all of the needed information. It should be noted that the additional tags will vary based on the view-type attribute specified earlier. The next tag encountered is called @ejb.pk with an attribute of class="int". You can probably guest that this tag is used to indicate the type for the primary key defined in our database table. In this case, the class is int.

Next, we define the characteristics of the home interface for our EJB as designated by the @ejb.home tag. For our example, we have only two attributes. The first attribute is generate="local", indicating the code generator should generate only a local home interface. The local-class="database.CommentHome" attribute tells the generator to output local home into the class CommentHome.

We also have a tag called @ejb.interface that indicates the type of interface to generate. Again we have only two attributes that closely match those found in the @ejb.home tag. The generate attribute is the same as before, but the localclass="database.Comment" attribute specifies the class to output the interface.

All of the tags just encountered set up the XDoclet generator along with the ejbdoclet and the Resin-specific doclet to output various files for our entity bean. We have placed all of the tags in the implementation file in order to keep the tags necessary for our bean in direct relationship with the implementation. Now we need to discuss the tags used within the implementation to define the set/get methods necessary for any entity bean.

First notice there are set/get methods for each of the columns in our database table. The only exception is the ID column. Notice there is only a get method for this column. The reason is the ID is autogenerated by the database when new rows are added to the table. Since we will not be manually setting the ID, we don't want to include a set method. For each of the set methods, you will see a consistent pattern of tags. These are:

```
@ejb.persistent-field
@ejb.interface-method
```

The @ejb.persistent-field tag tells the code generator that this field is persistent, and appropriate code needs to be generated to handle the persistence. The @ejb.interface-method instructs how the method will be exposed. The choices are local, remote, and both. You will also notice that the getlDO method includes a tag called @ejb.pk-field to indicate which of the fields is the primary key.

In the case of the get methods, there is just the single @ejb.interface-method tag to indicate the exposure level of the method. There really isn't any more code needed in order for our entity bean to be automatically created by XDoclet. The only thing left to do is build an appropriate build.xml Ant build file.

Sample Ant Build File

Earlier in the chapter we discussed how an Ant task is needed to invoke the XDoclet code generation. The following listing is a complete build.xml script which will take our implementation file and build our entity bean.

```
<project name="tutorial" default="all">
<property name="xdoclet.root.dir" value="c:\xdoclet-1.2"/>

<target name="xdoclet">
<taskdef name="ejbdoclet"
classname="xdoclet.modules. ejb.EjbDocletTask"
classpathref="xdoclet. lib.path"/>
</target>

<target name="generateEJB" depends="xdoclet">
<ejbdoclet destdir="ejbcode">
<fileset dir="ejbsrc">
<include name="* */*Bean.java"/>
</fileset>

<deploymentdescriptor destdir="deployment"/>

<homeinterface />
<localinterface />
<localhomeinterface />
</ejbdoclet>
</target>

<target name="build">
<mkdir dir=" {dest}"/>
<javac srcdir="${ src }"
classpathref="resinclasspath"
destdir=" {dest}"
</target>

<target name="all" depends="xdoclet, generateEJB, build"/>
</project>
```

As you can see there is quite a bit of additional information in a full build.xml build script. Let's start at the end of the file where we have a <target> element defined that depends on the xdoclet, generateEJB, and build targets. Look up at the top of the file, where the clean and xdoclet targets are defined. The xdoclet target will set up the environment needed to access the base XDoclet jars and classes. After the xdoclet target is accomplished, the generateEJB target will fire to handle all of our XDoclet code generation. The generateEJB task does almost all of the work by setting various environment variables and then executing several subtasks. Once the XDoclet and Resin class have done their work, the code for the entity bean will have been produced and it will be built.

XDoclet Tasks, Subtasks, and Templates

Now that you have a fairly good idea of what XDoclet is and how it can be used to generate code for your next project, let's look at some of the lower level details. There are three primary components to XDoclet: tasks, subtasks, and templates.

Core Tasks

The XDoclet tasks can be considered a modularization of the functionality available within XDoclet. Each defined task is specific to a domain such as EJB or Hibernate. All of the defined tasks inherit functionality from the <doclet> task. The current core XDoclet tasks are shown in this table:

Task Tag	Description
<ejbdoclet>	Tags for producing EJB code
<webdoclet>	Tags for producing servlets, tag libraries, etc.
<hibernatedoclet>	Tags for Hibernate
<mockdoclet>	Tags to produce mock objects
<jdodoclet>	Tags for JDO Persistence
<jmxdoclet>	Tags for JMX including interfaces and configs
<portletdoclet>	Tags for portlets

Because the tasks act as an encapsulation construct, it is only natural to expect that there are subcomponents or subtasks available within each of the core tasks.

Subtasks

Each task will have a number of subtasks that instruct XDoclet to invoke a specific template used in the code generation step. If you look back at our Ant build.xml script, you will find several subtasks listed for our EJB code generation. These subtasks were:

```
<localinterface/>
<localhomeinterface/>
<remoteinterface/>
<homeinterface/>
```

In order to help you understand what XDoclet is doing during the code generation, consider the code for the <localinterface> subtask found in the following listing. As you can see, the subtask relates to an actual class within the EJB module.

```
public class LocalInterfaceSubTask extends AbstractEjbCodeGeneratorSubTask
{
    public final static String DEFAULT_LOCAL_CLASS_PATTERN = "{0}Local";

    protected static String DEFAULT_TEMPLATE_FILE = "resources/local.xdt";

    /**
     * A configuration parameter for specifying the local interface name
pattern. By default the value is used for
     * deciding the local interface name. {0} in the value mean current
class's symbolic name which for an EJBean is the
     * EJB name.
     *
     * @see    #getLocalClassPattern()
     */
    protected String localClassPattern;


    /**
     */
    public LocalInterfaceSubTask()
    {
        setTemplateURL(getClass().getResource(DEFAULT_TEMPLATE_FILE));
        setDestinationFile(getLocalClassPattern() + ".java");
        addOfType("javax.ejb.EntityBean");
        addOfType("javax.ejb.SessionBean");
    }

...
```

In this partial code listing, we see the declaration of the LocalInterfaceSubTask that will be executed if the <localinterface> subtask element is found within our Ant build script. There are appropriate classes for all of the subtasks within XDoclet.

Templates

Templates are files that contain some code and some XML-like syntax used in the generation of the final source code. The following listing shows a template used in the <localinterface> subtask.

```
/*
 * <XDtI18n:getString bundle="xdoclet.modules.ejb.XDocletModulesEjbMessages"
resource="do_not_edit"/>
 */
package <XDtPackage:packageOf><XDtEjbIntf:componentInterface
type="local"/></XDtPackage:packageOf>;

/**
```

```
 * <XDtI18n:getString bundle="xdoclet.modules.ejb.XDocletModulesEjbMessages"
resource="local_interface_for" arguments="<XDtEjb:ejbName/>"/>
<XDtClass:classCommentTags indent="0"/>
*/
public interface <XDtClass:classOf><XDtEjbIntf:componentInterface
type="local"/></XDtClass:classOf>
    extends <XDtEjbIntf:extendsFrom type="local"/><XDtClass:ifHasClassTag
tagName="ejb:bean" paramName="local-business-interface">,
<XDtClass:classTagValue tagName="ejb:bean" paramName="local-business-
interface"/></XDtClass:ifHasClassTag>
{
  <XDtClass:ifDoesntHaveClassTag tagName="ejb:bean" paramName="local-
business-interface">
    <XDtMethod:forAllMethods>
     <XDtEjbIntf:ifIsInterfaceMethod superclasses="false" interface="local">
<XDtMethod:methodComment indent="3"/>
    public <XDtMethod:methodType/> <XDtMethod:methodName/>(
<XDtParameter:parameterList/> ) <XDtMethod:exceptionList/>;

    </XDtEjbIntf:ifIsInterfaceMethod>
    </XDtMethod:forAllMethods>
  </XDtClass:ifDoesntHaveClassTag>

  <XDtMerge:merge file="local-custom.xdt">
  </XDtMerge:merge>
}
```

As you see, the template includes common Java keywords and constructs intermixed with XML-like tags that are used by XDoclet to pull information from the source input files. It is important to understand that if the template doesn't like something needed by the developer, it won't appear in the resulting code. Code generation is still a fairly static process.

XDoclet Merging

Fortunately, there is one way to handle the static generation of the code. Looking at the previous listing, you will see tags such as the following:

```
<XDtMerge:merge file="local-custom.xdt">
   </XDtMerge:merge>
```

These tags represent merge points where the code generator will try to find the specified file, pull in all of the code verbatim from the file, and place it in the resulting source code.

To use the merge points, just place the code you want to have merged into the specified file. There are numerous merge points throughout the XDoclet template in order to provide a high level of developer customization of the resulting source code.

Summary

XDoclet is a technology that allows developers to increase their productivity by automatically generating code for many of the mundane tasks involved in EJB, Hibernate, or other technology development. When the XDoclet technology was first created, EJB development was its driving factor simply because of the numerous files needed for every EJB created. Clearly the developmental advantages of XDoclet caught on because numerous tasks were created to handle Hibernate, JDO, and others. This chapter presented an overview of XDoclet and a simple tutorial on using the technology.

Building J2EE Web Components with Ant and XDoclet

If you take a look at the current Internet software development arena, a good amount of the heavy lifting is still being accomplished with servlets. One of the reasons for this is the ability to use the advanced features of Java to handle the processing of information to and from the user. There are many commercial and open-source application servers to handle the servlets as well. One of the most important issues of servlet development is the creation of the web.xml file, which is the deployment descriptor for the Web application. Fortunately, XDoclet allows the automatic generation of the web.xml file using the webdoclet Ant task. In addition, we can use XDoclet to further configure the servlet using filtering and custom tags or tablibs.

Servlet Example

We will use a step-by-step process to show how to use XDoclet with servlets by creating a simple servlet and deploying it on an application server. For this example, we will be using Resin as the application server. First we will create a simple servlet, as shown inthe following listing. This servlet will query an account database, display the information in a table, and output some other simple text.

```
package example;

import javax.servlet.*;
import javax.servlet.http.*;
import javax.sql.*;
import java.sql.*;
import javax.naming.*;

public class SimpleServlet extends HttpServlet {

  public void init(ServletConfig config)
```

```
                throws ServletException {
            super.init(config);
    }

    protected void handleUser(HttpServletRequest request,
                             HttpServletResponse response)
                             throws ServletException }
        try {
          response.setContentType("text/html");
          java.io.PrintWriter out = response.getWriter();

          out.println("<html>");
          out.println("<head>");
          out.println("<title>My Simple Servlet" ),
          out.println("</head>");
          out.println("<body>");
          out.println("The current database is Production<br>");
          out.println("The username is 'accounts'<br><br>");

          displayTable(out);

          out.print In ("</body>");
          out.println("</html>");
          out.close();
        } catch (Exception e) {
          throw new ServletException (e);
        }
    }

    protected void doGet(HttpServletRequest request,
                         HttpServletResponse response)
                         throws ServletException {
        handleUser(request, response);
    }

    protected void doPost(HttpServletRequest request,
                          HttpServletResponse response)
                          throws ServletException {
        handleUser(request, response);
    }

    private void displayTable(java.io.PrintWriter out)
                             throws Exception {
        Object obj = new InitialContext().lookup("java:comp/en
v/jdbc/dbconnection");
        DataSource pool = (DataSource) obj;

        if (pool != null) {
          Connection connection = pool.getConnetion();
          out.println("<table>");
          out.println("<tr><td>description</td><td>price</td></tr>" );
          try {
            Statement statement = connection.createStatement();
            ResultSet rs = statement.executeQuery(
                "SELECT * FROM production WHERE username="accounts");
```

```
                while(rs.nextQ) {
                  out.println("<tr><td>" + rs.getString("description") +"</td><td>"
+
                            rs.getString(`price") + "</td></tr>");
                }
              } finally {
                connection.close();
              }
              out.println("</table>");
            }
         }
      }
```

For this servlet we will need to create a web.xml deployment descriptor, as shown in the following listing.

```xml
<?xml version="1.0" encoding="UTF-8"?>
<!DOCTYPE web-app PUBLIC "-//Sun Microsystems, Inc.
   //DTD Web Application 2.3//EN" http://Iava.sun.comldtd/web-app 2 3.dtd>

<web-app>
   <servlet servlet-name="SimpleServlet"
            servlet-class="example. SimpleServlet"
   />
   <load-on-startup>1</load-on-startup>

   <servlet-mapping>
     <servlet-name>SimpleServlet</servlet-name>
     <url-pattern>/Example/*</url-pattern >
   </servlet-mapping>

   <servlet-mapping>
     <servlet-name>SimpleServlet</servlet-name>
     <url-pattern>SimpleServlet</url-pattern>
   </servlet-mapping>

   <resource-ref>
     <description>JDBC Connection</description>
     <res-ref-name>jdbc/dbconnection</res-ref-name>
     <res-type>javax.sgl.DataSource</res-type>
     <res-auth>Container</res-auth>
   </resource-ref>
  </web-app>
```

If we deploy the code in the two previous listings on an application server and place the appropriate database table in our database, we will see an output page with the contents of the database table. Now, let's consider what the code is doing, even though it is just an example.

The primary purpose of this code example is to pull various rows from a database table based on an account name. During a production run, we want the table used to be called Production and have a user-name of Accounts. However, during development or testing work, we don't want to mess with trying to find the appropriate places within the code to make the changes. Instead, we'd like a common location.

Even more important, the deployment descriptor must be specifically designed for this servlet. There should be a way to automatically create the deployment descriptor from the servlet source code in order to keep like code with like code. We can accomplish both tasks using webdoclet XDoclet tags. As you know, XDoclet tags are added to code within the comments. So, we will change the code in the first listing to include a comment section with the XDoclet tags for the deployment descriptor and also change the code to use init-param tags for our database table and username. This following listing shows the new code.

```
package example;

/**
 *         @version 0.5
 *         @web.servlet name="SimpleServlet"
 *             display-name="Simple Servlet"
 *             load-on-startup=" 1"
 *
 *         @web-servlet-init-param name="table" value="production"
 *         @web-servlet-init-param name="account" value="accounts"
 *
 *         @web.resource-ref description="database connection"
 *                     name="jdbc/dbconnection"
 *                        type="javax.sql.DataSource"
 *                     auth="Container"
 *
 *         @web.servlet-mapping url-pattern ="/Example/*"
 *         @web.servlet-mapping url-pattern ="/SimpleServlet"
 */

import javax.servlet.*;
import javax.servlet.http.*;
import javax.sgl.*;
import java.sgl.*;
import javax.naming.*;

public class SimpleServlet extends HttpServlet {

  public void init(ServletConfig config)
                    throws ServletException {
    super.init(config);
  }

  protected void handleUser(HttpServletRequest request,
                             HttpServletResponse response)
                             throws ServletException {

    try {
      response.setContentType("text/html");
      java.io.PrintWriter out = response.getWriter();

      out.println("<html>");
      out.println("<head>");
      out.println("<title>My Simple Servlet");
      out.println("</head>");
      out.println("<body>");
      out.println("The current database is Production<br>");
      out.println("The username is `accounts'<br><br>");
```

```java
        displayTable(out);

        out.println("</body>");
        out.println("</html>");
        out.close();
      } catch (Exception e) {
      throw new ServletException (e);
      }
  }

  protected void doGet(HttpServletRequest request,
                       HttpServletResponse response)
                       throws ServletException {

    handleUser(request, response);
  }

  protected void doPost(HttpServletRequest request,
                        HttpServletResponse response)
                        throws ServletException {
    handleUser(request, response);
  }

  private void displayTable(java.io.PrintWriter out)
                            throws Exception {

  ServletConfig config = this.getServletConfig();
  String table = config.getInitParameter("table");
  String username = config.getln1tParameter("account");

  Object obj = new
InitialContext().lookup("java:comp/env/jdbc/dbconnection");
  DataSource pool = (DataSource) obj;

  if (pool != null) {
    Connection connection = pool.getConnection();
    out.println("<table>");
    out.print ln("<tr><td>description</td><td>price</td><Itr>");

    try {
      Statement statement = connection.createStatementO;
      ResultSet rs = statement.executeQuery(
        "SELECT * FROM " + table + " WHERE username="' + username + ""');

      while(rs.next()) {
        out.println("<tr><td>" + rs.getString("description") +"</td><td>" +
                    rs.getString("price") + "</td></tr>");
      }

    } finally {
      connection.close();
    }

    out.println("</table>");
  }
 }
}
```

There are two primary changes in this listing. The first is the comment section, and we will discuss that section in a moment. The second change occurred in the displayTable() method. In the function, we now pull the table and account name to use in the database query directory from the deployment descriptor because they will be declared as init parameters.

Webdoclet Tags

Let's take a moment and discuss the tags we've used in our servlet example shown in the previous listing. The first tag in our example is @web.servlet. This tag is designed to create the class-level <servlet> element within the deployment descriptor. For our servlet, we've defined the name, display-name, and load-on-startup attribute of the tag:

```
@web.servlet name="SimpleServlet"
        display-name="Simple Servlet"
            load-on-startup=" Y'
```

The result of the tag once processed by XDoclet will be:

```
    <servlet>

<servlet-name>SimpleServlet</servlet-name>
<display-name>Simple Servlet</display-name>
<servlet-class>example.SimpleServlet</servlet-class>
<load-on-startup>1</load-on-start up>

    </servlet>
```

The attributes available for the @web.servlet tag are shown in the following table.

Attribute	Description	Required
Name	Servlet name	T
display-name	Servlet display name	F
Icon	Servlet icon	F
Description	Servlet description	F
load-on-startup	The load order of this servlet – number where 1 is first	F
run-as	The role to run this servlet as	F

The next two webdoclet tags in our example use the @web-servlet-init-param to create the init-param tags within the deployment descriptor:

```
@web-servlet-init-param name="table" value="production"
@web-servlet-init-param name="account" value="accounts"
```

The result of these tags will be:

```
    <servlet>

  <servlet-name>

...

    <init-param>
      <param-name>table</param-name>
      <param-value>production</param-value>
    </init-param>

    <init-param>
      <param-name>table</param-name>
      <param-value>production</param-value>
    </init-param>

    </servlet>
```

The attributes available for the @web.servlet-init-param tag are shown in the following table.

Attribute	Description	Required
Name	Parameter value	T
Value	Parameter value	F
Icon	Servlet icon	F
Description	Servlet description	F

After creating the necessary parameters for the servlet, we can define any J2EE resources needed by the servlet. In our example servlet, we will be accessing a database to pull rows that will be displayed to the user based on the init-params:

```
    @web.resource-ref description="database connection"
                name=' jdbc/dbconnection"
                type="javax.sgl.DataSource"
                    auth="Container"
```

The result of this webdoclet tag will be:

```
    <resource-ref>

  <description>JDBC Connection</description>
  <res-ref-name>jdbc/dbconnection</res-ref-name>
  <res-type>javax.sgl.DataSource</res-type>
  <res-auth>Container</res-auth>

    </resource-ref>
```

The attributes available for the @web.resource-ref tag are shown in the following table.

Attribute	Description	Required
Name	Resource name	T
Type	Resource type	T
Auth	Resource authentication: Application or Container	T
Description	Resource description	F
Scope	Resource scope: Shareable Unshareable	F
Jndi-name	Resource Jndi-name	F

Finally, we can apply the necessary pattern-matching mappings necessary for launching the servlet. This is accomplished using the @web.servlet-mapping tag:

```
@web.servlet-mapping url-pattern="/Example/*"
@web.servlet-mapping url-pattern="/SimpleServlet"
```

These two tags will define the following mappings in our deployment descriptor:

```
    <servlet-mapping>

  <servlet-name>SimpleServlet</servlet-name>
  <url-pattern >/Example/* </url-pattern >

</servlet-mapping>

<servlet-mapping>

  <servlet-name>SimpleServlet</servlet-name>
  <url-pattern>SimpleServlet</url-pattem>

    </servlet-mapping>
```

The attribute available in the @web.servlet-mapping tag is shown in the following table.

Attribute	Description	Required
url-pattern	Pattern to match	T

Using Ant for the Configuration

Of course, just putting the tags in the comment section doesn't do much until we combine it with Ant and XDoclet. In fact, we will need a specific task called webdoclet and one of its subtasks called deploymentdescriptor. There are a couple paths that you will need to know before looking at the build script. These are:

- ❏ Location of the XDoclet install: on our test box it is /usr/local/xdoclet/lib
- ❏ Location of the deploy directory of your application server: /usr/local/resin/webapps
- ❏ Location of your application server's lib directory: /usr/localresin/lib

Here's an example task to handle the conversion of the deployment descriptor tags:

```xml
<'?xml version="1.0" ?>

<project name="webdoclet" default="deploy">

<path id="libpath">
<fileset dir="/usr/local/resin/lib"/> </path>

<path id="xdocpath">
<path refid="libpath">
<fileset dir="/usr/local/xdoclet/lib">
<include name="*.jar"/> </fileset>
</path>
<target name= "init">
<mkdir dir="./tmp/war" />
<mkdir dIi-"./web/WEB-INF/cl asses" /> </target>

<target name="compile">
<javac srcdir="./src" destdir="./web/WEB-INF/classes" debug="true"
deprecation="true"> <classpath refid="libpath"/>
</javac>
</target>

<target name="generateDD">
<taskdef name="webdoclet"
classname="xdoclet. moduels.web.WebDocletTask" classpathref="xdocpath"
<webdoclet destdir="./web/WEB -INF/classes"> <fileset dir="./src">
<include name="* */*Servlet.java" /> </fileset>
<deploymentdescriptor servletspec="2.3" destdir="./web/WEB-INF" />
</webdoclet>
<target>
<target name="package" depends="init, compile, generateDD">
<war defile="Jtmp/war/example.war" webxml="./web/WEB-INF/web.xml"> <fileset
dir="./web">
<exclude name="* */build.xml" /> <exclude name="**/*.bat" />
<exclude name="* */web.xml" /> <exclude name="**/*.java" />
<exclude name="**/*.class" /> </fileset>

<lib dir="./web/WEB-INF/lib"/>

<classes dir="./web/WEB-INF/classes"> <exclude name="* */*.Java"/> </classes>
</war>
</target>

<target name="deploy" depends="package">
<copy file="./tmp/war/example. war" todir="/usr/local/resin/webapps" />
</target>
```

So what have we done in this build script? First we needed to accomplish two tasks. The first was to generate the deployment descriptor using the <webdoclet> task. Since webdoclet isn't a common task with Ant, we needed to define it using the <taskdef> element. Next, we defined where XDoclet's library files can be found so that Ant will be able to find the class that actually implements webdoclet. Finally, we added the <webdoclet> task, which will process all files within the /src directory having Servlet.java as part of their filename. The resulting deployment descriptor will be placed in the directory ./web/WEB-INF.

After the deployment descriptor is created, the build script will compile the servlet, produce a WAR file, and deploy it to the webapps directory of the application server. Once Ant has finished with the processing of the files, you should have a successful build. At this point, you can browse to the application server and see the contents of your database displayed.

Using Ant Properties, Init-Params, and Filtering

If you consider the init-param values we added to the comments, we really didn't gain anything from a standpoint of making the necessary changes between a production and a development run. In either case, we need to open the source code to add the appropriate table and account values. However, we can use Ant to further abstract the init-param values. Remember that Ant and XDoclet have the ability to replace value based on the properties defined within an Ant build script. With this in mind, we could create a two properties such as the following in our Ant build script:

```
<property name="table" value="production"/> <property name="account" value="
accounts"/>
```

Now in the webdoclet tags for the servlet, the following tags

```
@web-servlet-init-param name="table" value="production" @web-servlet-init-
param name="account" value="accounts"
```

will be replaced with

```
@web-servlet-init-param name="table" value="$j table {"
@web-servlet-init-param name="account" value="${account
}"
```

When the Ant build script is executed, the task to create the deployment descriptor will automatically replace the ${table} and ${account} with the values set by the properties.

Creating Taglibs

Another feature of the webdoclet task is the ability to create custom tags using appropriate XDoclet tags. Custom tags provide a high level of reuse for the JSP page developer. In this section we will create an example custom tag and show how to use webdoclet to handle most of the details. Consider the custom tag defined in the following listing.

```
package customtag;

import java.io.*;
import javax.servlet.jsp.*;
import javax.servlet.jsp.taxext.*;

/**
* @jsp.tag name="NameTag"
* @jsp.variable name-given="currentTry"
*               class="java.lang.Integer"
*               scope="NESTED"
*               declare="true"
*/

public class NameTag implements Tag {

  private PageContext pc = null;
  private Tag parent = null;
  private String name = null;
  private int try = 0;

  public int doStartTag()
                    throws JspException {

    try {
      if (name != null) {
        pc.getOut().write("Your name is " + name);
        pc.setAttribute("currentTry", new Integer(0));
      } else {
        pc.getOut().write("You aren't using the tag correctly.
                You need to set the name attribute");
        try++;
        pc.setAttribute("currentTry", new Integer(try));
      }
    } catch(Exception e) {
      throw new JspException(e);
    }

    return SKIP BODY;
  }

  public int doEndTag()
            throws JspException {
    return EVAL PAGE;
  }

  /**
   * @jsp.attribute required="true"
   *                rtexprvalue=""
   *                descripton="The name of the thing"
   */
  public String getName() {
    return name;
  }

  public void setName(String s) {
    name = s;
```

```
    }

    public void setPageContext(PageContext p)
      pc = p;
    }

    public setParent(Tag t) {
      parent = t;
    }

    public Tag getParent() {
      return parent;
    }
    }
```

All custom tags must have a corresponding Tag Library Descriptor (TLD) in order for the engine to know about the tag. The next listing shows the start of the TLD for the simple tag above.

```
<taglib>

  <tlibversion>1.0</tlibversion>
  <jspversion>1.1</jspversion>
  <shortname>Tags</shortname>


  <tag>

    <name>NameTag</name>
    <tagclass>example.NameTag</tagClass>
    <bodycontent>empty</bodycontent>
    <info>First tag</info>

    <attribute>
      <name>name</name>
      <required>true</required>
...
```

Clearly, you can see why it is important that we have another option for creating the TLD. Although the file isn't complex, it can become quite large if you have many custom tags. It's easy to make mistakes. Our solution is to use Ant and webdoclet to generate the TLD for us. The next listing shows that task we will need to add to an Ant build script to handle the creation of our tag library. The subtask should be added to the GenerateDD target.

```
<webdoclet desdir="./web/WEB-INF">

<fileset dir="./src">
  <include name="* */*Servlet.java" />
  <include name="* */*Tag.j ava" />
</fileset>

<deploymentdescriptor
                        servletspec="2.3"
                        destdir="./web/WEB-INF" >

<taglib uri="mytablib"
        location="WEB-INF/tlds/mytablib.tld"
/>
```

```
<jsptaglib
            jspversion= 1.2"
            destdir="./web/WEB-INF/tlds"
            shortname="Tags"
            filename="mytablib.tld"
/>
```

Testing the Custom Tag

Now that we have a custom tag and an Ant build script that will handle the creation of the TLD as well as the custom tag class itself, it is time to write a JSP page to test the tag. The following listing shows an example JSP.

```
%@page contacntType="text/html"%
%@taglib uri="mytaglib" prefix="mytag"%

<html>
<head>
<title>JSP Tag</title>
</head>
<body>

<mytag:NameTag name="Jim">
  Total tries = <%=currentTry%> <br/>
</mytag:NameTag>

</body>
</html>
```

In this example JSP, we use the NameTag tag and supply a specific name for the name attribute. We also access the currentTry variable defined by the custom tag.

Using Eclipse with Webdoclet

Clearly the use of XDoclet makes the development of traditional Web-based applications easy and less prone to coding errors. When developing applications, there are those who use typical text-based editors such as vi and emacs and those who use an IDE. We aren't here to say which is more appropriate, but in this section we will show how the combination of Eclipse, Ant, and XDoclet can make building servlets even easier. We will use code from the third listing in this chapter.

Before we begin the process of building a new project, you need to make sure that you have Eclipse installed. For testing this code, we used Eclipse 2.1.1 and Tomcat. You will need to install the myeclipse plug-in found at www.myeclipseide.com. You will also need to register with the site in order to download the myeclipse plug-in.

Launch Eclipse to start the new project. The myeclipse plug-in will install itself as a perspective. Open the perspective by choosing Window > Open Perspective > Other > MyEclipse. Select File > New > Project > J2EE > Web Module Project and then click Next. Enter a project name of *SimpleProject*, and enter */SimpleProject* for the Context root URL. You should see the dialog shown in the following figure.

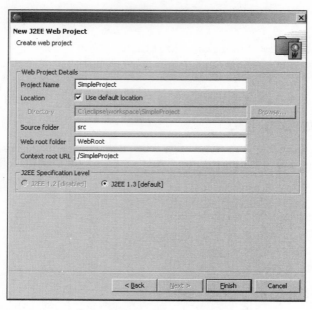

Click the Finish button to see a new project layout, as shown in this figure:

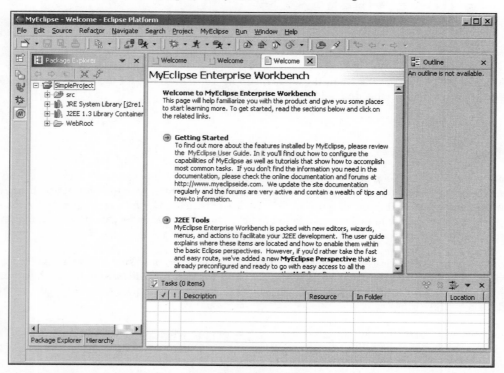

Now we need to create a new servlet. Click the SimpleProject entry in the Package Explorer and choose File > New > Servlet. In the Name field enter the value *SimpleServlet*. In the Package field enter the value *example*. Your dialog should appear as shown in the next figure.

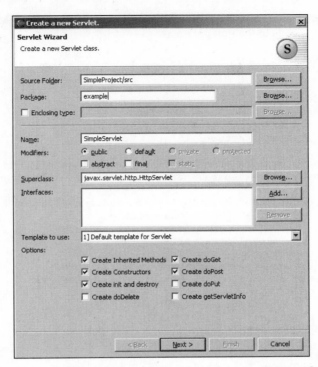

Click the Next button. The next wizard dialog will have the Generate/Map web.xml file checked. Uncheck this box because we want to use XDoclet to create our web.xml file. The dialog should now appear as shown in this figure:

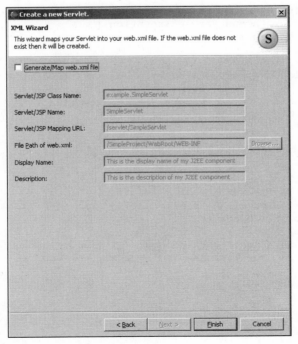

Click the Finish button to allow the IDE to create the servlet. You will be presented with an open Edit pane. Add the following code to the Edit pane:

```
package example;

/**
 *       @version 0.5
 *       @web.servlet name="SimpleServlet"
 *             display-name="Simple Servlet"
 *             load-on-startup=" 1"
 *
 *       @web-servlet-init-param name="table" value="production"
 *       @web-servlet-init-param name="account" value="accounts"
 *
 *       @web.resource-ref description="database connection"
 *                   name="jdbc/dbconnection"
 *                         type="javax.sql.DataSource"
 *                   auth="Container"
 *
 *       @web.servlet-mapping url-pattern ="/Example/*"
 *       @web.servlet-mapping url-pattern ="/SimpleServlet"
 */

import javax.servlet.*;
import javax.servlet.http.*;
import javax.sgl.*;
import java.sgl.*;
import javax.naming.*;

public class SimpleServlet extends HttpServlet {

  public void init(ServletConfig config)
                   throws ServletException {
    super.init(config);
  }

  protected void handleUser(HttpServletRequest request,
                            HttpServletResponse response)
                            throws ServletException {

    try {
      response.setContentType("text/html");
      java.io.PrintWriter out = response.getWriter();

      out.println("<html>");
      out.println("<head>");
      out.println("<title>My Simple Servlet");
      out.println("</head>");
      out.println("<body>");
      out.println("The current database is Production<br>");
      out.println("The username is `accounts'<br><br>");

      displayTable(out);

      out.println("</body>");
      out.println("</html>");
```

```
        out.close();
    } catch (Exception e) {
        throw new ServletException (e);
    }
}

protected void doGet(HttpServletRequest request,
                     HttpServletResponse response)
                     throws ServletException {

    handleUser(request, response);
}

protected void doPost(HttpServletRequest request,
                      HttpServletResponse response)
                      throws ServletException {
    handleUser(request, response);
}

private void displayTable(java.io.PrintWriter out)
                          throws Exception {

    ServletConfig config = this.getServletConfig();
    String table = config.getInitParameter("table");
    String usemame = config. getlnltParameter("account");

    Object obj = new
InitialContext().lookup("java:comp/env/jdbc/dbconnection");
    DataSource pool = (DataSource) obj;

    if (pool != null) {
      Connection connection = pool.getConnection();
      out.println("<table>");
      out.print ln("<tr><td>description</td><td>price</td><Itr>");

      try {
        Statement statement = connection.createStatement0;
        ResultSet rs = statement.executeQuery(
          "SELECT * FROM " + table + " WHERE username="' + username + ""');

        while(rs.next()) {
          out.println("<tr><td>" + rs.getString("description") +"</td><td>" +
                      rs.getString("price") + "</td></tr>");
        }

      } finally {
        connection.close();
      }

      out.println("</table>");
    }
  }
}
```

Now select the SimpleProject folder in the Package Explorer, and select File > New > Folder. In the Folder Name field, enter a value of *build*, as shown in the following figure.

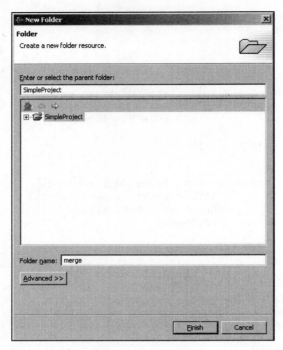

Click the Finish button. Then choose the SimpleProject/Merge entry in the Package Explorer, and select File > New > XML. Populate the dialog with field File Name: welcomefile.xml as shown in the next figure, and click Finish. When the file opens, replace the contents with the following:

```
<welcome-file-list>

<welcome-file>index.html</welcome-file>

</welcome-file-list>
```

Save the file. Now select the SimpleProject folder in the Package Explorer, and select File > New > File. In the File Name field, enter the name *xdoclet-build.properties*, as shown in the next figure, and click Finish.

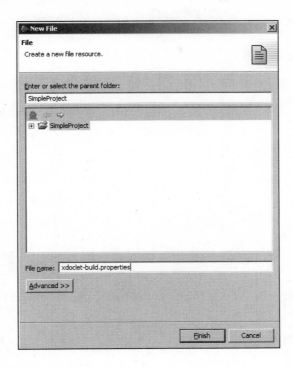

Replace the contents of the file with the following:

```
table = production
account = accounts
```

Now we need to deal with the XDoclet configuration. Right-click the SimpleProject folder in the Package Explorer. Select Properties > XDoclet Configurations to bring up the Properties dialog shown in the next figure.

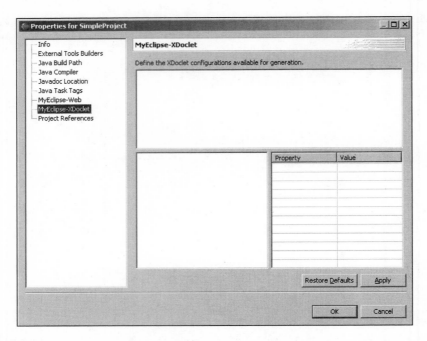

Right-click the dialog and select Add Standard; in this dialog select Standard Web. Your dialog should now look like this:

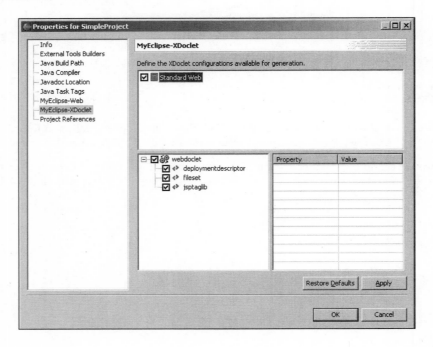

Select the deploymentdescriptor option in the list, and set the following values:

- ❑ Servletspec = 2.3
- ❑ destDir = WebRoot/WEB-INF
- ❑ displayName = Simple Project
- ❑ mergeDir = build

Your dialog should now look like this:

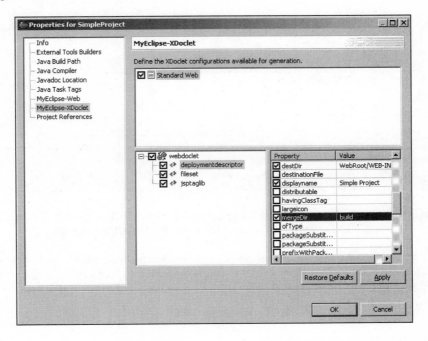

Now click OK to create an xdoclet-build.xml folder.

Next we need to set up Ant. Right-click the xdoclet-build.xml file in Package Explorer and select Run Ant. In the resulting dialog, choose the Properties tab. In the Property Files list, click the Add button. Browse to the SimpleProject folder and select xdoclet-build.properties. Your dialog should look like this:

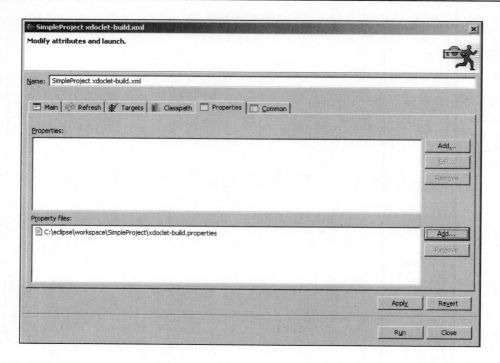

Click the Refresh tab and be sure that both checkboxes are checked. Click the Apply button and then click the Run button to let XDoclet do its job, and the web.xml file will be created.

Finally, let's add an HTML page for our servlet. Choose the SimpleProject folder in Package Explorer; right-click and select New > HTML. In the File Name field, enter the value *index.html* and click Finish. Add the following HTML to the opened page:

```html
<html>
 <head>
    <title>Simple Project</title>
  </head>
  <body>
    <br />
       <h3>Simple project</h3>
          <a href="SimpleServlet">Test Servlet</a>
  </body>
</html>
```

Save the file. Now let's set up the deployment. Right-click the SimpleProject project and select MyEclipse. Then choose Add And Remove Project Deployments. Click the Add button in the resulting dialog and select your server, as shown in the following figure.

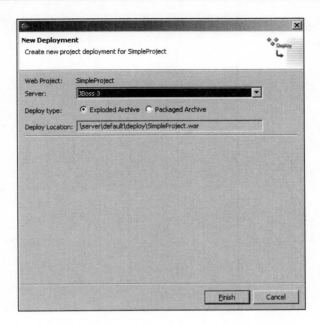

Click the Finish button and then click OK. Select the server and start it. Open a browser and test your servlet.

Summary

As developers, we are always looking for tools that will allow us to do more with less. XDoclet and the webdoclet task bring this ability to servlets. Instead of writing the deployment descriptor ourselves and potentially making errors, we can use just a few simple tags within the source code of our servlet and let the system do all the work. Not only do we eliminate the chance of additional errors, we keep similar information together in a single file. In addition, we can now use webdoclet to build JSP custom tags as well as incorporate Eclipse into the mix of technologies.

Building EJBs with Ant and XDoclet

In Chapter 6 we spent quite a bit of time developing Enterprise JavaBeans to support both an entity bean and a session bean. As you already know, building EJBs require quite a bit of work between several files. In this chapter, we continue with our use of XDoclet and see how to use it to build EJBs from the ground up. The topics we cover include database mappings, relationships, and primary keys.

Generating XDoclet EJBs

Now we will set up an example to illustrate how easily you can build EJBs when using XDoclet.Consider a sitaution where we have two container-managed persistence (CMP) entity beans called Student and Unit. There is a one-to-many relationship (a Unit can have many Students), and a session bean can be used to access the information within and between the Student and Unit beans.

Database Setup

Unlike in Chapter 6, we actually map the entity beans to a database so "real" information can be obtained. The database tables we will model are

```
CREATE TABLE unit (
  ID int not null auto_increment primary key,
 name varchar(64)
);

CREATE TABLE student (
```

```
        ID       INT            not null auto_increment  primary key,
        firstname          VARCHAR (80),
        lastname           VARCHAR (80),
        unitid      INT,
);
```

Each of the tables should be populated with appropriate data like the following:

```
INSERT INTO unit (NAME) VALUES ('CSC100');
INSERT INTO unit (NAME) VALUES ('ACC325');
INSERT INTO unit (NAME) VALUES ('EE785');
INSERT INTO unit (NAME) VALUES ('CE850');
INSERT INTO unit (NAME) VALUES ('MAT125');

INSERT INTO student VALUES('Jim', "Smith", 1);
INSERT INTO student VALUES('Jane', "Wellington", 3);
INSERT INTO student VALUES('Tim', "Docler", 2);
INSERT INTO student VALUES('Jim', "Smith", 4);
INSERT INTO student VALUES('John', "Doe", 2);
```

Creating Entity Beans

In our previous look at Enterprise JavaBeans, we were required to write code for three different files: the bean itself, a remote interface, and a home interface. If we made any change to the bean class, then both the remote and local interfaces had to change as well. This is of course a situation in which a typo results in a compile error and more than a bit of frustration. Since the bean class is the controlling feature of an EJB, it should be able to generate the other files, and this is what XDoclet does for us. In the following listing, consider the entity bean for the Unit database table.

```
package ejb;

import javax.ejb.EntityBean;
import javax.ejb.EntityContext;
import javax.ejb.CreateException;
import java.util.Collection;

/**
 * This entity bean maps to a Unit table and uses CMP version 2.x
 *
 * @ejb.bean
 *     type="CMP"
 *     cmp-version="2.x"
 *     name="UnitBean"
 *     schema="Unit"
 *     local-jndi-name="UnitBean"
 *     view-type="local"
 *     primkey-field="id"
 *
 *
 * @ejb.pk                     class="java.lang.Integer"
 *
 * @ejb.home generate="local" local-class="ejb.UnitHome"
 * @ejb.interface generate="local" local-class="ejb.Unit"
```

```
 *
 *
 * @ejb.finder
 *    signature="Dept findByUnitName(java.lang.String name)"
 *    unchecked="true"
 *    query="SELECT OBJECT(unit) FROM Unit unit where unit.name = ?1"
 *    result-type-mapping="Local"
 *
 * @ejb.finder
 *    signature="Collection findAll()"
 *    unchecked="true"
 *    query="SELECT OBJECT(unit) FROM unit unit"
 *    result-type-mapping="Local"
 *
 * @ejb.persistence          table-name="unit"
 *
 */
public abstract class UnitBean implements EntityBean {

    /**
     *
     * @ejb.create-method
     */
    public Integer ejbCreate(String name)
                                              throws CreateException {

        setName(name);

        return null;
    }

    public void ejbPostCreate(String name)
                throws CreateException{ }

       /**
        * This is a cmp field. The cmp field is read only.
        * And it is the primary key.
        *
        * @ejb.interface-method view-type="local"
        * @ejb.persistence       column-name="ID"
        */
    public abstract Integer getId();
    public abstract void setId(Integer id);

       /**
        * This is a cmp field. The cmp field is read/write.
        * @ejb.interface-method view-type="local"
        * @ejb.persistence       column-name="NAME"
        */
    public abstract String getName();
    public abstract void setName(String name);


       /**
        * @return return employees in this department
        *
```

```
    * @ejb.interface-method view-type="local"
    *
    * @ejb.transaction type="Required"
    *
    * @ejb.relation
    *     name="StudentsInAUnitRelation"
    *     role-name="UnitHasEmployees"
    *     target-role-name="StudentsInAUnit"
    *     target-cascade-delete="no"
    */
public abstract Collection getStudents();

    /** @ejb.interface-method view-type="local" */
public abstract void setStudents(Collection collection);


public void setEntityContext(EntityContext context){ }
public void unsetEntityContext(){ }
public void ejbRemove()throws javax.ejb.RemoveException{ }
public void ejbLoad(){ }
public void ejbStore(){ }
public void ejbPassivate(){ }
public void ejbActivate(){ }

}
```

All of the work for our EJBs is accomplished within the Bean class using a variety of XDoclet tags. With an appropriate Ant task, the deployment descriptor and other support files are created automatically.

Bean Class Tags

The XDoclet tags for generating EJBs appear in either the class or method level. In this section, we discuss those tags that appear in the comment above the actual Bean class definition.

@ejb.bean

The first and probably the most important tag is called ejb.bean. This tag allows the developer to specify the type of bean being created. In our example. there are seven attributes to the tag:

❑ **type:** This attribute specifies what kind of bean is being created. For this bean we create a CMP entity bean.

❑ **cmp-version:** Since we are creating a CMP entity bean, we need to specify the version.

❑ **name:** This is the name of the bean being created; it must match the name of the class where the ejb.bean tag is being used.

❑ **schema:** This is the name of the schema to be used in the bean; it is not the associated table, although it might have the same name.

❑ **local _jndi-name:** This is the JNDI name to use for the bean.

❑ **view-type:** This attribute specifies if this bean will be local, remote, or possibly both.

❑ **primkey-field:** If there is a primary key in the table being modeled with an entity bean, the field name is provided in this attribute.

When XDoclet executes the ejb.bean tag as we've defined it, the following information is contributed to the ejb-jar.xml file:

```
<entity>
 <ejb-name>UnitBean</ejb-name>
 <ejb-class>ejb.UnitBean</ejb-name>
 <reentrant>False</reentrant>
  <cmp-version>2.x</cmp-version>
  <abstract-schema-name>Unit</abstract-schema-name>
  <primkey-field>id</primkey-field>
</entity>
```

@ejb.pk

If you have a primary key for your table and resulting modeling EJB, you will need to specify the Java class type that directly relates to the type in the database. Since the most common type is an integer, the conversion from a database integer to a Java integer isn't too big a deal, but if you are using a compound key (not discussed in this chapter), you will need to give more thought to the class issue. We have a single attribute called class="java.lang.Integer" for the tag. When parsed, the following element is added to the ejb-jar.xml file:

```
<prim-key-class>java.lang.Integer</prim-key-class>
```

@ejb.home and @ejb.interface

As you might expect, XDoclet automatically creates the home and interface files for our entity bean. The names of the files and resulting code are specified using the @ejb.home and @ejb.interface tags. Here's the tags we used:

```
@ejb.home generate="local" local-class="ejb.UnitHome"
@ejb.interface generate="local" local-class="ejb.Unit"
```

We use the generate attribute to specify the type of home and/or interface. The values are local, remote, or both. XDoclet creates the appropriate classes using the values located in the local-class attributes. In addition to the classes, the following entries are added to the ejb-jar.xml file:

```
<entity>
<local-home>ejb.UnitHome</local-home>
 <local>ejb.Unit</local>
</entity>
```

Of course, if you specify a different generate value XDoclet adds the appropriate classes and entries to the XML file.

@ejb.finder

The finder methods are an important part of any entity bean, and XDoclet provides support for defining those methods within the bean. The signature of the finder is defined as well as the query to be used. Notice the use of the result-type-mapping attribute and its value of local.

XDoclet generates the finder methods in the home as well as appropriate elements in the deployment descriptor. The methods defined for our example are as follows:

```
public interface UnitHome extends javax.ejb.EJBLocalHomc {

        public ejb.Unit findByUnitName(java.lang.String name)
            throws javax.ejb.FinderException;

        public java.util.Collection findAll()
            throws javax.ejb.FinderException;

        public ejb.Unit findByPrimaryKey(java.lang.Integer pk)
throws javax.ejb.FinderException;
```

The resulting elements for the ejb-jar.xml file are as follows:

```
<query>

  <query-method>
        <method-name>findByUnitName</method-name>
        <method-params>
                <method-param>java.lang.String</method-param>
        </method-params>
  </query-method>

  <result-type-mapping>Local</result-type-mapping>

  <ejb-ql>SELECT OBJECT(unit) FROM Unit unit where unit.name =?1
  </ejb-ql>
</query>

<query>
  <query-method>
        <method-name>findAll</method-name>
        <method-params></method-params>

  </query-method>

  <result-type-mapping>Local</result-type-mapping>
  <ejb-ql>SELECT OBJECT(unit) FROM Unit unit</ejb-ql>
</query>
```

@ejb.persistence

Unfortunately, the EJB specification doesn't have a common Object/Relational mapping defined. For this reason, many application servers came up with their own spec and subsequently their own ejb tags. Resin is a good case in point. There are a few specific Resin ejb tags to handle the relationship between the EJB and the entity bean. However, most containers now map entities to classes and fields to columns. Recently the XDoclet specification has added a tag called @ejb.persistence that we can use to specify the table our entity bean relates to. In our example, the UnitBean has an entry called @ejb.persistence table-name="unit". The table-name attribute is the actual table name for our environment.

The resulting element in the ejb-jar.xml file is as follows:

```
<entity>
        <sql-table>unit</sql-table>
</entity>
```

When working with a specific application server, be sure to consult the product's documentation to determine if any specific tags are needed to handle the entity bean-table relationship.

Create Method Tags

An entity bean is required to have a create method. The code in our UnitBean is this:

```
/*
* @ejb.create-method
*/
public Integer ejbCrate(String name) throws CreateException setName(name);
return null;
```

The create tag doesn't require any attributes. This tag will use cause XDoclet to generate a corresponding create method in the home. For example:

```
public interface UnitHome
  extends javax.ejb.EJBLocalHome {
        public ejb.Unit create(java.lang.String name) ()
                throws javax.ejb.CreateException;
}
```

Getter/Setter Method Tags

For every field in the database table we are modeling, there will be corresponding getter/setter methods in the bean implementation. For the Unit table we have two different fields—the ID and the Name—so we need two pairs of setter/getter methods. Each of the pairs will have three XDoclet tags—persistence-field, method-view, and persistence—that could appear.

@ejb.persistence-field

The @ejb.persistence-field tag is used to designate the getter method as part of the CMP declaration and will subsequently signal XDoclet to produce an appropriate entry in the deployment descriptor. In our code, we have used this tag to specify that both the ID and Name fields are persistent. Notice that you don't put the name of the field with the tag. XDoclet determines the appropriate field based on the name of the getter method.

@ejb.persistence

If you have a situation where the getter/setter method signature doesn't relate to the name of the database field they represent or the vendor requires it, the @ejb.persistence tag can be used along with the column-name attribute. For example, we could have the following:

```
/**
*   @) ejb. persistence column-name="FULLID"
* */
public abstract Integer getId();
```

@ejb.interface-method

The @ejb.interface-method is used to specify the type of method for the appropriate getter/setter pairs and signal that the method should appear in the interface. The attribute for the tag is view-type. The value will be either local, remote, or both, and XDoclet creates the appropriate elements. For example, in the getID() method, we would see the following code in the interface:

```
public interface Unit
  extends javax.ejb.EJBLocalObject {
        public java.lang.Integer getId();
}
```

Relations

Probably one of the most difficult aspects of building EJBs is signaling to the beans the various relationships that exist within the relational database. In our example, there is a one-to-many relationship between the Unit and Student tables; there can be many Students to a Unit. Via the @ejb.relation tag, XDoclet allows you to define a CMR relationship.

@ejb.relation

For our code, the tags are defined as follows:

```
/**
 * @return return employees in this department
 *
 * @ejb.interface-method view-type="local"
 *
 * @ejb.transaction type="Required"
 *
 * @ejb.relation
 *     name="StudentsInAUnitRelation"
 *     role-name="UnitHasEmployees"
 *     target-role-name="StudentsInAUnit"
 *     target-cascade-delete="no"
 */
```

We have to give the relationship a name and then describe the role. Notice the use of the target-cascade-delete attribute. This attribute is used to determine whether, if a unit is deleted, all of the corresponding students should be deleted as well. In our case, we just use a value of no. As you will see in the StudentBean, we include another @ejb.relation tag because we need to specify each side of the relationship.

The result of both @ejb.relation tags is shown here:

```
<relationships >
 <ejb-relation >
       <ejb-relation-name>StudentsInAunitRelation</ejb-relation-name>
       <ejb-relationship-role >
             <ejb-relationship-role-name>StudentInAUnit</ejb-relationship-
          role-name>
             <multiplicity>Many</multiplicity>
             <relationship-role-source >
                   <ejb-name>StudnetBean</ejb-name>
             </relationship-role-source>

             <cmr-field >
                   <cmr-field-name>unit</cmr-field-name>
             </cmr-field>
       </ejb-relationship-role>
```

```
            <ejb-relationship-role >
                  <ejb-relationship-role-name>UnitHasStudents</ejb-relationship-
            role-name>
                  <multiplicity>One</multiplicity>
                  <relationship-role-source >
                        <ejb-name>UnitBean</ejb-name>
                  </relationship-role-source>

                  <cmr-field >
                        <cmr-field-name>students</cmr-field-name>
                        <cmr-field-type>java.util.Collection</cmr-field-type>
                  </cmr-field>
            </ejb-relationship-role>
      </ejb-relation>
</relationships>
```

@ejb.transaction

If your relationship requires a transaction to work properly, use the @ejb.transaction tag and its type attribute. In our case, we need to make sure that the unit isn't changed when a student is added to the table; therefore, we set the type attribute to required. The underlying database must support transactions in order for the process to work correctly.

Student Bean Code

We have another table to be modeled called Student, which contains all of the student information. Students are enrolled in a unit, and the relationship is kept between the two tables. The next listing shows the Student entity bean code along with its XDoclet tags. All of the tables are the same as described earlier.

```
package ejb;

import javax.ejb.EJBException;
import javax.ejb.EntityBean;
import javax.ejb.EntityContext;
import javax.ejb.CreateException;


import javax.naming.*;

/**
 * This entity bean represents Students in a table.
 *
 * @ejb.bean
 *     type="CMP"
 *     cmp-version="2.x"
 *     name="StudentBean"
 *     schema="Student"
 *     local-jndi-name="StudentBean"
 *     view-type="local"
 *     primkey-field="id"
 *
```

```
 *
 * @ejb.pk                    class="java.lang.Integer"
 *
 * @ejb.home generate="local" local-class="ejb.StudentHome"
 * @ejb.interface generate="local" local-class="ejb.Student"
 *
 * @resin-ejb.entity-bean
 *      sql-table="STUDENT"
 *
 *
 * @ejb.finder
 *    signature="Employee findByLastName(java.lang.String name)"
 *    unchecked="true"
 *    query="SELECT OBJECT(student) FROM Student student where
student.lastName = ?1"
 *    result-type-mapping="Local"
 *
 * @ejb.finder
 *    signature="Collection findAll()"
 *    unchecked="true"
 *    query="SELECT OBJECT(student) FROM Student student"
 *    result-type-mapping="Local"
 *
 *
 *
 */
public abstract class StudentBean implements EntityBean {

    /**
     *
     * @ejb.create-method
     */
    public Integer ejbCreate(
        String firstName,
        String lastName,
        Integer unitid)
        throws CreateException {
        setFirstName(firstName);
        setLastName(lastName);

        try {

            // The JNDI context containing local EJBs
            Context cmp = (Context) new
InitialContext().lookup("java:comp/env/ejb");;

            // Get the house stub
            DeptHome home = (DeptHome) cmp.lookup("UnitBean");
            setUnit(home.findByPrimaryKey(unitid));

        } catch (Exception e) {
            throw new EJBException(e);
        }

        return null;
    }
```

```
public void ejbPostCreate(
    String firstName,
    String lastName,
    Integer deptid)
    throws CreateException {
}

/**
 * This is a cmp field. The cmp field is read only.
 * And it is the primary key.
 *
 * @ejb.pk-field
 * @ejb.persistent-field
 * @ejb.interface-method view-type="local"
 * @ejb.persistence          column-name="ID"
 */
public abstract Integer getId();
public abstract void setId(Integer id);

/**
 * This is a cmp field. The cmp field is read/write.
 * @ejb.interface-method view-type="local"
 * @ejb.persistence          column-name="FIRSTNAME"
 */
public abstract String getFirstName();
public abstract void setFirstName(String name);

/**
 * This is a cmp field. The cmp field is read/write.
 * @ejb.interface-method view-type="local"
 * @ejb.persistence          column-name="LASTNAME"
 */
public abstract String getLastName();
public abstract void setLastName(String name);

/**
 * @return Return the group this user is in.
 *
 * @ejb.interface-method view-type="local"
 *
 * @ejb.transaction type="Required"
 *
 * @ejb.relation
 *    name="EmployeesInADeptartmentRelation"
 *    role-name="EmployeeInADept"
 *    target-role-name="DeptHasEmployees"
 *
 * @resin-ejb.relation    sql-column="UNITID"
 *
 */
public abstract Unit getUnit();
/** @ejb.interface-method view-type="local" */
public abstract void setUnit(Unit unit);

/** @ejb.interface-method view-type="local" */
```

179

```
    public Integer getUnitId() {
        return getUnit().getId();
    }

    public void setEntityContext(EntityContext context) {
    }
    public void unsetEntityContext() {
    }
    public void ejbRemove() throws javax.ejb.RemoveException {
    }
    public void ejbLoad() {
    }
    public void ejbStore() {
    }
    public void ejbPassivate() {
    }
    public void ejbActivate() {
    }

}
```

Creating a Session Bean

To use the two entity beans we have created, let's rely on our XDoclet experience to create a session bean as well. The next listing shows the code for the bean. For the most part, the tags are the same as those in the entity bean, but there are a few different ones. Within the @ejb.bean tag, a type attribute is available to let the system know whether the session bean is stateless.

In addition, there is a tag called @ejb.ejb-ref that adds a reference to each of the entity beans in our example. The ejb-name attribute is set to the class name of the bean, and the view-type attribute is set to local, remote, or both.

```
package ejb;

import javax.ejb.SessionBean;
import javax.ejb.SessionContext;


import java.util.*;
import util.*;

/**
 * Provides a session facade that works with cmp/cmr
 *
 * This bean uses container-managed transactions.
 * This bean does not maintain any state; thus, it can be stateless.
 *
 *
 * @ejb.bean name="StudentTest" type="Stateless"
 *     local-jndi-name="HRSystem"
 *
 *
 * @ejb.ejb-ref ejb-name="UnitBean" view-type="local"
 * @ejb.ejb-ref ejb-name="StudentBean" view-type="local"
```

```
 *
 */
public class StudentTest implements SessionBean {

    /**
     * Get a list of all the units.
     *
     * @ejb.interface-method view-type="local"
     * @ejb.transaction type="Required"
     */
    public String[] getUnits() {
        ArrayList unitList = new ArrayList();
        Collection collection = LocalFinderUtils.findAll("unitBean");
        Iterator iterator = collection.iterator();
        while (iterator.hasNext()) {
          unitList.add((Unit)iterator.next()).getName());
        }
        return (String[]) UnitList.toArray(new String[unitList.size()]);
    }

    /**
     *   The ejbActivate method.
     *   Since this is stateless, it should never get called.
     */
    public void ejbActivate() {
    }

    /**
     *   The ejbActivate method.
     *   Since this is stateless, it should never get called.
     */
    public void ejbPassivate() {
    }

    /**
     *   The ejbRemove method.
     *
     */
    public void ejbRemove() {
    }

    /**
     *   The ejbRemove method.
     *
     */
    public void ejbCreate() {
    }

    /**
     * Set session context — but it's stateless so don't implement
        */
    public void setSessionContext(SessionContext sc) {
    }
}
```

Ant Target for XDoclet

In order for the XDoclet tags to generate the necessary code for our EJBs, we need an appropriate Ant build script. Our example script is shown in the next listing.

The most important part of the build script is the element <target name="ejbdoclet">. Within this element, we define the EjbDoclet task as well as the subtasks that we want Ant to execute. As you can see, we've requested seven tasks: <localinterface/>, <localhomeinterface/>, <remoteinterface/>, <homeinterface/>, <entitypk/>, and <deploymentdescriptor>. Each of these subtasks will process the appropriate tags from the two entity and one session bean source code files. The result will be all of the bean code, support files, and deployment descriptor created automatically and configured for our example.

```xml
<?xml version="1.0"?>

<project name="baseline"  default="deploy">

    <property file="build.properties"/>

    <path id="cpath">
        <fileset dir="${lib}"/>
        <fileset dir="${WEBINF}/lib" />
    </path>

    <path id="xdocpath">
        <path refid="cpath"/>
        <fileset dir="${xdocletlib}">
            <include name="*.jar"/>
        </fileset>
    </path>

    <target name="init">
        <mkdir dir="${output}/war" />
        <mkdir dir="${dest}" />
    </target>

    <target name="clean">
        <delete dir="${output}/war" />

        <delete>
            <fileset dir="${dest}">
                <exclude name="**/*.java" />
                <exclude name="**/*.properties" />
            </fileset>
        </delete>

        <delete dir="${webapps}/${app}" />
        <delete dir="${webapps}/${app}.war" />

        <delete>
            <fileset dir="${gen.src}">
                <include name="**/*.java"/>
            </fileset>
        </delete>
</code>
```

```xml
        <delete>
            <fileset dir="META-INF">
                <include name="**/*.xml"/>
            </fileset>
        </delete>

        <delete>
            <fileset dir="${WEBINF}">
                <include name="**/cmp-xdoclet.ejb"/>
            </fileset>
        </delete>

        <delete>
            <fileset dir="${WEBINF}">
                <include name="**/resin.ejb"/>
            </fileset>
        </delete>

    </target>

    <target name="compile" depends="init">
        <javac destdir="${dest}" debug="true" deprecation="true">
            <src location="${gen.src}" />
            <src location="${src}" />
            <classpath refid="cpath"/>
        </javac>
    </target>

    <target name="package" depends="init,compile">

        <war destfile="${output}/war/${app}.war" webxml="${WEBINF}/web.xml">

                <fileset dir="${docroot}">
                    <exclude name="**/build.xml" />
                    <exclude name="**/*.bat" />
                    <exclude name="**/build.properties" />
                    <exclude name="**/web.xml" />
                    <exclude name="**/*.nbattrs" />
                    <exclude name="**/*.java"/>
                    <exclude name="**/*.class"/>
                    <exclude name="**/*.sql"/>
                    <exclude name="**/*.bat"/>
                </fileset>


                <lib dir="${WEBINF}/lib">
                    <exclude name="jdbc1.jar"/>
                </lib>

                <classes dir="${WEBINF}/classes">
                    <exclude name="**/*.java"/>
                    <exclude name="**/*.nbattrs" />
                </classes>
```

```
        </war>

    </target>

    <target name="deploy" depends="package">
        <copy file="${output}/war/${app}.war" todir="${webapps}" />
    </target>

  <target name="ejbdoclet" >

        <taskdef
            name="ejbdoclet"
            classname="xdoclet.modules.ejb.EjbDocletTask"
            classpathref="xdocpath"
            />

        <ejbdoclet
            ejbspec="2.0"
            mergeDir="${src}"
            destDir="${gen.src}"
        >

            <fileset dir="${src}">
                <include name="ejb/*Bean.java" />
            </fileset>

            <localinterface/>
            <localhomeinterface />
            <remoteinterface/>
            <homeinterface />

            <entitypk/>


            <deploymentdescriptor       destdir="META-INF"
                        destinationFile="ejb-jar.xml"
                        validatexml="true" />

            <deploymentdescriptor       destdir="${WEBINF}"
                        destinationFile="cmp-xdoclet.ejb"
                        validatexml="true" />

            <resin-ejb-xml destDir="${WEBINF}"/>

        </ejbdoclet>

    </target>

    <target name="all" depends="clean,ejbdoclet,compile,package,deploy" />

</project>
```

Summary

The complexity of writing EJBs can be drastically reduced with the help of Ant and XDoclet. In this chapter, we touched on building EJBs, both session and entity, using a single bean for each and one file for each. The XDoclet code and corresponding Ant task do the job of building the deployment descriptor and remaining support files.

10

Building Struts Apps with Ant and XDoclet

This chapter introduces Struts and shows how to use XDoclet to cut down on the work needed to use the framework. Struts, produced under Apache Jakarta, is probably the most well-known of the Web frameworks available today. In fact, entire books have been written on using Struts. Our goal in this chapter is to give you an introduction to using Struts without XDoclet in order to show the amount of work necessary to use the framework, and then we'll show how XDoclet can help with the situation. We will use an example registration system to illustrate the concepts.

Brief Introduction to Struts

As mentioned above, there are entire books written on the topic of Struts, so this section will be a short introduction to the major components of the system. Following is a flow diagram of what occurs within the Struts framework.

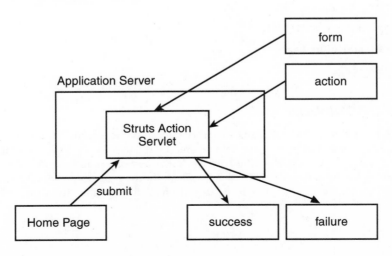

As you can see from this diagram, the entire process starts with a home page of sorts that presents the user with links or HTML forms to be filled out. In our example later in the book, we will be presenting the user with a form to register with a Web application. When the user clicks the link or the Submit button, the Struts ActionServlet will be invoked. This servlet is designed to take the URL specified in the action attribute of the HTML form or the link URL and determine an action to perform. The action is defined in a configuration file along with the Action class, action JavaBean, and the response HTML pages. The Action class is defined around the Action baseclass, and the form data is defined around the ActionForm. The HTML response pages are typically written in JSP.

Installing Struts

Struts is a framework and as such it relies on a few friends to accomplish its tasks. Those friends include:

❑   An application server such as Tomcat or Resin. We use Tomcat in this chapter.

❑   Ant to compile the source code for Struts.

❑   JDK, of course.

A Sample Application

In order to see how to use Struts, we will build a Web application that allows a user to log in and register using a username and password. The system will present a registration page with a form to gather a username, the password, and a copy of the password, which will be used to make sure the user typed in the right combination of characters.

The registration system consists of six steps. All of the steps relate to the Struts process diagrammed above. The steps are:

1. Create an ActionForm.
2. Build the action.
3. Modify the struts-config.xml file.
4. Create an appropriate web.xml file.
5. Create Success and Failure pages.
6. Create a Register page.

Creating the ActionForm

As you might expect, we will use an HTML form to gather the username, password, and second password. There will need to be a way of getting the data entered by the user into the system so it can be processed. In the "old" way, we would obtain the HttpServletRequest object and use the getParameter() method to get the values. Under Struts, we will use a JavaBean for the transport object. As you learned earlier, when a user clicks a Submit button in a form, the action attribute of the <form> tag will specify a

Struts action defined in the struts-config.xml file. Associated with the Struts action is an ActionForm. For our registration example, we will use the class defined in this listing:

```
import org.apache.struts.action.*;

public class RegisterForm extends ActionForm {
  protected String username;
  protected String password;
  protected String password2;

  public String getUsername() {
   return this.username;
  }

  public String getPassword() {
   return this.password;
  }

  public String getPassword2() {
    return this.password2;
  }

  public void setUsername(String username) {
    this.username = username;
  };

  public void setPassword(String password) {
    this.password = password;
  };

  public void setPassword2(String password) {
    this.password2 = password;
  };
}
```

The RegisterForm class is designed to handle all of the data that will be sent from our form. The class must inherit from ActionForm, which is a Struts base class. As you can see, the code in the class is what you would expect from a JavaBean. There are protected attributes and getter/setter methods for each of them. Both the system and the developer will use this Form class. The developer will access it from the Velocity templates here as well as in the action discussed next.

Building the Action

The action is where all of business work occurs, usually as a result of a user clicking a link or a Submit button of a form. Based on the Struts configuration file, an Action object will be put into play. The next listing shows the code for the RegisterAction class.

```
import org.apache.struts.action.*;
import javax.servlet.http.*;
import java.io.*;

public class RegisterAction extends Action {
```

```
public ActionForward perform(
      ActionMapping mapping,
      ActionForm form,
      HttpServletRequest request,
      HttpServletResponse response) {

  RegisterForm rf = (RegisterForm) form;

  String username = rf.getUsername();
  String password = rf.getPassword();
  String password2 = rf.getPassword2();

  if (password.equals(password2)) {
    try {
      return mapping.findForward("success");
    } catch(Exception e) {
      return mapping.findForward("failure");
    }
  }

  return mapping.findForward("failure");
  }
}
```

As you might expect, the RegisterAction class extends the Struts Action base class. The Struts system will call the perform() method providing a Form object if appropriate and the HttpServletRequest and Response objects. In our case, we immediately cast the Form class into RegisterForm and pull the values for the username, password, and second password.

The code will check to see if the two passwords match. If they do, we tell Struts to return a value of success, which is matched against the configuration file and the success.jsp template. Otherwise, a value of failure is returned for the failure.jsp template.

Configuring Struts Config

Most of the structure for a Struts Web application is found in the configuration file called struts-conf.xml, as shown in here:

```
<?xml version="1.0" encoding="ISO-8859-1" ?>

<!DOCTYPE struts-config PUBLIC
      "-//Apache Software Foundation//DTD Struts
         Configuration 1.0//EN"
      "http://jakarta.apache.org/struts/dtds/
         struts-config_1_0.dtd">

<struts-config>

  <form-beans>
    <form-bean name="registerForm" type="RegisterForm"/>
  </form-beans>

  <action-mappings>
```

```
<action      path="/struts"
             type="RegisterAction"
             name="registerForm">
   <forward name="success" path="/success.jsp"/>
   <forward name="failure" path="/failure.jsp"/>
</action>
</action-mappings>

</struts-config>
```

In the configuration file, we define the Form JavaBeans including their name, which is a reference for the <action> element, and the class name. Next, we define all of the actions that can occur in the application. We have only one, which we have called struts. When the struts action is called from a <form> or link, the framework will activate the RegisterAction action and use the RegisterForm form to pull the data from the <form> data. Also defined in the <action> element are the forwards, which represent the pages where results will be provided to the user.

Creating the Web.xml File

In addition to the Struts configuration file, we also need to include a web.xml file so the application server knows how to handle requests from the user:

```
<?xml version="1.0" encoding="ISO-8859-1"?>

<!DOCTYPE web-app
   PUBLIC "-//Sun Microsystems, Inc.//DTD Web Application 2.2//EN"
   "http://java.sun.com/j2ee/dtds/web-app_2_2.dtd">

<web-app>

  <!-- Action Servlet Configuration -->
  <servlet>

   <servlet-name>action</servlet-name>
    <servlet-class>org.apache.struts.action.ActionServlet</servlet-class>

    <init-param>
      <param-name>config</param-name>
      <param-value>/WEB-INF/struts-config.xml</param-value>
    </init-param>

    <init-param>
      <param-name>debug</param-name>
      <param-value>2</param-value>
    </init-param>

    <init-param>
      <param-name>detail</param-name>
      <param-value>2</param-value>
    </init-param>

    <init-param>
      <param-name>validate</param-name>
```

```
        <param-value>true</param-value>
      </init-param>

      <load-on-startup>2</load-on-startup>

   </servlet>

   <!-- Action Servlet Mapping -->

   <servlet-mapping>
     <servlet-name>action</servlet-name>
     <url-pattern>*.do</url-pattern>
   </servlet-mapping>


   <!-- Struts Tag Library Descriptors -->
   <taglib>
     <taglib-uri>/WEB-INF/struts-bean.tld</taglib-uri>
     <taglib-location>/WEB-INF/struts-bean.tld</taglib-location>
   </taglib>

   <taglib>
     <taglib-uri>/WEB-INF/struts-html.tld</taglib-uri>
     <taglib-location>/WEB-INF/struts-html.tld</taglib-location>
   </taglib>

   <taglib>
     <taglib-uri>/WEB-INF/struts-logic.tld</taglib-uri>
     <taglib-location>/WEB-INF/struts-logic.tld</taglib-location>
   </taglib>
</web-app>
```

The web.xml file consists of two important parts. The first is a definition of <servlet-mapping> and <servlet> elements for Struts. The configuration says that any URL with an ending of *.do will be redirected to the ActionServlet servlet provided with Struts. The second maps all *.jsp URLs to be directed to the VelocityViewServlet.

Building the Success and Failure Pages

When a user provides a username and two passwords that match, the RegisterAction class will instruct the Struts ActionServlet to use the success forward. The success forward, defined in the Struts configuration file, tells the system to use the success.jsp JSP to display output to the user. Following is the code for the template:

```
<HTML>
<HEAD>

  <TITLE>Success</TITLE>

</HEAD>
<BODY>

  Registration Success!
```

```
     Thanks for logging in.
     <P><A href="register.jsp">Try Another?</A></P>

</BODY>
</HTML>
```

The template is fairly basic, but you get the idea. If the user is successful in providing accurate information, we will pull the username from the RegisterForm object created when the RegisterAction action was executed by Struts. The result of this page is shown here:

The Failure page is similar to the Success template but tells the user to try again.

Building the Register Page

Throughout this discussion we have referenced the page where the user can provide information and submit it to the server. The following listing shows the Register template that provides this capability.

```
<%@ taglib uri="/tags/struts-bean" prefix="bean" %>
<%@ taglib uri="/tags/struts-html" prefix="html" %>
<%@ taglib uri="/tags/struts-logic" prefix="logic" %>

<HTML>
<HEAD>
<TITLE>Registration Page</TITLE>
<html:base/>
</HEAD>
<BODY>

<logic:present name="user">
  Hello <bean:write name="user" property="username" />
</logic:present>

<html:link forward="logon">Log in</html:link>
<logic:present name="user">

</BODY>
</HTML>
```

As you can see from the previous listing, we begin the code by determining if there is a user bean already stored in the current session for the user. If so, we display the name of the user and then a link to log into our system. The name of the actual login page is logon.jsp, and it is found here:

```
<%@ taglib uri="/tags/struts-html" prefix="html" %>

<HTML>

<HEAD>
<TITLE> Register Page</TITLE>
</HEAD>

<BODY>
  <html:form action="registerForm">

  <table>
  <tr>
    <td>username:</td>
    <td><html:text property="username"/></td>
  </tr>
  <tr>
    <td>password 1:</td>
    <td><html:text property="password1"/></td>
  </tr>
  <tr>
    <td>password 2:</td>
    <td><html:text property="password2"/></td>
  </tr>
  </table>

</BODY>
</HTML>
```

This code handles the form that will be used by the user to submit their username and two copies of their desired password. The most important part of the code is the <html:form> tag, which will use a mapping based on the registerForm entry. If you look back in the Struts configuration file, you will see that an action call to registerForm will execute the RegisterAction class.

Setup

The setup for the application is quite simple. Place all of the files based on this directory structure:

```
/webapps/struts
/webapps/struts/register.jsp
/webapps/struts/success.jsp
/webapps/struts/failure.jsp
/webapps/struts/WEB-INF/web.xml
/webapps/struts/WEB-INF/struts-config.xml
/webapps/struts/WEB-INF/classes/RegisterForm.java
/webapps/struts/WEB-INF/classes/RegisterAction.java
/webapps/struts/WEB-INF/lib/struts_1_0_2.jar
/webapps/struts/WEB-INF/lib/dom4j.jar
/webapps/struts/WEB-INF/lib/commons-collections.jar
```

Again, this structure is based on the Resin application server.

Compile

To compile the Action and Form classes, use the following command

```
javac "../lib/struts_1_0_2.jar;./;" *.java
```

or build an appropriate Ant build script. Once the .java source files have been compiled, you can restart the application server.

Run

Execute the application by browsing to the following URL or its equivalant, based on your application server:

```
http://localhost:8080/struts/register.jsp
```

You should immediately see a page asking you to log on to the system. After clicking the link, you will be presented with a form containing a username and two password fields as well as a Submit button. Enter the appropriate information in the fields and click Submit.

Struts and XDoclet

Now that you've seen how to create a simple Struts Web application, let's look at what needs to be done to reduce the amount of work in developing a Struts application. Let's begin with the bean we used to hold the username and password information (from the first code listing of this chapter). This bean is defined in the struts-config.xml file using the following code:

```
<form-beans>
    <form-bean name="registerForm" type="RegisterForm"/>
</form-beans>
```

You might be thinking, why use XDoclet to define the bean in the config file when it is just as simple as the declaration as above? The reasons are numerous, including making typos, remembering to remove the declaration if the bean is removed from the system, as well as others. The idea of XDoclet is simplity and not duplicating anything that shouldn't be duplicated. This means we can use an XDoclet tag to generate the <form-beans> element automatically. The tag is called @struts.form and is shown here:

```
/**
 * @struts.form name="RegisterForm"
 */
import org.apache.struts.validator.ValidatorForm*;

public class RegisterForm extends ValidatorForm {
```

```
    protected String username;
    protected String password;
    protected String password2;

    public String getUsername() {
     return this.username;
    }

    public String getPassword() {
     return this.password;
    }

    public String getPassword2() {
       return this.password2;
    }

    /**
     * @struts.validator type="required"
     */
    public void setUsername(String username) {
       this.username = username;
    };


    /**
     * @struts.validator type="required"
     */
    public void setPassword(String password) {
       this.password = password;
    };


    /**
     * @struts.validator type="required"
     */
    public void setPassword2(String password) {
       this.password2 = password;
    };
```

As you can see, the @struts.form tag is quite simple. Just assign the name attribute to the name of the bean being used in the application. Also notice that we changed the parent class from ActionForm to ValidatorForm. In the past, setting up a form for validation was a very time-consuming process. This isn't the case anymore with XDoclet. Just extend ValidatorForm and set a @struts.validator tag on the setter functions, as shown above. Now we don't need to worry about the <form-beans> element.

Another important part of the struct configuration file is the mapping necessary for the forms as well as the success/failure pages. The tags necessary are @struts.action and @struts.action-forward, and they are shown here:

```
    /**
     * @struts.action path="/struts"
     *                 name="registerForm"
```

```
 *                    scope="request"
 *                    input="/logon.jsp"
 *                    validate="true"
 *
 * @struts.action-forward name="success"
 *                        path= "/WEB-INF/success.jsp"
 *
 * @struts.action-forward name="failure"
 *                        path= "/WEB-INF/failure.jsp"
 *
 */

import org.apache.struts.action.*;
import javax.servlet.http.*;
import java.io.*;

public class RegisterAction extends Action {

  public ActionForward perform(
ActionMapping mapping,
ActionForm form,
HttpServletRequest request,
HttpServletResponse response) {

    RegisterForm rf = (RegisterForm) form;

    String username = rf.getUsername();
    String password = rf.getPassword();
    String password2 = rf.getPassword2();

    if (password.equals(password2)) {
      try {
        return mapping.findForward("success");
      } catch(Exception e) {
        return mapping.findForward("failure");
      }
    }

    return mapping.findForward("failure");
  }
}
```

In this code we have provided three mappings. The first is called the action mapping, and it handles the mapping from the RegisterForm to the RegisterAction class needed when the user enters her username and passwords. XDoclet is able to obtain the class when the RegisterForm name is used based on where the @struts.action tag is located. We also defined the two findForward strings, failure and success. These values are mapped to the appropriate .jsp files.

At this point in the development, we have eliminated the need to produce the validation configuration as well as the struts configuration file. Of course, we will need an appropriate Ant task to do the actual XDoclet work. The Ant task follows:

```
<target name="webdoclet" depends="init">

<mkdir dir="${build.dir}/web/WEB-INF"/>

<taskdef

    name="webdoclet"
    classname="xdoclet.modules.web.WebDocletTask">
    <classpath>
        <path refid="xdoclet.classpath"/>
        <path refid="web.compile.classpath"/>
    </classpath>

</taskdef>

<webdoclet destdir="${build.dir}/web/WEB-INF"
    force="${xdoclet.force}"
    mergedir="metadata">

    <fileset dir="src/web"/>

    <deploymentdescriptor validatexml="true"
                          distributable="false"
                          displayname="${app.name}"
                          mergedir="metadata/web"
    />

    <strutsconfigxml validatexml="true"
                     version="1.1"
                     mergedir="metadata/struts"
    />

    <strutsvalidationxml/>

</webdoclet>

</target>
```

The Ant task for <webdoclet> looks just like the other ones we've used in the past except we've added two additional subtasks: <strutsconfigxml> and <strutsvalidationxml>. These two subtasks do all of the work in generating the necessary support files for our application.

Summary

Struts is the premier MVC framework for the Java community. In this chapter, we've shown the vast amount of configuration needed for any Struts application. It you aren't careful, the information in the configuration will be tough to get right. XDoclet, however, provides simple tags that keep the work to a minimum for the developer.

Creating Custom Ant Tasks

As you've seen in the earlier chapters of this book, Ant is a valuable addition to the software development process and faciliates project bulding. Fundamentally, Ant is designed to execute tasks. We've seen tasks like compiling source code, automating code generation using XDoclet, and gathering code into a JAR, among others. What if we could create our own task for Ant to execute?

The key here is developing a task that isn't just a nice-to-have execution that could be accomplished with the standard <java> task. In other words, if we have an application that is launched by Java and just accepts a few command-line options, then we can use the <java> task instead. Suppose, however, we want to create a new <task> that can influence the application directly. This task might involve outputting results from the application in XML format. The output would be accomplished by an Ant task and not the application itself. In this chapter we look at an example task as well as how Ant works internally.

How Ant Works

When we create an Ant build script, we include some number of targets, which in turn include tasks. For example, consider the Ant build script in the following listing.

```
<?xml version="1.0 ?>
<property>

    <target name="clean"
                    description="clean up the output directories and
jar.">
        <delete dir="${local_outdir}" />
        <delete file="${model_jar}" />
    </target>

    <target name="prepare" depends="init"
                    description="prepare the output directory.">
```

```
            <mkdir dir="${build}" />
            <mkdir dir="${lib}" />
        </target>

        <target name="compile" depends="prepare"
                            description="compile the Java source.">
            <javac srcdir="./src" destdir="${build}" />
        </target>

        <target name="package" depends="compile"
                            description="package the Java classes into a jar.">
            <jar jarfile="${model_jar}"
                basedir="${build}" />
        </target>

        <target name="all" depends="clean,package"
                            description="perform all targets."/>

    </project>
```

Here we have several targets that will be executed in a specific hierarchy. The targets are designed for this purpose. What's important are the tasks within the targets, such as <jar>, <mkdir>, <delete>, and <javac>.

When the Ant build loop encounters a task, it relinquishes control to a specific class created for the task. In our example build script, the tasks are built into Ant itself; therefore, you don't see any <taskdef> elements, which would define a class to be used when evaluating the task. Ant just knows about <jar>, <mkdir>, <delete>, and <javac>. In the remainder of this chapter we show you how to build your own task.

An Example Task

Let's assume that we have a Java application that works in a peer-to-peer environment. The application is called TDSS, and it is made up of individual nodes. Each node is a separate class executing in a Java Virtual Machine (JVM). There are a few different parameters that our nodes can set, and we want the ability to gather statistics after the system has executed and output those results in a file. Based on the requirements of our applicaton, we might be able to configure everything using the Ant task. The next listing shows an example TDSS Ant task that would handle our requirements.

```
<TDSS
    TDSSDir="${buildDir}"
  displayoutput="${output}"
    verbose="true"
    outputfile="${buildDir}/output.txt" >
    <classpath refid="fullclasspath">
    <node
        id="1"
        username="node2"
        password="password"
        popularity="4"
        raid="true"
        if="devrun"
    />
    <node
```

```
        id="2"
        username="node3"
        password="password"
        popularity="14"
        raid="false"
        if="prodrun"
    />
</TDSS>
```

First, let's look at the options in the <TDSS> element itself. The options are considered global for the entire application. When the individual nodes are launched, they are provided with the value of the displayoutput and verbose attributes. The TDSSDir attribute is used to assemble any intermediate code, and the outputfile attribute is used to consolidate output from the application. The entire application consists of one or more <node> elements, which represent real Java applications running in their own VM. We have chosen to provide five different attributes for each of the nodes. The attribute is supplied on the command line of the running node. Notice the use of the if attribute to determine which nodes will execute for a given run of the application using the conditional attribute. Now we can begin the process of building our Ant task.

A Skeleton Task Example

As you might have guessed, all Ant tasks are just Java classes either built into Ant or specified by the <taskdef> element. The only requirement of the class is that it have an execute() method that can be called by the Ant application. So, we might design a new class like the following:

```
package com.company.ant;

public class NewTask {

  public void execute() {
    // do something

}
```

With this class we could have an Ant task like this:

```
<taskdef ame="todo" classname="com.company.ant.NewTask">
```

Of course, a real Ant task has various attributes and conditions, like unless, which we probably want to be able to access from the Ant build script. In order to have access to this information, we must extend org.apache.tools.ant.Task. For example:

```
package com.company.ant;

import org.apache.tools.ant.Task;

public class NewTask extends org.apache.tools.ant.Task{

  public void execute() {
    // do something

}
```

The Task class gives us the ability to access the varous attributes contained in the build script. The methods available in the Ant Task class are shown in the following table.

Method	Description
void execute()	Called by Ant to execute the work of the task.
java.lang.String getDescription()	Returns the description of this task.
Location getLocation()	Returns a Location object specifying where the Ant task appears in the build script.
Target getOwningTarget()	Returns a Target object containing the parent of this Ant task.
Project getProject()	Returns a Project object for this task.
java.lang.String getTaskName()	Gets the name of this task.
Void init()	Called by this Ant tasks project.
void log(String msg)	Logs a message.
void log(String msg, int msgLevel)	Logs a message.
void setDescription(String desc)	Sets the description.
void setLocation(Location location)	Sets the file location of this task.
void setOwningTarget(Target target)	Sets the target of this task.
void setTaskName(String name)	Sets the name of this task

As you've probably already seen in your Ant experience to this point, there are times when the Ant application will encounter an error in the build and halt the process. We can do the same things using the BuildException exception. Here is a more fully defined class:

```
package com.company.ant;

import org.apache.tools.ant.Task;
import org.apache.tools.ant.BuildException;

public class NewTask extends org.apache.tools.ant.Task{

  public void execute() throws BuildException  {
    try {
       // something
      } catch (Exception e) {
      throw new BuildException(e)
    }
  }
}
```

If there are any issues with the task, the BuildException exception is thrown and Ant terminates the build. This is all of the code that we need to use the use the new task. Here's an example build script:

```
<taskdef
name="NewTask"
classname="com.company.ant.NewTask"
classpath="${newtask.dir}"
/>
<NewTask>
</NewTask>
```

Of course, the task won't do anything, but Ant will do the necessary work of launching the task.

Building a New Task

Now let's start the process of building our new task for the TDSS application and its individual nodes. During the process, we will discuss how to access attributes, dealing with the unless condition and working with nested elements. First, we have the foundation of our example class:

```
package com.company.ant;

import org.apache.tools.ant.Task;
import org.apache.tools.ant.BuildException;

public class TDSSTask extends org.apache.tools.ant.Task{

  public void execute() throws BuildException {
    try {
        // something
        } catch (Exception e) {
        throw new BuildException(e)
    }
}
```

Accessing Properties

For each of the attributes within the <TDSS> node, we need to supply a setter method within our Task class. For example, we have an attribute called verbose that needs a setter, which should look like this:

```
Private boolean verbose = false;

Public void setVerbose(boolean verbose) {
  this.verbose = verbose;
}
```

As you can see, we've declared a boolean but the only value in the build script is a string. Fortunately, Java uses introspection to obtain the string value from the build script and then automatically expands the string into an appropriate data type. We need to add the following code needs to our class to handle all of the attributes in our task:

```
    private String TDSSDir = null;
  private boolean displayoutput = false;
    private boolean verbose = true;
```

```
    private String outputfile = "";

public void setTDSSDir(String TDSSDir) {
   this.TDSSDir = TDSSDir;
}


public void setVerbose (boolean verbose) {
   this.verbose = verbose ;
}


public void setDisplayoutput (boolean displayoutput) {
   this.displayoutput = displayoutput ;
}

public void setOutputfile (boolean outputfile) {
   this.outputfile = outputfile ;
}
```

At this point we just need to add as many setters as we have attributes in our task. For the moment we are going to ignore the attributes and the <node> element.

Working with <classpath>

As you will notice in the <TDSS> node, we have included a <classpath> element so we can have access to all of the classes available. There are a few specific methods for handling the class path:

```
public void setClasspath(Path classpath) {
   this.classpath = classpath;
}

public void setClasspathRef(Reference ref) {
   createClasspath().setRefid(ref);
}
```

The Ant system will call either the setClasspath or stClasspathRef method, depending on whether a specific path is supplied in the <classpath> element or a reference ID is specified.

Setting Up the Task

Within the execute() method are a few tasks that need to be handled in order to start the process of using the task. Ultimately, what we are trying to do is build a list of attributes and nodes for our application run. All of the node information will be passed to another class, which will launch TDSS, gather information, and produce our output file. With this goal in mind, we must consider how we are going to execute the overall application from our task. The asnwer is the Java class. We are basically going to build up a Java object that relates to a new class called TDSSLauncher. The TDSSLauncher will handle all of the details of running our actual application. Building the Java object will take place in the execute() method. The code to handle our launcher is as follows:

```
Java javaTask = null;

javaTask = (Java) getProject().createTask("java");
javaTask.setTaskName(getTaskName());
javaTask.setClassname("com.company.application.TDSSLauncher");

javaTask.setClasspath(classpath);

// Add command-line arguments
javaTask.createArg().setValue("-h");
javaTask.createArg().setFile(TDDSDir);

if (outputFile != null) {
  javaTask.createArg().setValue("-o");
  javaTask.createArg().setFile(outputFile);
}

if (showoutput) {
  javaTask.createArg().setValue("-d");
}

if (verbose) {
  javaTask.createArg().setValue("-v");
}

javaTask.setFork(true);
if (javaTask.executeJava() != 0) {
  throw new BuildException("Error from launching TDSSLauncher");
}
```

In this code, we begin by creating a Java object called javaTask, setting its name and, most important, setting the class to be executed. In our case, the class is called TDSSLauncher. We won't discuss TDSSLauncher here, but keep in mind that this class is designed to take all of the options specified in the build script, execute the TDSS application, and produce the appropriate output file. Each of the attributes set in the build script will call individual setters as we defined earlier. The setter just sets private variables within the TDSSTask class. Each of those private variables will be examined, and depending on their value, a command-line option to the TDSSLauncher will be set (or not). All we are doing in the execute() method is examining the attributes set by the user in the build script and executing another class to handle all of the work. The TDSSLauncher class is executed using the executeJava() method of the javaTask object. Notice we called the setFork() method to make sure that we don't stop the execution of our Ant task as well as the entire Ant build process. The TDSSLauncher and subsequently our TDSS application will run in a separate thread.

Using Nested Elements

One thing you will notice between the setters defined above and the <TDSS> element is the fact that we have not yet handled the <node> elements. Our system is designed so that we can have any number of nested <node> elements under the <TDSS> element. Just how does Ant hande this type of situation?

When the Ant process encounters a subelement, it attempts to find three different methods within the Task object representing the subelement. One of those methods is called addConfigured<element>.

This method is called with an argument of a configured <node> element. But what does that mean? Well, it means that we need to have another class defined called Node with the appropriate setters so Ant can fill out the values when the subelement is encountered. Here's an example of the Node class:

```java
public static class Node implements Serializable {

private int id = 0;
private String username;
private String password;
private int popularity = 0;
private boolean raid = false;
private String ifProperty;

public void setID(int id) {
   this.id = id;
}

public void setUsername(String username) {
   this.username = username;
}

public void setPassword(String password) {
   this.password = password;
}

public void setPopularity(int popularity) {
   this.popularity = popularity;
}

public void setRaid(boolean raid) {
   this.raid = raid;
}

public void setIf(String ifProperty) {
   this.ifProperty = ifProperty;
}

public int getID() {
   return id;
}

public String getUsername() {
   return username;
}

public String getPassword() {
   return password;
}

public int getPopularity() {
   return popularity;
}

public boolean getRaid() {
```

```
    return raid;
}

public String getIf() {
  return ifProperty;
}

}
```

As you can see, the Node class has all of the appropriate setters for the attributes within the <node> element. Now we must define the addConfiguredNode() method:

```
public void addConfiguredNode(Node n) {
    if (includeNode(n)) {
        nodes.add(robot);
    }
}
```

The Ant process calls addConfiguredNode() each time it encounters a <node> subelement. The Node object passed to the method will be already instantiated and filled with the values from the <node> element's attributes. Of course, we have the if property in the node attribute as well. We need to check this property before doing anything with the node object. The work of checking the if property is performed in the includeNode() method, which is defined as follows:

```
private boolean includeNode(Node node) {
  String ifProperty = node.getIf();
  Project p = getProject();

  if (ifProperty != null && p.getProperty(ifProperty) == null) {
    return false;
  }
  return true;

}
```

The includeNode() method obtains the boolean value associated with a particular node. It also pulls the ifProperty value from the Project to determine if it was set using –D or within the build script. If the property is not set, then we shouldn't include this node in our application run and thus a false value is returned; otherwise, we return true.

Looking back at the addConfiguredNode() method, we find that if the node should be included in the application, we add it to a private variable called nodes. The variable nodes is defined as

```
private ArrayList nodes = new ArrayList();
```

Well, we are getting close to completion. We have been able to obtain the attributes for the <TDSS> elements as well as all of the <node> elements. We've created a Java object that will execute a class called TDSSLauncher using all of the information gained from our own Ant task called TDSS. Our last step in the process is to let the TDSSLauncher have access to the Node list. We do this by serializing the ArrayList of nodes and place the resulting data stream into a file in the directory specified by TDSSDir. We accomplish all this using the execute() method. For example:

```
        FileOutputStream fo = null;
        ObjectOutputStream oo = null;

        try {
          fo = new FileOutputStream(TDSSDir + "/nodes.txt");
          oo = new ObjectOutputStream(fo);

          oo.writeObject(nodes);

          oo.close();
          fo.close();

        } catch(Exception fileE) {
        }
```

This code creates a file called nodes.txt within the directory specified by the TDSSDir defined within the <TDSS> Ant task. The ArrayList of nodes will be serialized and placed within the file. The TDSSLauncher application will be able to find the file because we pass the value of the TDSSDir to the class as a command-line option.

Using the New Task

As this point, we've written all of the code needed for our Ant task (following is the entire listing). The purpose of this Ant task example is to show how to get the appropriate attributes and subelements within a task, process the information, and do something with it. All of the built-in tasks for Ant work in the same manner. The goal is to have another class like TDSSLauncher that does most all of the work. Ant acts as a global parser and gathers all of the information to be processed by some outside applicaton. For our task, we are able to produce all of the information for a global environment and execute an application using the build script. Not only can the build script compile the code and deploy it, but also Ant can execute the code.

```
package com.company.ant;

import org.apache.tools.ant.BuildException;
import org.apache.tools.ant.DirectoryScanner;
import org.apache.tools.ant.Project;
import org.apache.tools.ant.Task;
import org.apache.tools.ant.taskdefs.Java;
import org.apache.tools.ant.types.Environment;
import org.apache.tools.ant.types.FileSet;
import org.apache.tools.ant.types.Path;
import org.apache.tools.ant.types.Reference;

import java.io.*;
import java.util.*;

public class TDSSTask extends org.apache.tools.ant.Task{

    private String TDSSDir = null;
  private boolean displayoutput = false;
    private boolean verbose = true;
```

```
      private String outputfile = "";
   private path classpath;
   private ArrayList nodes = new ArrayList();


   public void setTDSSDir(String TDSSDir) {
     this.TDSSDir = TDSSDir;
   }


   public void setVerbose (boolean verbose) {
     this.verbose = verbose ;
   }


   public void setDisplayoutput (boolean displayoutput) {
     this.displayoutput = displayoutput ;
   }

   public void setOutputfile (boolean outputfile) {
     this.outputfile = outputfile ;
   }

   public void setClasspath(Path classpath) {
     this.classpath = classpath;
   }

   public void setClasspathRef(Reference ref) {
     createClasspath().setRefid(ref);
   }


   public void execute() throws BuildException {
     try {

           FileOutputStream fo = null;
           ObjectOutputStream oo = null;
           try {
             fo = new FileOutputStream(TDSSDir + "/nodes.txt");
             oo = new ObjectOutputStream(fo);
             oo.writeObject(nodes);
             oo.close();
             fo.close();
           } catch(Exception fileE) {
           }

     Java javaTask = null;

     javaTask = (Java) getProject().createTask("java");
     javaTask.setTaskName(getTaskName());
     javaTask.setClassname("com.company.application.TDSSLauncher");

     javaTask.setClasspath(classpath);
```

```
      // Add command-line arguments
    javaTask.createArg().setValue("-h");
    javaTask.createArg().setFile(TDSSDir);

    if (outputFile != null) {
       javaTask.createArg().setValue("-o");
       javaTask.createArg().setFile(outputFile);
    }

    if (showoutput) {
       javaTask.createArg().setValue("-d");
    }

    if (verbose) {
       javaTask.createArg().setValue("-v");
    }

    javaTask.setFork(true);
    if (javaTask.executeJava() != 0) {
       throw new BuildException("Error from launching BattleRunner");
    }


       } catch (Exception e) {
       throw new BuildException(e)
    }
}


private boolean includeNode(Node node) {

    String ifProperty = node.getIf();
    Project p = getProject();

    if (ifProperty != null && p.getProperty(ifProperty) == null) {
       return false;
    }

    return true;
}


  public void addConfiguredNode(Node n) implements Serializable {
    if (includeNode(n)) {
       nodes.add(robot);
    }
  }

public static class Node implements Serializable {

private int id = 0;
private String username;
```

```
      private String password;
      private int popularity = 0;
      private boolean raid = false;
      private String ifProperty;

      public void setID(int id) {
        this.id = id;
      }

      public void setUsername(String username) {
        this.username = username;
      }

      public void setPassword(String password) {
        this.password = password;
      }

      public void setPopularity(int popularity) {
        this.popularity = popularity;
      }

      public void setRaid(boolean raid) {
        this.raid = raid;
      }

      public void setIf(String ifProperty) {
        this.ifProperty = ifProperty;
      }

      public int getID() {
        return id;
      }

      public String getUsername() {
        return username;
      }

      public String getPassword() {
        return password;
      }

      public int getPopularity() {
        return popularity;
      }

      public boolean getRaid() {
        return raid;
      }

      public String getIf() {
        return ifProperty;
      }

  }

      }
```

Summary

Just when you thought you had learned everything there is to know about Ant, you find out that Ant is an extensible application designed to handle just about any of your build and deployment needs. In this chapter, we've shown you how Ant deals with tasks and works to read the properties associated with a task. We've also created our own example task to perform operations for our application.

Creating XDoclet Custom Tags and Templates

As we've discussed throughout the book, XDoclet is a code generated engine that extends the concept of a Javadoc tag to other technologies. We can use XDoclet to produce code, text, HTML or just about any other type of output. There are a few different ways this works. First we have the tags which will be added to the source code to be parsed. It you visit xdoclet.sourceforge.net, you will find all of the tags available. The differences in the tags are usually found in the @ part. For example, we have @jsp, @servlet, @struts as well as others.

Of course, the tags won't really do anything until the Ant task is put into play. The various tasks and subtasks added in a build script will trigger a parsing of the source code and the individual tags pulled out. When a tag is found, a resulting template is pulled into the source code and the provided attributes replaced. In this chapter, we want to explore this process a little more and determine how to make our own tags and templates.

XDoclet Architecture

Before we start looking at a template, let's discuss the XDoclet architecture for a moment. XDoclet can be broken down into three primary components:

- ❑ XJavaDoc Engine
- ❑ XDoclet Engine
- ❑ Modules

In the very beginning of the XDoclet project, a high level of reuse was acheived by relying on the Javadoc to parse the Java source file and generate a tree of classes, language constructs and other metadate. As XDoclet began to become more popular, a need to have a much faster engine developed and the XJavaDoc engine is the result. The new engine does the same work as the Javadoc engine just faster and with a clean API.

Once the files have been parsed and "treed," the XDoclet engine reads tags from the metadata and the tree structure itself. The tags are matched with templates to generate code and other output as required by the template and context of the tags. All of the templating is accomplished in the XDoclet engine. Associated with XDoclet is the module which is dynamically loaded by the system. Modules are comprised of tasks, subtasks, tag handlers and template. A module is basically defined by its task. For example, we have the task webdoclet. Of course not much happens with just the task. We need to specify a sub-task like deploymentdescriptor. The sub-tasks job is to define the templates to be used when tags are encountered relating to the sub-task.

The templates are really the key to XDoclet. With the sub-tasks and tags, a template will be pulled within play and facilitate the output of specific text whether code or HTML. Fundamentally, all tags in XDoclet are custom tags in the same vein as JSP custom tags. The XDoclet engine has the responsibility to trigger specific tag handlers depending on the tag encountered in the source code. Reflection is used to invoke the handler. So our template tag XDtProperty:forAllClasses will require a method called forAllClasses.

A full mapping of tags is accomplished in the xdoclet.xml file found with the XDoclet distribution. The following listing shows an example of the core Ant Tasks.

```
<xdoclet-module>
  <taghandler namespace="Class"
class="xdoclet.tagshandler.ClassTagsHandler"/>
  <taghandler namespace="Comment"
class="xdoclet.tagshandler.CommentTagsHandler"/>
  <taghandler namespace="Config"
class="xdoclet.tagshandler.ConfigTagsHandler"/>
  <taghandler namespace="Constructor"
class="xdoclet.tagshandler.ConstructorTagsHandler"/>
  <taghandler namespace="Field"
class="xdoclet.tagshandler.FieldTagsHandler"/>
  <taghandler namespace="Id"
class="xdoclet.tagshandler.IdTagsHandler"/>
  <taghandler namespace="Merge"
class="xdoclet.tagshandler.MergeTagsHandler"/>
  <taghandler namespace="Method"
class="xdoclet.tagshandler.MethodTagsHandler"/>
  <taghandler namespace="Package"
class="xdoclet.tagshandler.PackageTagsHandler"/>
  <taghandler namespace="Parameter"
class="xdoclet.tagshandler.ParameterTagsHandler"/>
  <taghandler namespace="Property"
class="xdoclet.tagshandler.PropertyTagsHandler"/>
  <taghandler namespace="TagDef"
class="xdoclet.tagshandler.TagDefTagsHandler"/>
  <taghandler namespace="I18n"
class="xdoclet.tagshandler.TranslatorTagsHandler"/>
  <taghandler namespace="Type"
class="xdoclet.tagshandler.TypeTagsHandler"/>
  <taghandler namespace="Xml"
class="xdoclet.tagshandler.XmlTagsHandler"/>
</xdoclet-module>
```

In order to determine which of the handlers to use, the XDoclet engine will strip off the XDt string from the tag to obtain the namespace of the handler—in our tags so far, the result would be Property. As a result the class for the XDoclet engine to use is xdoclet.tagshandler.PropertyTagsHandler. The next listing shows a part of the PropertyTagsHandler handler.

```
public class PropertyTagsHandler extends AbstractProgramElementTagsHandler {
...
public void forAllPropertiesWithTag(String template, Properties attributes)
throws XDocletException
{
...

String requiredTag = attributes.getProperty("tagName");

if (requiredTag == null) {
throw new XDocletException("missing required tag parameter in
forAllPropertiesHavingTag");
}

XClass oldClass = getCurrentClass();
XClass superclass = null;
Collection already = new ArrayList();

// loop over superclasses
do {
XMethod oldCurrentMethod = getCurrentMethod();
Collection methods = getCurrentClass().getMethods();

for (Iterator j = methods.iterator(); j.hasNext(); ) {
XMethod currentMethod = (XMethod) j.next();
log.debug("looking at method " + currentMethod.getName());
if (currentMethod.getDoc().hasTag(requiredTag)) {
setCurrentMethod(currentMethod);
String propertyName =
currentMethod.getPropertyName();
log.debug("property identified " + propertyName);
if (!already.contains(propertyName)) {
generate(template);
already.add(propertyName);
    }
                    }
setCurrentMethod(oldCurrentMethod);
}

// Add super class info
superclass = getCurrentClass().getSuperclass();
if (superclass != null) {
    pushCurrentClass(superclass);
}
} while (superclass != null);

setCurrentClass(oldClass);
}
...
```

Just look at the snippet of code, you can see where the handler obtains the name of the current tag and starts looping over the classes.

A Simple Template

Let's continue by looking at a simple example. Imagine that we have a directory called /src which includes some number of java files. There are numerous files which represent either simple classes or those that extend other classes. There could also be a few classes that implement various interfaces. We'd like to design a template that will parrse through the files and return specific information about the classes back to us. Consider the following template:

```
<XDtClass:forAllClasses type="AbstractNode">

  Classname=<XDtClass:className/>

  <XDtProperty:forAllPropertiesWithTag tagName="node.attribute">
        Node Field = <XDtMethod:propertyName/>
  </XDtProperty:forAllPropertiesWithTag>

</XDtClass:forAllClasses>
```

This simple template includes two different types of template tags: block and content. The first tag <XDtClass:forAllClasses> is a block tag and is designed to parse through all of the files supplied to the template. The tag as displayed is designed to check all of the classes within the supplied files and remove all of these where the class is not of type AbstractNode. After the parsing, we will be a set of files with classes that are of type AbstractNode.

Next, a content tag <XDtClass:className> displays the name of the class. Then we have another block tag <XDtProperty:forAllPropertiesWithTag> that will parse through the remaining classes and display the name of all property with the tag @node.attribute. Thus, consider the following class snippet:

```
/**
 * @node.attribute name=popularity
 * @node.attribute name=raid
 *
 */
public class MyNode extends AbstractNode {
}
```

The result of this class will be the output

```
Classname = MyNode
Node Field = popularity
Node Field = raid
```

We can see the different levels of looping within the template. The forAllClasses acts as an outer loop and the forAllPropertiesWithTag is an inner loop because it appears within the forAllClasses tag. We can activate this template using the following Ant target:

```
<target name="nodetemplate" >

  <taskdef
        name="nodedoclet"
        classname="xdoclet.DocletTask"
classpathref="xdocpath"/>

  <templatedoclet destdir="test">
        <fileset dir="${src}">
```

```
                    <include name="**/*.java"/>
            </fileset>

            <template
                    templateFile="template/nodetemplate.xdt"
                    destinationfile="test.txt"/>

        </templatedoclet>

    </target>
```

This Ant task will use a generic XDoclet Task defined in xdoclet.DocletTask to execute our template. We've defined a <fileset> to only pass in files with a java extension. The template to use for the code generation is defined by the templateFile attribute of the <template> element. The result of the parse and applicatino of the template will be output into the file test.txt.

Building an XDoclet Template

In the previous section we saw how to create a simple template using a couple template tags. In this section of the chapter, we will develop a template that is a little more complex. The most important part of the template is deciding on the block and content tags that will produce the necessary output. A complete list of tags can be found in the installation directory of XDoclet: C:\\xdoclet-1.2\docs\ templates\index.html. You will find hundreds of block and content tags ready to be used. The output of the documentation is the familiar Javadoc output as shown in the following figure.

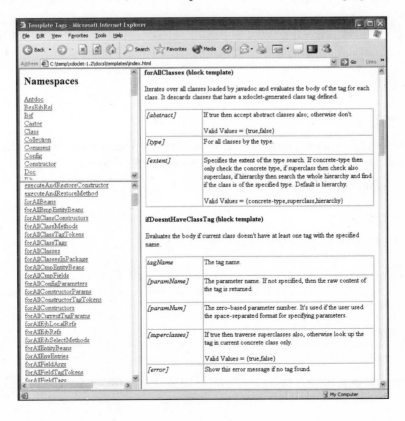

For our example template, we need to decide what the output is suppose to look like and then work backwards to the template and ultimately the tags that will be added to the source code. We are going to create a ficticous configuration for the TDSS application mentioned in Chapter 11. The format of the configuration file will be determined by the attributes available in each of the nodes. Here's an example of the output:

```xml
<?xml version="1.0" encoding="UTF-8"?>

<deployment>

  <attributes>

        <parameter name="raid" value="boolean"/>

      <parameter name="popularity" value="integer"/>

    <parameter name="cost" units="perMB"/>

    <parameter name="search" value="string"/>

  </attributes>

  <name>
        Name
  </name>

  <type>
        Remote
  </type>

  <db>
        mysql
  </db>

</deployment>
```

This information will be pulled from the source code of the individual node source code. The next listing shows an example of the template which will build the deployment file.

```xml
<?xml version="1.0" encoding="UTF-8"?>

  <deployment>

    <XDtClass:forAllClasses type="AbstractNode">

      <name>

        "<XDtClass:classTagValue tagName="tdss.name" paramName="name"/>"
      </name>

      <type>
        "<XDtClass:classTagValue tagName="tdss.type" paramName="type"/>"
      </type>

      <XDtClass:ifClassTagValueEquals tagName="tdss.type"
```

```
                                        paramName="client"
                                        value="local">

        <parameter name="cost"
                   units="<XDtClass:classTagValue
                                   tagName="tdss.cost"
                                   paramName="value"/>"
        />

        <parameter name="search"
                   value="<XDtClass:classTagValue
                                   tagName="tdss.search"
                                   paramName="class"/>"
        />


    </XDtClass:ifClassTagValueEquals>

    <XDtClass:ifClassTagValueEquals tagName="tdss.type"
                                    paramName="client"
                                    value="remote">

        <parameter name="raid"
                   value="<XDtClass:classTagValue
                                   tagName="tdss.raid"
                                   paramName="class"/>"
        />

        <parameter name="popularity"
                   value="<XDtClass:classTagValue
                                   tagName="tdss.popularity"
                                   paramName="class"/>"
        />

        <db>
             "<XDtClass:classTagValue
                        tagName="tdss.db"
                        paramName="class"/>"
        </db?


    </XDtClass:ifClassTagValueEquals>

   </XDtClass:forAllClasses>

 </deployment>
```

The template looks for a few custom tags:

- ❑ **@tdss.raid class=value:** Defines the type of class to use for raid.

- ❑ **@tdss.popularity class =value:** Defines the type of class to use for popularity.

- ❑ **@tdss.cost value=string:** Defines the type of cost structure.

❑ **@tdss.search class = value:** Defines the type of class to use for search.

❑ **@tdss.type client=remote/local:** Defines if the node type is local or remote.

❑ **@tdss.name name=value:** Defines the name of the node.

For example:

```
/**
* @tdss.type client = "local"
*
* @tdss.raid class = "boolean"
*
* @tdss.popularity class = "integer"
*
* @tdss.cost value = "perMD"
*
* @tdss.search class  = "string"
*
* @tdss.db class "mysql"
*/
```

The XDoclet engine will encounter the attribute tags and use them with the template in the third listing of this chapter to produce the deployment file needed for the application.

Summary

XDoclet is a comprehensive package for code generation using Javdoc like tags. There are many built-in tags and functions for developing the resulting code generation. In this chapter, we've taken the opportunity to create our own set of tags as well as develop a template to output a deployment configuration file.

13

Unit Testing with JUnit

This chapter discusses unit-level testing of Java classes with JUnit. Automated unit-level testing is an essential ingredient to continuous integration and XP; accordingly, several chapters in this book cover JUnit. This chapter is primarily a tutorial that introduces the JUnit framework. Chapter 14, "Load Testing with JUnitPerf" and Chapter 16, "Functional Testing with HttpUnit" illustrate techniques for using JUnit with other tools. Combined, these chapters provide thorough coverage of the JUnit framework.

If code has no automated test case written for it to prove that it works, it must be assumed not to work. An API that does not have an automated test case to show how it works must be assumed un-maintainable. Software without automated test cases cannot be economically refactored. Software that that cannot be refactored cannot be extended economically—and believe me, your code will likely be in circulation longer than you think. Your alternative to automated unit-level testing is writing expensive, un-maintainable, rigid, brittle software systems that cannot be easily extended or refactored. Your code base will go the way of the dodo bird or, worse, you will be stuck maintaining it forever—a fitting punishment! When you consider the alternatives, automated unit-level is not optional.

A common argument for not writing automated unit-level test cases is that you just don't have the time. Malarkey. This statement becomes a self-fulfilling prophecy. Productivity is directly related to the stability of your code base. The fewer test cases you write, the less stable your code base becomes. You spend all your time fixing unintended side effects and bugs that are coming out of the woodwork. Soon you have even less time to write tests, not to mention a stomach ulcer. Situation like this can have you running to be another member of the management ranks—and no good developer should want to do that. Get off the hamster wheel and take the time to write test cases.

In Chapter 1, "Introduction to Extreme Programming," we discussed the synergy between refactoring and unit-level testing at length. To sum up those thoughts, without refactoring your system becomes overly complex. Refactoring means keeping your code as simple as possible and yet providing all the features for that iteration of the release. Unit-level testing proves that the code you refactored did not break: The features still work. Testing enables you to have confidence in your ability to refactor and instills courage to refactor often, which keeps your code base solid and maintainable. Working under these conditions is fruitful and rewarding—you can achieve inner peace and contentment with your code.

Where to Get JUnit

JUnit was written by Erich Gamma and Kent Beck. Kent Beck defined the XP methodology and is the author of the first XP book, *Extreme Programming Explained: Embrace Change* as well as subsequent books about XP. JUnit is distributed on JUnit.org under the Common Public License Version 1.0:

www.junit.org/

It's hard to measure the progress of your project without testing. In this chapter, when we talk about *testing* we mean automated testing. Testing is not a metric that is typically tracked; however, it can tell you when something begins working or, more importantly, when something that used to work stops working. The next section will show you how to incrementally build a test suite full of test cases that will help you measure the progress of your project and identify unintended side effects of refactoring.

System.out.println Is Not Enough

To prove that their code works, some people watch the code using System.out.println or their IDE's debugger. This approach has three problems: scroll blindness, subjectivity, and lack of automation.

First, it is hard to tell if a complex system is working because so many System.out.println methods are printing so much garbage. Second (and this is very subjective), you must determine if something works by looking at a String scrolling by on a console. The string of text scrolling by may make sense the day you wrote it, but will it still make sense in three months? Third, when you make changes, things can break in unexpected ways. If you don't have an automated test, you may not test the subsystem that you broke. In fact, it may not be directly related to the subsystem you are working on for quite a while—long enough for the cobwebs of confusion to grow in your mind. Conversely, if you run an automated test several times a day or more, then you will find errors early and often. Simply put, you don't check your code into source control until all the tests run successfully.

Overview of JUnit

JUnit is a framework for writing unit tests. This section helps you focus your development efforts around proving that the code you wrote works and that later, when you refactor to add more features, it still works.

Let's clarify the following concepts: test case, test fixture, and test suite. A *test case* defines a fixture to run a related set of tests. Typically, every class that you write should have a test case. A *test fixture* provides resources: primitive variables and objects that tests need to run. A *test suite* is a collection of related test cases.

For example, if we write a HashMap class, we write a test case for it. The test case has a test fixture object for each test so that we can put objects into the map, pull them out of the map, and perhaps compare them as part of the test. However, if we write a library of collection objects, we write a test suite for it that contains the test case we wrote for the HashMap class—think of a test suite as a collection of test cases.

Let's put these concepts into practice. In order to write a test case, we do the following:

1. Subclass junit.framework.TestCase.

2. If we need fixture objects, override the setUp() method.

3. Define a number of tests that return void and whose method name begins with *test*, such as testAdd(), testPut(), and testIterator().

4. If we need to release resources that were part of the fixture, override the tearDown() method.

5. If we need to group a related set of test cases, define a suite of tests.

The next section discusses writing your own test case based on java.util.HashMap.

Writing a Test Case

An excellent example of creating a test case is provided in the samples that ship with JUnit. The example is called VectorTest, and it shows how you would go about writing a test case for java.util.Vector. The good thing about this example is that most people are familiar with the Vector class. In the same spirit, we created a simple example based on the java.util.HashMap (we will go through this example step by step):

```
/*
 * HashMapTest.java
 *
 * Created on February 8, 2004, 2:29 PM
 */

package xptoolkit.junit.example;

import junit.framework.*;
import java.util.Map;
import java.util.HashMap;
import junit.extensions.*;

/**
 *
 * @author  Rick Hightower
 * @version 1.0
 */
```

```java
public class HashMapTest extends TestCase {

    private Map testMap;
    private Map testMap2;

    public static Test suite() {
            return new TestSuite(HashMapTest.class);
    }

    public static void main (String[] args) {
        junit.textui.TestRunner.run (suite());
    }

    private static final String APPLE_KEY = "AppleCEO";
    private static final String APPLE_VALUE = "AppleCEO";

    protected void setUp() {
        testMap = new HashMap();
        testMap.put(APPLE_KEY, APPLE_VALUE);
        testMap.put("OracleCEO","Larry Ellison");

        testMap2 = new HashMap();
        testMap2.put("1", "1");
        testMap2.put("2", "2");

    }

    public void testPut(){
        String key = "Employee";
        String value = "Rick Hightower";

                //put the value in
        testMap.put(key, value);

                //read the value back out
        String value2 = (String)testMap.get(key);
        assertEquals("The value back from the map ", value, value2);
    }

    public void testSize(){
        assertEquals (2, testMap.size());
    }

    public void testGet(){
        assertEquals(APPLE_VALUE, testMap.get(APPLE_KEY));
        assertNull(testMap.get("JUNK_KEY"));
    }

    public void testPutAll(){
        testMap.putAll(testMap2);
        assertEquals (4, testMap.size());
        assertEquals("1", testMap.get("1"));
        testGet();
    }

    public void testContainsKey(){
```

```
            assertTrue("It should contain the apple key",
                       testMap.containsKey(APPLE_KEY));

    }

    public void testContainsValue(){
        assert(testMap.containsKey(APPLE_VALUE));
    }

    public void testRemove(){
        String key = "Employee";
        String value = "Rick Hightower";

                //put the value in
        testMap.put(key, value);

                //remove it
        testMap.remove(key);

                //try to read the value back out
        assertNull(testMap.get(key));

    }


}
```

Let's break down the example based on the steps we defined in the last section for writing a test case. Step 1 is to define a class that derives junit.framework.TestCase, as follows:

```
import junit.framework.*;
...
public class HashMapTest extends TestCase {
```

Next, if our test case needs a fixture, we override the setUp() method (Step 2), which the HashMapTest does as follows:

```
        protected void setUp() {
            testMap = new HashMap();
            testMap.put(APPLE_KEY, APPLE_VALUE);
            testMap.put("OracleCEO","Larry Ellison");

            testMap2 = new HashMap();
            testMap2.put("1", "1");
            testMap2.put("2", "2");
        }
```

Here we see that the fixture the test case sets up is actually instances of the class under test: the HashMap class. In addition, the test fixture adds some objects (int wrapper) to the HashMap instance. Because the objects that the setUp() method creates will be garbage-collected when we are done with them, we don't have to write a tearDown() method (Step 4). If the setUp() method allocated resources like network connections or database connections, then we would override the tearDown() method to release those resources (Step 4).

Next, the HashMapTest class defines several tests to test the HashMap class, as follows (Step 3):

```java
public void testPut(){
    String key = "Employee";
    String value = "Rick Hightower";

            //put the value in
    testMap.put(key, value);

            //read the value back out
    String value2 = (String)testMap.get(key);
    assertEquals("The value back from the map ", value, value2);
}

public void testSize(){
    assertEquals (2, testMap.size());
}

public void testGet(){
    assertEquals(APPLE_VALUE, testMap.get(APPLE_KEY));
    assertNull(testMap.get("JUNK_KEY"));
}

public void testPutAll(){
    testMap.putAll(testMap2);
    assertEquals (4, testMap.size());
    assertEquals("1", testMap.get("1"));
    testGet();
}

public void testContainsKey(){
    assertTrue("It should contain the apple key",
            testMap.containsKey(APPLE_KEY));
}

public void testContainsValue(){
    assertTrue(testMap.containsKey(APPLE_VALUE));
}

public void testRemove(){
    String key = "Employee";
    String value = "Rick Hightower";

            //put the value in
    testMap.put(key, value);

            //remove it
    testMap.remove(key);

            //try to read the value back out
    assertNull(testMap.get(key));
}
```

Note that each test method becomes a test. The JUnit framework uses reflection to look for methods whose names begin with *test* and uses them as test cases. It does this when we invoke the TestSuite constructor in the static suite() method, as follows:

```
public static Test suite() {
        return new TestSuite(HashMapTest.class);
}
```

A test suite (TestSuite) is a collection of test cases. The test cases themselves can be other test suites. Thus the test suite is a composite of tests using the composite design pattern.

Notice that each test performs an operation on one or both of the HashMaps and then asserts that some condition is true, as follows:

```
public void testPutAll(){
    testMap.putAll(testMap2);
    assertEquals (4, testMap.size());
    assertEquals("1", testMap.get("1"));
    testGet();
}
```

The assertTrue() method asserts that a condition is true; if you are an old C/C++ programming dog, this assert works similar to the one in assert.h. If the condition is not true, then the assert method throws an AssertionFailedError, which is an unchecked exception that causes the test to fail. The JUnit API includes various forms of assert methods; for example, we could put a description of the assertion as in the testContainsKey() method, as follows:

```
public void testContainsKey(){
    assertTrue("It should contain the apple key",
                        testMap.containsKey(APPLE_KEY));
}
```

Or we can opt to leave it out, as follows:

```
public void testContainsValue(){
    assertTrue(testMap.containsKey(APPLE_VALUE));
}
```

Note that the setUp() and tearDown() methods are called before and after every textX() method that is run. Because the setUp() method does not allocate any resources that need to be released, the HashMapTest does not need to override the tearDown() method. If it did, the code would look something like this:

```
protected void setUp() {
        //get db connection
    connection = DriverManager.getConnection();
    statement = connection.createStatement();
    results = statement.executeQuery("select count(*) from Pet");

}
protected void tearDown() {
        //get db connection
```

```
            results.close();
            statement.close();
            connection.close();
    }
```

So far, we've created a test case and fixture objects and tested with assert, but how do we group these test cases into a suite of related test cases? The authors of JUnit have also provided an example of how to do this. They define two tests in the JUnit samples directory: VectorTest and MoneyTest. Then, they define a test suite to run the test cases in the class AllTest, defined in the next listing.

```
package junit.samples;

import junit.framework.*;
import junit.samples.money.MoneyTest;


/**
 * TestSuite that runs all the sample tests
 *
 */
public class AllTests {

        public static void main (String[] args) {
            junit.textui.TestRunner.run (suite());
        }
        public static Test suite ( ) {
            TestSuite suite= new TestSuite("All JUnit Tests");
                suite.addTest(VectorTest.suite());
                suite.addTest (new TestSuite(MoneyTest.class));
                suite.addTest(junit.tests.AllTests.suite());
            return suite;
        }

}
```

The code in this listing compiles several suites of test into one suite. Notice that the main method calls junit.textui.TestRunner.run, passing it the returned value from the static suite() method. The suite() method creates an instance of TestSuite and then adds suites of tests from VectorTest, MoneyTest, and junit.tests.AllTests. Notice that when the AllTest suite() method adds the VectorTest, it calls the VectorTest's suite() method, which is defined as follows:

```
public static Test suite() {
    return new TestSuite(VectorTest.class);
}
```

As you can see, the VectorTest's static suite() method creates a new TestSuite instance by passing itself as a class. TestSuite uses reflection to extract the test methods that make up the suite. The end effect is that you can group related tests into larger and larger test suites. Thus, you could have suites of tests nested in a larger suite. The alternative would be to run every TestCase independently, which would take a long time and would be tedious. Nesting suites of tests enables you to test large portions of code quickly.

We have now covered the basics of JUnit. In the next section, we integrate the test suite with Ant.

Integrating JUnit with Ant

JUnit and Ant go together like a horse and carriage. Ant automates the build-and-deploy process. JUnit automates testing. Put them together, and Ant can automate the build, deploy, and test process. Ant has several tags to support JUnit.

For the integration to work, we need the Extensible Style Language Transformation (XSLT) transform engine JAR file installed; refer to the Ant User Manual documentation for more information. We also need to put the JAR file for JUnit on the Ant classpath, and we must download the optional.jar file from the Apache site (go to http://jakarta.apache.org/ant/index.html and select the "download" option). The easiest way to put these JAR files on the Ant classpath is to copy them to the lib directory in the ANT_HOME directory (ANT_HOME/lib).

Once we have the required JAR files, we can build and test the last example with the following Ant buildfile, which we put in the ANT_HOME directory:

```
<project name="junitSample" default="test">

        <target name="init">
                <property name="outdir" value="/tmp/junitSample" />
        </target>

        <target name="prepare" depends="init">
                <mkdir dir="${outdir}" />
        </target>

        <target name="compile" depends="prepare">
                <javac srcdir="." destdir="${outdir}"
                                    classpath="junit.jar"/>
        </target>

        <target name="test" depends="compile">

            <junit printsummary="true" >
                    <test name="junit.samples.AllTests" />

                    <classpath>
                            <pathelement location="${outdir}" />
                    </classpath>

            </junit>

        </target>


    </project>
```

Let's quickly break down this buildfile. The name of the project is junitSample, and it has the typical targets, as follows: init, prepare, compile, and test. The test target is the default target of the junitSample project's buildfile. The init target creates an "outdir" property that holds the location of the output directory. The prepare tag creates the output directory (outdir). The compile tag builds the Junit sample source code (discussed in the last section) to the output directory (outdir). The interesting target is the test target, as follows:

```
<target name="test" depends="compile">

        <junit printsummary="true" >

                <test name="junit.samples.AllTests" />

                <classpath>
                        <pathelement location="${outdir}" />
                </classpath>

        </junit>
</target>
```

The test target depends on the compile target. The test target uses the junit task defined in the optional.jar file—note that you must have junit.jar on the classpath in order for this task to work. The junit task can run a test created with the junit framework, such as junit.samples.AllTest, described in the last section. The junit task has a sub-element called test. We use the sub-element test to set the classname of the test case we are going to run. In addition, we set up the classpath for JUnit so that it can find the sample classes we compiled in the compile target. Running the code yields these results:

```
C:\tools\junit> ant
Buildfile: build.xml

init:

prepare:

compile:

test:
    [junit] Running junit.samples.AllTests
    [junit] Tests run: 86, Failures: 0, Errors: 1, Time elapsed: 0.911 sec
    [junit] TEST junit.samples.AllTests FAILED

BUILD SUCCESSFUL

Total time: 2 seconds
```

The sample test for our JUnit distribution failed! This event is a nice segue to our next point. As you can see, the summary report for running the test is not very verbose—in fact, it's terse. It is hard to tell which test failed. This result may not be what you want. In fact, we are sure that in the real world, you probably want to know which test failed. All we have to do is add a formatter sub-element that directs JUnit to print out a more detailed report. To do so, we add the following to the test target under the junit task (<formatter type="plain" usefile="false"/>):

```
<target name="test" depends="compile">

        <junit printsummary="true" >
                <formatter type="plain" usefile="false"/>

                <test name="junit.samples.AllTests" />

                <classpath>
```

```
                        <pathelement location="${outdir}" />
                </classpath>

        </junit>
    </target>
```

Now we get much more detailed information, as follows:

```
Buildfile: build.xml

init:

prepare:

compile:

test:
    [junit] Running junit.samples.AllTests
    [junit] Tests run: 86, Failures: 0, Errors: 1, Time elapsed: 0.941 sec
    [junit] Testsuite: junit.samples.AllTests
    [junit] Tests run: 86, Failures: 0, Errors: 1, Time elapsed: 0.941 sec
    [junit]
    [junit] Testcase: testCapacity took 0 sec
    [junit] Testcase: testClone took 0 sec
    [junit] Testcase: testContains took 0 sec
     . . .
     . . .
    [junit] Testcase: testFailAssertNotNull took 0 sec
    [junit] Testcase: testSucceedAssertNotNull took 0 sec
    [junit] Testcase: testFilter took 0 sec
    [junit]     Caused an ERROR
    [junit] null
    [junit] java.lang.NullPointerException
     . . .
     . . .

    [junit] Testcase: testJarClassLoading took 0.01 sec
    [junit] TEST junit.samples.AllTests FAILED

BUILD SUCCESSFUL
```

We can clearly see that the testFilter failed. What a bummer! But let's not leave this section on a bad note. We'll change the Ant buildfile to build and test the VectorTest described in the previous section so we can show a test that passes. The test target changes as follows:

```
<target name="test" depends="compile">

    <junit printsummary="true" >

        <formatter type="plain" usefile="false"/>

        <test name="junit.samples.VectorTest" />

        <classpath>
```

```
                        <pathelement location="${outdir}" />
                </classpath>

        </junit>

    </target>
```

Then we run it as follows:

```
Buildfile: build.xml

init:

prepare:

compile:

test:
    [junit] Running junit.samples.VectorTest
    [junit] Tests run: 6, Failures: 0, Errors: 0, Time elapsed: 0.01 sec
    [junit] Testsuite: junit.samples.VectorTest
    [junit] Tests run: 6, Failures: 0, Errors: 0, Time elapsed: 0.01 sec
    [junit]
    [junit] Testcase: testCapacity took 0 sec
    [junit] Testcase: testClone took 0 sec
    [junit] Testcase: testContains took 0 sec
    [junit] Testcase: testElementAt took 0 sec
    [junit] Testcase: testRemoveAll took 0 sec
    [junit] Testcase: testRemoveElement took 0 sec

BUILD SUCCESSFUL

Total time: 1 second
```

Perhaps you were hoping for a little more from your reporting. It would be nice if you could display the results in a Web page. Then you could have an automated build that would run every night, send out a status email, and post the results on your department's intranet Web site. You can do that with the JUnitReport junitreport task.

First we must change the formatter sub-element's "type" attribute to "xml"; it was set to "plain". This setting outputs the test information in XML format. We also need to set the "usefile" attribute to "true"; for the last example, it was "false". The default "usefile" attribute value is "true", so we will remove it altogether. Here is the updated test target:

```
<target name="test" depends="compile">

    <junit printsummary="true" >
```

```
            <formatter type="xml" />

            <test name="junit.samples.VectorTest" />

            <classpath>
                    <pathelement location="${outdir}" />
            </classpath>

        </junit>

    </target>
```

Now, when we run the buildfile, it creates an XML file named TEST-junit.samples.VectorTest.xml. The contents of the XML file are as follows:

```
<?xml version="1.0"?>
<testsuite errors="0" failures="0" name="junit.samples.VectorTest" tests="6"
time="0.201">
  <testcase name="testCapacity" time="0"></testcase>
  <testcase name="testClone" time="0"></testcase>
  <testcase name="testContains" time="0"></testcase>
  <testcase name="testElementAt" time="0"></testcase>
  <testcase name="testRemoveAll" time="0"></testcase>
  <testcase name="testRemoveElement" time="0"></testcase>
</testsuite>
```

Because we now have the output in XML, we can use the junitreport task, which takes the XML and transforms it to HTML using XSLT. You don't have to know XSLT to use the junitreport task. There are two types of reports: those with frames and those without. We add the junitreport task tag after the junit task tag, as follows:

```
        <junitreport todir="./reports">

            <fileset dir=".">

                <include name="TEST-*.xml"/>

            </fileset>

            <report format="frames" todir="./report/html"/>

        </junitreport>
```

When we run this buildfile it generates the report shown on the next page.

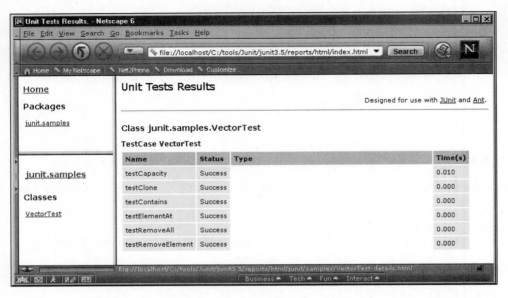

As you can see from this figure, the report that is generated allows you to navigate the tests that were run. Therefore, instead of building large suites, you may want to use Ant and the junit task and just specify the tests you want to run as file sets; you will be able to generate really nice reports.

Case Study: Adding an Entity Bean to the Pet Store

This section explains the test cases for the baseline version of the pet store. We discuss adding an entity bean and Web form to manage product data over the Web (that is, to add, delete, and modify product data). Once we add the entity bean, we add more test cases to test it, and then we integrate those tests into the test buildfile. Thus we will cover building and deploying an entity bean to our EJB server. Before we talk about including EJBs, let's look at what we already have for testing the system. Remember, before you refactor, you should have tests set up so you know that what you refactor does not break.

Overview of Existing JUnit Tests

The test buildfile runs four JUnit tests, as follows:

- ❑ CategorySystemTest
- ❑ CategoryTest
- ❑ SubcategoryTest
- ❑ ProductTest

Each test class tests its corresponding counterpart in the model—that is, the public interface to the system. Complete code listings for these tests and their interfaces can be found in Appendix A. Because the structure of these four tests are very similar, this section describes only two of them in detail for purposes of illustrating unique elements and techniques. These tests are run by the test project buildfile, demonstrated with this test buildfile snippet (the complete code will be discussed later):

```
<target name="test" depends="compile">
. . .

        <test  name="test.xptoolkit.model.CategorySystemTest"
               todir="${reports}" />

        <test  name="test.xptoolkit.model.CategoryTest"
               todir="${reports}" />

        <test  name="test.xptoolkit.model.SubcategoryTest"
               todir="${reports}" />

        <test  name="test.xptoolkit.model.ProductTest"
               todir="${reports}" />

. . .
```

The tests are designed to test all the functionality of the public interface—everything that could possibly break. The following listing for CategorySystemTest tests the CategorySystem.

```
package test.xptoolkit.model;
import xptoolkit.petstore.model.CategorySystem;

import junit.framework.*;

public class CategorySystemTest extends TestCase {
    CategorySystem system;

    public static void main(java.lang.String[] args) {
        junit.textui.TestRunner.run(suite());
    }

    public static Test suite() {
        TestSuite suite = new TestSuite(CategorySystemTest.class);

        return suite;
    }

    protected void setUp()throws Exception {
        system = new CategorySystem();
    }


    /** Test of getCurrentCategory method, of class
        xptoolkit.petstore.model.CategorySystem. */
    public void testGetCurrentCategory() throws Exception{
        assertNotNull(system.getCurrentCategory());
    }
```

```
    /** Test of getSubcategory method, of class
        xptoolkit.petstore.model.CategorySystem. */
    public void testGetSubcategory() throws Exception{
        assertNotNull(system.getSubcategory(111));
    }

    /** Test of getProduct method, of class
        xptoolkit.petstore.model.CategorySystem. */
    public void testGetProduct() throws Exception {
        testGetSubcategory();
        assertNotNull(system.getProduct(1));
    }

        /** Test of getCurrentSubcategory method, of class
            xptoolkit.petstore.model.CategorySystem. */
    public void testGetCurrentSubcategory() throws Exception{
        testGetSubcategory();
        assertNotNull(system.getCurrentSubcategory());
    }

    /** Test of getCurrentProduct method, of class
        xptoolkit.petstore.model.CategorySystem. */
    public void testGetCurrentProduct() throws Exception{
        testGetSubcategory();
        testGetProduct();
        assertNotNull(system.getCurrentProduct());
    }
}
```

As you may remember from Chapter 5, we populate the database with default values. The JUnit tests use that information to navigate the category hierarchy (for example, the following listing shows the CategoryTest).

```
package test.xptoolkit.model;

import java.util.*;
import junit.framework.*;

import xptoolkit.petstore.model.Category;
import xptoolkit.petstore.model.Product;
import xptoolkit.petstore.model.Subcategory;


public class CategoryTest extends TestCase {

    Category category; //object under test

    public static void main(java.lang.String[] args) {
        junit.textui.TestRunner.run(suite());
    }

    public static Test suite() {
        TestSuite suite = new TestSuite(CategoryTest.class);

        return suite;
```

```
        }

        public void setUp()throws Exception{
            category = Category.getCategory();
            category.setId(777);
        }

        /** Test of getCategory method, of class
            xptoolkit.petstore.model.Category. */
        public void testGetCategory() throws Exception{
            System.out.println("testGetCategory");
            Category category = Category.getCategory();
            category.setId(777);
            this.assertNotNull("category", category);

        }

        /** Test of getSubcategories method, of class
            xptoolkit.petstore.model.Category. */
        public void testGetSubcategories() throws Exception {
            Subcategory [] categories = category.getSubcategories();
            assertNotNull("categories", categories);
            for (int index=0; index < categories.length; index++){
                assertNotNull("subcategory", categories[index]);
            }
        }

            /** Test of getSubcategory method, of class
                xptoolkit.petstore.model.Category. */
        public void testGetSubcategory() throws Exception {
            Subcategory [] categories = category.getSubcategories();
            assertNotNull("categories", categories);
            for (int index=0; index < categories.length; index++){
                Subcategory subcat=categories[index];
                int id = subcat.getId();
                assertNotNull("subcategory", category.getSubcategory(id));
            }
        }


        public void testGetters() throws Exception {
            assertNotNull("name", category.getName());
            assertNotNull("description", category.getDescription());

        }

    }
```

There are four tests to test the public interface of xptoolkit.petstore.model.Category, as follows:

- ❏ testGetCategory
- ❏ testGetSubcategories
- ❏ testGetSubcategory
- ❏ testGetters

The setUp() method creates a category instance and sets it to the main test category.

```
category = Category.getCategory();
category.setId(777);
```

Remember, setUp() is called for each test. Thus, each test gets its own copy of category. For example, testGetSubcategories gets its own copy of category, which it uses to test the getSubcategories() method of xptoolkit.petstore.model.Category as follows:

```
public void testGetSubcategories() throws Exception {
    Subcategory [] categories = category.getSubcategories();
    assertNotNull("categories", categories);
    for (int index=0; index < categories.length; index++){
        assertNotNull("subcategory", categories[index]);
    }
}
```

Because the test data is known, we could check for specific values of subcategories in specific locations. For example, look at testGetters() from the ProductTest class:

```
/** Test of getters method of class
                    xptoolkit.petstore.model.Product. */
public void testGetters() {
    this.assertEquals("name", product.getName(), "Poodle");
    this.assertEquals("description", product.getDescription(),
                                        "Poodle description");
    testSetters();
    this.assertEquals("name", product.getName(), "Boo");
    this.assertEquals("description", product.getDescription(),
                                        "Designer");

}
```

Note that each main model class in the model project has a corresponding test class in the test project:

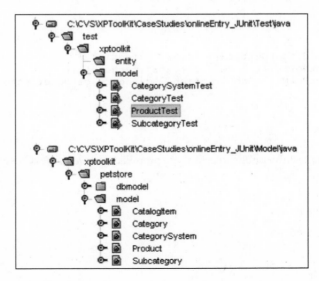

The test buildfile is responsible for executing the tests in an automated fashion (see the following listing). Typically, you write the tests as you develop your classes. Once you are done writing your tests and using them to incrementally test your code as you write it, you put them in your test buildfile so they are included in your automatic build and deploy. Then, not only can you break the build by checking in code that does not compile, you can break the build by writing code that breaks the tests.

```xml
<project name="test" default="all" >
    <target name="setProps" unless="setProps"
                        description="setup the properties.">
        <property name="outdir" value="/tmp/petstore" />

    </target>


    <target name="init" depends="setProps"
                        description="initialize the properties.">
        <tstamp/>
        <property name="local_outdir" value="${outdir}/pettest" />
        <property name="lib" value="${outdir}/lib" />
        <property name="dist" value="${outdir}/dist" />
        <property name="reports" value="${outdir}/reports" />
        <property name="build" value="${local_outdir}/testclasses" />
        <property name="build_lib" value="./../lib" />
        <property name="test_lib" value="./../testlib" />
        <property name="test_jar" value="${lib}/pettest.jar" />
    </target>


    <target name="clean" depends="init"
                        description="clean up the output directories.">
        <delete dir="${local_outdir}" />
        <delete dir="${reports}" />
    </target>


    <target name="prepare" depends="init"
                        description="prepare the output directory.">
        <mkdir dir="${build}" />
        <mkdir dir="${dist}" />
        <mkdir dir="${reports}" />
        <mkdir dir="${reports}/html" />
    </target>


    <target name="compile" depends="prepare"
                        description="compile the Java source.">

        <javac srcdir="./java" destdir="${build}">
            <classpath >
                <fileset dir="${lib}">
                    <include name="**/*.jar"/>
                </fileset>

                <fileset dir="${build_lib}">
```

```
                    <include name="**/*.jar"/>
            </fileset>

            <fileset dir="${test_lib}">
                <include name="**/*.jar"/>
            </fileset>

        </classpath>
    </javac>
</target>

<target name="package" depends="compile">

    <jar jarfile="${test_jar}"
        basedir="${build}" />

</target>

<target name="test" depends="compile">

    <junit printsummary="true" fork="yes">

        <formatter type="xml" />

        <test  name="test.xptoolkit.model.CategorySystemTest"
                todir="${reports}" />

        <test  name="test.xptoolkit.model.CategoryTest"
                todir="${reports}" />

        <test  name="test.xptoolkit.model.SubcategoryTest"
                todir="${reports}" />

        <test  name="test.xptoolkit.model.ProductTest"
                todir="${reports}" />


        <classpath>
            <fileset dir="${lib}">
                <include name="**/*.jar"/>
            </fileset>

            <fileset dir="${build_lib}">
                <include name="**/*.jar"/>
            </fileset>

            <fileset dir="${test_lib}">
                <include name="**/*.jar"/>
            </fileset>

            <fileset dir="/tools/ant/lib">
                <include name="**/*.jar"/>
            </fileset>
```

```
            <fileset dir="${build}" />

        </classpath>

    </junit>

    <junitreport todir="${reports}">

        <fileset dir="${reports}">

            <include name="TEST-*.xml"/>

        </fileset>

        <report format="frames" todir="${reports}/html"/>

    </junitreport>
</target>


<target name="cleanTest" depends="clean,package,test" />

<target name="all" depends="package,test"
                    description="perform all targets."/>

</project>
```

The focal point of the test buildfile is the test target. The test target runs each of the tests that we defined, such as test.xptoolkit.model.CategoryTest. The test target uses the junit and junitreport tasks as follows:

```
<target name="test" depends="compile">

    <junit printsummary="true" fork="yes">

        <formatter type="xml" />

        <test  name="test.xptoolkit.model.CategorySystemTest"
               todir="${reports}" />

. . .
        <classpath>
. . .

            <fileset dir="${test_lib}">
                <include name="**/*.jar"/>
            </fileset>

. . .

        </classpath>

    </junit>

    <junitreport todir="${reports}">
```

```
<fileset dir="${reports}">

    <include name="TEST-*.xml"/>

</fileset>

<report format="frames" todir="${reports}/html"/>

    </junitreport>
</target>
```

Notice that the classpath sub-element of the JUnit class uses the JAR files in ${test_lib}. This is where we store the JAR file (junit.jar) that contains the JUnit framework classes.

The junitreport task specifies the output directory as "${reports}/html" and the input test files that are the XML files generated from the output of the junit task. The junitreport task also specifies the output directory in which to put the report HTML files. (You can see examples of the output HTML displayed in a browser in Chapter 5.) The following figure shows the output of this test.

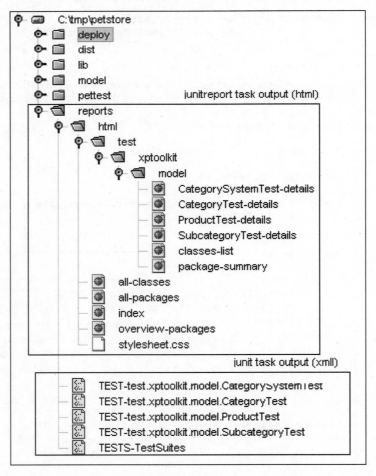

Adding an Enterprise JavaBean to the Pet Store

This section adds a feature to the baseline pet store application: the ability to add, edit, and delete products from the Web. We have decided to use a container-managed entity EJB. Thus, we need to do the following:

1. Create the product entity bean.
2. Add a new subproject buildfile for EJBs.
3. Add a new test case class to test our Product EJB.
4. Update our categorySystem class.
5. Create an HTML form.
6. Add additional JSPs to handle the form submission and the backend navigation.

The next figure shows a block diagram of how the output will look when we are done.

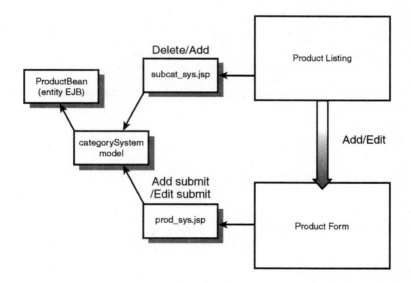

Security and Authentication

In the real world, you should password-protect your product entry management. Servlets 2.3 enables you to do this with a servlet filter. Or, you can do this with Web authentication provided by your application server or Web server. This example does not demonstrate authentication, but you can add it without changing the JSPs introduced with any of the methods we use.

The entity bean is fairly simple, because it is uses container managed persistence (CMP). The container takes care of persisting the bean to the database. See the next three listings for the complete product entity bean: its interface, implementation, and home, respectively. With this product entity bean we add, delete, and edit product entries. You can use a number of techniques and design patterns to reduce the number of remote procedure calls; for simplicity, we don't use them here.

```
package xptoolkit.petstore.entity;

import javax.ejb.*;
import java.rmi.RemoteException;

public interface Product extends EJBObject {

    public String getDescription()throws RemoteException;
    public String getName()throws RemoteException;
    public Integer getId()throws RemoteException;
    public int getSubcategoryId()throws RemoteException;
    public int getQty()throws RemoteException;
    public java.math.BigDecimal getPrice()throws RemoteException;


    public void setDescription(String description)throws RemoteException;
    public void setName(String name)throws RemoteException;
    public void setId(Integer ID)throws RemoteException;
    public void setSubcategoryId(int subcat)throws RemoteException;
    public void setQty(int qty)throws RemoteException;
    public void setPrice(java.math.BigDecimal price)throws RemoteException;


}



package xptoolkit.petstore.entity;

import javax.ejb.*;

public class ProductBean implements EntityBean {

    EntityContext ctx;
    public String description;
    public String name;
    public Integer id;
    public int subcategoryId;
    public int qty;
    public java.math.BigDecimal price;

    public Integer ejbCreate (Integer id, String name, int qty,
                    String description, int subCat,
                    java.math.BigDecimal price){
        this.id = id;
        this.name=name;
        this.description=description;
        this.qty=qty=0;
```

```
            subcategoryId=subCat;
            this.price= price;
            return null;
        }

        public void ejbPostCreate(Integer _id, String name, int qty,
                        String description, int subCat,
                        java.math.BigDecimal price){
            id = (Integer)ctx.getPrimaryKey();
            System.out.println("Product ID " + id);
        }

        public String getDescription(){return description;}
        public String getName(){return name;}
        public Integer getId(){return id;}
        public int getSubcategoryId(){return subcategoryId;}
        public int getQty(){return qty;}
        public java.math.BigDecimal getPrice(){return price;}

        public void setDescription(String description)
                                {this.description =description;}
        public void setName(String name){this.name=name;}
        public void setId(Integer id){this.id=id;}
        public void setSubcategoryId(int subcategoryId)
                                {this.subcategoryId=subcategoryId;}
        public void setQty(int qty){this.qty=qty;}
        public void setPrice(java.math.BigDecimal price){this.price=price;}

        public void setEntityContext(EntityContext ctx) { this.ctx = ctx; }
        public void unsetEntityContext() { ctx = null; }
        public void ejbActivate() { }
        public void ejbPassivate() { }
        public void ejbLoad() { }
        public void ejbStore() { }
        public void ejbRemove() { }

    }



package xptoolkit.petstore.entity;

import javax.ejb.*;
import java.util.*;

import java.rmi.RemoteException;

public interface ProductHome extends EJBHome {


    public Product create(Integer id, String name, int qty,
                    String description, int subCat,
                    java.math.BigDecimal price)
                        throws RemoteException, CreateException;
```

```
     Product findByPrimaryKey(Integer key)
                          throws RemoteException, FinderException;

     Collection findAll()throws RemoteException, FinderException;

     Collection findBySubcategoryId()throws RemoteException, FinderException;

}
```

```
<ejb-jar>

<description>
This ejb-jar files contains the Enterprise beans for the
Petstore Case Study
</description>
<enterprise-beans>
  <entity>
    <ejb-name>ProductBean</ejb-name>
    <home>xptoolkit.petstore.entity.ProductHome</home>
    <remote>xptoolkit.petstore.entity.Product</remote>
    <ejb-class>xptoolkit.petstore.entity.ProductBean</ejb-class>
    <persistence-type>Container</persistence-type>
    <prim-key-class>java.lang.Integer</prim-key-class>
    <primkey-field>id</primkey-field>
    <reentrant>False</reentrant>
    <cmp-field><field-name>description</field-name></cmp-field>
    <cmp-field><field-name>name</field-name></cmp-field>
    <cmp-field><field-name>id</field-name></cmp-field>
    <cmp-field><field-name>subcategoryId</field-name></cmp-field>
    <cmp-field><field-name>qty</field-name></cmp-field>
    <cmp-field><field-name>price</field-name></cmp-field>
  </entity>

</enterprise-beans>
<assembly-descriptor>
   <container-transaction>
      <method>
        <ejb-name>ProductBean</ejb-name>
        <method-name>*</method-name>
      </method>
      <trans-attribute>Required</trans-attribute>
   </container-transaction>
</assembly-descriptor>
</ejb-jar>
```

The new ProductTest (test.xptoolkit.petstore.entity.ProductTest) is used to test the entity bean (xptoolkit.petstore.entity.Product). The ProductTest simulates a client; thus, it must import the needed client-side EJB classes. It must import the Java Naming and Directory Interface (JNDI) support and the RMI PortableRemoteObject as follows:

```
import javax.rmi.PortableRemoteObject;
import javax.naming.*;
```

Of course, it must import the bean's home and remote interface, as follows:

```
import xptoolkit.petstore.entity.Product;
import xptoolkit.petstore.entity.ProductHome;
```

Because every test needs to access the home interface to create, find, and delete Products, we locate an instance of the home interface using JNDI in the setUp() method as follows:

```
protected void setUp()throws Exception{
    Object ref;
    InitialContext jndiContext=null;
    jndiContext = new InitialContext(env);
    ref  = jndiContext.lookup("ProductBean");
    home = (ProductHome)
            PortableRemoteObject.narrow (ref, ProductHome.class);
}
```

This is fairly standard client-side EJB code. The first test uses the home interface to create a product entity with test data.

```
public void testCreate()throws Exception{
    product = home.create(new Integer(876662), "Rick", 5, "you ", 555,
            new java.math.BigDecimal(1200));
    assertNotNull("product", product);
    assertEquals("name", "Rick", product.getName());

}
```

As you can see, the first and second tests depend on each other; they are order dependent. The scenario works because the test framework uses reflection, and reflection uses the methods in the order they are declared. This code is brittle and depends on some minutia in the Java reflection API. You can ensure the order of execution by explicitly setting it in the suite() method instead of relying on the generic reflection-based methods. The TestSuite has an addTest() method that lets you add test cases to it. You could also use OrderedTestSuite, which is available in junit-addons (http://sourceforge.net/projects/junit-addons).

The second test finds the entity created with the first test and then deletes that entity by calling the product entities' remove() method. Then, to make sure the entity was removed, the test tries to find it again. If the home interface's findByPrimaryKey() method does not find the object, we return; otherwise, we force a fail by calling fail(), as follows:

```
public void testRemove()throws Exception{
    product = home.findByPrimaryKey(new Integer(876662));
    product.remove();

    try{
        product = home.findByPrimaryKey(new Integer(876662));
    }
    catch(javax.ejb.ObjectNotFoundException e){
```

```
        return;

    }

    fail("Product entity should already be gone and not findable.");
}
```

The other methods test the setter and getter methods of the product, as follows:

```
/** Test of setter methods, of class
                    xptoolkit.petstore.model.Product. */
public void testSetters() throws Exception{
    testCreate();
    product.setName("Boo");
    product.setDescription("Designer");
    product.setQty(5);
    testRemove();
}

/** Test of getter methods, of class
                  xptoolkit.petstore.model.Product. */
public void testGetters() throws Exception{
    testCreate();
    this.assertEquals("name", product.getName(), "Rick");
    this.assertEquals("description", product.getDescription(),
                                                "you ");

    product.setName("Boo");
    product.setDescription("Designer");
    product.setQty(5);


    this.assertEquals("name", product.getName(), "Boo");
    this.assertEquals("description", product.getDescription(),
"Designer");
    testRemove();

}
```

The tests in ProductTest are quite simple. They ensure that we have set up and created our entity bean correctly. See the following list for the complete ProductTest code.

```
package test.xptoolkit.petstore.entity;
import junit.framework.*;
import java.util.Properties;
import javax.rmi.PortableRemoteObject;
import javax.naming.*;

import xptoolkit.petstore.entity.Product;
import xptoolkit.petstore.entity.ProductHome;


public class ProductTest extends TestCase {
```

```
Product product;
ProductHome home;

protected void setUp()throws Exception{

  Object ref;
  InitialContext jndiContext=null;
  jndiContext = new InitialContext(env);
  ref  = jndiContext.lookup("ProductBean");
  home = (ProductHome)
         PortableRemoteObject.narrow (ref, ProductHome.class);
}


public static void main(java.lang.String[] args) {
    junit.textui.TestRunner.run(suite());
}

public static Test suite() {
    TestSuite suite = new TestSuite(ProductTest.class);

    return suite;
}

public void testCreate()throws Exception{
    product = home.create(new Integer(876662), "Rick", 5, "you ", 555,
            new java.math.BigDecimal(1200));
    assertNotNull("product", product);
    assertEquals("name", "Rick", product.getName());

}

public void testRemove()throws Exception{
    product = home.findByPrimaryKey(new Integer(876662));
    product.remove();

    try{
        product = home.findByPrimaryKey(new Integer(876662));
    }
    catch(javax.ejb.ObjectNotFoundException e){
        return;

    }

    fail("Product entity should already be gone and not findable.");
}


/** Test of getSetter methods, of class
                            xptoolkit.petstore.model.Product. */
public void testSetters() throws Exception{
    testCreate();
    product.setName("Boo");
```

```
        product.setDescription("Designer");
        product.setQty(5);
        testRemove();
    }

    /** Test of getter methods, of class
                                  xptoolkit.petstore.model.Product. */
    public void testGetters() throws Exception{
        testCreate();
        this.assertEquals("name", product.getName(), "Rick");
        this.assertEquals("description", product.getDescription(), "you ");

        product.setName("Boo");
        product.setDescription("Designer");
        product.setQty(5);
        this.assertEquals("name", product.getName(), "Boo");
        this.assertEquals("description", product.getDescription(),
                                                     "Designer");

        testRemove();

    }

    static Properties env = new Properties();
    static {
        env.setProperty("java.naming.factory.initial",
                        "org.jnp.interfaces.NamingContextFactory");
        env.setProperty("java.naming.provider.url",  "localhost:1099");
        env.setProperty("java.naming.factory.url.pkgs",
                                    "org.jboss.naming");
    }
}
```

IDEs Support JUnit and Ant

Plug-ins are available for Eclipse, Forte, NetBeans, TogetherSoft ControlCenter, JBuilder, and so on for both JUnit and Ant. We create many of our tests by generating the tests' started code in the NetBeans IDE. The ProductTest started code was initially generated with NetBeans support for JUnit. You specify the class, and NetBeans generates the started skeleton to test your class. Cool beans!

It's our considered opinion that no JSP should know whether you are using JDBC, flat files, or entity beans to manage the persistence of the system. Thus, we decided to add support for adding and removing products behind the CategorySystem façade class. In fact, the implementation of the client-side piece of the Product entity is in CategoryDB, and the public interface is defined in the Category abstract class.

Here are the additional methods that we added to the CategorySystem class (xptoolkit.petstore.model .CategorySystem):

```
    public void createProduct(Product product) throws Exception{
        currentCategory.createProduct(product);
        if(currentSubcategory!=null)currentSubcategory.invalidate();
```

```
    }
    public void editProduct(Product product) throws Exception{
        currentCategory.editProduct(product);
        if(currentSubcategory!=null)currentSubcategory.invalidate();
    }
    public void deleteProduct(int id) throws Exception{
        currentCategory.deleteProduct(id);
        if(currentSubcategory!=null)currentSubcategory.invalidate();
    }
```

Here are the corresponding methods we added to the Category class:

```
    public abstract void createProduct(Product product) throws Exception;
    public abstract void editProduct(Product product) throws Exception;
    public abstract void deleteProduct(int id) throws Exception;
```

The actual implementation of these methods is in the CategoryDB class, as follows:

```
    public void createProduct(Product product) throws Exception{
        getHome().create(new Integer(product.getId()),
                        product.getName(),
                        product.getQty(),
                        product.getDescription(),
                        product.getFkSubcategoryId(),
                        new java.math.BigDecimal(product.getPrice()));
    }
    public void editProduct(Product product) throws Exception{
        xptoolkit.petstore.entity.Product p
                    =getHome().findByPrimaryKey(
new Integer(product.getId()));
        p.setName(product.getName());
        p.setDescription(product.getDescription());
        p.setPrice(new java.math.BigDecimal(product.getPrice()));
        p.setQty(product.getQty());
    }

    public void deleteProduct(int id) throws Exception{
        getHome().findByPrimaryKey(new Integer(id)).remove();
    }

    private ProductHome getHome() throws Exception{
      Object ref;
      InitialContext jndiContext=null;
      jndiContext = new InitialContext(env);
      ref  = jndiContext.lookup("ProductBean");
      return (ProductHome)
              PortableRemoteObject.narrow (ref, ProductHome.class);
    }
```

This code should look familiar. It is much like the code in our test, except that now we are using it to implement the public interface to our Web application. You should add tests at the boundary points to every tier in an n-tier architecture. That way, you test the public interface of each tier. This approach becomes particularly useful if things begin to go wrong; when debugging a distributed multitiered application, it's helpful to be able to test access to each tier independently from the rest of the added business logic in the encapsulating tier.

Because the CategorySystem is a very thin wrapper in the case of adding, removing, and editing products, we decided to add the tests in the CategoryTest as follows:

```
public void testCreateDeleteProduct() throws Exception {
    . . .
    Product p = new Product(){};
    p.setId(1119996);
    p.setFkSubcategoryId(111);
    p.setName("Test1");
    p.setDescription("Test1 Description");
    p.setPrice(11);
    p.setPrice(6);
    category.createProduct(p);

    Product p2 = category.getProduct(1119996);
    assertEquals("name after create",p2.getName(), p.getName());

    p.setName("Test2");
    category.editProduct(p);
    Product p3 = category.getProduct(1119996);
    assertEquals("name after edit", p3.getName(), p.getName());


    category.deleteProduct(p.getId());
    Product p4 = category.getProduct(1119996);
    this.assertEquals("product should be gone", -1, p4.getId());
}
```

This code is fairly simple, because the actual product implementation is tested thoroughly in the entity ProductTest. Essentially, the test creates a product, edits it, and deletes it. It makes sure the product data is added, edited, and removed. Here the test creates the product by calling the category createProduct() method:

```
Product p = new Product(){};
p.setId(1119996);
p.setFkSubcategoryId(111);
p.setName("Test1");
p.setDescription("Test1 Description");
p.setPrice(11);
p.setPrice(6);
category.createProduct(p);
```

Next, the test makes sure that the product actually was created by looking it up:

```
Product p2 = category.getProduct(1119996);
assertEquals("name after create",p2.getName(), p.getName());
```

Here the test edits the product by changing the product object and then submitting it. Then, the test makes sure the product was edited:

```
p.setName("Test2");
category.editProduct(p);
Product p3 = category.getProduct(1119996);
assertEquals("name after edit", p3.getName(), p.getName());
```

Finally, the test removes the product, as follows:

```
category.deleteProduct(p.getId());
Product p4 = category.getProduct(1119996);
this.assertEquals("proudct should be gone", -1, p4.getId());
```

One thing is wrong with this test. It should be further functionally decomposed. For example, let's say the create part fails or the delete part fails. The output of the test will not make clear which functionality was not working. There is a fine line between being over-cautious and sloppy. The more you functionally decompose, the better your reports will be able to point you to the correct failure point.

So, let's decompose the test a little further. We can see that we are doing four things: creating a product, getting a product from the data store, editing a product, and deleting a product from the data store. We begin by moving the test data that the tests will share to the setUp() method, as follows:

```
Product p;

public void setUp()throws Exception{
    . . .
    . . .
    p = new Product(){};
    p.setId(1119996);
    p.setFkSubcategoryId(111);
    p.setName("Test1");
    p.setDescription("Test1 Description");
    p.setPrice(11);
    p.setPrice(6);

}
```

Notice that the test object p is now an instance variable, so it can be used in all four tests. The next step is to break the method testCreateDeleteProduct() into four methods. We add the product from the setUp() method:

```
public void testCreateProduct() throws Exception {
    category.createProduct(p);
}
```

The next test tests the ability to get the product out of the database. Notice that you could combine this get-product test and the previous test, because this one validates the create-product test:

```
public void testGetProduct()throws Exception {
    Product p2 = category.getProduct(1119996);
    assertEquals("name after create",p2.getName(), p.getName());
}
```

The next test tests the ability to edit an existing product:

```
public void testEditProduct() throws Exception {
    p.setName("Test2");
    category.editProduct(p);
    Product p3 = category.getProduct(1119996);
    assertEquals("name after edit", p3.getName(), p.getName());
}
```

Finally, we test the deletion of the product as follows:

```
public void testDeleteProduct()throws Exception {
    category.deleteProduct(p.getId());
    Product p4 = category.getProduct(1119996);
    this.assertEquals("proudct should be gone", -1, p4.getId());
}
```

You really need to endeavor to keep tests small and as atomic in operation as possible. If something breaks in the future, the test will identify exactly what broke. If we had left the test as it was and something broke, it would be hard to tell what broke—not impossible, but difficult. Plus, these methods describe exactly what we are testing.

Creating an Ant Buildfile to Deploy Our Entity Bean

Just like the Hello World example, the EJB source, libraries, and buildfile are self-contained in their own directory structure:

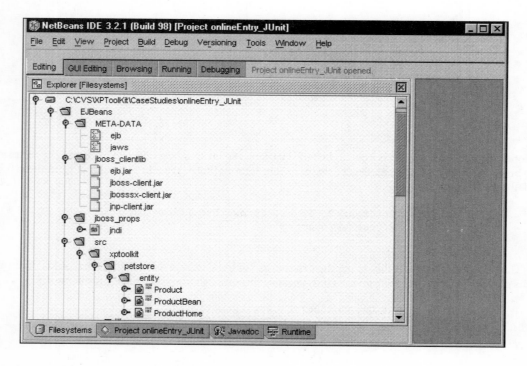

The src directory holds the source files. The jboss-clientlib directory holds the library files needed by JBoss (the EJB server). The META-DATA directory holds the deployment descriptor and the entity property to SQL table field mapping file. The buildfile project name is enterprise_beans; refer to this listing:

```xml
<project name="enterprise_beans" default="all" >


    <target name="setProps" unless="setProps"
                        description="setup the properties.">
        <property name="outdir" value="/tmp/petstore" />
        <property name="jboss" value="/tools/jboss/jboss/deploy" />
    </target>

    <target name="init" depends="setProps"
                        description="initialize the properties.">
        <tstamp/>
        <property name="ejbout" value="${outdir}/ejbs" />
        <property name="build" value="${ejbout}/ejb-jar" />
        <property name="client" value="${ejbout}/ejb-jar-client" />
        <property name="dist" value="${outdir}/dist" />
        <property name="lib" value="${outdir}/lib" />
        <property name="meta-data" value="${build}/META-INF" />
        <property name="build_lib" value="./../lib" />
        <property name="jar_name" value="petbeans.jar" />
    </target>

    <target name="clean_jboss" if="jboss">
        <delete file="${jboss}/${jar_name}" />
    </target>

    <target name="clean" depends="init,clean_jboss"
                        description="clean up the output directories.">
        <delete dir="${build}" />
        <delete dir="${meta-data}" />
        <delete dir="${client}" />
        <delete dir="${dist}/${jar_name}" />
    </target>


    <target name="prepare" depends="init"
                        description="prepare the output directory.">
        <mkdir dir="${build}" />
        <mkdir dir="${lib}" />
        <mkdir dir="${meta-data}" />
        <mkdir dir="${client}" />
        <mkdir dir="${dist}" />
    </target>

    <target name="compile" depends="prepare"
                        description="compile the Java source.">
        <javac srcdir="./src" destdir="${build}" >
            <classpath >
                <pathelement location="." />
```

```xml
                    <fileset dir="${build_lib}">
                        <include name="**/*.jar"/>
                    </fileset>

                    <fileset dir="${lib}">
                        <include name="**/*.jar"/>
                    </fileset>

            </classpath>
        </javac>
    </target>

    <target name="config_jboss_jndi" if="jboss">
        <copy todir="${client}" >
            <fileset dir="./jboss_props" />
        </copy>

    </target>

    <target name="config_jndi" depends="config_jboss_jndi" />


    <target name="package" depends="compile,config_jndi"
                        description="package the Java classes into a jar.">
        <copy todir="${client}" >
            <fileset dir="${build}" excludes="**/*Bean*"
                                    includes="**/*.class*" />
        </copy>

        <jar jarfile="${lib}/client-${jar_name}"
          basedir="${client}" />


          <copy file="./META-DATA/ejb.xml"
                        tofile="${meta-data}/ejb-jar.xml"/>
          <copy file="./META-DATA/jaws.xml"
                        tofile="${meta-data}/jaws.xml" />

         <jar jarfile="${dist}/${jar_name}"
           basedir="${build}" />


    </target>

    <target name="deploy_jboss" depends="package" if="jboss">
        <copy file="${dist}/${jar_name}" todir="${jboss}" />
        <copy todir="${lib}"  >
            <fileset dir="./jboss_clientlib" />
        </copy>
    </target>

    <target name="deploy" depends="package,deploy_jboss"
                    description="deploys the jar file to the ejb server.">
    </target>
```

```
<target name="all" depends="clean,deploy"
                    description="perform all targets."/>

</project>
```

Let's break down the buildfile and explain the important parts step by step. The setProps task defines a property called "jboss", which it sets to the deploy directory of JBoss as follows:

```
<target name="setProps" unless="setProps"
                    description="setup the properties.">
    <property name="outdir" value="/tmp/petstore" />
    <property name="jboss" value="/tools/jboss/jboss/deploy" />
</target>
```

JBoss has a deploy directory; any Enterprise JavaBean copied to the deploy directory will be automatically read and deployed by the JBoss server. The buildfile uses this property to conditionally delete the EJB JAR file during a clean, to copy the JNDI properties needed for JBoss during a package, and to copy the EJB JAR file to the JBoss deploy directory during a deploy, as follows:

```
<target name="clean_jboss" if="jboss">
    <delete file="${jboss}/${jar_name}" />
</target>

. . .

<target name="config_jboss_jndi" if="jboss">
    <copy todir="${client}" >
        <fileset dir="./jboss_props" />
    </copy>

</target>

. . .

<target name="deploy_jboss" depends="package" if="jboss">
    <copy file="${dist}/${jar_name}" todir="${jboss}" />
    <copy todir="${lib}" >
        <fileset dir="./jboss_clientlib" />
    </copy>
</target>
```

Obviously, your application server may need extra tasks executed. If you have several application servers to deploy to, you can use this technique to create tasks that are executed conditionally.

The compile target of this application is fairly vanilla—that is, it is a lot like the other subprojects. However, the package is interesting because we have to create two JAR files: one for clients and one for the EJB server, as follows:

```
<target name="package" depends="compile,config_jndi"
                    description="package the Java classes into a jar.">
    <copy todir="${client}" >
```

```
                    <fileset dir="${build}" excludes="**/*Bean*"
                                           includes="**/*.class*" />
        </copy>

        <jar jarfile="${lib}/client-${jar_name}"
          basedir="${client}" />


         <copy file="./META-DATA/ejb.xml"
                              tofile="${meta-data}/ejb-jar.xml"/>
         <copy file="./META-DATA/jaws.xml"
                              tofile="${meta-data}/jaws.xml" />

        <jar jarfile="${dist}/${jar_name}"
          basedir="${build}" />



    </target>
```

The package task first creates a client-side JAR file by copying the needed files to a staging area and then jarring them. The first step to create a client-side JAR is to use the copy task to copy all the class files except the implementation to a temporary staging directory, as follows:

```
        <copy todir="${client}" >
            <fileset dir="${build}" excludes="**/*Bean*"
                                    includes="**/*.class*" />
        </copy>
```

Notice how this copy task uses the excludes pattern **/*Bean* to exclude any class file containing the substring *Bean*. This step effectively excludes the product implementation class (ProductBean), which is not needed for the client-side JAR. Now that all the needed client-side files are in the ${client} directory, the buildfile can jar the client-side files, as follows:

```
        <jar jarfile="${lib}/client-${jar_name}"
          basedir="${client}" />
```

The client JAR file is put in the output directory lib where the Web application buildfile can get it and put it in the WAR file.

The JAR file for the EJB server must contain not only the implementation class but also the deployment descriptor and the CMP mappings file. (Note that we copy in a mapping file specific to JBoss. In a real buildfile, you may want to do this in a target that is executed only if the "jboss" property is set.) Here are the tasks to build the server EJB JAR file:

```
        <copy file="./META-DATA/ejb.xml" tofile="${meta-data}/ejb-jar.xml"/>
        <copy file="./META-DATA/jaws.xml" tofile="${meta-data}/jaws.xml" />

        <jar jarfile="${dist}/${jar_name}"  basedir="${build}" />
```

When this buildfile executes, we get a JAR file in lib (client-petbeans.jar) and a JAR file in the distribution directory (petbeans.jar):

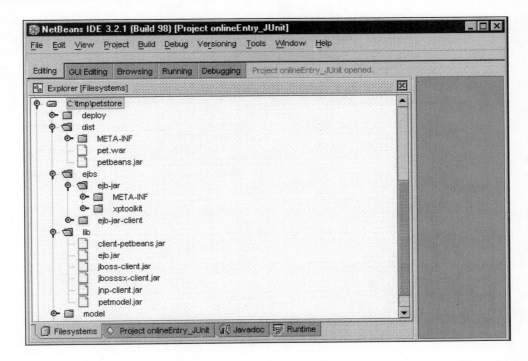

In addition to the client-side JAR file, in the case of JBoss the Web application needs the following: naming, RMI, and EJB support libraries (the JAR files ejb.jar, jboss-client.jar, and jbosssx.jar, shown in the following figure. Thus the deploy target depends on the jboss_deploy target, which copies the files to the lib directory where they can be picked up by the Web application buildfile and packaged in the WAR file, as follows:

```
<target name="deploy_jboss" depends="package" if="jboss">
    <copy file="${dist}/${jar_name}" todir="${jboss}" />
    <copy todir="${lib}"  >
        <fileset dir="./jboss_clientlib" />
    </copy>
</target>

<target name="deploy" depends="package,deploy_jboss"
                description="deploys the jar file to the ejb server.">
</target>
```

When the WAR file is deployed, the needed libraries are in the WEB-INF/lib directory where they can be used by the Web applications class loader:

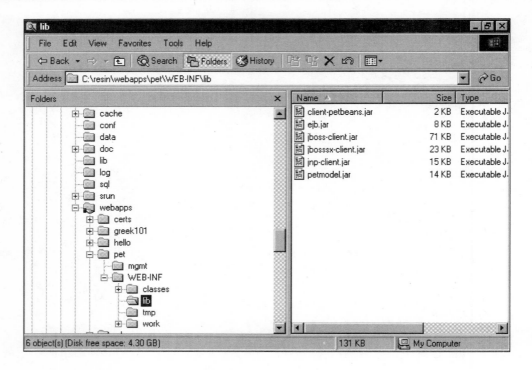

Now that we have created the classes, tests, and buildfiles to build and deploy the features to add, edit, and delete products, let's update the test buildfile so that it can automatically test the files.

Modifying the Test Buildfile to Test Our Entity Bean

In the following code, we added the lines in bold to the test target of the test buildfile:

```
<target name="test" depends="compile">

    <junit printsummary="true" fork="yes">

        <formatter type="xml" />

        <test  name="test.xptoolkit.model.CategorySystemTest"
               todir="${reports}" />

        <test  name="test.xptoolkit.model.CategoryTest"
               todir="${reports}" />

        <test  name="test.xptoolkit.model.SubcategoryTest"
               todir="${reports}" />

        <test  name="test.xptoolkit.model.ProductTest"
               todir="${reports}" />
```

```
            <test   name="test.xptoolkit.petstore.entity.ProductTest"
                    todir="${reports}" />


        <classpath>
           <fileset dir="${lib}">
               <include name="**/*.jar"/>
           </fileset>

           <fileset dir="${build_lib}">
               <include name="**/*.jar"/>
           </fileset>

           <fileset dir="../EJBeans/jboss_clientlib">
               <include name="**/*.jar"/>
           </fileset>


           <fileset dir="${test_lib}">
               <include name="**/*.jar"/>
           </fileset>

           <fileset dir="/tools/ant/lib">
               <include name="**/*.jar"/>
           </fileset>


           <fileset dir="${build}" />

        </classpath>

    </junit>

    <junitreport todir="${reports}">

        <fileset dir="${reports}">

            <include name="TEST-*.xml"/>

        </fileset>

        <report format="frames" todir="${reports}/html"/>

    </junitreport>
  </target>
```

Note that we didn't add much, because the additional test methods were added to CategoryTest and CategorySytemTest. The only test we have to add is the entity ProductTest, as follows:

```
<test   name="test.xptoolkit.petstore.entity.ProductTest"
            todir="${reports}" />
```

Because the junitreport task uses a file set, the output from the entity ProductTest is automatically included with the rest. The important point here is that once the testing buildfile is set up, adding new tests and reports is easy. Please look at the output for the entity ProductTest in the following figure.

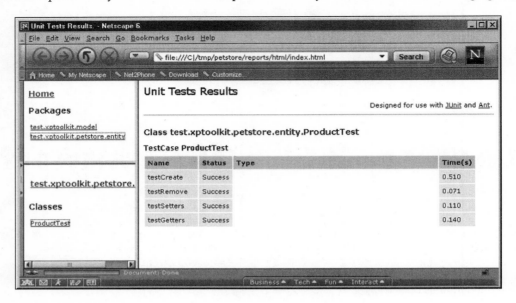

Case Study Conclusion

This case study included test cases used for the baseline version of the pet store. We added an entity bean and Web form to manage product data over the Web (add, delete, and modify product data). Once we added the entity bean, we added test cases to test it, and then we integrated them into the test build-file. Using this example, we more realistically demonstrated building and deploying an entity bean to our EJB server.

Summary

This chapter covered the basics of using JUnit (a framework for writing automated unit tests) to create automated testing for your project. We discussed some of the reasons why you would want to use automated testing. Unit-level testing shows that the code you just refactored did not break. Automated testing gives you confidence in your ability to refactor. Ant and JUnit together can automate the build, deploy, and test process, which is essential for continuous integration and refactoring. In addition, Ant allows you to create snazzy HTML reports on your project using the junit and junitreport tasks. This reports allows you to see the state of your project at a glance.

Load Testing with JUnitPerf

As part of the planning phase of any project, you should be given performance criteria for the completed system. By using JUnitPerf to decorate your existing JUnit test cases, you can ensure that your system meets its performance criteria. For example, you can test each Web page to ensure that it loads in 10 seconds or less and that the average load time is less than 5 seconds while the site is handling 1,000 concurrent users.

JUnitPerf 1.9 is the latest release. It requires the use of Java 2 and JUnit 3.2 or higher. JUnitPerf consists of a small set of test decorators and related classes that extend the JUnit API; thus JUnitPerf tests extend a JUnit test by using the decorator pattern. You must have pre-existing JUnit tests to use JUnitPerf. JUnitPerf allows you to easily load tests and have tests fail if they do not respond in a certain time. You should be judicious in deciding when to use JUnitPerf. Using JUnitPerf to test every line of code is usually time-consuming and unnecessary. JUnitPerf is most effective in situations where you have specific performance criteria to meet. It is often a good idea to first use a performance-profiling tool, such as JProbe, to identify areas of code that have the highest potential for scalability and performance issues. Then you can focus your JUnitPerf tests on those relatively few bottleneck class methods.

You can use JUnitPerf in conjunction with HttpUnit and JMeter to test performance of a Web site under load. For example, write a set JUnit test that uses HttpUnit tests that simulate a user navigating to a product in a Web catalog. Use JMeter to flood the site with requests, while you run a navigation test under a JUnitPerf timed test and set the test to fail if it does not navigate the site to the product page in 15 seconds.

Where To Get JUnitPerf

JUnitPerf was developed by Mike Clark from Clarkware Consulting, Inc. and is distributed under the BSD license. You can download JUnitPerf at www.clarkware.com/software/JUnitPerf.html.

JUnitPerf Concepts

There are two major types of tests for JunitPerf: the timed test and the load test, defined by the TimedTest class and LoadTest class, respectively.

When you create a TimedTest test decorator, you pass it an existing JUnit test and a maximum elapsed time in milliseconds. A TimedTest is a JUnit TestDecorator, which fails the decorated test after a specified time. You can use the TimedTest in two ways: Wait until the test completes and check the elapsed time, or fail immediately if the elapsed time exceeds the maximum.

A LoadTest is also a test decorator that runs a test with a number of simulated users for a certain amount of iterations. You can slowly ramp the load or turn it on all at once.

TimedTest Example

To show the concepts of the TimedTest put into practice, we'll create a simple JUnit test case and then decorate it with a TimedTest (see the following listing). We will step through this test in the remainder of this section.

```
package xptoolkit.junitperf;
import junit.framework.TestCase;
import junit.framework.Test;
import junit.framework.TestSuite;
import junit.textui.TestRunner;


import java.util.Random;
import java.util.Vector;
import java.util.Iterator;
import com.clarkware.junitperf.TimedTest;



public class SimpleTest extends TestCase{
    public SimpleTest(String testName){
        super(testName);
    }

    private final static int MAX_STRINGS = 55555;
    private final static String hiddenString = 'Hi Mom';
    private final static int LENGTH = hiddenString.length();
    private static String [] strings = new String[MAX_STRINGS];
    private static Vector vector = new Vector();
    private static int hiddenLocation;

    static {
        Random random = new Random();
        for (int index=0; index < MAX_STRINGS; index++){
            strings[index]=random.nextLong() + ' Not Mom';
            vector.add(strings[index]);
        }
```

```
            hiddenLocation= MAX_STRINGS-1;
            strings[hiddenLocation]=hiddenString;
            vector.setElementAt(hiddenString,hiddenLocation);

    }

    public final void testForLoop(){
        boolean found = false;
        char [] chars = null;
        int index;
        for (index=0; index < strings.length; index++){
            chars = strings[index].toCharArray();
            if (chars.length != LENGTH) return;
            if(chars[0]!='H') continue;
            if(chars[1]!='i') continue;
            if(chars[2]!=' ') continue;
            if(chars[3]!='M') continue;
            if(chars[4]!='o') continue;
            if(chars[5]!='m') continue;
            found =  true;
            break;
        }
        assertEquals('Index', hiddenLocation, index);
        assertEquals('Found', true, found);
    }

    public final void testIteration(){
        boolean found=false;
        Iterator iterator = vector.iterator();
        int index=0;

        while(iterator.hasNext()){
            String string = (String) iterator.next();
            if (string.equals(hiddenString)){
                found = true;
                break;
            }
            index++;
        }
        assertEquals('Index', hiddenLocation, index);
        assertEquals('Found', true, found);
    }

    public final void testVector(){
        boolean found=false;
        Object [] items = vector.toArray();

        int index;
        String string;

        for (index=0; index < items.length; index++){
            string = (String)items[index];
            if (string.length() != LENGTH) return;
            if (string.equals(hiddenString)){
```

```
                found = true;
                break;
            }
            index++;
        }
        assertEquals('Index', hiddenLocation, index);
        assertEquals('Found', true, found);
    }


    static final int TIMES = 2000;

    public void testForLoopAlot(){
        for(int index=0; index < TIMES; index++){
            testForLoop();
        }
    }

    public void testVectorAlot(){
        for(int index=0; index < TIMES; index++){
            testVector();
        }
    }


    public void testIterationAlot(){
        for(int index=0; index < TIMES; index++){
            testIteration();
        }

    }

    public static Test suite2() {
        TestSuite suite= new TestSuite();
        suite.addTest(new SimpleTest('testIterationAlot'));
        return suite;
    }

    public static Test suite1() {
        TestSuite suite= new TestSuite();
        suite.addTest(new SimpleTest('testForLoopAlot'));
        return suite;
    }

    public static void main(String [] args){
        TestRunner.run(suite1());
        TestRunner.run(suite2());
        TestRunner.run(new SimpleTest('testVectorAlot'));

        long maxElapsedTime = 5000;
        Test testCase = suite1();
        Test timedTest = new TimedTest(testCase, maxElapsedTime);
        TestRunner.run(timedTest);

        testCase = suite2();
```

```
        timedTest = new TimedTest(testCase, maxElapsedTime);
        TestRunner.run(timedTest);

        timedTest = new TimedTest(new SimpleTest('testVectorAlot'),
                                  maxElapsedTime);
        TestRunner.run(timedTest);


    }
}
```

The JUnit test case has two tests that iterate through a list of strings in two different ways searching for a target string. For this scenario, we decided that a vector should be passed around; after some performance analysis, we decided that the test of the code must execute in five seconds or less so that the code will not be a bottleneck in the system's performance. The first test gets an Iterator object from a vector collection, casts each element to a string, and then checks to see if the string is equal to the hidden string as follows:

```
public void testIteration(){
    boolean found=false;
    Iterator iterator = vector.iterator();
    int index=0;

    while(iterator.hasNext()){
        String string = (String) iterator.next();
        if (string.equals(hiddenString)){
            found = true;
            break;
        }
        index++;
    }
    assertEquals('Index', hiddenLocation, index);
    assertEquals('Found', true, found);
}
```

Notice that the test asserts that the index is the same as the hiddenLocation, and that it asserts that the string was found.

The second test has the same functionality as the first, but it tries to reduce the number of method calls, casts, and lines of executed code, as follows:

```
public void testForLoop(){
        boolean found = false;
        char [] chars = null;
        int index;
        for (index=0; index < strings.length; index++){
            chars = strings[index].toCharArray();
            if (chars.length != LENGTH) return;
            if(chars[0]!='H') continue;
            if(chars[1]!='i') continue;
            if(chars[2]!=' ') continue;
            if(chars[3]!='M') continue;
            if(chars[4]!='o') continue;
```

```
            if(chars[5]!='m') continue;
            found = true;
            break;
        }
        assertEquals('Index', hiddenLocation, index);
        assertEquals('Found', true, found);
    }
```

Because the testForLoop() method runs extremely fast, we put the tests in another loop that executes 2,000 times, as follows:

```
static final int TIMES = 2000;

public void testForLoopAlot(){
    for(int index=0; index < TIMES; index++){
        testForLoop();
    }
}

public void testIterationAlot(){
    for(int index=0; index < TIMES; index++){
        testIteration();
    }

}
```

Now that we have created the tests, we need to give the tests enough data so that they will register a measurable time (this was not an issue when we all had 8080 PCs).

The code to set up the test data is not in the setUp() method as you might expect, because code in the setUp() and tearDown() methods is counted by the TimedTest decorator class. So, when we decorate this JUnit test with a JUnitPerf TimedTest, the setup code will not be counted in the test, which makes the test of our code more accurate. The code to set up the test data is therefore all initialized in a static initializer block, as follows:

```
private final static int MAX_STRINGS = 55555;
private final static String hiddenString = 'Hi Mom';
private final static int LENGTH = hiddenString.length();
private static String [] strings = new String[MAX_STRINGS];
private static Vector vector = new Vector();
private static int hiddenLocation;

static {
    Random random = new Random();
    for (int index=0; index < MAX_STRINGS; index++){
        strings[index]=random.nextLong() + ' Not Mom';
        vector.add(strings[index]);
    }
    hiddenLocation= MAX_STRINGS-1;
    strings[hiddenLocation]=hiddenString;
    vector.setElementAt(hiddenString,hiddenLocation);

}
```

To run the previous test, we use JUnit TestRunner. We added the following code to use the TestRunner (you may recall that the TestRunner's run() method runs a suite of tests and reports status via stdio). Notice that the main method calls junit.textui.TestRunner.run, passing it the returned value from the static suite() method:

```
public static Test suite2() {
    TestSuite suite= new TestSuite();
    suite.addTest(new SimpleTest('testIterationAlot'));
    return suite;
}

public static Test suite1() {
    TestSuite suite= new TestSuite();
    suite.addTest(new SimpleTest('testForLoopAlot'));
    return suite;
}

public static void main(String [] args){
    TestRunner.run(suite1());
    TestRunner.run(suite2());
}
```

The default behavior of the test runner prints out the time it takes to run the test. The results from running this test are as follows:

```
Time: 0.01

OK (1 tests)


.
Time: 26.071

OK (1 tests)
```

As you can see, the testForLoop executes a lot faster than the testIteration. Now that we have two working JUnit tests, let's decorate them with a JUnitPerf TimedTest. As you have likely realized by now, these two JUnits tests are supercilious. However, let's pretend for the sake of learning that it is not, and that we want to get the execution time so that the test always runs in less than five seconds. To do this, we create a JUnitPerf TimedTest. First we import the TimedTest class as follows:

```
import com.clarkware.junitperf.TimedTest;
```

Then we run the forLoopTest through the TimedTest decorator, as follows:

```
long maxElapsedTime = 5000
Test testCase = suite1();
Test timedTest = new TimedTest(testCase, maxElapsedTime);
TestRunner.run(timedTest);
```

Notice that we pass the timedTest the TestSuite that has the testForLoop in it, and we tell it to fail if the operation takes longer than five seconds. Next we run the test for the testIteration:

```
    testCase = suite2();
    timedTest = new TimedTest(testCase, maxElapsedTime);
    TestRunner.run(timedTest);
```

Because we know that suite2(), the testForIteration test, takes about 28 seconds, we know that it will fail. Here is the output from this test:

```
. . .
.TimedTest (WAITING): junit.framework.TestSuite@5debc3: 0 ms
. . .

.TimedTest (WAITING): junit.framework.TestSuite@218aa2: 26187 ms
1) junit.framework.TestSuite@218aa2 'Maximum elapsed time exceeded!
Expected 5000ms, but was 26187ms.'

FAILURES!!!
Tests run: 1,  Failures: 1,  Errors: 0
```

We can see that the test failed. Just for kicks, let's try to optimize the test to pass. Suppose it would make the code much simpler if we were able to use a vector. However, instead of grabbing the iterator, we decide to see how much faster would it be if we get the array from the vector. Here is the code we add to try this new search function:

```
    public final void testVector(){
        boolean found=false;
        Object [] items = vector.toArray();

        int index;
        String string;

        for (index=0; index < items.length; index++){
            string = (String)items[index];
            if (string.length() != LENGTH) return;
            if (string.equals(hiddenString)){
                found = true;
                break;
            }
            index++;
        }
        assertEquals('Index', hiddenLocation, index);
        assertEquals('Found', true, found);
    }

. . .

    public void testVectorAlot(){
        for(int index=0; index < TIMES; index++){
            testVector();
        }
    }
. . .
        TestRunner.run(new SimpleTest('testVectorAlot'));
. . .
        timedTest = new TimedTest(new SimpleTest('testVectorAlot'),
```

```
        maxElapsedTime);
            TestRunner.run(timedTest);
```

We set up JUnitPerf as before, but notice when we run this test it now passes, and we are still using a vector. Here is the output from this code:

```
.
Time: 4.617


.
TimedTest (WAITING): testVectorAlot(xptoolkit.junitperf.SimpleTest): 4606 ms

Time: 4.606

OK (1 tests)
```

Just to cap off what we have done, we created a simple JUnit test that showed different ways to loop through a list of string searching for a string. We set up a JUnitPerf test for each test to see if each test could finish the test in under five seconds. We had two extreme version of the search. One version used a String array and a for loop, and it was really fast. The other version used the iterator utility to iterate through the strings in a vector and search for the string. In our contrived example, we decided that we had to use a vector, so we wrote another loop that met the criteria (and was a lot more readable than the really fast version), and then we used JUnitPerf TimedTest to prove that the new loop met the criteria.

LoadTest Example

Like the TimedTest, a LoadTest is a test decorator. The LoadTest runs a test with a number of simulated concurrent users and iterations. When you create a LoadTest class instance, you pass it a number of concurrent users. Each user runs the test once, unless you set the iteration higher when you construct a LoadTest.

First, to see a simple usage of the LoadTest, let's take our testVectorAlot and this time load-test with five threads. Because we are running this test on a machine with one processor, we expect the time to go up by a factor of five or so. Here is the code to run the LoadTest:

```
int users = 5;
Test loadTest = new LoadTest(
                new SimpleTest('testVectorAlot'), users);
TestRunner.run(loadTest);
```

Notice that the LoadTest constructor is a lot like the TimeTest constructor in the last section when we wrapped the SimpleTest in the TimedTest. Now, instead of using the TimedTest and passing the max time out, we are using the LoadTest class and passing the number of user threads to simulate.

Here is the output from this test:

```
.....
Time: 27.75

OK (5 tests)
```

271

The JUnit framework uses the decorator design pattern to add additional functionality to tests dynamically. Thus, you can nest a test inside a decorator test that adds additional functionality but still has the same public interface as the nested test. You can nest the test to decorate the nested test. If we wanted a test where each user ran 5 tests, the test had to complete in 150 seconds, and the test failed as soon as 150 seconds passed, we could create it as follows.

We first import the RepeatedTest from JUnit (we could have used this approach instead of the forXXXAlot tests earlier):

```
import junit.extensions.RepeatedTest;
```

Next, we create the simpleTest to run the testVector as follows:

```
Test simpleTest = new SimpleTest('testVector');
```

We create the repeated test to execute 2,000 iterations:

```
int iterations = 2000;
Test repeatedTest = new RepeatedTest(simpleTest, iterations);
```

Notice that the simpleTest is passed to the repeated test constructor, along with the number of iterations that we want the test run. We decorated the simple test with a repeated test.

Next, we decorate the repeated test with a load test:

```
int users = 5;
Test loadTest = new LoadTest(repeatedTest, users);
```

Finally, we decorate the loadTest with the timedTest and run the timedTest as follows:

```
long maxElapsedTime = 150 * 1000;
Test timedTest = new TimedTest(loadTest, maxElapsedTime);
TestRunner.run(timedTest);
```

In this section, we covered how to decorate test with different tests. As we can see, you can nest these tests pretty deep.

Case Study

This case study gives you a quick peek at the case studies in the rest of the book. Instead of leaving the best for last, we give the whole shebang here. In this case study, we will incorporate JUnitPerf, HttpUnit, and JMeter. Basically, we pound on the site with JMeter at the same time we run an HttpUnit test decorated with a JUnitPerf timed test. We essentially scale up the user until we no longer meet the timed requirement.

Of course, we have not covered JMeter or HttpUnit yet, but this case study will give you a taste of how to use those tools.

HttpUnit Test

Remember that JUnitPerf is a sort of parasite; it needs a host JUnit test to work. Thus, the first part of this case study is writing an HttpUnit test that will test the site. For this case study, we borrowed the code for the pet store HttpUnit Case study, which we discussed in Chapter 13, in a section called "Case Study: Adding an Entity Bean to the Pet Store." We won't cover the code in detail because it we'll present it later; briefly, the test code performs navigation and form entry. Here is a real brief overview of the code to test the site. First, we import the needed HttpUnit and support classes as follows:

```
import com.meterware.httpunit.*;
import java.io.IOException;
import java.net.MalformedURLException;
import org.xml.sax.*;
import org.w3c.dom.*;
import junit.framework.*;
```

Next, we define some constants that point to our site:

```
protected static String HOST = 'http://localhost/pet/';
protected static String MGMT = 'mgmt/';
protected static String INDEX_PAGE = 'index.jsp';
protected static String SUBCATEGORY_PAGE = 'subcategory.jsp?id=222';
```

In the real world, you may make the host a command-line argument. For this example, we just hard-coded it. Let's look at the navigation tests.

Here is the code to test the main page:

```
public void testIndex() throws Exception {
    WebConversation wc = new WebConversation();
    WebResponse resp = wc.getResponse(HOST+INDEX_PAGE);
    WebTable table = resp.getTables()[2];

    assertEquals('# of tables', 3, resp.getTables().length);
    assertEquals('message in third table',
'Welcome to AAA Pets',
table.getCellAsText(0,0));
    }
```

This code verifies that the index page has exactly three HTML tables and displays the message "Welcome to AAA Pets" in the body of the third table.

Here is the code to test the subcategory page. This test verifies that there are three links corresponding to the products (breeds) associated with the subcategory 'cats':

```
public void testSubCategory() throws Exception {
    WebConversation wc = new WebConversation();
    WebResponse resp = wc.getResponse(HOST + SUBCATEGORY_PAGE);

    assertNotNull('Cat Breed #1', resp.getLinkWith('Calico'));
    assertNotNull('Cat Breed #2', resp.getLinkWith('Jaguar'));
    assertNotNull('Cat Breed #3', resp.getLinkWith('Siamese'));
    }
```

Notice that the test checks for the data that was populated with the sample data from the buildDB.xml ant buildfile discussed in the last case study on JUnit. There is also a test on Product (testProduct) that we haven't listed here, because we will discuss it in the HttpUnit case study.

In addition to these navigation tests, three tests examine the form entry on the product management price (testCreate, testDelete, and testEdit). For example, here is the code to test creating a product:

```
/**
 * Verifies that it can create a new product.
 */
public void testCreate() throws Exception {

    WebConversation wc = new WebConversation();
    WebResponse    resp = wc.getResponse(
                                HOST + MGMT + SUBCATEGORY_PAGE);

    WebForm form = resp.getForms()[0];
    WebRequest req = form.getRequest('add');
    resp = wc.getResponse(req);

    form = resp.getForms()[0];
    req = form.getRequest();
    req.setParameter('name', 'Persian');
    req.setParameter('price', '$10.00');
    req.setParameter('qty', '2');

    resp = wc.getResponse(req);
    resp = wc.getResponse(HOST + MGMT + SUBCATEGORY_PAGE);

    assertNotNull('link for 'Persian'', resp.getLinkWith('Persian'));
}
```

Now that you get the gist of the HttpUnit test for the Web navigation and product management, let's look at the JMeter test.

JMeter Configuration

For the JMeter configuration, like HttpUnit, we will navigate the site and manage products (add, delete, edit) on the backend. For this test, we will set up the back end with one simulated users that edits a site randomly distributed every 30 seconds with a standard deviation of 5 seconds using the Gaussian random timer. A front-end user will hit the site every three seconds with a standard deviation of five seconds using the Gaussian random timer.

In Chapter 17, "Performance Testing with JMeter," we'll explain in depth how to set up JMeter to perform this magic. For completeness, the following figure shows the configuration panel for adding a test product to the Web site using JMeter.

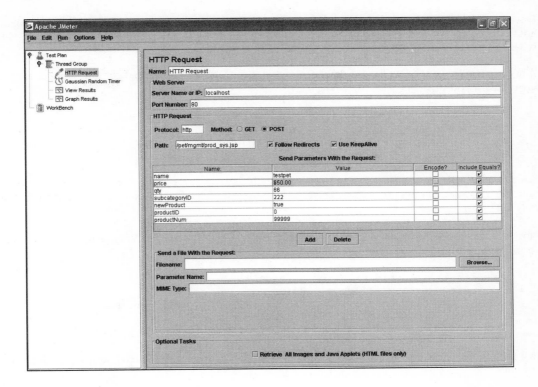

This figure also shows that we have two thread groups, one to perform product management and one to handle front-end navigation of the site similar to testProduct, testIndex, and testSubcategory in the earlier HttpUnit test. Notice that even though the figure shows the Product Management thread group and the Navigation thread group in the same JMeter instance, we run them into two different instances because JMeter sums the times; we want the simulated users that are navigating to be faster than the simulated users that are performing product management.

Putting It All Together

Now that we have the JMeter test and the HttpUnit test, let's require the test that navigates and edits a product to complete in less that five seconds. In addition, we want to determine how many simultaneous users we can have and still meet this threshold. After viewing the Web logs of an existing site, we model the behavior of the existing site and create a JMeter test (from the previous section).

We will decorate the HttpUnit test with a JUnitPerf timed test. The existing HttpUnit test starts its test as follows:

```
public static void main(String args[]) {
    junit.textui.TestRunner.run(suite());
}
```

```
        public static Test suite() {
            return new TestSuite(HttpUnitTest.class);
        }
```

When we run this test a few times to make sure that Resin (the servlet engine) compiles the JSPs, we get the following output:

```
......
Time: 1.202

OK (6 tests)
```

Keep in mind that we are running Resin, JBoss (the EJB server), and SQL Server 2000 on the same box (a laptop). If you are running in a more distributed environment or a beefier box (like a real server), you may get better results.

Now that we know the baseline test, let's decorate the test with the TimedTest class to execute in five seconds as follows:

```
        public static void main(String args[]) {
            int maxElapsedTime = 5000;
            Test timedTest = new TimedTest(suite(), maxElapsedTime);
            junit.textui.TestRunner.run(timedTest);
        }
```

Just for a baseline, we run both thread groups for a while with one thread each and get the following results:

```
......TimedTest (WAITING): test.xptoolkit.petstore.httpunit.HttpUnitTest:
1292 ms

Time: 1.302

OK (6 tests)
```

Now, we increase the number of front-end simulated users in JMeter to five. We stop and start the Navigation thread group and rerun the JUnitPerf-decorated HttpUnit test. We get the following results:

```
......TimedTest (WAITING): test.xptoolkit.petstore.httpunit.HttpUnitTest:
1232 ms

Time: 1.232

OK (6 tests)
```

We run this test a few times to make sure we get the same results. Now, we crank up the number of users to 50, because we want to see some action. We also notice that we're running the TimedTest several times, so we decide to decorate it with a RepeatedTest as follows:

```
        public static void main(String args[]) {
            //junit.textui.TestRunner.run(suite());
            int maxElapsedTime = 5000;
```

```
                Test timedTest = new TimedTest(suite(), maxElapsedTime);
                Test repeatTest = new RepeatedTest(timedTest,5);
                junit.textui.TestRunner.run(repeatTest);
        }
```

The results with 50 users are as follows:

```
......TimedTest (WAITING): test.xptoolkit.petstore.httpunit.HttpUnitTest:
1382 ms
......TimedTest (WAITING): test.xptoolkit.petstore.httpunit.HttpUnitTest:
501 ms
......TimedTest (WAITING): test.xptoolkit.petstore.httpunit.HttpUnitTest:
591 ms
......TimedTest (WAITING): test.xptoolkit.petstore.httpunit.HttpUnitTest:
500 ms
......TimedTest (WAITING): test.xptoolkit.petstore.httpunit.HttpUnitTest:
461 ms

Time: 3.435

OK (30 tests)
```

As you can see, the overall performance has improved after the first iteration because the test class was created already.

Now it's time to get nasty. We increase the JMeter test to run 5,000 simulated users with the Navigation Thread group. We get the following results:

```
......TimedTest (WAITING): test.xptoolkit.petstore.httpunit.HttpUnitTest:
3305 ms
......TimedTest (WAITING): test.xptoolkit.petstore.httpunit.HttpUnitTest:
6670 ms
F......TimedTest (WAITING): test.xptoolkit.petstore.httpunit.HttpUnitTest:
420 ms
......TimedTest (WAITING): test.xptoolkit.petstore.httpunit.HttpUnitTest:
301 ms
......TimedTest (WAITING): test.xptoolkit.petstore.httpunit.HttpUnitTest:
330 ms

Time: 11.026
There was 1 failure:
1) test.xptoolkit.petstore.httpunit.HttpUnitTest 'Maximum elapsed time
 exceeded! Expected 5000ms, but was 6670ms.'

FAILURES!!!
Tests run: 30,   Failures: 1,   Errors: 0
```

As we can see, on our lowly laptop we can handle around 5,000 users attacking the site before we start to fail the test and go over five seconds (we are still under five seconds on average). Of course, because everything is running on a laptop, there is no network latency. The same techniques could be used on a real Web application with real requirements to help you determine what hardware you need, how to partition your Web application, and so on.

> **Real Test**
>
> For a real test, you should increase the number of users at a slower pace and have the JUnitPerf test repeat 30 times. If any of the 30 times failed, then the test would fail. This way, passing the test would not be a fluke fluctuation of system performance, but a realistic result.

In the case studies throughout the book, you earn the ins and outs of HttpUnit and JMeter. We incorporated JUnitPerf, HttpUnit, and JMeter in this case study to pound on the site with JMeter and measure performance of the site under load; JUnitPerf wrapped a test done in HttpUnit that navigated the site and edited the back end. We essentially scaled the simulated navigation users until we no longer met the timed requirement.

Summary

This chapter demonstrated the extensibility of the JUnit framework by showing several test decorators from JUnitPerf and the JUnit extensions. We also gave a real-world example of how to create TimedTest for code that is about to be optimized or code that has a strict requirement to be optimized.

JUnitPerf works with existing JUnit tests. If you have performance criteria for a certain piece of code, then create a JUnitPerf test to show your code meets the criteria and continues to meet the criteria after you refactor the code.

Defect Tracking with Bugzilla

Why does a project need defect-tracking software? Requirements can be vague or misunderstood, and even the best developers make mistakes when creating a module. Modules that work perfectly well in isolation often prove to need bug fixes when system and integration testing begins. Users often wish to request new features as well.

Defect-tracking software packages can create a central repository to maintain a running list and status of the software shortcomings mentioned above. Good defect-tracking software can also serve as a conduit of communication between the members of a project team.

The original defect-tracking mechanism for high-tech projects was probably a stack of Post-it notes or a small spreadsheet maintained by the project lead. In this chapter you will learn to use the Bugzilla package to facilitate defect tracking for your projects.

Where to Get Bugzilla

Bugzilla was created by mozilla.org to replace the bug tracking software that had been in use at Netscape. Bugzilla is both free and open source; it is available under a combination of Mozilla and Netscape public licenses, as well as GPL. You can download the software at:

www.bugzilla.org/

Enter Bugzilla

Bugzilla is open source, Web-based, defect-tracking software. Bugzilla is created in Perl CGI and HTML, and like CVS you are most likely to encounter it running on a Linux or UNIX system.

Bugzilla began in the early days of Mozilla.org, the open source development center for the code behind Netscape browsers. The Mozilla browser project became the first project to use Bugzilla for defect tracking. Bugzilla was shown to lend itself quite well to a distributed development project such as Mozilla, and since then many commercial and open source projects have adopted Bugzilla for defect tracking.

What features of Bugzilla make it suitable for open source and distributed projects?

❑ **Communication:** Bugzilla makes it easy for all the stakeholders of a project to communicate over an open system. By stakeholders we mean anyone who is interested; software developers, users of the system being developed, and management responsible for steering the project can benefit from Bugzilla. Bugzilla relies on e-mail notification to inform interested parties of significant events such as a bug being assigned to a developer, the status of a bug changes, etc.

❑ **Internet based:** Unlike many commercial defect-tracking programs, Bugzilla uses a database-backed Web site to handle defect tracking. No software (other than a browser) need be installed; Bugzilla is inherently cross-platform.

❑ **Task management:** Bugzilla can help developers track their time.

How Does Bugzilla Work?

Bugzilla ties the developers, users, and modules of a project together. How? Bugzilla uses a Web-based administration piece to create users and projects—and ultimately bugs in the system. The Bugzilla administrator, a role you will fulfill for this appendix, creates users and takes note of e-mail addresses. The administrator also sets up projects, modules within those projects, and milestones for those projects.

Once these things are entered into the Bugzilla system, bug entry may begin. Bugzilla makes it easy for *everyone* involved with a project to enter bugs. The Bugzilla administrator can create login IDs for quality assurance team members, end users, project managers, and, of course, all the developers, since Bugzilla is able to track defects for many projects simultaneously.

Now that we have a general idea of the benefit Bugzilla will provide, it's time to install Bugzilla.

Bugzilla Setup

We will use Bugzilla version 2.16, the current stable release at the time of this writing, for the examples. Bugzilla is freely available under the GPL from http://www.bugzilla.org/. Once you have downloaded the gnu zipped tar, installation can begin.

Installation

First, there are some dependencies to be resolved before installing Bugzilla itself. These are a Web server, a database, and the Perl scripting language. Bugzilla highly recommends the most current version of

Perl, the Apache Web server, and the MySQL database (There are many MySQL-specific function calls and data types buried in the Bugzilla code.)

MySQL

Currently Bugzilla is closely tied to the MySQL database, so if your server does not already have MySQL installed, you should install it before you attempt to install Bugzilla itself.

MySQL is a freely available RDBMS that is available through http://www.mysql.com. For the purposes of this appendix we will install the MySQL server and the basic client tools. Make sure to download the following files:

❑   MySQL-3.23.52-1.i386.rpm

❑   MySQL-client-3.23.52-1.i386.rpm

Install the server and client tools using the Package Manager by typing the following, as root:

```
rpm -i MySQL-3.23.52-1.i386.rpm MySQL-client-3.23.52-1.i386.rpm
```

The installation should produce output something like the following:

```
Preparing db table
Preparing host table
Preparing user table
Preparing func table
Preparing tables_priv table
Preparing columns_priv table
Installing all prepared tables
020929 15:56:33  /usr/sbin/mysqld: Shutdown Complete


PLEASE REMEMBER TO SET A PASSWORD FOR THE MySQL root USER !
This is done with:
/usr/bin/mysqladmin -u root  password 'new-password'
/usr/bin/mysqladmin -u root -h linuxserver  password 'new-password'
See the manual for more instructions.

Please report any problems with the /usr/bin/mysqlbug script!

The latest information about MySQL is available on the web at
http://www.mysql.com
Support MySQL by buying support/licenses at https://order.mysql.com

Starting mysqld daemon with databases from /var/lib/mySQL
```

So, we should set the MySQL root user password immediately before trying to use MySQL. We'll set the password to "wrox" for our purposes here.

```
/usr/bin/mysqladmin -u root  password 'wrox'
```

MySQL should now be up and running. Verify this by typing *ps aux | grep mysqld* or using the MySQL status command mysqladmin -u root -p status. Once the MySQL installation is complete, we can move onto Bugzilla proper.

Bugzilla

Now that we have a Bugzilla-compatible system, its time to install the Perl modules needed for Bugzilla. We can do this automatically using CPAN. CPAN (Comprehensive Perl Archive Network) is a site that Perl will connect to and automatically get all the Perl modules needed for Bugzilla to run. This is the best way to begin configuration.

Note: If you are not a Perl expert, you may wish to upgrade to the latest version of the CPAN module first, in order to avoid possible pitfalls later.

```
perl -MCPAN -e 'install Bundle::CPAN'
```

Then:

```
perl -MCPAN -e 'install "Bundle::Bugzilla" '
```

When CPAN starts, it will ask if you'd like to use manual configuration or autoconfiguration. If you don't want CPAN to use its defaults, enter the manual setup; otherwise type *no* for autoconfiguration and let CPAN autoconfigure itself.

Once CPAN is configured, it will begin downloading and building the Perl modules needed. The output is verbose and may require minimal user interaction. For example, it will ask to delete temporary files used during the install process, etc. Once all of the builds are complete, it's time for the next step.

CPAN is usually very good about resolving dependencies and installing the modules you ask for. However, *usually* does not mean *always*. The most common error message for a missing dependency reports is "Module *Module.pm* could not be found in @INC. @INC contains…." In this case, resolve the dependency by going to http://www.cpan.org and finding the module.

Apache

There are some Apache settings needed for Bugzilla to run. Since Bugzilla functions as a series of CGI scripts, Apache must be set up to allow .cgi execution. Using your favorite editor, open /etc/httpd/conf/httpd.conf. Most Apache distributions will contain the following lines, commented out by default. If your httpd.conf file does not contain them, add the following lines:

```
# To use CGI scripts:
#
AddHandler cgi-script .cgi
```

Again, make sure the AddHandler line is not commented out. Now we need to set up the directory to hold the Bugzilla files. Create or alter an Apache Directory tag as shown below:

```
<Directory "/var/www/html/bugzilla">
  Options ExecCGI
</Directory>
```

Change the directory path within the opening Directory tag to point to the Bugzilla directory underneath your site root location. In newer distributions this is most likely /var/www/html, but it may be found beneath /home/httpd or some other location for older versions of Apache.

MySQL

First, you will need to create a database that Bugzilla can use for storing defects and a user that Bugzilla can connect as. Connect to the MySQL command-line interface and create the database using the following commands:

```
mysql -u root -p
```

Once you have logged in, create the bugs database and the bugzilla user with the following two SQL commands:

```
mysql>create database bugs;
mysql> insert into user (Host, User, Password) values ('%', 'bugzilla',
'wrox');
```

Some additional configuration needs to occur on the MySQL side for Bugzilla to be able to use it. We must create a user that Bugzilla will connect as and give that user access to the MySQL bugs database. We'll give the user the name bugzilla and the password wrox. To do this, we need to enter the MySQL command-line tool and issue two SQL statements, as shown below:

```
[root@linuxserver bin]# mysql -u root -p
Enter password:
Welcome to the MySQL monitor. Commands end with ; or \g.
Your MySQL connection id is 10 to server version: 3.23.52

Type 'help;' or '\h' for help. Type '\c' to clear the buffer.

mysql> GRANT SELECT,INSERT,UPDATE,DELETE,INDEX, ALTER,CREATE,DROP,REFERENCES
ON bugs.* TO bugzilla@localhost IDENTIFIED BY 'wrox';
Query OK, 0 rows affected (0.00 sec)

mysql> flush privileges;
Query OK, 0 rows affected (0.00 sec)

mysql>
```

Now the database is ready. Note that we gave the database the name "bugs," the user "bugzilla," and the password "wrox." We will need to know these in the final section.

Bugzilla

At last it's time to untar Bugzilla and complete the installation. Copy the bugzilla-2.16.tar.gz file downloaded at the beginning of the chapter into the site root directory. Now issue the command to expand the .tar file:

```
tar zxvf bugzilla-2.16.tar.gz
```

This creates a directory called bugzilla-2.16. Rename the directory to "bugzilla" instead. Make sure the user that the Apache Web server runs as on your system has write access to this directory.

Determine the location of the Perl executable on your server with the command which perl. The Bugzilla .cgi files contain references to /usr/bonsaitools/bin/perl for the Perl executable. In order to point this to your own Perl executable, create a symbolic link in this directory. Assuming your Perl executable is found in /usr/bin/perl, you can do this by first creating the /usr/bonsaitools/bin directory, changing to it, and issuing the following command to create the symbolic link:

```
ln —s /usr/bin/perl perl
```

Bugzilla comes with a Perl file called checksetup.pl to finalize the installation; this file should be in our Bugzilla root directory created earlier. You will need to run this program twice, once as root and once as the user that Apache runs as. After the first time, the file will create a settings file called localconfig. Add the Bugzilla database and user settings defined above into this file. Run the file again, restart Apache, and Bugzilla should be ready to go. By browsing to http://yourServerAndPort/bugzilla, you should be greeted with the following screen.

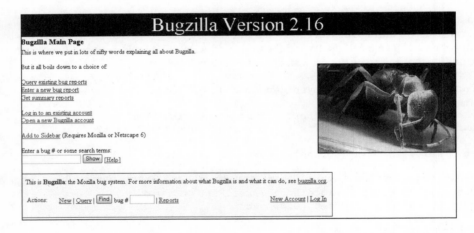

Click the Log In link in the lower right-hand corner of the yellow box at the bottom of the page. Enter the e-mail address and password you created when checksetup.pl prompted you for them. You are now ready to begin setting up Bugzilla for your project!

Configuration

There are a few things you'll want to configure right away. Once you have logged in as the administrator account, the yellow box near the bottom of the screen should contain many more options, as shown here:

Edit prefs, parameters, users, products, attachment statuses, groups, keywords | Sanity check | Log out

Click Parameters first. In order for Bugzilla to be useful, you must assign meaningful values to the following options right away:

- ❑ **maintainer:** This should probably be your e-mail address. If something goes wrong with Bugzilla, the user will be shown this e-mail address as a contact.

- ❑ **urlbase:** This parameter is important because when Bugzilla sends automated e-mails, it uses this as the URL base. This will be useful when users forget their passwords or in other situations where Bugzilla builds a link.

- ❑ **cookiepath:** Change this to indicate the proper installation directory. In the examples, this value should be /Bugzilla.

Submit the form. You are now ready to move on to bug management.

Bugs in Bugzilla

Now that Bugzilla is up and running with some basic configuration settings, we can begin using it to track project defects. Before there can be bugs and feature requests, there must be a development effort created in Bugzilla. In the following sections we show how Bugzilla represents a development effort, and then we walk through the life cycle of a bug.

Setting Up the Sample Product

In order to demonstrate how you might use Bugzilla on a real project, we will set up a sample product for which to track defects.

The Product

The first step in tracking defects for a software project is to create it in Bugzilla. Bugzilla calls this a *product*. Bugzilla can store many products. To learn how to have some isolation between the stakeholders of multiple products in the same Bugzilla instance, see the section on security later. In these examples, we'll be able to create a product complete with versions and components and begin entering bugs.

The Component

Bugzilla calls all the pieces of a software development project *components*. The granularity of a component in Bugzilla deserves some attention.

Remember that Bugzilla supports open communication very well, and in an ideal situation end-users and quality assurance professionals will be using Bugzilla to communicate with the software development team. Therefore, it makes the most sense for a component to be a unit of functionality that a non-programmer can relate to and comment on without talking about code. That said, the development team might also wish to create components that are strictly programming constructs so that Bugzilla can help keep track of tasks and defects on those modules. Refer to the table below to get an idea of how to represent components in Bugzilla.

Programmer Components	End-User Components
Build script	Login screen
DB Connection Manager	Update employee records form
JUnit tests	

Step 1–Create a Product

Select Products from the list of Edit links, as shown previously. This brings you to a screen showing a list of products in the system. Right now the screen contains only a test product, but there is a link to add a new product. Select that link, and enter the information for our sample product, as shown below.

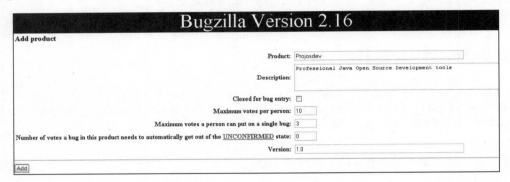

The Product and Description fields cannot be explained better than their names do. Leave Closed For Bug Entry unchecked so we can enter some defects against some components in this product a little later. And finally, ignore the three settings related to voting for now. An in-depth voting example will be covered later in this appendix. Enter *1.0* in the Version box. This is the only product version we'll need for these examples, but you are free to enter more versions to coincide with important milestones for your real-world products. Click Add to save the product, and move on to Step 2.

Step 2–Create a Component

Return to the product screen and you should now see the newly created Projosdev product. The first column shows Edit Product, and the product name is a hyperlink. Follow this hyperlink and you will see a screen similar to the one shown previously, with some additional options. Near the bottom of the Edit Product area is another hyperlink called Edit Components, which is followed by the red text Missing. Following the Edit Components hyperlink leads to a screen with the heading Select Components Of Projosdev right below the Bugzilla heading. At the right of this table is a hyperlink called Add A New Component. Following this leads finally to another administration screen used to create the details of the component. Enter the data for a login screen, as shown in the next figure.

Bugzilla Version 2.16

Add component of Projosdev

Component: Login Page

Description: Logs the user in to the system

Initial owner: admin@yoursite.com

[Add]

Since there is currently only one user in the system, enter the administrator e-mail address as Initial Owner of the component. Click the Add button to save the component. Bugzilla confirms that the component was added to Projosdev. Follow the steps above and add another example component to the product. Enter *Employee Dependents Page* and *Administer Family Coverage Information* for the Component and Description, respectively.

Entering Bugs

With a product and two child components created in the system, defect tracking can at last begin. Navigate back to the Bugzilla home screen, and take a look at the Actions menu, shown in the next figure. For non-administrative tasks this is where most of the interaction with Bugzilla will take place.

Usually you must be logged in to enter bugs. You can also create a login on the fly as you create the bug, and Bugzilla will send a password to the e-mail address entered. Once you use this e-mail address to enter the bug, you will be notified of changes to the bug in the future. If this is not what you want, Bugzilla clearly gives you the option to change the kinds of e-mails you get from Bugzilla when you perform actions.

Select New from the Actions menu. You are greeted with a screen showing the available products in the system. Select Projosdev from the list of available projects to view the bug entry screen. Enter the information as shown in the next figure, and click Commit. Be sure to enter the administrator e-mail address you used to set up Bugzilla in the Assigned To field.

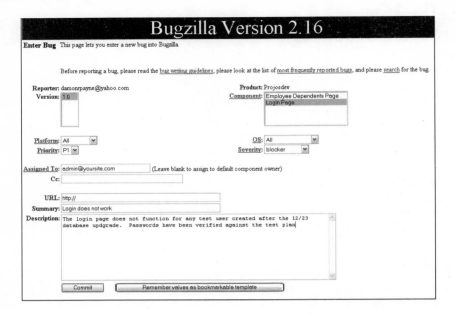

There are a few other interesting parts to this screen other than the bug entry itself. At the top are three links of interest:

❑ Bug Writing Guidelines is a link to advice on writing better bugs. In general it says that bugs should contain the most specific information possible and be reproducible.

❑ The Search hyperlink leads to the bug search screen, explained in detail below. The theory is that by putting the link here, users will be more likely to check for a bug matching theirs and not re-enter the same bugs.

❑ The links in front of bug information fields, such as Platform, lead to pages describing what that field means.

The bug entry fields on this screen should be fairly self-explanatory. Select the product and version on which the bug was encountered, and fill in the rest of the information. The most important fields are the Summary and Description fields. These will help developers supporting the product re-create and eventually fix the bug. Once you select Commit, the page redirects you to the screen shown below, where you can enter more detailed information about the defect.

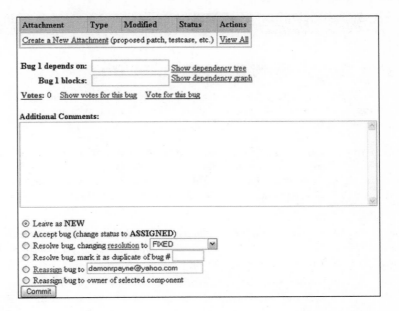

Once the bug has been created there are more options here. Try creating two or three more bugs for both of the components defined under our Projosdev project. Leave them assigned to the default owner for now.

With the default settings, Bugzilla will not send any e-mail based on the bugs created here because they are assigned to the default user. However, if you change these settings or use Bugzilla on a project where bugs are being assigned to you, Bugzilla will send you e-mail. Here is an example Bugzilla e-mail:

```
Date: Mon, 26 Jan 2004 22:33:20 -0500
From: bugzilla-daemon@localhost.localdomain
To: your@email.com
Subject: [Bug 3] New: Icons
        http://www.yourbugzilla.com/bugzilla/show_bug.cgi?id=3
          Summary: Icons
          Product: Projosdev
          Version: 1.0
         Platform: PC
       OS/Version: Windows XP
           Status: NEW
         Severity: enhancement
         Priority: P5
        Component: Employee Dependents Page
       AssignedTo: you@yahoo.com
       ReportedBy: someone-else@yahoo.com

Can we change the color of the icons to Cornflower Blue?

------- You are receiving this mail because: -------
You are the assignee for the bug, or are watching the assignee.
You reported the bug, or are watching the reporter.
```

The e-mail contains a summary of the bug parameters entered. Below the ReportedBy field is the description the bug reporter entered when creating the bug.

Maintaining Bugs–The Lifecycle of a Bug

Each new bug in Bugzilla is assigned to a user in the system or the administrator if the bug enterer did not choose another user to assign the bug to. The recipient then receives an e-mail from Bugzilla with the bug summary shown above.

From this point, there are three main phases that a bug goes through in Bugzilla. First, the bug enters an investigation phase, where the project team determines what to do with the bug. Next, the bug enters its active phase, during which a resolution is sought for the defect. Finally, the bug enters the resolution phase, where the bug is put to rest and notes are taken as to the solution to the defect:

1. Once a bug has been entered, the assignee investigates the bug. The assignee may know immediately that the bug is invalid or that it has already been reported as another bug. One of several things will occur in the investigation stage:

   ❏ The assignee determines that the bug has already been reported. The assignee edits the bug definition, changing its status to Duplicate of Bug # X.

   ❏ The assignee determines that the bug may or may not be valid, but another person on the project team is best equipped to answer that question. The assignee chooses either to reassign the bug giving the e-mail address of the person best able to handle it or, if the owner of the component is not known, to select Reassign Bug To Owner Of Selected Component upon determining which component of the product the bug deals with. The new assignee is notified and begins investigating the bug.

   ❏ The assignee accepts responsibility for the defect, and the bug enters the active phase.

2. The active phase of a bug is really the time during which the assignee attempts to resolve the defect. This may require fixing code, clarifying requirements, or proving that the bug was never really a bug in the first place. Also during this phase, voting can occur. We discuss voting in detail a little later.

3. The bug is resolved when the assignee feels that a conclusion has been reached regarding the defect. The most obvious way to resolve a bug is to change some code and verify that the undesired behavior no longer exists. This may be the most common solution. Assignees do have at their disposal other ways of responding to defects entered. The assignee can resolve the bug as INVALID, meaning the bug isn't a bug—perhaps it's a feature? Upon investigation the assignee can also resolve the bug as status WONTFIX, meaning that for some reason he has no intention of ever addressing the defect. A status of LATER indicates the problem is real but may be intended to be addressed in the future; the same goes for REMIND. Last, the status WORKS-FORME indicates that the bug may or may not be valid but was unable to be reproduced by the assignee.

When the resolution status of a bug changes, interested parties such as the original bug parties have a chance at recourse. When the status of a bug is changed to RESOLVED, that does not necessarily mean its life is over. Rather, the bug resolution is awaiting approval of some sort. The bug can be reopened, indicating to the assignee that the resolution was unsatisfactory. The bug would then reenter the bug life cycle, most likely in the active phase. The status of the bug can also be changed to VERIFIED, indicating that the solution was satisfactory and the bug is dead.

You control the lifecycle of the bug by changing its status near the bottom of the Show Bug page (see the previous figure).

Searching for Bugs

There are several ways to search for bugs in Bugzilla. Some are easy, and some, like the full query screen shown in the next figure, can be quite daunting. In this section you will learn how to look for bugs in Bugzilla.

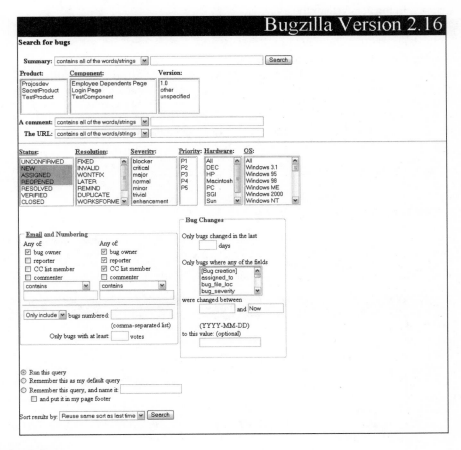

By Bug Number

This is the easiest method. If you already know the bug number because you have been working with it before, go to the Actions menu pictured in previous figures, and enter the bug number to bring up the screen containing all the necessary data.

The Full Query Screen

At first sight the Bugzilla Search for Bugs screen can be somewhat daunting because of the number of fields. It is easy to master this screen by deconstructing it into its components (see the last figure). Here is a brief explanation of the search fields.

❑ Summary refers of course to the Summary field.

❑ Product, Component, and Version should be self-explanatory. These fields are all multiple select. All of these fields refer to the product to search bugs for, not any attributes of the bugs themselves.

❑ Status, Resolution, Severity, Priority, Hardware, and OS refer to attributes of the bug you are searching for and are also multi-select.

❑ In the Email And Numbering field, you query instead based on which Bugzilla users may be involved in the life cycle of the bug.

❑ In the Bug Changes field, queries are based on when bugs have undergone a change.

One question may arise by looking at all of these fields: Is this a large AND query or a large OR query? The answer is both. All of the query options are ANDed together to create the Bugzilla search. Multiple-select fields such as Status and Resolution are appended as AND parameters created as aggregates of all selected values. So, to get a feel for how Bugzilla is going to search, navigate to the query screen shown in the following figure. If you enter a product of Projosdev, a component of Login Page, a Status of NEW, ASSIGNED, and REOPENED, and a Severity of Critical and Trivial, you can expect the query logic to look something like the following query pseudocode:

```
Select * from bugs where product='projosdev'
AND component='LoginPage'
AND (status='NEW' OR status='ASSIGNED' OR status='REOPENED')
AND (severity='critical' OR severity='trivial')
```

Any fields left out won't be included; so in the example shown in the next figure, bugs would be returned for all versions of Projosdev and so on. Following the hyperlink in the ID column will lead to the bug maintenance screen for that bug.

By Preset Queries

Bugzilla allows you to save this query to be used again in the future from the query.cgi page. This allows you to create a shortcut to avoid the hassle of entering all the search criteria again.

By default, Bugzilla installs one preset query titled My Bugs. This query returns all bugs of any open status for all products, components, versions, etc. that belong to the currently logged-in user.

When would you want to create more preset queries? Any particularly evil set of criteria is worth saving a query for. Also, if you are responsible for mentoring other developers and keeping track of their progress, you could save a preset query for their bugs. The same is true for tracking bug traffic for an entire product you might be responsible for.

Security

As we have mentioned, Bugzilla can track many projects at once. However, it may not make sense to allow users of the Employee Self Services system to enter bugs for the Cafeteria Inventory Management system, for example. You may also run a services company with many clients and use Bugzilla to track bugs for all projects, but you would not want different clients to know about one another. Bugzilla supports basic user and group-level security for these needs. This section describes how to configure Bugzilla for bug groups.

Step 1–Create a New User

In order to test security, we'll first need to add a non-administrator user to Bugzilla.

1. From the main menu, log out.

2. The menu will now include a New Account option. Select this link and create a new account with an alternate e-mail address you have access to. Bugzilla creates a random password and sends it to the e-mail address given.

3. Log in as the new user and change the password to something you will remember, using the Prefs hyperlink.

4. Log out, and log back in as the administrator account.

Step 2–Configure Bugzilla

Logged in as the administrator account, we can now configure Bugzilla. From the Actions menu, choose the Parameters option. Near the top of the page are two options that need to be set to On for bug groups, as shown in the next figure.

usebuggroups: If this is on, Bugzilla will associate a bug group with each product in the database, and use it for querying bugs.
☐ Reset ⦿ On ○ Off

usebuggroupsentry: If this is on, Bugzilla will use product bug groups to restrict who can enter bugs. Requires usebuggroups to be on as well.
☐ Reset ⦿ On ○ Off

Save the Parameters page. Bugzilla has now created bug groups. What does this mean? Whenever a new product is added, Bugzilla automatically creates a bug group for that product. Users must be members of these groups in order to see the products in the system and, therefore, to enter or search for bugs related to that product. The administrator user will automatically be able to see bugs for all products.

In many cases this setting may be turned on after there are already products in the system. To handle this, create a new group with a group name exactly matching the product name. This is explained in Step 3 below.

Step 3—Administer Groups

First, we will verify that by default, users cannot see bugs for products they do not have access to. Create a new product called SecretProduct in Bugzilla. Be sure to leave the User Regex field blank so that no users are added to the bug group that will be automatically created. Log out of the administrator account, and log in as the user created in Step 1. The user is greeted with the Search For Bugs screen upon a successful login. However, SecretProduct does not appear as a product that may be searched. The user has no access to this bug group.

To grant access, log the test user out and reenter Bugzilla as the administrator account. In the Edit menu at the bottom of the Bugzilla screen, select the Users hyperlink to make some changes to the test user. This leads to a search screen allowing you to look for users to edit. Type in the e-mail address of the test user and click Submit. The next screen contains the results of the search. Follow the hyperlink containing your test user's name to edit that user. In the middle of the resulting screen, shown in the next figure, is a list of groups to which you can add users.

Group Access: Can turn this bit on for other users
| User is a member of these groups
☐ ☐ **Developers**: programmers
☐ ☐ **Projosdev**: Projosdev Bugs Access
☐ ☐ **SecretProduct**: SecretProduct Bugs Access
☐ ☐ **Test Product**: Test Product Access

Select SecretProduct to add the user to the bug access group, and save the user by clicking the Update button. Log back in as the test user, and you should now be able to see the product, its components, and its bugs!

Advanced Configuration

In addition to the parameters immediately set up upon installation, you may want to consider changing some other Bugzilla configuration options:

❑ **sendmailnow:** Bugzilla by default will spool mail messages and not send them immediately. For quicker communication turn this setting on.

❑ **shutdownhtml:** If you are upgrading Bugzilla (see below) or performing MySQL administration or just want to turn Bugzilla off for a while, you can create some HTML in this setting. Users attempting to use Bugzilla will see this HTML instead of any Bugzilla page. The only page that can still be navigated to is editparams.cgi, so remember that you may need to manually type the URL when it's time to turn Bugzilla back on. Erase the HTML to reenable Bugzilla.

❑ **usertargetmilestone:** Often on an open-source project such as Mozilla, the project lists some features it expects to introduce or bugs it intends to fix by a certain milestone. By turning on this setting, you can let Bugzilla can track this information for you. You will now have options to edit milestones for products.

Another advanced configuration option is keeping up with the Bugzilla code base itself. The Bugzilla code exists in a CVS repository with anonymous access. Current information on the location of the repository and how to update it can be found at http://www.bugzilla.org/download.html. For detailed information on CVS commands, see Chapter 3.

Voting

Voting is a feature fairly unique to Bugzilla, and it suits open-source projects with somewhat decentralized management quite well. The basic premise of voting is that each Bugzilla user will have a certain number of votes to put toward bugs.

To turn on and configure voting, navigate to the Edit Parameters page and make sure the usevotes parameter is on. Voting is now configured on a product-by-product basis. Navigate to the Edit Products screen and select the Projosdev example product. There are three settings for voting on each product, as shown below:

Maximum votes per person:	10
Maximum votes a person can put on a single bug:	3
Number of votes a bug in this product needs to automatically get out of the UNCONFIRMED state:	0

The Maximum Votes Per Person setting indicates the most times a person can vote *on this project*. People can vote for the same bug more than once, up to the number of votes they have or the number specified in the second setting. Votes are really like a point system that allows the project team and its users to weight defects and enhancements and try to get the owners of the components in question to address these items sooner rather than later. You should configure these settings based on the estimated number of bugs in the product. For example, a product with, say, 30 modules should have a proportionally large number of votes allowed. The number of bugs currently active for the product is shown at the bottom of this screen.

Bugzilla users can vote for bugs on the Bug Detail screen. Choosing Vote For This Bug takes the users to a screen where they may assign as many votes to the bug as they like, up to the maximum number allowed for the product.

Summary

Having a central defect management repository for a project carries with it many of the benefits of source code versioning. Bugzilla creates an audit trail of what was worked on and when, and in which versions of the product. Bugzilla facilitates communication between developers and between developers and end users in a way not seen in other defect-tracking systems. For large distributed products, Bugzilla might be the best bug-tracking system available. What other bug-tracking software offers the community that Bugzilla can offer? With Bugzilla you gain the ability for any product user around the world to create an account without an administrator interceding and to take part in the improvement of software. The unique voting system also lends itself to project self-management, with the project team itself determining the priorities.

16

Functional Testing with HttpUnit

The chapter explains the techniques for performing functional testing of Web applications with the HttpUnit framework. The chapter opens with a consideration of the role of functional testing in XP; it then explains how to use the HttpUnit tool. The chapter concludes with a case study covering the development of a link-checking spider using HttpUnit.

Why Functional Testing?

HttpUnit is not unit testing at all. HttpUnit more closely approximates functional testing, or black-box testing. Web application tests written using HttpUnit do not test *pieces* of the application code but rather query the Web server externally and examine the responses received. Extreme Programming does not usually focus on this sort of testing, because of its inherent complexities. Testing an entire Web application can be a daunting task; many different combinations of user behavior exist, and attempting to replicate them all seems difficult. Faced with the challenge of writing code that verifies each possible permutation of "The system could not process your request because…," programmers will hide out in the nearest dark room and attempt to port Linux to the Sega Dreamcast, instead. So XP focuses on unit testing—testing small, manageable pieces of code so that each building block of the system is verified as being good.

However, functional testing holds an important place in Extreme Programming. XP stresses that functional tests are written for (and largely *by*) the customer so that they receive high-level feedback about the state of the system. Because functional tests verify the whole system, they can catch subtle bugs that emerge only in a close-to-production environment (server configuration issues, subsystem-interaction bugs, user-experience issues, and so on). As a system matures (and XP says that the natural state of a project is in deployment), it becomes more possible (and necessary) to devote time to ensuring that the system performs as expected. Automated functional tests relieve someone (even, gasp!, a developer) of the grim duty of manually inspecting unchanged areas of the site before a new build is released to production.

Furthermore, in a Web environment, the line between unit and functional testing blurs. Because each request-response cycle is somewhat atomic, a page view can be treated as a "unit" of code. Testing that sales_report.jsp returns a view of sales reports is a legitimate verification of a component. Also, when using technologies such as JSP, testing the raw HTML output may be the only useful way to determine whether a component has behaved as expected.

Where to Get HttpUnit

HttpUnit is an open source, automated Web site testing tool created by Russell Gold. HttpUnit is written in Java and is distributed for free on SourceForge at:

http://sourceforge.net/projects/httpunit/

Why HttpUnit?

Plenty of functional testing products for Web applications clutter the market. Most of them are aimed at Quality Assurance engineers looking for graphical automation tools. Given that HttpUnit is competing in the same space as all these fine beasts, why should an XP developer turn to HttpUnit?

One obvious answer is price. HttpUnit is an open source API that can be put into place without licensing fees or concerns about software piracy. Another advantage is HttpUnit's simplicity. The HttpUnit classes encapsulate in Java the basic mechanisms of maintaining client state, sending requests, retrieving responses, and following links. In addition, they provide handy shortcut methods to extract meaningful elements from an HTTP response (headers, tables, and so on). That's about all. HTTPUnit offers no proprietary GUI, automated test scheduling, graphical reports, or similar features.

Although these might seem like arguments against the software, they also mean that developers are free to provide their own customized solutions for these areas. For instance, HttpUnit tests could be combined with JUnitPerf's test decorators to provide a quick load-test. In addition, because HttpUnit tests are written in Java, they can be structured in almost any imaginable way. With other testing tools, test choices are limited to those anticipated by the team who wrote the tool. Finally, HttpUnit does not directly extend JUnit—meaning that it can be put to use outside of a testing context (perhaps posting HTTP requests to a remote server from within a Java application).

HttpUnit provides fertile ground on which to build complex test suites; however, this flexibility comes at a price. A typical test case for a Web page that contained a form might be to fill out the form in several wrong ways, verifying that validation worked in each case, and then to fill it out correctly, checking that the appropriate subsequent page was displayed. Writing the Java code to perform this test could become cumbersome, because much of it would be repeated with minor changes (which form fields to fill out, which failure message was returned, and so on). Ideally, testing applications would be developed on top of HttpUnit to address some of these issues. One interesting technique (still in its early stages) is to create XML "scripts" for HttpUnit tests. The script defines which pages were consulted in what order and which assertions were performed on the results. New scripts could be written as new functionality arose, and the test suite would execute one test for each script. One such system has already been developed, based on JXUnit (http://jxunit.sourceforge.net/).

Because much of the value of functional testing comes in its thoroughness and scope (testing every user-visible feature of the whole application), and because the tests cannot be incrementally developed with the same ease as unit tests (many smaller components must be assembled before the test can be written), HttpUnit tests are not as lightweight or critical to XP as other types of tests. However, they can be deployed somewhat incrementally, and the features that HttpUnit provides to aid assertion writing (the ability to easily find hyperlinks in a response, for example) are unparalleled. It's worth considering HttpUnit as a developer if you have to write any assertions against a returned HTML page for any reason or if you need automated functional tests for your Web site and wish to leverage the flexibility of a framework instead of a tool.

HttpUnit vs. Cactus

HttpUnit and Cactus overlap each other's functionality. However, the basic difference is clear: HttpUnit performs functional tests, whereas Cactus performs unit/integration tests. See Chapter 18, "Cactus Primer," for a more complete delineation of the frameworks' respective roles, as well as for instructions on how use them together.

HttpUnit Basics

HttpUnit can be thought of as two clusters of functionality:

❑   A Web client that maintains state and provides the facility to send requests and retrieve responses

❑   A variety of methods that simplify the verification of response content

The first cluster of functionality allows for the basics of talking to a Web server and is easily explained. The second cluster allows for the unit testing of individual pages. Used together, the clusters can verify complex behavior such as page flow. The rest of this section will explain how to employ the basics of HttpUnit.

WebClient Functionality

HttpUnit's WebClient class, appropriately enough, models a Web client. (Actually, WebClient is an abstract class; WebConversation provides the implementation that test developers will use.) WebClient/WebConversation acts basically like a standard Web browser: It maintains client state—including persistent response headers such as cookies, relative URLs, and frame sets—and allows a user to send requests for specific resources and retrieve the responses.

Natural collaborators with WebConversation are WebRequest and WebResponse. WebRequest (naturally) represents a request to a remote server, and WebResponse encapsulates the reply. Using these classes is simple:

```
WebConversation conversation = new WebConversation();
WebRequest simpleRequest =
    new GetMethodWebRequest("http://httpunit.sourceforge.net/");
WebResponse response = conversation.getResponse(simpleRequest);
```

Note that GetMethodWebRequest is a subclass of the abstract class WebRequest (specifically one that uses HTTP GET). The last two lines occur so often that WebConversation implements a convenience method to shorten them into one line:

```
WebResponse response =
    conversation.getResponse("http://httpunit.sourceforge.net/");
```

Building on these core classes, HttpUnit provides the facility to follow links contained in WebResponses:

```
WebLink link = response.getLinkWith("automated web site testing");
WebRequest request = link.getRequest();
response = conversation.getResponse(request);
```

Note that the text searched for in getLinkWith is the clickable text, not the value of the "href" attribute. Also, getLinkWith will return the first link that contains the matching text. HttpUnit provides other methods for link searching via its API.

Response Inspection and Multiple Pages

Requesting and retrieving pages is great—but how do you use HttpUnit to verify that the responses are in order? Several methods on the WebResponse object are designed to allow easy inspection of the response. These run the gamut from the quick and dirty (return the response as text with response.getText()) to the specific (find a table with response.getTableWithSummary()) to the ultrapowerful (get the XML DOM for the Html page with response.getDOM()). The results of these methods can be used in combination with JUnit assertions to check that the requested pages are as expected.

The following example introduces a fully working functional Web test. You can download the JSPs and HTML files that serve as the application under test, as well as the test itself, from the book's Web site at www.RickHightower.com/JavaXP. The folder on this chapter contains a short read-me file describing how to download and set up the example code. The component under test is the annual sales report page (presumably generated dynamically from the database). Because sales reports are naturally sensitive matter, a login page protects the page. To test this component, the test developer might decide that the following facts should be verified:

❑ **Login**

    1. The sales report page will redirect to the login page if the user is not logged in.

    2. The login page will redirect to the private page if filled out correctly.

    3. The login page will display a message if the username and/or password are entered incorrectly.

❏ **Sales Report Page**

    1. The sales report page will contain two tables: projected and current sales.

    2. Each table will contain dollar amounts representing the sales for a given year.

    3. The sales report page will contain a list of the board of directors.

❏ **Feedback**

    1. The feedback form on the bottom of each page is structured correctly.

    2. The feedback form submits correctly.

It's easy to see how many different testable facts can be contained in a relatively simple set of user actions. This is only natural, and it makes thorough functional testing somewhat daunting. Still, the task of functional testing with HttpUnit can be made easier with good design. The first step is to try to break down the testable facts into small groups that can be unit tested.

For this example, the entire test will be contained inside a JUnit TestCase (see Chapter 13, "Unit Testing with JUnit," if you are unfamiliar with its functionality). Each of the groups of facts will be verified with its own test method—for example, testLogin(). The setUp() method will initialize the instance variable conversation with a new WebConversation to avoid having to create one in each test method.

Login Testing

The test method for the login page will verify the testable fact summarized under "Login" in the previous section. The test simulates the following page flow: A user attempts to access a private page. She is redirected to the login page and fills it out incorrectly. Her login is processed, and the application takes her back to the login page, displaying an error message. Finally she logs in correctly and arrives at the private page. The following listing contains the code for login testing.

```
public void setUp(){
  conversation = new WebConversation();
}

private WebResponse goToPrivatePage() throws Exception{
  /*try to get to a protected page*/
  return conversation.getResponse(
      "http://localhost:8080/examples/private.jsp");
}

public void testLogin() throws Exception{
  WebResponse response = this.goToPrivatePage();
  /*verify that we are at the login page*/
  assertLoginPage(response);

  /*try to login with a bad username and password*/
  response = login(response, "xxx", "notAPassword");
  assertLoginPage(response);

  /*check that an error message has been displayed*/
  String pageStr = response.getText();
  assertTrue(pageStr.indexOf("Password or User name not correct.")>-1);
```

```
    /*login correctly*/
    response = login(response, "user", "muffinWaste77");
    assertTrue(!response.getTitle().equals("Login"));
}

public void assertLoginPage(WebResponse response)throws Exception{
    /*
    page title is often a quick verification that the correct page is
    being examined.
    */
    assertEquals("redirected successfully to login",
                "Login", response.getTitle());
}

public WebResponse login(WebResponse loginPage, String userName,
                         String pass) throws Exception{
    /* since the forms are not named, get the first form on the page */
 WebForm form = loginPage.getForms()[0];

    /*Get the request from the form*/
    WebRequest loginRequest = form.getRequest();

    /*set the user name and password*/
    loginRequest.setParameter("userName", userName);
    loginRequest.setParameter("password", pass);

    /*return the response for the login*/
    return conversation.getResponse(loginRequest);
}
```

Notice that this listing breaks the code into four separate methods (in addition to setUp). login() and goToPrivatePage() were originally inlined. After we began work on the other two tests (which needed similar tasks performed), we devised separate methods to avoid code duplication (one of the cardinal rules of code design in XP). Eventually, as the testing application grew, methods such as these would probably find a home in a separate utility class. Another note on design: Almost all the methods in this TestCase declare Exception in the throws clause. HttpUnit classes declare some exceptions that are somewhat difficult to deal with (SAXException, IOException, and MalformedURLException). In most cases there is nothing that a test can do about the underlying cause, aside from bringing it to a developer's attention. Therefore, it makes sense to allow the JUnit framework to handle and log the errors as test failures once they bubble up past the TestCase. Later on, if one of the exceptions becomes meaningful, this behavior can be changed; but for now it makes sense to throw most exceptions through our TestCase.

The first method, goToPrivatePage(), uses HttpUnit functionality covered earlier in the chapter and serves mostly to save some tying. assertLoginPage() simply asserts that the page title retrieved with reponse.getTitle() is equal to "Login". These utility methods (along with login()) support testLogin(), which simulates requesting a protected page, logging in incorrectly, and then logging in correctly and being directed to the originally requested resource.

The login() method submits a login request and introduces form handling in HttpUnit. The first step is to obtain a WebForm from the WebResponse that simulates the login page. This is taken care of with:

```
WebForm form = loginPage.getForms()[0];
```

getForms() returns an array, and we select its first member, corresponding to the first form on the page. WebForm supports the verification of its contents (which we will cover later in this example), but in order to submit it, we first have to get a request that corresponds to a submission of this form:

```
WebRequest loginRequest = form.getRequest();
```

Now, form parameters for the username and password are set in the request:

```
loginRequest.setParameter("userName", userName);
```

Finally, the request is submitted to the server with conversation.getResponse(request).

The testLogin() method contains barely any new HttpUnit code. It uses the utility methods to simulate page flow, and uses JUnit asserts to verify that the results are correct. The only new feature employed is response.getText(), which returns a String equivalent to what View Source would return for the same page in a Web browser. A quick way to check for simple HTML out put is to use String.indexOf() to search the returned text for the specified content:

```
String pageStr = response.getText();
assertTrue(pageStr.indexOf("Password or User name not correct.")>-1);
```

Testing the Sales Report Page

Now that the login feature has been tested, we will dive into table manipulation with HttpUnit. The sales report page is laid out (minus the feedback form at the bottom) in one top-level table with two rows (see the following figure). The first row contains two other tables, each contained in a cell, that display the report information. We also know that the sales report page has a complex table layout based on figures retrieved from the company database. This means that we cannot assert the specific textual contents of the page, only its general form. We begin by examining the output of the sales report page contained in the following listing.

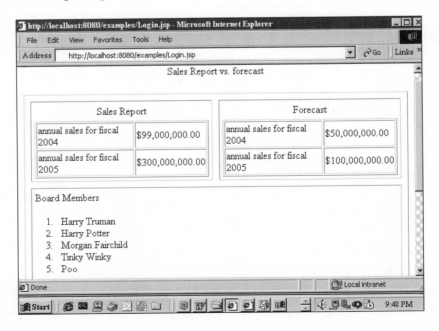

```
<!-- head and body tags skipped -->
<table border='true' cellspacing='10' cellpadding='5'>
<caption>
Sales Report vs. forecast
</caption>
<tr>
 <td width="50%">
    <table border='true' title='Sales Report'>
        <caption>
            Sales Report
        </caption>
        <tr>
            <td width='40%'>
                annual sales for fiscal 2004
            </td>
            <td width="20%">
                $99,000,000.00
            </td>
        </tr>

        <tr>
            <td width='40%'>
                annual sales for fiscal 2005
            </td>
            <td width='20%'>
                $300,000,000.00
            </td>
        </tr>
    </table>
 </td>

<td width="50%">
    <table title='forecast' border="true">
        <caption>
            forecast
        </caption>
        <tr>
            <td width='40%'>
                annual sales for fiscal 2004
            </td>
            <td width='20%'>
                $50,000,000.00
            </td>
        </tr>

        <tr>
            <td width='40%'>
                annual sales for fiscal 2005
            </td>
            <td width='20%'>
                $100,000,000.00
            </td>
        </tr>
    </table>
```

```
          </td>
        </tr>
        <tr>
          <td colspan='2'>
            Board Members <br />
            <ol title='Board Members'>
                <li>Harry Truman</li>
                <li>Harry Potter</li>
                <li>Morgan Fairchild</li>
                <li>Tinky Winky</li>
                <li>Poo</li>
            </ol>
            <br/>
            Note that the actual sales are a lot higher than the projected sales.
          </td>
        </tr>
        </table>
        <!--Feedback form follows-->
```

HttpUnit recognizes the importance of tables as a page-structuring tool and gives you several handy tools for interacting with them. This example uses verifies three facts:

❑   There will be current and forecast sales report tables.

❑   Each table will contain sales data for a number of years.

❑   A list of the Board of Directors will appear on the page.

In order to test the first of these, we need to access each table individually. The WebResponse class has several methods for retrieving tables:

```
public WebTable[] getTables()
public WebTable getTableStartingWith(String text)
public WebTable getTableStartingWithPrefix(String text)
public WebTable getTableWithID(String text)
public WebTable getTableWithSummary(String text)
```

Of these, only getTables() will return an array of the top-level tables on this page. This seems like a good way to narrow the results. However, the getTableWithXXX() methods will recurse into tables in search of a match. It would be nice to use one of those methods. The getTableStartingWithXXX() methods return tables based on the text of their first (non-empty) cell. These methods do not suit our needs because the two tables begin identically ("Sales report", and "forecast" are contained in the <caption> tag). The other two methods will search for a table based on the "id" and "summary" attributes of the table. However, upon examination of the HTML output, the page designers have included neither attribute in their tables. According to XP's principle of common code ownership, we should change the class that generates this page. If the tables are summarized or given IDs, they are easier to test. In the real world, we would consider this refactoring. For the purposes of our example, we will leave the page design alone in order to explore more of HttpUnit's functionality.

Because the page includes only one top-level table, we go ahead and get it:

```
WebTable topLevelTable = response.getTables()[0];
```

WebTable represents an HTML table and has a method that returns a specific cell: getTableCell(int row, int column). We use this to get the first cell of the first row (which contains the sales report table):

```
TableCell reportCell = topLevelTable.getTableCell(0,0);
```

TableCell is in turn an object representation of an HTML table cell. It shares many of the methods of WebResponse (in fact, they share an interface, HTMLSegment), including the ability to retrieve contained tables. At this point we want to verify that we have two distinct tables, the report and the forecast. Examining the HMTL, we see that the tables are identified only by their captions. Again, if we had summaries or IDs, we could make short work of this problem. However, none exist, and we have no quick way to determine a specific subtag (we could access the HTML DOM, but let's leave that for later in the chapter). So, we decide again to use a quick substring search that verifies the caption exists in the cell at all:

```
String cellStr = cell.asText();
assertTrue(cellStr+ "contained " +caption,cellStr.indexOf(caption)>-1);
```

Now that we have checked to be sure we are seeing the cell containing the correct table, we can get the actual cell and verify its structure:

```
WebTable table = cell.getTables()[0];
this.assertGenericSalesTable(table);//a custom method
```

The assertGenericSalesTable() method uses a for loop to iterate over the contents of one of the sales tables. It also uses WebTable.asText(), which returns the table as a two-dimensional String array. (This is only a convenience, because the same result can be obtained with TableCell.asText()—in fact, WebTable uses TableCell.asText() internally.) Each row in the table is checked—the first cell must start with "annual sales for fiscal ", and the second cell must begin with a dollar sign.

The following listing contains the full code for this portion of the test.

```
/*
  Sets up the sales report page to be checked by
  assertSalesReportPage(WebResponse response)
*/
public void testReportsPage() throws Exception{

  WebResponse response = this.goToPrivatePage();

  /*redirected automatically to login page, so attempt to log in*/
  response = login(response, "user", "muffinWaste77");

  /*now we should be on the sales report page*/
  assertSalesReportPage(response);
}

public void assertSalesReportPage(WebResponse response) throws Exception{
  /*will return null--designers have unhelpfully forgotten to specify
    'summary' attribute!
  */
  //response.getTableWithSummary("Sales Report");
```

```
    /*
      Also unusable--both the "Forecast" and "Sales Report" tables
      start with the same cell!
    */
    //response.getTableStartingWith("Annual sales for fiscal 2004");

    WebTable topLevelTable = response.getTables()[0];
    TableCell reportCell = topLevelTable.getTableCell(0,0);
    assertSalesCell("Sales Report", reportCell);
    //WebTable reportTable = reportCell.getTables()[0];
    TableCell forecastCell = topLevelTable.getTableCell(0,1);
    assertSalesCell("Forecast", forecastCell);

    TableCell boardCell = topLevelTable.getTableCell(1,1);
    assertBoardCell(boardCell);
  }

  public void assertSalesCell(String caption, TableCell cell)throws Exception{
    /*verify the cell contains the caption*/
    String cellStr = cell.asText();
    assertTrue(cellStr+ "contained " +caption,cellStr.indexOf(caption)>-1);

    /*get the table and verify its structure*/
    WebTable table = cell.getTables()[0];
    this.assertGenericSalesTable(table);
  }

  public void assertGenericSalesTable(WebTable table) throws Exception{
    String[][] tableArray = table.asText();
    for(int i =0; i< tableArray.length; i++){
      assertTrue("row correctly captioned",
              tableArray[i][0].startsWith("annual sales for fiscal "));
      assertTrue("row contains dollar figure",
              tableArray[i][1].startsWith("$"));
    }
  }

  public void assertBoardCell(TableCell cell) throws Exception{
    /*should span 2 columns*/
    assertEquals(2, cell.getColSpan());

    /*
      Turn the cell into text and verify that it contains "Board Members"
    */
    String cellStr = cell.asText();
    assertTrue(cellStr.indexOf("Board Members ") > -1);
  }
```

At this point, the sales report page is all but verified. Verifying that the board member list exists involves only another substring search through a text rendering of a cell. All that remains in this TestCase is to check on the feedback form at the bottom of the page:

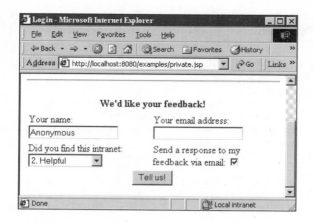

To complete our functional test of this component of the Web application, we have to check that the form at the bottom of the page is structured correctly and that it will accept average user input. The page designers have named this form so that it can be retrieved with this simple code:

```
WebForm feedbackForm = response.getFormWithName("feedback");
```

WebForm (naturally) represents an HTML form. If we examine the page's HTML, we can see that this form is laid out internally using a table—this layout should not affect anything we are doing, because WebForm models the form itself, not the exact HTML on which it is based. The first check we can run is that the form contains all of the possible parameters we expect. First we retrieve the possible parameters with:

```
String[] parameters = feedbackForm.getParameterNames();
```

Then we can check these versus our expectations with a custom assert function:

```
String[] expected = {"name", "email", "reply", "usefulness"};
assertArraysEqual(expected, parameters);
```

Now we can verify that the "usefulness" dropdown box contains the correct parameters using a similar technique:

```
String[] usefulnessValues  = feedbackForm.getOptionValues("usefulness");
String[] expectedValues  = {"1","2","3"};
assertArraysEqual(expectedValues, usefulnessValues);
```

We can also assert that a given parameter has a default value:

```
assertEquals("2", feedbackForm.getParameterValue("usefulness"));
```

Once we have checked on the state of the form in the received page, we can fill it out and submit it. We have already covered the basics of form submission with the login page; only a couple of wrinkles remain undiscussed. First, all form parameters are set with request.setParameter(). Parameters that accept more than one value (multiple select boxes, for instance) can be set with request .setParameter(String name, String[] values). By default, parameters are checked against the acceptable values in the underlying form. Attempting to set the "usefulness" parameter to "600" would yield an IllegalRequestParameterException. Checkboxes and other request parameters can be removed from the request with request.removeParameter(String name). Note that HttpUnit does *not* check whether you are removing a parameter that could not be removed from the browser. The statement

```
feedbackRequest.removeParameter("usefulness");
```

would be just fine by HttpUnit. Once all the request parameters are set, the request can be submitted in the usual manner.

Advanced Topics in HttpUnit

If you have gotten this far in the chapter, you already know enough about HttpUnit to begin developing. With the source code and the reference chapter at your side, you should be able to write some mean Web testing code. The rest of this chapter will be devoted to giving an overview of the remaining issues in the HttpUnit framework and developing a more sophisticated testing program that leverages the power of HttpUnit's Java base. This section covers topics in HttpUnit such as DOM inspection, headers and validation, and HttpUnit's configurable options.

DOM Inspection

HttpUnit provides the ability to inspect an HTML document or part of an HTML document as a DOM. The Document Object Model (DOM) is a standard developed by the World Wide Web Consortium (www.w3.org/DOM/) that treats documents as objects that can be manipulated. DOM was developed to allow programmatic access to data in languages such as XML and HTML. A full discussion of DOM lies outside the scope of this book; if you need a primer, everyJava journal with online archives is sure to have several articles on XML and its two common program interfaces, DOM and SAX (Simple API for XML). What you need to know about DOM and HttpUnit is that HttpUnit uses JTidy—an HTML parser—to turn a server response into an in-memory DOM whose contents can be accessed at random. Almost all of HttpUnit's powerful assertion capabilities (WebResponse.getTables(), for instance) rely on DOM manipulation under the hood. For instance, WebResponse.getLinks() uses

```
NodeList nl = NodeUtils.getElementsByTagName( _rootNode, "a" );
Vector list = new Vector();
for (int i = 0; i < nl.getLength(); i++) {
  Node child = nl.item(i);
  if (isLinkAnchor( child )) {
    list.addElement( new WebLink( _baseURL, _baseTarget, child ) );
  }
}
```

to find all the Nodes (roughly corresponding to tags, in this case) with the name "a" (as in <a href="blah">) in the underlying HTML.

Using the DOMs provided by HttpUnit can be somewhat difficult, simply because DOM programming can be difficult. The DOM API (the Javadocs can be found at www.w3.org/DOM/2000/12/dom2-javadoc/index.html) was designed to be language independent and thus doesn't jibe with Java as well as it might.

Manipulating the HTML DOM can yield information that would otherwise be unavailable for assertion. As an example, let's return to our earlier test of the sales report page. The sales report tables were labeled with captions, an element not specifically searched for or returned by HttpUnit. Let's say that it becomes essential to validate these captions. The following DOM code could find the value of the <caption> element for inspection:

```
/**
 * @param cell A table cell containing a single nested table.
 */
private String findCaption(TableCell cell) throws Exception{
  Node node = cell.getDOM();
  Element elem = (Element)node;
  NodeList listOfCaptions = elem.getElementsByTagName("caption");

  /*presume only 1*/
  Node firstCaption = listOfCaptions.item(0);

  /*contents are actually contained in a child node of the caption Node*/
  Node contents = firstCaption.getFirstChild();
  return contents.getNodeValue();
}
```

As you can see, DOM code can get a bit involved. But, on the bright side, our sales report test is now more accurate!

Headers and Cookies

HttpUnit's WebConversation class internally stores all the headers that will be sent to the Web server with each request. Naturally, this storage covers cookies, authentication headers, and various other request headers. In order to set a header for transmission to the server with all future requests, use WebConversations's setHeaderField(String fieldName, String fieldValue) method. Shortcut methods exist for commonly used headers, such as authorization headers: setAuthorization(String userName, String password). Setting a header field to null will remove the header from all subsequent requests.

Cookies are handled slightly differently. WebConversation has methods (getCookieNames() and getCookieValue()) that return all of the cookies names to be sent as well as an individual cookie's value. addCookie(String name, String value) adds a cookie to the list of cookies to send. Unlike with header fields, there is no way to remove an individual cookie from the list.

As for server-defined cookies, the WebResponse class allows inspection of new cookies through two methods: getNewCookieNames() and getNewCookieValue(). For example, the following code would print all the new cookies set in a Web server response:

```
for(int i =0; i < names.length; i++){
  System.out.print(names[i] + " -- ");
  System.out.println(response.getNewCookieValue(names[i]));
}
```

This facility allows verification that the server has tried to set a specific cookie in the response.

Frames

HttpUnit handles frames in a straightforward manner; the WebClient stores a Hashtable of frames internally. The contents of a given frame can be accessed by name with

```
WebResponse response = WebClient.getFrameContents("someFrameName")
```

If a test follows a link from within one frame that updates another frame, the response from the WebConversation will be the contents of the target frame (which will also be accessible through getFrameContents).

SSL

HttpUnit can test sites that use Secure Sockets Layer (SSL), but doing so is somewhat involved. The process requires two basic steps: The server must have an SSL certificate installed, and the JVM used by HttpUnit must trust the installed certificate. (Certificates from Verisign or Thawte are automatically trusted.) A number of technical details surround SSL support in Java/HttpUnit, most of which are covered in the SSL FAQ hosted on HttpUnit's SourceForge site (http://httpunit.sourceforge.net/doc/sslfaq.html).

HttpUnitOptions

The HttpUnitOptions class provides a series of static properties that configure the behavior of HttpUnit. HttpUnitOptions provides options that determine whether link searches are case-sensitive, whether to follow page refresh requests automatically, and whether to print headers to the System.out stream as they are sent and received. It is worth noting that because these properties are merely static variables, you need to exercise some care in using them in a multithreaded testing environment (such as running JUnitPerf with HttpUnit) if the options are set to conflicting values in different tests.

Technical Limitations

HttpUnit provides much of the functionality of a Web browser from within a Java application. However, a number of things remain outside its purview. JavaScript is an obvious example. Currently, HttpUnit offers very limited JavaScript support. Russell Gold, the developer of HttpUnit, has stated that he plans on building in full JavaScript 1.1 support in the future, but currently only a subset of JavaScript DOM elements are usable, as well as inline and included scripts. If JavaScript does not function at all, make sure that you have the Rhino JAR (js.jar) in your classpath.

HttpUnit does not forgive bad HTML. This feature can cause problems when you test pages that display correctly in major browsers but do not strictly adhere to the HTML specification. Frequently, the problem has to do with <form> tags, which must be nested correctly within tables. Unfortunately, the HTML must be corrected to fix this problem, although calling HttpUnitOptions.setParserWarnings Enabled(true) will at least indicate HTML problems encountered during parsing.

Spider Example

HttpUnit's Java foundations mean that it's possible to devise all sorts of interesting testing applications. The API merely offers objects for test developers to employ at their convenience. In fact, verifying page output from individual requests (as we did with the sales report page in our previous examples) is perhaps the lowest-order use of the framework. The code for verifying three simple pages was over 100 lines long. Writing a test like that could take several hours, especially as you slowly tweak it to account for wrinkles in the underlying site. To quote one developer I worked with, "You could check the output manually in three seconds." Clearly, writing code like that is not the best option. Instead, test developers should seek ways to automatically verify portions of Web applications without manually asserting every single page. The spider example illustrates this approach by attempting to solve a common problem: how to quickly verify that a new site deployment has no major errors.

Spider Development: First Iteration

Our criteria for basic verification of a deployment is that each user-accessible link will display a page without an exception (HTTP code 500 Internal Server Error). HttpUnit helpfully turns these exceptions into HttpInternalErrorExceptions, which will fail tests for us. So, we have a starting point. If we can retrieve a response for every link on the site without an exception, the site must at least be up and running.

> **Is This a Valid Test?**
>
> **Checking all the internal links is not a thorough test for most sites because it omits things like user-interaction, customization, correct page sequence (private.jsp should redirect to the login page), and so on. However, imagine a dynamically generated catalog site. The on-line catalog contains more than 10,000 products. A link-checking spider could automatically verify that all the product pages are at least displaying—something that even the most dedicated tester would be loath to do. Some added logic to verify the general structure of a product display page could provide testing coverage for more than 90 percent of the accessible pages on such a site.**

Using HttpUnit's classes, coding such a spider becomes easy. All we need to do is start at the front page and try to go to every internal link on it. If we encounter a link we have checked before, we ignore it. For each page we successfully retrieve, we check all the links on it, and so on. Eventually, every link will have been checked and the program will terminate. If any page fails to display, HttpUnit will throw an exception and stop the test.

We begin by initializing a WebConversation to handle all the requests and a java.util.HashSet to keep track of which links we have followed so far. Then we write a test method that gets the response for a site's homepage and checks all the links on it:

```
private WebConversation conversation;
private Set checkedLinks;
private String host = "www.sitetotest.com";
```

```
public void setUp(){
        conversation = new WebConversation();
        checkedLinks = new HashSet();
}

public void testEntireSite() throws Exception{
  WebResponse response = conversation.getResponse("http://"+host);
  checkAllLinks(response);
  System.out.println("Site check finished. Link's checked: " +
        checkedLinks.size() + " : " + checkedLinks);
}
```

The checkAllLinks() method is also simple:

```
private void checkAllLinks(WebResponse response) throws Exception{
  if(!isHtml(response)){
    return;
  }
  WebLink[] links = response.getLinks();
  System.out.println(response.getTitle() + " -- links found = " +
        links.length);
  for(int i =0; i < links.length; i++){

    boolean newLink = checkedLinks.add(links[i].getURLString());
    if(newLink){
      System.out.println("Total links checked so far: " +
                      checkedLinks.size());
      checkLink(links[i]);
    }
  }
}

private boolean isHtml(WebResponse response){
  return response.getContentType().equals("text/html");
}
```

The isHtml() method checks to be sure that the response in which we are checking the links is in fact HTML (HttpUnit doesn't parse Flash content, for instance). After the available links in the response have been retrieved, checkAllLinks() iterates over the link array and attempts to put the text of each link into the checkedLinks set. If it is successful (indicating a new link), then checkAllLinks() attempts to verify the link with checkLink():

```
private void checkLink(WebLink link) throws Exception{
  WebRequest request = link.getRequest();
  java.net.URL url = request.getURL();
  System.out.println("checking link: " + url);
  String linkHost = url.getHost();
  if(linkHost.equals(this.host)){
    WebResponse response = conversation.getResponse(request);
    this.checkAllLinks(response);
  }
}
```

The java.net.URL is retrieved from the link through getRequest().getURL() (shown in expanded form). If the host part of the URL matches the host under test, then checkLink() retrieves the response (here is where an exception would be thrown) and then attempts checkAllLinks() in it. Finally, all of the links will be checked and the test will terminate.

At this point, the spider is perfectly usable. However, it has one major flaw: All the testing is carried out in one test method. That means that if one link fails, the entire test fails. This approach does not granularize the test output—if .1 percent of product pages (10 of 10,000) in a hypothetical catalog test suffer from a rare bug because of bad data in the database, we don't want the whole test to fail. We want to record the error, but have the test results reflect that 99.9 percent of the site is working.

Spider Development: Second Iteration

Because the spider is a testing class, our benchmark for the newly added functionality is that given the same input as our first iteration, it should yield the same results. With that quick and dirty test in mind, we begin integrating the HttpUnit spider into JUnit's framework. The integration shouldn't affect the core logic of the spider; it will still use a Set to keep track of already spidered links, ignore links outside a specified host, and so on. However, the test we ran as a method will be refactored into a separate object. The setup for the test (which we ran in testEntireSite) now exists in a separate class:

```
public class SpiderSiteTest {

public static Test suite(){
    String host = "www.eblox.com";
    TestSuite suite = new TestSuite();
    WebRequest homePage = new GetMethodWebRequest("http://" + host);
    SpiderPageTest test =
            new SpiderPageTest(homePage, new HashSet(), host);
    suite.addTest(test);
    return suite;
}

    public static void main(String[] args){
      /*
        junit.swingui.TestRunner.main(
            new String[]{"xptoolkit.httpUnitSpiderSiteTest"}
      );
      */
      junit.textui.TestRunner.run(suite());
    }
}
```

The class declares a static suite method, which allows it to be accessed by JUnit's test runners as demonstrated in the main() method. The suite consists of a single instance of SpiderPageTest—the object that performs all the logic of spidering pages, checking results, and so on. SpiderSiteTest merely serves as a convenient test launcher. It could be replaced with a more sophisticated launcher class that, say, read in the host initial page from a properties file or some such.

The SpiderPageTest object is the critical piece of the testing application. Its public interface consists of two constructors that parameterize the behavior of the test as well as the methods specified in junit.framework.Test. The constructors specify the WebRequest (or, for convenience, the WebLink from which the request is derived), a java.util.Set of links that have already been tested, and the host of the site to test (offsite links are ignored).

The Test interface specifies two methods: run(junit.framework.TestResult result) and countTestCases(). run() is supposed to execute the Test and report the outcome to the TestResult. We will cover this method in a moment. countTestCases() returns the total number of TestCases run by this Test. In this case, we have to cheat and return 1, because we have no way of knowing in advance how many pages will be tested and, hence, how many tests will run. This clues us in to imperfect integration with JUnit. JUnit's designers expected TestCases to be the objects that actually execute a test (as opposed to aggregate or modify tests). Perhaps SpiderPageTest should be a TestCase. We write this down on our task list as something to investigate after our SpiderSiteTest runs. Once we have all the logic, we may be able to see how to reshape SpiderPageTest for better integration. See the following listing for the constructors and class initialization.

```
private WebConversation conversation = new WebConversation();
private WebRequest request;
private WebLink link;
private Set alreadyChecked;
private String host;

public SpiderPageTest(WebRequest request, Set alreadyChecked, String host) {
  this.request = request;
  this.alreadyChecked = alreadyChecked;
  this.host = host;
}

public SpiderPageTest(WebLink link, Set alreadyChecked, String host) {
  request = link.getRequest();
  this.alreadyChecked = alreadyChecked;
  this.host = host;
}
```

JUnit's TestRunners (and, later on, the class itself) will call the run() method of SpiderPageTest to execute the object's testable behavior, so it makes sense to examine this method first:

```
public void run(TestResult result) {
  if(notSameHost()){
    System.out.println(this + " not run because host for test (" +
                        host + ") does not match URL being tested.");
    return;
  }

  WebResponse response = runTest(result);

  if(response != null){
    try{
      spiderPage(response, result);
    }
    catch(SAXException e){
      result.addError(this, e);
    }
  }
}
```

Its first step is to verify that the host of the request matches the host under test. If it does not, the method returns; external links are neither failures nor successes—they are simply ignored. Then, the runTest() method checks the page and reports the outcome to the test result. If this step is successful, the response from that page is sent to spiderPage(), which acts almost exactly like checkAllLinks() in the first iteration of the spider (we will cover this method in detail in a moment).

The runTest() method takes care of accessing the page and logging exceptions (read test failures) that occur in the process:

```
private WebResponse runTest(TestResult result){
  WebResponse response = null;

  result.startTest(this);
  try{
    response = this.accessPage();
  }
  catch (ThreadDeath e) { throw e; }
  catch (AssertionFailedError e) {
    result.addFailure(this, e);
  }
  catch (Throwable t) {
    result.addError(this, t);
  }
  /*furture requests are wrapped in their own test,
    so this test ends here*/
  result.endTest(this);

  return response;
}

private WebResponse accessPage() throws Exception{
  return conversation.getResponse(request);
}
```

First, the start of the test is registered with the result using result.startTest(this). Then the test() method is run and the errors (if any) are registered with the result using the result.addError() and result.addFailure() methods. Finally, result.endTest(this) is called to signal test completion to the result.

> ### Errors or Failures?
>
> **Should we log HttpUnitExceptions (that is, page failures, commonly 404 or 500 status responses) as errors (unanticipated) or failures (anticipated)? There are reasons for either approach. Logging them as failures seems proper because the test is meant to check for exactly this type of exception. Logging them as errors is easier, and we did not specifically raise an AssetionFailedError with an assertion, so the exception could be regarded as unexpected.**

The run() method calls spiderPage()if there are no failures in runTest(). The only difference between spiderPage() and its earlier incarnation (checkAllLinks()) is that instead of executing a method on each link it finds, it instantiates a new SpiderPageTest and calls run() on it:

```
SpiderPageTest linkTest =
        new SpiderPageTest(links[i], alreadyChecked, host);
linkTest.run(result);
```

Thus, a call to the run() method of a SpiderPageTest will probably execute calls to the run() methods of several SpiderPageTests. For this reason, SpiderPageTest is more like a combination of a test runner and a test than a pure test. The full code for spiderPage() appears in here:

```
private void spiderPage(WebResponse response, TestResult result)
                    throws SAXException{

  if(!isHtml(response)){
    return;
  }
  WebLink[] links = response.getLinks();

  for(int i =0; i < links.length; i++){

    boolean newLink = alreadyChecked.add(links[i].getURLString());

    if(newLink){
      System.out.println("Total links checked so far: "
                          + alreadyChecked.size());

      SpiderPageTest linkTest =
          new SpiderPageTest(links[i], alreadyChecked, host);
      linkTest.run(result);
    }
  }
}

private boolean isHtml(WebResponse response){
        return response.getContentType().equals("text/html");
}
```

Future Work on the Spider

As we discovered in implementing countTestCases with a "cheat" return value, this example still has wrinkles to be ironed out. Tighter integration with JUnit would probably be beneficial. Also, we could extend the spider with new launchers. For example, imagine a site where a logged-in user is able to access more or different areas than a non-authenticated user. With a few lines of HttpUnit code, we might write a launcher that spidered the site, logged in, and then spidered the site again.

Summary

HttpUnit provides a flexible Java API for interacting with Web servers while maintaining client state and a powerful set of utilities that make writing assertions against HTTP responses easy. This chapter has covered the mechanics of writing basic HttpUnit code; explored the specifics of interacting with forms, tables, cookies, and opened the door to sophisticated automated testing with the development of a link-checking spider.

Functional testing with HttpUnit is more complex than unit testing with JUnit. Web site tests must be carefully structured, and you must strike a constant balance between thoroughness and time spent in test development. Writing a generic test framework like the link checker in this chapter can increase coverage without increasing time spent. The best argument in favor of the framework is that HttpUnit's flexibility lends itself to this type of development.

17

Performance Testing with JMeter

Ideally, during the design phase of a project, you will receive important performance criteria such as the target number of simultaneous users the system should support and the hardware the system will run on. Of course, we don't always live in an ideal world, but you will still be responsible for delivering an application that meets all performance criteria. Don't wait until the end of the project to begin measuring performance.

You should build tracer bullets for the system incrementally—single slices of business value that utilize major pieces of your expected final architecture—and then measure performance of those tracer bullets. If you don't, expect to work some late hours and weekends the first few weeks after product launch. The faster you can identify potential bottlenecks, the quicker you can re-architect and avoid them.

Where To Get JMeter

JMeter is distributed by The Apache Software Foundation, under The Apache Software License, Version 1.1, at:

http://jakarta.apache.org/site/binindex.cgi

Overview of JMeter

JMeter 1.9.1, from The Apache Software Foundation, is a 100% pure Java desktop application created to load-test and measure system performance. It originally focused on Web applications but was made extensible and extended. Thus, JMeter can load and performance-test HTTP, FTP, and RDBMS with its support for Java Database Connectivity (JDBC). And, you can write pluggable samplers that perform tests, pluggable timers, and data analysis and visualization plugins.

For example, you could write a plugin that allows you test Enterprise JavaBeans (EJBs), Simple Object Access Protocol (SOAP), or Common Object Request Broker Architecture (CORBA) by writing your own custom sampler.

Typically, you use JMeter to measure your system performance. At first it may seem that JMeter overlaps with JUnitPerf or HttpUnit. Rather, it complements these tools: You can use JMeter to simulate load while you use JUnitPerf in conjunction with HttpUnit to ensure that your Web application still responds in a timely manner.

You can use JMeter to simulate a heavy load on a your system, server, and network. JMeter has a full multithreading framework that allows concurrent sampling by many threads and simultaneous sampling of different functions by separate ThreadGroups. Thus, you can also use JMeter to test system performance under different load types, such as heavy updates, heavy browsing, heavy transactions, or under different combination of load profiles simultaneously. An advantage of using JMeter is that you get instant visual feedback of system performance with its graphs and splines.

Because JMeter can load test a site using HTTP, it can be used to test performance of both static and dynamic resources: files, Java servlets, Perl CGI, Python CGI, PHP, JavaServer Pages (JSP), Cold Fusion, Active Server Pages, and more.

Being a Hero Is No fun

One company hired me three days before launch. I spent the first three days untangling a connection-pooling problem. The product (an e-commerce Web site) launched the same day the customer company was showing the Web site at a convention. You could say the Web site was the star of the show. Expectations grew.

Unfortunately, the Web site did not scale. I spent the month working 100-hour weeks in an effort to re-architect a site that was in production, making many patch releases. We made steady improvements, and before the end of the month the site was performing very well. Then, without warning, the customer company did a major marketing blitz and the site got twice as many hits as before in a matter of days. At this point, I began sleeping at work because I was there so much.

It took another month of 100-hour+ work-weeks to get the site up to speed again. The moral of the story is that a little planning and performance monitoring up front can save you a lot of heartache and late nights, and you may avoid angering your customer and burning out your employees.

JMeter Concepts

To use JMeter, you must construct and then run a TestPlan. A *TestPlan* consists of one to many ThreadGroups. You can think of a thread as a simulated user, and a ThreadGroup as a list of simulated users. The general rule is that the more threads you add, the harder your system resources will get hit.

Once you create all the elements in the TestPlan, you begin your test. JMeter then compiles your test elements and creates a single TestPlan object. From the TestPlan, a JMeterEngine is formed. The JMeterEngine creates threads, and each thread iterates through the test cases.

When you start JMeter, you see two top-level nodes in its tree: the TestPlan node and the WorkBench node. The TestPlan node holds the active TestPlan you are ready to run. In the WorkBench area, you can construct and configure tests. You must move the test elements and configuration to the TestPlan node before you actually run it. The following figure shows an active test loaded in the TestPlan node and a test under construction in the WorkBench node.

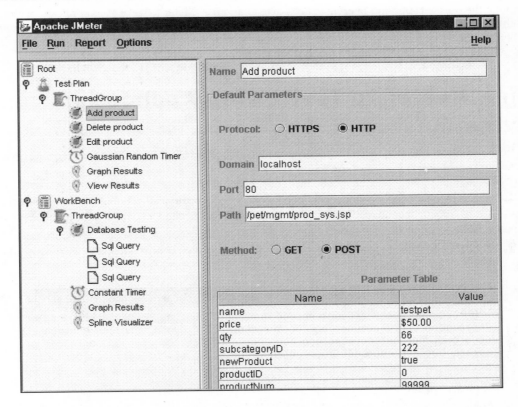

A *timer* is a simple element that is added to a ThreadGroup. Remember, we said that a thread is like a simulated user; without a timer, that thread becomes a hyper user. If you do not add a timer, the simulated user will keep hitting the site with no delay; however fun this scenario might be, it rarely simulates a real-world user. Thus you add timers to slow down the simulated users (threads) so they behave like real-world users. JMeter has three types of timers: constant timer, Gaussian random timer, and uniform random timer. We typically use the constant timer to create a repeatable test, and we use a Gaussian random timer to simulate real-world user activity.

Another element you'll typically add to a ThreadGroup is a *controller*. JMeter uses two types of controllers: testing and logic. You use a testing controller to test your system with various protocols (JDBC, HTTP, FTP, and so on). The testing controller does the sampling, but it does not record the results—for that, you need to add something else. A logical controller controls the flow. It controls the iterative behavior of sub-controllers.

A controller may contain many config elements that help you configure the controller. When you run a test, every element in the TestPlan receives every config element that is above it. For example, a timer inserted into the TestPlan at the highest level applies to all testing controllers.

You'll also typically add a listener to a ThreadGroup. A *listener* receives sampling data and either graphs it or stores it. Thus JMeter uses two types of listeners: visualizers and reporters. A testing controller collects sampling data and publishes it to one or more listeners, which may store the data in a file or display it in a graph. The View Results listener shows the text returned from a Web site. We use it to make sure the Web application is returning real HTML and not an error page.

Enough theory, concepts, and overview: Let's dive in and use JMeter to test a Web application; then, later in this chapter, we'll test some JDBC queries. The following sections walk step by step through building a TestPlan that first tests navigating through our pet store example and then tests filling out forms on the backend management piece created in the JUnit chapter.

Using JMeter to Test a Web Application Navigation

In this example, we'll set up a ThreadGroup, add Web-test controllers to the ThreadGroup, set up a timer, and set up a graph listener. We follow these steps:

1. Start JMeter. After installing JMeter, you will see a directory called bin in the JMeter home directory. Go to bin and type "jmeter"; this script will work under Unix and Windows because the makers of JMeter created both types of start-up scripts.

2. We'll add a ThreadGroup to the TestPlan. Right-click on the TestPlan node, select Add, and select ThreadGroup from the pop-up menu:

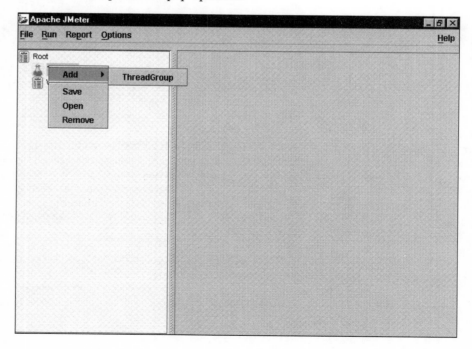

3. Expand the TestPlan node and select the ThreadGroup node. Note that the number of threads is set to 1. Although one thread is not a realistic load test, it's great when we are developing a test. We don't want to launch 100 simulated users (threads) when we don't know if our TestPlan works.

4. Change the name of the ThreadGroup to Navigation, because we're going to set up this type of test.

5. In order for the test to do something, we need to add a controller. Right-click the ThreadGroup node and add a WebTesting Controller, as shown here:

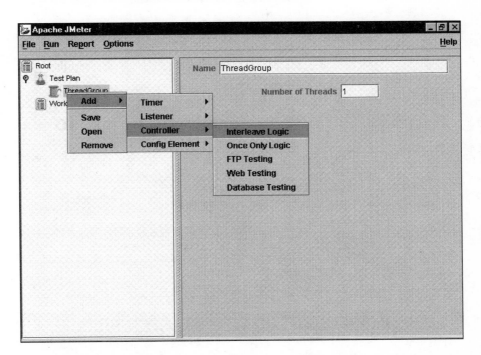

6. We need to configure the Web-testing controller. We will set up several Web-testing controllers to simulate navigating down the Web application from the home page to the product page of the pet store sample application. Set up the first controller as follows:

   ❑ Set the name to HomeWebTest.

   ❑ Set the domain to localhost (or wherever petstore is running).

   ❑ Set the port to 80, which is the default (or whatever port the Web application server is set to run on).

   ❑ Set the path to pet (as in http://localhost/pet).

7. Set up the ability to access the subcategory, as in http://localhost/pet/subcategory.jsp?id=222. Add another Web-testing controller as follows:

   ❑ Set the name to SubcategoryWebTest.

   ❑ Set the domain to localhost.

   ❑ Leave the port at 80.

   ❑ Set the path to pet/subcategory.jsp (as in http://localhost/pet/subcategory.jsp?id=222).

8. Add the "id" parameter and set it to a valid subcategory id. Note that 222 should be a valid subcategory identifier, but we need to check the DB just in case we deleted it. To add an "id" parameter, click on Add in the Web-controller configuration pane. Type "id" for the name and "222" for the value. In the next two figures, the first displays the pane and the second shows the corresponding browser view of the same URL.

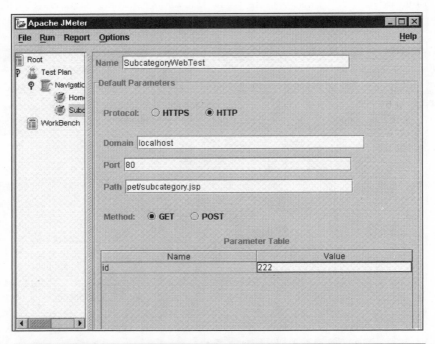

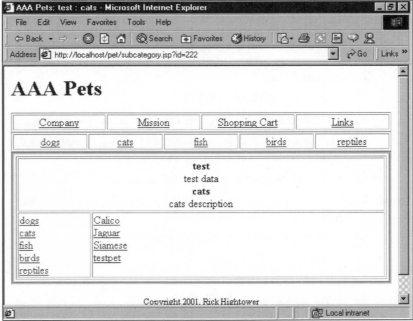

9. Repeat the last step for the product page test. That is, set up the ability to access the product, as in http://localhost/pet/product.jsp?id=2221. Add another Web-testing controller as follows:

❑ Set the name to ProductWebTest.

❑ Set the domain to localhost.

❑ Leave the port at 80.

❑ Set the path to pet/product.jsp (as in http://localhost/pet/product.jsp?id=2221).

❑ Add an "id" parameter set to "2221".

10. Now that the Web controllers are set up, we'll set up a timer. For this example, we will use a constant timer. Go to the Navigation ThreadGroup node, right-click it, and choose Add, Timer, Constant Timer from the pop-up menu. When we are setting up a test, we like to slow down the timer so we can see if the test is really doing what we expect it to. To set the timer interval to 3 seconds, use a value of 3000 (the timer works with milliseconds).

11. We need a way to view our results. Right-click the Navigation ThreadGroup, and choose Add, Listener, Graph Results from the pop-up menu. As we stated earlier, the first time a test runs, it is good to see the real HTML flying by; so, add a View Results listener, as well (select Add, Listener, View Results from the pop-up menu).

Now that we can see the results, let's run the test. Select the Navigation ThreadGroup and then select Run, Start from the main menu bar.

There are two ways to know the test is working: We can look at the View Results listener and see the pages of HTML, or we can look at the data being spit out to the console by JMeter, as follows:

```
Sampling url: http://localhost:80/pet
Original location=http://localhost/pet/
Modified location=http://localhost/pet/
Sampling url: http://localhost:80/pet/
Sampling url: http://localhost:80/pet/subcategory.jsp?id=222
```

The console indicates test errors on the product.jsp because the current subcategory is in the Web application session information. We have not set up JMeter to track session information. The error when trying to load product.jsp is as follows:

```
Sampling url: http://localhost:80/pet/product.jsp?id=2221
java.io.FileNotFoundException:
http://localhost:80/pet/product.jsp?id=2221
        at sun.net.www.protocol.http.HttpURLConnection.getInputStream
(Unknown Source)
        at java.net.HttpURLConnection.getResponseCode
(Unknown Source)
        at org.apache.jmeter.protocol.http.sampler.HTTPSampler.getErrorLevel
(HTTPSampler.java:191)
        at
org.apache.jmeter.protocol.http.sampler.HTTPSampler.sample(HTTPSample
```

This happened quite by mistake. Remember, we said the pet store Web application was not robust. Well, we did not lie; as it happens, the pet store Web application needs session data to traverse to the products correctly. You don't want this feature in a real Web application, but this Web application is non-robust by design.

However, a real Web application may hold important session information like user id, preferences, affiliations, and so on. This information may provide a customized view or provide some filtering on a per-user/per-session basis. Therefore, this snafu lends an excellent opportunity to show you how JMeter can track session information.

The default behavior of many JSP and Servlet engines is to send a special cookie to the client to track session information. A *cookie* is a name/value pair that is stored on the client's machine. The cookie is associated with a particular URL, and it's sent when you access pages under that URL. Thus, we must set up JMeter to receive and transmit the cookie back to Web application server. Fortunately, this is easy to do with JMeter: All we have to do is add a cookie manager to the thread navigation ThreadGroup (Add, Config Element, Cookie Manager), and JMeter does the rest. When we rerun the test, it will work this time.

So far we've been lobbing softballs at our Web application. Now that we know it runs, it's time to play hard ball. Set the thread count to 100 on the Navigation ThreadGroup, and reduce the time to 300 milliseconds on the timer. Save any work in open programs before starting this test. Run the test—let 'er rip!

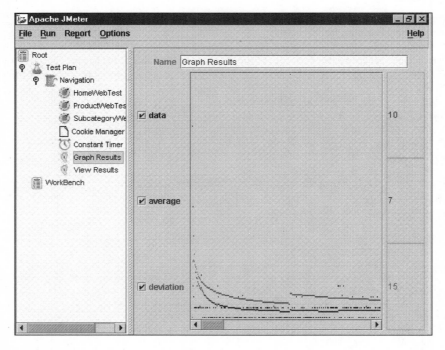

We find the graph useful, but we also like to dump the data out to a file and read it in with a spreadsheet application (Excel) and some Python stats package we wrote. In addition, we find the spline visualizer useful in seeing the runtime performance of the system. Add the spline visualizer to the Navigation ThreadGroup by right-clicking and choosing Add, Listener, Spline Visualizer from the pop-up menu.

Now, add the file reporter to the Navigation ThreadGroup (select Add, Listener, File Reporter). Click on the File Reporter element and set the output file location (for example, /tmp/output.log). Now, let's run it again.

After running the spline visualizer, we can see that the average access time is around 444 milliseconds, and we get a very interesting view of the runtime data:

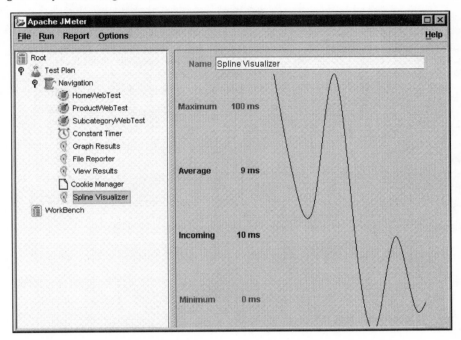

In addition to the data shown in the previous figure and the graph from the first run, we can import the output data recorded by the File Reporter into our favorite spreadsheet or other analysis software and create a custom report. Here is a sample file listing of the date in verbose mode:

```
http://localhost:80/pet/product.jsp?id=2221   200
http://localhost:80/pet/subcategory.jsp?id=222   220
http://localhost:80/pet/subcategory.jsp?id=222   230
http://localhost:80/pet/   220
```

In this example, we set up a ThreadGroup; added Web-test controllers to the ThreadGroup; set up a timer; added a cookie manager; and set up a graph, file reporter, and spline visualizer listener. In the next section, we'll create a script that can simulate form entry.

Using JMeter to Test the Web Application's Form Entry

In this example, we will test the back-end product form entry. In Chapter 13 we created a case study that added to the pet store example the functionality to add, delete, and edit products. In this section, we will write code that tests this feature. Then, we will combine this test with the last test so we can simulate customers browsing the Web site at the same time we simulate the pet store clerk adding new pets, to see what happens to performance.

First we will add a Web-application test that tests adding products. If we open the backend product page (http://localhost/pet/mgmt/product.jsp?id=2221) in a browser and view the source, the form looks like this:

```
<form method="POST" action="prod_sys.jsp">
  <p>Name: <input type="text" name="name" value="" size="20"></p>
  <p>Price: <input type="text" name="price" value="$0.00" size="20"></p>
  <p>Qty: <input type="text" name="qty" value="0" size="20"></p>
  <input type="hidden" name="subcategoryID" value="222" size="20">
  <input type="hidden" name="productNum" value="4" size="20">
  <input type="hidden" name="newProduct" value="true" size="20">
  <input type="hidden" name="productID" value="0" size="20">


  <p>Description:</p>
  <p><textarea rows="8" name="description" cols="84" ></textarea></p>
  <p> </p>
  <p><input type="submit" value="Submit" name="submit"><input type="reset"
                  value="Reset" name="reset"></p>
</form>
```

All we have to do with JMeter is simulate adding a product with this form. Thus we need to fill in the form parameters:

❑ **"name"** is the name of the new product we are creating.

❑ **"price"** can be set to any valid price.

❑ **"qty"** can be set to any valid quantity.

❑ **"subcategoryID"** must be set to a valid subcategory id. Consult the ID field of the subcategory table to see a valid id. If the test data hasn't changed, "222" is the subcategory id for Cats.

❑ **"productNum"** is the number of products in the current subcategory. We don't have to know how many products are in the subcategory; instead, we just make productNum really large—in this case, "99999".

❑ **"newProduct"** should be set to "true", which just means that we are adding a new product rather than editing an existing product.

❑ **"productID"** can be set to "0" because this value simulates adding a new product. (This parameter really is not used.)

❑ **"description"** can be any value.

We add all these parameters to the Web-application controller we added, and then change the method from GET to POST to match the HTML form. We set everything else just as we did in the earlier example, and we set the path to pet/mgmt/prod_sys.jsp to match the "action" attribute in the HTML form. Our Web controller configuration panel looks like this:

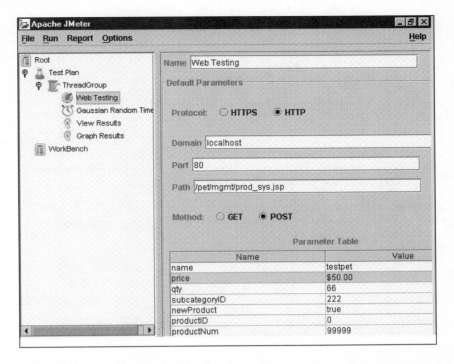

We can run this test now, but we will only be able to run it once—the test is essentially hard-coding the primary key of the product, which must be unique. To run the test many times, we need to create another test to delete the product we set up in this test. So, we add another Web-testing controller to delete the one we just added.

The form we are trying to simulate is the backend subcategory form (http://localhost/pet/mgmt/subcategory.jsp?id=222) shown below. The HTML for the form we are tying to simulate is as follows:

```
<form method="POST" action="subcat_sys.jsp">
  <table border="1" width="100%">



    <tr>
      <td width="9%">
         <input type="checkbox" name="delete_2221" value="OFF">delete</td>
      <td width="86%">
        <a href="product.jsp?id=2221" target="_blank">Calico</a>
       <br>
    </td>
    </tr>
```

```
<tr>
  <td width="9%">
     <input type="checkbox" name="delete_2222" value="OFF">delete</td>
  <td width="86%">
     <a href="product.jsp?id=2222" target="_blank">Jaguar</a>
   <br>
  </td>
  </tr>


  <tr>
    <td width="9%">
        <input type="checkbox" name="delete_2223"
            value="OFF">delete</td>
    <td width="86%">
     <a href="product.jsp?id=2223" target="_blank">Siamese</a>
     <br>
  </td>
  </tr>


  <tr>
    <td width="9%">
     <input type="checkbox" name="delete_22299999"
            value="OFF">delete</td>
    <td width="86%">
     <a href="product.jsp?id=22299999" target="_blank">testpet</a>
     <br>
  </td>
  </tr>

  </table>
  <p>
      <input type="submit" value="Submit" name="submit">
      <input type="reset" value="Reset" name="Reset">
      <input type="submit" value="Add" name="add"></p>
</form>
```

If we examine the JSP code to which we need to submit this form, we see that the id is embedded in the name of the check box in bold, as follows:

```
<input type="checkbox" name="delete_22299999"
        value="OFF">delete</td>
```

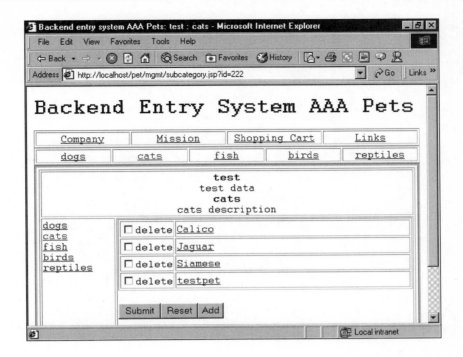

We need to add a parameter to our Web testing controller, as follows:

- ❑ Set the name to "Delete product".
- ❑ Set the domain to localhost.
- ❑ Leave the port at 80.
- ❑ Set the path to pet/mgmt/subcat_sys.jsp.
- ❑ Change the method to POST (default is GET).
- ❑ Add a parameter to delete_22299999 and set the value to "ON".

When we are done, the configuration panel looks like this:

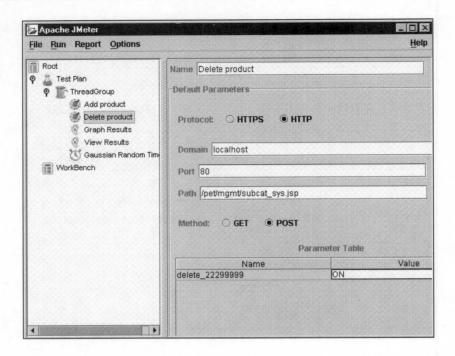

Finally, for completeness, let's add the ability to test editing a product. We'll set up two of these tests: one to edit a product and one to change it back. To set up the editing test, we add a new Web-controller tester and configure it as follows:

❑ Set the name to "Edit product".

❑ Set the domain to localhost.

❑ Leave the port at 80.

❑ Set the path to pet/mgmt/prod_sys.jsp.

❑ Change the method to post (default is get).

❑ Add the following name/value pairs to the parameter list:

      ❑ "name"="Calico"

      ❑ "price"="$500"

      ❑ "qty"="5"

      ❑ "subcategoryID"="222"

      ❑ "newProduct"="false"

      ❑ "productNum"="0"

      ❑ "description"="Calico data has been edited!"

When we are done, the configuration panel looks like the following.

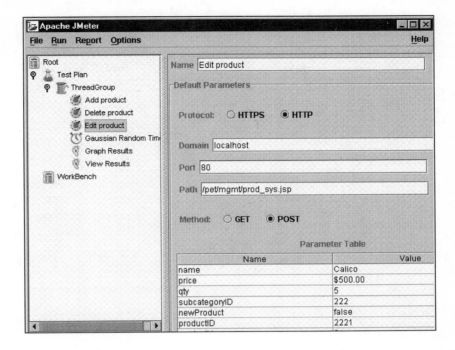

We recommend setting the thread count to 1 and then using the timer to adjust the frequency of edits, because these tests should execute in order. Before running the test, add some listeners and a timer as in the last example. Go ahead and run the test and examine the results.

Notice that we can save any node. Let's save this test and create or reload the last test, and then save it at the ThreadGroup node. Then we can load both the front-end browsing and the backend product management into the test case by selecting Open from the popup-menu, and they will run at the same time.

Because the nodes are saved as XML, we could write a program that reads the test data or that generates it quite easily. The next figure shows the XML text for the test we just created as displayed in Internet Explorer.

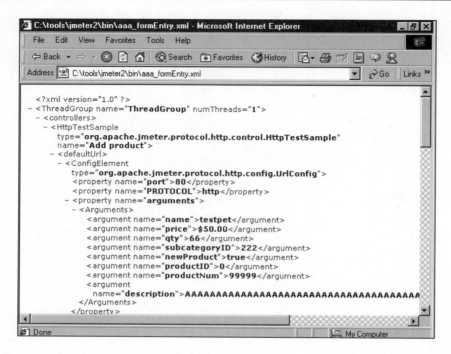

JMeter has other ways of creating the setup XML for tests. We can set up a proxy server that listens to requests and records them in an XML text that we can use for test cases. Refer to the user guide under Recording Browser Activity to learn how to do this. This technique can shave off some of the time it takes to create tests. In the next section, we will create a JDBC test.

Using JMeter to Test Performance of Our RDBMS

For completeness, we want to add a test to test the RDBMS server for our pet store application. If your system was experiencing some lag, you could rule out the RDBMS system by load testing. Perhaps you need to adjust some indexes or add a vertical or horizontal split to reduce lock contention and dead-locks. After you do this, you want to be sure your throughput is what you expect—that you got the improvements you were hoping for.

Start JMeter as before and add a new ThreadGroup. Then, add a database testing controller to the ThreadGroup (right-click the ThreadGroup and select Add, Controller, Database Testing). Now, configure the controller as shown here:

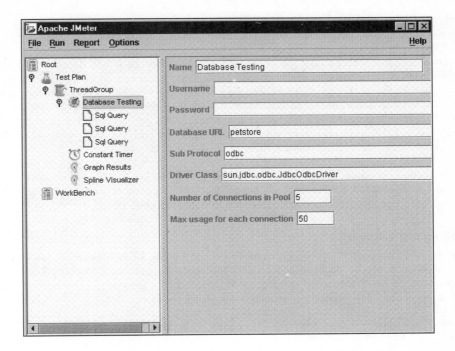

Right-click the Database Testing controller and add three SQL queries to it with the following SQL query statements:

```
select name, description, id from category where ID = 777
select name, description, id, fk_category_id from subcategory
where ID = 111
select name, description, price, id, fk_subcategory_id from product
where id = 1
```

These queries essentially test navigation of the front-end pet store. To complete the test, we need to add a timer and a listener. When we are done we can run the test, and the JMeter instance will look like the one in the previous illustration.

Case Study: The Pet Store

We will use JMeter to gather performance metrics on a new prototype of the AAA Pet Store and compare the performance of a new technology (XML/XSLT) to the existing technology (straight JSP). These numbers will help us decide whether to make the switch in the near future.

Business Need

XML and Extensible Style Language Transformation (XSLT) have garnered a lot of media attention recently. Therefore, let's imagine that our chief technology strategist has suggested that the design team look into porting the AAA Pet Store's presentation logic to this new technology. Always cautious, the engineering team decided that before they could create any estimates related to XML use, we had to know more.

So, we went ahead and built a prototype of the pet store that converts model data into XML using an open-source API called JDom. One of our enterprising design team members learned XSL and wrote style sheets to turn the XML into HTML. Then, we used Apache's Xalan engine to perform the transformation. Voilà! We had a working prototype. Management was ready to move again, but a couple of programmers had doubts. Something bothered us about the prototype—it seemed as though we were just adding the XML/XSLT on top of our existing code. After all, we still had JSPs pushing out HTML; they were just going through some extra steps. XP says, "Listen to your gut."

Before management commits us to a new schedule involving XML, we decide to do some quick performance analysis to see what kind of price we are paying for these extra steps. It may be that the prototype, while functional, doesn't represent a design that will work under load.

Prototype Architecture

Let's take a look at the prototype's structure so we can get a better sense of what we are about to test. The new interface reuses the application's model code, so there's nothing new there. The changes begin to happen at the JSP level. Instead of spitting out HTML, the JSPs generate XML elements using JDOM (www.jdom.org). The XML generation looks like this (from productlist.jsp):

```
Element eProduct = new Element("CURRENT_PRODUCT");
  Element id = new Element("ID");
    id.addContent(String.valueOf(product.getId()));
  eProduct.addContent(id);

  Element name = new Element("NAME");
    name.addContent(product.getName());
  eProduct.addContent(name);

  Element description = new Element("DESCRIPTION");
    description.addContent(product.getDescription());
  eProduct.addContent(description);

  Element ePrice = new Element("PRICE");
    ePrice.addContent(price);
  eProduct.addContent(ePrice);

root.addChild(eProduct);
```

This page looks like a good candidate for refactoring. Perhaps if we pursue this architecture, we can write use some object-to-XML mapping tools. Also, this code probably should execute in a separate class so that we can test it more easily. We take down these ideas as notes for later. The XML that this page produces looks something like the following:

```
<CURRENT_PRODUCT>
  <ID>1</ID>
  <NAME>Poodle</NAME>
  <DESCRIPTION>Poodle description</DESCRIPTION>
  <PRICE>$1.00</PRICE>
</CURRENT_PRODUCT>
```

After all, the XML has been modeled in JDOM objects; the JSP writes the XML out to a String and then pass it to Xalan's XSLT processing engine. We note this operation as a potential performance bottleneck. JDOM may already represent its object in a form that an XSLT engine can read—reading from and writing to Strings could be unnecessary. The XSLT engine uses a style sheet specified by the JSP to transform XML output of the page into HTML. Here is the XSL for the product element:

```
<xsl:if test="CURRENT_PRODUCT">
  <table width="100%" cellpadding="0" cellspacing="0" border="0">
    <tr>
      <td align="center">
        <b>
          <xsl:value-of select="CURRENT_PRODUCT/NAME" />
        </b>
        <br />
        <xsl:value-of select="CURRENT_PRODUCT/DESCRIPTION" />
        <br />
        <b>
          <xsl:value-of select="CURRENT_PRODUCT/PRICE" />
        </b>
      </td>
    </tr>
  </table>
</xsl:if>
```

The end result is a page that mimics the page created by the regular pet store application (we could even use HttpUnit to verify that they are structurally identical). However, with some refactoring, XML data generated by the page could be transformed in a number of different ways, or even sent to partners without transformation. If those are pressing business needs, maybe this will be a viable architecture. We have to weigh these potential advantages (and XP says we should treat *potential* advantages with suspicion) against the results of our JMeter testing in order to give management good feedback about the decisions they make.

Creating the Test

We decided to compare the XSL prototype's performance against that of the existing system. By taking this as our goal, we simplify our task. Real-world performance conditions can be hard to replicate, making absolute performance difficult to measure. By testing two alternatives side by side, we develop an idea of their *relative* worth. When deciding between the two options, that's all the data we need.

The Test Plan

We decide to subject both Web applications to the same series of tests. Several simulated users will access a series of pages over and over again. While the system is under this load, we will gather its performance metrics. We will test each application four times: with 10, 30, 100, and 500 users. We know that the AAA Pet Store gets an average of 10 to 30 concurrent users during the day, but the customer worries about the potential increase in use connected to their upcoming promotional campaign.

We model the test case after typical user behavior: We enter at the index page, go to a pet category, and then view a couple of animals within the category. This test exercises every major page in the prototype—another excellent feature. We note a couple of complicating factors: The Web server, the database, and the testing application (JMeter) are collocated. This fact eliminates one type of test noise (data transfer over an open network) but generates another: If the load becomes too high, the three applications might begin to compete with one another for scarce resources, increasing test times artificially. We decide to accept this risk, especially in light of the fact that Distributed JMeter (http://jakarta.apache.org/jmeter/user_manual/ rmi.html) was developed precisely to eliminate uncertain network bottlenecks. Also, we are testing two applications side by side, and any box issues should affect both equally. Still, we minimize our risk by reducing the number of extraneous processes running on the test box.

The simulated users will hit an average of one page per second, with a variation of one second (users might request another page immediately, or could wait two seconds before doing so). Real users are probably more variable, but we choose to ignore that fact for this test. Without research, have no idea what a real use pattern would look like, and (again) the side-by-side test minimizes risk.

Creating the Test in JMeter

We create a ThreadGroup in JMeter's test tree area and set the initial number of threads to 10. We will go back and manually edit this value before each test run. Then, we add a Web Testing controller to the ThreadGroup. (By the way, you can see the final test configuration in the sidebar of any of the screenshots in this section.) To the Web Testing controller, we add URL samples for each page we want a test user to visit (index, product, and so on). A Cookie Manager element takes care of maintaining client state for the entire test (important for the pet store's navigation system). Right before the listeners, we add a Gaussian random timer. We set the values as decided earlier.

The Listeners

We add several listeners to the test, each with a different purpose. The View Results listener allows us to verify that all the pages are coming through OK. After we are sure the test works, we remove this listener because it clutters the interface and adds a slight performance drag to the test. The three main visualizers we employ are the graph, the spline visualizer, and the file reporter. The graph is our best friend: It provides a quick visual analysis while also providing a running average and deviation count along its side. It also automatically scales its view of the data to keep the data in eyesight. This works for a quick check, but it prevents good visual comparisons between systems under different loads (a heavily loaded system might appear to have better response times because its response times vary so widely—to keep the data in view, JMeter shrinks the Y axis of the graph). The spline visualizer tracks minimum and maximum response times for us, and also provides a picture of the performance relative to time. This is handy, but because response times can vary so widely (under heavy load, both applications have occasional sharp spikes), the spline visualizer's averaging behavior can create a strange picture of the data. We keep it in this test only for its quick statistics.

The file reporter is probably our biggest asset in the long term. We use it to store all the response times from each test. Then, we can run a more detailed analysis if the data warrants (if both systems perform identically, we can probably skip this step). We manually change the output file for each test run to keep the data for different loads and applications separate (we use names like XSLT_100.txt).

Execution

Executing the tests is as simple as clicking on Start and then clicking on Stop after enough data has been gathered. We do not enforce any particular policy on the length of test runs--average behavior interests us more, and without a few hours for each test run, a real-world test length cannot be simulated. To switch test applications, we remove the Web testing controller from the TestPlan and replace it with a new one. This leaves the listeners, timer, and cookie manager properly configured.

Results

Even under the lightest load, the XSLT prototype takes longer to respond. As the user load increases, the XSLT times increase more rapidly than do those of the plain-JSP application. We punch the numbers we gathered (by simply writing down JMeter's analyses) into a table as shown here (all times are shown in milliseconds). Note that the minimum time was usually for the first request, before the system became loaded, and so was always near 0.

	10 Users		30 Users		100 Users		500 Users	
	Plain JSP	XSLT	Plain JSP	XSLT	Plain JSP	XSLT	Plain JSP	XSLT
Maximum	20	891	51	851	991	6019	39000	33408
Average	0	58	2	195	66	3324	584	8233
Deviation	3	151	7	151	82	1260	784	11000

As you can gather from the statistics, the JSP version of the site with 100 users performs much like the XSLT version with 10.

The next two figures show two of the test graphs. We discard most of the graphs generated by JMeter during the test because they are so difficult to compare visually. If we need valid graphs later, we will generate them from the report files.

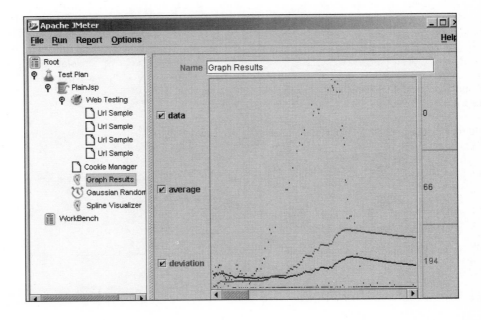

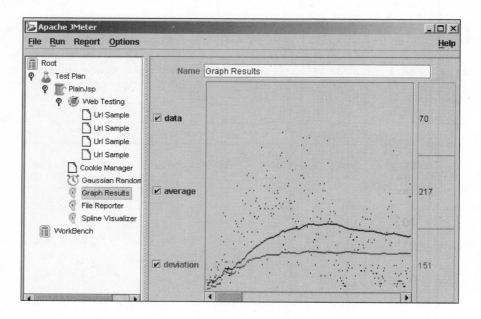

Both graphs reveal a strong tendency to have occasional response times much higher than the average response time (the light gray line). The next figure shows how response times degrade as users are added to the load (this naturally happens as JMeter starts more threads.)

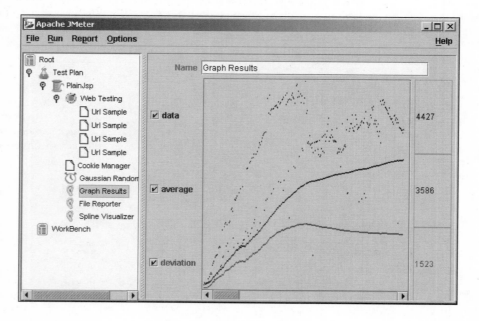

Analysis

Obviously, the XSLT prototype does not scale as well as the plain JSP solution. However, this is just the first step of a comprehensive evaluation. We begin by determining the actual performance needs of the client. Yes, the JSP version outperforms the XSLT version, but the difference between the two implementations barely registers to the end user under light load. A careful analysis of the pet store's current usage (and/or future projections) could define how *much* worse XSLT must perform to be ruled out. We also know that the tests do not accurately model user behavior—more time could be spent on that issue. Also, what other performance issues might affect the end user's experience? If the time to retrieve data from a production database (as opposed to a collocated one) adds a reliable one second to every response, the page-view time could change from acceptable to unacceptable. Finally, what is acceptable or unacceptable to a user? How many seconds or milliseconds occupy the space between "zippy" and "I'll take my business elsewhere"? Any or all of these questions could yield avenues for further research.

What Do We Do?

If all the questions have been resolved and the client decides that AAA Pet Store must go forward with XSLT, and that it must handle 100 concurrent users at one second per page or less, then we need to examine what can be done to speed things up. The JMeter tests we ran could be rewritten in HttpUnit and turned into functional tests for the customer—then they would know when we had achieved their performance goals. After that, we could use profiling tools to expose bottlenecks in the system. With the bottlenecks in sight, we could refactor components, testing our performance expectations with JUnitPerf. Our prototype isn't necessarily fatally flawed—some caching and refactoring might bring it well within the functional test's "pass" range.

One thing is certain: A sensible team would not build new functionality around the unaltered prototype without at least devoting some resources to the task of improving performance. Even in that situation, the client would have to hear that there was significant risk in going forward without more exploratory development.

Conclusion

We developed a "rubber to the road" prototype of a proposed redesign of AAA Pet Store using XSLT. Along the way, we (re)learned the value of XP's *rapid feedback* principle. A half-day's worth of testing with JMeter was enough to give the team some solid data about the relative performance characteristics of the two frameworks. Real numbers (even if gathered quickly) are worth a thousand conversations like this:

- ❏ **XSL Enthusiast:** "XML-based technology performs just fine! You just have to make sure you're using the right Fozzenbanger."

- ❏ **XSL Naysayer:** "XSLT will never be fast enough for a high-performance site because of the inherent performance penalties associated with glazing the wondabanger."

Imagine that the XSLT prototype was constructed to model the future architecture of a multimillion-dollar Web site. Using JMeter to gather feedback about its potential performance could save someone a costly mistake. An XP team always looks for hidden difficulties and lurking problems so they can be avoided. JMeter is a good flashlight to shine into the dark crannies of performance.

Summary

In this chapter, we discussed testing our Web application with JMeter. We used JMeter to test the front end of the pet store: the navigation. And, we used JMeter to test the back end of the pet store: the product management piece to add, delete, and edit products. We also set up a test to work with JDBC testing.

Because JMeter makes performance testing so easy, you won't do what some developers do—you won't wait until the end of the project to measure performance. You can now incrementally build tracer bullets of the system and measure performance of the tracer bullets. You can identify major bottlenecks before they become the overriding architecture for your system.

To use JMeter, you must construct and run a TestPlan that consists of one to many ThreadGroups. A thread is like a simulated user. JMeter forms a JMeterEngine from the TestPlan. Then, the JMeterEngine creates threads, and each thread iterates through the test cases that you set up. The test cases are stored in simple XML.

You can use JMeter to post and get pages. You can also send HTML parameters to simulate a form post. Sometimes you may want to manage the session information cookie with a JMeter cookie manager. We needed to do this to navigate to the Product page of the pet store, because the current subcategory was stored in the session information.

Cactus Primer

This chapter shows how to use Cactus for in-container testing, a vital concern of any XP/J2EE developer. To phrase it another way, this chapter attempts to answer "How do I do unit tests on servlets and other J2EE components?" We assume that you are familiar with JUnit and J2EE components—especially servlets and JSPs.

> **Where to Get Cactus**
>
> Originally, Cactus was called J2EEUnit, a name that captured the intent of the framework nicely. However, Sun owns the J2EE trademark, so the Apache Software Foundation changed the framework's name to Cactus. Cactus 1.5 is a top-level project under Jakarta and is distributed under the Apache Software License, Version 2.0. It can be downloaded at
>
> http://jakarta.apache.org/cactus/downloads.html

Why In-Container Testing?

You need a framework like Cactus to test J2EE code. Why? Because of the special relationship that J2EE code—servlets, JSPs, EJBs, and so on—holds with its *container*. Naturally, unit testing focuses on *units* of program code. However, no code exists in a vacuum. Even the simplest program is dependent on other units of code (any Java program, for instance, depends on the JVM). One of the biggest challenges of unit testing is how to "tease" the unit apart from its context so that its behavior can be asserted independently.

Testing in Isolation: Mock Objects

The idea behind mock object testing, or endo-testing, is to define "mock objects" that test cases can pass to the code being exercised. These mock objects take the place of domain objects and have dummy behavior that test cases can configure at runtime. A typical mock object interaction might go something like this:

```
public void testFilter() {
  mockFilter.setExpectedFilterCalls(1);
  filterableObject.apply(mockFilter);
  mockFilter.verify();
}
```

The verify() method would ensure that the expected calls to the filter's filter() method occurred.

Endo-testing solves the problem of code in context by providing an ultra-lightweight emulation of that context on a per-test basis. The mock object passed to code under test should encompass all of the state that the code needs to operate correctly.

Advantages to Mock Objects

Using mock objects refines the practice of unit testing by ensuring almost totally independent operation of the code under test. This provides a variety of advantages. Certain application states may be impossible, difficult, or time consuming to reproduce. Mock objects avoid this problem by keeping all of the "state" set up in the mock object. Mock objects also improve code design, according to the authors of *Endo-Testing: Unit Testing with Mock Objects* (a paper presented by Tim Mackinnon, Steve Freeman, and Philip Craig at "eXtreme Programming and Flexible Processes in Software Engineering—XP2000"). An isolating unit test "improves domain code by preserving encapsulation, reducing global dependencies, and clarifying the interactions between classes."

Disadvantages of Using Mock Objects

Mock objects require some effort to design and implement. Mackinnon et al. point to this difficulty: "In some cases it can be hard to create Mock Objects to represent types in a complex external library. The most difficult aspect is usually the discovery of values and structures for parameters that are passed into the domain code." In the case of J2EE container services, the complexity and scope of the libraries can be very high. With time, as the Java community develops reusable mock libraries and perfects code-generation tools for mock objects, this disadvantage will lessen. Several projects dedicated to these goals already exist, such as EasyMock (http://www.easymock.org/) and DynaMock. DynaMock is part of the Mock Objects Framework (http://www.mockobjects.com), an open source project with contributors from the Cactus team. Another promising tool is MockMaker (http://www.mockmaker.org/), which has plug-ins for most popular IDEs, including Eclipse and JBuilder.

Testing in Context: Integration Testing

Integration, or in-container, J2EE testing eliminates the problem of isolating tests by embracing it. Integration tests attempt to test the domain code (as far as is possible) from within the context provided by the container. For instance, an in-container test for a servlet would exercise its doGet() method by passing it actual or thinly wrapped versions of real ServletRequest and ServletResponse objects.

Advantages to Integration Testing

The chief advantage to in-container testing is verification of the interaction between domain code and container services. J2EE containers grow in complexity and scope every year, providing such diverse services as object life-cycle maintenance, security, transactions, object persistence, and so on. Containers rely on declarative deployment descriptors to specify and configure many of these services. Although many J2EE services are governed by the specifications released through the Java Community Process, the specifications leave many implementation details to container providers. Furthermore, there are no guarantees that a given container will be bug-free or that it will implement the specification exactly.

A Real-World example

I worked on a project where we wanted to take advantage of some new features of the EJB 2.0 specification. We were working with a small application server (Resin), which had recently implemented the parts of the specification (specifically container-managed persistence) that we were interested in. Using integration tests helped us refine our understanding of the domain because we had to precisely specify our expectations about the container, and it helped us uncovered some pitfalls early. We were getting an intermittent error that showed up in about one out of three test runs.

It turned out that the service we were requesting needed to be isolated in a transaction to avoid modification to underlying database tables while the service was running. Integration tests helped us focus our attention on the specific container service that we were calling——without the surrounding context of an application to distract us.

Integration testing allows developers to verify all the aspects of testing that elude verification in the domain code. Proper in-container tests can validate assumptions about the way the application is configured (is such-and-such a servlet mapped correctly?)and whether services perform as expected, and helps track down bugs that result from component interaction.

Disadvantages of Using Integration Testing

By its nature, integration testing is less "unit" than mock object testing. Although it helps verify interaction with the container, it does not provide especially good verification of domain code. Integration testing generates less pressure to refine the underlying design, since integration tests work perfectly well with systems of interdependent components. On the flip side, the context that in-container tests provide cannot be exactly identical to the code's production context. Integration testing is white-box testing—it gets inside the container to test pieces of logic. The intrusion of test code into the container must necessarily alter the surrounding context. As an example, Cactus provides wrappers for several container objects. Although the extra behavior added by these wrappers should not affect testing adversely, it could cause results that would not occur in a normal context. Black-box testing (with a framework such as HttpUnit) that calls an application externally can replicate a production environment more closely.

A Blend of Approaches

Ideally a full test suite would include verification of the domain logic with mock objects, integration testing with Cactus, and functional tests with a framework such as HttpUnit. However, integration testing is a critical part of this picture. J2EE applications rely can on container services so heavily that not having at least a "smoke test" of interaction with the deployment container amounts to a significant project risk.

Why Cactus?

Cactus is an open source framework that provides in-container testing services for servlets, JSP custom tags, and servlet filters. Other container components, such as connection pools or EJBs, can also be easily tested through Cactus.

Cactus works by providing objects called "redirectors" that serve as points of entry to the container. These redirectors execute test cases written for Cactus in the container and provide access to container objects such as HttpServletRequest, PageContext, and FilterChain. There is one proxy per directly supported API: one for servlets, one for filters, and one for custom tags. More are planned for the future. Developers who wish to work with components that are indirectly supported can choose the most appropriate redirector (usually ServletRedirector) to gain access to the container.

In addition to providing an entry into the container and access to the implicit objects, Cactus integrates with the JUnit framework and makes the business of talking to the redirector transparent to the user (well, almost transparent). Writing Cactus test cases can be as easy as extending a Cactus base class and using the objects that Cactus provides.

Cactus vs. HttpUnit

Cactus and HttpUnit both test Web application components, so questions naturally arise about their relationship and respective domains. Although there is some overlap, the basic difference is that Cactus is the more unit-oriented of the two. Cactus tests are designed to exercise the behaviors of specific classes and methods, whereas HttpUnit is designed to exercise requests to specific resources on a server.

A Cactus test might target the behavior of HelloWorldServlet, whereas an HttpUnit test might target http://myserver.com/hello/HelloWorldServlet. Depending on the server configuration, this path could invoke several filters and/or kick the user out to a login page before allowing access to HelloWorldServlet. Cactus tests *pieces* of the chain of objects that generate a response, and HttpUnit tests the *whole* chain. Although each tool has its separate place (Cactus for unit testing and HttpUnit for functional testing), the line sometimes blurs. For instance, a simple servlet might be in charge solely of writing some data to the response. In this case, inspection of the servlet response is all the testing the servlet needs. HttpUnit, Cactus, or a combination of the two would serve.

HttpUnit ships with an interesting companion API called ServletUnit. This framework essentially provides a stub container for servlets to reside in and allows these servlets to be accessed as if they were running in a remote Web server. Although ServletUnit could be useful, it still leans toward the functional end of testing--its domain does not overlap that of Cactus.

Installing Cactus

Installation involves the coordination of the two halves of the Cactus equation: the client side, where requests are composed and sent to the Web container, and the server side, where the tests are actually executed. (This is a simplified explanation. The exact relationship between the server and client sides of Cactus is explored in a later section, "Cactus Architecture.") The prerequisites for a Cactus installation are trivial (for anyone intending to write code that Cactus would test): a JVM capable of running JDK 1.2 and a servlet engine compliant with the Servlet 2.2 (or better) specification.

Open-source development moves fast, and the Cactus user community constantly suggests improvements to the installation process. Furthermore, Cactus currently integrates with several tools, such as Ant, Maven, and Eclipse, to simplify the building and test-deployment process.

An overview of how to deploy and run Cactus tests with Ant is given in the section "Cactus with Ant."

Server-Side Installation

Installing Cactus components on the server involves the following steps:

1. Put the Cactus libraries on the server's class path. In most cases, this means you must put these JAR files into the WEB-INF/lib folder of the Web application that will contain your Cactus tests.

2. Put the test classes on the server's class path. This step is necessary because Cactus executes any given test case both on the server and on the client. Omitting this step will cause a ClassNotFoundException when the redirector servlet attempts to load a test case that is not on the server. It is important not only to put tests on the server initially but also to keep them up to date. If a test is changed and the server is not updated with a new copy of the test, it will continue to use the old one—causing unexpected results. For this reason, an automated build and deployment tool such as Ant is a practical necessity for development with Cactus.

3. Put the classes under test on the server's class path. Naturally, the latest copy of all the code that the tests depend on also needs to reside on the server for the tests to run.

4. Map URLs to the various Cactus redirectors. Ordinarily, doing so will involve adding mappings to the web.xml file of the Web application that contains the Cactus tests. Cactus operates by calling these redirectors with HTTP requests from the client; they must have URL mappings so they can be called externally. The following code listing shows the web.xml file that we will be using for the first example (assuming the Web application is named cactus-tests); its general form should be familiar to anyone who has worked with servlets before. This example includes mappings for the servlet, JSP custom tag, and filter redirectors.

```
<?xml version="1.0" encoding="ISO-8859-1"?>

<!DOCTYPE web-app
    PUBLIC "-//Sun Microsystems, Inc.//DTD Web Application
2.2//EN"
    "http://java.sun.com/j2ee/dtds/web-app_2.2.dtd">

<web-app>

    <!- Mappings for the Servlet Redirector ->
    <servlet>
```

```
        <servlet-name>ServletRedirector</servlet-name>
        <servlet-class>
            org.apache.cactus.server.ServletTestRedirector
        </servlet-class>
    </servlet>

<servlet-mapping>
        <servlet-name>ServletRedirector</servlet-name>
        <url-pattern>/ServletRedirector/</url-pattern>
    </servlet-mapping>

    <!-- Mappings for the FilterRedirector -->
    <filter>
        <filter-name>FilterRedirector</filter-name>
        <filter-class>
            org.apache.cactus.server.FilterTestRedirector
        </filter-class>
    </filter>

    <filter-mapping>
        <filter-name>FilterRedirector</filter-name>
        <url-pattern>/FilterRedirector/</url-pattern>
    </filter-mapping>

    <!-- Mappings for the JspRedirector -->
    <servlet>
        <servlet-name>JspRedirector</servlet-name>
        <jsp-file>/redirector.jsp/</jsp-file>
    </servlet>

    <servlet-mapping>
        <servlet-name>JspRedirector</servlet-name>
        <url-pattern>/JspRedirector/</url-pattern>
    </servlet-mapping>
</web-app>
```

If custom tag tests are on the horizon, add redirector.jsp (the JSP redirector) to your Web application in the location specified in the previous step. (In the example, this will be the root of the Web application.) This step is necessary because the cactus JAR that contains the classes for the other redirectors cannot contain JSPs.

Client-Side Installation

Client-side setup involves less work. First, make sure that Cactus JARs are on the client's class path (along with your Cactus test cases, of course). Second, create a properties file called cactus.properties and put it on your class path. cactus.properties will contain entries that correspond to the URL of the test Web application and the names of the redirectors that were mapped during the server-side installation. Cactus needs these properties set so that it can direct requests to the server-side test runners from within the client test runners.

Here are the contents of the cactus.properties file we will use to develop our first example:

```
cactus.contextURL=http://localhost:8080/cactus-tests

cactus.servletRedirectorName=ServletRedirector

cactus.jspRedirectorName=JspRedirector

cactus.filterRedirectorName=FilterRedirector
```

The entries for the names of the redirectors are optional, and you can skip them if the redirectors are mapped in web.xml with the default names (i.e., ServletRedirector, JspRedirector, and FilterRedirector, respectively).

With some help from Ant, the cactus.properties file can be generated just before test suite execution. Generating the file allows for on-the-fly customization of the redirector URLs to account for differences between local and integration servers.

A Simple Example

Now that Cactus is installed in a Web application called cactus-tests on our Web server, let's try to run a test to prove that it works. The class we want to test is simple: It maps all the request parameter into session attributes (and returns a java.util.Map of the parameters and values). It has a single static method:

```
public static Map mapRequestToSession(HttpServletRequest request){
  HttpSession session = request.getSession();
  Map paramsMap = new HashMap();
  for(Enumeration e = request.getParameterNames(); e.hasMoreElements();){
    String paramName = (String)e.nextElement();
    String paramValue = request.getParameter(paramName);
    session.setAttribute(paramName, paramValue);
    paramsMap.put(paramName, paramValue);
  }
  return paramsMap;
}
```

Our Cactus test for the SessionMapper class follows the standard JUnit test case template. It has a couple of differences: The class descends from org.apache.cactus.ServletTestCase, and there is another method in addition to the testSessionMapper()—beginSessionMapper(WebRequest request). Here is the code for the test case:

```
package xptoolkit.cactus;
import org.apache.cactus.*;
import junit.framework.*;

public class MapperTest extends ServletTestCase{
  /*standard constructor omitted */

  public void beginSessionMapper(WebRequest clientSideRequest){
    clientSideRequest.addParameter("xp", "rules!");
  }

  public void testSessionMapper(){
    Map map = SessionMapper.mapRequestToSession(request);
```

```
        String val = (String)session.getAttribute("xp");
        assertEquals("rules!", val);
        val = (String)map.get("xp");
        assertEquals("rules!", val);
    }

    /*standard main and suite methods omitted */
}
```

The beginSessionMapper() method is executed on the client, and it sets up the request that will eventually arrive at the redirector servlet and thereby at the SessionMapper class. We'll cover this type of method in more detail in the next section.

The testSessionMapper() method passes the request instance variable inherited from ServletTestCase into mapRequestToSession(HttpServletRequest request). The request variable implements the HttpServletRequest interface because it wraps an instance of the request generated by the Web server. Once mapRequestToSession() has completed its work, we expect to find a session attribute mapped under the key XP. ServletTestCase also provides an instance variable session (type HttpSession). We pull our value from this variable, assert that it is equal to the String we expect, and voilà! Our test is complete.

To execute the test, first we make sure that the server has the latest version of both SessionMapper and MapperTest. Once the server has been made aware of the new classes, we use one of the usual JUnit test runners to execute the test normally on the client side. When the test executes, Cactus automatically sends an HTTP request to the servlet redirector specifying that MapperTest should be instantiated and that its testMapRequestToSession() method should be invoked. The server runs the test and returns the results to the client for Cactus to interpret. Barring any setup issues, the test should run. As pair programming partners, we give each other a high-five and begin integrating our test and code into the system.

Cactus Architecture

To generate the implicit objects available in a Web server, Cactus needs to replicate the request-response cycle of HTTP communication. To do this (and also to allow verification of the response returned by the Web server), Cactus test cases are fully executed in two instances that pretend to run as one—the first on the client side and the second on the server side. The framework authors made this decision to simplify the creation of test cases: the alternative would be to have one class for the server and one for the client. This process operates so smoothly that it often appears that Cactus test cases are standard JUnit test cases. Occasionally, test execution can produce unexpected behavior because, although the two objects operate as one, they do not actually share a common state. However, with caution and a solid understanding of the Cactus architecture, writing test cases that execute in the container is a snap.

In this section, we'll give you an in-depth look at the various pieces of a Cactus test case and show you how Cactus goes about executing a test case (including which steps happen where).

Extending the Appropriate Class

Cactus tests are JUnit tests. Their execution is started using JUnit's TestRunners outside the container, and in format they follow the basic JUnit test case. There are a couple of key differences, however. The most obvious is that Cactus tests extend one of the three types of Cactus TestCases (ServletTestCase, FilterTestCase, or JspTestCase). These base classes provide hooks into the Cactus framework for remote execution and specify several instance variables (such as request and response) that correspond to objects that are readily available to the redirector during execution. The presence of these objects allows you to test methods that depend on these portions of the API in question.

Beginning Execution

A Cactus test is started from a usual JUnit test runner; following is a diagram of the first stage of Cactus test case execution.

Client Side

FooTest instance

(testDoSomething selected)

An instance of the test case is instantiated, and its test method is selected by the name passed into the constructor.

The beginXXX() Method

Based on the name of the test method (a method named testXXX()), Cactus will look for and execute a method in the TestCase named beginXXX() as shown in the following illustration. For example, if Cactus were executing the testFoo() method of your test case, it would execute your beginFoo() method during this step. The beginXXX() method must accept one argument—an org.apache.cactus.WebRequest. The WebRequest represents a client-side request that the ServletTestCase will send to the redirector servlet, and that will eventually (in a modified form) be copied into the test case's request instance variable. The beginXXX() method serves primarily to add parameters and other information to this request object. Because beginXXX() is executed in a different copy of the test case from the one that runs on the server, its only method of communicating with the server-side test execution code is through the WebRequest.

Client Side

FooTest instance

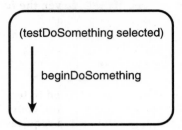

(testDoSomething selected)

beginDoSomething

Adding Information to the Request

The WebRequest defines several methods that set up the state of the request. The Cactus API documentation contains more detailed descriptions of these methods; however, they are worth outlining here. addCookie(), addHeader(), and addParameter() add request cookies, headers, and parameters, respectively. These can be retrieved from the request variable during server-side execution with the methods defined in the HttpServletRequest interface. setMethod() sets the HTTP method (GET or POST) that the request will use. setAutomaticSession() determines whether a session will automatically be created for this request; the default value is true. If beginXXX() calls setAutomaticSession(false), the session instance variable in the server-side TestCase (if any) called with this request will be null. setURL() sets the simulated URL of the HTTP request. If the code under test does URL processing, setURL() allows for a mock URL.

The following example illustrates how to add setup information for a specific testXXX method to the request that will be sent to the server.

```
public void beginGoOnVisionQuest(WebRequest request) {
   /* The URL being constructed is: http://nationalparks.org/organ-pipe-
monument/long_walk.do
   */
   request.setURL("nationalparks.org",
                          "/organ-pipe-monument",
                          null,
                          "/long_walk.do",
                          null);
   /*multiple values for same key*/
   request.addParameter("SPIRIT_GUIDES", "Coyote");
   request.addParameter("SPIRIT_GUIDES", "Snake");

   request.addCookie("PREPARED", "true");
}
```

A Possible Trap

The beginXXX() method seems like an ideal place to do method-specific setup above and beyond request parameters. However, the following beginXXX() method will not work:

```
public void beginCyborgAttack{
    someImportantInstanceVariable = someSpecificSetupMethod();
}
```

If someImportantInstanceVariable is referenced in testCyborgAttack, a NullPointerException will result because beginCyborgAttack() executes in a different copy of the test case. If a test method requires specific setup, you should use the following code instead:

```
public void testCyborgAttack{
    someImportantInstanceVariable = someSpecificSetupMethod();
    //..rest of testMethod
}
```

Calling the Redirector Servlet

After beginXXX() completes, the Cactus TestCase opens an HTTP connection to the redirector servlet as shown in the next illustration. In addition to sending any request parameters added in, beginXXXCactus sends some internal parameters that specify which test (and which test method) to execute on the server.

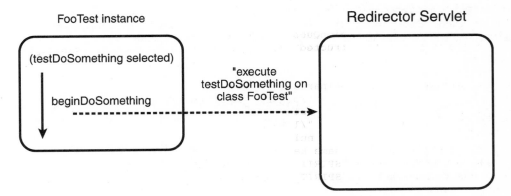

Server-Side Setup

When the redirector servlet receives the request, it inspects the internal parameters and instantiates a new copy of the correct test case on the server as shown in the following illustration. Once the class is instantiated, the redirector servlet uses reflection to copy the standard servlet variables (request, response, and so on) into the new test case instance. These variables are wrapped versions of the variables available to the redirector servlet and are covered in detail in the next section.

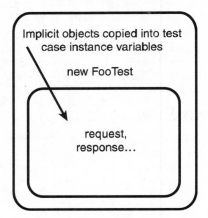

The Implicit Objects

A major feature of Cactus is the presence of implicit objects as public member variables of its TestCases. Server-side methods can pass these variables as parameters to tested methods that require them. Available to all three types of Cactus TestCases (ServletTestCase, FilterTestCase, and JspTestCase) are the following implicit objects: request, response, and config. These variables are initialized just prior to the calling of setUp() and are available only in the copy of the test case that runs on the server. (They contain null on the client.) Each implicit object is either the exact version or a thinly wrapped version of the same object available to the redirector servlet. The reasons for the wrapping are explored under the individual section.

request

The request variable implements HttpServletRequest. Its actual class is org.apache.cactus.server .HttpServletRequestWrapper, which delegates almost all its calls to the original HttpServletRequest. This means that the wrapper contains all of the request parameters that were specified in beginXXX(). The only exceptions are the methods that return information about the URL. These methods return the simulated URL specified with WebRequest.setURL in beginXXX(). The request variable also returns a Cactus-wrapped version of a RequestDispatcher from getRequestDispatcher() to avoid problems resulting from the mocked URL.

response

This variable is set to the actual response object passed into the redirector servlet's doGet()/doPost() method.

config

This variable contains a wrapped version of the ServletConfig object returned by a call to getServletConfig() in the redirector. The wrapper delegates almost all its methods; the key difference is its handling of initialization parameters. In addition to being able to return init parameters of the redirector servlet (as mapped in the deployment descriptor), you can set further init parameters with setInitParameter(). The values set with this method take precedence over the values of the redirector servlet.

The config object also returns a wrapped ServletContext from getServletContext(). The ServletContext wrapper handles forwards and includes correctly (additional logic is needed to cope with the simulated URL of the HttpServletRequestWrapper); it also saves all calls to its logging methods so that they can be easily retrieved and inspected by test code.

Server-Side Execution

Once the server-side test case has been fully initialized, server-side execution begins as shown in the following illustration. The setUp(), testXXX(), and tearDown() methods are executed at this point. (Note that these are executed only in the copy of the test case that runs on the server.) The results of the test (including errors or failure, if any) are captured and stored in an application scope variable.

Client Side

FooTest instance

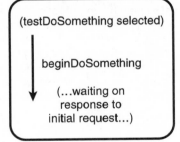

(testDoSomething selected)

beginDoSomething

(...waiting on
response to
initial request...)

Redirector Servlet

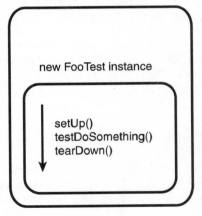

new FooTest instance

setUp()
testDoSomething()
tearDown()

setUp() and tearDown()

The setUp() and tearDown() methods mark the beginning and end of server-side execution, respectively. The use of these methods is analogous to their use in regular JUnit. They are not specific to any test method and are the ideal place to construct a test fixture. All the implicit objects are available in setUp() and tearDown().

In the following example, setUp() sets an init parameter on the config object to simulate the expected initialization parameters for the FooServlet. Then setUp() creates an instance of FooServlet, and it is initialized with the modified config object. Notice that this is done manually by the setUp() method; ordinarily, the servlet engine would handle this housekeeping chore. Here, the "unit" nature of Cactus becomes more apparent. The framework does not invoke servlets; it merely provides access to the container:

```
public void setUp() {
  config.setInitParameter("loginPage","/login.jsp");
  servlet = new LoginServlet();
  servlet.init(config);
}
```

testXXX()

The test method, as in JUnit, defines the meat of the testing logic. In the following example, it consists of passing two of the implicit objects to the servlet under test and then running assertions against other implicit objects to verify that they were modified correctly:

```
public void testDoGet() throws Exception{
  servlet.doGet(request, response);
  String value = (String)session.getAttribute("name");
  assertEquals("request param not mapped into session", "siegfried", value);
}
```

However, the implicit objects do not need to be used. The test method can verify any code that relies on container services. Imagine the following static method, which performs a JNDI lookup:

```
public static XAConnection connectionLookup() throws Exception {
  InitialContext ctx = new InitialContext();
  XADataSource src =
      (XADataSource)ctx.lookup("java/comp/env/webDatabase");
  return src.getXAConnection();
}
```

This method could be tested in a Cactus test case as follows:

```
public void testJNDILookup()throws Exception{
  javax.sql.XAConnection conn = JNDILookup.connectionLookup();
  assertNotNull(conn);
}
```

Results Collection and Postprocessing

Once the test has finished executing, the copy of the test on the client makes another request to the redirector servlet asking for the results, as shown in the next illustration. The redirector servlet pulls the results from the application scope variable where they were stored and sends them to the client. If any exceptions or failures were stored in the results, they are rethrown so the JUnit test runner will log them normally. If the result was successful, a final endXXX() method is executed on the client.

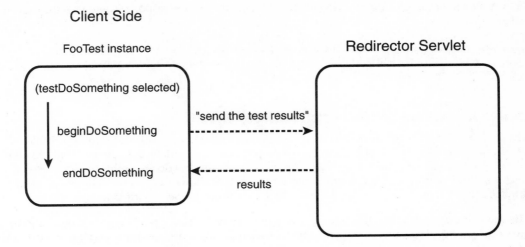

The endXXX() takes a WebResponse parameter. The WebResponse object contains response data written to the client, if any. The endXXX() method can perform assertions against contents of the response using the methods of the WebResponse object. Test execution is complete after endXXX() returns. Note that there are actually two types of WebResponse objects—we will cover these in the next section.

endXXX()

The final (optional) method that ServletTestCase expects subclasses to define is endXXX(). This method is called only after the results of the server-side execution have been retrieved from the server. If the results do not contain any failures or errors, endXXX() is called. This method is used to verify the final output sent by the server. This can be useful for cases where to code under test generates a full HTML response, as well as cases (such as custom tags) where only a small amount of data is written to the client. Needless to say, the servlet implicit objects are not available in endXXX(); nor are any variables that were set during server-side execution.

You can define endXXX() with one of two signatures, which differ based on the type of the single parameter they accept. The two possible parameter types are org.apache.cactus.WebResponse and com.meterware.httpunit.WebResponse. Each one provides different assertion capabilities, detailed in the following subsections.

Basic Assertions: Cactus's WebResponse

The Cactus version of WebResponse supports simple assertions. It allows the transformation of the server's response into a searchable String with getText() or into an array of Strings with getTextAsArray(). It also provides facilities for retrieving and performing assertions on cookies returned with the response by the server; this can be done by using getCookies() and getCookie(String).

In the following example, the endFoo() method checks whether the response contains the String "siegfried":

```
public void endFoo(WebResponse response) {
    assertEquals("siegfried not found in response", "siegfried",
response.getText());
}
```

Complex Assertions: HttpUnit's WebResponse

The alternate signature for endXXX is endXXX(com.meterware.httpunit.WebResponse). HttpUnit's WebResponse class supports significantly more sophisticated assertions but operates primarily on HTML documents. For plain-text or XML responses, for example, you are probably better off with Cactus's WebResponse. Using the two frameworks together allows easy access to these powerful assertion facilities without tying test development to the black-box model of HttpUnit.

Using the HttpUnit WebResponse class is a piece of cake. The HttpUnit API reference details the available methods, but a few examples here will illustrate their general capabilities. getLinks() returns an array of WebLink objects, which provide accessors for their target URLs. getDOM() returns the org.w3c.dom.Node corresponding to the underlying HTML document, and getText() returns a String containing the raw HTML. In order to access these features, the content type of the response must be set to "text-html"; however, a suggestion has been submitted to the HttpUnit team to allow this to be assumed if necessary (although the response will still have to contain HTML).

An Example of endXXX() Using HttpUnit

The following listing contains the source of a simple servlet that prints a link into the response object.

```
public class HappyServlet extends javax.servlet.http.HttpServlet {

   public void doGet(HttpServletRequest request,
                    HttpServletResponse response)throws IOException{
      response.setContentType("text/html");
      PrintWriter writer = response.getWriter();
      writer.println("<a href='http://www.happypuppy.com/'>");
      writer.println("I'm so happy!</a>");
   }
}
```

The following listing contains the relevant methods of a Cactus test that verifies the output of our HappyServlet by using HttpUnit.

```
private HappyServlet servlet;

public void setUp()throws Exception{
   servlet = new HappyServlet();
   servlet.init(config);
}

/** Test of doGet method, of class xptoolkit.cactus.HappyServlet. */
public void testDoGet()throws Exception{
   System.out.println("testDoGet");
   servlet.doGet(request, response);
```

```
  }

  public void endDoGet(com.meterware.httpunit.WebResponse response)
                                              throws Exception{
    WebLink link = response.getLinkWith("I'm so happy!");
    assertNotNull(link);
  }
```

Cactus with Ant

If you've already read the sections on Ant and J2EE application assembly, then you probably have an idea of how you might use Ant to get test code onto the server for execution. Deploying test cases with Ant requires no new technical knowledge, but rather some strategic knowledge and some organization. The Cactus Web site (http://jakarta.apache.org/cactus/index.html) provides an in-depth tutorial on Ant integration and supplies custom tasks suited for Ant deployment (such as starting the server if it isn't already running). It's worth checking out these tutorials because this section will give you an overview of strategy rather than specific instructions.

The Strategy

To run Cactus tests, you must have several pieces in place, namely:

- ❑   The code under test must be deployed in the container.

- ❑   The test cases themselves (including the Cactus and JUnit JARs) must also be deployed on the server.

- ❑   If the server does not support hot deployment, the server must be restarted after a deployment.

- ❑   Before test execution, the server must be running.

- ❑   A test runner must call the Cactus test cases on the client side (thereby activating the server-side test code).

Ant is a natural choice for automating these tasks. In fact, if you accomplish all these steps, and the test suite exercises all the code, then you are practically in the presence of continuous integration! Of course, although the strategy appears simple, the execution is slightly more complex. In particular, the deployment of test code raises the question of how to deploy it in relation to the tested code.

A Web Application Just for Testing

The Ant integration tutorial on the Cactus Web site suggests creating a separate WAR file used only for testing purposes. The advantage to this approach is that it is self-contained. The testing WAR can be deployed easily alongside a production Web application, and builds and execution of test code will have their own space to run in. JARs used only by test cases (the Cactus and JUnit JARs spring to mind) don't pollute the class path of the working application. The chief drawback is having to pull all the code under test into the testing application.

Testing as Part of the Production Application

An alternate strategy is to build the testing into the application that it tests. This avoids duplication of code in two different WAR files. Also, test cases may be harder to separate from their code than to keep together. However, the production Web application will be laden with unexecuted test code. Of course, you could modify the Ant script so that a release build excluded the test code, but at the cost of added build script complexity.

The best solution is probably to experiment with different organization patterns and see which ones work and which don't. Unlike bare JUnit tests, Cactus tests demand at least deployment automation, and at that point it's worth going the extra mile to achieve continuous integration.

Summary

This chapter examined the importance of in-container integration testing and the role the Cactus framework plays in implementing it. Cactus enables extreme programming on the J2EE platform by providing tests with access to the inner workings of a J2EE container. By doing so, Cactus allows and encourages scores of unit tests that might not otherwise have been written. The test cases it enables are often those that most need to be run—tests of code that intertwines with container services. Also, because it allows access to the real thing rather than mock objects or the stub framework, you can gain valuable insight into your container as well as into your application.

With Cactus, when you feel tempted to grouse about the application server, you can write a quick test case to prove yourself wrong (or right!). Personally, we couldn't live without Cactus—unit tests of server-side code should be easy to write, and Cactus makes that a reality.

Testing Servlets and Filters with Cactus

If you read the previous chapter, then you saw how the various pieces of a Cactus test fit together. This chapter shows you how to use Cactus to test specific J2EE components, such as servlets and filters. Later chapters cover testing JSP custom tags, and EJBs.

Testing Servlets

As you saw in the previous chapter, developers extend one of the three Cactus TestCases (ServletTestCase, FilterTestCase, or JspTestCase) to create their own test case.

Testing servlets with Cactus requires that you extend ServletTestCase. ServletTestCase adds features to support the testing of methods that depend on objects made available in the servlet container. Note that most of the principles that apply to writing a ServletTestCase apply to the other types of Cactus TestCases.

In order for any Servlet tests to run, you need to map the ServletRedirector in web.xml:

```
<filter>
    <filter-name>ServletRedirector</filter-name>
    <filter-class>
        org.apache.cactus.server.ServletTestRedirector
    </filter-class>
</filter>

<filter-mapping>
    <filter-name>ServletRedirector</filter-name>
    <url-pattern>/ServletRedirector</url-pattern>
</filter-mapping>
```

The Code Under Test

The code under test is a servlet that wraps the behavior of the SessionMapper class as seen in the "Installing Cactus" section in Chapter 18. The following listing contains the code for the MapperServlet. In addition to mapping the results of the request into the session, this servlet prints each request parameter to the response in a separate HTML table cell in the format "key=value". We need Cactus to ensure that the request parameters are appropriately mapped into the session. The MapperServlet also responds to initialization parameters (specifically, it varies the capitalization of its output if the ALL_CAPS parameter is set to "true"). With Cactus, we can set different initialization parameters without having to modify the deployment descriptor for the Web application.

```java
package xptoolkit.cactus;
import javax.servlet.http.HttpServlet;
import javax.servlet.http.HttpServletRequest;
import javax.servlet.http.HttpServletResponse;
import java.util.*;
import java.io.PrintWriter;
import java.io.IOException;

public class MapperServlet extends HttpServlet{

  public void doGet(HttpServletRequest request,
                    HttpServletResponse response)throws IOException{

    Map paramMap =  SessionMapper.mapRequestToSession(request);
    PrintWriter writer = response.getWriter();

    writer.println(<TABLE>);
    writer.println(<TR>);

    Set mapEntries = paramMap.entrySet();
    for(Iterator iter = mapEntries.iterator(); iter.hasNext();){
      Map.Entry entry = (Map.Entry)iter.next();
      String entryStr = entry.getKey() + "=" + entry.getValue();
      if(useAllCaps()){
        entryStr = entryStr.toUpperCase();
      }
      writer.println("<TD>");
      writer.println(entryStr);
      writer.println("</TD>");
    }

    writer.println("</TR>");
    writer.println("</TABLE>");
  }

  public boolean useAllCaps(){
    String useAllCapsStr =getServletConfig().getInitParameter("ALL_CAPS");
    return useAllCapsStr.equalsIgnoreCase("true");
  }
}
```

Before the execution of the test proper, Cactus looks for any beginXXX() methods. As you remember from Chapter 18, beginXXX methods are used to set up any request parameters required by the test.

Remember that Cactus looks for and executes a beginXXX() method only if it matches with a testXXX() method. In our test we use the beginDoGet() method to add a single parameter "foo" with the value "manchu" to the request:

```
public void beginDoGet(WebRequest request){
        request.addParameter("foo","manchu");
}
```

As with JUnit tests, the object under test must be created and initialized manually. We do this in the setUp() method:

```
public void setUp()throws Exception{
        config.setInitParameter("ALL_CAPS","true");
        servlet = new MapperServlet();
        servlet.init(config);
}
```

First the "ALL_CAPS" init parameter is set to "true", via the implicit object config, so the test can evaluate the servlet's capitalization handling. An instance of the MapperServlet is then created and initialized with the modified config object.

We are now prepared to test that the request parameter "foo" gets correctly mapped into the session:

```
public void testDoGet() throws Exception{
        servlet.doGet(request, response);
        /*maps the parameters into the session as a side effect*/
        String value = (String)session.getAttribute("foo");
        assertEquals("request param not mapped into session",
                     "manchu", value);
}
```

First the servlet method doGet() is called with two implicit objects. Then we assert that the session attribute "foo" has the expected value of "manchu".

With a ServletTestCase you can also have an optional endXXX() method. In the endDoGet() method, we verify that the output sent to the client is what we expect:

```
public void endDoGet(WebResponse response) throws Exception{
    String responseString = response.getText();
    System.out.println(responseString);
    boolean paramInResponse =
            responseString.indexOf("FOO=MANCHU") > -1;
    assertTrue("param not found in response",  paramInResponse);
}
```

The getText() method of the Cactus WebResponse returns a String. Then it is searched for the occurrence of the capitalized request parameters. Conversely, we can use HttpUnit to check the response. Cactus, as seen in Chapter 18 supports an alternate signature for the endXXX() method using the com.meterware .httpunit.WebResponse:

```
public void endDoGet(com.meterware.httpunit.WebResponse response) throws
Exception{
```

```
        assertEquals("number of tables", 1, response.getTables().length);
        assertEquals("number of rows", 1,
response.getTables()[0].getRowCount());
        assertEquals("number of columns", 1,
response.getTables()[0].getColumnCount());
        assertEquals("FOO=MANCHU",
response.getTables()[0].getCellAsText(0, 0));
            }
```

HttpUnit's WebResponse class allows for very fine-grained assertions against a returned HTML page. For more information on HttpUnit, see Chapter 16, "Functional Testing with HttpUnit."

In addition, we test the useAllCaps() method in the servlet:

```
        public void testUseAllCaps(){
            assertTrue("servlet not set to use all
            caps",servlet.useAllCaps());
        }
```

The following listing contains the complete code for MapperServletTest.

```
    package xptoolkit.cactus;
    import org.apache.cactus.*;

    import junit.framework.*;

    public class MapperServletTest extends ServletTestCase{

        private MapperServlet servlet;

        public MapperServletTest(String name) {
            super(name);
        }

        public void setUp()throws Exception{
            config.setInitParameter("ALL_CAPS","true");
            servlet = new MapperServlet();
            servlet.init(config);
        }

        public void beginDoGet(ServletTestRequest request){
            request.addParameter("foo","manchu");
        }

        public void testDoGet() throws Exception{
            servlet.doGet(request, response);
            /*maps the parameters into the session as a side effect*/
            String value = (String)session.getAttribute("foo");
            assertEquals("request param not mapped into session",
                        "manchu", value);
        }

        public void endDoGet(WebResponse response) throws Exception{
```

```
        String responseString = response.getText();
        System.out.println(responseString);
        boolean paramInResponse =
                responseString.indexOf("FOO=MANCHU") > -1;
        assertTrue("param not found in response", paramInResponse);
    }

    public void testUseAllCaps(){
        assertTrue("servlet not set to use all
        caps",servlet.useAllCaps());
    }

    public void tearDown(){
        /*no significant server-side resources to release*/
    }

    public static TestSuite suite(){
        TestSuite suite = new TestSuite(MapperServletTest.class);
        return suite;
    }

    public static void main(String[] args){
        junit.textui.TestRunner.run(suite());
    }
}
```

Testing Filters

The Servlet 2.3 specification introduced the concept of filters, reusable components that would execute before and/or after a given resource. Cactus, since version 1.2, includes a redirector and TestCase to facilitate the testing of filters and other components that depend on the implicit objects available in a filter.

Before any filter tests can begin, the FilterRedirector must be mapped into the web.xml file:

```
<filter>
    <filter-name>FilterRedirector</filter-name>
    <filter-class>
        org.apache.cactus.server.FilterTestRedirector
    </filter-class>
</filter>

<filter-mapping>
    <filter-name>FilterRedirector</filter-name>
    <url-pattern>/FilterRedirector</url-pattern>
</filter-mapping>
```

Writing a Filter test case is, for the most part, straightforward. Complications arise from the fact that filters are meant to be executed in a chain. Each filter has the option of continuing the chain of execution by calling doFilter() on the FilterChain object that the container passes to it. Continuing (or discontinuing) the chain is an important part of filter behavior—good unit tests should verify that the chain of filters is handled correctly. At the time of this writing, the preferred method of verifying the chain behavior of the filter is to pass it a mock FilterChain and assert that the mock did or did not receive a call to its doFilter() method. The following example illustrates how to create and work with a mock FilterChain.

An Example

The code under test is a simple filter that verifies that a user is logged onto the server (it checks that a "User" object exists in the session). If the user record exists in the session, the filter continues the chain. If not, the filter breaks the chain and forwards to a login page specified in an initialization parameter.

```java
package xptoolkit.cactus;

import java.io.IOException;

import javax.servlet.*;
import javax.servlet.http.*;
import javax.servlet.http.HttpServletRequest;
import javax.servlet.http.HttpServletResponse;

public class AuthFilter implements Filter {
    private FilterConfig config;

    public void init(FilterConfig config) throws ServletException {
        this.config = config;
    }

    public void doFilter(
        ServletRequest request,
        ServletResponse response,
        FilterChain chain)
        throws IOException, ServletException {

        String loginPage = config.getInitParameter("LOGIN_PAGE");
        HttpSession session = ((HttpServletRequest)request).getSession();
        Object user = session.getAttribute("USER");

        if(user != null) {
            chain.doFilter(request, response);
        } else {
            RequestDispatcher rd = request.getRequestDispatcher(loginPage);
            rd.forward(request, response);
        }
    }

    public void destroy() {}
}
```

The basics of writing a FilterTestCase are almost the same as those for writing a ServletTestCase. As with servlets, the filter in question must be created and initialized manually (usually in the setUp() method):

```java
public void setUp()throws Exception {
  filter = new AuthFilter();
```

```
      filter.init(config);
      config.setInitParameter("LOGIN_PAGE", "/login_test.html");
      recordingChain = new RecordingChain();
   }
```

The config variable of FilterTestCase stores the filter redirector's FilterConfig object (in wrapped form). The wrapper allows us to specify the initialization parameter "LOGIN PAGE" without having to add it to the web.xml entry for the FilterRedirector.

In the case of AuthFilter, we need to verify the filter's behavior in two states: user logged in and user not logged in. Here are the two test methods:

```
   public void testDoFilter() throws Exception{
      RecordingChain recordingChain = new RecordingChain();
      /*put "user" in session*/
      request.getSession().setAttribute("USER", "not a real user");
      filter.doFilter(request, response, recordingChain);
      assertTrue(recordingChain.verify());
   }


   public void testNoUser() throws Exception{
      RecordingChain recordingChain = new RecordingChain();
      /*no user in session*/
      filter.doFilter(request, response, recordingChain);
      assertTrue(!recordingChain.verify());
   }
```

In both cases, we create an instance of a RecordingChain, which is a mock-type object invented for this test. FilterChain is easy to mock up because the interface contains only one method: doFilter(). RecordingChain implements FilterChain and adds a verify() method, which returns true or false depending on whether doFilter() was called on the chain. Both test methods call verify() to discover whether the chain was continued. Here is the source code:

```
   class RecordingChain implements FilterChain{
      boolean doFilterInvoked = false;
      public void doFilter(ServletRequest servletRequest,
                           ServletResponse servletResponse) {
         doFilterInvoked = true;
      }

      public boolean verify(){
         return doFilterInvoked;
      }
   }
```

One final method asserts that the forward to the login page actually occurred. This is done by running assertions in endXXX() on the response returned from the testNoUser method:

```
   public void endNoUser(WebResponse response){
      String text = response.getText();
      assertEquals("test login page contents", text);
   }
```

Alternatively, we can use the Cactus HttpUnit integration to check the response:

```
public void endNoUser(com.meterware.httpunit.WebResponse response){
  /*
   page title is often a quick verification that the correct page is being
examined.
  */
  String pageTitle = response.getTitle();
  assertEquals("Login Page", pageTitle);
}
```

If you need to test more complex behavior, you are free to implement FilterChain in such a way that it emulates more complex behavior (perhaps it writes some data to the response).

The following listing contains the complete code for AuthFilterTest.

```
package xptoolkit.cactus;
import org.apache.cactus.*;

import junit.framework.*;

public class AuthFilterTest extends FilterTestCase{

    private AuthFilter filter;

    public AuthFilterTest(String name) {
        super(name);
    }

    public void setUp()throws Exception {
      filter = new AuthFilter();
      filter.init(config);
      config.setInitParameter("LOGIN_PAGE", "/login_test.html");
      recordingChain = new RecordingChain();
    }

    public void testDoFilter() throws Exception{
      RecordingChain recordingChain = new RecordingChain();
      /*put "user" in session*/
      request.getSession().setAttribute("USER", "not a real user");
      filter.doFilter(request, response, recordingChain);
      assertTrue(recordingChain.verify());
    }


    public void testNoUser() throws Exception{
        RecordingChain recordingChain = new RecordingChain();
        /*no user in session*/
        filter.doFilter(request, response, recordingChain);
          assertTrue(!recordingChain.verify());
    }

    public void endNoUser(WebResponse response){
        String text = response.getText();
```

```
            assertEquals("test login page contents", text);
        }

        public void tearDown(){
            /*no significant server-side resources to release*/
        }

        public static TestSuite suite(){
            TestSuite suite = new TestSuite(AuthFilterTest.class);
            return suite;
        }

        public static void main(String[] args){
            junit.textui.TestRunner.run(suite());
        }
    }
```

Summary

Cactus allows developers to write in-container tests for J2EE components. In this chapter, we covered testing two of these components, servlets and filters, respectively. Both ServletTestCase and FilterTestCase provide a set of implicit objects, such as request, response, and config, which can be used to simulate the context of a container in our tests. Again, most of the principles that apply to writing a ServletTestCase apply to the other types of Cactus TestCase. For details on JspTestCase, check out the next two chapters on testing JSPs and custom tags.

20

JspTestCases and Testing Custom Tags with Cactus

JspTestCase was designed to exercise code that depends on the JSP API, specifically that require the pageContext and out objects available in every JSP. This chapter covers testing of JSP custom tags, the main type of J2EE component that uses these objects.

> ### Then How Can I Test My JSPs?
>
> Cactus can be used to test actual JSPs as well as JSP components. Essentially, you can have JspTestCase map mock versions of objects that the JSP depends on into the appropriate scopes and then forward control to the tested JSP. The output of the JSP can then be verified in endXXX() .
>
> In any case, you should be working to minimize the need for JSP testing. JSPs should contain very little logic, so that you can concentrate on testing the classes the JSPs depend on and still ensure good coverage. The output of a JSP should not vary *radically* depending on its context—at least not unless the radical variation is encapsulated in a bean or a custom tag. If it the output *does* vary, maybe the page needs some refactoring.

Custom tags are both powerful and complicated. A custom tag consists of a *tag handler* class combined with entries in a deployment descriptor file (and possibly a TagExtraInfo class that specifies additional features of the tag). Like a servlet or an applet, tags have a specific life cycle that is maintained by the container. In the case of custom tags, the tag handler class is deeply intertwined with the container code. Because of this complexity, test developers can struggle with creating proper unit tests—after all, how do you unit-test a deployment descriptor? However, in a complicated situation, unit testing increases in importance. You can ferret out subtle container-interaction bugs with ease if you are confident that your code behaves as expected.

Spending the time to understand how a custom tag works, so that this behavior can be replicated in isolation (in other words, in a test), pays off. This section illustrates how to use the context provided by JspTestCase to exercise different types of custom tags, but it is beyond the scope of this book to examine the nuances of, say, the custom tag life cycle in detail. One of the easiest and most practical ways of deciphering custom tag behavior is to examine the generated servlet for a JSP that uses custom tags. Many IDEs offer JSP translation and compilation, along with the ability to view the translated servlet. Also, most servlet containers keep a copy of the JSP servlets somewhere close to the original (usually in some sort of working directory). If your IDE won't translate your JSPs, look for these files. Once you have the translated servlets, spend some time putting in custom tags, recompiling, and examining the generated code. Although the generated code is implementation specific, there are only so many ways to conform to the JSP specification. Examine the output from a couple of different servlet engines and cross-reference your findings with the J2EE tutorial, a reference work, and/or the JSP specification.

Testing Simple Tags

You can quickly put together a unit test for a simple tag. Let's start with the equivalent of "hello world," a custom tag that prints one line of output to the page's JspWriter and ignores any body. The tag handler class appears in the following listing.

```java
public class ExampleTag extends BodyTagSupport {

  public int doStartTag() {
    try {
      JspWriter out = pageContext.getOut();
      out.print("simple tag");
    } catch(IOException ioe) {
      throw new RuntimeException(ioe.toString());
    }
    return(SKIP_BODY);
  }
}
```

This tag submits to Cactus testing without a whimper. Because the tag handler implements only one method, all we have to do is initialize the custom tag, call its one method (doStartTag ()), and inspect the results.

We begin creating the test case by extending JspTestCase. JspTestCase operates like ServletTestCase, except that it uses a JSP to execute the test methods and provides two additional implicit variables available in JSPs: pageContext and out. These variables are simply set to the variables of the same name in redirector.jsp. To test our tag, we initialize it in the setUp() method. The initialization consists of two steps: instantiating the tag and setting the pageContext:

```java
public void setUp(){
  tag = new ExampleTag();
  /*pageContext set with the JspTestCase instance variable*/
  tag.setPageContext(this.pageContext);
}
```

The pageContext object grants the tag access to all the servlet implicit objects, as well as the output writer from the page.

Once the test case has initialized the tag, we exercise its behavior in our test method. In this case, we call doStartTag() and verify that it returns the SKIP_BODY constant from the javax.servlet.jsp.tagext.Tag interface:

```
public void testDoStartTag() {
    System.out.println("testDoStartTag");
    int result = tag.doStartTag();
    assertEquals(tag.SKIP_BODY, result);
}
```

But wait! How do we verify that the String "simple tag" was written to the output? Easy enough: We simply use the endXXX() method and inspect the response. Because doStartTag() is the only candidate for writing to the output, it must be responsible for anything that shows up in the response. Here is the endDoStartTag() method:

```
public void endDoStartTag(WebResponse resp) throws Exception{
    String response = resp.getText();
    boolean containsText = response.indexOf("simple tag") > -1;
    assert(containsText);
}
```

These are the basic steps in any tag test: Set up the tag according to the specification, call the tag handler's life-cycle method in isolation, and inspect the response if necessary. Of course, a test like this will not verify the whole tag because it does not interact with the tag deployment descriptor and/or TagExtraInfo class. See the "Testing Auxiliary Tag Components" section for strategies related to these extra elements of a custom tag.

Testing Tag Attributes and Page Interaction

Attributes of a custom tag are implemented as setter methods on the tag handler class, to be called before the tag's processing methods begin. The mapping of tag attributes to methods is specified in the tag library descriptor file, which includes an "attribute" element for each tag attribute, with subelements specifying the name, whether the attribute is required, and whether its value can be specified as a run-time expression. To examine how to test a tag that uses attributes, we'll look at a simple tag. The ifParameterEquals tag checks the request for a named parameter and evaluates the tag body if the parameter is equal to a specified value. In the following snippet, ifParameterEquals prints "Consuelo Jones" to the page writer if the "iWantConsuelo" request parameter is set to "true":

```
<example:ifParameterEquals name="iWantConsuelo" value="true">
    Consuelo Jones
</example:ifParameterEquals>
```

The following listing contains the tag handler class for ifParameterEquals.

```
public class IfParameterEqualsTag extends TagSupport {
    protected String name = null;
    protected String value = null;

    public String getName() {
```

```
          return (this.name);
      }

      public void setName(String name) {
        this.name = name;
      }

      public String getValue() {
        return (this.value);
      }

      public void setValue(String value) {
        this.value = value;
      }


      /**
       * Compare the specified parameter to the specified value, and decide
       * whether or not to include the body content.
       *
       * @exception JspException if a JSP exception has occurred
       */
      public int doStartTag() throws JspException {

        // Retrieve the value of the specified parameter
        HttpServletRequest request =
          (HttpServletRequest) pageContext.getRequest();
        String compare = request.getParameter(name);
        if (compare == null)
          compare = "";

        // Conditionally evaluate the body of our tag
        if (compare.equals(value))
            return (EVAL_BODY_INCLUDE);
        else
            return (SKIP_BODY);

      }


      public void release() {
        super.release();
        name = null;
        value = null;
      }

  }
```

A quick examination of the generated servlet shows us how Tomcat would set up the tag:

```
    xptoolkit.cactus.IfParameterEqualsTag
                _jspx_th_example_ifParameterEquals_0 =
                    new xptoolkit.cactus.IfParameterEqualsTag();
_jspx_th_example_ifParameterEquals_0.setPageContext(pageContext);
```

```
_jspx_th_example_ifParameterEquals_0.setParent(null);
_jspx_th_example_ifParameterEquals_0.setName("iWantConsuelo");
_jspx_th_example_ifParameterEquals_0.setValue("true");
```

Our test case will attempt to replicate this. First, we add the required parameter to the request:

```
public void beginPresent(ServletTestRequest request){
  request.addParameter("iWantConsuelo", "true");
}
```

Then, we initialize the tag's attributes in setUp(). Notice that we do not have to write special steps to allow the tag access to the request; the pageContext variable takes care of that for us:

```
public void setUp(){
  tag = new IfParameterEqualsTag();
  tag.setPageContext(this.pageContext);
  tag.setName("iWantConsuelo");
  tag.setValue("true");
}
```

We write the test method to call doStartTag() and check that it returns EVAL_BODY_INCLUDE:

```
public void testPresent() throws Exception{
  assertEquals(tag.EVAL_BODY_INCLUDE, tag.doStartTag());
}
```

This verifies that the tag will include the body—we don't need to add body content and check that it shows up in the response. In order to verify that the tag works when the request does not contain the expected parameter, we write another test method:

```
public void testNotPresent()throws Exception{
  assertEquals(tag.SKIP_BODY, tag.doStartTag());
}
```

Because we have not specified a beginNotPresent() method, no parameters will be added to the request.

Managing Information in Scopes

Tag handler classes have access to information in four possible scopes: page, request, session, and application. As we saw in the previous example, the pageContext object manages access to these scopes. The pageContext view of the scopes is *live*, so that anything set in, say, the request object immediately becomes available through a call to pageContext.getAttribute("name", PageContext.REQUEST_SCOPE). This relationship works in reverse as well, so you can use it to verify that your tags are properly modifying the various implicit objects. For instance, to check that a tag has mapped a String into the session under the key "hotProductChoice," you could use this:

```
tag.doStartTag()//or the appropriate tag lifecycle method
assertNotNull(session.getAttribute("hotProductChoice"));
```

See "Testing Auxiliary Tag Components" for a more involved example.

Testing Body Tags

Tags that perform processing on their body use a BodyContent object to access their page content. BodyContent extends JspWriter and nests within another JspWriter, possibly another BodyContent object. You should keep these facts in mind; they indicate that the BodyContent object contains the *result* of the evaluation of the body, not the unaltered content of the body as it appears on the JSP page. Imagine that one tag nests within another like this:

```
<parent>
  <child/>
</parent>
```

In this situation, *child* is evaluated first and simply writes its output (if any) into the BodyContent object of parent. When *parent* begins execution, its BodyContent object only contains the String results of *child*'s processing. Although the concept may elude immediate understanding, it simplifies the testing of BodyTags. To test a tag that processes its body, simply write some test data into a BodyContent object and pass it to the tag in question. See the section "Working with Nested Tags" for further information.

To obtain a suitable BodyContent, use pageContext.pushBody(). This method returns a new BodyContent object nested within the previous JspWriter. This operation also updates the value of the JspWriter contained in the page scope (available with pageContext.getOut()) to the new BodyContent. Most translated servlets perform the operation like this:

```
out = pageContext.pushBody();
tag.setBodyContent((BodyContent) out);
```

(out is the standard JSP implicit variable.) Let's look at an example.

productLink Tag Example

The productLink tag turns its contents into a hyperlink that points to the product page on the current Web site. The product page requires an ID in the request, so the productLink tag accepts an "id" attribute. JSP designers use productLink tags like this:

```
<example:productLink productId="3">
    Check out the Bastion of Fun (TM)
</example:productLink>
```

The tag handler class is simple. It writes out the opening <a> tag, then the content of the tag, and finally the closing </a>. The following listing displays the code.

```
public class ProductLinkTag extends BodyTagSupport{

  private String productId;

  public void setProductId(String id) {
    this.productId = id;
  }

  public int doAfterBody()throws JspTagException{
```

```
      try{
        JspWriter writer = bodyContent.getEnclosingWriter();
        writer.print("<a href='product.jsp?id="+productId+"'>");
        bodyContent.writeOut(writer);
        writer.println("</a>");
      }
      catch(java.io.IOException e){
        throw new JspTagException(e.toString());
      }
      return BodyTag.EVAL_PAGE;
    }
  }
```

The test case builds upon the other test cases designed so far. A couple of extra steps are included to deal with the BodyContent object. Here is the setUp() method:

```
  public void setUp() throws Exception{
    tag = new ProductLinkTag();
    tag.setPageContext(this.pageContext);
    out = pageContext.pushBody();
    tag.setBodyContent((BodyContent)out);
    /*not necessary since product link tag does not implement it,
      but this is where it would go in the standard lifecycle*/
    tag.doInitBody();
  }
```

Once the out variable is converted to an instance of BodyContent and registered with the tag, the test method can write sample content to it to be processed by the tag. In testDoAfterBody(), we print a manifest constant (for easy assertions later) as the body of the tag. Then we call doAfterBody() (which handles the body processing) and verify that it returns SKIP_BODY:

```
  public void testDoAfterBody() throws Exception{
    /*violates strict life cycle order...but that should not have any
      effect on this tag, and results in better separation between setUp and
      test method*/
    tag.setProductId(TEST_PRODUCT_ID);

    out.println(TEST_LINK_TEXT);
    int afterBodyResult = tag.doAfterBody();
    assertEquals(tag.SKIP_BODY, afterBodyResult);
  }
```

endDoAfterBody()does most of the assertion work for us. First, we define the signature that uses HttpUnit's WebResponse, and then we use the convenience method getLinkWith(String) on WebResponse to search for the link with the text we specified earlier. If the search succeeds, we verify that the "href" attribute of the link indeed points to the product page:

```
  /*using HttpUnit's WebResponse*/
  public void endDoAfterBody(WebResponse resp)throws Exception{
   WebLink link = resp.getLinkWith(TEST_LINK_TEXT);
   assertNotNull(link);
   String pointsTo = link.getURLString();
   assertEquals(TEST_LINK_TARGET, pointsTo);
  }
```

Testing Iteration Tags

The iteration tag life cycle specified by JSP 1.2 can be roughly represented with the following boilerplate code (ignoring extra stages that might occur because the tag might also be a BodyTag):

```
if(tag.doStartTag() != SKIP_BODY){
  do{
    /*body processing*/
  }while(tag.doAfterBody() == EVAL_BODY_AGAIN);
}
/*evaluate doEndTag*/
```

To test an iteration tag, all we have to do is replicate this type of loop in a test method. If possible, we should also attempt to verify each life-cycle method in isolation. For instance, if the tag stops iterating after a certain variable in the page scope reaches a certain value, we could design a test method to verify that this was the case:

```
public void testAfterBodyConditions(){
  pageContext.setAttribute("shouldStop", new Boolean(true));
  assertEquals(tag.SKIP_BODY, tag.doAfterBody());
}
```

However, the boundary conditions of the loop may depend on an unexposed internal state. Although the tag under test can be modified to expose state, doing so may violate encapsulation. In these cases, the best option is to re-create the entire loop and verify that the tag body was processed the expected number of times.

Repeat Tag Example

We use this method to verify the behavior of a simple repeat tag. The tag takes a single attribute, "repetitions", which governs the number of times the tag body repeats without modification. This is how the repeat tag might appear in a JSP:

```
<%int count = 0;%>
<example:repeat repetitions="3">
    <%count++;%>
    Some content: <%=count%>
</example:repeat>
```

The following listing shows the code for the handler class.

```
public class RepeatTag extends javax.servlet.jsp.tagext.BodyTagSupport{
  private int repetitions;
  private int count;

  public void setRepetitions(String repetitions) {
    this.repetitions = Integer.parseInt(repetitions);
  }

  public void doInitBody(){
```

```
      /*doStartTag dicatates that the tag body will always be processed at
       *least once.
       */
      count = 1;
    }

  public int doStartTag(){
    if(repetitions > 0){
      return EVAL_BODY_INCLUDE;
    }
    return SKIP_BODY;
  }

  public int doAfterBody(){
    if(++count < repetitions){
      return EVAL_BODY_AGAIN;
    }
    return SKIP_BODY;
  }
}
```

Testing an iteration tag requires no special setup (beyond that required for any custom tag). First we verify that doStartTag() will go forward only if the number of repetitions has been set to a number greater than zero:

```
public void testDoStartTag() {
  tag.setRepetitions("0");
  int result = tag.doStartTag();
  assertEquals(tag.SKIP_BODY, result);
  tag.setRepetitions("2");
  result = tag.doStartTag();
  assertEquals(tag.EVAL_BODY_INCLUDE, result);
}
```

The second test method will validate the tag's behavior in the standard iteration loop:

```
public void testDoAfterBody() throws Exception {
  tag.setRepetitions("3");
  int count = 0;
  do{
    count++;
    out.print("Some content: " + count);
  }while(tag.doAfterBody() == tag.EVAL_BODY_AGAIN);
  assertEquals(3, count);
}
```

Before anything else, testDoAfterBody() sets the tag's repetitions attribute to a reasonable value. Then the method declares a local count variable to keep track of the number of loop executions. After running the do-while loop (terminated by the return value of doAfterBody()), the method verifies that the loop body has executed the expected number of times. The out.print(…) statement was inserted for illustration; because the tag includes the body without performing any tag-specific processing, it does not matter what goes on within the loop—only that it exists.

Server-Side Assertion Facilities

JspTestCase provides an instance variable, out, that corresponds to the JSP implicit variable of the same name. out is an instance of JspWriter, which declares no methods that allow the inspection of the underlying buffer. However, the BodyContent class (which extends JspWriter) explicitly allows the inspection of its contents. Because of its subclass relationship to JspWriter, the contents of out in JspTestCase could be replaced with a BodyContent object without necessitating changes in usage. Doing so would allow us to inspect the response without waiting to return the output to the client. For example, the out object could be examined and cleared after each call to a doAfterBody() method, thereby making the test method more isolated.

We can obtain a BodyContent object through a call to pageContext.pushBody(). As we saw in the "Testing Body Tags" section, this method call also updates the out object stored in the pageContext object. Therefore, any custom tags that, for instance, call pageContext.getOut() will automatically be using the new BodyContent object instead of the standard JspWriter. Further calls to pushBody() will function transparently. The only problem so far relates to the buffered nature of the BodyContent object. Because BodyContent was intended for use with tags that might never want to write the contents to the client, using pushBody() to replace the out instance variable in JspTestCase prevents any data written to out from reaching the response unless special steps are taken.

To write the data to the underlying servlet response, we use BodyContent.writeOut(Writer) to copy the buffer of the BodyContent object into the specified writer. We can combine this with BodyContent's getEnclosingWriter() method to print the BodyContent's data back into the original JspWriter object. A typical usage pattern might go something like this:

```
private BodyContent tempOut;

public void setUp(){
  tag = new TestedTag();
  tag.setPageContext(pageContext);
  tag.setSomeAttribute("testValue");
  tempOut = pageContext.pushBody();
}

public void testDoStartTag()throws Exception {
  /*produces some output based on attribute set above*/
  tag.doStartTag();
  String result = tempOut.getString();
  assertTrue(result.indexOf("testValue ") > -1);
}

public void tearDown()throws Exception{
  tempOut.writeOut(tempOut.getEnclosingWriter());
}
```

If you are testing nested tags, you need to watch out for the creation of new BodyContent objects with subsequent calls to PageContext.pushBody(). In the examples thus far, we have omitted calls to PageContext.popBody() because after the test method finishes executing, no code remains to make use of the writers. However, if you adopt this trick to simplify your assertions, you will have to be sure that each *further* pushBody() call is balanced by a popBody() after the test finishes using the BodyContent object.

Working with Nested Tags

The JSP specification allows tags to be nested within other tags. Most of the time, nested tags operate independently. However, tag designers can build child tags that interact with their enclosing parent tags. (The relationship does not work the other way; enclosing tags cannot act on their children unless they communicate through shared page data.) To adequately test this complex situation, we need two sets of tests. First, simulate the effects of the child on the parent and verify that the parent behaves as expected. Second, test the child tag to be sure that the parent tag provides access to the correct services or data. This section will walk through both sets of tests.

Two tags form the basis for our example: parent and child. The parent element (taking a single attribute, "name") simply prints out a message stating its name and whether it contains children. The child elements each obtain the name of their parent and print a message declaring who they belong to. The tag might be used like this:

```
<example:parent name="Papa Smurf">
    <example:child/>
    <example:child/>
</example:parent>
```

The generated output would be

```
Child tag nested within parent named 'Papa Smurf'. Child tag nested
within parent named 'Papa Smurf'. Parent tag named 'Papa Smurf' does contain
children.
```

The tag handler classes (minus class imports) is shown in the following listing.

```
public class ParentTag extends TagSupport{

  private boolean containsChildren;
  private String name;

  public boolean getContainsChildren() {
    return containsChildren;
  }

  public void setContainsChildren(boolean containsChildren) {
    this.containsChildren = containsChildren;
  }

  public String getName() {
    return name;
  }

  public void setName(String name) {
    this.name = name;
  }

  public int doAfterBody() throws JspTagException{
    JspWriter out = pageContext.getOut();
    try{
```

```
        out.print("Parent tag named '" + name + "' does ");
        if(!containsChildren){
          out.print("not ");
        }
        out.print("contain children.");
      }
    catch(java.io.IOException e){
      throw new JspTagException(e.toString());
    }
    return this.SKIP_BODY;
  }

}

public class ChildTag extends TagSupport{
  public int doStartTag() throws JspTagException{
    JspWriter out = pageContext.getOut();
    ParentTag parent =
      (ParentTag)TagSupport.findAncestorWithClass(this, ParentTag.class);

    parent.setContainsChildren(true);
    String parentName= parent.getName();
    try{
      out.print("Child tag nested within parent named '" +
                parentName+"'.");
    }
    catch(java.io.IOException e){
      throw new JspTagException(e.toString());
    }
    return this.EVAL_BODY_INCLUDE;
  }
}
```

The child tag interacts with the parent by setting a property in the parent tag (containsChildren). Depending on the value of containsChildren, the message printed from ParentTag's doAfterBody() method will differ. Instead of attempting to test a full nested interaction right off the bat, we begin by testing this interaction. The following listing shows the setUp() method (the test uses the BodyContent trick discussed in the section "Server-Side Assertion Facilities") and two test methods (each exercising a different state of the ParentTag class).

```
public void setUp(){
  tag = new ParentTag();
  tag.setPageContext(pageContext);
  tag.setName("testName");
  tempOut = pageContext.pushBody();
}

public void testNoKids()throws Exception {
  tag.setContainsChildren(false);
  tag.doAfterBody();
  String result = tempOut.getString();
  /*should print "does not contain children"*/
  assertTrue(result.indexOf("not") > -1);
}
```

```
public void testKids()throws Exception{
  tag.setContainsChildren(true);
  tag.doAfterBody();
  String result = tempOut.getString();
  /*should print "does contain children"*/
  assertTrue(result.indexOf("not") == -1);
}
```

Once we verify the basic mechanism of interaction, we can move on to the ChildTag class. The setUp() method performs some extra steps:

```
private ChildTag tag;
private ParentTag p;
private BodyContent tempOut;

public void setUp()throws Exception{
  startParentTag();
  tag = new ChildTag();
  tag.setPageContext(this.pageContext);
  tag.setParent(p);

  /*the BodyContent trick*/
  tempOut = pageContext.pushBody();
}

public void startParentTag() throws Exception{
  p = new ParentTag();
  p.setPageContext(this.pageContext);
  p.setName("test parent name");
  p.doStartTag();
}
```

As you can see, setUp() creates both a ParentTag and a ChildTag class. setUp() instantiates and initializes ParentTag first, including a call to doStartTag() (which remains the default implementation in this case). Once setUp() has reached the point in parent tag's life cycle where its body would be processed, it creates the child tag and sets p (the instantiated ParentTag object) as the child tag's parent. ChildTag now awaits testing.

The test method calls doStartTag() (the only implemented life-cycle method) on the child and then checks the containsChildren property of the parent tag—tag.doStartTag() should have changed the property to "true":

```
public void testDoStartTag() throws Exception{
  tag.doStartTag();
  /*child's doStartTag method should have modified the parent's
    containsChildren property.
    */
  assertTrue(p.getContainsChildren());
  String outputOfDoStartTag = tempOut.getString();
  assertEquals("Child tag nested within parent named '"+ p.getName()+"'.",
               outputOfDoStartTag);
}
```

Assuming that this first assertion passes, testDoStartTag() uses the BodyContent trick (see the section "Improving the Assertion Facilities") to obtain the output from the child tag. The test method uses a call to assertEquals() to verify that the output contains the name of the parent tag and is formatted correctly.

Having simulated the effects of the child tag upon the parent and also verified that the child tag was finding and using the parent tag correctly, our test cases cover most of the territory available to them. However, nested tag interactions can get very complex. Creating several actual-use examples in a real JSP and then examining the translated servlet yields valuable insight into how to model tag interactions in a test context.

Testing Auxiliary Tag Components

The definition of a custom tag extends beyond the behavior of the tag handler class. In order to test a custom tag thoroughly, we need test cases to verify that the tag library descriptor entry and/or the TagExtraInfo class perform as expected.

TagExtraInfo Classes

The tag element in the tag library descriptor file contains an optional <tei-class> subelement. The tei-class element contains the fully qualified name of a subclass of javax.servlet.jsp.tagext.TagExtraInfo. The TagExtraInfo class for a given tag provides two possible services: specifying scripting variables to be defined as part of the tag's execution (with getVariableInfo()) and providing translation-time validation of a tag's attributes (with isValid()). Both methods surrender to testing without complaint; in fact, TagExtraInfo tests do not need to be run in the container. Both methods depend on a single TagData object, which you can construct manually from a Hashtable or Object[][] (the TagData object represents name-value pairs for all of the attributes used in a given tag at translation time). Simply construct a TagData object and pass it to the method, then assert that the result is as expected.

Tag Library Descriptor Testing

Because deployment descriptors are declarative specifications of container behavior rather than executable program code, they evade most Java-based unit-testing techniques. However, creating a simple JSP that uses a tag in its intended manner provides a common-sense check that no major errors have crept in. Making this sanity-check JSP part of a unit-testing suite takes a small amount of effort and provides important test coverage. If you need to change the deployment descriptor to support a new feature, these JSP-based tests allow rapid discovery of any incompatibilities. Let's examine JSP-based descriptor tests by applying them to a common problem in tag testing: verifying the creation of a scripting variable.

Scripting variables can be defined by a tag either in its TagExtraInfo class or in the tag's <variable> subelements in the tag library descriptor (in JSP 1.2). Both methods of defining a scripting variable rely on the container to generate the necessary servlet code. For example, the custom tag var specifies VarTei as its TagExtraInfo class in the deployment descriptor. According to the JUnit test, VarTei behaves correctly: specifying a single scripting variable var, to be newly created and available from the beginning of the tag onward. To test the container-generation process, we give the container a JSP that depends on the presence of var. Here is what such a page might look like:

```
<%@page import="junit.framework.Assert"%>
<%@taglib uri="WEB-INF/example.tld" prefix="example"%>
<example:var/>
<%
  Assert.assertNotNull(var);
  Assert.assertEquals("foo", var);
%>
```

If the container does not create var correctly, the attempt to access it in the scriptlet will cause a compilation error. So, this JSP constitutes a test. The value of the scripting variable (set in the VarTag handler class with pageContext.setAttribute("var", "foo")) is verified with assertions called directly from junit.framework.Assert. These assertions round out this sanity test, but we sense it's a bad idea to put *too* many assertions in the JSP-based test—it's probably better to use actual test cases because of the greater control they afford.

To provide error logging and to make these hybrid tests part of the regular suite, we call the test JSPs from within ordinary Cactus tests. We begin by extending JspTestCase to provide access to the pageContext implicit object. Then, we implement a test method that calls pageContext.include() with an argument specifying the JSP test we want to run:

```
public void testVarCreate() throws Exception{
  pageContext.include("/var_create.jsp");
}
```

Any uncaught exceptions (including compilation exceptions!) are propagated up the stack to the test method where they are trapped and logged by the Cactus error handler.

This method of verifying the tag library descriptor may be useful, but it may also possess some problems. We don't guarantee perfect results, and you may need to pursue a variety of strategies to ensure that the container does not use older JSP translations. (For instance, occasionally you need restart some versions of Resin to ensure that it will retranslate JSPs.) That being said, we feel more comfortable with a unit test verifying that our code works as intended—and creating a sample JSP that illustrates possible tag configurations fulfills one of the most important functions of automated tests: serving as executable documentation.

Case Study: The Pet Store with Custom Tags

So far, we have explored the access Cactus provides to the servlet container and the ways in which Cactus test cases can be leveraged to unit- or integration-test various J2EE components. Now it's time to put the rubber to the road and see how Cactus-based unit tests can verify our code and speed the refactoring process on a sample application. We will use Cactus to test a custom tag we develop to simplify the JSPs used in the front end of the AAA Pets online store.

The Business Need

Let's suppose that the developers who designed the JSPs for the front end of the AAA pet store were more concerned with getting a site up and running than with design. Now, several months after the initial launch, the AAA marketing director has authorized a redesign. Furthermore, in the time since development began, our shop has adopted extreme programming. As a result, our XP coach reminds us constantly of the value of adding unit tests to the existing code. The original JSPs contain a lot of logic, and a few near-disasters have reminded us of the fragility of untested code. This week, we are scheduled to refactor the JSPs to use custom tags, separating some of the logic so that we can test it.

Finding a Starting Point

We begin looking over the JSPs. The J2EE blueprints available on Sun's Web site suggest that "JSP pages should contain no code written in the Java programming language (that is, no expressions or scriptlets). Anything a JSP page needs to do with Java code can be done from a custom tag" (http://java.sun.com/j2ee/blueprints/web_tier/qanda/index.html). We ponder that for a while and begin to wonder at the enormity of our task. We decide to keep the blueprint's suggestion as our eventual goal and tackle a small chunk first. After an examination of the main navigation pages, we find a for loop whose basic structure appears on two separate pages. The loop iterates through all the subcategories available in the current category and prints out a link to each one. The following listing displays the code fragment from header.jsp.

```
<%
  Category category = categorySystem.getCurrentCategory();
  Subcategory [] subcategories = category.getSubcategories();
  for (int index=0; index < subcategories.length; index++){
    Subcategory subcategory = subcategories[index];
%>
  <td width="20%" align="center">
    <a href="subcategory.jsp?id=<%=subcategory.getId()%>">
      <%=subcategory.getName()%>
    </a>
    <br />
  </td>
<%}%>
```

subcategory.jsp creates a similar loop (the contents do not include table cells) that displays the subcategories in the sidebar. The IterationTag interface provides easy hooks into just this sort of functionality. This seems to be a likely place to begin our refactoring, and we sit down to work.

The TestCase

We begin by writing the test first, a practice recommended by XP that helps us think through the problem domain before attempting to solve it. "What will our custom tag have to accomplish?" we ask ourselves. We decide that the custom tag should assume responsibility for obtaining a valid list of subcategories. Then, the tag should step through the subcategories and print the body of the tag once for each member of the array. However, we need to vary some elements of the body on each pass. The old solution does this by making method calls in scriptlets:

```
<%=subcategory.getName()%>
```

We decide to move this Java code into the custom tag and create a couple of temporary variables that exist strictly within the body of the tag and change their values with each body iteration.

The setUp() Method

To test custom tags, we extend JspTestCase. Then, we proceed with the setup code that is common to almost all custom tags: creating the tag, setting its page context, and calling doStartTag(): (We don't know that we'll need doStartTag for sure, but doStartTag often serves to initialize the "first pass" of the tag—we guess we'll need it in a minute.)

```
private SubcategoryListTag tag;
private CategorySystem categorySystem;

public void setUp()throws Exception{
  categorySystem = new CategorySystem();
  session.setAttribute("categorySystem", categorySystem);
  tag = new SubcategoryListTag();
  tag.setPageContext(this.pageContext);
  tag.doStartTag();
}
```

In addition to the tag setup, we map an instance of the CategorySystem model object into the session. We allow this dependency because most of the existing pages do this already using a <jsp:useBean> tag.

The Tag Loop

Now that our tag is ready to run, we need to write code that verifies its entire life cycle. Because we know it will iterate, we type in the standard tag do-while loop used by most servlet containers:

```
do{

}while(tag.doAfterBody() == tag.EVAL_BODY_AGAIN);
```

Now we ask "What do we need to test? " We must check if we have created our scripting variables, and according to the JSP specification, these variables are made available to the container by nesting them in one of the accessible scopes (usually the PAGE scope). This approach seems promising, so we code to pull the variables from where they should have been placed by the tag:

```
do{
  pageContext.getAttribute("subCatId");
  pageContext.getAttribute("subCatName");
}while(tag.doAfterBody() == tag.EVAL_BODY_AGAIN);
```

"But how," we wonder, "will we verify that these objects are correct? " We could set up an array that parallels the one used by the loop, and we could even get the data the same way. This seems like a good verification, so we implement this logic and add a final check to verify that the tag iterates once per element in the array (lest the test terminate prematurely). Now that we've completed the test, it's time to write the actual code. The next listing contains the final version of the test method.

```
public void testList() throws Exception{
  Category category = categorySystem.getCurrentCategory();
  Subcategory [] subcategories = category.getSubcategories();
```

```
        int count = 0;
        do{
          Subcategory subCat = subcategories[count++];

          int id = subCat.getId();
          assertEquals(""+id, pageContext.getAttribute("subCatId"));

          String name = subCat.getName();
          assertEquals(name, pageContext.getAttribute("subCatName"));
        }
        while (tag.doAfterBody() == tag.EVAL_BODY_AGAIN);

        /*tag has repeated as many times as there are array members*/
        assertEquals(count,subcategories.length);
    }
```

Writing the Tag

Writing the test simplifies writing the code. We have the following facts clearly in mind:

❑   We must set up the initial tag state in doStartTag(), including retrieval of the data and preparation for the first evaluation.

❑   The container calls doAfterBody() once after each body evaluation to determine whether to continue processing.

We begin to brainstorm about code that fulfills these criteria. An iterator would keep track of our position, and it has a handy hasNext() method that we can use to determine the return value for doAfterBody(). Using this utility class prevents us from having to maintain an internal count and do numeric comparisons.

My first impulse had been to use the array without the iterator, since that's what the original JSP did. Because we have a test to validate the class, we don't feel so bound to the previous implementation. Already the tests have helped. We set to work.

We write a private helper method to initialize our iterator (stored in an instance member variable). Aside from some exception checking, the method is straightforward: First, we pull a CategorySystem object from the session scope using pageContext. Then, we retrieve an array of subcategories to iterate over. Finally, we use the static method asList() from java.util.Arrays to turn the array into a java.util.List, and from there we get its iterator. The code for the helper method is shown here:

```
    private Iterator iter;

    public int doStartTag() throws JspTagException{
      initializeIterator();
      if(!iter.hasNext()){
        return SKIP_BODY;
      }

      updatePageVariables();
      return EVAL_BODY_INCLUDE;
    }
```

```
private void initializeIterator() throws JspTagException{
  CategorySystem categorySystem =
    (CategorySystem) pageContext.getAttribute("categorySystem",
                                      pageContext.SESSION_SCOPE);
  if(categorySystem == null){
    throw new JspTagException("categorySystem not found in session");
  }

  Category category = categorySystem.getCurrentCategory();
  Subcategory [] subcategories = null;
  try{
    subcategories = category.getSubcategories();
  }
  catch(Exception e){
    throw new JspTagException("subcategories cannot be retrieved: " + e);
  }
  //iter is an instance variable.
  iter = Arrays.asList(subcategories).iterator();
}
```

We use another private helper method to update the scripting variables in the pageContext, and we use Iterator.hasNext() to determine the return value of doAfterBody():

```
public int doAfterBody(){
  if(iter.hasNext()){
    updatePageVariables();
    return EVAL_BODY_AGAIN;
  }
  return SKIP_BODY;
}

private void updatePageVariables(){
  Subcategory subCat = (Subcategory)iter.next();
  /*new values repalce previous ones, if any*/
  pageContext.setAttribute("subCatId", String.valueOf(subCat.getId()));
  pageContext.setAttribute("subCatName", subCat.getName());
}
```

Now all we have to do is build and run the tests. We discover that they all pass! Next, we ask ourselves, "Have we tested everything that could possibly break? " We haven't put the tag into its native JSP context yet, and until we do we can't be sure of it. We whip up a one-tag JSP to demonstrate use and verify that our tag library descriptor also works. We use the method outlined in the section "Tag Library Descriptor Testing" earlier in this chapter—using pageContext.include() to load and process the JSP. The following listing gives the test method from the JspTestCase as well as the test JSP itself.

```
/*test method from Catus test case*/
public void testListWithJsp() throws Exception{
  pageContext.include("subcategory_list_test.jsp");
}

/**** subcategory_list_test.jsp ****/
<%@taglib uri="WEB-INF/petstore-taglib.tld" prefix="petstore"%>
```

```
<petstore:subcategoryList>
  Name = <%= subCatName%>.<br>
  ID = <%= subCatId %>
</petstore:subcategoryList>
```

The error message Cactus dumps when we run the improved test reveals that we never wrote the tag library descriptor entry! (Unit tests are great for catching coarse errors as well as subtle ones.) We quickly write the deployment descriptor entry:

```
<tag>
  <name>subcategoryList</name>
  <tagclass>xptoolkit.petstore.tag.SubcategoryListTag</tagclass>
  <info>
    Iterates over all of the available subcategories. Provides two
    nested variables, "subCatName" and "subCatId" corresponding to
   same attributes of current subcategory.
  </info>
  <bodycontent>JSP</bodycontent>
  <variable>
    <name-given>subCatId</name-given>
    <declare>true</declare>
    <!-- default is nested -->
  </variable>
  <variable>
    <name-given>subCatName</name-given>
    <declare>true</declare>
    <!-- default is nested -->
  </variable>
</tag>
```

Once we verify that our code passes all our automated tests, we begin adding the tag to our JSPs. Here is the end result of one such replacement:

```
<petstore:subcategoryList>
        <a href="subcategory.jsp?id=<%= subCatId%>"><%= subCatName %></a>
        <br>
</petstore:subcategoryList>
```

One minor issue crops up while we are manually verifying that the pages do indeed still work (in a way, we are testing our tests). The variable names we have defined inside the subcategoryList tag conflict with other variables in the JSPs. We make the change (a very minor one), run our tests, and redeploy. Now all the modified pages (along with our tag code) have become production candidates. Because our tests let an error through, however, we are not content. We decide to add a link-checking spider to the suite of tests that are run with each build. I concur, and we add functional testing to our list of tasks.

Review of the Case Study

During this refactoring episode, we pulled code out of JSPs (the view in an MVC architecture) and encapsulated it in JSP custom tags. In the process, we made portions of the site's logic amenable to testing. This result represents a victory. Every piece of code that is paired with a unit test is a safe piece of code—one that you're not afraid to touch and redesign. Would we have written these tests without Cactus? Maybe not. Faced with mocking up portions of the servlet specification (and JSP, and custom tag specifications to boot!), even the most dedicated programming pair might have released their inner pig and relied on total visual inspection. Not only do we have better code for the future, but the test helped us write our tag today. Because we were forced to think through what defined a successful tag execution, we were able to meet that definition all the more rapidly.

Summary

JSP custom tags pose a few challenges to test developers with their complexity. For testing the logic of the tag handler class, we used Cactus's JspTestCase. JspTestCase provides access to JSP implicit objects (pageContext and out) as member variables in addition to the implicit objects of ServletTestCase. In order to thoroughly test a custom tag, we must also test the tag's library descriptor and/or its TagExtraInfo class. For this we used a JSP-based testing method. Although not entirely bulletproof, this method has the benefit of serving as executable documentation for our code.

Testing EJBs with Cactus

This chapter demonstrates the techniques for unit-testing Enterprise JavaBeans (EJBs) using Cactus. At the time of this writing, Cactus does not include any EJB redirectors. However, you can use any of its TestCases (ServletTestCase, FilterTestCase, or JspTestCase) for testing EJBs.

Cactus offers powerful incentives for testing EJBs. Although there are alternate ways that can be used to test EJBs, such as JUnit or mock objects, the following benefits are a direct result of using Cactus:

- ❏ **Testing of Enterprise Beans with local interfaces:** Because local EJBs can be accessed only inside of a container, you need a framework like Cactus for testing.

- ❏ **Continuous integration:** Cactus provides a set of Ant tasks to help automate EJB tests. Using these tasks, you can start the EJB server, run the tests, and stop the server. For more information on integrating Cactus and Ant see http://jakarta.apache.org/cactus/integration/ant/index.html.

- ❏ **Consistent test coverage:** Applications for EJBs often include servlets, JSPs, and other such container components. With Cactus you can thoroughly test these components and avoid inconsistencies by running your tests within the same environment as your container.

Let's now take a look at a simple local stateless session bean (local SLSB). The following listing gives the code for the OrderReportBean. The OrderReportBean SLSB returns a list of orders placed within a given date range:

```
public class OrderReportBean implements SessionBean {
    private String queryStatement = "SELECT ID, " +
                                    "TOTAL " +
                                    "FROM ORDER order " +
                                    "WHERE order.ORDER_DATE BETWEEN ?
    AND ? ";
```

```
    public List ordersByDateRange(java.util.Date startDate, java.util.Date
endDate) throws EJBException{
        ResultSet rs = null;
        PreparedStatement stmt=null;
        Connection conn = null;
        List records = null;

        try {
            conn = getConnection(); //getConnection() not listed here
            stmt = conn.prepareStatement(queryStatement);
            stmt.setDate(1, new java.sql.Date(startDate.getTime()));
            stmt.setDate(2, new java.sql.Date(endDate.getTime()));
            rs = stmt.executeQuery();
            records = new ArrayList();
        Map record = new HashMap();
            while(rs.next()){
                        record.put(rs.getInt(1), rs.getDouble(2));
records.add(record);
            }
        }
        catch (SQLException e){
            throw new RuntimeException(e, "unable to get orders by date
range. " + queryStatement);
        }
        finally{
            try {
                if (rs!=null)rs.close();
                if (stmt!=null)stmt.close();
                if (conn!=null)conn.close();
            }
            catch (SQLException e){
                throw new RuntimeException(e, "unable to get orders by date
range. " + queryStatement);
            }
        }
        return records;
    }

    public void ejbActivate() throws EJBException{}
    public void ejbPassivate() throws EJBException {}
    public void ejbCreate() throws EJBException {}
    public void ejbRemove() throws EJBException {}
    public void setSessionContext(javax.ejb.SessionContext context) throws
EJBException {}
}
```

Writing a test for the OrderReportBean is straightforward. First, we extend ServletTestCase. Then, we perform a lookup on our EJB in the setUp() method. OrderReportBeanTest gets its environment properties from the container; thus we do not specify any JNDI properties before calling new InitialContext():

```
public void setUp()throws Exception{
    OrderReportHome home = (OrderReportHome)new
InitialContext().lookup("ejb/xptoolkit/OrderReport");
  orderReport = home.create();
        start = formatter.parse("01/01/2001");
```

```
        end = formatter.parse("01/01/2035");
    createTestOrders(); // insert some test orders
}
```

We test the ordersByDateRange method in our EJB by verifying that it returns a non-empty list:

```
    public void testOrdersByDateRange() {
   List records = orderReport.ordersByDateRange (start, end);
        assertTrue(records.size() > 0);
        }
```

At last, we clean up the test data:

```
    public void tearDown()throws Exception{
   deleteTestOrders(); //delete test orders


    }
```

The following listing contains the complete code for OrderReportBeanTest.

```
package xptoolkit;
import java.text.SimpleDateFormat;
import java.util.Date;

import junit.framework.Test;
import junit.framework.TestSuite;

import org.apache.cactus.ServletTestCase;

public class OrderReportBeanTest extends ServletTestCase {
    private OrderReport orderReport;
    private Date start;
    private Date end;
    private SimpleDateFormat formatter = new SimpleDateFormat("MM/dd/yyyy");

    public OrderReportBeanTest(java.lang.String testName) {
        super(testName);
    }

    public void setUp()throws Exception{
    OrderReportHome home = (OrderReportHome)new
InitialContext().lookup("ejb/xptoolkit/OrderReport");
  orderReport = home.create();
        start = formatter.parse("01/01/2001");
        end = formatter.parse("01/01/2035");
    createTestOrders(); //create test data — code not shown
    }

    public void testOrdersByDateRange() {
   List records = orderReport.ordersByDateRange (start, end);
        assertTrue(records.size() > 0);
        }

    public void tearDown()throws Exception{
    deleteTestOrders(); //delete test data - code not shown
```

```
        }

    public static void main(java.lang.String[] args) {
        junit.textui.TestRunner.run(suite());
    }

    public static Test suite() {
        TestSuite suite = new TestSuite(OrderReportBeanTest.class);

        return suite;
    }
}
```

Creating an Ant Buildfile to Run the Test

To run the test, we use the Ant tasks from the Cactus-Ant integration project. First, we "cactify" the WAR and update the EAR:

```
...
<cactifywar version="2.3" destfile="${build.dir}/project.war">
<classes dir="${build.dir}"/>
</cactifywar>

<ear update="true" destfile="${build.dir}/project.ear">
<fileset dir="${build.dir}">
<include name="project.war"/>
</fileset>
</ear>

...
```

The <cactifywar> task adds definitions for the Cactus test redirectors, deployment descriptors, and server-side JARs.

To run the test, we use the <cactus> task. The <cactus> task extends the standard <junit> task, and thus inherits all its attributes. In addition, it deploys the EAR, starts the container, runs the tests, and then stops the container.

```
...
    <cactus earfile="${build.dir}/ejb.ear" fork="yes"
        printsummary="yes" haltonerror="true"
        haltonfailure="true">

            <formatter type="plain" usefile="false"/>
            <containerset>
                <jboss3x dir="${jboss.home}"
                output="serveroutput.txt"/>
            </containerset>
            <test name="xptoolkit.OrderReportBeanTest"/>
            <classpath>
                <pathelement location="${build.dir}"/>
            </classpath>
    </cactus>
...
```

For complete details on the Cactus-Ant integration, please see http://jakarta.apache.org/cactus/integration/ant/index.html.

In the next section, we go over the process of adding an entity bean to the PetStore application from the previous chapter. The case study also shows how to unit-test an entity bean that uses container-managed persistence (CMP).

Case Study: Adding an Entity Bean to the Pet Store

In this section of the chapter we add an Enterprise JavaBean to our pet store application and step through the process of deployment.

Adding an Enterprise JavaBean to the Pet Store

This section adds a feature to the baseline pet store application: the ability to add, edit, and delete products from the Web. We have decided to use a container-managed entity EJB. Thus, we need to do the following:

1. Create the product entity bean.
2. Add a new subproject buildfile for EJBs.
3. Add a new test case class to test our Product EJB.
4. Update our categorySystem class.
5. Create an HTML form.
6. Add additional JSPs to handle the form submission and the back-end navigation.

Following is a block diagram of how the output will look when we are done.

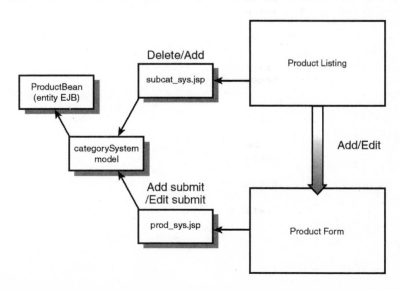

Security and Authentication

In the real world, you should password-protect your product entry management. Servlets 2.3 enables you to do this with a servlet filter. Or you can do this
with Web authentication provided by your application server or Web server.
This example does not demonstrate authentication, but you can add it without
changing the JSPs introduced with any of the methods we use.

The entity bean is fairly simple, because it is uses container-managed persistence (CMP). The container
takes care of persisting the bean to the database. The next three listings contain the complete product
entity bean: its interface, implementation, and home, respectively. With this product entity bean we add,
delete, and edit product entries. You can use a number of techniques and design patterns to reduce the
number of remote procedure calls; for simplicity, we don't use them here.

```java
package xptoolkit.petstore.entity;

import javax.ejb.*;
import java.rmi.RemoteException;

public interface Product extends EJBObject {

    public String getDescription()throws RemoteException;
    public String getName()throws RemoteException;
    public Integer getId()throws RemoteException;
    public int getSubcategoryId() throws RemoteException;
    public int getQty()throws RemoteException;
    public java.math.BigDecimal getPrice()throws RemoteException;


    public void setDescription(String description)throws RemoteException;
    public void setName(String name)throws RemoteException;
    public void setId(Integer ID)throws RemoteException;
    public void setSubcategoryId(int subcat)throws RemoteException;
    public void setQty(int qty)throws RemoteException;
    public void setPrice(java.math.BigDecimal price)throws RemoteException;

}
```

```java
package xptoolkit.petstore.entity;

import javax.ejb.*;

public class ProductBean implements EntityBean {

    EntityContext ctx;
    public String description;
    public String name;
    public Integer id;
    public int subcategoryId;
```

```java
    public int qty;
    public java.math.BigDecimal price;

    public Integer ejbCreate (Integer id, String name, int qty,
                    String description, int subCat,
                    java.math.BigDecimal price){
        this.id = id;
        this.name=name;
        this.description=description;
        this.qty=qty=0;
        subcategoryId=subCat;
        this.price= price;
        return null;
    }

    public void ejbPostCreate(Integer _id, String name, int qty,
                    String description, int subCat,
                    java.math.BigDecimal price){
        id = (Integer)ctx.getPrimaryKey();
        System.out.println("Product ID " + id);
    }

    public String getDescription(){return description;}
    public String getName(){return name;}
    public Integer getId(){return id;}
    public int getSubcategoryId(){return subcategoryId;}
    public int getQty(){return qty;}
    public java.math.BigDecimal getPrice(){return price;}

    public void setDescription(String description)
                                    {this.description=description;}
    public void setName(String name){this.name=name;}
    public void setId(Integer id){this.id=id;}
    public void setSubcategoryId(int subcategoryId)
                                    {this.subcategoryId=subcategoryId;}
    public void setQty(int qty){this.qty=qty;}
    public void setPrice(java.math.BigDecimal price){this.price=price;}

    public void setEntityContext(EntityContext ctx) { this.ctx = ctx; }
    public void unsetEntityContext() { ctx = null; }
    public void ejbActivate() { }
    public void ejbPassivate() { }
    public void ejbLoad() { }
    public void ejbStore() { }
    public void ejbRemove() { }

}


package xptoolkit.petstore.entity;

import javax.ejb.*;
import java.util.*;
```

```java
import java.rmi.RemoteException;

public interface ProductHome extends EJBHome {

    public Product create(Integer id, String name, int qty,
                          String description, int subCat,
                          java.math.BigDecimal price)
                            throws RemoteException, CreateException;

    Product findByPrimaryKey(Integer key)
                            throws RemoteException, FinderException;

    Collection findAll()throws RemoteException, FinderException;

    Collection findBySubcategoryId()throws RemoteException, FinderException;

}
```

```xml
<ejb-jar>

<description>
This ejb-jar files contains the Enterprise beans for the
Petstore Case Study
</description>
<enterprise-beans>
  <entity>
    <ejb-name>ProductBean</ejb-name>
    <home>xptoolkit.petstore.entity.ProductHome</home>
    <remote>xptoolkit.petstore.entity.Product</remote>
    <ejb-class>xptoolkit.petstore.entity.ProductBean</ejb-class>
    <persistence-type>Container</persistence-type>
    <prim-key-class>java.lang.Integer</prim-key-class>
    <primkey-field>id</primkey-field>
    <reentrant>False</reentrant>
    <cmp-field><field-name>description</field-name></cmp-field>
    <cmp-field><field-name>name</field-name></cmp-field>
    <cmp-field><field-name>id</field-name></cmp-field>
    <cmp-field><field-name>subcategoryId</field-name></cmp-field>
    <cmp-field><field-name>qty</field-name></cmp-field>
    <cmp-field><field-name>price</field-name></cmp-field>
  </entity>

</enterprise-beans>
<assembly-descriptor>
  <container-transaction>
    <method>
      <ejb-name>ProductBean</ejb-name>
      <method-name>*</method-name>
    </method>
    <trans-attribute>Required</trans-attribute>
```

```
    </container-transaction>
  </assembly-descriptor>
</ejb-jar>
```

The new ProductTest (test.xptoolkit.petstore.entity.ProductTest) is used to test the entity bean (xptoolkit.petstore.entity.Product).

ProductTestCase extends Cactus's ServletTestCase and thus gets its JNDI properties from the container. In order to create, find, and delete Products, we first need to locate an instance of the home interface as follows:

```
protected void setUp()throws Exception{
    Object ref;
    InitialContext jndiContext= new InitialContext();
    ref = jndiContext.lookup("ProductBean");
    home = (ProductHome)
            PortableRemoteObject.narrow (ref, ProductHome.class);
}
```

This is fairly standard client-side EJB code. The first test uses the home interface to create a product entity with test data:

```
public void testCreate()throws Exception{
    product = home.create(new Integer(876662), "Rick", 5, "you ", 555,
new java.math.BigDecimal("1200"));
    assertNotNull("product", product);
    assertEquals("name", "Rick", product.getName());

}
```

As you can see, the first and second tests depend on each other; they are order dependent. The scenario works because the test framework uses reflection, and reflection uses the methods in the order they are declared. This code is brittle and depends on some minutia in the Java reflection API. You can ensure the order of execution by explicitly setting it in the suite() method instead of relying on the generic reflection-based methods. The TestSuite has an addTest() method that lets you add test cases to it. You could also OrderedTestSuite available in junit-addons (http://sourceforge.net/projects/junit-addons).

The second test finds the entity created with the first test and then deletes that entity by calling the product entities' remove() method. Then, to make sure the entity was removed, the test tries to find it again. If the home interface's findByPrimaryKey() method does not find the object, we return; otherwise, we force a fail by calling fail(), as follows:

```
public void testRemove()throws Exception{
    product = home.findByPrimaryKey(new Integer(876662));
    product.remove();

    try{
        product = home.findByPrimaryKey(new Integer(876662));
    }
    catch(javax.ejb.ObjectNotFoundException e){
        return;
    }

}
```

```
            fail("Product entity should already be gone and not findable.");
    }
```

The other methods test the setter and getter methods of the product, as follows:

```
    /** Test of setter methods, of class
                        xptoolkit.petstore.model.Product. */
    public void testSetters() throws Exception{
        testCreate();
        product.setName("Boo");
        product.setDescription("Designer");
        product.setQty(5);
        testRemove();
    }

    /** Test of getter methods, of class
                        xptoolkit.petstore.model.Product. */
    public void testGetters() throws Exception{
        testCreate();
        this.assertEquals("name", product.getName(), "Rick");
        this.assertEquals("description", product.getDescription(),
                                                    "you ");

        product.setName("Boo");
        product.setDescription("Designer");
        product.setQty(5);


        this.assertEquals("name", product.getName(), "Boo");
        this.assertEquals("description", product.getDescription(),
"Designer");
        testRemove();


    }
```

The tests in ProductTest are quite simple. They ensure that we have set up and created our entity bean correctly. Please see the following listing for the complete ProductTest code.

```
package test.xptoolkit.petstore.entity;
import org.apache.cactus.*;
import java.util.Properties;
import javax.rmi.PortableRemoteObject;
import javax.naming.*;

import xptoolkit.petstore.entity.Product;
import xptoolkit.petstore.entity.ProductHome;


public class ProductTest extends ServletTestCase {

    Product product;
    ProductHome home;

    protected void setUp()throws Exception{
```

```java
        Object ref;
        InitialContext jndiContext = new InitialContext();
        ref  = jndiContext.lookup("ProductBean");
        home = (ProductHome)
                PortableRemoteObject.narrow (ref, ProductHome.class);
    }


    public static void main(java.lang.String[] args) {
        junit.textui.TestRunner.run(suite());
    }

    public static Test suite() {
        TestSuite suite = new TestSuite(ProductTest.class);

        return suite;
    }

    public void testCreate()throws Exception{
        product = home.create(new Integer(876662), "Rick", 5, "you ", 555,
                new java.math.BigDecimal(1200));
        assertNotNull("product", product);
        assertEquals("name", "Rick", product.getName());


    }

    public void testRemove()throws Exception{
        product = home.findByPrimaryKey(new Integer(876662));
        product.remove();

        try{
            product = home.findByPrimaryKey(new Integer(876662));
        }
        catch(javax.ejb.ObjectNotFoundException e){
            return;

        }

        fail("Product entity should already be gone and not findable.");
    }


    /** Test of getSetter methods, of class
                                xptoolkit.petstore.model.Product. */
    public void testSetters() throws Exception{
        testCreate();
        product.setName("Boo");
        product.setDescription("Designer");
        product.setQty(5);
        testRemove();
    }

    /** Test of getter methods, of class
                                xptoolkit.petstore.model.Product. */
```

```
public void testGetters() throws Exception{
    testCreate();
    this.assertEquals("name", product.getName(), "Rick");
    this.assertEquals("description", product.getDescription(), "you ");

    product.setName("Boo");
    product.setDescription("Designer");
    product.setQty(5);
    this.assertEquals("name", product.getName(), "Boo");
    this.assertEquals("description", product.getDescription(),
                                                "Designer");
    testRemove();

}
}
```

IDEs support JUnit and Ant

Plug-ins are available for Eclipse, Forte, NetBeans, TogetherSoft ControlCenter, JBuilder, and so on for both JUnit and Ant. We create many of our tests by generating the tests' started code in the NetBeans IDE. The ProductTest started code was initially generated with NetBeans support for JUnit. You specify the class, and NetBeans generates the started skeleton to test your class. Cool beans!

It's our considered opinion that no JSP should know whether you are using JDBC, flat files, or entity beans to manage the persistence of the system. Thus, we decided to add support for adding and removing products behind the CategorySystem façade class. In fact, the implementation of the client-side piece of the Product entity is in CategoryDB, and the public interface is defined in the Category abstract class.

Here are the additional methods that we added to the CategorySystem class (xptoolkit.petstore.model .CategorySystem):

```
public void createProduct(Product product) throws Exception{
    currentCategory.createProduct(product);
    if(currentSubcategory!=null)currentSubcategory.invalidate();
}
public void editProduct(Product product) throws Exception{
    currentCategory.editProduct(product);
    if(currentSubcategory!=null)currentSubcategory.invalidate();
}
public void deleteProduct(int id) throws Exception{
    currentCategory.deleteProduct(id);
    if(currentSubcategory!=null)currentSubcategory.invalidate();
}
```

Here are the corresponding methods we added to the Category class:

```
public abstract void createProduct(Product product) throws Exception;
public abstract void editProduct(Product product) throws Exception;
public abstract void deleteProduct(int id) throws Exception;
```

The actual implementation of these methods is in the CategoryDB class, as follows:

```
public void createProduct(Product product) throws Exception{
    getHome().create(new Integer(product.getId()),
                        product.getName(),
                        product.getQty(),
                        product.getDescription(),
                        product.getFkSubcategoryId(),
                        new java.math.BigDecimal(product.getPrice()));
}
public void editProduct(Product product) throws Exception{
    xptoolkit.petstore.entity.Product p
                =getHome().findByPrimaryKey(
new Integer(product.getId()));
        p.setName(product.getName());
        p.setDescription(product.getDescription());
        p.setPrice(new java.math.BigDecimal(product.getPrice()));
        p.setQty(product.getQty());
}

public void deleteProduct(int id) throws Exception{
        getHome().findByPrimaryKey(new Integer(id)).remove();
}

private ProductHome getHome() throws Exception{
    Object ref;
    InitialContext jndiContext = new InitialContext();
    ref  = jndiContext.lookup("ProductBean");
    return (ProductHome)
                PortableRemoteObject.narrow (ref, ProductHome.class);
}
```

This code should look familiar. It is much like the code in our test, except that now we are using it to implement the public interface to our Web application. You should add tests at the boundary points to every tier in an n-tier architecture. That way, you test the public interface of each tier. This approach becomes particularly useful if things begin to go wrong; when debugging a distributed multi-tiered application, it's helpful to be able to test access to each tier independently from the rest of the added business logic in the encapsulating tier.

Because the CategorySystem is a very thin wrapper in the case of adding, removing, and editing products, we decided to add the tests in the CategoryTest as follows:

```
public void testCreateDeleteProduct() throws Exception {
    . . .
    Product p = new Product(){};
    p.setId(1119996);
    p.setFkSubcategoryId(111);
    p.setName("Test1");
    p.setDescription("Test1 Description");
    p.setPrice(11);
    p.setPrice(6);
    category.createProduct(p);
```

```
Product p2 = category.getProduct(1119996);
assertEquals("name after create",p2.getName(), p.getName());

p.setName("Test2");
category.editProduct(p);
Product p3 = category.getProduct(1119996);
assertEquals("name after edit", p3.getName(), p.getName());


category.deleteProduct(p.getId());
Product p4 = category.getProduct(1119996);
this.assertEquals("product should be gone", -1, p4.getId());
    }
```

This code is fairly simple, because the actual product implementation is tested thoroughly in the entity ProductTest. Essentially, the test creates a product, edits it, and deletes it. It makes sure the product data is added, edited, and removed. Here the test creates the product by calling the category createProduct() method:

```
Product p = new Product(){};
p.setId(1119996);
p.setFkSubcategoryId(111);
p.setName("Test1");
p.setDescription("Test1 Description");
p.setPrice(11);
p.setPrice(6);
category.createProduct(p);
```

Next, the test verifies that the product was actually created by looking it up:

```
Product p2 = category.getProduct(1119996);
assertEquals("name after create",p2.getName(), p.getName());
```

Here the test edits the product by changing the product object and then submitting it. Then, the test makes sure the product was edited:

```
p.setName("Test2");
category.editProduct(p);
Product p3 = category.getProduct(1119996);
assertEquals("name after edit", p3.getName(), p.getName());
```

Finally, the test removes the product, as follows:

```
category.deleteProduct(p.getId());
Product p4 = category.getProduct(1119996);
this.assertEquals("proudct should be gone", -1, p4.getId());
```

One thing is wrong with this test. It should be further functionally decomposed. For example, let's say the create part or the delete part fails. The output of the test will not make clear which functionality was not working. There is a fine line between being overly cautious and sloppy. The more you functionally decompose, the better your reports will be able to point you to the correct failure point.

So, let's decompose the test a little further. We can see that we are doing four things: creating a product, getting a product from the data store, editing a product, and deleting a product from the data store. We begin by moving the test data that the tests will share to the setUp() method, as follows:

```
Product p;

public void setUp()throws Exception{
        .  .  .
        .  .  .
        p = new Product(){};
        p.setId(1119996);
        p.setFkSubcategoryId(111);
        p.setName("Test1");
        p.setDescription("Test1 Description");
        p.setPrice(11);
        p.setPrice(6);

}
```

Notice that the test object p is now an instance variable, so it can be used in all four tests. The next step is to break the method testCreateDeleteProduct() into four methods. We add the product from the setUp() method:

```
public void testCreateProduct() throws Exception {
        category.createProduct(p);
}
```

The next test tests the ability to get the product out of the database. Notice that you could combine this get-product test and the previous test, because this one validates the create-product test:

```
public void testGetProduct()throws Exception {
    Product p2 = category.getProduct(1119996);
    assertEquals("name after create",p2.getName(), p.getName());
}
```

The next test tests the ability to edit an existing product:

```
public void testEditProduct() throws Exception {
    p.setName("Test2");
    category.editProduct(p);
    Product p3 = category.getProduct(1119996);
    assertEquals("name after edit", p3.getName(), p.getName());
}
```

Finally, we test the deletion of the product as follows:

```
public void testDeleteProduct()throws Exception {
    category.deleteProduct(p.getId());
    Product p4 = category.getProduct(1119996);
    this.assertEquals("proudct should be gone", -1, p4.getId());
}
```

You really need to try and keep tests as small and atomic in operation as possible. If something breaks in the future, the test will identify exactly what broke. If we had left the test as it was and something broke, it would be hard to tell what broke—not impossible, but difficult. Plus, these methods describe exactly what we are testing.

Summary

In this chapter, we saw that testing EJBs with Cactus is a straightforward process. Cactus offers a comprehensive framework for testing J2EE components. With Cactus, we are guaranteed consistent results by running our tests within the same execution environment as our container. In addition, the Cactus-Ant integration helps automate testing, thus lessening the burden of building, deploying, and running the tests as well as having to manually start and stop the container.

22

Code Coverage with jcoverage

Code coverage represents a new facet of test driven development (TDD), that is moving many developers to write their tests first and their classes to fit the tests. Code coverage aids this philosophy by ensuring that you are indeed testing what you think you are testing. It also allows you to quickly fix your tests for new pieces of functionality, by highlighting new or changed code that may not be properly tested. This enables developers to move forward with confidence that their code is fully tested.

As part of any unit testing implementation you should seriously consider adding code coverage to your toolbox. jcoverage is one such tool. There are other options: Quilt, another open source project, offers the same kind of reports; and there is Clover, which is a closed source but open source project-friendly tool. Of these tools, though, we use jcoverage for several reasons: it is code-complete, it is available under the GPL license for free use, and there is a closed source version with advanced features also available.

So, what does jcoverage offer you? jcoverage uses byte-code manipulation or enhancement to hook into your base classes for unit testing analysis. jcoverage refers to this as *instrumentation*, and it uses this instrumentation along with your unit tests to generate reports. The reports list classes that you haven't completely tested, as well as problematic areas in your code that could cause you grief later on. By doing this it can ensure that you are indeed properly testing all of your code— you are "test-infected" aren't you? After all, code that isn't properly tested is potentially buggy code, and that is something that none of us wants.

> **Where to Get jcoverage**
>
> jcoverage was created by jcoverage ltd. It is available in two versions jcoverage+ which is a commercial product or jcoverage which is licensed under the GNU Public License and is available as a free download. jcoverage+ adds in quite a few features and is worth checking out if you like the open source version. Both versions can be downloaded from:
>
> http://www.jcoverage.com/

Why Code Coverage?

While code coverage is not a strictly a necessity for most projects, it is highly desirable and adds very little overhead. Projects that are developed using an Agile methodology should definitely add a code coverage tool to its toolbox. No matter how well you think you are testing, there is always something you have missed. The first time I ran jcoverage against one of my projects, I was astonished at the little things I hadn't even thought about. In going through the report and thinking about it, though, it all made sense. Code coverage helps you become a better programmer. Like unit testing, code coverage can greatly improve the quality of your projects. You may be thinking "I've only got a 10 file project, why should I use code coverage?" I would counter with these reasons:

1. Small projects often turn into bigger projects as people make requests or new functionality is added.

2. You may move on, leaving the project, and someone else will have to pick the project up. By adding code coverage you ensure that what you have written is properly tested and that any changes future developers make will also have to be tested. This ensures that they write code that is properly tested.

3. Agile projects are constantly refactored to make them better. By using a code coverage tool you ensure that your refactorings are properly covered through your tests.

Code coverage is something that can become invaluable for a larger project. If your project has been performing unit tests for awhile, code coverage can illuminate holes in your tests so that you can go back incrementally and fix those tests until you achieve 100% coverage. Code coverage isn't an all-or-nothing deal. Like unit tests, it can be added at any time to ensure a higher-quality, better tested, and easier to understand application.

How does it work? Coverage analyzers add instrumentation. There are three types of instrumentation that can be added: source code instrumentation through a code pre-processor, byte-code instrumentation through a tool like cglib, and running code through a modified JVM.

Byte-code manipulation/enhancement occurs is the process by which a program takes the class file that your compiler produces and inserts new code into your methods. The inserted code could be aspect-oriented in nature, like adding a logging call into each method, or the code might enhance your class by dynamically adding properties to it. Bytecode enhancement appears to be gaining popularity for a wide variety of tasks. Currently you will see a type of enhancement in AspectJ (http://www.eclipse.org/aspectj) that takes custom aspects and merges them with existing code after the code has been compiled. Tapestry uses bytecode enhancement through JavAssist (http://www.csg.is.titech.ac.jp/~chiba/javassist/) when it automatically extends abstract classes and provides implementations of abstract methods you have declared, thereby simplifying the development process.

Until bytecode manipulation becomes more standardized, however, we may run into future problems with doing too much to pre-compiled classes. Some projects are already colliding and will not work together properly. For example you may have difficulty running jcoverage on classes that have had aspects added to them through AspectJ.

Types of Coverage

There are several types of code coverage that tools offer these are:

- ❑ **Statement or line coverage:** Indicates the degree to which individual statements are getting executed during test execution.

- ❑ **Basic block coverage:** Considers each sequence of non-branching statements as its unit of code instead of individual statements.

- ❑ **Branch coverage:** Indicates whether decision points such as if and while statements are executed through their corresponding branches with the tests.

- ❑ **Path coverage:** Indicates whether each possible path from start of the method to the end of the method is getting exercised—this is different from Branch coverage in that Branch coverage considers each individual branch, whereas Path coverage looks at the logic paths altogether.

- ❑ **Function coverage:** Indicates whether each function is called during the test.

- ❑ **Race coverage:** Indicates when multiple threads are run what resources are shared amongst the threads and can indicate a possible race condition.

- ❑ **Relational operator coverage:** Iindicates the amount of coverage you have on operators such as a < 4; for instance, have you tested all the possibilities (such as 2, 3, 4, and 5)?

jcoverage Primer

There are three ways to run jcoverage on your project: from the command-line, as an Ant script, or as a Maven plugin. We are going to cover how to run and interpret jcoverage reports as an Ant script and cover any issues with running it as a Maven plugin.

jcoverage as an Ant task

Adding jcoverage reports to your Ant buildfile is relatively easy. First you need to download the jcoverage/gpl JAR file and its third-party JAR files to your local hard drive. Place these files where your Ant project can find it— typically this means that you can add it to your project's lib directory and reference it using your Ant buildfile (for more information about Ant, see Chapter 4). Once you have done that, you can add the JAR file to your build.xml:

```
<path id="jcoverage.path">
 <fileset dir="${lib.dir}">
        <include name="jcoverage.jar"/>
        <include name="log4j*.jar"/>
        <include name="bcel.jar"/>
        <include name="jakarta-oro*.jar"/>
        <include name="java-getopt*.jar"/>
 </fileset>
</path>
<taskdef classpath="jcoverage.path" resource="tasks.properties"/>
```

This adds the following tasks to your Ant build file:

❑   **instrument:** Instructs jcoverage what classes to add to the instrumentation and where to put the instrumented classes.

❑   **jtestrun:** This will run your tests through jcoverage so that jcoverage can analyze the tests and their coverage.

❑   **report:** Allows you to create custom reporting, such as xml and html.

❑   **merge:** Allows you to merge multiple jcoverage runs together into one comprehensive report.

❑   **check:** Specifies a pain threshold for coverage testing. If your project falls below a certain coverage percentage on either line or branch testing, check will fail and send up a red flag.

jcoverage puts all the information that it uncovers into a serialized file (.ser). You can specify additional files that can be merged together for different testing types (such as unit and functionality testing). In this way you create one comprehensive coverage report, instead of dealing with multiple ones.

Adding the Necessary Pieces to Your buildfile

Once you have added the jars as classpath references, you then add the taskdef element (as seen above). The next step is to make sure that you are running your JUnit tests correctly. This means that we need to instrument the classes first so that jcoverage can collect the information that it needs to build a report. This requires some setup first as we need to tell Ant where we want all the files to go first.

```
<property name="build.dir" value="${basedir}/build/"/>
<property name="build.classes.dir" value="${build.dir}/classes"/>
<property name="build.test-classes.dir" value="${build.dir}/test-classes"/>
<property name="build.instrumented-classes.dir"
value="${build.dir}/instrumented-classes"/>
<property name="build.coverage.dir" value="${build.dir}/coverage"/>
<property name="build.reports.dir" value="${build.dir}/reports"/>
<property name="lib.dir" value="${basedir}/lib"/>
<property name="src.dir" value="${basedir}/src/java"/>
<property name="test.dir" value="${basedir}/src/test"/>
```

Here is a brief description of the properties shown above:

❑   **build.dir:** The location we will build our application and tests to.

❑   **build.classes.dir:** The location our main classes that get built compile to.

- ❑ **build-test-classes.dir:** The location our test classes that get built compile to.
- ❑ **build-instrumented-classes.dir:** The location our modified classes (application only, not test) get compiled to.
- ❑ **build.coverage.dir:** The location our coverage reports that are created are sent to.
- ❑ **build.reports.dir:** The location our test reports that are created are sent to.
- ❑ **lib.dir:** The libraries directory; this is where jcoverage and other third-party JARs are placed.
- ❑ **src.dir:** The java source directory.
- ❑ **test.dir:** The test source directory.

Ok, so we have now defined all of our directories. Just like any build file we need to specify an init target that will create some of these directories that we need.

```
<target name="init">
    <mkdir dir="${build.dir}"/>
    <mkdir dir="${build.classes.dir}"/>
    <mkdir dir="${build.test-classes.dir}"/>
    <mkdir dir="${build.coverage.dir}"/>
    <mkdir dir="${build.instrumented-classes.dir}"/>
    <mkdir dir="${build.reports.dir}"/>
</target>
```

Next we need to compile our source files and then instrument them.

```
<target name="compile" description="compile all classes">
    <javac srcdir="${src.dir}" destdir="${build.classes.dir}"
failonerror="yes" debug="yes"/>
</target>
<target name="instrument" description="Add jcoverage instrumentation">
    <instrument todir="${build.instrumented-classes.dir}">
        <ignore regex="org.apache.log4j.*"/>
        <fileset dir="${build.classes.dir}">
          <include name="**/*.class"/>
        </fileset>
    </instrument>
</target>
```

This is fairly straightforward, but some explanation is warranted. First we call compile, which compiles the java files into class files. We then have the instrument target which calls its own task of instrument. The instrument task takes a todir argument to tell jcoverage where we wish to place the modified files—it's important that this be done to a separate directory as you don't want to distribute instrumented classes to your users (they are only meant for test coverage purposes). The body of the tag takes an Ant fileset specifying which classes to instrument. You can also specify packages to ignore using the ignore with a regex option; in this case we are telling jcoverage to ignore any line with a reference to log4j.

Now that we have instrumented our classes we want to run our unit tests on them.

```
<target name="test" description="Unit test the application">
<javac srcdir="${test.dir}" destdir="${build.test-classes.dir}"
failonerror="yes" debug="yes">
 <classpath refid="junit"/>
```

```
        <classpath location="${build.classes.dir}"/>
    </javac>
```

First we compile the test classes to the test-classes directory under build. Next we run the tests using junit. When running the tests we need to specify the instrumented classes prior to the real classes so that the instrumented classes are called first.

```
    <junit fork="yes" dir="${basedir}" errorProperty="test.failed"
  failureProperty="test.failed">
        <!--
          note the classpath order, instrumented classes are before the
          original (uninstrumented) classes.
        -->
        <classpath refid="junit"/>
        <classpath location="${build.instrumented-classes.dir}"/>
        <classpath location="${build.classes.dir}"/>
        <classpath location="${build.test-classes.dir}"/>
        <!--
          the instrumented classes reference classes used by the
          jcoverage runtime.
        -->
        <classpath refid="jcoverage.path"/>
        <formatter type="xml"/>

        <test name="${testcase}" todir="${build.reports.dir}" if="testcase"/>

        <batchtest todir="${build.reports.dir}" unless="testcase">
          <fileset dir="${build.test-classes.dir}">
            <include name="**/*Test.class"/>
          </fileset>
        </batchtest>
    </junit>
  </target>
```

This executes a standard unit test, but because we are using the instrumented classes it requires that we have the jcoverage jars in the testing classpath; otherwise our tests will fail. Upon completion of the unit testing, jcoverage will have collected all of its data in jcoverage.ser, which it will then use to create the coverage reports:.

```
  <target name="coverage" description="HTML and XML coverage reports can be
  found in build/coverage">
      <report srcdir="${src.dir}" destdir="${build.coverage.dir}"/>
      <report srcdir="${src.dir}" destdir="${build.coverage.dir}"
  format="xml"/>

      <echo>
  jcoverage reports have been generated.
  The HTML report is ${build.coverage.dir}/index.html
  The XML report is ${build.coverage.dir}/coverage.xml
          </echo>
  </target>
```

jcoverage creates two kind of reports: HTML and XML. In this example we specified that we want to see both. Now that we have built our reports, what do they look like? Here they are—the first figure shows the overall coverage report, and the second shows a class coverage report:

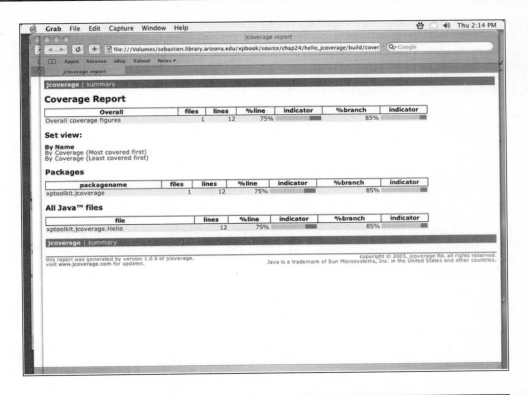

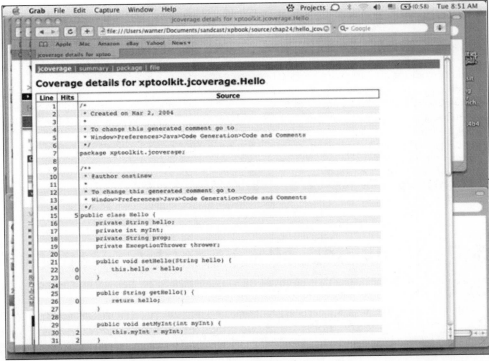

As you can see with our test class, we do not have 100% coverage, this is intentional to show what it looks when you don't have everything covered properly. We will examine what to do a little later in our case study.

jcoverage as a Maven Plugin

Installing the jcoverage Maven plugin is relatively easy; by default jcoverage is included as one of the optional plugins. If you want to use the latest jcoverage plugin, you will need to manually download it from http://maven.apache.org/reference/plugins/jcoverage/. Please follow the manual plugin installation instructions found in Chapter 26, "Managing Projects with Maven" of this book.

Once you have installed the plugin version you wish to use, you can set up jcoverage to be used in your Maven project. As with the Ant build file, there are a number of properties we can use to configure the plugin.

❑ **maven.jcoverage.dir:** Specifies the root directory for the jcoverage report output and defaults to ${maven.build.dir}/jcoverage. This property should not need to be changed.

❑ **maven.jcoverage.instrumentation:** Specifies where you would like the instrumented files to live and defaults to ${maven.jcoverage.dir}/classes, it also should not need to be changed.

❑ **maven.jcoverage.junit.fork:** Specifies whether or not to fork junit into a separate JVM; it defaults to yes.

❑ **maven.jcoverage.merge.instrumentedFiles:** Specifies the instrumented files list to be merged as a comma-seperated list. Necessary only if you have several types of unit testing that need one report.

❑ **maven.jcoverage.merge.outputDir:** Specifies where the resulting jcoverage.ser file will be placed upon completion.

To call jcoverage you simply type

```
maven jcoverage or jcoverage:html-report
```

which will generate the HTML report that we saw above in the Ant section. To include this as one of the default reports for your project, you will need to add the following to the reports section of your Maven project.xml file:

```
<report>maven-jcoverage-plugin</report>
```

Now when you generate your Web site, this will automatically include the jcoverage reports for your project.

100% Go Code and 80% Exception Handling

What do we mean by this, exactly? One of your project goals should be that line and branch code coverage should be at 100% so that you do not have any obvious coverage holes. You should also be checking to make sure that you have at least 80% exception handling in your code; otherwise exceptions might get lost and go out to the user directly, rather than being captured by the application and showing something usable.

Now that we know this is our goal, how does jcoverage assist us in achieving it, and what are some of the weaknesses of the methods it uses so that we are aware of them and can work around them?

Statement or Line Coverage

As we discussed earlier, statement or line coverage is the indication of the degree to which individual statements or lines are called during a test execution; you can see this when you look at an individual class report:

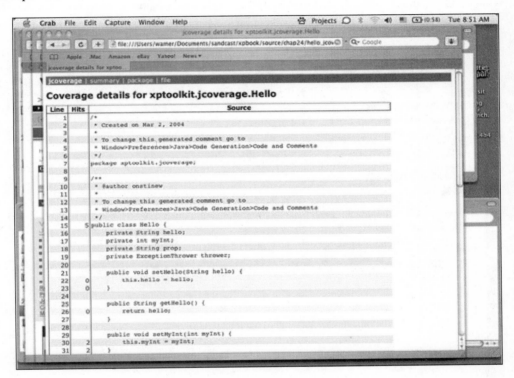

This report shows us how often a particular line was called during the test execution. jcoverage will show 0 counts and highlight the fact that the line has yet to be called. This is a very handy feature that enables you to quickly verify how your code is being called in tests.

One of the drawbacks of line coverage is that it doesn't indicate how much of your logic has been tested, only the particular lines that have been executed. This is where branch coverage steps in.

Branch Coverage

Branch coverage gives an indication of how our logic does or does not get called during tests. If we look at our example again, we see that by changing the addInt function to something like this:

```
public int addInt(int newInt) {
    if(newInt > 0) {
        return myInt + newInt;
    } else {
        return myInt;
    }
}
```

that our test code will not sufficiently capture the less than 0 conditional. jcoverage indicates this by showing a 0 line count in our class coverage report, and by decreasing our branch coverage percentage to 85%.

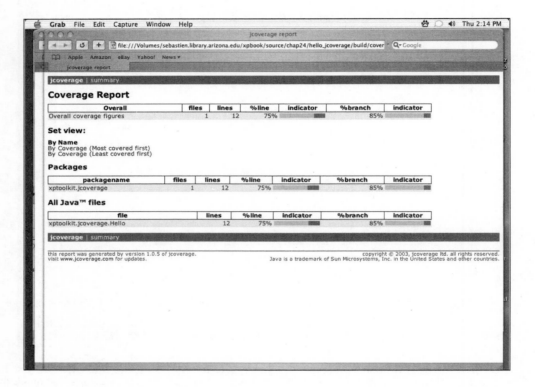

As we can see from this report screen we have now reduced our overall coverage by missing this simple branch test. But, some of the drawbacks of Branch coverage are that it may not capture the conditional coverage properly. We see that here when we change the setProperty method to look at different string types.

```
public void setProperty(String prop) {
        if(prop == "mystring" || prop == "someotherstring") {
                this.prop = prop;
        } else {
                this.prop = "mystring" + prop;
        }
}
```

Here is our corresponding jcoverage output:

As you can see, this does not truly capture our possible condition coverage. We are not testing all three conditions, but jcoverage only counts the two as missing (one for the "mystring" check, and the other for everything else), not the third option of "someotherstring".

Exception Handling

Here are the two classes in question—you will see the highlighting to indicate the Exception being thrown, and highlighting again where it is caught:

```
 2        * Created on Mar 4, 2004
 3        *
 4        * To change this generated comment go to
 5        * Window>Preferences>Java>Code Generation>Code and Comments
 6        */
 7       package xptoolkit.jcoverage;
 8
 9       /**
10        * @author onstinew
11        *
12        * To change this generated comment go to
13        * Window>Preferences>Java>Code Generation>Code and Comments
14        */
15       public class ExceptionThrower {
16
17           private String prop;
18
19           public ExceptionThrower(){
20    1          super();
21    1      }
22
23           public void setSomeOtherProp(String myProp) throws Exception {
24    1          if(!myProp.equalsIgnoreCase("my property")) {
25    0              throw new Exception("Incorrect property set!");
26               } else {
27    1              prop = myProp;
28               }
29    1      }
30
31           public String getSomeOtherProp() {
32    1          return prop;
33           }
34    }
```

jcoverage | summary | package | file

```
38    1          if(newInt > 0) {
39    1              return myInt + newInt;
40               } else {
41    0              return myInt;
42               }
43
44           }
45
46           public void setProperty(String prop) {
47    1          if(prop == "mystring" || prop == "someotherstring") {
48    1              this.prop = prop;
49               } else {
50    0              this.prop = "mystring" + prop;
51               }
52    1      }
53
54           public String getProperty() {
55    1          return this.prop;
56           }
57
58           public void setExceptionThrower(String prop) {
59    1          thrower = new ExceptionThrower();
60               try {
61    1              thrower.setSomeOtherProp(prop);
62    1          } catch (Exception e) {
63                   //do nothing
64    0          }
65    1      }
66
67           public String getExceptionThrowerProperty() {
68    1          return thrower.getSomeOtherProp();
69           }
70    }
```

jcoverage | summary | package | file

By changing the way our test runs, we can easily test whether or not an exception will get thrown, but it is the base code in Hello.java that needs to be changed in order to do something with the exception once it is caught. Another item that jcoverage doesn't completely pick up on is the branch coverage for the exception. Even though it shows 100% branch coverage, we have not exercised the two possible branches here to the greatest conclusion. jcoverage does pick up on the line coverage for the unexercised branch.

It can be very tricky to decipher what any ccoverage tool is telling you about exception handling. In our simple case it's rather straightforward. We are not exercising the Exception code either in the throwing stage or in catching. Unfortunately jcoverage does not have a built-in function to check that all exception code is exercised; it can only perform the more general line and branch coverage, but this it does well. Paying attention to when you should be doing something with an exception and when you aren't fully exercising all of your code will help you in determining whether or not your code is ready to go.

Diminishing Return

Now let's try and improve our percentage rating by testing our addInt() branch with a negative number.

```
assertEquals(7, hello.addInt(-1));
```

So, what does this get us?

As you can see from this, jcoverage thinks that we are completely covering our addInt() method, increasing our percentage to 90%, however we haven't fully tested this method, we are missing the newInt == 0 condition.

```
public int addInt(int newInt) {
        if(newInt > 0) {
                return myInt + newInt;
        } else {
                return myInt;
        }
}
```

Adding this method into our testing might increase our code coverage percentage, but jcoverage does not seem to catch this possible one-off error that we have run into. Our code coverage percentage stays at 90%. What to do? Do we stop writing tests simply because the coverage tool tells us we've reached our goal? My answer, of course, is no. By writing complete tests we again ensure that we are testing everything. The coverage tool is just there to help catch it before it becomes a big problem, or to put forward a goal for you to attain. And, if you aren't happy with one coverage tool, try another—perhaps it will use a different algorithm that catches more.

Setting Goals

One of the nice things that you can do using jcoverage is to set absolute percentage goals using the check ant target.

```
<check branch="95" line="95"/>
```

By adding this into the report target, or the test target, we are able to send up a flare warning developers that their intended goals have not been met. jcoverage does this by failing the test class for whichever class falls below the defined percentages you have indicated are acceptable. You can also set goals on a per-package basis that look like this:

```
<check branch="95" line="95">
 <regex pattern="xptoolkit.jcoverage.*" branch="85" line="95"/>
</check>
```

This would verify that everything that wasn't covered by the regex statement would be at 95% for branch coverage and 95% for line coverage, and that the particular package would be at 85% for branch and 95% for line. This is particularly useful if you have an old package that is slowly getting tests added to it—you can ensure that your tests still pass, but you will be made aware of the deficiency if you suddenly stop writing new tests for it.

Other Tools: GroboUtils

The list of useful code coverage tools continue to grow. GroboUtils is very similar to setting up jcoverage, with the exception of the Ant task names that need to be called when instrumenting your classes and running the reports. One drawback is that GroboUtils is not yet a Maven plugin. GroboUtils is an Open Source product licensed under the MIT Open Source License and can be downloaded from http://groboutils.sf.net.

Conclusion

This chapter addressed why code coverage is important to your project and how to use jcoverage to achieve the goals of 100% coverage and 80% exception handling. We have showed how to configure and use jcoverage in the Ant build tool and the Maven project management tool.

23

Swing Testing with Jemmy

In the world of Swing GUI testing, Jemmy has a unique position. While, at a core level, it does the same thing that the other Swing testers do, it goes about it in a very atypical fashion. It isn't a JUnit extension. Its methods don't return values that can easily be put in an assert statement. And, at first, it seems like it had been written by aliens. But, once you get past the initial learning curve, Jemmy becomes one of the easiest swing testers to implement in Java code.

Where to Get Jemmy

Jemmy can be found at http://jemmy.netbeans.org/.

I highly recommend getting the source because the documentation is, well, not a bad reason to buy this book. Don't count on the Javadocs, either. I've found them to be missing, misleading, self-contradictory, and occasionally just plain wrong. The only drawback to Jemmy is that it lacks any method to automatically record tests by having it watch and remember your interactions with the Swing app you want to test.

It's a lot harder to make the case for Jemmy than it should be. Jemmy is a good choice when you want to write your test cases in Java. Once you get your head around Jemmy, you'll be able to write tests very quickly and with very little code. Sadly, Jemmy is not a good choice if you need to get your tests written yesterday. Or if you're not willing to have to occasionally poke through source code to figure out what it's doing, or why. It's not a good choice if you're looking for something that works like everything else, or gives you simple return values that you can stick into JUnit assert statements. In fact, at first glance, Jemmy seems like far more trouble than it's worth. But trust me, it can be worth it. Hopefully, this chapter will help to bring its worth to light, and minimize the need for any future code-poking.

When the NetBeans (http://www.netbeans.org/) people decided that they needed a tool to test their Swing apps, they sat down and wrote Jemmy. Jemmy was not designed from the ground up to work with JUnit, but using Jemmy in JUnit isn't hard at all; it's just not what you'd expect. Instead of testing the output of a method call against a known value, you simply execute the method. If it didn't work, Jemmy will throw an exception, which your TestCase will catch and record as a failed test, just as surely as a failed assertion would. There is no need to write explicit try/catch blocks to handle these exceptions.

The next departure from the norm is that you rarely deal directly with the Swing objects you're testing. Instead, you deal with Jemmy's Operator classes. For example, if you wanted to test if a button were functioning correctly, you would instantiate a JButtonOperator with some arguments to help it find the JButton you're interested in. The naming convention is pretty simple. It's the name of the class of the Swing object you're working with, followed by *Operator*.

Jemmy Primer

The first thing you have to do when using Jemmy, like any Swing tester, is find the primary frame of the application you're dealing with. Since we're looking for a JFrame object, we use a JFrameOperator to find it. Windows are particularly simple to find since we just need to give our JFrameOperator the title of the window we're looking for in its constructor. In the SwingSet test application that title is, unsurprisingly, SwingSet.

```
private JFrameOperator getOuterFrameOperator(){
  // We'll need this object later to drill down to our widgets
  if (outerFrameOperator == null){
        outerFrameOperator = new JFrameOperator("SwingSet");
  }
  return outerFrameOperator;
}
```

We'll be using that outerFrameOperator as the source from which Jemmy will navigate to whatever object we're interested in working with. Once we've got that, we can then drill down to the widgets we *really* care about. First, though, we need to find the right tab. It's crucial that we select the correct tab because, in Swing, you can't access any object that hasn't been displayed yet. And if we don't select the tab we're interested in, then its components won't be displayed. So we set up a JTabbedPaneOperator:

```
private JTabbedPaneOperator getTabbedPaneOperator(){
  if (jtpo == null){
      jtpo = new JTabbedPaneOperator(getOuterFrameOperator());
  }
  return jtpo;
}
```

We're setting the JFrameOperator and JTabbedPaneOperator up in "get" methods so we won't need to instantiate them again and again throughout the code. You'll notice that the constructor here took our outerFrameOperator as an argument. This tells the JTabbedPaneOperator to drill down from the JFrame object referenced by the JFrameOperator until it hits a JTabbedPane. What if you have more than one JTabbedPane? Operator classes generally have a variety of constructors at your disposal with enough arguments to let you tell the Operator exactly which component to drill down to.

Here are JTabbedPaneOperator's:

1. JTabbedPaneOperator(ContainerOperator cont)

2. JTabbedPaneOperator(ContainerOperator cont, ComponentChooser chooser)

3. JTabbedPaneOperator(ContainerOperator cont, ComponentChooser chooser, int index)

4. JTabbedPaneOperator(ContainerOperator cont, int index)

5. JTabbedPaneOperator(ContainerOperator cont, java.lang.String text)

6. JTabbedPaneOperator(ContainerOperator cont, java.lang.String text, int index)

7. JTabbedPaneOperator(ContainerOperator cont, java.lang.String text, int tabIndex, int index)

8. JTabbedPaneOperator(javax.swing.JTabbedPane b)

While the constructors available differ from Operator to Operator, JTabbedPaneOperator gives us a good selection to walk you through. If the object you're trying to find can have a title, you're generally going to want to use 5 from the list above. This basically says, "Start here and use the first one you find with this title." Usually you will only have one object with a given title, but just in case you have more than one, you can use number 6. The int you're passing is the zero-based index of the object you're looking for. For example, if there were two items with the title "foo" then you would write the following to get the second one:

```
new JTabbedPaneOperator(myJFrameOperator, "foo", 1);
```

When you're hunting for objects with unknown titles or that have no title, you can use number 4.

You'll notice that a number of the constructors take a ComponentChooser as one of their parameters. Different ComponentChoosers take different arguments depending on the type of object they're trying to find. In the case of the JtabbedPaneOperator, you should use a JTabbedPaneOperator .JtabbedPaneByItemFinder, which takes a String and int, and optionally, an Operator.StringComparator. It uses the String and int to compare to the titles of JTabbedPane objects it encounters at the index denoted by the int. Other ComponentChoosers work differently based on the type of Swing object they're testing, but they all essentially take the parameters you give them and use them to compare against objects of the appropriate type that it finds. In general, you don't have to do this because the object will just create, and use, a ComponentChooser for you.

Testing a Swing Application with Jemmy

Now that we've set up the basic tools, we'll need to navigate to the components we really want to test. So, let's go test some buttons.

```
public void testButton(){
        getTabbedPaneOperator().selectPage("Buttons");
        JButtonOperator jbo = new JButtonOperator(getOuterFrameOperator(),
0);
        assertTrue(jbo.getText().equals("One"));
        // get the JButton the JButtonOperator refers to and set its action
```

```
            ((JButton)jbo.getSource()).setAction(new
    SimpleButtonAction((JButton)jbo.getSource()));
            assertTrue(jbo.getText().equals("Action Set"));
                    // tells us that the action has been set correctly and that
                    // the buttons text has been changed successfully
            jbo.push();
            // push()is a blocking method. if the action triggered a modal dialog
    we would use .pushNoBlock();
            assertTrue(jbo.getText().equals("I've been clicked"));
            // click it again to reset it to the original state
            jbo.push();
            assertTrue(jbo.getText().equals("One"));
    }
```

The first thing we need to do is select the appropriate tab. JTabbedOperator refers to the tabs as "pages." After calling ourGetTabbedPaneOperator() method, we call selectPage("Buttons") on it because "Buttons" is the title of the tab we want. Behind the scenes, Jemmy finds the tab in question and executes a mouse click to bring it to select it.

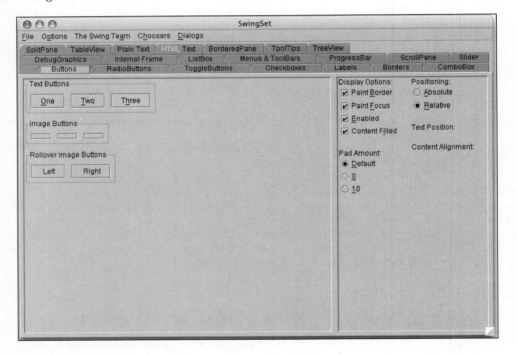

Next up we select the first button with:

```
    JButtonOperator jbo = new JButtonOperator(getOuterFrameOperator(), 0);
```

If we had passed in a 1 instead of the 0, we would have gotten the second button. Since we're going for the first button, we could have actually just left that second parameter off entirely. If you're not specific (and this applies to all operators,) Jemmy will give you the first instance of the type of object you're looking for. If for some reason Jemmy can't find the object you specify in any constructor, it will throw an exception. Which, while an atypical way of handling such a situation, helps us to minimize the code in our test since we won't need to bother testing if the constructor worked (which, if we make it to the next line of code, it did.)

Now that we've gotten the button, we should make sure it's the right one. Our JButtonOperator extends AbstractButtonOperator which has a bunch of methods that just pass through to the underlying button object, getText() being a prime example. We know that the button we're hoping we have has "One" as its text. So, we can just put that in a standard JUnit assertion.

```
assertTrue(jbo.getText().equals("One"));
```

As mentioned before, you don't normally deal with the actual underlying Swing object directly, but sometimes you need to. In this case we do because the buttons in the SwingSet don't actually do any-thing by default. This makes it difficult to test because clicking on them did the appropriate thing. So, we're going to give our button an action to perform; first, though, we need to get the actual JButton object:

```
((JButton)jbo.getSource()).setAction(new
SimpleButtonAction((JButton)jbo.getSource()));
```

The getSource() method of an Operator will get you the underlying Swing object. Once we get it, we then assign it a new SimpleButtonAction as its action. SimpleButtonAction is an action written for this test that just changes the text of a button when you click on it. Calling setAction(...) on a JButton also sets the text of the button. If our action assignment goes well, then the text of the button will be "Action Set", which leads us to our next assertion:

```
assertTrue(jbo.getText().equals("Action Set"));
```

With that in place, we need to "push" the button to see if it is functioning correctly. You can "press" a but-ton or you can "push" it. Pressing is equivalent to executing a mouse down. Pushing is the same as click-ing. Nothing special happens when our button is pressed, so we won't bother testing that. Pushing it couldn't be simpler.

```
jbo.push()
```

If our action worked correctly, the button's text will have changed to "I've been clicked".

```
assertTrue(jbo.getText().equals("I've been clicked"));
```

Now, just to make sure that our button hasn't gotten itself into some funky state as a result of our press-ing it, let's press it again to make sure it's still working.

```
jbo.push();
assertTrue(jbo.getText().equals("One"));
```

Clicking again should reset the text to "One", and if our assertion passes, it has.

Next, let's test a JTable.

```
public void testTable(){
```

```
        getTabbedPaneOperator().selectPage("TableView");
        JTableOperator jto = new JTableOperator(getOuterFrameOperator());
        TableModel tm = jto.getModel();
        assertTrue(tm.getRowCount() == 32);
        assertTrue(tm.getColumnCount() == 6);
        assertTrue(String.valueOf(jto.getValueAt(0,0)).equals("Mike"));
        jto.selectCell(0,0);

assertTrue(((String)jto.getValueAt(jto.getSelectedRow(),jto.getSelectedColumn
())).equals("Mike"));
    }
```

The JTable we're testing has 32 rows and 6 columns. The first cell should have a value of "Mike". With these things in mind we can proceed to test the table.

You'll notice that we leave out the int parameter when we instantiate our JTableOperator. There's only one in this tab, so we don't have to worry about providing any parameters other than a starting point. The contents of the table are, of course, stored in its TableModel, so we call one of JTableOperators pass-through methods to get that:

```
TableModel tm = jto.getModel();
```

Afterwards, we just go through a short series of assertions to confirm that the table we got was the table we were expecting. The only thing left to test is that we are able to correctly select a cell, which we do with the selectCell(int, int) method. The ints being the indexes into the rows and columns of the cell we want selected.

```
jto.selectCell(0,0);
assertTrue(((String)jto.getValueAt(jto.getSelectedRow(),jto.getSelectedColumn(
))).equals("Mike"));
```

The next test, testDialog(), will be testing a JDialog by way of a JMenuItem. Selecting menuItems is trickier than it really ought to be. This is partially due to the fact that Swing's JMenu is actually a subclass of JmenuItem, which is amazingly counterintuitive and problematic, because when you try and get Jemmy to find a JmenuItem, it will try and give you the first one it finds, (which is actually a Jmenu.) To complicate matters even more, the JMenuItems aren't actually contained in the JMenu—they're in its JPopupMenu. Fortunately, Jemmy's developers have given us some convenience methods to make our lives a bit easier.

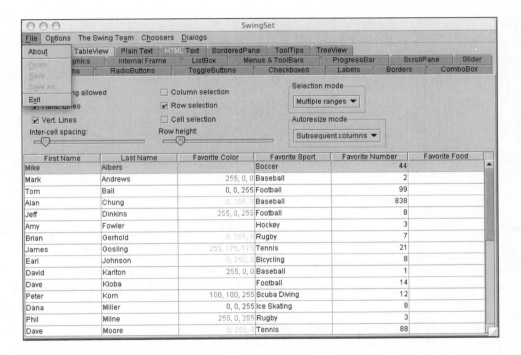

```
public void testDialog(){
        JFrameOperator jfo = getOuterFrameOperator();
        JMenuBarOperator jmbo = new JMenuBarOperator(jfo); // there's only
one menubar

        jmbo.pushMenu("File/About", "/");

        JDialogOperator jdo = new JDialogOperator("About Swing!");
        JButtonOperator jbo = new JButtonOperator(jdo, "OK");
        jbo.push(); // close the dialog

        jmbo.pushMenu("File");
        // select the about menu item
        JMenuOperator jmo = new JMenuOperator(jmbo, "File");
```

```
        //jmo.pushMenu("File/About", "/");  // would work here too.
        JPopupMenu jpm = jmo.getPopupMenu();
        JMenuItem firstMenuItem = (JMenuItem)jpm.getComponent(0);
        assertTrue(firstMenuItem.getText().equals("About"));
        JMenuItemOperator jmio = new JMenuItemOperator(firstMenuItem);
        jmio.push();

        jdo = new JDialogOperator("About Swing!");
        jbo = new JButtonOperator(jdo, "OK");
        jbo.push();

        jmbo = new JMenuBarOperator(jfo);
        jmbo.pushMenu("File");
        jmo = new JMenuOperator(jmbo, "File");
        jmo.pushKey(KeyEvent.VK_T);

        jdo = new JDialogOperator("About Swing!");
        jbo = new JButtonOperator(jdo, "OK");
        jbo.push();

        /*from the docs: http://jemmy.netbeans.org/faq.html#awtmenu
         *
         *        The only way [to interact with AWT menus] is to use keyboard
shortcuts, or
         * Alt key sequences (using [Alt], arrows  and [Enter]).
         */
    }
```

You access a menu by selecting the menu bar, which is always visible, then pushing a menu that you specify by its title. There are quite a few ways to do that, so we'll go through three of them here. After each push we'll have to close the resulting dialog box so that we can get back to the menu again. We'll cover the dialog bit after discussing the ways to open it. The simplest way is to just call its pushMenu(String, String) method. The first string is the path to the menu you want to click on, including all of its submenus. The second tells it what delimiter you used in the preceding string. So, in our example we'll use the following lines:

```
JMenuBarOperator jmbo = new JMenuBarOperator(jfo);
jmbo.pushMenu("File/About", "/");
// or…
jmbo.pushMenuNoBlock("File/About", "/");
```

If we were opening a modal dialog, we'd have to use the NoBlock variant. This is because unless otherwise specified, *all Jemmy operations are blocking*. If we don't use a non-blocking variant with a modal dialog, the thread will get caught up waiting for the dialog to go away and time out. Whenever a Jemmy operation times out it will throw an org.netbeans.jemmy.TimeoutExpiredException exception (we'll cover timeouts later), which will cause your test to fail, which is what you want when things take longer than they should. In the following examples we won't be using the NoBlock variants because this particular dialog isn't modal.

The next way is to actually drill our way down to the menu item we want manually and then click it.

```
JMenuOperator jmo = new JMenuOperator(jmbo, "File");
//jmo.pushMenu("File/About", "/");  // would work here too.
JPopupMenu jpm = jmo.getPopupMenu();
JMenuItem firstMenuItem = (JMenuItem)jpm.getComponent(0);
assertTrue(firstMenuItem.getText().equals("About"));
JMenuItemOperator jmio = new JMenuItemOperator(firstMenuItem);
// the first menu item is the "About" menu, which is the one we want.
jmio.push();
```

In this example we've instantiated the JMenuItem by passing it an actual Swing object. Doing it that way might be atypical, but sometimes it's a useful way of instantiating an Operator class. It is worthwhile to note that JMenuOperators also have a pushMenu(String, String) method just like the JmenuBarOperator, but this example is about drilling down to the actual menu item we want to click on, so we'll do it the long way. The "About" menu item is in the JPopupMenu in the "File" JMenu. We'll use a typical Jemmy constructor to find that, then use it's getPopupMenu() method to get the JpopupMenu, and then grab the first component out of that because the "About" menu is the first one. After verifying that we have the correct menu item, we now instantiate a JmenuItemOperator so that we can actually perform operations (like clicking on it.) Then it's just a matter of calling push() or pushNoBlock().

The last way we'll explore is the use of keystrokes to select the menu item. It's important to know how to do this so that your menuitems have the appropriate key commands associated with them. You'll also need to know this if you're using AWT menus because Jemmy can't find mouse coordinates for AWT menus and thus can't click on them.

In the SwingSet, pressing Alt+f doesn't always activate the File menu even though it has that key binding, which is a great example of why you should have tests like this. If the SwingSet's creators had tested navigating menus with key commands, they would have noticed that sometimes it does one thing (the "Paint Focus" action) and sometimes it does another (opening the File menu). Anyway, we'll click on the File menu to get it in focus, and then we'll execute a java.awt.KeyEvent on it. In this case, we're just typing *T*, which is bound to the About menu item. We could have also typed a down arrow, followed by the Enter key.

```
jmbo = new JMenuBarOperator(jfo);
jmbo.pushMenu("File");
jmo = new JMenuOperator(jmbo, "File");
jmo.pushKey(KeyEvent.VK_T);
```

And now, as promised, we'll deal with that dialog box. It's pretty simple, and if you've looked at that part of the code already, you've probably figured it out.

```
JDialogOperator jdo = new JDialogOperator("About Swing!");
JButtonOperator jbo = new JButtonOperator(jdo, "OK");
jbo.push();
```

You instantiate a JdialogOperator, just like a JframeOperator, by passing it the title of the window you want. The dialog contains an OK button, which we grab by specifying its text. We could have specified its index, or not specified anything at all, because this is the only JButton in this window and Jemmy's default behavior is to give you the first one it finds. Clicking this OK button will close the dialog.

Closing that dialog brings us to the end of our example code. There are, however, a few specific Jemmy things we still need to cover. The first of which is Timeouts. Assuming you're not running these tests on an 8086, you haven't had any timeouts, so increasing the timeout hasn't been needed. Also, none of the tests we ran resulted in time-consuming operations, but sometimes a click can be telling the system to go off and perform some massive calculation that will just take a bit longer than most.

Timeouts are handled by the org.netbeans.jemmy.Timeouts class, which is essentially just a wrapper around a HashTable. In order to set a timeout, you have to know its key. Unfortunately, those keys don't appear to be documented in any central location, so you need to look in the javadocs of the class in which you need to modify a timeout. Each class that has particular timeouts generally has them listed and explained. To make your life a bit easier, we've included a list of the documented timeouts in the current version of Jemmy (see below).

The easiest way to set a timeout is by calling this method:

```
JemmyProperties.setCurrentTimeout(String arg0, long arg1);
```

If you want to set a number of timeouts at once, you can call this method:

```
JemmyProperties.setCurrentTimeouts(Timeouts arg0);
```

Timeouts can be stored in a properties file and loaded via the Timeouts.load(...) and Timeouts .loadDefaults(...) methods which will make your life much easier if you need to use a common set in multiple tests. You can set a timeout globally or locally via Timeouts' setDefault(String name, long newValue) and setTimeout(String name, long newValue) methods, respectively.

ComponentOperator has a setTimeouts(Timeouts) method which is inherited by all of its children. Unfortunately, you have to instantiate an object, which causes it to try an find the swing object in question before you can have access to its setTimeouts(Timeouts) method. The easiest way is to just set the timeout globally before you instantiate the Operator you need and then set it back afterwards.

The following list contains the timeouts we were able to find by digging through the source code. It should not be considered exhaustive. Don't let its size intimidate you, because you rarely ever use them, and when you do need one you can just pull up the Javadocs for that class.

- ❑ **AbstractButtonOperator.PushButtonTimeout:** Time between button pressing and releasing.
- ❑ **ButtonOperator.PushButtonTimeout:** Time between choice pressing and releasing.
- ❑ **ComponentOperator.AfterDragTimeout:** Time to sleep after drag'n'drop operations.
- ❑ **ComponentOperator.BeforeDragTimeout:** Time to sleep before drag'n'drop operations.
- ❑ **ComponentOperator.MouseClickTimeout:** Time between mouse pressing and releasing.
- ❑ **ComponentOperator.PushKeyTimeout:** Time between key pressing and releasing.
- ❑ **ComponentOperator.WaitComponentEnabledTimeout:** Time to wait choice enabled.
- ❑ **ComponentOperator.WaitComponentTimeout:** Time to wait until choice is displayed.
- ❑ **ComponentOperator.WaitFocusTimeout:** Time to wait until component has focus.
- ❑ **ComponentOperator.WaitStateTimeout:** Time to wait for the component to be in some state.
- ❑ **DialogWaiter.AfterDialogTimeout:** Time to sleep after the dialog has been displayed.

- ❑ **DialogWaiter.WaitDialogTimeout:** Time to wait until the dialog is displayed.

- ❑ **EventDispatcher.RobotAutoDelay:** Unknown.

- ❑ **EventDispatcher.WaitComponentUnderMouseTimeout:** Unknown.

- ❑ **EventDispatcher.WaitQueueEmptyTimeout:** Unknown.

- ❑ **EventTool.EventCheckingDelta:** Unknown.

- ❑ **FrameWaiter.AfterFrameTimeout:** Time to sleep after frame has been displayed.

- ❑ **FrameWaiter.WaitFrameTimeout:** Time to wait until the frame displayed.

- ❑ **JComboBoxOperator.BeforeSelectingTimeout:** Time to sleep after list has opened and before an item is selected.

- ❑ **JComboBoxOperator.WaitListTimeout:** Time to wait until the list has opened.

- ❑ **JComponentOperator.ShowToolTipTimeout:** Time to show the tool tip.

- ❑ **JComponentOperator.WaitToolTipTimeout:** Time to wait until the tool tip is displayed.

- ❑ **JMenuOperator.WaitBeforePopupTimeout:** Time to sleep before a popup expands.

- ❑ **JMenuOperator.WaitPopupTimeout:** Time to wait until the popup is displayed.

- ❑ **JMenuItemOperator.PushMenuTimeout:** Time between pressing and releasing a button.

- ❑ **JScrollBarOperator.OneScrollClickTimeout:** Time for one scroll click.

- ❑ **JScrollBarOperator.WholeScrollTimeout:** Time for the whole scrolling.

- ❑ **JSplitPaneOperator.BetweenClickTimeout:** Time to sleep between scroll clicks.

- ❑ **JSplitPaneOperator.ScrollClickTimeout:** Time for a simple scroll click.

- ❑ **JSplitPaneOperator.WholeScrollTimeout:** Time for the whole scrolling.

- ❑ **JTextComponentOperator.BetweenKeysTimeout:** Time to sleep between typing two chars.

- ❑ **JTextComponentOperator.ChangeCaretPositionTimeout:** Maximum time to change the caret position.

- ❑ **JTextComponentOperator.PushKeyTimeout:** Time between a keys press and release during text typing.

- ❑ **JTextComponentOperator.TypeTextTimeout:** Maximum time to type text.

- ❑ **JTreeOperator.WaitAfterNodeExpandedTimeout**

- ❑ **JTreeOperator.WaitNodeExpandedTimeout:** Maximum time to wait next for a node to be loaded during tree operations.

- ❑ **QueueTool.InvocationTimeout:** Time for and action that was put into queue to be started.

- ❑ **QueueTool.LockTimeout:** Time to wait for the queue to be locked after lock action has been put there.

- ❑ **QueueTool.WaitQueueEmptyTimeout:** Timeout to wait until the queue is emptied.

- ❑ **Test.WholeTestTimeout:** Unknown.

- ❏ **TextComponentOperator.BetweenKeysTimeout:** Unknown.
- ❏ **Waiter.TimeDelta:** Default time to sleep between attempts.
- ❏ **Waiter.WaitingTime:** Unknown.
- ❏ **WindowWaiter.AfterWindowTimeout:** Time to sleep after a popup window has been displayed.
- ❏ **WindowWaiter.WaitWindowTimeout:** Time to wait until a popup window is displayed.

The last issue to cover in Jemmy is how to suppress its rather verbose output to Standard Out. The FAQ indicates that it's generated by the org.netbeans.jemmy.Test class, but it actually seems to be coming from the TestOut class. Luckily, suppressing it is very simple. Just call add the following line to the setUp() method of your or anywhere else that is executed before you start using Jemmy objects.

```
JemmyProperties.getProperties().setOutput(TestOut.getNullOutput());
```

JemmyProperties and TestOut are both in the org.netbeans.jemmy package; if you only want to suppress some of the output, TestOut has a variety of constructors that will let you control exactly where all that output will go.

That's it! There are of course a variety of tests you can perform on Swing object with Jemmy that we don't cover here, as doing so would take up an entire book in itself. But hopefully what we've covered here will be enough to get you moving.

Summary

In this chapter we've covered how to use Jemmy in a JUnit test, pointed out some of its quirks, and covered in depth how to work with Frames, Dialogs, Buttons, Menus, and TabbedPanes. We've explored the variety of ways to select a particular object, how to use the Operator classes that perform actions on your objects, and how to get at the Swing objects that Operators encapsulate. Jemmy is probably the fastest way to write Swing tests in Java code, but it's unique structure takes a little getting used to.

Swing Testing with jfcUnit

jfcUnit is a Swing testing framework built on top of JUnit. As we saw in Chapter 13, JUnit allows us to do unit testing of our application's individual classes to ensure that they are performing as designed. jfcUnit extends that functionality to Swing-based applications, allowing us to test our user interfaces as well as our application interfaces.

Currently it supplies support for:

❑ Obtaining window and dialog handles.

❑ Locating specific components inside of a window, including components inside of components (a component hierarchy).

❑ Raising events on the found components, e.g. clicking a button, or typing text in a text field.

❑ Handling testing of components in a thread-safe manner.

❑ XML recording of events for playback testing.

The version of jfcUnit that we will be covering in this chapter is 2.0.2. Earlier versions do not have the XML support for recording and playback that this version has.

So, why would you want to test your Swing application—why not just test the classes that it uses? In order to properly ensure that your application functions properly under all circumstances, you should perform as many tests as possible. By providing a Swing test framework, the makers of jfcUnit have made it possible to not only test the underlying classes but also the user interface. By testing the user interface you ensure that your users will always see what they should be seeing, and that your application receives the proper input to its underlying classes.

Testing with jfcUnit is rather straightforward. Because jfcUnit offers an extension of the normal JUnit test case, you can simply integrate it with your normal test cases as either its own test suite or as a member of an existing suite. The primary difficulty that you may encounter when using a tool like jfcUnit is ensuring that you are finding the correct component for testing. We will show you how to do this in the next section.

jfcUnit Primer

How does jfcUnit work? First, it extends the JUnit test case in the JFCTestCase class; this class enables us to interact with the AWT thread so that we can start the application and run the tests interactively. If we attempted to do this with a standard JUnit test, we would run into the primary problem of waiting for the Swing application to start and interact with the right thread (JUnit tests typically execute in a separate thread). We might be able to do this with the Robot class that Sun provides in jdk1.3 and above (java.awt.Robot), but it is very limited in its capabilities. jfcUnit takes advantage of this by extending the Robot class in its RobotTestHelper class.

JfcUnit also has two classes that assist us in discovering components and in performing actions on those components: Finder and TestHelper, respectively. A TestHelper instance (or one of its subclasses JFCTestHelper or RobotTestHelper) is created within the setUp() method, or outside of it in a private variable, so that it is available throughout the tests. An appropriate Finder class is instantiated like so:

```
Finder jTableFinder = new ComponentFinder(JTable.class);
```

This enables us to find the component that we want to test or contains sub-components we also want to interact with. Now let's take a look at one of TestHelper's subclasses JFCTestHelper and see what it does.

Creating an instance of the helper is simple:

```
JFCTestHelper helper = new JFCTestHelper();
```

This essentially starts up the helper and keeps it in memory, ready to simulate a user's actions on your Swing application. Some of these methods are:

- ❑ **enterClickAndLeave:** Simulates a user clicking a component and leaving it.
- ❑ **enterDragAndLeave:** Simulates a user dragging a component and leaving it.
- ❑ **enterMouseWheel:** Simulates a user using a Mouse wheel on your application.

More fine-grained methods, for handling key presses and mouse movements.

- ❑ **isBounded:** Checks to see if a value is bounded by maximum and minimum values.
- ❑ **keyPressed:** Processes a key pressed event for your application.
- ❑ **keyReleased:** Processes a key released event for your application.

❏ **mouseMoved:** Processes a mouse moved event for your application.

❏ **mousePressed:** Process a mouse pressed event for your application.

These are just a few of the methods in the TestHelper and JFCTestHelper sub-class; other methods include helper methods for getting all the dialogs open on the screen or all the currently open windows.

So, how do these two work together? Simply use an appropriate Finder class for the type of component you are testing, in general this will be a ComponentFinder. Once you have found the appropriate component (a Swing component will get returned to you), you then use the JFCTestHelper to send events to it. So, a full round-trip would look something like this in your JUnit test class:

```
private JFCTestHelper helper = new JFCTestHelper();
 protected void setUp() throws Exception {
        super.setUp();
        AllTests.startSwingSet();
 }
public void testTable(){

        JTabbedPane tabbedPane = selectTab("TableView");
        Finder finder = new ComponentFinder(JTable.class);
        JTable table = (JTable)finder.find(tabbedPane, 0);
        JTableMouseEventData jtmed = new JTableMouseEventData(this, table, 0,
0, 1);
        …
        helper.enterClickAndLeave(jtmed);
        awtSleep();
        assertTrue(((String)table.getValueAt( table.getSelectedRow(),
table.getSelectedColumn())).equals("Mike"));
 }
```

As you can see it's relatively straightforward, but I'll walk through this a little bit. First, we set up our test by creating a JFCTestHelper, and then in the setUp() method we go ahead and start up our Swing application for testing. Next we step into the first test, testTable(), which we will go into further detail in the next section, "Testing a Swing application with jfcUnit." The first thing we do in the test is to select the appropriate tab name, "TableView", then we instantiate a new Finder for the JTable that contains that tab. Once we have the finder instantiated we use it to find the tabbedPane we previously defined and the first component in this tab, which is a JTable. This returns the JTable that we are looking to test, enabling us to now perform some action on it, such as an enterClickAndLeave. The JTableMouseEventData is another class that assists us with testing our Swing application by passing in the appropriate data to the AWT event stream for processing. awtSleep is called to pause the test so that the AWT event queue can process the event. Then we test to make sure that the proper value has been processed.

Testing a Swing Application with jfcUnit

Now that we've reviewed the fundamentals, let's get down to testing our application. We are going to be using the SwingSet.jar that came from the original Swing demo that Sun and Netscape put together to demonstrate how to use Swing. An updated version of this jar is available, but quite honestly is more than we need for our purposes.

The first test that we will look at will be the testButton unit test. This tests the simple click and press of a JButton in our application, but before we do that I want to show one of our private methods that we will be using throughout the test process, selectTab().

```java
private JTabbedPane selectTab(String tabName){
    Finder finder = new ComponentFinder(JTabbedPane.class);


    JTabbedPane tabbedPane = (JTabbedPane) finder.find(getOuterFrame(), 0);

    assertNotNull("Could not find tabbed pane", tabbedPane);
    helper.enterClickAndLeave(new JTabbedPaneMouseEventData(this, tabbedPane,
-1, tabName, 1));
    awtSleep(); // suspends the thread to give the tab a chance to load up

    return tabbedPane;
}
```

What does this do for us? Essentially it makes it easier for us to activate the appropriate tab in our application. It does this by first grabbing the outer frame (discussed later in this section) and then making sure that we did not receive an error in doing so. After that it attempts to click on the appropriate tab, and then it puts the AWT thread to sleep so that it has a chance to respond to the action.

Now onto testButton, which tests the simple click and press of a JButton:

```java
public void testButton(){

    JTabbedPane tabbedPane = selectTab("Buttons");
    Finder finder = new ComponentFinder(JButton.class);
    JButton button = (JButton)finder.find(tabbedPane, 0);

    assertTrue(button.getText().equals("One"));
    button.setAction(new SimpleButtonAction(button));

    assertTrue(button.getText().equals("Action Set"));
        // tells us that the action has been set correctly and that
        // the buttons text has been changed successfully

    helper.enterClickAndLeave(new MouseEventData(this, button));

    assertTrue(button.getText().equals("I've been clicked"));
    // click it again to reset it to the original state
    helper.enterClickAndLeave(new MouseEventData(this, button));

    assertTrue(button.getText().equals("One"));

}
```

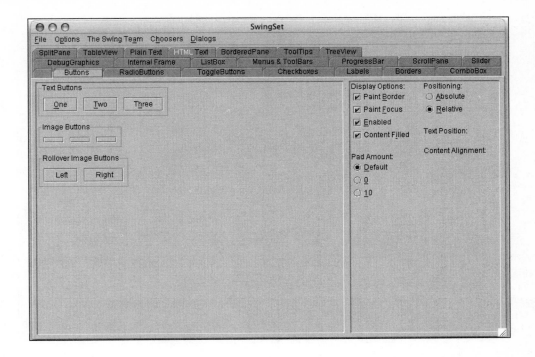

First we set up the proper tab in our application (Buttons in this case), and then we instantiate a ComponentFinder for the component we wish to test, a JButton. Once we have set that up we need to find the first button in our component layout and ensure that it has the proper labeling "One". Then we attempt to change the button's defined action to one that we control (ButtonAction in this case), and then we assert that that change has been made to the button.

Now for the fun part! We call on the helper that we instantiated earlier, and tell it to perform some actions for us. In this case we perform a click action on the button, which in turn should fire off an event that changes the button's text to "I've been clicked". If all goes well, then this test should pass. Next, we perform the same test again, which should reset it to its original state of "One".

That's about it for the button test. What else could we have done? If the button updated text in a separate area, we could have used another Finder to grab that and then check the values that it contained with what should have been there. Essentially, any interaction that the button has with the rest of the application can be checked in this fashion: a reset button could turn all TextFields empty, so we could check for that, or it could turn some fields on and off.

The next test that we will build is testTable. Our goal is to test a JTable to ensure that it is laid out the way that we want it and that we can click into the appropriate column and row.

```
public void testTable(){

    JTabbedPane tabbedPane = selectTab("TableView");
    Finder finder = new ComponentFinder(JTable.class);
    JTable table = (JTable)finder.find(tabbedPane, 0);

    // we've got the table. now let's make sure it is set up correctly.
    // this assumes that nobody has touced any of the controls in this tab.
    // They modify the table.


    // confirm the number of rows (32), columns (6), and the contents of the
first cell (Mike)
    assertTrue(table.getRowCount() == 32);
    assertTrue(table.getColumnCount() == 6);
    assertTrue(((String)table.getValueAt(0,0)).equals("Mike"));

    // the constructor we're using here:
    // JTableMouseEventData(JFCTestCase _testCase, JTable _table, int
_rowIndex, int _columnIndex, int _numberOfClicks)
    JTableMouseEventData jtmed = new JTableMouseEventData(this, table, 0, 0,
1);
```

```
    helper.enterClickAndLeave(jtmed);
    awtSleep();
    assertTrue(((String)table.getValueAt( table.getSelectedRow(),
table.getSelectedColumn())).equals("Mike"));


}
```

Again we define the appropriate tab that our component exists on, and then instantiate a finder for the JTable that we are going to be acting on. Once we have found the JTable we want to test, we start looking at the layout of the table itself to ensure that it is correct; we do this by performing some assertions on the JTable component and what it contains ("Mike" in our case).

Then we use the helper to perform a click action on a particular cell in the table. We pause the test for a moment, and then we check to make sure that the first cell still contains its default value of "Mike".

So, what else could we do here? We could further test our table by changing values in cells or its layout to make sure it is working properly. We could also lock down our table and attempt to make changes on it to see if those succeed. Another option is to use the drag methods to simulate changing the size of a column or row, which could be an interesting exercise on its own.

The final test that we will investigate is to test launching a dialog box using the menu system. Additional examples using the menu system can be found in the jfcUnit distribution under MenuNavigationTestCase. This is a little more involved so we are going to step through this.

```
public void testDialog(){
    JFrame outerFrame = getOuterFrame();
    //get the first menu
    Finder menuFinder = new ComponentFinder(JMenu.class);
    JMenu jm = (JMenu)menuFinder.find(getOuterFrame(), 0);
assertNotNull(jm);
```

First, we need to find our menu, this is accomplished using a private method we have defined called getOuterFrame(), here is the code for this method:

```
private JFrame getOuterFrame(){
    if (outerFrame == null){
        FrameFinder ff = new FrameFinder("SwingSet");
        Set set = ff.findAll();
        outerFrame = (JFrame)set.toArray()[0];
        //outerFrame
        assertNotNull("Could not find frame: SwingSet", outerFrame);
    }
    return outerFrame;
}
```

This method creates a new FrameFinder for the "SwingSet" frame, then it finds all components that match this finder. Once it has done this we are assuming that only one frame was found and that we only care about the first one in that set and assign it to the outerFrame variable. If it doesn't find the appropriate frame it fails with an assertion failure.

Ok, so we have found the outer frame and aren't afraid to use it, once we have that outer frame we instantiate a regular ComponentFinder for our JMenu, in this case the first menu available to us, and ensure that it is not an empty JMenu. Now for the next step, selecting the "File" menu using jfcUnit and the "About" menu item.

```
// select and click the file menu
helper.enterClickAndLeave(new MouseEventData(this, jm));

    // select the About menu item
    Finder menuItemFinder = new JMenuItemFinder("About");

    JMenuItem jmi = (JMenuItem)menuItemFinder.find(jm.getPopupMenu(), 0);

assertNotNull(jmi);

// clicks the about menu item
helper.enterClickAndLeave(new MouseEventData(this, jmi));
```

So, again this is relatively straightforward. We use the helper to click the File menu (the first menu element) and use another jfcUnit class called JMenuItemFinder to find the appropriate menu item, About.

Once we have found the appropriate menu item, we go ahead and click on it using the enterClickAndLeave method; this launches our dialog box.

```
    // a dialog is launched
    List showingDialogs = TestHelper.getShowingDialogs();


    JDialog jd = (JDialog)showingDialogs.get(0);
    assertNotNull(jd);
    Finder buttonFinder = new ComponentFinder(JButton.class);

    // it has an ok button which you should click to make it go away
    JButton jb = (JButton)buttonFinder.find(jd, 0);

    assertNotNull(jb);
    helper.enterClickAndLeave(new MouseEventData(this, jb));

assertTrue(! jd.isVisible());
...
```

We have now launched a dialog box, so we want to make sure that it is the correct one. We do this using a static method in the TestHelper class called getShowingDialogs(). TestHelper has a number of these methods that enable us to get open windows and dialog boxes that have popped up on the screen. It also has methods that aid in destroying open windows so that we can continue on with testing. It is possible that these methods will be moved into a separate class or classes as the find methods were moved into the Finder class—just something to be aware of.

Now on with the testing. By using getShowingDialogs we have a java.util.List of dialogs, but we only want the active one. Again, we assume that there is only one dialog, so we grab the first element off of the list and then check to make sure that it isn't null. Once we have our dialog box, we want to find the OK button. In our case this is the first button element on the dialog box, so we instantiate a finder for it and then click it. Finally, we check to make sure that the dialog box is no longer visible to the user.

As you can see there is quite a bit to jfcUnit, and we've only scratched the surface a bit. Each application will be different and need to test different UI elements, I highly recommend taking a look at the jfcUnit API to see what will be useful for your project. As with any pre-existing project the best way to add unit testing is to add a unit test any time you change existing code, that way you gradually add your tests plus you ensure that the new code works the way that it should.

Summary

Now that we've taken a look at jfcUnit and what it can do, what does it offer over the other testing frameworks?

- ❑ **Tight JUnit integration:** jfcUnit extends the JUnit TestCase class and adds in the necessary pieces for you to test your Swing application right JUnit.

- ❑ **Ease of use:** As we've seen, it is relatively easy to grab the appropriate component using the ComponentFinder.

❏ **Easy component testing:** jfcUnit's TestHelper class offers us several methods to aid us in testing our interfaces with mouse clicks and drags, mouse wheel movements, and text entry. This wide variety of simulations is enough to perform most test cases available.

❏ **XML Tests:** jfcUnit also offers the ability to record and perform tests on your classes using an XML testing file. We didn't cover here because we felt the support for pure Java is currently superior to the XML support; hopefully this will improve in future releases of jfcUnit. For more information on the XML part of jfcUnit go to http://jfcunit.sourceforge.net/jfcunitxml.htm

What are some of the disadvantages of jfcUnit?

❏ **Functionality Testing:** If you are looking for more functionality testing versus unit testing, Jemmy may be a better choice.

25

Swing Testing with Abbot

Abbot is the final Swing testing framework that we will discuss in this section of the book. The primary difference between Abbot and the other two (Jemmy and jfcUnit) is that Abbot provides test recording functionality and playback through Costello (get it, Abbot and Costello?). This functionality makes it easier for us to write tests for a pre-existing application by simply firing up Costello and our application and manually recording the tests. Costello also offers us the ability to edit saved test scripts as well as allowing us to separate our tests into discrete units and then aggregate them.

Another difference between Abbot and the others is that it is based off of the java.awt.Robot class—this class was created by Sun to aid in remotely interacting with Swing applications, but is rather low level. Abbot has extended Robot and added more usable interfaces to it for Swing testing. This comes through specifically in the naming of Abbot, which stands for "A better 'bot".

Where to Get Abbot and Its Required JARs

Abbot is an open source project hosted at Sourceforge, and it is available under the Common Public License at http://abbot.sourceforge.net/.

Abbot also requires other packages which are not included in its source download:

❑ JUnit: http://junit.org

❑ jdom: http://jdom.org

❑ Xerces parser: http://xml.apache.org/xerces2-j/index.html

❑ GNU RegExp: www.cacas.org/java/gnu/regexp/ (version 1.1.0)

❑ MRJ Toolkit: http://developer.apple.com/samplecode/Sample_Code/QuickTime/QuickTime_for_Java/MRJToolkitStubs.htm (this ZIP file is not included in either the source or ZIP distribution, so you will need to download it)

These capabilities are highlighted in the goals of Abbot:

❑ **Scripted control of actions and inspection:** Test scripts are dynamically interpreted rather than using compiled tests, allowing users the ability to quickly edit and execute tests.

❑ **Loose component bindings:** Rather than binding to a specific component by location, Abbot allows us to bind to the component's name. This enables users to rely on the naming convention of the component itself rather than its location, which can change over time.

❑ **High-level semantic actions, bound to low-level events:** Abbot builds on top of the Robot class to aid in testing Swing applications by providing a wrapper around it, easing the use of the Robot class.

❑ **Support live recording of high-level semantic actions:** Using Costello a user can easily record just about any event one would like to test for in their application.

❑ **Extensible user action recording and generation:** The core Tester and Recorder objects are easily extended to make new ones for more extensive or custom testing.

Abbot and Costello Primer

Abbot is essentially a two-part framework: the first part, Abbot, allows us to test our Swing applications using standard Java; the second part, Costello, allows us to record our tests manually and then replay them in JUnit. Now let's look at how to record a test using Costello. At the moment, Costello has no documentation (another great reason to buy this book!).

The primary use of Costello is to record a series of actions performed on some Swing application, and then to play them back. To record a script with Abbot you need to make sure that your test application is in Costello's classpath. Once you've done that you can either type

```
java -jar abbot.jar // launches costello
```

or call

```
abbot.editor.Costello.main(new String[]);
```

If you're running Costello from within Eclipse, you'll probably want to just make a new Run configuration that calls the latter. Everything in your project's classpath will be in Costello's, which makes life that much easier. Once you've launched Costello, choose File > New Script... and save it somewhere in your project. Select the first line in the list "Insert your launch information here" and an editor frame will appear on the right.

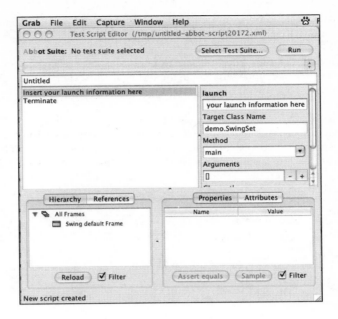

So, what do we see here?

- ❑ **The "launch" field:** A description of what you're launching.

- ❑ **Target Class Name:** The fully qualified name of the class you want to call some method in. Usually this is the class with the main method in it.

- ❑ **Method:** The method you want to call in the previously specified class; usually just "main".

- ❑ **Arguments:** The arguments you're passing to the method; "" for a main method that doesn't take any arguments.

Now you're ready to actually record something. Just to make sure everything you need is ready, click Run and make sure the widgets you want to test load up correctly. Your app will most likely launch and then close immediately.

Once you know that Costello has everything in its classpath and was able to find the method you were hoping it would, you can choose Capture > All Actions (no motion) or Capture > All Actions. The former is generally what you want as it will capture all the significant events but won't bother to record the actual MouseEvent.MOUSE_MOVED events. And no, if you play back a recording that saved mouse events, your pointer won't start zooming around your screen all by itself!

Now select Start Recording, click on the important items, type where you need to, Drag, etc..

One thing to be aware of here is that dragging requires Robot mode. If you see a "Robot non-functional, falling back to AWT mode" message while starting Costello, then any dragging events won't work. Clicking and typing will continue to function as normal, though.

Also be aware of how Costello treats key modifiers: when trying to record Alt+f Costello only recorded the f without the Alt modifier. Hopefully the developers will fix this soon.

Once you have finished recording you can close your application and switch back to Costello to finish the recording sequence. When you want to run the test again, just click Run; Costello will load up your application, perform all your operations, and terminate it.

What happens when things don't go as they should? An easy way to test this is to just change the arguments to one of your actions. When Abbot gets to that point in the script, the line will turn red and processing will stop. Considering that this is a functional test and not a unit test, it makes sense to stop processing since one function is generally dependant upon the previous one. You might expect that it would just cancel operation on the current sequence, but instead it cancels all upcoming events and leaves your application open.

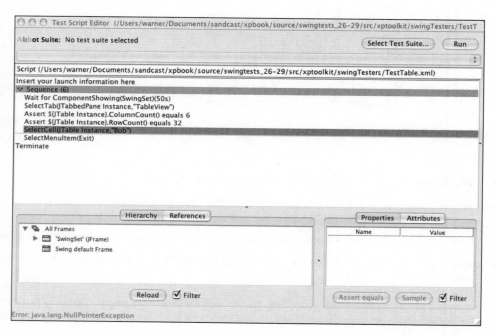

A couple other oddities: While there is a Cut option in the Edit menu, there's no Paste, so it is really more of a misnamed Delete. Also, Costello can have a tendency to spit out copious errors to STDOUT. Just ignore them. That's normal.

Now, onto using Abbot to replay our test in a JUnit TestCase. First we start with the Abbot ScriptFixture (junit.extensions.abbot.ScriptFixture) which extends the JUnit TestCase class to allow us to interact with our application and the Costello tests we write.

To integrate our test (which is now stored as an XML file), we simply extend the ScriptFixture class and load the XML files in the suite() method.

```
public class ExampleTest extends ScriptFixture {
 public static Test suite() {
        return new ScriptTestSuite(ExampleTest.class,
"src/example/scripts/ExampleTest");
```

Then, in our main method we call

```
TestHelper.runTests(args, ExampleTest.class);
```

What does all of this do? Basically the ScriptTestSuite function accepts a class (this test) and a pointer to the XML file in the classpath, and then it runs that test. Pretty simple, huh? Now let's take a peek at the XML file that gets generated by Costello to get a feel for things:

```
<AWTTestScript>
  <component class="javax.swing.JLayeredPane" id="JLayeredPane Instance"
index="1" parent="JRootPane Instance" window="SwingSet" />
  <component class="javax.swing.JPanel" id="JPanel Instance" index="0"
parent="JLayeredPane Instance" window="SwingSet" />
  <component class="javax.swing.JRootPane" id="JRootPane Instance" index="0"
parent="SwingSet" />
  <component class="javax.swing.JTabbedPane" id="JTabbedPane Instance"
index="1" parent="Main SwingSet Panel" window="SwingSet" />
  <component class="demo.SwingSet" id="Main SwingSet Panel" index="0"
name="Main SwingSet Panel" parent="JPanel Instance" window="SwingSet" />
<component class="javax.swing.JFrame" id="SwingSet" root="true"
title="SwingSet" />
```

First, Abbot defines the components that we are interacting with; this includes the Frames and Panels that are visible during our test.

```
<launch args="[]" class="demo.SwingSet" classpath="." desc="Insert your launch
information here" method="main" threaded="true" />
```

Next, it defines our launch arguments for the Swing class that we are testing. Nothing too fancy here.

```
  <sequence>
    <action args="JTabbedPane Instance,&quot;SplitPane&quot;"
class="javax.swing.JTabbedPane" method="actionSelectTab" />
    <action args="JTabbedPane Instance,&quot;TableView&quot;"
class="javax.swing.JTabbedPane" method="actionSelectTab" />
  </sequence>
<terminate />
```

Now, the fun bits—interaction with our application. As you can see here we have two actions, both of which were selectTab. First we selected the SplitPane tab and then the "TableView" tab, both of which were recorded by Costello for playback. Now let's run through some more real-world type tests to see what happens.

Recording and Using Our Test

The first test that we will investigate is TestTable.xml, where we test a JTable and ensure that it is laid out the way that we want it and that we can click into the appropriate column and row.

```
<AWTTestScript>
   <component class="javax.swing.JMenuItem" id="Exit" index="6"
parent="JPopupMenu Instance" text="Exit" window="SwingSet" />
   <component class="javax.swing.JMenu" id="File" index="0" parent="JMenuBar
Instance" text="File" window="SwingSet" />
   ...
<component class="demo.TablePanel" id="TablePanel Instance" index="16"
parent="JTabbedPane Instance" window="SwingSet" />
```

Again we see a listing of all the components that we deal with in our test.

```
  <sequence>
     <wait args="SwingSet" class="abbot.tester.ComponentTester"
method="assertComponentShowing" />
     <wait args="Frame Creator" class="abbot.tester.ComponentTester"
invert="true" method="assertComponentShowing" />
     <action args="Frame Creator,270,250" class="javax.swing.JInternalFrame"
method="actionResize" />
     <action args="Frame Creator,360,10" class="javax.swing.JInternalFrame"
method="actionMove" />
     <action args="SwingSet,117,109" class="java.awt.Window"
method="actionMove" />
     <action args="SwingSet,790,550" class="java.awt.Frame"
method="actionResize" />
     <action args="JTabbedPane Instance,&quot;TableView&quot;"
class="javax.swing.JTabbedPane" method="actionSelectTab" />
     <action args="JTable Instance,&quot;Mike&quot;"
class="javax.swing.JTable" method="actionSelectCell" />
     <action args="Exit" method="actionSelectMenuItem" />
  </sequence>
  <terminate />
</AWTTestScript>
```

And we see a listing of our sequence actions. Initially we fire up the SwingSet demo and wait for that window to show (assertComponentShowing). Then we wait for all of the windows, frames, and internal frames to show as well. Finally, we access the TableView tab, then click in the first table cell which contains the string "Mike". Next we want to add some assertions to ensure that Abbot will capture what we want to test for. To add an assertion to a script, open the Costello script editor and the TestTable.xml script file, and move down to select the SelectCell action. Now we are ready to add our first assertion.

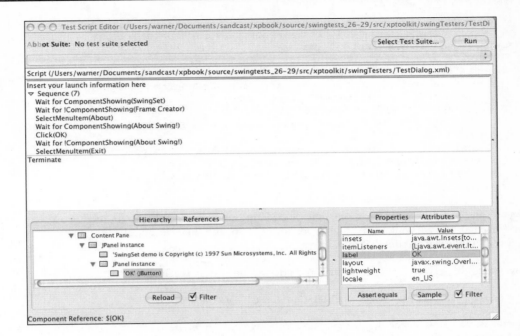

Adding assertions is a little odd in Costello, so let's walk through it step-by-step. If we are dealing with an existing script that we just loaded, we need to load our application first. The easiest way to do that is through Test->Load. Then we need to determine what we want to add the assertion to—in this case it's the JTable that we've been dealing with. Once our test script is running we go ahead and bring the SwingSet application in front.

To add a particular assertion—verify the row size, for instance—we place our mouse over one of the cells, hold down the shift key, and press F1. Going back to Costello we should see the component hierarchy has changed a bit, and the JTable instance is selected. Going over to the right we see a listing of all the properties for that instance. Scroll down on the right until we see columnCount; selecting that gives us the option of adding an assertEquals. We go ahead and do that for both columnCount and rowCount, with the following results:

```
<assert component="JTable Instance" method="getColumnCount" value="6" />
<assert component="JTable Instance" method="getRowCount" value="32" />
```

Not too bad. Where we run into an issue is in checking other items like the actual cell value. What we might need to do in that case is to use the JTable or it's model to gain access to the operator and then to the value contained therein.

The final test that we will investigate is to test launching a dialog box using the menu system. This is actually quite easy in Costello.

```
<sequence>
    <wait args="SwingSet" class="abbot.tester.ComponentTester"
method="assertComponentShowing" />
    <wait args="Frame Creator" class="abbot.tester.ComponentTester"
invert="true" method="assertComponentShowing" />
    <action args="About" method="actionSelectMenuItem" />
    <wait args="About Swing!" class="abbot.tester.ComponentTester"
method="assertComponentShowing" />
    <action args="OK" class="javax.swing.AbstractButton" method="actionClick"
/>
    <wait args="About Swing!" class="abbot.tester.ComponentTester"
invert="true" method="assertComponentShowing" />
    <action args="Exit" method="actionSelectMenuItem" />
</sequence>
```

As you can see, all we need to do is actionSelectMenuItem and select the About menu item. Once we have selected that we wait for the dialog box to show up, and then click on the OK button to close the window. Finally we call the Exit menu item.

Now we could get a little more complex and add in some assertions like

```
<assert component="OK" method="getLabel" value="OK" />
```

which basically says: check this component (which we have referenced above) and make sure that it's label says OK.

Cleaning Up

As you record scripts you may notice items like this:

```
<action args="Frame Creator,270,250" class="javax.swing.JInternalFrame"
method="actionResize" />
```

If it isn't something that is needed as part of the test (i.e., it was part of the recording but not something you need to test), you can safely remove it. To delete unintended results, either use your favorite text editor to delete the line, or remove them from inside the Costello script editor by using Edit->Cut. You may also wish to move actions around inside of the sequence; to do this inside of Costello, highlight the line you wish to move, and then select edit->move up or down. This reorders the sequence of events that your script runs.

Putting it All Together

Now that we have everything cleaned up and have tested it inside of Costello to make sure it's running, we need to create a test suite to execute it all. Unlike the other frameworks we do not need to actually start the Swing application as Abbot takes care of this for us. So that just leaves us to finding the XML scripts and running them. As before, this is very easy:

```
public static Test suite() {
  return new ScriptTestSuite(AbbotTest.class, "src/xptoolkit/swingTesters") {
        public boolean accept(File file) {
                String name = file.getName();
```

```
                    return name.endsWith("xml");
            }
    };
    }
```

Here we go ahead and go through our source directory and look for all of our XML script files; this of course could be a bit more robust depending on your needs. Once we have located all of the files, we pass them into the ScriptTestSuite for execution. Abbot then runs through each test and returns with either success or errors in a standard JUnit report.

Now that you have gotten a taste of what Costello does and how Abbot works with the scripts it creates, we hope you have enough information (and inclination) to pick up that dusty Swing application and see what you can test on it.

Advantages of Abbot

Now that we've taken a look at Abbot and what it can do, what does it offer over the other testing frameworks?

❑ **Good JUnit integration:** while most of the test themselves are XML Abbot utilizes JUnit under the covers for it's assertions and failures.

❑ **Good UI for Recording/Playback:** Costello offers a nice user interface for designing and interacting with recorded tests, it isn't the best that it could be, but it is pretty good for what it does.

❑ **Java-only support:** Abbot also offers the ability to code your Swing tests only in Java, while we didn't investigate this in this chapter, it is a fairly complete package, comparable with JFCUnit or Jemmy's capabilities.

What are some of the disadvantages of jfcUnit?

❑ **Costello UI could be better:** There's always room for improvement, especially in the realm of user interface design.

❑ **Recording could be better:** Some of the initial scripts that you create add in extra methods for no apparent reason.

❑ **Costello class access:** It is unclear on how to gain access to some of the other elements present in a Swing application that are not directly tied to a component, such as the TableOperator through Costello's interface.

26

Managing Projects with Maven

Maven started life as a subproject of Turbine (http://jakarata.apache.org/turbine), a Web application framework. It was born out of the need of its lead developer, Jason Van Zyl, to easily add in new pieces of functionality to his build process, such as unit testing or source metrics, both of which can be extremely important to a large project. The first iterations used Ant as the build system, but then Maven moved away from Ant to use Jelly as its primary scripting engine to build the plug-in architecture that is there today.

There is currently talk on the mailing list about making plug-ins scriptable with a variety of languages, notably using Groovy or BeanShell with Object-Graph Navigation Language (OGNL). Originally Maven started out as a solution to the multitude of copying tasks required to move Ant files from project to project, and the plethora of dependent JAR libraries that would change on a regular basis. Its primary goal has always been to make it easy for developers to follow agile methods and to make it a little difficult to step out of those methods (like unit testing). Among those goals are the following:

- ❏ Making the build process easy.
- ❏ Providing a uniform build system.
- ❏ Supplying quality project information.
- ❏ Providing clear development process guidelines.
- ❏ Offering guidelines for thorough testing practices.
- ❏ Enabling coherent visualization of project information.
- ❏ Allowing transparent migration to new features.

Maven satisfies these goals and continues to improve its feature set through the plug-in architecture.

Where to Get Maven

Maven is a top-level project hosted by Apache and is available under the Apache License at http://maven.apache.org

Its core plug-ins are part of the initial download and installation. Some projects (such as XDoclet) are hosting their own plug-ins, or you need to build and install other plug-ins yourself. But once installed, plug-ins can be used by any project requiring them, one of the key benefits of Maven. Some additional plug-ins (including a reference to the XDoclet plug-in) can be found at

http://maven.apache.org/reference/plugins/index.html

Maven makes it relatively easy to get a new project up and running. If you stick with the defined project layout (which makes a lot of sense), you can have a bare-bones project built with Maven in about half an hour to an hour. You can even have a simple project Web site with all of your reports and related documents up and running within a couple of hours or less, depending on how your documentation is formatted and how much you want to put online.

The following are some of the benefits of Maven:

❑   **Well-defined project layout:** Most Maven projects stick with the basic layout of a project, which makes it easy for you to look for items.

❑   **Built-in unit testing:** Maven's JUnit plug-in provides most of the hooks needed for thorough testing of your project.

❑   **Built-in code visualization and reporting:** Maven has a number of built-in, ready-to-run reports to help your team focus on the project. All of these reports can be integrated into the project Web site build.

❑   **Integration with other agile technologies:** Maven includes plug-ins for code coverage, CVS check-in, code formatting, code style violations, and bug tracking.

❑   **Project Web sites:** Maven has several plug-ins to help you build and maintain your project Web site, including all of the generated project reports like code coverage, source cross reference, JavaDoc, CVS activity, and code style violations.

Maven Primer

The easiest way to get started with Maven is to first download and install the latest version; as of right now that is Maven-1.0-rc1. A final release is expected soon. First go to the Maven Web site and click on the download link at the top. From there you can choose the most appropriate download for your platform (EXE for easy Windows install, zip for Windows DIY install, and Tar-gzip for Unix). Once you've downloaded the file you can either extract the Zip or Tar-gzipped file onto your system or double-click the EXE file for installing. Instructions for installing each of these can be found at http://maven.apache.org/start/install.html. If you wish you can also install Maven from source, but depending on the status of the project this can be a painful process. Instructions for installing from source can be found on the Maven site at http://maven.apache.org/start/bootstrap.html.

Installing on Unix

To install Maven on Unix or a Unix-friendly operating system (OS X, Linux), retrieve the tar.gz file from the download section. Once you have downloaded the tar.gz file (tape archive, gnu zipped) to your local machine, unpack it using either gnutar or your favorite archive-handling software (OS X comes equipped with StuffIt, which will automatically unzip and untar your downloaded files for you). Once you have unarchived the file, you should be left with a folder called maven-1.0-rc1 (or another name that reflects the version you downloaded). You can place this folder anywhere on your system that you have read and write access to. Note the location for the next step.

At this point you should add an environment variable called MAVEN_HOME to your startup or login shell script. We leave this exercise to since different shells have different methods. In OS X, you do this by adding a setenv command to your .tcshrc file (if you are using tc shell), which looks something like this:

```
setenv MAVEN_HOME /Users/me/maven-1.0-rc1
```

Then you may also wish to add this to your PATH statement like so:

```
setenv PATH ${PATH}:${MAVEN_HOME}/bin
```

This line adds the Maven binaries to your executable path for the user that you are logged in as.

Installing on Windows

If you are running Windows 95/98/2000 or XP, then you should download the Windows executable. It essentially does the same thing as the tar.gz file, but the EXE places Maven in your Program Files directory for you, rather than having you choose where to put it. You may also choose to download the zip file; if you go this route, then follow the directions for the Unix installation given earlier.

Adding system environment variables will vary depending on which version of Windows you are running. For Windows 2000 you can add system variables by right-clicking on My Computer and choosing Properties. From there select the Advanced tab and then click the Environment Variables button. Now you have two options: System variables or User variables. For ease of use, I recommend choosing System variables just to make sure that the command-line sees the variable properly (this may vary from version to version). To add the Maven binaries to your PATH statement, double-click on the PATH entry and go to the end of the line. Add the following after typing a semicolon to end the previous PATH statement:

```
%MAVEN_HOME%\bin
```

Verifying the Install

To verify that you have Maven installed properly, go to a command line, change to your project directory, and type *maven –g*. This command runs Maven and outputs all the goals available to you. You can think of goals as Ant targets, except that these goals are available to all of your projects, not just to some custom-defined target that you created for Ant. You should see something like this:

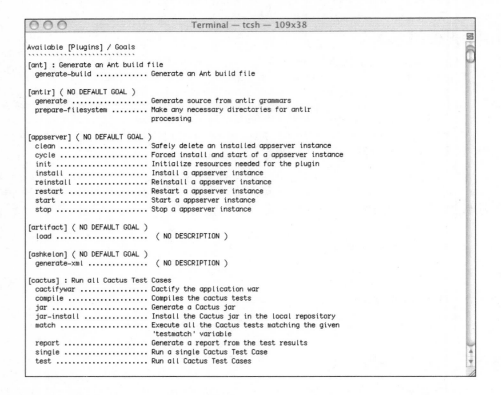

If you experience connection problems, perhaps you aren't actually connected, in which case you want to run Maven in offline mode, or maybe you are connected through a proxy server. The easiest way to run Maven in offline mode is to specify it on the command line using the –o modifier, so it would look like *maven –o*. To specify a proxy server, the best thing to do is to specify a build.properties file in your user home directory. In this file, specify the following properties:

- ❑ **maven.proxy.host:** The IP or address of your proxy.
- ❑ **maven.proxy.port:** The port number of your proxy.
- ❑ **maven.proxy.username:** The username if your proxy requires authentication.
- ❑ **maven.proxy.password:** The password if your proxy requires authentication.

What was all that stuff about downloading? Didn't Maven come with everything already? Well, yes and no. What you downloaded was the skeleton of Maven. To keep it small and easy to install, it has been stripped down to exactly what it needs to run. That's not to say that what you downloaded isn't usable—it is. But a number of plug-ins are downloaded the first time you run Maven, so it's best if you're connected when you do it. Maven also checks for the latest of a particular internal dependency or plug-in and downloads that the first time it runs.

Now that it has downloaded everything, Maven needs a place to put it. It handles this by default by placing your repository and extracted plug-ins into your user home (on Windows this is Documents and Settings/*username*; on OS X and other Unix-like operating systems it is in /etc/home/*username* or /Users/*username*) underneath the directory .maven. Calling the directory with a dot (.) in front of it hides it by default in most Unix environments (including OS X) but doesn't do anything in a Windows environment.

Once you have Maven installed and you've verified that it's running, we can now dig into the fun stuff! Maven uses three files to define your project, additional properties, and custom goals. These files are:

❑   **project.xml:** Where you place the project descriptor or Project Object Model (POM).

❑   **project.properties:** Where you can override Maven and plug-in properties.

❑   **maven.xml:** Where you define custom Maven goals using Jelly (which we will discuss later in this chapter).

Installing Plug-ins

If you wish to install other plug-ins not available through the Maven distribution or want to install newer versions of them, there are a few ways to go about it:

1.   Manually download and install.

2.   Install through Maven itself.

3.   Declare the plug-in as a dependency.

Manual Download and Install

To perform a manual install of a plug-in, simply download the plug-in JAR file in question and place it in the MAVEN_HOME/plug-ins directory. Maven should then automatically unjar the file and deploy it to your local .maven/plugins directory. If it does not do this, see the "Gotchas" section.

Installing Through Maven

To install a plug-in through Maven, make sure that the repository that contains the plug-in is specified in your maven.repo.remote project property. If it isn't Maven won't know where to find the plug-in.

```
maven plugin:download -DartifactId=cactus-maven -DgroupId=cactus
-Dversion=1.6dev-20040226
```

This code tells Maven that we want to download the cactus-maven plug-in, version 1.6dev-20040226, and install it to our local repository.

Declaring the Plug-in as a Dependency

By declaring a plug-in as a dependency, you enable Maven to download and install it into your plug-ins directory as long as it can find the dependency to download. If a plug-in is stored at another repository make sure that repository location is added to your maven.repo.remote property in project.properties; otherwise Maven will not be able to find it.

```
<dependency>
    <groupId>xdoclet</groupId>
    <artifactId>maven-xdoclet-plugin</artifactId>
    <type>plugin</type>
    <version>1.2b3</version>
</dependency>
```

As you can see, this is rather straightforward: We are telling Maven that we need the maven-xdoclet-plug-in, version 1.2b3, installed as a plug-in so that we can use it. Once it has downloaded and installed the dependency, we can use this plug-in throughout our code (including other projects as well).

Gotchas

Here are some items to be aware of once you have downloaded and installed the plug-ins:

❑ **Older versions of the same plug-in:** Browse the plug-ins directory and look for previous versions of the downloaded plug-in. These will need to be removed.

❑ **Cached data:** Maven caches data when it runs builds so it doesn't constantly have to read the plug-in goals and properties. These are called .cache files. Remove all of these once old plug-ins have been removed or new ones have been added, if you are having problems.

❑ **Plug-ins not extracted:** If you did a manual install, the plug-in JAR file may not have extracted itself. This will require a manual unjar: jar –xvf jarname.jar.

Now let's look at the Project Object Model (POM). First we focus on the elements inside it that are most important to us right now, and then we look at how a Maven project is structured.

The Project Object Model (POM)

The POM is an XML file called project.xml that describes your project to Maven so that it can build the project, run the appropriate tests, and build reports. All of these are core plug-ins for Maven so there is no extra coding or tweaking you need to do; you just supply the appropriate information in the POM for Maven to get ready to go. When you run Maven in a directory that contains a project.xml file, it attempts to use that as the POM, just as Ant looks for a build.xml file in the current directory it is being run in. Here is a sample project.xml file:

```
<?xml version="1.0"?>
<project>
  <pomVersion>3</pomVersion>
  <name>XPToolkit Maven Test Project</name>
  <id>test</id>
  <groupId>xptoolkit</groupId>
  <currentVersion>1.0-b1</currentVersion>
  <organization>
    <name>Wrox</name>
    <url>http://wrox.com/</url>
  </organization>
  <inceptionYear>2004</inceptionYear>
  <package>com.wrox.xptoolkit</package>

  <shortDescription>Test Project for Java Tools for Extreme Programming 2nd
Edition</shortDescription>
```

```xml
<description>
    This is a simple test project to highlight the structure of a Maven
project for the 'Java Tools for Extreme Programming' 2nd Edition book
published by Wrox in its Professional series.
</description>

<url>http://www.wrox.com/javatools/</url>
<issueTrackingUrl/>
<siteAddress/>
<siteDirectory/>
<distributionSite/>
<distributionDirectory/>

<repository/>
<versions/>
<mailingLists/>
<developers>
  <developer>
    <name>Rick Hightower</name>
    <id>rick</id>
    <email>rick@arc-mind.com</email>
    <organization>Arc-Mind</organization>
  </developer>

  <developer>
    <name>Warner Onstine</name>
    <id>warner</id>
    <email>warner@sandcastsoftware.com</email>
    <organization>Sandcast Software</organization>
  </developer>
</developers>

<contributors/>
<licenses/>

<dependencies>
  <dependency>
    <groupId>test-dependency</groupId>
    <artifactId>test-dependency</artifactId>
    <version>1.0</version>
    <url>http://www.test.org/</url>
  </dependency>
</dependencies>

<build>
  <nagEmailAddress/>
  <sourceDirectory>src/java</sourceDirectory>
  <unitTestSourceDirectory>src/test</unitTestSourceDirectory>
  <aspectSourceDirectory/>

  <!-- Unit test cases -->
  <unitTest>
    <includes>
      <include>**/*Test.java</include>
```

```
      </includes>
      <excludes>
        <exclude>**/ExcludedTest.java</exclude>
      </excludes>
    </unitTest>

    <!-- J A R   R E S O U R C E S -->
    <!-- Resources that are packaged up inside the JAR file -->
    <resources>
      <resource>
        <directory>${basedir}/src/resources/misc</directory>
        <includes>
          <include>*.xsd</include>
        </includes>
      </resource>
      <resource>
        <directory>${basedir}/src/resources/logging</directory>
        <includes>
          <include>log4j.properties</include>
        </includes>
      </resource>
    </resources>

    <jars/>
  </build>
  <reports/>
</project>
```

So, what does this all mean? Starting from the top level we have the project element as the root element. Every POM file needs to have this as the root element.

The project Element

Under the project element we have several top-level elements:

- ❑ **pomVersion:** This is the version of POM we are adhering to. Currently it is at version 3. It should not be necessary to change this once you have set it. When you upgrade your instance of Maven, it will automatically update this reference for you if necessary.

- ❑ **groupId:** The groupId element is the short, Unix-like version of the group name. Say your company is the one sponsoring this project; then the name could be the company name. Or the name could be the parent project name. This element may change in the near future since it is potentially confusing.

- ❑ **id:** This is the artifact's ID, or what will be generated from this particular project. When a build is done, the name of the JAR, WAR, or EAR file will be groupId-id-version.jar (.war or .ear).

- ❑ **name:** This element contains the full version of the project's name.

- ❑ **version:** This element specifies the current version of this project's artifact, in our case 1.0-b1, which is shorthand for version 1.0 beta release 1. However, you can put whatever you want in here. So our final artifact that will be generated would be xptoolkit-test-1.0-b1.jar (.war or .ear).

- ❑ **organization:** This element describes what organization this project belongs to. The URL and text information will be used in generating the site generation as well as JavaDoc.

- ❑ **inceptionYear:** This element specifies when this particular project started. It is also used in site generation and JavaDoc.

- ❑ **package:** This element contains the main package that this project builds under, used in generating the JavaDoc.

- ❑ **shortDescription and description:** These elements are used for generating the site's home page (they can be replaced by creating an index.xml file with more information in the xdocs directory, which we cover later).

- ❑ **url:** This element contains the project page URL used for site generation.

- ❑ **issueTrackingUrl:** This element specifies the issue tracking URL (for example, the Web site address for your BugZilla, Scarab, or Jira installation for this project).

- ❑ **siteAddress/siteDirectory:** This element specifies the hostname of the Web server and the directory where you want to deploy the generated Web site.

- ❑ **distributionSite/distributionDirectory:** This element specifies the hostname of the server and the directory where you want to deploy released distributions. It is very useful if you are using your own repository and need to keep things internal.

- ❑ **repository:** This element specifies information regarding the type of source code management software you are using for this project (CVS, SourceSafe, SVN, etc.).

- ❑ **versions/version:** This element provides information on previous versions and their tags so that it is easy to check out and build a previous release.

- ❑ **mailingLists/mailingList:** This element provides information regarding mailing lists that are devoted to this project. Use this element when generating your Web site.

- ❑ **developers/developer:** This element lists the developers who have active commit status on the project along with their contact information.

- ❑ **contributors/contributor:** This element lists the contributors and their roles in the project.

- ❑ **licenses:** This element describes all the licenses for this project. Use it when generating the license page of your Web site. These licenses are typically only for this project and not its dependencies.

- ❑ **dependencies/dependency:** This element contains all the dependencies of the project needed in order to build and/or deploy it.

- ❑ **build:** This element describes the build environment of the project: source locations, test locations, unit test flags, etc.

- ❑ **reports:** We examine reports in more detail in the case study later in this chapter.

The dependencies Element

The dependencies and build elements are the biggest part of any Maven POM. The dependencies element describes to Maven what JARs you will need when building and distributing your project. If you have no dependencies for your project, you can simply make this an empty XML element <dependencies/>. Most won't be that fortunate, so let's look at the subelement of dependencies, dependency, and what is required in that element.

One of the best things about dependencies is that the majority of them probably already reside on the Maven repository, which has been graciously hosted on Ibiblio (http://ibiblio.org). If the dependency isn't hosted and the license allows for it to be freely downloaded, then a simple request to the Maven developers will generally get the dependency installed on the repository.

So, how do we describe a dependency so that Maven knows where to get it?

❑ **artifactId (formerly id):** This element contains the unique ID for an artifact produced by the project group.

❑ **groupId:** This element provides unique ID for the group that created this dependency (i.e., jboss for the jBoss group).

❑ **version:** This element specifies the version of the dependency that your project relies on.

❑ **jar:** This element is useful if the dependency doesn't follow the <artifactId>-<version>.jar pattern.

❑ **type:** This element specifies the type of dependency. Allowed values are jar, ejb, and plugin. It is not a required element.

❑ **url:** This element specifies the alternate location for the download if it cannot be found on the Maven repository.

❑ **properties:** This element contains properties about the dependency. Some plug-ins allow you to set their properties in the POM, and you would do so here. One plug-in that does allow this is the WAR plug-in, which we will look at in greater detail when we discuss the case study.

The build Element

The build element is the other critical section of the POM. It contains several elements that describe the build environment to Maven:

❑ **nagEmailAddress:** This element provides an e-mail address where you want to send build status. This element is useful to plug-ins that perform automatic integration builds, such as AntHill, CruiseControl, or Gump.

❑ **sourceDirectory:** This element specifies the directory beneath this one that contains your Java source files. Typically this directory is src/java (we discuss the proposed project layout shortly).

❑ **sourceModifications:** This element is used to look for a particular class, and if that class cannot be loaded, it includes or excludes certain classes from your build and tests.

❑ **unitTestSourceDirectory:** This element specifies the directory beneath this one that contains your standard unit tests. Typically, this directory is src/tests.

❑ **aspectSourceDirectory:** This element specifies the directory containing Aspect sources of the project. The build will compile the Aspects in this directory using the AspectJ plug-in.

❑ **unitTest:** This element specifies which unit tests should be included or excluded from running.

❑ **resources:** This element describes any resources that you need included in the final distribution. The unitTest element also contains a similar element for defining specific resources or files specific to testing.

Project Properties

The project.properties file resides at the same level as the project.xml file. This file allows you to override specific Maven properties and plug-in properties for your project to use. One common property that is typically used is maven.repo.remote, which allows you to specify where your remote repository resides as an HTTP address. When overriding this property, you must separate the repositories with commas. Use the Maven repository first and then any custom repositories afterwards.

The code looks like this:

```
maven.repo.remote=http://www.ibiblio.org/maven,http://mywebsite.com/path/to
/repo
```

Before setting up a custom repository, make sure you understand what structure Maven expects the filesystem to follow in order for it to find any JARs that you have placed there.

maven.xml

This file describes additional goals that you may want to execute before others, such as custom goals or custom Ant tasks that have not been created as plug-ins yet. This file is a Jelly file (which we discuss later in the chapter). A maven.xml file includes several elements, starting with the top-level project element. In this element you define the default goal of your project. Here is a bare-bones maven.xml file that tells Maven to build your project by default whenever you simply type *maven* in your project directory:

```
<project default="java:compile"/>
```

Project Layout

Now we're going to take a look at a basic project structure that Maven recommends:

```
LICENSE.txt
project.properties
project.xml
maven.xml
build.properties
src
    test
    java
    announcements (optional)
xdocs
    navigation.xml
```

The basic structure of a Maven project is a very well-defined layout. You can customize the layout to a certain degree by specifying items in the build element in addition to setting custom properties in the project.properties file. The src directory is where all of your source and configuration code will go. Place all of your custom documentation for the project in the xdocs directory. Maven automatically converts this documentation to HTML or PDF format, depending on which Maven goal you execute (either site:generate or pdf:pdf goal). Now let's examine the src directory a bit more.

The src directory typically consists of at least two subdirectories: java and test. The java directory contains all of your base code for the project, and the test directory contains all of your JUnit unit tests. You can also place a conf directory in here for storing things like additional properties files or configuration files that you need copied into your final JAR or testing JAR.

When Maven executes a JAR goal it will always run through the tests in the test directory. You can control what files are executed by modifying the excludes element in the unitTest section of your POM. You can optionally turn off running the tests entirely by adding a maven.test.skip=true or maven.test.failure .ignore=true property in your project.properties file. Neither of these is recommended for obvious reasons—by turning off testing you run the risk of failing code.

Maven generates the following when building distributions, the project Web site, and other documentation:

```
target
    classes
    test-classes
    iutest-classes
    generated-docs
    test-reports
    docs
        index.html
        apidocs
        xref
        xref-test
        mail-lists.html
        team-list.html
        dependencies.html
        changelog.html
        file-activity-report.html
        developer-activity-report.html
        jdepend-report.html
        junit-report.html
        checkstyle-report.html
```

The target directory is where everything that gets built (source, tests, documentation, and reports) end up. Most of these can also be controlled either by setting properties for specific plug-ins or by changing elements in your POM. Maven generates a number of these documentation and report files automatically for you when you run a site:generate or pdf:pdf goal. Most of these files and folders, such as apidocs, xref, mail-lists.html, and dependencies.html, are pulled directly from the POM. Others, such as developer-activity-report.html and junit-report.html, are generated from plug-ins such as changelog and test.

As you can see, there isn't too much to setting up a project to use Maven initially. The real fun comes afterwards when you want to start doing some customization, like separating your project into discrete modules, specifying new reports to run, or adding in Ant tasks that haven't been turned into plug-ins yet. Next we're going to look at the architecture a bit so that you understand how Maven works with those files you've just supplied to it.

Maven Architecture

Maven at its core is based around its plug-in architecture and the POM. This architecture uses the Jelly scripting language (which we examine in the next section) for its goal processing. The POM, as the project descriptor, controls what features your project will use, what libraries it depends on, who is working on the project, project mailing lists, and so forth. All installed plug-ins are stored in your MAVEN_HOME directory. Each plug-in that is deployed is in a named directory, such as maven-java-plugin-1.3, and under that directory are a number of files, such as plugin.jelly, plugin.properties, project.properties, and project.xml. A Maven plug-in is similar to a Maven project.

Each plug-in consists of two items: goals and properties. *Goals* are items that you as a developer can execute to perform an action on your project. Some example goals are:

❑   **jar:install:** Builds your JAR file and places it in your local Maven repository for use among other projects locally.

❑   **war:war:** Builds a Web application and packages it into a WAR file for you.

❑   **test:test:** Builds and executes your JUnit unit tests, outputting test results as XML and text files for easy perusal.

Every plug-in has executable *goals*. To see what each goal does, you can either look at the plug-in documentation on the Maven Web site or type *maven –g* (which displays all available goals for installed plug-ins). Most goals are not stand-alone, which means they rely on other goals being executed before them. To better understand this, let's look at one of the core plug-ins and examine its goals:

```
Java plugin.jelly file
<?xml version="1.0"?>

<project
  xmlns:j="jelly:core"
  xmlns:ant="jelly:ant"
  xmlns:define="jelly:define"
  xmlns:maven="jelly:maven">
  <goal name="java:prepare-filesystem"
        description="Create the directory structure needed to compile">
    <ant:mkdir dir="${maven.build.dest}"/>
  </goal>

  <goal name="java:compile"
        description="Compile the project"
        prereqs="java:prepare-filesystem">
  ....
  </goal>
```

As you can see from this Jelly file, the plug-in is essentially an XML file with custom processing that will be interpreted by the Jelly engine. First we start with a project element, which allows you to create namespace declarations. These declarations are then interpreted by Jelly, and it loads those tag files. For right now, don't worry about these too much; we discuss them in more detail in the "Understanding Jelly" section. Now we need to concentrate on the java:compile goal. As you can see, there is a prereqs attribute that describes what goals need to execute prior to this goal being attained. There is also a description attribute that will display when you type *maven –g* on the command line. Later we use a similar technique when we write our maven.xml file to execute a custom goal of our definition.

Plug-in properties allow you to modify the default behavior or to specify things like additional source directories specific to that plug-in. Most of the plug-ins properties that can be set are documented on the Maven site (if they are distributed with Maven) or in the plug-in's own documentation. If neither of these is available, you can go into the plug-in's directory and view its plugin.properties file. This file should not be modified. Here is an example of one from the CruiseControl plug-in:

```
maven.cruisecontrol.config=${basedir}/cruisecontrol.xml
maven.cruisecontrol.schedule.interval=300
maven.cruisecontrol.checkout.dir=${basedir}/checkout
maven.cruisecontrol.logs.dir=${basedir}/target/cc-logs
maven.cruisecontrol.goals=scm:update|clean test|site:deploy
maven.cruisecontrol.home=CC_HOME_NOT_SET
maven.cruisecontrol.mail.host=localhost
maven.cruisecontrol.mail.defaultsuffix=DEFAULT_SUFFIX_NOT_SET
maven.cruisecontrol.mail.subjectprefix=[BUILD]
```

These are all properties that you can set in your own project.properties file. In fact, a number of these are required to be set, such as the cruisecontrol.home property, to tell the plug-in where you have installed CruiseControl (see chapter 27 for more information about CruiseControl).

Now that we've examined some of the Maven underpinnings, the next step is to look at how Maven works. The easiest way to do this is to run Maven in debug mode by typing *maven –X jar:jar*. This executes the jar command, which first builds your classes, then runs the unit tests and finally jars your project for deployment or distribution, as shown below.

```
○ ○ ○              Terminal — tcsh — 109x38
[main-lib-dhcp47:chap28/case_study/model] warner% maven -X

 __  __
|  \/  |__ _Apache__ ___
| |\/| / _` \ V / -_) ' \    ~ intelligent projects ~
|_| |_\__,_|\_/\___|_||_|  v. 1.0-rc1-SNAPSHOT

[DEBUG] Adding reference: maven.dependency.classpath -> /Users/warner/.maven/repository/hsqldb/jars/hsqldb-1.
7.2-rc1.jar
        [available] [VERBOSE] Found: src/java
        [available] [VERBOSE] Found: src/test
[DEBUG] Adding reference: maven-classpath ->
[DEBUG] Adding reference: maven.compile.src.set ->
[DEBUG] Adding reference: maven.test.compile.src.set ->
[DEBUG] Adding reference: maven.dependency.classpath ->
[DEBUG] Adding reference: maven-classpath ->
[DEBUG] Adding reference: maven.compile.src.set ->
[DEBUG] Adding reference: maven.test.compile.src.set ->
[DEBUG] Adding reference: maven.dependency.classpath -> /Users/warner/.maven/repository/ant/jars/ant-1.5.3-1.
jar:/Users/warner/.maven/repository/commons-jelly/jars/commons-jelly-tags-antlr-20030211.143720.jar:/Users/wa
rner/.maven/repository/commons-lang/jars/commons-lang-1.0.1.jar:/Users/warner/.maven/repository/antlr/jars/an
tlr-2.7.2.jar
[DEBUG] Adding reference: maven-classpath ->
[DEBUG] Adding reference: maven.compile.src.set ->
[DEBUG] Adding reference: maven.test.compile.src.set ->
[DEBUG] Adding reference: maven.dependency.classpath ->
[DEBUG] Adding reference: maven-classpath ->
[DEBUG] Adding reference: maven.compile.src.set ->
[DEBUG] Adding reference: maven.test.compile.src.set ->
[DEBUG] Adding reference: maven.dependency.classpath -> /Users/warner/.maven/repository/junit/jars/junit-3.8.
1.jar:/Users/warner/.maven/repository/xml-apis/jars/xml-apis-1.0.b2.jar:/Users/warner/.maven/repository/xerce
s/jars/xerces-2.4.0.jar
[DEBUG] Adding reference: maven-classpath ->
[DEBUG] Adding reference: maven.compile.src.set ->
[DEBUG] Adding reference: maven.test.compile.src.set ->
[DEBUG] Adding reference: maven.dependency.classpath -> /Users/warner/.maven/repository/maven/jars/maven-1.0-
beta-10.jar:/Users/warner/.maven/repository/commons-io/jars/commons-io-20030203.000550.jar:/Users/warner/.mav
en/repository/commons-net/jars/commons-net-1.0.0.jar:/Users/warner/.maven/repository/commons-httpclient/jars/
commons-httpclient-2.0-beta1.jar:/Users/warner/.maven/repository/commons-lang/jars/commons-lang-1.0.1.jar:/Us
```

You should see a lot of text flying by as the debug output goes to the console. I'll walk through some of the initial phases of Maven:

1. **Sets references**: Maven sets up all of its internal references, including the JAR dependency locations, test source, Java source, and whatever other references you have defined specific to your project. These also include project and personal properties files.

2. **Downloads dependencies:** If there are missing dependencies in the local repository, Maven attempts to download these, according to your maven.repo.remote property (which defaults to ibiblio.org/maven).

3. **Updates plug-in dependencies:** Maven updates the class path dependencies with internal dependencies required by installed plug-ins.

4. **Prepares filesystem:** If the target directory has not been created, Maven creates it and populates it with required directories according the plug-in's goals.

5. **Scans files:** Maven scans for package.html in the source tree to exclude automatically.

6. **Builds:** It builds the Java source.

7. **Unit-tests:** It compiles and runs unit tests.

8. **Jars:** It jars classes for deployment and places them in the target directory.

Maven processes the following properties files in this order:

1. ${project.home}/project.properties

2. ${project.home}/build.properties

3. ${user.home}/build.properties

So, each project can override Maven properties, and each user can override project and Maven properties.

Maven Properties

There are a number of properties specific to Maven that you can override to provide a custom look and feel for your generated site, to turn on and off XML declarations in HTML headers, and other behavior. Here are some of the properties that you may want to change depending on your needs:

- **maven.build.dest:** Contains the directory where generated classes go.

- **maven.build.src:** Specifies the directory where the generated source goes.

- **maven.conf.dir:** Specifies the directory that holds configuration files.

- **maven.docs.dest:** Indicates the output directory for the generated HTML from reports.

- **maven.docs.omitXmlDeclaration:** Specifies whether generated documentation should have an XML declaration, e.g., <?xml version="1.0"?>.

- **maven.docs.outputencoding:** Indicates the character encoding for generated documentation.

- ❑ **maven.docs.src:** Contains the directory for user-supplied documentation.

- ❑ **maven.gen.docs:** Specifies the directory where generated XDocs that need to be changed to HTML are placed.

- ❑ **maven.home.local:** Indicates the directory on the local machine Maven uses to write user-specific details to, such as expanded plug-ins and cache data.

- ❑ **maven.mode.online:** Indicates whether you are connected to the Internet.

- ❑ **maven.plugin.dir:** Indicates where Maven can find its plug-ins.

- ❑ **maven.plugin.unpacked.dir:** Specifies where Maven expands installed plug-ins for processing.

- ❑ **maven.repo.central:** Specifies the host that Maven will attempt to deploy the distribution to during a dist:deploy.

- ❑ **maven.repo.central.directory:** Specifies the directory that Maven will copy the distribution to during a dist:deploy.

- ❑ **maven.repo.local:** Indicates the repository on the local machine Maven should use to store downloaded artifacts (JARs, etc.).

- ❑ **maven.repo.remote:** Specifies the repository Maven should use to download artifacts (JARs, etc.) that it can't find in the local repository.

- ❑ **maven.repo.remote.enabled:** Indicates whether or not a remote repository should be used.

- ❑ **maven.scp.executable:** Indicates the executable to use for secure copies.

- ❑ **maven.src.dir:** Contains the base directory for the source code.

- ❑ **maven.ssh.executable:** Specifies the executable to use for executing commands remotely.

- ❑ **maven.proxy.host:** Contains the IP or address of your proxy.

- ❑ **maven.proxy.port:** Contains the port number of your proxy.

- ❑ **maven.proxy.username:** Specifies username if your proxy requires authentication.

- ❑ **maven.proxy.password:** Specifies password if your proxy requires authentication.

Understanding Jelly

Jelly is an XML scripting language written by James Strachan and Bob McWhirter (who are also members of another scripting language project, Groovy, http://groovy.codehaus.org/), and Geir Magnusson (project lead on an excellent templating language project, Velocity, http://jakarta.apache.org/velocity). Jelly consists of a series of tag libraries similar to JSP tag libraries. The core tag libraries offer support for coding logic, including files, object creation, and script threading for spawning other Jelly scripts in a new thread.

> ### Where to Get Jelly
>
> **If you want to try Jelly out for other projects, then you can download it as a stand-alone application here:**
>
> **http://jakarta.apache.org/commons/jelly/**

The real joy of Jelly is when you get to the non-core tag libraries. Jelly provides a number of tag libraries that perform additional tasks. Some of these tag libraries are

- ❑ **Ant:** Allows Ant scripts to be run inside Jelly.
- ❑ **BeanShell:** Allows BeanShell scripts to be run inside Jelly.
- ❑ **Email:** Contains various tags for dealing with e-mail.
- ❑ **Validate:** Allows for XML validation of XML files and snippets.

There are many, many tag libraries, and to realize the full power of Jelly you should take a look at the core tags (http://jakarta.apache.org/commons/jelly/tags.html) and the optional tags (http://jakarta .apache.org/commons/jelly/libs/index.html). An additional tag library specifically written for Maven can be found here: http://maven.apache.org/tags.html. One of the primary reasons why Maven switched to Jelly was the ability to code logic into plug-ins (which Ant currently lacks) and the ability to reuse Ant tasks inside Jelly. This allows users to easily migrate their custom Ant files over to use Maven with a minimal amount of rewriting.

So, how can we use Jelly in Maven? Well, the good news is, you already are. The POM file is actually a Jelly script; it's just hidden from your view. But if we want to add some custom Ant tasks into our Maven project, we need to create a maven.xml file and place it at the top level of our project, at the same level as our project.xml.

Let's take a look at how to add an existing Ant task into our maven.xml file:

```
<project
default="java:compile"
xmlns:j="jelly:core"
    xmlns:maven="jelly:maven"
    xmlns:deploy="deploy">
    <preGoal name="java:compile">
        <attainGoal name="plugin:goal"/>
    </preGoal>
    <taskdef name="anttask"
        classname="com.company.AntTask">
        <classpath>
            <path refid="maven.dependency.classpath"/>
            <pathelement path="${maven.build.dest}"/>
        </classpath>
    </taskdef>

    <goal name="myAntGoal">
        <attainGoal name="plugin:goal"/>
```

```
            <attainGoal name="java:compile"/>
            <anttask
                var1="myvariable"
                var2="secondvar to pass to ant task">
                <fileset dir="${maven.build.dir}/classes">
                    <include name="**/*.xml"/>
                </fileset>
            </anttask>
        </goal>
    </project>
```

Let's walk through this a bit so you can get the feel for things. First we have the project element. This element allows us to define the default goal for this project. The goal attribute can be any valid goal you can execute on the command line. We have chosen java:compile as the default goal, which will build our class files. You will also see a number of XML namespace declarations here; these are required if you wish to use some of the optional Jelly tag libraries. The Ant tag library and Werkz tag library (which is specific to Maven) are the only two libraries that are registered with an empty namespace element. This allows us to more easily copy over custom Ant scripts and use them in Maven, without having to edit all the elements by hand and add in a namespace declaration.

The second element you will notice is the preGoal element. This is part of the Werkz tag library and tells Maven to execute the body inside this element prior to the named goal. So, in our case we want a plugin:goal to execute prior to java:compile being executed. This gives us some incredible control over our build process—if we wanted to copy some files into a specific directory, or perform some file filtering on those files before execution, this is how we would do it.

Next we find an Ant task declaration, and as you will notice, this is almost unchanged from a normal Ant task declaration. The only two differences are the variables that you want to pass into the classpath statement. In our case we are passing in two arguments: a reference to maven.dependency.classpath and the classes directory property.

Now we get to the fun part! This is where we can define our own goals to execute. All we need here is a goal name. The only caveat is that this name must not conflict with any existing names, which shouldn't be a problem as long as you don't prefix your goals with an existing plug-in name, such as jar:, java:, or test:. We have named our goal myAntGoal, which allows us to type *maven myAntGoal* on the command line and have this custom goal be executed. Inside this goal we have two elements that define what goals we want to attain prior to executing anything else in our goal. The first one calls a fictitious plugin:goal, and the second calls the java:compile goal. Once these two goals have executed successfully, we want to run our custom Ant task we defined earlier. This is, again, almost identical to the way a custom Ant task would be called in Ant. Here we are calling our Ant task and passing in custom variables needed to run it, along with where we want our XML files to be placed once we have generated them.

That's about it when it comes to Jelly. You can, of course, use any number of additional tag libraries that come with Jelly to perform other tasks. To use it effectively, though, it is helpful to know what some of the Maven properties and references are.

Project Management with Maven

Now that we've seen all the pieces of Maven, where is a good place to start with your project? First, there are several questions you need to ask yourself:

1. Does my project produce multiple artifacts?

If your project produces a JAR file, an EAR file, and a WAR file, then the answer to this is yes. If it produces several JAR files that each do different things or contain different items, then the answer is yes. If you produce only a JAR file or a WAR file, then you are producing only one artifact for users.

2. If the above answer is yes, then can you easily separate your project into discrete modules, like core/model, web, ear, etc.?

❏   What are my projects dependencies?

❏   What does your project require in order to build?

❏   What does your project require to run?

❏   What does your project require to test?

3. What plug-ins will your project make use of?

Will your project use Cactus, XDoclet, jcoverage, Hibernate? Make note of these and what versions of the plug-ins you wish to use.

4. What reports do you want to generate for your project when you build your Web site?

5. Do you want Cactus reports, jcoverage reports, Checkstyle reports? Make note of these to include in the reports section of your project descriptor.

Defining Your Project Structure

Once you have these questions answered you can now start with your first task: creating your project directory structure. I highly recommend following the standard structure that we discussed earlier. If you do decide to stick with your own, just make sure that you set all the appropriate elements in the project descriptor for the source directories and build directories.

So a simple structure might look like this:

```
project.xml
project.properties
maven.xml
src
    java
    test
target (generated by Maven)
```

A more complex structure might look like this:

```
project.xml
project.properties
```

```
maven.xml
src
    java
    test
core
    project.xml
project.properties
maven.xml
    src
        java
        test
    target (only for core)
web
    project.xml
project.properties
maven.xml
    src
        java
        webapp (for use with the war goal)
    target
target (generated by Maven)
```

Defining Your Root Project Descriptor

The next step is to begin creating your main project descriptor (project.xml). As you were thinking about the items above, you may have formed an idea as to how you will structure your projects directory. If you are dealing with a multimodule project, you should create a subdirectory for each artifact under your main directory. For example, if you have a core module and a web module, you should create a directory for each of these under your root directory. Alternatively, you could keep your core code in the main directory (and not separate it out into its own directory) and put the Web code in a separate directory.

I recommend starting with one of the sample POMs we have provided or building one from scratch. The file will need to be called project.xml and live in the root of the project tree. Once you have started you should decide on a group name and a project name. These respective names go in groupId and id elements. For a more descriptive name, use the name element. You will also need to choose a currently released version of the code; typically this will be something like 1.0-b1, 2.0, 3.1.1, or whatever your chosen versioning scheme is. If you haven't released anything yet, choose an appropriate number like .0.8.1-b45, which denotes that the project has not had a final release and is beta-quality software. Still in the top portion of the descriptor, we come to the organization element, which stores the information about what organization is the primary producer of this project. This element is used in the copyright and Web site creation. Along with this is the inception year of the project and the project's package, both of which are used in the JavaDoc creation.

The next two items are the short description and description elements. If you want, you can leave them empty for the time being as they are only used in generating the Web site documentation. You should fill them in at some point, just to give your users more information about the project. In addition, there are other elements below these that are optional, such as url (the Web site's URL), issue tracking url (where bugs are filed), site address and directory (for uploading the built Web site), distribution site and directory (for artifact distribution), repository (the source code management repository descriptor string, typically CVS, but SVN will be available), versions (tagged versions that users can check out from SCM), and mailing lists (mailing lists, either external or internal, that users and developers can subscribe to).

Now we come to the developers and contributors section. I recommend filling in the primary developers' information here. Primarily, this section is used for SCM and reporting, but it's always good to know who is working on the project and what role everyone plays in it. It is also nice to showcase contributors, so that they feel a sense of accomplishment from having contributed something back to the project.

Following this is the licenses section, which allows you to specify what licenses this project is distributed under, be it Apache, GPL, LGPL, BSD-Style, or whatever. A copy of each license should also live in the root of the project directory and be referenced here. If you haven't chosen a license yet, I highly recommend doing so prior to releasing any code to steer clear of any ambiguity. If the project is a commercial one, then you will need to consult with your project leader or supervisor to determine what the license document needs to say. Several licenses are available for open-source projects (if yours is one); you can find these licenses at http://www.opensource.org/licenses/. These are strictly for the project itself and not for the dependencies, which we will get to shortly. Choosing an appropriate license may not be easy—you need to determine what your goals and needs are, so choose wisely.

Now, we come to what can be one of the meatiest sections of any project descriptor: the dependencies. Pull out your list of JARs, EARs, or WARs that you wrote down earlier. These are dependencies that your project relies on, not what plug-ins you are utilizing rely on (those should be defined by the plug-in itself). First, determine whether or not a dependency is available on Ibiblio. To do so, visit the Maven repository on Ibiblio at http://ibiblio.org/maven. There you will see a directory listing of several projects; scan the list for the name of the project or a close approximation. If you don't see it initially, don't worry; next you look for the group name of the project (such as Avalon, which houses several subprojects). If you still can't find it, then you have three choices: download the JAR and place it on your own repository (this repository must mimic the layout that you see on Maven's repository); ask the Maven developers to upload the JAR to the repository (this is only an option if the JAR is freely available and its license allows it to be distributed elsewhere); or if the JAR is not freely available (such as many Sun-supplied JARs that require implicit license agreement), you can supply a URL for the dependency for end users to download and install into their own local repository.

Once you have determined exactly what JARs, EARs, and WARs you need and where they are located, you still must determine what version you need. Unfortunately, making this decision is not the simplest task in the world. Several projects do not number their releases. The closest you can get at times will be a date of release. My best advice is to pick the closest number that you feel is right. It may take a few tries to get the right combination of JARs (some JARs rely on others with specific versions as well). Another option is to look at other projects, also using Maven, that rely on the same JARs you do and copy their dependencies.

Now that we have our dependencies defined, we must define the rest of our project structure, specifically the source directory locations and what files we are going to include. The two primary elements we need to define are sourceDirectory and unitTestSourceDirectory. Then we should define what a test class looks like with respect to file naming. This step is identical to what you would do in an Ant build file when telling JUnit what to run. In addition, you can also define other resources that are necessary during unit testing; these can include property and configuration files, test data files, or other items you might need. After we have defined all of the unit test specifics, we can now define specific resources that the application needs in order to run. They can be identical to the resources that you just defined for unit testing or they can be completely different—it's all up to you.

There are also several other elements in here that may or may not be required, depending on your project: the nag e-mail address (when a build fails, Maven can be configured to automatically send an e-mail to this address), the aspect source directory (for AspectJ aspects that will need to be woven into your code just after building the code), source modifications (which define when and if a source should be included or excluded, depending on the class being loaded, and finally the reports element. If you want specific reports to be run, you must define them. The default reports that will run automatically are JUnit tests, dependency, and source cross reference. You can run a test build to determine what the default reports are.

Your project.properties File

Depending on what plug-ins you have decided to use in your project, you may have some very different properties in this file. One that is common, if you are hosting your own repository or you need to download a JAR from someone else's repository, is maven.repo.remote. This is a comma-separated list of HTTP-accessible repositories. The first repository should almost always be http://ibiblio.org/maven, followed by any other repositories that should be checked. Maven will look for all of your dependencies on Ibiblio first, and if it cannot find them it will move on to the next repository in the list until it does find them. There are several properties that you can set, so I encourage you to review the current Maven documentation to see what each of them does prior to changing them.

Your maven.xml File

Initially, your maven.xml file may define only your project's default goal, typically java:compile or jar:jar. A simple maven.xml file is shown here:

```
<project default="java:compile"/>
```

This tells Maven that when you type *maven* on the command line you want it to compile your project. You can change this to any of the goals that you see when you type *maven –g*. So, if you always want your project to be jar'ed for distribution you would change this to jar:jar, and then Maven would compile your code, run your unit tests, and then jar your project in the target directory.

In addition, if you want to specify some actions be taken before jar'ing your project, you would do so using some of the Jelly tags that we spoke of earlier. Primarily you want to focus on the preGoal, postGoal, and attainGoal tag elements.

Maven multiproject (reactor) and Subprojects

One of the core plug-ins that comes with Maven is the multiproject, or reactor, plug-in. This plug-in allows you to create a modularized project. Originally it was called reactor, but the name has recently been changed to multiproject; however, you will still find some documentation referring to it as the reactor plug-in. The plug-in, when called, analyzes all of the subprojects and determines which ones need to be built first. Whenever you extend a project file, you are implicitly using the multiproject plug-in each time you build that subproject.

Calling Subprojects from the Main Project Using reactor

For each subdirectory that you have created you will need to add the following to its project.properties file, specifying what artifact type will be the default:

```
maven.multiproject.type={war, jar, ear, ejb}
```

That way, when you run from the root of the project directory it knows exactly what type of artifact you wish to deploy from each subproject. Some of the built-in goals that you can automatically run on each subproject are

- ❑ **multiproject:deploy and deploy-snapshot:** Deploys the respective artifact or artifact-snapshot to a server.

- ❑ **multiproject:install and install-snapshot:** Installs the respective artifact or artifact-snapshot for each subproject.

- ❑ **multiproject:site:** Generates the main site for the project, including all the subprojects in its generation.

- ❑ **multiproject:clean:** Cleans all the subprojects' target directories.

Running other goals on your respective subprojects is a little more involved, but not much. To call a specific goal on each subproject you must use the multiproject:goal goal. For example, to run clean and java:compile on each subproject use this:

```
maven -Dgoal=clean,java:compile multiproject:goal
```

This runs the clean goal and then the java:compile goal. If you wanted to add more goals, just specify them before or after these, separated by commas.

Building the Web Site

Now we have come to the final step in our project: creating the documentation and Web site. Honestly it shouldn't be the last thing that you think of, but most often it is. Maven steps in to help you out with this as well. All the documentation that Maven generates is processed as XML files, so if you want to change the files from HTML to PDF just grab your local PDF plug-in (http://maven.apache.org/reference/plugins/pdf/). Maven can also handle documentation in other formats depending on the platform. Some of these are DocBook (all platforms: http://maven.apache.org/reference/plugins/docbook/), Word for Windows (Windows only: http://maven.apache.org/reference/plugins/word2html/), or Tasklist (all platforms: http://maven.apache.org/reference/plugins/tasklist/). Primarily, though, most of the documentation you write will be in the XDoc format (http://jakarta.apache.org/site/jakarta-site-tags.html). XDoc was defined as a way to easily categorize information for the Jakarta project site and then attracted more widespread use. Unfortunately, not all of its XML elements are clearly defined as there is no schema or DTD to constrain what is and is not a valid element. Only the program parsing the file knows what it will and will not accept.

Before I digress much further, all of your .xdoc files belong in the xdocs directory, and from there Maven grabs the files and transforms them along with the rest of the Maven-generated content to produce your site. If you run the DocBook plug-in as well, then those files will be processed along with everything else. To generate your site, it is simply another goal in Maven:

```
maven site:generate
```

This goal will parse through your XDocs and generated JUnit reports, jcoverage reports, and whatever else happens to be lying around in the target directory waiting to be turned into documentation.

Case Study: Managing Our Pet Store Project with Maven

Now let's look at how to convert our project using Maven. First we examine the new directory structure and its relevant files.

The New Directory Structure

We have decided to create a new structure instead of trying to change our existing structure to reflect how Maven works. We did this for a variety of reasons, which we discuss here.

First, the test directory contains the unit tests for our application. However, the only portion tested is the model, not the Web application. Second, this application has two distinct deliverables: a JAR file for the models, and a WAR file for the Web application. Now, we could have put the model and model tests in the root directory, but one of the things I want to show you is how to modularize our application, so I chose to split the tests into separate directories as well. What does that leave us in the root directory then?

```
project.xml
project.properties (if needed)
maven.xml (if needed)
model
web
target
```

Next let's look at the model directory. Essentially this is the same directory as before; however, we have now added in a test directory, where we have moved the tests. Since we are no longer relying on using Test as a package, we can do a simple refactor and change the package to xptoolkit.petstore.model (or dbmodel). So, what does the model directory look like now?

```
project.xml
project.properties
maven.xml
src
    java
    test
```

The project.xml file extends the existing root project.xml through this definition:

```
<extend>${basedir}/../project.xml</extend>
```

This tells Maven to grab the dependencies from the parent before the child, allowing us to store dependencies specific to this subproject without polluting the parent or other children with that dependency.

The Web subproject is similar in layout to the model subproject, with a few changes:

```
project.xml
project.properties
maven.xml
```

```
src
    java
    webapp
```

As you will notice there is a new directory here called webapp. This directory stores all of your information relating to the deployment of a Web application. Underneath it you will place your JSP files, WEB-INF directory, web.xml file, and basically anything that needs to go in the WAR or EAR file, except for JAR files, which are determined elsewhere, and class files, which are built by Maven and placed inside at artifact creation time. We show you how to define these a little later on.

Defining Our Dependencies

There are essentially two dependencies that we need to worry about: the hsqldb JAR file and the Servlet API JAR file. Both of these are available on the Maven repository at Ibiblio (respectively at http://www.ibiblio.org/maven/hsqldb/ and http://www.ibiblio.org/maven/servletapi/).

In addition, we have an interproject dependency between the model and the Web subprojects, so we need to define that dependency in the project descriptor for the Web subproject. The main project descriptor will look like this:

```xml
<?xml version="1.0"?>
<project>
  <pomVersion>3</pomVersion>
  <name>XPToolkit Petstore</name>
  <id>petstore</id>
  <groupId>xptoolkit</groupId>
  <currentVersion>1.0</currentVersion>
  <organization>
    <name>Wrox</name>
    <url>http://wrox.com/</url>
  </organization>
  <inceptionYear>2004</inceptionYear>
  <package>xptoolkit.petstore</package>

  <shortDescription>XPToolkit Petstore demo application</shortDescription>

  <description>
    This is a simple Petstore application to demonstrate the techniques in
the Java Tools for Extreme Programming 2nd edition.
  </description>

  <url>http://www.wrox.com/javatools/</url>
  <issueTrackingUrl/>
  <siteAddress/>
  <siteDirectory/>
  <distributionSite/>
  <distributionDirectory/>

  <repository/>
  <versions/>
  <mailingLists/>
  <developers>
```

```
        <developer>
          <name>Rick Hightower</name>
          <id>rick</id>
          <email>rick@arc-mind.com</email>
          <organization>Arc-Mind</organization>
        </developer>

        <developer>
          <name>Warner Onstine</name>
          <id>warner</id>
          <email>warner@sandcastsoftware.com</email>
          <organization>Sandcast Software</organization>
        </developer>
      </developers>

      <contributors/>
      <licenses/>

      <dependencies>
        <dependency>
          <groupId>hsqldb</groupId>
          <artifactId>hsqldb</artifactId>
          <version>1.7.2-rc1</version>
          <properties>
              <war.bundle>true</war.bundle>
          </properties>
        </dependency>
      </dependencies>

      <build/>
      <reports/>
    </project>
```

As you can see, everything is rather straightforward. Since the main project does not have any source to compile (remember, we moved that to the model and Web subprojects), we do not have to define anything in the build section. We currently aren't going to define any specific reports other than the defaults, so we don't need anything in that element either.

Now, when we run java:compile on one of our subprojects, it will automatically check the dependencies here first, download them if necessary, and add them to the class path. We have also defined something new here called war.bundle, which will be explained in just a second when we look at the Web subproject.

The New Project Descriptors and How They Work

First we look at the model subproject's project descriptor:

```
<project>
<extend>${basedir}/../project.xml</extend>
  <pomVersion>3</pomVersion>
  <name>Petstore-Model</name>
  <id>petstore-model</id>
```

```
      <groupId>xptoolkit</groupId>
      <currentVersion>2.0</currentVersion>
      <build>
        <sourceDirectory>src/java</sourceDirectory>
        <unitTestSourceDirectory>src/test</unitTestSourceDirectory>
        <!-- Unit test cases -->
        <unitTest>
          <includes>
            <include>**/*Test.java</include>
          </includes>
        </unitTest>
      </build>
    </project>
```

Note that this subproject has id and name elements that are different from the parent. This is to distinguish its artifacts from the parent and other children. In this case it is petstore-model, which denotes that it is the model for the pet store project. We will do something similar to the Web subproject. Also notice that this has a test directory specified; we will not have one specified for the Web subproject since we don't have any unit tests for that one.

The Web subproject is similar but with some new elements in the dependencies we will be discussing shortly:

```
<project>
  <extend>${basedir}/../project.xml</extend>
  <pomVersion>3</pomVersion>
  <name>Petstore-Web</name>
  <id>petstore-web</id>
  <groupId>xptoolkit</groupId>
  <currentVersion>2.0</currentVersion>

  <dependencies>
    <dependency>
        <groupId>xptoolkit</groupId>
        <artifactId>petstore-model</artifactId>
        <version>2.0</version>
          <properties>
            <eclipse.dependency>true</eclipse.dependency>
            <war.bundle>true</war.bundle>
          </properties>
    </dependency>
    <!-- non-war dep -->
    <dependency>
      <groupId>servletapi</groupId>
      <artifactId>servletapi</artifactId>
      <version>2.3</version>
      <type>jar</type>
    </dependency>
   </dependencies>
   <build>
     <sourceDirectory>src/java</sourceDirectory>
   </build>
</project>
```

There is quite a bit more going on here. First let's tackle the petstore-model dependency. This basically tells Maven that you require that this JAR be built and in the local repository before you start the build. And there is something new here as well: a properties element. This element is used for placing plug-in properties in the project.xml file. In our case we have two plug-ins: the WAR plug-in and the Eclipse plug-in. The war.bundle property tells the WAR plug-in that we want this JAR file to be included in the lib directory of our final WAR file. The eclipse.dependency property tells the Eclipse plug-in to create an interproject dependency in Eclipse to make coding easier inside the Eclipse IDE.

Using the Eclipse Plug-in

If you use Eclipse as your IDE, then this plug-in will be of great use to you. It maintains and updates your .project and .classpath files for you. So, if you add a new project dependency, or remove one, then by running the plug-in on the appropriate project you can remove that dependency from the .project and .classpath files—and then refresh your project in Eclipse and you're off and running.

So, how do you use this plug-in? First, make sure you have specified all of your dependencies in your project.xml file. Then you need to set a custom variable in Eclipse to point to your Maven repository. Do this in Eclipse by selecting the Window menu and choosing Preferences. In the resulting dialog box, select the Java node and then Classpath Variables. Create a new variable named MAVEN_REPO that points to your local Maven repository, which will typically be at /user_home/.maven/repository. Once you have that set, you can either add this as a new project to Eclipse (if it isn't already) or refresh the project by right-clicking on the project name and choosing Refresh.

Building the Respective Pieces

Now that we have everything defined, we are ready to build our project. There are a couple of ways to do this: First, we could build each project separately by changing to the subproject directory and running jar:install, or running war:war on the Web subproject. In order for this to work properly, we need to run the jar:install first, and then switch to the Web directory and run the war:war goal. Or we could let Maven handle it for us.

To tell Maven that we want to build both subprojects' artifacts, we have to let Maven know what artifacts those are by using the respective project.properties of each subproject:

First, for the model's project.properties file:

```
maven.multiproject.type=jar
```

This tells Maven that for the model subproject we want it to build the JAR as the artifact. Now, let's take a look at the Web subproject's project.properties file:

```
maven.multiproject.type=war
```

This tells Maven that for the Web subproject we want it to build a WAR file. Depending on the artifact, Maven will automatically choose the right goal to run on each subproject. So, for the model it will run jar:jar, and for Web it will run war:war.

Now that we have those defined, we can simply type

```
maven multiproject:install
```

This will run the respective {artifact}:install goal, jar:install for model, and war:install for the Web sub-project. There are more options that we discussed earlier for running specific goals on subprojects. I invite you to review the Maven multiproject section and try them out yourself.

Adding In Custom Deployment Options Using Jelly

Say that every time we built the Web subproject we wanted to deploy it to a container. What steps would we need to take to make that happen? The first step is determining when in the build process we want that to happen—ideally, right after the war:war goal. So, our code might look something like this:

```
<postGoal name="war:war">
        <copy file="${maven.war.final.name}"
todir="my/tomcat/directory/webapps/" />
</postGoal>
```

This code tells Maven that, after we WAR a file, we want to copy that file (identified by the group and project IDs) to our local Tomcat webapps directory. This should work great, as long as Tomcat is not running; otherwise we will receive an error that Maven couldn't overwrite the file. Not good. So, what are some of our other options? We could look at calling Tomcat through Ant—there are several scripts out there that do this already for starting and stopping Tomcat. Basically anything that you can already do in Ant, you should be able to do in Maven with little or no trouble.

Luckily for us, someone has already done this and created a Tomcat plug-in. You can download this plug-in from http://www.codeczar.com/products/tomcat/ and install it in your MAVEN_HOME/plugins directory. The next time you run Maven it should pick up on the new plug-in and automatically extract and install it for you.

In our original Ant build we copied over the database to the container, and we need to do the same for the new Maven-handled code. The easiest way for us to do this is to include the database code as part of the Web application, so copy it into the final build for the Web application with something like this:

```
<preGoal name="war:war">
    <copy todir="${maven.war.build.dir}/WEB-INF/data">
        <fileset dir="../src/data/">
            <include name="**/petstore.*"/>
        </fileset>
    </copy>
</preGoal>
```

This code copies over all of the data files into the WEB-INF directory underneath the data directory. Of course, in a real application we would not want this—it would be better to have a running database to hit against rather than an in-memory one.

Deploying the Web Application to Tomcat or Other Containers

As we have just seen, someone has already written a plug-in for Tomcat deployment. By examining this plug-in we might also be able to write one for deploying to something like Resin. But to keep things simple we have specified only two properties, one for Resin and the other for Tomcat. To ensure that the files are copied over correctly, make sure that your instance of Resin or Tomcat is properly shut down. Let's specify two new goals, one for Tomcat and one for Resin, that you can use:

```
<goal name="deploy-tomcat">
    <attainGoal name="war:war"/>
    <copy file="${maven.war.final.name}" todir="${tomcat.deploy.dir}/webapps"
/>
</goal>
<goal name="deploy-resin">
    <attainGoal name="war:war"/>
    <copy file="${maven.war.final.name}" todir="${resin.deploy.dir}/webapps"
/>
</goal>
```

To execute either of these tasks, all you need to do is type *maven deploy-tomcat* or *maven deploy-resin*, but make sure that you have set the deploy directories in the master project.properties file first; otherwise Maven will complain that it can't find the files.

Building the Web Site

The last item I want to show you is how to build the Web site, which includes all of the reports. Basically to build the Web site for our project you go to the top-level of the project and type

```
maven multiproject:site
```

This code generates our site as shown in the next three figures, with some of the built-in reports.

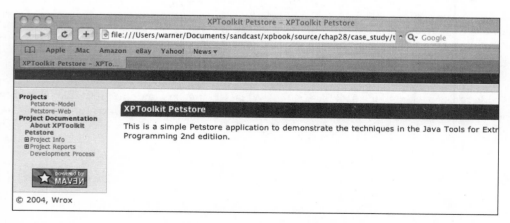

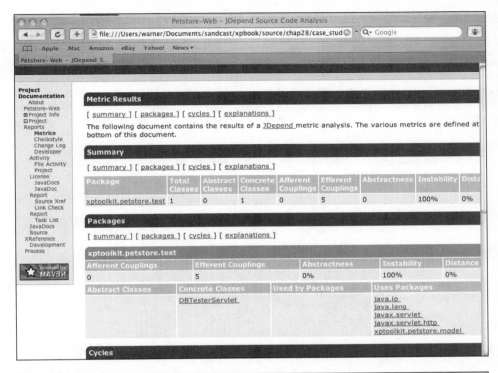

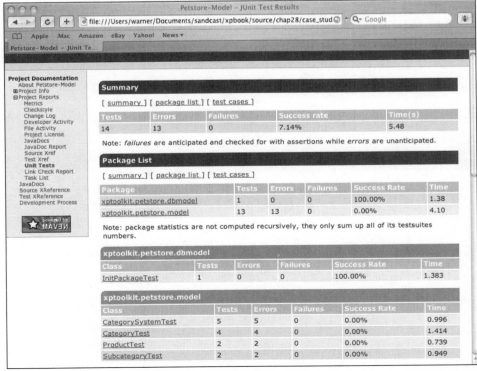

Summary

In this chapter you learned about the Maven project management tool. On its own, it is quite powerful, but combined with the myriad of plug-ins available you have a real powerhouse of a tool. No longer are you bogged down with trying to determine what version of a particular JAR you are using—the answer is right there in your descriptor. As more and more projects move to Maven, versions will become easier to identify. To get the most out of Maven, you need to start using it and conversing with other users, a group that is growing larger every day. Getting up and running with Maven shouldn't take too long—I find that I spend the most time actually tracking down dependencies, as many of these are not well documented in the projects that I rely on, which is distressing. But once I've done it, I don't have to worry about it (until the next release). So, in closing, good luck with your project, and I'm sure that you'll enjoy using Maven as much as I have.

27

Automating Continuous Integration with CruiseControl

In this chapter we introduce you to CruiseControl and show you how to use this tool to assist with continuous integration. CruiseControl is an automated build tool that leverages your Ant build scripts and your version control systems to ensure that your projects are continually integrated. CruiseControl is written in Java, and so has the same cross-platform benefits that tools such as Ant and JUnit provide.

Where to Get CruiseControl

CruiseControl was originally developed by Thoughtworks Inc. to assist its developers on a large development project. It was then released as open source in early 2000 and developed a large following. CruiseControl is distributed under a BSD-style license and can be downloaded at http://cruisecontrol.sourceforge.net/download.html.

At the time of this writing, the current version of CruiseControl is 2.1.5.

CruiseControl comes in a "source-only" distribution; you will have to run the build scripts provided before using it.

CruiseControl is based on a simple concept. A CruiseControl instance is normally set up to watch a version control repository, and to detect changes to the files in the repository. When changes are detected, the instance will update a local copy of a project from the repository, and then invoke the build script for the project. After the build is complete (either successfully or unsuccessfully), the CruiseControl instance will publish various user-specified artifacts (including the log of the build), and inform the project members of the success or failure of the build.

This tool offers a lot of flexibility in how it achieves these tasks. A number of types of version control repositories are supported, including CVS, Subversion, ClearCase, and Visual SourceSafe. These repositories can be monitored at regular intervals or at preset times. Although CruiseControl was built to use Ant build scripts, it also comes with support for Maven, another Java-based build tool. Results can be published to a Web site, or sent out via e-mail, or copied to another machine. Finally, CruiseControl comes with a fully functional sample Web application that you can use to view the build logs.

Like Ant, CruiseControl was designed to be extended. All of the components it uses are built around a plug-in architecture (inspired by a similar mechanism in Ant), and writing your own plug-in to support your own environment is easy. Several of the components in the CruiseControl distribution have been contributed to the project by members of the community.

CruiseControl supports a team practicing *continuous integration* by ensuring that builds are performed on a regular basis as your project evolves. This is similar to the concept of the *nightly build* that many companies (such as Microsoft) practice but occurs even more often. CruiseControl supports continuous integration by ensuring that the builds are performed, even when we fallible humans forget. In addition, the tool can make it feasible to reduce the amount of effort required by developers for their local builds; developers can, for example, run only tests relevant to the work they were doing, and rely on the CruiseControl server to detect if a change has broken an unrelated area. Finally, CruiseControl can be used to run tests and tools that would not normally be run by developers.

CruiseControl is only as effective as your build script, however. To leverage CruiseControl, you must have an effective build script. On the plus side, having a good build script has lots of other benefits, as discussed elsewhere in this book.

What Do Your Build Scripts Do?

Developing effective build scripts is very much a learning experience. Build scripts will vary between projects, sometimes quite dramatically, based on the needs of each project.

As a rule of thumb, however, your build scripts should do a minimum of two things. They should "build" the project, and they should "verify" the result of the build. Building the project involves compiling source code, packaging it up into a distributable file, and completing the various other steps involved in getting from input to output. Verifying the result includes such activities as running code analyzers (like Checkstyle and PMD), unit tests, and integration tests.

The "holy grail" of automated builds is a result you can use with confidence and as few steps as possible. For a J2EE application, this would be an EAR file and possibly configuration scripts for targeted application servers. For a client-side application, this would be a set of files ready to burn to a CD and install.

How close do your build scripts get to this?

There are alternatives to CruiseControl, naturally. A number of places have "rolled their own" build systems, based on their own build scripts. The UNIX cron command works well for scheduling builds, as does the Windows at command. Another example of a continuous build system based on Ant is AntHill.

In the next section, we describe how to configure CruiseControl for an existing project.

Basics of Using CruiseControl

This section is a quick tutorial demonstrating how to get CruiseControl up and running over an existing project, with an existing Ant build script. You will learn how CruiseControl can detect changes, how it can invoke build scripts, and how you can publish the results. Upon completion of this chapter, you should understand CruiseControl well enough to use it with your own projects.

As an example, we create a CruiseControl configuration file for the MVCHelloWorld project described earlier. We describe what we are doing at each step, and we then give a more thorough explanation later on.

The MVCHelloWorld Project

Let's create a CruiseControl configuration file for the MVCHelloWorld file, with some assumptions. The main one is that we are using CVS as a source control system.

The Configuration File

The first step is to create the configuration file. CruiseControl uses an XML-based configuration file format, and by convention, the configuration file is normally called cruise-config.xml. An otherwise empty configuration file would look like this:

```
<?xml version="1.0"?>

<cruisecontrol>
</cruisecontrol>
```

Inside the <cruisecontrol> tag, you can define projects. A single CruiseControl configuration file can hold details about many projects, and as you will see later, these projects can interact. For now, however, we have only one:

```
<?xml version="1.0"?>

<cruisecontrol>
    <project name="helloWorld" >
    </project>
</cruisecontrol>
```

> Project entries in CruiseControl must have a unique name. By convention, this is typically the same as the name given to the Ant project (if Ant is used).

Inside the <project> tag, we define many other tags. These can be entered in any order, but it is easiest to describe them in a logical order. The first of these is the <modificationset> element, which tells CruiseControl where to look for changes. A project can have only one <modificationset>, but it can contain a number of places to look. For this project, we assume that we are using CVS, and that the local copy already has all the details needed (in the CVS subdirectories):

```
<modificationset quietperiod="30" >
    <cvs localWorkingCopy="." />
</modificationset>
```

The quietperiod parameter is extremely important. It specifies how long ago (in seconds) the most recent change has been made. This allows people to commit related changes to the repository in several steps. If you make this value too low, you will sometimes get builds occurring that are inconsistent, with only some of the recently applied changes present. If you make the value too high, then you may have difficulty getting a build to occur, because of developers checking code in frequently.

If the most recent change is within the quiet period, CruiseControl will wait until enough time has passed and then look again. As an example, if the most recent change occurred 10 seconds ago, then with the setting in the example, CruiseControl would wait for 20 seconds, and then look for changes again.

Timing Difficulties

The way CruiseControl works out when the most recent change was made is typically based on the source code control server's clock, but the decision as to how long to wait is based on the CruiseControl server's clock. It is important to ensure that your CruiseControl server and your source code control server have reasonably synchronized clocks. If, for example, your CruiseControl machine is a few hours behind the source code control server, then you will see CruiseControl sleeping for hours every time it detects changes.

Keeping machine clocks synchronized is an easy task these days. Modern operating systems can easily be configured to obtain their current time from a Network Time Protocol (NTP) server. Nonetheless, synchronization remains a common source of problems.

Having decided where CruiseControl will look for changes, our next step is to configure how often it will look, and what it will do when it detects changes. This is done via the <schedule> element:

```
<schedule interval="30" >
    <ant antscript="build.sh" target="cruise-build" />
    <pause startTime="2100" endTime="0300" />
</schedule>
```

The interval attribute states how long (in seconds) CruiseControl should wait between builds before checking again. Nested inside of the <schedule> element are one or more types of builders. In this case, we have an Ant builder that will invoke the provided build.sh shell script (telling it to build the cruise-build target), and a Pause builder that stops this project between 9 p.m. and 3 a.m. every night (so that it doesn't interfere with backups).

Use "Antscript" by Preference

The Ant builder for CruiseControl can actually launch Ant "in-process." This approach provides a slightly faster build time, but it leads to some serious complications. The most annoying one is that Ant, or rather, some Ant tasks, might have some slight memory leaks. In typical Ant usage, these leaks don't cause problems. However, when you run it inside a long-lived process, they add up over time. Another issue is that you have to supply the class path required for your Ant build script when launching CruiseControl.

One common misconception about CruiseControl is that the <modificationset> element, in addition to detecting the changes, will obtain the latest version. This turns out not to be the case. It is obviously going to be necessary to get the latest version of files before doing a build. The <bootstrappers> element provides this functionality:

```
<bootstrappers>
    <currentbuildstatusbootstrapper file="logs/helloWorld/currentbuild.txt"
/>
    <cvsbootstrapper localWorkingCopy="." />
</bootstrappers>
```

This example shows two pieces of functionality. The first is that a file will be updated to show that a build is being started. The second invokes CVS to obtain an up-to-date version of the project.

Keeping Track of Your Builds

An easy way to monitor the progress of your builds is to output messages into the build status file. The Ant <echo> task can be used to achieve this.

Another more complicated way is to use a tool that will observe your build. The Dashboard project (dashboard.sourceforge.net) is one such tool.

After the build is complete, CruiseControl stores the build log away for you. This build log is then used by the publishers to announce the success or failure of the build:

```
<log dir="../logs/helloWorld">
</log>
```

The log file is created in the specified directory. The name of the log file is a combination of a date-timestamp indicating when the build was done and, if the build was successful, a label for the build. A typical log name is log20040304093642LhelloWorld.1.xml.

The log file is an XML-based format, and it contains various data about the build. The log file would include, at a minimum, the set of detected changes, information about the build, and the Ant (or Maven) build log. Also, it is possible to specify in the <log> element additional XML-based files to be included in the log. This makes it easy to merge in reports generated as part of the build.

> **What Sort of Information Do You Want in Your Builds?**
>
> CruiseControl can merge any XML-based data into its log files. A good question, then, is what sort of data would you want to merge. One excellent example is JUnit results. When a test failure breaks the build, having the information of the failure present in the CruiseControl log makes it easy to see what broke. The Ant JUnit task has support for supplying output in an XML format.

This log file will later be transformed using Extensible Style Sheet Language Transformations (XSLT) style sheets. CruiseControl comes with style sheets for displaying information about several common Ant tasks, as well as support for JUnit and Checkstyle XML log files. Assuming you know XSLT, it is relatively easy to create additional style sheets to display other information that you want to see.

The last step involved in creating the configuration file is to enter how you want the results published. CruiseControl has support for many ways of publishing build information. For this example, let's send an e-mail notification as well as update the build status file:

```
<publishers>
    <currentbuildstatuspublisher file="logs/helloWorld/currentbuild.txt" />
        <email mailhost="localhost" returnaddress="cruise@localhost"
               defaultsuffix=""

buildresultsurl="http://localhost:8080/cruisecontrol/buildresults/helloWorld"
>
        <failure address="buildmaster@localhost" />
    </email>
</publishers>
```

This code creates a very simple e-mail message, which is sent to the people who made changes in the build. For this example, information on failed builds is also sent to the "buildmaster." CruiseControl can also be configured to send messages on successful builds in a similar manner, or simply send include an address on all notices.

The e-mail sent by this publisher is a simple one-line message, with a hyperlink to the reporting page (as specified in the buildresultsurl attribute). The subject of the message indicates success or failure, allowing developers to use the filter rules in their e-mail client to sort messages appropriately.

> **Where's the Address Book?**
>
> When CruiseControl gets the list of changes from the source control system, it also gets the user IDs of the people who made the changes. The assumption made here is that the user ID in the source control system will be a valid local e-mail address.
>
> That isn't always the case. Fortunately, you can use CruiseControl to map user IDs to e-mail addresses. You can also sometimes get the source control system to do it for you. For CVS, this is done using the special CVSROOT/users admin file.

Other ways of publishing results include using a fancier e-mail message, with an HTML view of the log file included, or announcing the build results using an instant messaging server (support for IBM's SameTime software is included in CruiseControl). In addition, publishers can be used to transfer the build log, and artifacts of the build process, to another location (for example, to be published via a Web server).

That's the complete configuration file. To make the picture a bit clearer, this is what it looks like now it's finished:

```xml
<?xml version="1.0"?>

<cruisecontrol>
    <project name="helloWorld">
        <bootstrappers>
            <currentbuildstatusbootstrapper
file="logs/helloWorld/currentbuild.txt" />
        <cvsbootstrapper localWorkingCopy="." />
        </bootstrappers>
        <modificationset quietperiod="30" >
            <cvs localWorkingCopy="." />
        </modificationset>
        <schedule interval="30" >
            <ant antscript="build.sh" target="cruise-build" />
            <pause startTime="2100" endTime="0300" />
        </schedule>
        <log dir="../logs/helloWorld">
        </log>
        <publishers>
            <currentbuildstatuspublisher
file="logs/helloWorld/currentbuild.txt" />
            <email mailhost="localhost" returnaddress="cruise@localhost"
                    defaultsuffix=""

buildresultsurl="http://localhost:8080/cruisecontrol/buildresults/helloWorld"
>
                <failure address="buildmaster@localhost" />
            </email>
        </publishers>
    </project>
</cruisecontrol>
```

The order of the elements inside the project directory is not important; the order that is presented is a common one, largely because it is the order used in the examples provided with CruiseControl.

Tying Up the Loose Ends

There are still some loose ends we need to tie up. The first one is that the Ant target that we want to run (cruise-build) does not exist in the build.xml file yet. It is not a complex task, but it needs to do the basic steps common to all automated builds: clean the environment, build from scratch, then verify the build. Targets exist in the build.xml file for each of these, but there isn't any single target that will do it all. Adding this target is a simple step, however:

```xml
<target name="cruise-build" depends="clean,package,test" />
```

The second loose end is that we do not yet have an easy way to run CruiseControl. The most common way to do this include creating a shell script or batch file that lets us invoke CruiseControl. Fortunately, example scripts are included with the CruiseControl distribution. For the sake of this example, we've provided a simple UNIX shell script:

```
#!/bin/bash
# The root of the CruiseControl directory.  The key requirement is that this
is the parent
# directory of CruiseControl's lib and dist directories.
CCDIR=../cruisecontrol/main

LIBDIR=$CCDIR/lib
DISTDIR=$CCDIR/dist

CRUISE_PATH=$DISTDIR/cruisecontrol.jar:$LIBDIR/log4j.jar:\
$LIBDIR/jdom.jar:$LIBDIR/mail.jar:$LIBDIR/activation.jar

EXEC="java -cp $CRUISE_PATH CruiseControl $@"
echo $EXEC
$EXEC
```

Running CruiseControl

To run CruiseControl, all you need to do is invoke the shell script and tell it where the configuration file is:

```
sh ./cruisecontrol.sh -configfile cruise_config.xml
```

You can also supply a port address that can be used by an in-built HTTP server. This allows the CruiseControl service to be controlled remotely:

```
sh ./cruisecontrol.sh -configfile cruise_config.xml -port 8180
```

Cruise RemoteControl

The in-built HTTP server uses the HTTP Java Management Extensions (JMX) adapter supplied by Sun Microsystems. It is also possible to use Remote Management Interface (RMI), and in future versions of CruiseControl, full support for JMX Remoting will be included.

When first run, CruiseControl creates a label for the project based on the project name; for our example, the first label would be helloWorld.1, the second label would be helloWorld.2, and so forth. It also assumes that the last build (for modification purposes) was performed at midnight. Both of these options can be changed via the Web interface, if desired. These values (and other dynamic values about each project) are saved in a [project].ser file, after the first build attempt (though you can force the serialization through the Web interface).

Typically, CruiseControl will be run as a service in the background, similar to how a Web server is run. On UNIX or Linux machines, this is easy to do; simply add the shell script to the appropriate runlevel.

For Windows, it is somewhat more complicated. One program to assist with this is JavaService, from Alexandria Software Consulting (http://www.alexandriasc.com/software/JavaService/index.html); however, there are a number of other options, and no particular solution is recommended.

CruiseControl has extensive logging built into it, using the Jakarta log4J libraries. An example log4j configuration file is included in the CruiseControl distribution.

Viewing the Logs

The CruiseControl log files, while very detailed, are not exactly easily readable. Fortunately, CruiseControl comes with two ways of viewing them in a human-readable form. The HTML e-mail publisher has already been discussed. The other is a Web application that can index the logs and display them in a human-readable format.

The first step in installing the Web application is to compile it; just like the main CruiseControl program, the Web application comes in source-only form. This is simple enough; all that you need to do is go into the directory and run the build script. You can take advantage of this process to customize the Web application slightly for your own environment:

```
cd ../cruisecontrol/jsp
sh ./build.sh -Duser.log.dir=/path/to/logs \
-Duser.build.status.file=currentbuild.txt \
-Dcruise.build.artifacts.dir=/path/to/artifacts war
```

> You can insert the properties you are overriding into an override.properties file, so that you do not have to enter them again if you rebuild.

The user.log.dir property must match that used in the cruise-config.xml file, with the project name stripped (this is part of the multiproject support in CruiseControl). Similarly, if you have used an ArtifactPublisher in your cruise-config.xml file, the cruise.build.artifacts.dir property must match this path (if you haven't used an ArtifactPublisher, you can enter any value). The user.build.status property should be the path to the build status file, *relative to the project log directory*.

The result of this build process is a WAR file that can be deployed into any Java Web Application Server, such as Tomcat. Assuming that it is deployed into Tomcat running on port 8080, the URL to the reporting Web application will be http://localhost:8080/cruisecontrol/buildresults/helloWorld; note that this matches the buildresultsurl property specified in the e-mail publisher in the cruise-config.xml file.

Wrapping It Up

With the CruiseControl service installed and running, and the Web application built, the helloWorld project is ready to go. To trigger some builds, however, you need to have some activity in the CVS repository. That's where your developers come in, and where we leave you to it.

CruiseControl Components

In this section, we cover the standard components that come with CruiseControl, and describe in general the architecture of CruiseControl. Instructions on how to configure each component are included in the tool's documentation.

Source Control Systems

CruiseControl uses components called *source control systems* to detect changes to projects. These components go into the <modificationset> element in the CruiseControl configuration file. Not all of these components actually talk to version control systems, but most do and so the name has stuck.

❑ **BuildStatus:** Used to watch the status of another project. It allows builds of one project to trigger another; very useful when dealing with related projects.

❑ **ClearCase:** Monitors a ClearCase repository for changes. It uses the cleartool lshistory command to obtain the list of changes.

❑ **CVS:** Monitors a CVS repository for changes. It uses the cvs log command to obtain the list of changes.

❑ **FileSystem:** Watches a specified file or directory for changes. Changing the modification date of the file(s) (e.g., by editing it) triggers a new build. One limitation of this method is that it is unknown who changed the file.

❑ **MKS:** Monitors an MKS repository for changes. It uses the rlog command to obtain the list of changes.

❑ **P4:** Monitors a Perforce repository for changes. It uses the p4 changes command to obtain the list of changes.

❑ **PVCS:** Monitors a PVCS repository for changes. It uses the vlog command to obtain the list of changes.

❑ **StarTeam:** Monitors a StarTeam repository for changes. It uses the StarTeam Java API to obtain the required information. This requires the StarTeam SDK to be present when building CruiseControl as well as when running it.

❑ **VSS:** Monitors a Visual SourceSafe repository for changes. It uses the ss history command to obtain the list of changes.

❑ **VSSJournal:** Monitors a Visual SourceSafe repository for changes, using the Visual SourceSafe journaling facility. This works by reading the journal file directly.

❑ **SVN:** Monitors a Subversion repository for changes. It uses the svn log command to obtain the list of changes. This component is not enabled in the default distribution of CruiseControl, because Subversion had not been finalized. In future releases, it will be enabled. In the interim, to enable it you need to enter the following into your configuration file, inside a <project> element:

```
<plugin name="svn"
classname=:"net.sourceforge.cruisecontrol.sourceontrols.SVN" />
```

Bootstrappers

Bootstrappers are components used to update some or all of your project before the build officially kicks off. They were introduced to get around a significant problem: if you use the build script to obtain the latest version of your project, what do you do when the build script changes?

At the very least, you should use a bootstrapper to update your build script. Bootstrappers also provide a convenient way to perform any other "pre-build" activity.

You enter bootstrappers within the <bootstrappers> element.

> The word "bootstrapper" is a common term used in computing to describe a process that is done to enable another process. The term comes from the phrase "to pull yourself up by your bootstraps."

In theory, there should be a bootstrapper to match each supported version control system. However, only some of the version control systems have bootstrappers at this time.

❑ **ClearCaseBootStrapper:** Uses ClearCase to update the specified files or directory.

❑ **CurrentBuildStatusBootStrapper:** Not really a bootstrapper, this component updates the specified status file to indicate that a build is starting.

❑ **CVSBootStrapper:** Uses CVS to update the specified files or directory.

❑ **P4BootStrapper:** Uses Perforce to update the specified files or directory.

❑ **StarTeamBootStrapper:** Uses StarTeam to update the specified files or directory. It requires the StarTeam SDK, just like the StarTeam source control component.

❑ **VSSBootStrapper:** Uses Visual SourceSafe to update the specified files or directory.

❑ **CurrentBuildStatusFTPBootStrapper:** Similar to the CurrentBuildStatusBootStrapper; however, this component then transfers the status file to a remote server via FTP. This component is not enabled in the default distribution of CruiseControl. In future releases, it will be enabled. In the interim, to enable it you must enter the following into your configuration file, inside a <project> element:

```
<plugin name="currentbuildstatusftpbootstrapper"
classname="net.sourceforge.cruisecontrol.bootstrappers.CurrentBu
ildStatusFTPBootStrapper.SVN" />
```

❑ **SVNBootStrapper:** Uses Subversion to update the specified files or directory. This component is also not enabled in the default distribution of CruiseControl, since Subversion had not been finalized. In future releases, it will be enabled. In the interim, to enable it you must enter the following into your configuration file, inside a <project> element:

```
<plugin name="svn"
classname="net.sourceforge.cruisecontrol.bootstrappers.SVNBootSt
rapper" />
```

Builders

Builder components are what CruiseControl actually uses to build the project. In theory, any sort of mechanism could be used to build a project, but in practice it is only feasible to make a builder for a mechanism that can produce an XML log file. There is no requirement that the build mechanism be Java based; for example, both the Ant and Maven builders can (and should) be run by a supplied batch script.

Although a CruiseControl configuration file can define many projects within it, at this time there is support for only one project to be built at a time. As such, there is only one active builder.

In addition to building at regular intervals, as already demonstrated, builders can be supplied for timed builds or to be run at particular intervals. For example, a common usage is to supply a <schedule> element like this:

```
<schedule interval="30" >
    <ant antscript="build.sh" target="cruise-build" multiple="1" />
    <ant antscript="build.sh" target="full-cruise-build" multiple="5" />
    <ant antscript="build.sh" target="nightly-cruise-build" time="0830" />
    <ant antscript="build.sh" target="weekly-cruise-build" time="0305"
day="Saturday" />
    <pause startTime="2100" endTime="0300" />
</schedule>
```

As you can see, this schedule runs the cruise-build task normally, but every fifth build will run the full-cruise-build. The nightly and weekly tasks provide for still more flexibility. These tasks are useful for running Ant tasks that are not desirable to run every build (presumably because they take too long to complete).

You enter builder components within the <schedule> element.

❑   **Ant:** Invokes an Ant build script.

❑   **Maven:** Invokes a Maven build script.

❑   **Pause:** Forces the project to pause during the specified hours.

BuildLoggers

BuildLoggers are used to supplement the log file that CruiseControl produces. By default, CruiseControl includes information on the build, along with information supplied by the source control components and the builder components.

You enter BuildLoggers components within the <log> element.

The only BuildLogger to ship with CruiseControl is the Merge logger. This component merges the specified XML file (or XML files in the specified directory) into the log file.

LabelIncrementers

LabelIncrementers are used to determine the next label to be used on a project. You enter them within the <project> element. If you do not include one, the default incrementer is used.

Getting the Build Label

The build label that will be applied to the project (if it is successfully built) is available to the build scripts as a property called label. However, it will be applied only if the build is successful. Other properties of interest are cctimestamp (the time of this build), cclastbuildtimestamp (the time of the last build), and cclastgoodbuildtimestamp (the time of the last known good build).

❑ **LabelIncrementer:** The default label incrementer. It produces labels like Project.1. By default, the last numeric component is incremented following a successful build (which means that there may be a number of failed builds between Project.1 and Project.2), but it can be configured to increment before the build. If it increments before the build, the build number will increase even if the build fails, thus reflecting build attempts.

❑ **CVSLabelIncrementer:** This is exactly like the default label incrementer, except that it uses a -character instead of a period to separate the text of the label from the numeric extension. This allows the label to be used as a CVS tag. By default, it is not enabled. To enable it, simply register the label as follows:

```
<plugin name="cvslabelincrementer"
classname="net.sourceforge.cruisecontrol.labelincrementers.CVSLa
belIncrementer" />
```

❑ **EmptyLabelIncrementer:** This incrementer always returns an empty string for the label. By default, it is not enabled. To enable it, simply register the label as follows:

```
<plugin name="emptylabelincrementer"
classname="net.sourceforge.cruisecontrol.labelincrementers.Empty
LabelIncrementer" />
```

When you're registering a LabelIncrementer, it is possible to set it as the default incrementer (thus allowing it to be omitted, if you're happy with its default behavior). To do this, simply name the plug-in labelincrementer. This trick works for overriding the behavior of any component; however, it is normally more sensible to use a different name for the overriding component. The LabelIncrementer is a special case, due to the fact that it can be omitted.

Publishers

Publisher components are run after the build is complete, and after the resulting log file is finalized. The intent of these components is to publish the results of the build.

You enter publisher components within the <publishers> element.

❑ **ArtifactsPublisher:** Copies build products to a unique destination directory based on the build timestamp. This publisher is good for preserving the results of builds (such as the distributable files).

❑ **CurrentBuildStatusPublisher:** Updates the build status file with an indicator of when the next build attempt will be made.

❑ **Email:** Sends an e-mail to the list of users detected by the source control components. In addition, users can be entered to receive notification of successful or failed builds, or both. The e-mail will consist of a link to the reporting application, plus a subject line indicating the success or failure of the build. Successful builds will include the build label in the subject line.

❑ **Execute:** Executes a shell command.

❑ **HTMLEmail:** Sends an e-mail to the list of users detected by the source control components. In addition, users can be entered to receive notification of successful or failed builds, or both. The e-mail will contain the XML log file, *after* selected style sheets have been applied to it. The default style sheets result in an HTML message, similar to the Web application report. The subject of the e-mail will indicate success or failure, and successful builds will include the build label in the subject.

❑ **SCP:** This uses SCP (Secure Copy Protocol) to transfer a selected file to another machine.

❑ **XSLTLogPublisher:** Applies an XSLT style sheet to the log file, and saves the result.

❑ **CurrentBuildStatusFTPPublisher:** This is similar to the CurrentBuildStatusPublisher, but it will then transfer the status file via FTP to another server. By default, it is not enabled. To enable it, simply register the component as follows:

```
<plugin name="currentbuildstatusftppublisher"
classname="net.sourceforge.cruisecontrol.publishers.CurrentBuild
StatusFTPPublisher" />
```

❑ **FTPPublisher:** This is similar to the SCP publisher, but it uses FTP to transfer the file. By default, it is not enabled. To enable it, simply register the component as follows:

```
<plugin name="ftppublisher"
classname="net.sourceforge.cruisecontrol.publishers.FTPPublisher
" />
```

❑ **SameTimeAnnouncementPublisher:** This works similar to the Email publisher, but instead of sending an e-mail, it sends a SameTime announcement (SameTime is an instant messaging product from IBM). By default, it is not enabled. To enable it, simply register the component as follows:

```
<plugin name="sametimeannouncementpublisher"
classname="net.sourceforge.cruisecontrol.publishers.SameTimeAnno
uncementPublisher" />
```

CruiseControl Life Cycle

Upon starting, CruiseControl goes through the configured projects and loads in the saved state information for each project (if any). It then determines when the next build for each project will occur, and enters a wait cycle.

Whenever a project is scheduled to be built (as determined by the information in the <schedule> element), the project is placed into a *build queue*. A separate thread of execution monitors the build queue, and is responsible for actually building the projects. Once the project is built, the next build is scheduled; if it would have occurred in the past, the project goes straight back into the build queue (at the end).

> **Although CruiseControl supports only one thread accessing the build queue at the moment, future versions are planned to have a configurable number of build threads.**

When the build thread starts building a project, the first step taken is to "bootstrap" the project, by invoking the bootstrappers associated with the project. After that is complete, the project looks for modifications, using the source control components. Assuming that modifications are found, the project is built by invoking the builders (with the label being calculated either before or after the build attempt).

After the project is built, the log is created. The project state is then saved to disk (where it will be used to recover the project if the CruiseControl service is restarted), and finally the project results are published. The project then goes back into the idle mode, until the next scheduled build.

Multiproject Support

One of the nicer (and newer) features of CruiseControl is support for multiple projects. There are two aspects to this: support for multiple projects within a CruiseControl server instance (i.e., in the configuration file), and support for multiple projects within the Web application.

By defining multiple projects within a single CruiseControl instance, you are explicitly catering for a single server building two or more projects. While there is a limit on how many actively developed projects a CruiseControl instance can effectively manage, this solution works very well for projects with relatively low activity (such as projects in "maintenance" mode).

> **Resource Management**
>
> A single CruiseControl instance cannot effectively serve a large number of active projects because it can build only one at a time. Consequently, the amount of time that developers will have to wait before a build result is increased, possibly quite significantly. This issue can be addressed somewhat by having multiple instances per machine, but resource limits on the server will still pose a hard limit. It is difficult, for example, for even a four-CPU server to build eight projects concurrently. Nor will the addition of multiple build threads to CruiseControl address this issue. The solution will be a distributed build system—far from an easy task.

One nice feature of defining multiple projects in the one configuration file is to be able to have builds of one project trigger other builds, via the BuildStatus source control component. This approach allows projects to be updated when common components change, promoting reuse between projects and a core set of common code.

The CruiseControl reporting service provides support for multiple projects as well. As noted in the installation section, the Web application is provided with a path to a log directory, minus the project name. This is because the Web application assumes that all the directories beneath the log directory are distinct projects. The Web application provides a nice summary page so that the state of all the projects can be seen at a glance

If you have multiple CruiseControl services, there is no reason why they cannot save their log files into the same base directory. This allows you to use one Web application to report on multiple CruiseControl services. You can even have the CruiseControl services on different machines; they just need to be able to publish their logs back to the reporting server.

Enhancing Your Build Scripts

Having established your CruiseControl service, the next step is to go back to your build script. There are a number of features that are useful in a script (which is automatically built) that you probably wouldn't bother putting into a script that is run only by humans.

Cleanliness Is Next To...

Automated scripts must start from a clean base. You must include a target that cleans out the project work area, removing all generated artifacts. Naturally, this should be the first target invoked by the build target.

An exception occurs when you use CruiseControl to do partial builds and only do full builds periodically. In this case, the partial builds need only remove the artifacts that will later be regenerated.

Document Thyself

A common use of an automated build is to generate (and publish) documentation, particularly JavaDoc. This is an excellent task to do in a nightly build, for example.

Testing Times

While every good build script should include unit tests (and developers should run those tests themselves!), automating other tests, such as integration, performance, and acceptance tests, can pay off in an automated environment. Although developers won't normally run them since they can often be quite time consuming, it doesn't matter that much if your nightly build takes an hour longer than your daytime builds. Performance tests, in particular, are often run overnight, with endurance tests performed over weekends.

Latest and Greatest

You could create a nightly task to migrate the latest working release up to a user acceptance or testing region. This would allow testers to start each day with a fresh version.

Who Goes There?

With automated builds, particularly automated builds that deploy to servers by themselves, it is a good idea to embed the build label into the generated files in some manner. The Ant <propertyfile> task provides a good way to do this, as you can put the label property into a property file. All you need then is to provide a way to find out the label in your application. (Hint: About pages are a good place for this sort of data.)

Navel Gazing

It is worthwhile spending time putting analytical tools into your build scripts. Such tools can analyze your project and give back some metrics, some meaningful, others not so good. There are a number of such tools, and some good open-source tools are Checkstyle, PMD, JDepend, JavaNCSS, and JCoverage. These reports can be used both to examine your project for problems right now and to discover trends over time.

Summary

This chapter covered the installation and use of CruiseControl, and the various facilities it provides. While not intended to be a complete reference, this introduction should be sufficient for you to be able to see what CruiseControl can provide for you and how to go about using it.

This chapter demonstrated how you can take an existing Ant project and turn it into a regularly occurring automated build, providing the developers on the project with a safety net that will support them in their use of continuous integration. Armed with this information, you should be able to install CruiseControl in your own organization.

Finally, we've given some suggestions on how you can gain the most out of regular automated builds. The rest is up to you.

Wait! I've Still Got Some Questions!

You can ask your questions on the CruiseControl Users mailing list, cruiscontrol-users@lists.sourceforge.net. If you are interested in extending CruiseControl, and want help, or wish to contribute to the CruiseControl project, you should direct your correspondence to the CruiseControl Developers mailing list, cruisecontrol-devel@lists.sourceforge.net. Details on how to subscribe to these mailing lists can be found at http://cruisecontrol.sourceforge.net/contact.html.

There is also a Wiki devoted to all things CruiseControl, which can be found at http://c2.com/w4/cc/wiki.cgi. If you haven't been exposed to a Wiki before, a Wiki is a collaborative Web site, which provides an easy way to document and publish questions and answers.

28

Automating Continuous Integration with AntHill

As the complexity of software development continues to grow, a project team needs to be aware of the processes and practices used in its software development methodology. Whether waterfall or Extreme Programming, all software must be compiled, integrated, and tested. In many projects, this process of compiling, integrating, and testing is performed on an ad hoc basis triggered when a team leader or manager dictates that it is time to begin pulling the new release together. However, many of projects and most of the software configuration management literature will tell you that "building" the software should take place on a nightly basis at a minimum and potentially several times a day. In this chapter, we introduce the open-source product AntHill developed by urban{code} and show how to use AntHill to fully automate the build process. Further, we will show how to use AntHill with the Petstore project.

Where to Get AntHill

AntHill is both a commercial and an open-source product. The open-source product can be obtained from the following URL: http://www.urbancode.com/ projects/anthill/download.jsp. There are both binary and source download files available. For the sake of this chapter, we will assume that you are downloading the binary file.

AntHill Primer

In an effort to help the open source community and promote the idea of continuous integration, urban{code} has released a slimmed-down version of its AntHill Pro package called AntHill OS. The OS stands for open source. AntHill is a continuous integration tool designed to provide the following:

Chapter 28

- ❑ A controlled build process.
- ❑ The ability to track and reproduce builds.
- ❑ Signal a build status through e-mail, CM labels, etc.
- ❑ Fully automate the build process, run tests, and generate metrics.

These tasks are important to the development of a successful project because without them the project pieces would be working a vacuum.

If you are new to software development or haven't been a part of a medium/large project, this idea of continuous integration might seem like a foreign topic when, in fact, the idea of doing automatic nightly builds and running a smoke test after a successful build has been around for just about as long as software development itself. Consider as an example a very large project I worked on several years ago. In this project, we had roughly 50 developers working in five major areas, with most of the developers dedicated to a single component within the areas. These developers were slinging code on a daily basis. Each night the developers who thought their code was ready for the build as well as developers who were just making maintenance changes would check their code into the CM repository. At some magical time during the night, a build would be fired off on a dedicated build machine. If the build was successful, it would be automatically copied to a test machine and an informal smoke test would be executed on the code.

A good deal of the fun in our project was the morning after a build failure. A build failure occurred when either the compiling/linking failed or the smoke test failed. In either case, the developer who caused the failure would receive a traveling trophy. For the most part, the embarrassment of the trophy was a joke, but there was also the serious side of knowing that the newly checked-in code had caused a failure in the system. When the failure was addressed in the morning, the build would be fired off again to make sure the code was again in a stable state. So you can see that continuous integration is important, but what are some of the benefits?

First, bugs are introduced into code on a daily basis but might not be caught for weeks or months. Consider the times when code is being integrated from a variety of sources. At one point during the initial process, an entity might reveal the API of a key component to others in the team but not readily supply the code behind the interface. Since there is no code, there is no reason to compile, right? Well, what happens when the API changes and those changes aren't communicated? If we were under a strict build process, this situation would be immediately caught because the code wouldn't compile. The interface could be put through the build process by using stubs, with the stubs slowly replaced with real code. The point here is that API changes from one entity to another need to be communicated quickly, and if the project waits until integration, there will be a large amount of time needed to resolve the situation. Many projects will schedule a significant amount of time just for this integration because they know problems will exist simply because this would be the first time the different pieces of code would have been compiled together.

Second, when a continuous integration system has been set up and working successfully, developers have a faster and better mechanism to verify that changes they have just made to the code are successful. We all know that developers do a good job of writing their own unit test cases and thoroughly testing their code, but in those rare cases where this doesn't occur, the night build will catch the problem before it manifests itself too far into the project.

Third, the build system will be designed in such a manner that developers are able to access the most up-to-date code possible when making changes. This helps the process because developers won't make a code change to a piece of source code just lying around in their home directory.

It is clear that a continuous integration system can be an important element of a software development process, but what's involved? There are many different components necessary for a successful system. The components include:

- Successful build process definition
- Configuration management (CM) software
- Build scripts
- Automated testing
- Controlling server

The build process definition tells the project and its team what constitutes a successful build. The definition is likely to be different for each project, but one definition might be the following: In order for a build process to be successful, it must obtain fresh copies of all source code, compile the code without errors and warnings (yes, there are projects that allow production code to have warnings), process the results of the compile into a deployment format, deploy the newly compiled software, run a series of system tests on the code, and report the results.

A configuration management system handles the safekeeping of the code. Developers are required to check out any code they wish to make changes to and then check the same code back in when they have finished. The CM system will keep track of the changes and provide a way of always being able to view and access older pieces of code. Further, the system will be able to track who made changes, so faulty source code can be traced to the person who made the coding mistake.

Scripts to automate the build are important because we don't want to hire a person to "do the build" during the night. The system should be able to automatically perform the build without human intervention.

Testing is important because the system isn't successful just because it was built. We don't believe in the statement, "Hooray, it compiled. Ship it!" All of the tests on the code that will be performed by the continuous integration process need to be of the automated variety. If inputs are needed, then automated testing tools might need to be employed, but there shouldn't be the need for a human to do the testing.

Finally, the controlling server is a software process that pulls together each of the components listed above. It is responsible for obtaining the latest source code from the configuration management system, compiling the code, putting together an appropriate deployment package, testing the deployment, and finally generating any necessary statistics or alerts.

Now where does AntHill come into play? The answer is the controlling server. AntHill provides the process through which a comprehensive continuous integration system can be built.

Obtaining and Installing AntHill

There are a few key questions to ask yourself when installing AntHill. The first is where to host the system. Since AntHill is designed to act as a central server that handles the nightly builds, it is a good idea to install the software on a machine divorced from the development platform itself. This machine should probably be considered a separate build machine and labeled as such. AntHill requires the use of an application server such as Tomcat, Resin, or JBoss, so make sure one of those is available on the build machine. It should be noted that AntHill has been tested only on Tomcat versions 3.2.2, 3.3.1, and 4.0.2. We used Resin 3.0 for this chapter during testing as well.

Once the binary AntHill file has been downloaded, you will need to determine where to install AntHill. The recommended location is /usr/local/anthill. One of the directories extracted from the tar is called /dist. Within the /dist directory is a file called anthill.war. This file should be placed in the webapps directory of your application server.

After the .war file has been transferred to the webapps directory of your application server, open a browser and browse to your application server and the directory /anthill, for example, http://localhost:8080/anthill. The result should look something like this:

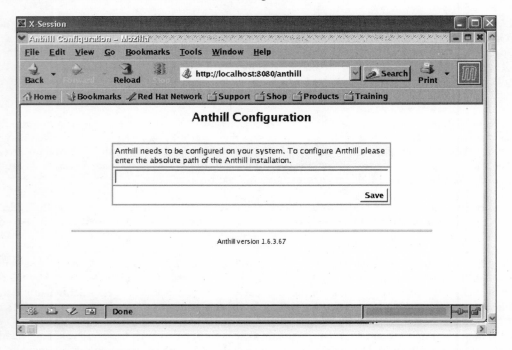

The AntHill Configuration page requires that you enter the path where you installed AntHill. If you installed it in /usr/local/anthill, just enter this path into the page's edit line. Once you've entered the path, click the Save button. The installation path will be saved, and the primary AntHill Administration screen will be displayed, as shown below.

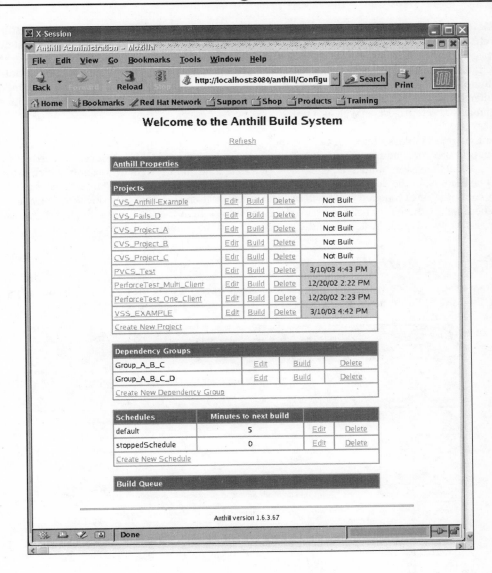

Let's take a moment and discuss the various parts of the Administration page, since it will be an important part of getting our continuous integration system up and running. As you can see from the previous image, there are five different functional areas for administrating a build system. These areas are:

❏ AntHill Properties

❏ Projects

❏ Dependency Groups

❏ Schedules

❏ Build Queue

When the Administration page is first opened, it shows the examples preconfigured for AntHill. Later in this chapter, we will run through the example build before building our own system. The first option on the page is for the AntHill properties. In the next section we will look at this link in detail. Next on the page is a table of projects showing the name of the project, the time it was last built, and the outcome of the build. When you view the Administration page on your computer, you will see that the build status is either red or green, indicating whether or not the build was successful. There are three options links available for each project, as well as a link to add a new project.

After the project table is a table for dependency groups. The dependency groups are used to create a hierarchy of projects. For example, we might have three projects, A, B, and C, where project B needs to be build before A and C. We can build a dependency group to tell the build system the order in which the projects must be built. After the dependency group table is the schedule. The schedule table includes a list of the different times the automated build will be kicked off. There can be more than one time when a build will be scheduled, so there may be more than one entry in the schedule table. Finally, the Build Queue area of the page shows all of the builds currently being built and those in the queue to be built.

Configuring AntHill

Before we start working with AntHill, let's take a moment and review the properties needed to use AntHill. Click the AntHill Properties link at the top of the Administration page to reveal the page found below.

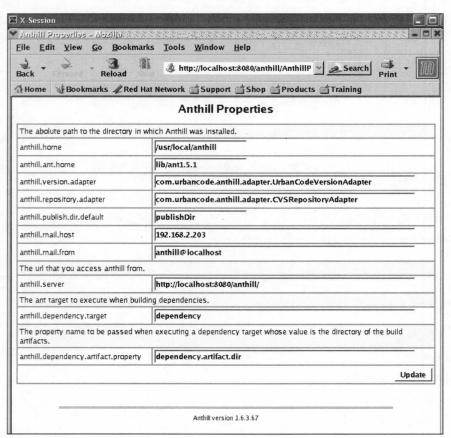

There are a total of 10 different configuration options to be set in AntHill, which are outlined here:

❏ **anthill.home:** This option is the same as the directory added when we first accessed the system. If you move the location of the AntHill application directory, you will need to change this option as well.

❏ **anthill.ant.home:** As you might expect, AntHill uses Ant to perform the actual builds. You need to set this option to the current server's Ant application directory.

❏ **anthill.version.adapter:** When builds are fired off by AntHill, the version number of the build needs to be increased. The version adapter handles the incrementing of the build version automatically. Currently, AntHill ships with only a single adapter called com.urbancode.anthill .adapter.UrbanCodeVersionAdapter, and this value should not be changed. As you will see shortly, the build version number appears as major.minor.build. The default adapter will increase only the build number. To increase either the major or minor version, an unscheduled build must take place. Also, if you are building within a branch, only a single build number is used, which is appended to the branch label name.

❏ **anthill.repository.adapter:** AntHill is required to pull current source files from a repository. This option is used to set the default adapter for your specific CM system. Note: This option is used to set only the adapter type for your CM repository software but not the actual values for the repository. You will set the repository options when you add a project to the system.

The current options available are:

- ❏ com.urbancode.anthill.adapter.CVSRepositoryAdapter
- ❏ com.urbancode.anthill.adapter.PVCSRepositoryAdapter
- ❏ com.urbancode.anthill.adapter.PerforceRepositoryAdapter
- ❏ com.urbancode.anthill.adapter.VSSRepositoryAdapter
- ❏ com.urbancode.anthill.adapter.MKSIntegrityRepositoryAdapter
- ❏ com.urbancode.anthill.adapter.FileSystemRepositoryAdapter

❏ **anthill.publish.dir.default:** The Publish Directory option prompts the user to specify a directory where all of the artifacts from a build will be placed and subsequently accessed by the Administration page. The default location is the publishDir directory of the primary AntHill installation directory.

❏ **anthilll.mail.host:** AntHill will send e-mails to appropriate people based on the build. In this option, you will need to set up the host of the mail system to be used to send those e-mails.

❏ **anthill.mail.from:** This option sets the mail-from text value for the e-mails sent by the system.

❏ **anthill.server:** In the default case, the AntHill Administration page is accessed from the URL http://localhost:8080/anthill. If you need to access the page through a different URL, make the appropriate change here.

❏ **anthill.dependency.target:** When a dependency has been created for several projects, the system will use a specific target for Ant to designate the dependency. The default task name is dependency.

❏ **anthill.dependency.artifact.property:** When a dependency target is executed, the name of the build artifacts directory will be passed in the property name of this option.

Experimenting with AntHill

Before we start the process of setting up our own projects in AntHill, we have the opportunity to see how the system works using an example project hosted by urban{code}. In order to use the example in its fullest, set the e-mail server to your server name. You will also need to set up a CVS repository for the example project. Since you are setting up a build server, we are going to assume that you already have a repository set up in your organization. However, for the AntHill example, you will need CVS installed. If you don't have CVS installed, you can obtain it from http://www.wincvs.org. Once it is installed, you will need to execute the following command:

```
cvs —d :pserver:anthill-example@cvs2.urbancode.com:/usr/local/anthill-test
login
```

The urban{code} CVS repository will return with a password. Type in the value *anthill-example*. Now we also want the example project to send us notification e-mails. Click the Edit link next to the Anthill-Example project. Locate the option for anthill.users, and enter your e-mail address, as shown below.

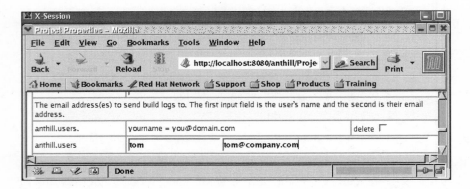

At this point, you are ready to begin using the example. Find the entry called CVS_Anthill-Example link in the Projects part of the AntHill Administration page, and click the Build link to reveal the image shown here:

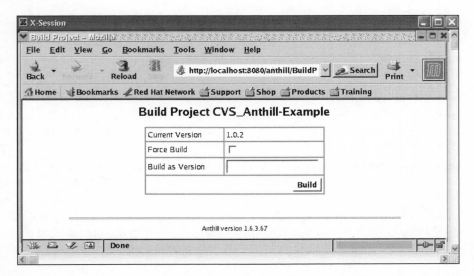

Now enable the checkbox for Force Build to tell the system to force a build of this project. Notice that we could place a specific value in the Version field; otherwise, we will just let AntHill use the version it finds appropriate. Now click the Build button. After you do, the Build Queue will have an entry called CVS_Anthill-Example – Being Built. The CVS_Anthill-Example row under Projects will update to show the current data and time. After some time, the Administration page will automatically update to show a successful build, or you can just click the Refresh button at the top of the Administration page. Once the example project is successful, as shown by the green highlighting of the Time/Date field, click the CVS_Anthill-Example link to reveal the project artifacts, as shown below.

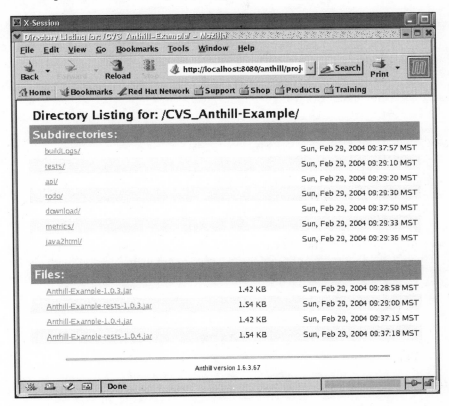

When the example project has been built, you should receive an e-mail showing the status of the build. Notice that there are a number of subdirectories created from the Ant build script as well as AntHill itself. Click the first directory link called buildLogs. Within this directory you will find the logs from the various builds that have been performed on the project. If you click one of the log links, you will see the output from the Ant build.xml script.

An AntHill HelloWorld

With the AntHill example project experience under our belt, let's work on a HelloWorld-type example to see how to use AntHill within the scope of a new project. We'll start the process by creating a new software project based on the familiar HelloWorld code.

Creating the Project

For this project, we are are going to assume that you have acccess to AntHill as well as a working CVS repository. Within your home directory, create a new directory called helloworld and a subdirectory called src, and within the subdirectory, create a new file called HelloWorld.java and type in the following code:

```
import java.io.*;

public class HelloWorld {

  String myHello;

  public void buildString(String s) {
    myHello = s;
  }

  public String getString() {
    return myHello;
  }

  public static void main (String [] args) {
    HelloWorld hw = new HelloWorld();

    hw.buildString("Fancy HelloWorld");
    System.out.println(hw.getString());
  }
}
```

Next we need to create a simple build.XML Ant script to handle the compiling of our HelloWorld class. The following listing shows the simple Ant script that we need to put in the directory with our Java code.

```
<?xml version="1.0"?>
<project name="HelloWorld" default="all" basedir=".">
        <target name="init">
                <mkdir dir="dist"/>
                <mkdir dir="dist/classes"/>
                <mkdir dir="dist/lib"/>
        </target>

        <target name="build-src">
                <javac  srcdir="src"
                                destdir="dist/classes"
                                classpath="${build-classpath}"
                                debug="on"
                                deprecation="off"/>
        </target>

        <target name="build" depends="init,build-src">
        </target>

        <target name="jar" depends="build">
                <jar    jarfile="dist/lib/HelloWorld.jar"
                                basedir="dist/classes"/>
        </target>

        <target name="clean">
                <delete dir="dist"/>
        </target>
```

```
      <target name="all">
        <antcall name="init"/>
        <antcall name="clean"/>
        <antcall name="build"/>
        <antcall name="jar"/>
      </target>
</project>
```

Impounding the Project

In order for our system to ultimately build fresh source code, we need to have our code within the configuration system. In this example, we will be using CVS as our repository of choice. Let's impound the code into CVS with a command like the following:

```
cvs -d ~/repository import -m "" hello hello initial
```

The result of the import should be:

```
N hello/build.xml
cvs import: Importing /home/node2/repository/hello/src
N hello/src/HelloWorld.java

No conflicts created by this import
```

At this point we are ready to test whether our code and Ant build script are set up correctly before working with AntHill to automate the process.

Doing a Test Build Using Ant

Before setting up a project within AntHill it is important to make sure that our Ant build.xml script and environment are set up properly to ensure that the code will build and that we have an issue only with the code. The following shows an example of what we should see when we execute Ant on our build script and the HelloWorld source code:

```
[node2@node2 helloworld]$ ant
Buildfile: build.xml

clean:
    [delete] Deleting directory /home/node2/helloworld/dist

init:
    [mkdir] Created dir: /home/node2/helloworld/dist
    [mkdir] Created dir: /home/node2/helloworld/dist/classes
    [mkdir] Created dir: /home/node2/helloworld/dist/lib

build-src:
    [javac] Compiling 1 source file to /home/node2/helloworld/dist/classes

build:

jar:
      [jar] Building jar: /home/node2/helloworld/dist/lib/HelloWorld.jar

all:

BUILD SUCCESSFUL
Total time: 16 seconds
```

Of course, the magic words from this build are BUILD SUCCESSFUL. If you see these words, we can move to the AntHill project.

Creating an AntHill Project

Now that we know that our build process is successful, we want to move closer to a continuous integration system by allowing AntHill to automatically handle all of the tasks necessary for a successful build. Remember that a successful build is determined by the project itself. If you need to accomplish Javadocs, PDF output, testing, and other processes, just include them in your project build.xml script. For this example, we've removed all of the projects and dependencies from the AntHill Administration page by clicking the Delete links.

Now let's create a new AntHill project. Click the Create New Project link from the Administration page. You will receive a page like this:

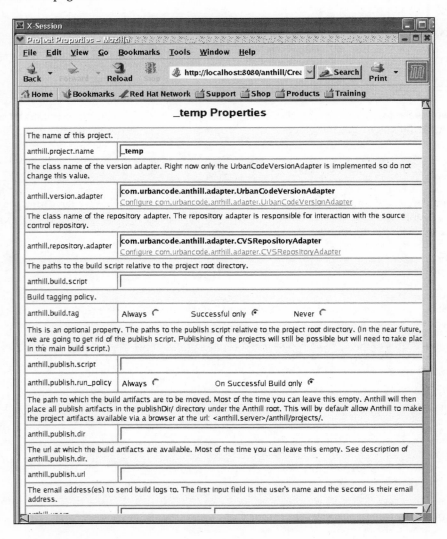

The options available for a new project are the following:

❏ **anthill.project.name:** The name of the project. This value will display on the AntHill Administration page.

❏ **anthill.version.adapter:** The version adapter to use for this project. The default value entered for AntHill will be displayed. You don't want to change this adapter, but it can be configured. Click the Configure link to display the page shown below.

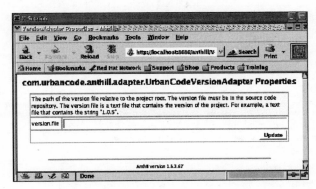

For every project in the AntHill system, there needs to be a version file within that contains the current version of the software. In the Properties line of the Version Adapter, enter the name of the file relative to the root directory of the project. For example, we might enter the filename of *version* and place it in the root of our project. Within the file, put a starting string such as 1.0.0.

❏ **anthill.repository.adapter:** The default repository adapter for the project will be displayed in each part of the Project page. You cannot change the repository adapter, but you can configure it for this specific project. The followingfigure shows an example of the options available for the repository adapter:

For each of the various repository adapters, there will be options to determine the access specifics for the current project. You will need to update which user to use when accessing the respository as well as the project directory specifics.

❏ **anthill.build.script:** AntHill needs to know where the Ant build.xml script is located within the project directory. Put the path relative to the root directory of the project along with the build script name in this field.

❏ **anthill.build.tag:** When a build is performed, the system will generally assign a build tag to the code within the repository. The options available are Always, Successful Only, and Never. The default is Successful Only. It is generally a good idea to have a build tag on all successful builds in order to have a history and be able to re-create the build as needed.

❏ **anthill.publish.script;** Within the current version of AntHill, publishing is a separate process and requires a different script. The script path should be added into this field. The current release notes indicate that this process will change to be accomplished within the main build script. If you don't put a script in this field, AntHill will not perform a publish and you will need to put the publishing steps in your build.xml script.

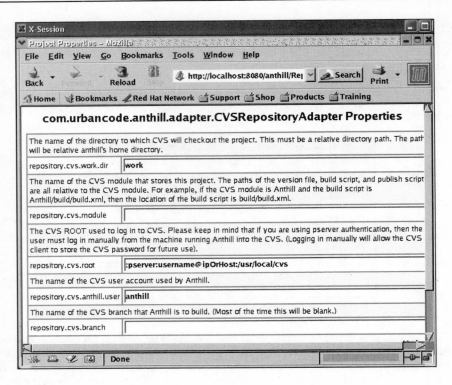

❑ **anthill.publish.run_policy:** The policy for the publish script can be either Always or On Successful Build only.

❑ **anthill.publish.dir:** During the build process, various artifacts will be created such as the logs. If this field is empty, AntHill will automatically place the artifacts in the /publishDir of the root. If you change this directory, the artifacts won't be automatically available.

❑ **anthill.publish.url:** If you change the location of the artifact directory, you will need to put the URL of the directory in this field.

❑ **anthill.users:** The name of the user or users to which an e-mail will be sent after the build. There are two fields in the users area. The first is just a name and the second is an e-mail address.

❑ **anthill.mail.policy:** The policy to use when sending an e-mail to the above users. The options are Always and Failed Builds Only. The default is to always send an e-mail.

❑ **anthill.build.ant.params:** Additional parameters to be sent to Ant when this project is executed.

❑ **anthill.publish.ant.params:** Additional parameters to be sent to the publish Ant script.

❑ **anthill.java.extra.options:** Additional parameters to be sent to Java.

❑ **anthill.schedule:** The current schedule to use for this project.

For our HelloWorld project, we filled the New Project options with the following values:

❑ **Anthill.project.name:** Used the name of HelloWorld.

❑ **Anthill.version.adapter:** Added a file called version containing the text 1.0.0. Also impounded the file to CVS.

❑ **Anthill.repository.adapter:** Added the name of the directory for the AntHill to build within— hello. Added the name of the CVS project—hello. Added the username of a CVS user. It is important if you are using CVS that you have the specified user log in to the build machine so that CVS can remember the user's password since AntHill doesn't have the ability to handle passwords.

❑ **Anthill.build.script:** Our build.xml script is located in the root directory of the project, so we added build.xml to this field.

❑ **Anthill.build.tag:** Left this field at the default.

❑ **Anthill.publish.script:** Didn't enter one.

❑ **Anthill.publish.run_policy:** Left at the default.

❑ **Anthill.publish.dir:** Left at the default.

❑ **Anthilll.publish.url:** Left at the default.

❑ **Anthill.users:** Added a single user—tom – tom@yahoo.com.

❑ **Anthill.mail.policy:** Left at Always.

❑ **Anthill.build.ant.params:** Left empty.

❑ **Anthill.publish.ant.params:** Left empty.

❑ **Anthill.java.extra.options:** Left empty.

❑ **Anthill.schedule:** Set to default (we will change this later).

Once we have entered all of the fields, the new project will appear on the AntHill Administration page and we will be ready for a build.

Doing a Build

After the new project has been created, you will have an option to Edit, Build, or Delete it. Let's manually build the project to be sure that our project properties are accurate. To build the project, just click the Build link. Be sure to enable the Force Build checkbox when prompted. If you have filled out everything correctly, the build will be successful and you will see a green field; otherwise you will see red. If the field is red, click the name of the project and view the buildLog to see what the problem was during the build. In most cases it will be an issue with the repository settings.

This task has shown that we can use the AntHill system to accomplish a forced build just like we would have done by executing Ant within the directory of our project. Looking in the logs, we find that the build was successful and it was provided the appropriate label 1.0.1 based on the version of 1.0.0 that we supplied in the version file.

If you take a close look at the output produced when you click the HelloWorld project name, you will see that there is no /dist directory. If you look back at our Ant build script, you will see that a /dist directory is supposed to be created. Let's take a moment to understand what we are looking at when we click on a project's name from the Administration page. Open a terminal window and browse to where you installed AntHill. The path might be something like /usr/local/anthill. Within the installation directory there will be another directory called publishDir. This is where AntHill puts all of the files produced from the build. Recall that during the setup of the HelloWorld project and the discussion of the deployDir property, this property will be passed to the Ant build script with the location of the directory where the project will be published by AntHill. In our case, the property will have the value /usr/local/anthill/publishDir/HelloWorld. It is within this directory that we want to put our .jar file. Clearly the build.xml script we developed earlier won't do. So consider the following script:

```xml
<?xml version="1.0"?>
<project name="HelloWorld" default="all" basedir=".">
        <property name="deployDir" location="dist"/>
        <property name="dist.dir" location="${deployDir}"/>

        <target name="build">
                <mkdir dir="classes"/>
                <javac  srcdir="src"
                                destdir="classes"
                                classpath="${build-classpath}"
                                debug="on"
                                deprecation="off"/>
        </target>

        <target name="jar" depends="build">
                <mkdir dir="${dist.dir}/lib"/>
                <jar jarfile="${dist.dir}/lib/HelloWorld.jar"
                        basedir="classes"/>
        </target>

        <target name="clean">
                <delete dir="classes"/>
        </target>

        <target name="all">
          <antcall target="clean"/>
          <antcall target="build"/>
          <antcall target="jar"/>
        </target>
</project>
```

Notice at the top of the script that we have two new property tags:

```xml
<property name="deployDir" location="dist"/>
<property name="dist.dir" location="${deployDir}"/>
```

AntHill will pass in the value for the deployDir, and we will use that value in the jar <target> element so that we will have a specific place to put the results of our project. Now we need to set up a specific schedule for performing nightly scheduled builds.

Scheduling a Nightly Build

When we created a new project, we chose a schedule to use called default. If you take a look at the Administration page, you will see an entry for a schedule called default. Click the Edit link next to the schedule. Each schedule will have a specific name, the total number of minutes between builds, and the time when the build will actually start. The default build schedule is quite aggressive at a build every 30 minutes. All of the projects that are currently using a specific schedule will be shown at the bottom of the Schedule page.

If you click the Back button, you will also see that there is a link to create a new schedule. When you click the link, you will be required to enter a schedule name, interval, and start time. To use the new schedule, edit a specific project and select the newly entered schedule; then click Update.

Adding More Builds

If you have a situation where there is a need to have builds at a specific time of the day, you will need to have multiple schedules. For example, let's say we would like to have a build at 11:00 A.M. and 3:00 P.M. each day but also a nightly build at 2:00 A.M. Since the times aren't separated by equal intervals, we will need to create three different schedule tasks as well as three different projects. The reason is that the projects are able to be associated with only a single schedule.

So we might ultimately have the following projects and their associated schedules:

- ❏ HelloWorld_1100am
- ❏ HelloWorld_300pm
- ❏ HelloWorld_nightly

These three builds will have all of the necessary support for our project by allowing the developers to submit code throughout the day and be sure that they don't break the build.

Working with Dependencies

Of course, there are many times when a single project just doesn't handle all of the situations necessary. Let's work with a couple of new projects to support our need for a dependency. First, create two new projects called HelloWorld_B and HelloWorld_C. Now click the Create New Dependency Group link on the main Administration page to reveal the page shown below.

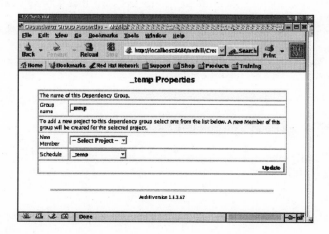

To build a new group, enter an appropriate name and then select the first member of the group as well as the schedule. The system will return you to the Administration page. Click the Edit link of the new group to add another project to the group. After the second project has been added to the dependency group, click the Edit link again and add the final project. At this point in our example, we have the situation shown below.

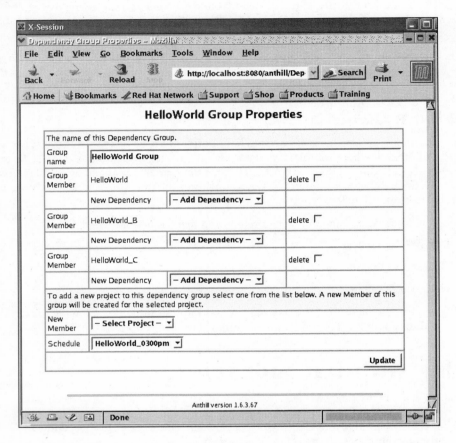

Now it's time to create the dependencies within the group. Let's say that we have a situation where we want HelloWorld_B to be built once HelloWorld has been built, but HelloWorld_C must be built first. To accomplish this dependency hierarchy, click the New Dependency combo box for HelloWorld_B and select HelloWorld. Then click the New Dependency combo box for HelloWorld and select the HelloWorld_C project. Click the Update button, and your dependency will be configured and ready to be triggered based on the projects' specific schedules.

Using AntHill with Petstore

Now that we have a good idea of how to use AntHill for a project, let's look at how to put our Petstore application into AntHill. The first step is to impound the Petstore application in the repository. Before actually impounding the code, add a text file to the root directory of your Petstore code called version, and set the version within to 0.5.0 or some other text. Change to the root directory of the Petstore code and issue a command like the following:

```
cvs -d ~/repository import -m "" petstore petstore initial
```

As you might expect, we are going to have to do a little surgery on the build.xml file to make sure the artifacts for the Petstore are placed in the right directory once it is built. The first step in the process is to include the following <property> tags in the build.xml file:

```
<property name="deployDir" location="dist"/>
<property name="dist.dir" location="${deployDir}"/>
```

There are two different places where the deployDir needs to be used. The first is within the <target name=" "> element. The code is:

```
<target name="prepare" depends="init"
                        description="prepare the output directory.">
    <mkdir dir="${lib}" />
    <mkdir dir="${dist}" />
    <mkdir dir="${deployDir}" />
</target>
```

Simply change the ${deploy} variable to ${deployDir}. The same thing needs to be done in the <target name="package"> element.

```
<target name="package" depends="build">
    <copy file="./META-INF/application.xml" todir="${dist}/META-INF" />

    <jar jarfile="${deployDir}/pet.jar"
         basedir="${dist}" />
</target>
```

Once the build.xml file has been changed, commit the changed file to the source code repository.

Creating a Project

With the code committed to the repository and the build file changed, it's time to create an appropriate project. The changes necessary are as follows:

1. Set anthill.project.name to an identifier such as Petstore.

2. Configure anthill.repository.adapter for the username and project under which the Petstore code was impounded.

3. Set anthill.build.script to build.xml.

4. Set the e-mail address as needed and any of the other optional parameters, and update the project. If successful, the project will appear in your Project list.

Doing a Build

Now it's time to check to see if things worked out. Click the Build link for the Petstore project. Be sure to enable the Force Build checkbox. After some time, you should see a successful build. If not, check the buildLogs and make any appropriate changes. Again, most problems with the build will be related to the source code repository if the build.xml script works outside the AntHill system.

29

Ant Tag Reference

Another Neat Tool (Ant), despite its modest name, is a powerful platform-independent build tool. By creating XML files to develop build tasks, you can extend Ant to solve a host of problems, taking it far beyond simple code compilation. Ant's focus on code completion and application building is its strength and weakness. Ant does solve some problems programmatically. However, it is not intended to be a programming language. This reference covers most of Ant's built-in tasks and a few optional tasks that relate to the content of this book. The task descriptions are concise and organized into logical groupings for easier reference.

Ant Command Line Options

After following Ant's installation instructions, you can execute build.xml files by simply typing "ant" at the command prompt. If you're using someone else's buildfile, you should investigate its purpose and functionality before running it. If the creator of the buildfile has described its main tasks, that extended help/usage will be available using the projecthelp switch.

> **Throughout this chapter, an asterisk (*) after a parameter name indicates that this is a required parameter in the task's simplest form.**

The general syntax for the ant command line is as follows:

```
ant [options] [target [target2 [target3] ...]]
```

Simple buildfiles won't require most of these switches. However, if your buildfile is not named build.xml, you will need to specify the buildfile's name by using the -buildfile option; to execute a target other than the default, use the following:

```
ant -buildfile [ANT file] [target]
```

Command line options displayed from Ant's help option are as follows:

```
-help                  print this message
-projecthelp           print project help information
-version               print the version information and exit
-quiet                 be extra quiet
-verbose               be extra verbose
-debug                 print debugging information
-emacs                 produce logging information without adornments
-logfile [file]        use given file for log output
-logger [classname]    the class that is to perform logging
-listener [classname]  add an instance of class as a project listener
-buildfile [file]      use specified buildfile
-find [file]           search for buildfile towards the root of the
                       filesystem and use the first one found

-Dproperty=[value]     set property to value
```

XML Tag

Ant uses XML files to execute. The default name of Ant's XML file is build.xml. If an Ant user types "ant" with no other commands, Ant will attempt to open build.xml. Ant's build.xml file must contain the XML version and encoding:

```
<?xml version="1.0" encoding="UTF-8"?>
```

If you are not familiar with XML encoding, be aware that comments are written as follows:

```
<!-- comment goes here -->
```

Ant Parent Elements

There are many parent tags in Ant, which are described in this section.

Project Tag

All targets are nested within a parent tag that defines the Ant project:

```
<project basedir="[working directory]" default="[default task]"
name="[project name]">

        <!--All tasks will be nested within targets here-->

</project>
```

Parameters

❑ **name:** Name of the project.

❑ **default*:** The target to use when one is not specified in the Ant command line execution.

❑ **basedir:** The working directory for the project or root path for the project; defaults to the parent directory of the build file.

Target Tag

All of Ant's tasks fit into a parent target element:

```
<target name="[target name]"/>
```

All tasks reside within target tags. The parent target tag defines the order of execution by declaring dependences. All dependent tasks will then execute before the task that defined it. This relationship is the primary way to define execution order within Ant files. Alternatively, the antcall and ant tasks can be used to execute tasks by target name. For more information, refer to these tasks under the section "Ant's Key Tasks" later in this chapter for more detail.

Parameters

❑ **name*:** Name of the target.

❑ **depends:** A comma-separated list of tasks that must execute all of their task's dependences, listed in their task parameter, before the task will execute:

```
<target name="[target name]" depends="[dependent target name]"/>
```

When the target is called, the dependent target will execute will execute first. For example, consider the following usage:

```
<target name="A"/>
<target name="B" depends="A"/>
<target name="C" depends="B"/>
<target name="D" depends="C,E"/>
<target name="E" depends="C,B,A"/>
```

If we execute the following command, the order of execution will be A, B, C, E, and then D:

```
ant d
```

If we execute the following command, the order of execution will be A, B, C, and then E. No dependency is defined for D, so target D will not execute:

```
ant e
```

❑ **if:** Name of a property that must exist in order for the task to run. It does not evaluate against the value of a property, it only checks to see if the property exists:

```
<target name="[target name]" if="[property name]"/>
```

When the target executes, it looks to see if a property with that name exists. If it does, the task will execute.

❑ **unless:** Name of a property that must not be set in order for the task to execute. The "unless" parameter does not depend on the "if" parameter. It only evaluates that a property does not exist; it does not evaluate against the value of a property:

```
<target name="[target name]" unless="[property name]"/>
```

When the target executes, it will look to see if a property with that name exists. If it does, the task will not execute.

❑ **description:** A short description of the task.. These descriptions do not print to the screen:

```
<target name="[target name]" description="[task description]"/>
```

When you use Ant's command line option –projecthelp, all the tasks and their descriptions will be printed to the screen.

Path Tag

The path element allows for paths to be used by many tasks:

```
<path id=[property] path="[path]"/>
```

Parameter

❑ **id*:** Property to represent many path and class path references. The property is referred to as a *reference id*. Many tasks allow the use of a path task via the reference id.

Nested Parameters

❑ **pathelement:** A class used to specify both paths and class paths. It is often used as a child of a project to create a set of reusable paths and class paths:

```
<path>
    <pathelement path="[path]"/>
</path>
```

❑ **path:** A comma-separated list of paths:

```
<path>
    <pathelement path="[path]"/>
</path>
```

❑ **location:** A comma-separated list of paths relative to the base directory of the project:

```
<path>
    <pathelement location="classes"/>
</path>
```

❑ **fileset:** Groups a set of files and directories. The following buildfile snippets groups all jar files in the /cvs/jars directory as follows:

```
<path>
    <fileset dir="/cvs/jars" >
        <include name="**/*.jar"/>
    </fileset>
</path>
```

Filter Tag

Filters can be used for file-copying tasks. All instances of a specified token can be replaced with a specified value.

A *token* is a value that can be automatically expanded in a set of text files when they are copied. Tokens are encased in the @ character as in @filename@. If a token exists in a file but no token is defined in the buildfile then no action will be taken, i.e., the token defined in the file will not be changed.

You define a token using the filter tag as follows:

```
<filter token="filename" value="autoexec.bat"/>
```

Later if you copied a text file with that contained the text "@filename@" and filtering is on, the text "@filename@" is replaced with "autoexec.bat". Demonstrated as follows:

```
<copy todir="/tmp" filtering="true">
  <fileset dir="/src/config"/>
</copy>
```

Parameters

❑ **token*:** Value of the string of text to be replaced in the file. An at sign (@) will be placed around this value automatically.

❑ **value*:** Replacement value to be applied to the token in the file.

❑ **filtersfile:** File containing one name/value pair per line. This file creates filters for every entry in the properties file.

❑ **filtersfile*:** A properties file from which to read the filters.

Tstamp Tag

The tstamp task sets several properties to the current date and time. From the system time:

❑ **DSTAMP:** The date formatted as "yyyymmdd".

❑ **TSTAMP :**The time formatted as "hhmm".

❑ **TODAY:** The current date formatted as "month day year".

The tag is as follows:

```
<tstamp/>
```

Nested Parameters

❑ **property:** A property to set to a particular time/date format.

❑ **pattern:** Time/date pattern to use:

```
<tstamp>
    <format property="TODAY_UK" pattern="d MMMM yyyy">
</tstamp>
```

Ant Key Tasks

A key task is something that must be done for Ant. In contrast, most other tasks have more to do with accomplishing things for the application we are building.

Ant Task

The ant task executes an Ant buildfile from the currently executing Ant script:

```
<ANT antfile="[ant file name]"/>
```

It will execute the project's default target.

Parameters

❑ **antfile***: The name of the Ant file to execute; defaults to build.xml.

❑ **dir:** The directory where the Ant file is located The root path of this file is specified in the project tag's basedir parameter, at the beginning of the Ant file.

```
<ANT antfile="[ant file] dir="[location of ant file]"/>
```

❑ **target:** A specific target to be run, located in the Ant file:

```
<ANT antfile="[ant file] target="[target]"/>
```

❑ **output:** A file to hold the output of the Ant script:

```
<ANT antfile="[ant file] output="[log file]"/>
```

Antcall Task

The antcall task executes an Ant target:

```
<antcall target="[target]"/>
```

All of the dependent Ant targets will execute, followed by the specific target specified.

Parameters

❑ **target***: The target name that antcall will execute.

Nested Parameters

❑ **param:** A property to be set before running the tasks in the target.

❑ **name:** Name of a property to be assigned a value.

❑ **value:** Value to assign to the property.

This example will set a property to a value when the antcall task is executed:

```
<antcall target="[target name]">
<param name="[property]" value="[property value]"/>
</antcall>
```

Available Task

You can use the available task to determine if a file, class, or Java Virtual Machine (JVM) system property is available. If it is not present, the task sets the value of a given property to "false" (the value defaults to "true").

In the following example, if the file is not available, the property will be set to "false":

```
<available file="[resource]" property="[property]"/>
```

Parameters

❑ **property*:** Name of the property to set, as defined by the property task.

❑ **value:** The text that will be assigned to the property if the resource is available. The default value is "true":

```
<available file="[file name]" property="[property]" value="[property
    value]"/>
```

❑ **classname:** Name of a class file; used to determine if the class file is available:

```
<available classname="[class file]" property="[property]"/>
```

❑ **resource:** Name of a JVM resource; used to determine if the resource is available:

```
<available resource ="[JVM Resource]" property="[property]"/>
```

❑ **file*:** Name of a file; used to determine if the file is available.

❑ **classpath:** A class path to use when looking up class files with the classname attribute:

```
<available classpath="[class path]" classname="[class file]"/>
```

❑ **classpathref:** A classpathref is used to look into a classpath that has already been defined with a path element demonstrated in the buildfile snippet below.

The following example will determine if a class file within a given path exists, by using the property that references a path:

```
<project...
    <path id="[property]">
        <pathelement path="[path]/"/>
    </path>

    <task...
        <available classname="[class file]" classpathref="[property
            of path]"/>
    </task>
```

Nested Parameter

❑ **classpath:** Allows tasks to use paths and class paths efficiently (see section "Frequently Used Nested Parameters and Elements" at the end of this chapter).

Echo Task

The echo task sends message to Ant's system output or to a specified file:

```
<echo message="Hello world"/>

<echo>
This is a longer message stretching over
two lines.
</echo>
```

Parameters

- ❑ **message***: Text of the message to display.

- ❑ **file:** Name of a file to direct output to.

- ❑ **append:** Boolean value of "true" or "false". When set to "true", output will be appended to a file specified by the file element. Defaults to "false".

Fail Task

The fail task stops execution of the current build:

```
<fail/>
```

Parameter

- ❑ **message:** Text of a message to be displayed when the fail task is executed.

Property Task

The property task creates properties by assigning values to names. Properties set outside the current Ant project cannot be reassigned in the current Ant project:

```
<property name="[property]" value="[property value]"/>
```

Parameters

- ❑ **name***: A name to be assigned to a name/value pair.

- ❑ **value***: A value to be assigned to a name/value pair.

- ❑ **refid:** A name used in referring to an attribute specified by the "id" parameter of a path structure (see the path element in the section "Ant Parent Elements"):

  ```
  <property refid="[property]"/>
  ```

- ❑ **file:** A reference to an external properties file in which each line specifies a new key value pair:

  ```
  <property file="[file name]"/>
  ```

- ❑ **location:** A reference to an external properties file with an absolute path, in which each line specifies a new key value pair in the file:

  ```
  <property location="[absolute path]"/>
  ```

- ❑ **environment:** A prefix to be assigned to the property used to get the current systems properties:

  ```
  <property environment="[property]"/>
  ```

  The following line will return the value of the system property:

  ```
  <echo message="[environment property].[system property]"
  ```

- ❑ **classpath:** The class path used to determine the properties file for the java.util.Properties class in Sun's JDK.

- ❑ **classpathref:** The class path defined in Ant's path element that is used to determine the properties file for the java.util.Properties class in Sun's JDK.

Nested Parameter

- ❑ **classpath:** Allows tasks to use paths and class paths efficiently (see section "Frequently Used Nested Parameters and Elements" at the end of this chapter).

Taskdef Task

The taskdef task creates a custom task by executing Java classes:

```
<taskdef name="[task]" classname="[java class]"/>
```

Parameters

- ❑ **name*:** The name of the task.

- ❑ **classname*:** The full class name.

- ❑ **classpath:** The class path used when looking up the class name:

  ```
  <taskdef name="[task]" classname="[java class]" classpath"[classpath]"/>
  ```

Directory and File System Tasks

These are tasks focusing on file-based issues.

Chmod Task

The chmod task changes file permissions on Unix systems:

```
<chmod file="[file]" perm="[permissions]"/>
```

Parameters

❑   **file*:** File or directory on which to alter permissions.

❑   **dir:** Directory whose files and directories are targeted to have their permissions changed:

```
<chmod dir="[path]" perm="[permissions]"/>
```

❑   **perm*:** Value to which the targeted files' or directories' permissions will be set. On Unix systems, there are typically three groups: User, Group, and Other. The three values used most often to set these values are Read, Write, and Execute.

❑   **defaultexcludes:** A value of "yes" or "no". Indicates whether default excludes are used.

❑   **includes:** A comma-separated list of patterns to include in the file set. All other files are excluded.

❑   **includesfile:** A file source of patterns to include in the file set. All other files will be excluded.

❑   **excludes:** A comma-separated list of patterns to exclude in the file set. All other files are included.

❑   **excludesfile:** A file source of patterns to exclude in the file set. All other files will be included.

❑   **parallel:** If "false", more then one chmod command can be used. Defaults to "true".

❑   **type:** A value of "file", "dir", or "both"; defaults to "file". The file command sends only file names as system commands. The dir command sends the directory name to be used to determine what files to execute. The both command uses the file names and directory names.

Nested Parameters

❑   **fileset:** Specifies a collections of files (see section "Frequently Used Nested Parameters and Elements" at the end of this chapter for more information).

Copy Task

The copy task attempts to create a copy of a file/directory structure and place it in a specified directory:

```
<copy file="[file name]" todir="[directory]"/>
```

Source files that are older then the destination files are not copied unless otherwise specified with the "overwrite" parameter. You can also use this command to copy a source file to a destination of a different name.

Parameters

❑   **file*:** File name of the source target file. When you're using a nested file set, the "todir" or "tofile" parameter is required, instead.

❑   **preservelastmodified:** Boolean value of "yes" or "no". It gives the destination files the same creation dates as the source files.

❑   **tofile:** Name of the destination file name target:

```
<copy file="[file name]" tofile="[file name]"/>
```

- ❑ **todir*:** Name of the destination directory target.

- ❑ **overwrite:** When set to "yes", older source files will overwrite newer files in the destination. Defaults to "no".

- ❑ **filtering:** When set to "yes", turns on token filtering (for more information, see the section "Ant Parent Elements" earlier in this chapter.) Defaults to "no".

- ❑ **flatten:** When set to "yes", the target is identical to the source name and the directory structure is stripped off, effectively making the branch of the directory tree flat. Defaults to "no".

- ❑ **includeEmptyDirs:** When set to "no", the empty directories in a file set are not created in the destination target. Defaults to "yes".

Nested Parameters

- ❑ **fileset:** Specifies a collections of files (see section "Frequently Used Nested Parameters and Elements" at the end of this chapter for more information).

- ❑ **mapper:** A definition can be found under the "Frequently Used Nested Parameters" section at the end of this chapter.

Delete Task

The delete task removes a file or a file structure from a directory structure:

```
<delete file="/lib/foo.jar"/>
```

If the file or directory does not exist, execution is halted, unless the "quiet" parameter is set to "true".

Parameters

- ❑ **file*:** File name of the target to be removed.

- ❑ **dir:** Directory name of the target to be removed:

  ```
  <delete dir="../foo"/>
  ```

- ❑ **verbose:** When set to "false", deleted files will not be written out during execution. Defaults to "true".

- ❑ **quiet:** When set to "true", the build won't fail if the item does not exist when delete is called. Error messages pertaining to files or directories that don't exist will also be suppressed. Defaults to "false".

- ❑ **includeEmptyDirs:** When set to "true" while using a fileset, empty directories will be deleted. Defaults to "false".

Nested Parameters

- ❑ **fileset:** Specifies a collections of files (see section "Frequently Used Nested Parameters and Elements" at the end of this chapter for more information).

- ❑ **mapper:** A definition can be found under the "Frequently Used Nested Parameters" section at the end of this chapter.

Mkdir Task

The mkdir task creates a directory structure, adding directories when needed:

```
<mkdir dir="[directory]>
```

Parameter

❑ **dir***: The directory structure to create.

Move Task

The move task attempts to delete the source file or single directory while creating a copy of that file or directory in a new location:

```
<move file="[file]" todir="[directory]"/>
```

Using move in conjunction with a "fileset" parameter enables you to move groups of files and directory structures. This command can also be used to move a source file to a destination with a different name.

Parameters

❑ **file***: The file name of the source target file to be removed.

❑ **tofile**: The name that the file will have when written:

```
<move file="[file]" tofile="[file]"/>
```

❑ **todir***: The name of the destination directory.

❑ **overwrite**: When set to "yes", older source files will overwrite newer files in the destination. Defaults to "no".

❑ **filtering**: When set to "on", token filtering is used. Defaults to "off".

❑ **flatten**: When set to "yes", the target is identical to the source name and the directory structure is stripped off, effectively making the branch of the directory tree flat. Defaults to "no".

❑ **includeEmptyDirs**: When set to "no", the empty directories in a file set will not be created in the destination target. Defaults to "yes".

Nested Parameters

❑ **fileset**: Specifies a collections of files (see section "Frequently Used Nested Parameters and Elements" at the end of this chapter for more information).

❑ **mapper**: A definition can be found under the "Frequently Used Nested Parameters" section at the end of this chapter.

Touch Task

The touch task changes the modification time of existing files to the current time, unless a time is specifically stated. If the file does not exist, it is created:

```
<touch file="[file]"/>
```

Parameters

- ❏ **file*:** Name of the file to manipulate or create.
- ❏ **millis:** The modification time in seconds since Jan 1 1970.
- ❏ **datetime:** The modification time in the format "MM/DD/YYYY HH:MM AM":

```
<touch file="[file]" datetime="01/01/2000 12:00 am"/>
```

External Execution Tasks

External execution tasks enable you to invoke other programs and shell scripts.

Apply Task

The apply, exec, and execon tasks all have similar functions, but it is useful to review their capabilities before you decide which one to use. Apply is the most complex of the three. It executes the specified program using both file sets and mappers. The file sets define a group of files that will be applied to the executable. The mapper allows for time and date checking to compare the source files times against the destination files, avoiding unnecessary execution of unwanted sources. The apply task is as follows:

```
<apply executable="[command]" dest="[path]"/>
```

Parameters

- ❏ **executable*:** File name of the executable.
- ❏ **dest*:** Directory that holds the target files.
- ❏ **dir:** The working directory of the system command.
- ❏ **os:** List of operating systems on which the command will run.
- ❏ **output:** A file to store the output of the command.
- ❏ **timeout:** Amount of time after which execution will be halted, specified in milliseconds.
- ❏ **failonerror:** If the program returns a code other then 0, the build will fail.
- ❏ **parallel:** When set to "true", files are appended as arguments rather than being executed individually. Defaults to "false".
- ❏ **type:** Value of "file", "dir", or "both". The "file" command sends only file names as system commands. The "dir" command sends the directory name to be used to determine what files to execute. The "both" command uses file names and directory names. Defaults to "file".

Nested Parameters

- ❏ **fileset:** Specifies a collections of files (see section "Frequently Used Nested Parameters and Elements" at the end of this chapter for more information).
- ❏ **arg:** Comand line arguments for the command.

❑ **srcfile:** In cases where some arguments come befor and some are after the name of the soure files name, it's relative poison can be marked with the srcfile tag.

```
<apply executable=[file name]>
  <arg value=[argument]/>
  <srfile/>
  <arg value=[argument]/>
  <fileset dir=[path]/>
</apply>
```

❑ **targetfile:** Uses the dest parameter of the apply task to find files to be used as targets. Like the srcfile nested task is marks the location of the targeted files within command line arguments.

❑ **env:** Specifies values available at run time.

> ❑ **key:** Name of the environmental variable.
>
> ❑ **value:** Value of the environmental variable.
>
> ❑ **path:** A path value to use with a key.
>
> ❑ **file:** A file to use with a given command.
>
> ❑ **mapper:** A definition can be found under the "Frequently Used Nested Parameters" section at the end of this chapter.

Exec Task

As we mentioned earlier, the apply, exec, and execon tasks have similar functions. Exec is the simplest of the three—it simply executes the specified program:

```
<exec executable="[commad and switches]"/>
```

Parameters

❑ **command*:** The whole command line as it would be executed, with all its parameters, on the system.

❑ **executable:** File name of the executable.

❑ **dir:** Working directory of the system command.

❑ **os:** List of operating systems on which the command will run.

❑ **output:** File to store the output of the command.

❑ **timeout:** Amount of time after which execution will be halted, specified in milliseconds.

❑ **failonerror:** If the program returns a code other then 0, the build will fail.

❑ **newenvironment:** When new environment variables are specified, does not propagate the old environment. Defaults to "false".

Nested Parameters

❑ **arg:** Comand line arguments for the command.

❑ **env:** Specifies values available at run time.

  ❑ **key:** Name of the environmental variable.

  ❑ **value:** Value of the environmental variable.

  ❑ **path:** A path value to use with a key.

  ❑ **file:** A file to use with a given command.

  ❑ **mapper:** A definition can be found under the Frequently Used Nested Parameters section.

Execon Task

As we've mentioned, the apply, exec, and execon tasks have similar functions. Execon's complexity falls between the other two. It executes the specified program and allows for filesets to be used. The filesets define a group of files that can be applied to the executable:

```
<execon executable="[command]">
  <fileset dir="[directory]" includes="[pateren set]"/>
</apply>
```

Parameters

  ❑ **executable*:** File name of the executable.

  ❑ **dir:** The working directory of the system command.

  ❑ **os:** List of operating systems on which the command will run.

  ❑ **output:** File to store the output of the command.

  ❑ **timeout:** Amount of time after which execution will be halted, specified in milliseconds.

  ❑ **failonerror:** If the program returns a code other then 0, the build will fail.

  ❑ **newenvironment:** When new environment variables are specified, does not propagate the old environment. Defaults to "false".

  ❑ **parallel:** When set to "true", files are appended as arguments rather than being executed individually. Defaults to "false".

  ❑ **type:** Value of "file", "dir", or "both". The "file: command sends only file names as system commands. The "dir" command sends the directory name to be used to determine what files to execute. The "both" command uses file names and directory names. Defaults to "file".

Nested Parameters

  ❑ **fileset:** Specifies a collections of files (see section "Frequently Used Nested Parameters and Elements" at the end of this chapter for more information).

  ❑ **arg:** Comand line arguments for the command.srcfilecom. In cases where some arguments come befor and some are after the name of the soure files name, it's relative poison can be marked with the srcfile tag.

```
<apply executable=[file name]>
  <arg value=[argument]/>
  <srfile/>
  <arg value=[argument]/>
  <fileset dir=[path]/>
</apply>
```

❑   **targetfile:** Uses the dest parameter of the apply task to find files to be used as targets. Like the srcfile nested task is marks the location of the targeted files within command line arguments.

❑   **env:** Specifies values available at run time.

> ❑   **key:** Name of the environmental variable.
>
> ❑   **value:** Value of the environmental variable.
>
> ❑   **path:** A path value to use with a key.
>
> ❑   **file:** A file to use with a given command.
>
> ❑   **mapper:** A definition can be found under the Frequently Used Nested Parameters section.

Java Task

The java task executes a Java class:

```
<java classname="java class" />
```

This method of invoking the compiler has many useful options you can use to invoke a new JVM for the Java application to run in. In most cases, it is more robust to invoke a new JVM.

Parameters

❑   **classname*:** The Java class to execute.

❑   **classpath:** The class path for the Java program execution.

❑   **classpathref:** A reference id to a class path for the Java program execution.

❑   **fork:** Boolean value of "yes" and "no". When set to "yes", a new JVM will be instantiated. Defaults to "no".

❑   **jvm:** Used with the "fork" parameter. Invokes the Java compiler. Defaults to "java".

❑   **jvmargs:** Used with the "fork" parameter. Specifies parameters to pass when invoking the JVM.

❑   **maxmemory:** Used with the "fork" parameter. The maximum amount of memory allocated to theJVM.

❑   **failonerror:** Available only if "fork" is "yes" (true). Stops the build process if the command exits with a returncode other than 0.

❑   **dir:** Used with the "fork" parameter. The working directory for the JVM.

❑   **output:** A file to which to write the output of the JVM.

Nested Parameters

❑   **arg:** Comand line arguments for the java application.

❑   **jvmarg:** Comand line arguments for the JVM.

❑   **sysproperty:** Specifies values available at run time.

❏ **key:** Name of the environmental variable.

❏ **value:** Value of the environmental variable.

❏ **path:** A path value to use with a key.

❏ **file:** A file to use with a given command.

❏ **mapper:** A definition can be found under the "Frequently Used Nested Parameters" section at the end of this chapter.

❏ **classpath:** Allows tasks to use paths and class paths efficiently (see section "Frequently Used Nested Parameters and Elements" at the end of this chapter).

Javac Task

This command is used to compile Java source code using the JVM in which Ant is running:

```
<javac srcdir="[directory]"/>
```

Parameters

❏ **src*:** The directory where the Java packages to be compiled are located.

❏ **dirdestdir:** The location where the class files will be placed after they are successfully compiled.

❏ **includes:** Comma-separated list of patterns to use with the src parameter.

❏ **includesfile:** File in which each new line lists patterns to use with the src parameter.

❏ **excludes:** Comma-separated list of patterns not to use with the src parameter.

❏ **excludesfile:** File in which each new line lists patterns not to use with the src parameter.

❏ **defaultexcludes:** A value of "yes" or "no". "Yes" sets the default excludes to be used. Defaults to "no".

❏ **classpath:** Class path to be used by the compiler.

❏ **bootclasspath:** Location of the bootstrap class files.

❏ **classpathref:** Class path to be used by the compiler, specified as a reference ID.

❏ **bootclasspathref:** Location of the bootstrap class files, specified as a reference ID.

❏ **extdirs:** Location of installed extensions.

❏ **encoding:** Encoding of source files.

❏ **debug:** When set to "no", debug information from the compiler will be shown as output. Defaults to "off".

❏ **optimize:** When set to "on", the compiler is set to optimize its execution. Defaults to "off".

❏ **deprecation:** When set to "on", deprecation information from the compiler will be shown as output. Defaults to "off".

❏ **target:** Tells the compiler to generate class files for a JVM version.

- ❏ **verbose:** Tells the compiler to use verbose output.

- ❏ **depend:** Tells the compiler to use dependency tracking, if it supports it.

- ❏ **includeANTRuntime:** When set to "no", the lib directory in the ANT_HOME directory will not be used as part of the class path. Defaults to "yes".

- ❏ **includeJavaRuntime:** When set to "yes", the lib directory in the JAVA_HOME directory will be used as part of the class path. Defaults to "no".

- ❏ **failonerror:** When set to "false", the compiler will continue even when it fails to compile a class. Defaults to "true".

Nested Parameters

- ❏ **fileset:** Specifies a collections of files (see section "Frequently Used Nested Parameters and Elements" at the end of this chapter for more information).

- ❏ **src:** Same as srcdir in the javc task.

- ❏ **classpath:** Same as classpath in the javac task.

- ❏ **bootclasspath:** Same as bootclasspath in the javac task.

- ❏ **extdirs:** Same as extdirs in the javac task.

Sql Task

The sql task executes SQL statements using a JBDC source:

```
<sql
    driver="[java class]"
    url="[database url]"
    userid="[user]"
    password="[password]"
    src="[file]"
/>
```

Commands can be executed without an src parameter file, as follows:

```
<sql
    driver=[java class]
    url="[database url]"
    userid="[user]"
    password="[password]"
    >
select *
from tablefoo

insert into table foo values (1,2,3)
</sql>
```

Parameters

- ❏ **driver:** Java class name of the Java Database Connectivity (JDBC) driver.

- ❏ **url:** Database connection URL.

❏ **userid:** Database user name.

❏ **password:** Database password.

❏ **src:** File containing SQL statements separated by semicolons and commented with double slashes (//) or double dashes (--).

❏ **autocommit:** When set to "true", the transactions are committed after execution. Defaults to "false".

❏ **print:** When set to "true", the output returned from the execution of the SQL statement is displayed. Defaults to "false".

❏ **showheaders:** When set to "false", the headers will not be displayed out. Defaults to "true".

❏ **output:** File to write system out information to. Defaults to System.out.

❏ **classpath:** Class path used to load the driver.

❏ **onerror:** Value of "continue", "stop", or "abort". Tells Ant how to handle errors. "Continue" shows the error, and execution is not interrupted. "Stop" halts execution of Ant, and transactions are committed. "Abort" stops execution of Ant, and transactions are not committed.

❏ **rdbms:** Executes commands only if the JBDC driver returns that the RDBMS (Remote Database Message System) is equal to a given value.

❏ **version:** Executes commands only if the JBDC driver returns that the RDBMS(Remote Database Message System) version is equal to a given value.

Nested Parameters

❏ **transaction:** Executes several commands using the same connection.

❏ **src:** File containing SQL statements separated by semicolons and commented with double slashes (//) or double dashes (--).

❏ **classpath:** Allows tasks to use paths and class paths efficiently (see section "Frequently Used Nested Parameters and Elements" at the end of this chapter).

File Library Tasks

Ant's file library tasks enable you to bundles classes and other files into library files such as JARs and WARs.

Jar Task

The jar task creates a Java type Java Application Resource (JAR) file:

```
<jar jarfile="[jar]" basedir="[directory]"/>
```

Parameters

❏ **jarfile*:** Name of the JAR file to create.

❏ **basedir:** The directory from which to recursively make the JAR.

- ❑ **compress:** Boolean value of "true" or "false". When set to "false", compression won't be used. Defaults to "true".

- ❑ **includes:** Comma-separated list of patterns to use with a basedir parameter.

- ❑ **includesfile:** File in which each new line lists patterns to use with a basedir parameter.

- ❑ **excludes:** Comma-separated list of patterns not to use with a basedir parameter.

- ❑ **excludesfile:** File in which each new line lists patterns not to use with a basedir parameter.

- ❑ **defaultexcludes:** A value of "yes" or "no". "Yes" sets the default excludes to be used. Defaults to "no".

- ❑ **manifest:** The name of the manifest file to use.

- ❑ **whenempty:** If set to "skip", the JAR file is not made if no files match the pattern. Defaults not to skip.

Nested Parameters

- ❑ **fileset:** Specifies a collections of files (see section "Frequently Used Nested Parameters and Elements" at the end of this chapter for more information).

War Task

The war task creates a Java type Web Application Resource (WAR) file.

```
<war warfile="[file name]" webxml="[file name]">
  <fileset dir="[path]"/>
    <lib dir="[path]">
    </lib>
  <classes dir="[path]"/>
</war>
```

Parameters

- ❑ **warfile:** The name of the WAR (Web Application Resource) file the task will create.

- ❑ **webxml:** The web.xml file to be used as a deployment descriptor for the WAR file.

- ❑ **basedir:** The directory that contains the files to put into the Zip. Defaults to the base directory defined in the project.

- ❑ **compress:** Boolean value of "true" or "false". When set to "false", the files will not be compressed in the Zip. Defaults to "true".

- ❑ **includes:** Comma-separated list of patterns to use with a directory parameter.

- ❑ **includesfile:** File in which each new line lists patterns to use with a directory parameter.

- ❑ **excludes:** Comma-separated list of patterns not to use with a directory parameter.

- ❑ **excludesfile:** File in which each new line lists patterns not to use with a directory parameter.

- ❑ **defaultexcludes:** When set to "yes", default excludes are to be used. Defaults to "no".

- ❑ **manifest:** A manifest to use in the WAR file.

- ❑ **whenempty:** If set to "skip", the Zip is not made when no files match the pattern. Defaults to not skip.

Nested Parameters

- **lib:** Specifies files to go in the WEB-INF/LIB directory of the WAR. All files in the LIB directory will be available when the Web application runs.
    - **fileset:** Specifies a collections of files (see section "Frequently Used Nested Parameters and Elements" at the end of this chapter for more information).

- **classes:** Specifies files to go in the WEB-INF/CLASES directory of the WAR. All files in the CLASSES directory are the compiled source of the Web application.
    - **fileset:** Specifies a collections of files (see section "Frequently Used Nested Parameters and Elements" at the end of this chapter for more information).

- **webinf:** Specifies files to go in the WEB-INF directory of the WAR.
    - **fileset:** Specifies a collections of files (see section "Frequently Used Nested Parameters and Elements" at the end of this chapter for more information).

- **zipfileset:** See section "Frequently Used Nested Parameters and Elements" at the end of this chapter for a definition.

Zip Task

The zip task creates a compressed file library of the Zip type.

```
<zip zipfile="[file]"
     basedir="[path]"
/>
```

Parameters

- **zipfile*:** The name of the Zip file the task will create.
- **basedir:** The directory that contains the files to put into the Zip. Defaults to the base directory defined in the project.
- **compress:** When set to "false", the files will not be compressed in the Zip. Defaults to "true".
- **includes:** Comma-separated list of patterns to use with a directory parameter.
- **includesfile:** File in which each new line lists patterns to use with a directory parameter.
- **excludes:** Comma-separated list of patterns not to use with a directory parameter.
- **excludesfile:** File in which each new line lists patterns not to use with a directory parameter.
- **defaultexcludes:** When set to "yes", default excludes are to be used. Defaults to "no".
- **whenempty:** If set to "skip", the Zip file is not made if no files match the pattern. Defaults not to skip.

Nested Parameters

- **fileset:** Specifies a collections of files (see section "Frequently Used Nested Parameters and Elements" at the end of this chapter for more information).
- **zipfileset:** See section "Frequently Used Nested Parameters and Elements" at the end of this chapter for definition.

Unjar, Unzip, and Unwar Tasks

The unzip task expands file libraries of the Zip type, including WARs and JARs:

<unzip src="[file]" dest="[directory]"/>

Parameters

❑   **src:** The file library to expand.

❑   **dest:** The directory in which to expand the files.

File Readers, Writers, and Tokenizers

This section covers tasks that manipulate the content of text files.

Replace Task

The replace task finds and replaces a string or strings of text within a text file:

```
<replace file="[file]" token="[replacement value]"/>
```

Parameters

❑   **file*:** Specific file in which to replace the tokens.

❑   **dir:** Directory in which to find the files whose tokens will be replaced.

❑   **token:** Value of the string of text to act as an indicator for replacement.

❑   **value:** Text with which to replace the token. Defaults to an empty string.

❑   **propertyFile:** A file containing one name/value pair per line. This file is used by the "replace-filter" nested parameter tag to replace multiple strings at one time with values that can be different.

❑   **includes:** Comma-separated list of patterns to use with a directory parameter.

❑   **includesfile:** File in which each new line lists patterns to use with a directory parameter.

❑   **excludes:** Comma-separated list of patterns not to use with a directory parameter.

❑   **excludesfile:** File in which each new line lists patterns not to use with a directory parameter.

❑   **defaultexcludes:** When set to "yes", default excludes are to be used. Defaults to "no".

❑   **token*:** The value of the string of text to be replaced in the file.

❑   **value:** Replacement value to be applied to the token in the file.

❑   **property:** Replacement value as a property for the token to be replaced in the file:

```
<replace dir="${../mailTemplates}" value="foo@bla.org"
includes="**/*.template" token="&mailAddress&"/>
```

or

```
<replace
    file="mailTemplate.txt"
    value="foo"
    propertyFile="../mailTemplates/mail.properties" >
  <replacefilter
    token="$project.name$" />
  <replacefilter
    token="$email.link$"
    value="http://www.fooBuildStatus.com"/>
  <replacefilter
    token="$build.time$"
    property="build.time"/>
</replace>
```

Nested Parameters

❑ **fileset:** Specifies a collections of files (see section "Frequently Used Nested Parameters and Elements" at the end of this chapter for more information).

❑ **replacefilter:** Defines tokens and replacement values.

    ❑ **ftoken:** Value of the string of text to act as an indicator for replacement.

    ❑ **fvalue:** Text with which to replace the token. Defaults to an empty string.

    ❑ **fproperty:** Property that defines text with which to replace the token.

Mail Task

The mail task sends Simple Mail Transfer Protocol (SMTP) email:

```
<mail from="foo" tolist="bla" subject="Your code doesn't compile bla"
      files="error.log"/>
```

Parameters

❑ **from:** Email address of sender.

❑ **tolist:** List of recipients separated by commas.

❑ **message:** Text for the body of the email.

❑ **files:** List of files to use that contain the text for the body of the email.

❑ **mailhost:** Host name of the mail server.

❑ **subject:** Text for the subject of the email.

Source Control Tasks

Ant's source control tasks enable you to manage Java source and related development files using systems like CVS.

Cvs Task

The cvs task name is based on the acronym for Concurrent Versioning System. (CVS is a source control system; you can learn more about it at www.cvshome.org.) This task allows for the handling of CVS modules that contain source files.

Parameters

- ❏ **command:** CVS command to be executed, and parameters provided with that command.
- ❏ **cvsRoot:** Root directory of the remote CVS server.
- ❏ **dest:** Directory other than the project's root directory, where files are checked out locally.
- ❏ **package:** CVS module to check out.
- ❏ **tag:** Tag of the CVS module to check out.
- ❏ **date:** Date which the most recent version of the CVS module to be checked out must be equal to or earlier than.
- ❏ **quiet:** Boolean value of "true" or "false". When set to "true", prevents CVS information from printing out on the terminal. Defaults to "false".
- ❏ **noexec:** Boolean value of "true" or "false". When set to "true", only reports will be generated— no files will be modified. Defaults to "false".
- ❏ **output:** File to which the command's standard output should be output. Defaults to Ant's log MSG_INFO.
- ❏ **error:** File to which the command's standard error should be output. Defaults to Ant's log MSG_WARN.

Get Task

The get task downloads a file from a URL.

Parameters

- ❏ **src*:** URL from which to download a file.
- ❏ **dest*:** File name and location to write the file to.
- ❏ **verbose:** Boolean value of "on" or "off". When set to "on", messages will be suppressed. Defaults to "off".
- ❏ **ignoreerrors:** Boolean value of "true" or "false". When set to "true", the build will not fail when errors occur. Defaults to "false".
- ❏ **usetimestamp:** Boolean value of "true" or "false". When set to "true", the file time and date are compared. If the file is newer than a file specified in the dest parameter, it will be downloaded.

Some Key Optional Tasks

Junit Task

The junit task runs unit-level tests developed in Junit's testing framework.

Parameters

- ❑ **printsummary:** When set to "on", prints one line of statistics for each test case.
- ❑ **fork:** When set to "on", runs the test in a JVM separate from the one in which Ant is running.
- ❑ **haltonerror:** When set to "on", fails the build if an error occurs during the testing.
- ❑ **haltonfailure:** When set to "on", fails the build if a test fails.
- ❑ **timeout:** Skips a test if it doesn't finish in a given amount of time. Specified in milliseconds.
- ❑ **maxmemory:** Maximum amount of memory for the new JVM.
- ❑ **jvm:** Command used to invoke a new JVM. Default value is "Java".
- ❑ **dir:** The directory to invoke a new JVM.

Nested Parameters

- ❑ **classpath:** Allows tasks to use paths and class paths efficiently (see section "Frequently Used Nested Parameters and Elements" at the end of this chapter).
- ❑ **jvmarg:** Allows properties to be passed to the new JVM:

  ```
  <jvmarg value="-Dfoo=baz"/>
  ```

  - ❑ **value:** The property key and value specified for the new JVM's use:

    ```
    -D<key>=<value>
    ```

- ❑ **sysproperty:** Allows properties to be used by the test classes as they run:

  ```
  <sysproperty key="foo" value="bla"/>
  ```

  - ❑ **key:** Name of the property.
  - ❑ **value:** Text associated with the key.

- ❑ **formatter:** Prints test results with a specified format

  - ❑ **type*:** Either "xml" or "plain"; "plain" outputs a text file, and "xml" outputs XML.
  - ❑ **classname:** Name of a custom formatter class.
  - ❑ **extension:** Extension on the file name for use with the custom class.
  - ❑ **usefile:** When set to "false", the output won't go to a file.

❑ **test:** Runs a single Junit test.

  ❑ **name*:** Name of the test class to run.

  ❑ **fork:** When set to "yes", a new JVM will be used.

  ❑ **fork:** When set to "on", runs the test in a separate JVM from the one in which Ant is running.

  ❑ **haltonerror:** When set to "on", fails the build if an error occurs during the testing.

  ❑ **haltonfailure:** When set to "on", fails the build if a test fails.

  ❑ **todir:** Directory the reports will write to.

  ❑ **outfile:** Base name of the report file.

  ❑ **if:** Evaluates whether a property exists before running a test.

  ❑ **unless:** Evaluates whether a property does not exists before running a test.

❑ **batchtest:** Runs many Junit test with a nested file set.

  ❑ **fork:** When set to "on", runs the test in a JVM separate from the one in which Ant is running.

  ❑ **haltonerror:** When set to "on", fails the build if an error occurs during the testing.

  ❑ **todir:** Directory the reports will write to.

  ❑ **if:** Evaluates whether a property exists before running a test.

  ❑ **unless:** Evaluates whether a property does not exist before running a test.

JunitReport Task

The junitreport task transforms the XML output from a Junit task's tests into an HTML-based report:

```
<junitreport todir="./foo">
  <fileset dir="./bla">
    <include name="TEST-*.xml"/>
  </fileset>
  <report format="frames" todir="./reports"/>
</junitreport>
```

Parameters

❑ **tofile:** File name to hold a list of all the files generated by the Junit task; defaults to TESTS-TestSuites.xml.

❑ **todir :**Directory to which to write the file specified in the tofile parameter.

Nested Parameters

❑ **fileset:** Specifies a collections of files (see section "Frequently Used Nested Parameters and Elements" at the end of this chapter for more information).

- ❏ **report:** Generates reports for the JUnit tests.
  - ❏ **format:** Set to "frames" or "no frames"; defaults to "frames".
  - ❏ **styledir:** Directory where style sheets are defined; defaults to embedded style sheets.
  - ❏ **todir:** Directory where the final HTML files are written.
  - ❏ **extension:** Extension for the final reports; defaults to HTML.

Frequently Used Nested Parameters and Elements

Nested parameters can be used within certain tasks tags, as children. Some of the most frequent ones are listed below in order to shorten the definition a tasks, by avoiding repetition.

Classpath Element

The classpath task allows tasks to use paths and class paths efficiently:

```
<classpath path="[path]"/>
```

Nested Parameters

- ❏ **pathelement:** Class used to specify both paths and class paths. Pathelement is used as a nested element for many other tasks:

  ```
  <classpath>
  <pathelement path="[path]"/>
  </classpath>
  ```

  - ❏ **path:** A comma-separated list of paths:

    ```
    <classpath>
    <pathelement path="[path]"/>
    </classpath>
    ```

  - ❏ **location:** A comma-separated list of paths, relative to the base directory of the project:

    ```
    <classpath>
    <pathelement location="classes"/>
    ```

    ```
    </classpath>
    ```

- ❏ **fileset:** Specifies a collections of files (see section "Frequently Used Nested Parameters and Elements" at the end of this chapter for more information).

  ```
  <fileset dir="/src/java" >
      <include name="**/*.java"/>
      <exclude name="**/*Test*"/>
  </fileset>
  ```

The above example includes all Java source except those with the substring "Test" in their filename.

Mapper Element

The mapper task simply maps a file to a target. Keep in mind that this task is used in conjunction with other tasks.

```
<mapper type="identity"/>
```

In the above the to and from are ignored and the files are copied into a parallel subdirectory hierarchy as the source to the destination (e.g., c:\src\xptool\Hello.java copied to d:\backup\src\xptool\Hello.java).

```
<mapper type="flatten"/>
```

Unlike the first example, copy all the files from the source to the destination, but all in the source directory with no subdirectory hierarchy (e.g., c:\src\xptool\Hello.java copied to d:\backup\Hello.java).

```
<mapper type="glob" from="*.java" to="*.java.bak"/>
```

Copy *.java files to *.java.bak files (e.g., c:\src\xptool\Hello.java copied to d:\backup\src\xptool\Hello.java.bak).

Parameters

❑ **type:** Several types have been defined internally to this class:

   ❑ **identity:** The target is identical to the source name.

   ❑ **flatten:** The target is identical to the source name and is stripped of any directory structure, effectively making the branch flat.

   ❑ **merge:** The type will map all entries to the same target using the mapper's "to" parameter.

   ❑ **glob:** Patterns will be matched using the mapper's "to" and "from" parameters. The "to" parameter will be used to specify the pattern-matching names. The "from" parameter will be used to specify the target pattern.

   ❑ **regexp:** Patterns will be evaluated against a regular expression using the mapper's "to" and "from" parameters. The "to" parameter will be used to specify the regular expression to match names. The "from" parameter will be used to specify the regular expression for the target pattern.

❑ **classname:** Specifies the implementation by class name.

❑ **classpath:** The class path to use when looking up the class name.

❑ **classpathref:** A class path used in looking up a class specified by the reference id of one of the build files elements:

```
<project ... >
  <path id="project.class.path">
    <pathelement location="lib/"/>
    <pathelement path="${java.class.path}/"/>
  </path>

<available classname="Foo" classpathref="project.class.path"/>
```

- **from:** Refer to the earlier implementations of the "type" parameter of the mapper task to see how and when "from" is used.

- **to:** Refer to the earlier implementations of the "type" parameter of the mapper task to see how and when "to" is used.

Nested Parameters

- **classpath:** A definition was listed above.

Fileset Element

The fileset task defines groups of files in a branch of a directory structure:

```
<fileset dir="src/" >
```

Parameters

- **dir*:** Base of the branch in the directory structure from which the fileset will be built.

- **defaultexcludes:** Value of "yes" or "no"; specifies whether default excludes are used.

- **includes:** Comma-separated list of patterns to include in the file set. All other files are excluded.

- **includesfile:** File source of patterns to include in the file set. All other files will be excluded.

- **excludes:** Comma-separated list of patterns to exclude in the file set. All other files are included.

- **excludesfile:** File source of patterns to exclude in the file set. All other files will be included.

Nested Parameters

- **patternset:** A definition can be found defined above at the start of the section "Frequently Used Nested Parameters."

Patternset Element

The patternset task provides a way to group patterns for later use. It is commonly used nested in a fileset task:

```
<patternset id="junit.test.sources" >
<include name="**/*Test*.java" />
    <exclude name="**/AllTests.java" />
</patternset>
```

Parameters

- **includes:** Comma-separated list of patterns to include in the file set. All other files are excluded.

- **includesfile:** File source of patterns to include in the file set. All other files will be excluded.

- **excludes:** Comma-separated list of patterns to exclude in the file set. All other files are included.

- **excludesfile:** File source of patterns to exclude in the file set. All other files will be included.

Zipfileset Element

The zipfileset task defines groups of files in a branch of a directory structure:

```
<zipfileset dir="src/" >
```

Parameters

- ❑ **prefix:** File that specifies the path of a Zip archive where files will be added.

- ❑ **fullpath:** Directory in which a single file is added to an archive.

- ❑ **src:** Zip file whose extracted contents should be included in the archive.

- ❑ **dir*:** Base of the branch in the directory structure from which the file set will be built.

- ❑ **defaultexcludes:** Value of "yes" or "no"; specifies whether default excludes are used.

- ❑ **includes:** Comma-separated list of patterns to include in the file set. All other files are excluded.

- ❑ **includesfile:** File source of patterns to include in the file set. All other files will be excluded.

- ❑ **excludes:** Comma-separated list of patterns to exclude in the file set. All other files are included.

- ❑ **excludesfile:** File source of patterns to exclude in the file set. All other files will be included.

Ant API Reference

This purpose of this chapter is to summarize the part of the Ant API that developers can use to customize an individual build process. The Ant classes documented in this chapter are as follows:

- ❏ AntClassLoader
- ❏ BuildEvent
- ❏ BuildException
- ❏ BuildListener
- ❏ BuildLogger
- ❏ DefaultLogger
- ❏ DesirableFilter
- ❏ DirectoryScanner
- ❏ FileScanner
- ❏ IntrospectionHelper
- ❏ Location
- ❏ Main
- ❏ PathTokenizer
- ❏ Project
- ❏ ProjectHelper
- ❏ RuntimeConfigurable
- ❏ Target
- ❏ Task

Chapter 30

- ❏ TaskAdapter
- ❏ UnknownElement
- ❏ XmlLogger

Package org.apache.tools.ant

Class AntClassLoader

```
public class AntClassLoader
```

Inheritance Information

Extends: java.lang.ClassLoader

Description

This class is used to load a class in Ant if that class exists within a classpath different from the one used to start Ant.

A helper method (forceLoadClass) allows classes to be loaded from the system classpath of the machine running Ant.

Constructors

```
public AntClassLoader(Project project, Path classpath)
```

When constructing a new classloader, you must specify both the Ant project it should be associated with and the classpath from which it will load classes.

```
public AntClassLoader(Project project, Path classpath,
                      boolean systemFirst)
```

The alternate constructor for an AntClassLoader takes a true or false flag indicating whether the system classpath should also be used. This information is helpful if the classloader needs to access classes (or dependencies to classes) loaded in your system path (for example, JUnit).

Methods

```
public void setIsolated(boolean isolated)
```

This method forces Ant to look only in this classloader's classpath (as opposed to also including the base classloader or other loaded classloaders). If isolated mode is turned on, then any classes referenced and not found in this classloader will throw a java.lang.classNotFoundException.

```
public void addSystemPackageRoot(java.lang.String packageRoot)
```

This method adds a new directory (or Java package) to the default path for the system path classloader. Any subdirectories will also be included.

```
public void addLoaderPackageRoot(java.lang.String packageRoot)
```

This method adds a new directory (or Java package) to the default path for this classloader. Any subdirectories will also be included.

```
public java.lang.Class forceLoadClass(java.lang.String classname)
```

This method loads this classloader even if that class is available on the system classpath. Any future class loaded by this object will be loaded using this classloader. If those classes are not available in its classpath, they will throw a java.lang.ClassNotFoundException.

```
public java.lang.Class forceLoadSystemClass(java.lang.String classname)
```

This method loads a class but defers to the system classloader. You use this method to ensure that any objects created by the class will be compatible with the system loader.

```
public java.io.InputStream getResourceAsStream(java.lang.String name)
```

You use this class to get an InputStream to a named resource.

```
protected java.lang.Class loadClass(java.lang.String classname,
                                     boolean resolve)
```

This method loads a given class using this classloader. If the requested class does not exist on the system classpath or this loader's classpath, the method will throw a java.lang.ClassNotFoundException.

```
public java.lang.Class findClass(java.lang.String name)
```

This method finds and loads a given class using this classloader. If the requested class does not exist on the system classpath or this loader's classpath, the method will throw a java.lang.ClassNotFoundException.

Class BuildEvent

```
public class BuildEvent
```

Inheritance Information

Extends: java.util.EventObject

Constructors

```
public BuildEvent(Project project)
public BuildEvent(Target target)
public BuildEvent(Task task)
```

Methods

```
    public void setMessage(java.lang.String message, int priority)
```

This method sets the default logging message for this event.

```
    public void setException(java.lang.Throwable exception)
```

This method specifies a custom exception you want this event to throw.

```
    public Project getProject()
```

This method returns the Project that fired this event.

```
    public Target getTarget()
```

This method returns the Target that fired this event.

```
    public Task getTask()
```

This method returns the Task that fired this event.

```
    public java.lang.String getMessage()
```

This method returns the logging message.

```
    public int getPriority()
```

This method returns the priority value associated with the logging message.

```
    public java.lang.Throwable getException()
```

This method returns the exception that was thrown, as a Throwable. This field will be set only for taskFinished, targetFinished, and buildFinished events.

Interface BuildListener

```
    public Interface BuildListener
```

Inheritance Information

Extends: java.util.EventListener

Description

Classes that implement this interface will be notified of events happening in a build.

Methods

```
    public void buildStarted(BuildEvent event)
```

This method is called before any events are started.

```
    public void buildFinished(BuildEvent event)
```

This method is called after the last target has finished. It will still be called if an error occurs during the build.

```
    public void targetStarted(BuildEvent event)
```

This method is called before the target's execution is started.

```
    public void targetFinished(BuildEvent event)
```

This method is called after the target has finished. It will still be called if an error occurs during the execution of the target.

```
    public void taskStarted(BuildEvent event)
```

This method is called before the task's execution is started.

```
    public void taskFinished(BuildEvent event)
```

This method is called after the task has finished. It will still be called if an error occurs during the execution of the task.

```
    public void messageLogged(BuildEvent event)
```

This method is executed whenever a message is logged.

Interface BuildLogger

```
    public Interface BuldLogger
```

Inheritance Information

Extends: BuildListener

Description

Ant uses this interface to log the output from the build. A build logger is very much like a build listener with permission to write to the Ant log, which is usually System.out (unless redirected by the -logfile option).

Methods

```
    public void setMessageOutputLevel(int level)
```

This method sets the msgOutputLevel for this logger. Any messages with a level less than or equal to the given level will be logged. The constants for the message levels are in Project.java. The order of the levels, from least verbose to most verbose, is MSG_ERR, MSG_WARN, MSG_INFO, MSG_VERBOSE, MSG_DEBUG.

```
public void setOutputPrintStream(PrintStream output)
```

This method sets the output stream this logger will use.

```
public void setEmacsMode(boolean emacsMode)
```

This method sets this logger to produce emacs-compatible output.

```
public void setErrorPrintStream(java.io.PrintStream err)
```

This method sets the output stream this logger will use for errors.

Class DefaultLogger

```
public class DefaultLogger
```

Inheritance Information

Extends: java.lang.Object

Implements: BuildLogger

Description

This class writes a build event to a PrintStream. Note that DefaultLogger only writes which targets are being executed and any messages that are logged.

Fields

```
protected java.io.PrintStream out
```

```
protected java.io.PrintStream err
```

```
protected int msgOutputLevel
```

```
protected static java.lang.String lSep
```

```
protected boolean emacsMode
```

Methods

```
public void setMessageOutputLevel(int level)
```

This method sets the msgOutputLevel for this logger. Any messages with a level less than or equal to the given level will be logged. The constants for the message levels are in Project.java. The order of the levels, from least verbose to most verbose, is MSG_ERR, MSG_WARN, MSG_INFO, MSG_VERBOSE, MSG_DEBUG.

```
public void setOutputPrintStream(java.io.PrintStream output)
```

This method sets the output stream this logger will use. It is specified by setOutputPrintStream in interface BuildLogger.

```
public void setErrorPrintStream(java.io.PrintStream err)
```

This method sets the output stream this logger will use for errors. It is specified by setErrorPrintStream in interface BuildLogger.

```
public void setEmacsMode(boolean emacsMode)
```

This method sets this logger to produce emacs-compatible output. It is specified by setEmacsMode in interface BuildLogger.

```
public void buildStarted(BuildEvent event)
```

This method executes before any targets are started. It is specified by buildStarted in interface BuildListener.

```
public void buildFinished(BuildEvent event)
```

This method executes after all other activity in the build and prints the build's success status and any errors. It is specified by buildFinished in interface BuildListener.

```
public void targetStarted(BuildEvent event)
```

This method executes when a target is started. It is specified by targetStarted in interface BuildListener.

```
public void targetFinished(BuildEvent event)
```

This method executes when a target is complete, whether errors occurred or not.

```
public void taskStarted(BuildEvent event)
```

This method executes when a task is started.

```
public void taskFinished(BuildEvent event)
```

This method executes when a task has finished, whether errors occurred or not.

```
public void messageLogged(BuildEvent event)
```

This method executes when a message is logged.

Class DesirableFilter

```
public class DesirableFilter
```

Inheritance Information

Extends: java.lang.Object

Implements: java.io.FilenameFilter

Description

This class is designed to filter filenames to determine their desirability.

Methods

```
public boolean accept(java.io.File dir, java.lang.String name)
```

This method tests the given filename to determine whether it's desirable. It helps tasks filter temporary files and files used by Concurrent Versioning System (CVS). It is specified by accept in interface java.io.FilenameFilter.

Class DirectoryScanner

```
public class DirectoryScanner
```

Inheritance Information

Implements: FileScanner

Description

This class is designed to scan a directory for specific files and subdirectories.

Fields

```
protected static final java.lang.String[] DEFAULTEXCLUDES
```

This field is a string array to hold patterns that should be excluded by default.

```
protected java.io.File basedir
```

This field is the base directory from which to scan.

```
protected java.lang.String[] includes
```

This field is a string array to hold patterns that should be included by default.

```
protected java.lang.String[] excludes
```

This field is a string array to hold patterns that will be excluded.

```
protected java.util.Vector filesIncluded
```

This field specifies all files that were found and matched one or more includes, and matched no excludes.

```
protected java.util.Vector filesNotIncluded
```

This field specifies the files that were found and matched zero includes.

```
protected java.util.Vector filesExcluded
```

This field specifies the files that were found and matched one or more includes, and also matched at least one exclude.

```
protected java.util.Vector dirsIncluded
```

This field specifies the directories that were found and matched one or more includes, and matched zero excludes.

```
protected java.util.Vector dirsNotIncluded
```

This field specifies the directories that were found and matched zero includes.

```
protected java.util.Vector dirsExcluded
```

This field specifies the files that were found and matched one or more includes, and also matched one or more excludes.

```
protected boolean haveSlowResults
```

This field is a true or false value indicating whether the vectors holding results were built by a slow scan.

Methods

```
protected static boolean
matchPath(java.lang.String pattern, java.lang.String str)
```

This method matches a path(str) against a pattern.

```
protected static boolean match(java.lang.String pattern,
                               java.lang.String str)
```

This method matches a path(str) against a pattern.

```
public void setBasedir(java.lang.String basedir)
```

This method sets the basedir from which to scan.

```
public void setBasedir(java.io.File basedir)
```

This method sets the basedir from which to scan.

```
public java.io.File getBasedir()
```

This method returns the basedir from which to scan.

```
public void setIncludes(java.lang.String[] includes)
```

This is the setter method for the includes array.

```
    public void setExcludes(java.lang.String[] excludes)
```

This is the setter method for the excludes array.

```
    public void scan()
```

This method scans the basedir for files that match one or more include patterns and zero exclude patterns.

```
    protected void slowScan()
```

This method invokes a scan.

```
    protected void scandir(java.io.File dir, java.lang.String vpath, boolean fast)
```

This method scans the passed dir for files and directories. Found files and directories are placed in the respective collections, based on the matching of includes and excludes. When a directory is found, it is scanned recursively.

```
    protected boolean isIncluded(java.lang.String name)
```

This method returns true or false if a name matches at least one include pattern.

```
    protected boolean couldHoldIncluded(java.lang.String name)
```

This method returns true or false if a name matches the start of at least one include pattern.

```
    protected boolean isExcluded(java.lang.String name)
```

This method returns true or false if a name matches at least one exclude pattern.

```
    public java.lang.String[] getIncludedFiles()
```

This is the getter method for the included-files array.

```
    public java.lang.String[] getNotIncludedFiles()
```

This is the getter method for the not-included-files array.

```
    public java.lang.String[] getExcludedFiles()
```

This is the getter method for the excluded-files array.

```
    public java.lang.String[] getIncludedDirectories()
```

This is the getter method for the included-directories array.

```
    public java.lang.String[] getNotIncludedDirectories()
```

This is the getter method for the not-included-directories array.

```
    public java.lang.String[] getExcludedDirectories()
```

This is the getter method for the excluded-directories array.

```
public void addDefaultExcludes()
```

This method adds the array with default exclusions to the current exclusions set.

Interface FileScanner

```
public Interface FileScanner
```

Description

This is an interface that describes the actions required by any type of directory scanner.

Methods

```
public void addDefaultExcludes()
```

This method adds an array with default exclusions to the current exclusions set.

```
public java.io.File getBasedir()
```

This method gets the basedir to use for scanning.

```
public java.lang.String[] getExcludedDirectories()
```

This method gets the names of the directories that matched one or more of the include patterns and also matched one or more of the exclude patterns.

```
public java.lang.String[] getExcludedFiles()
```

This method gets the names of the files that matched one or more of the include patterns and matched also one or more of the exclude patterns.

```
public java.lang.String[] getIncludedDirectories()
```

This method gets the names of the directories that matched one or more of the include patterns and matched none of the exclude patterns.

```
public java.lang.String[] getIncludedFiles()
```

This method gets the names of the files that matched one or more of the include patterns and matched zero of the exclude patterns.

```
public java.lang.String[] getNotIncludedDirectories()
```

This method gets the names of the directories that matched zero of the include patterns.

```
public java.lang.String[] getNotIncludedFiles()
```

This method gets the names of the files that matched zero of the include patterns.

```
public void scan()
```

This method scans the basedir for files that match one or more include patterns and zero exclude patterns.

```
public void setBasedir(java.lang.String basedir)
```

This method sets the basedir from which to scan, given a String.

```
public void setBasedir(java.io.File basedir)
```

This method sets the basedir from which to scan, given a file.

```
public void setExcludes(java.lang.String[] excludes)
```

This method sets the array of exclude patterns.

```
public void setIncludes(java.lang.String[] includes)
```

This method sets the array of include patterns.

Class IntrospectionHelper

```
public class IntrospectionHelper
```

Description

IntrospectionHelper collects the methods a task or nested element holds to set or create attributes or elements.

Methods

```
public static IntrospectionHelper getHelper(java.lang.Class c)
```

This method implemente the FactoryMethod design pattern for helper objects.

```
public void setAttribute(Project p,  java.lang.Object element,
                         java.lang.String attributeName,
                         java.lang.String value)
```

This method sets the named attribute to the given value.

```
public void addText(java.lang.Object element, java.lang.String text)
```

This method adds PCDATA areas.

```
public java.lang.Object createElement(java.lang.Object element,
                                      java.lang.String elementName)
```

This method creates a nested element with the given name.

```
public java.lang.Class getElementType(java.lang.String elementName)
```

This method returns the type of the nested element with the given name.

```
public java.lang.Class getAttributeType(java.lang.String attributeName)
```

This method returns the type of an attribute with the given name.

```
public boolean supportsCharacters()
```

This method returns a true or false value indicating whether the introspected class supports PCDATA.

```
public java.util.Enumeration getAttributes()
```

This is the getter method for an Enumeration of all attributes supported by the introspected class.

```
public java.util.Enumeration getNestedElements()
```

This is the getter method for an Enumeration of all nested elements supported by the introspected class.

Class Main

```
public class Main
```

Description

This class acts as the command-line entry point into Ant and assembles and executes an Ant project.

Field

```
public static final java.lang.String DEFAULT_BUILD_FILENAME
```

This field is the default name of the buildfile.

Methods

```
protected Main(jatva.lang.String[] args)
```

```
public static void main(java.lang.String[] args)
```

This method executes a build using either a given target or the default target.

Class PathTokenizer

```
public class PathTokenizer
```

Description

A PathTokenizer returns the components that make up a path. The path can use either colons (:) or semi-colons (;) as path separators and slashes (/) or backslashes (\) as file separators.

Constructor

```
public PathTokenizer(java.lang.String path)
```

Methods

```
public boolean hasMoreTokens()
```

This method returns true or false indicating whether the string has more tokens.

```
public java.lang.String nextToken()
```

This method returns the next token.

Class Project

```
public class Project
```

Inheritance Information

Extends: java.lang.Object

Description

The Project class is the main focus of an Ant project and represents the build XML file. This class defines a Ant project with all of its targets and tasks. It also has the ability to execute a build given a specific target name.

Project has a single parameterless constructor, so it can be instantiated with the following syntax:

```
Project proj = new Project();
```

Programmatically, the Project class can be used to create an object that will automatically run a set of Ant tasks.

Methods

```
public void init()
```

This method initializes the project. This process involves setting the default task definitions and loading the system properties.

```
public void log(java.lang.String msg)
```

This method writes the given message to the log.

```
public void log(java.lang.String msg,int msgLevel)
```

This method writes the given message to the log at the given message level.

```
public void log(Task task, java.lang.String msg,  int msgLevel)
```

This method writes the given message to the log for the given task at the given message level.

```
public void log(Target target, java.lang.String msg, int msgLevel)
```

This method writes the given message to the log for the given target at the given message level.

```
public void setProperty(java.lang.String name, java.lang.String value)
```

This is the setter method for a property in an Ant project given the name and value. For example:

```
<property name="phase3.src.dir"          value="../phase3/src"/>
```

sets a property called "phase3.src.dir" to the String value "../phase3/src"".

```
public void setUserProperty(String name, String value)
```

This is the setter method for the UserProperty, given a name and value.

```
public java.lang.String getProperty(java.lang.String name)
```

This is the getter method for a property with the given name.

```
public java.lang.String getUserProperty(java.lang.String name)
```

This is the getter method for a UserProperty with the given name.

```
public java.util.Hashtable getProperties()
```

This method gets a hashtable of the properties belonging to the project.

```
public java.util.Hashtable getUserProperties()
```

This method gets a hashtable of the UserProperties belonging to the project.

```
public void setDefaultTarget(java.lang.String defaultTarget)
```

This method sets the default target for a project.

```
public java.lang.String getDefaultTarget()
```

This method returns a String representation for the default target for a project.

```
public void setDefault(java.lang.String defaultTarget)
```

This method sets the default target for a project.

```
public void setName(java.lang.String name)
```

This method sets the name for a project.

```
public java.lang.String getName()
```

This method gets the name of the project.

```
public void addFilter(java.lang.String token,  java.lang.String value)
```

This method adds a filter to the given project.

```
public java.util.Hashtable getFilters()
```

This method returns a hashtable of the filters belonging to the project.

```
public void setBasedir(java.lang.String baseD)
```

This method sets the "baseDir" property of the project to a file resolved to the given String.

```
public void setBaseDir(java.io.File baseDir)
```

This method sets the "baseDir" property of the project to a file resolved to the given file.

```
public java.io.File getBaseDir()
```

This method returns a file representation of the project's "baseDir" property.

```
public static java.lang.String getJavaVersion()
```

This method returns the Java version property of the project.

```
public void setJavaVersionProperty()
```

This method sets the Java version property of the project.

```
public void addTaskDefinition(java.lang.String taskName,
                              java.lang.Class taskClass)
```

This method adds a task to the project based on the "name" and "class" parameters.

```
public java.util.Hashtable getTaskDefinitions()
```

This method returns a hashtable of the TaskDefinitions belonging to the project.

```
public void addDataTypeDefinition(java.lang.String typeName,
                                  java.lang.Class typeClass)
```

This method adds a DataTypeDefinition to the collection belonging to the project.

```
public java.util.Hashtable getDataTypeDefinitions()
```

This method gets a hashtable of the DataTypeDefinitions belonging to the project.

```
public void addTarget(Target target)
```

This method adds a target to the project, matching the parameter.

```
public void addTarget(java.lang.String targetName, Target target)
```

This method adds a target to the project, matching the parameter.

```
public void addOrReplaceTarget(Target target)
```

This method adds a target to the project, matching the parameter, or replaces it if it already exists.

```
public void addOrReplaceTarget(java.lang.String targetName, Target target)
```

This method adds a target to the project, matching the parameters, or replaces it if it already exists.

```
public java.util.Hashtable getTargets()
```

This method returns a hashtable of the Target objects belonging to the project.

```
public Task createTask(java.lang.String taskType)
```

This method returns a new task of the given task type within the scope of the project.

```
public void executeTargets(java.util.Vector targetNames)
```

This method calls execute() on each target within the given collection.

```
public void executeTarget(java.lang.String targetName)
```

This method calls execute() on the given target.

```
public static java.lang.String translatePath(java.lang.String to_process)
```

This method translates a path into its native (platform-specific) format using a PathTokenizer.

```
public void copyFile(java.lang.String sourceFile,
                     java.lang.String destFile)
```

This is a convenience method to copy a file from a source to a destination without filtering.

```
public void copyFile(java.lang.String sourceFile,
                     java.lang.String destFile, boolean filtering)
```

This is a convenience method to copy a file from a source to a destination given a Boolean to indicate whether token filtering must be used.

```
public void copyFile(java.lang.String sourceFile,
                     java.lang.String destFile,
                             boolean filtering, boolean overwrite)
```

This is a convenience method to copy a file from a source to a destination given Booleans to indicate whether token filtering must be used and whether source files may overwrite newer destination files.

```
public void copyFile(java.lang.String sourceFile,
                     java.lang.String destFile,
                         boolean filtering, boolean overwrite,
                         boolean preserveLastModified)
```

This is a convenience method to copy a file from a source to a destination given Booleans to indicate whether token filtering must be used, whether source files may overwrite newer destination files, and whether the last modified time of destFile file should be made equal to the last modified time of sourceFile.

```
public void copyFile(java.io.File sourceFile, java.io.File destFile)
```

This is a convenience method to copy a file from a source to a destination without filtering.

```
public void copyFile(java.io.File sourceFile,
                     java.io.File destFile,
                     boolean filtering)
```

This is a convenience method to copy a file from a source to a destination given a Boolean to indicate whether token filtering must be used.

```
public void copyFile(java.io.File sourceFile,
                     java.io.File destFile,
                     boolean filtering, boolean overwrite)
```

This is a convenience method to copy a file from a source to a destination given Booleans to indicate whether token filtering must be used and whether source files may overwrite newer destination files.

```
public void copyFile(java.io.File sourceFile,
                     java.io.File destFile,
                     boolean filtering, boolean overwrite,
                     boolean preserveLastModified)
```

This is a convenience method to copy a file from a source to a destination given Booleans to indicate whether token filtering must be used, whether source files may overwrite newer destination files, and whether the last modified time of destFile file should be made equal to the last modified time of sourceFile.

```
public static boolean toBoolean(java.lang.String s)
```

This method returns the Boolean equivalent of a String, which is considered true if "on", "true", or "yes" is found, ignoring case.

```
public void runTarget(Target target)

public final java.util.Vector topoSort(java.lang.String root,

java.util.Hashtable targets)
```

This method returns a Vector that is a topologically sorted set of targets given a root (the [String] name of the root target). The sort is created in such a way that the sequence of targets until the root target is the minimum possible such sequence.

```
public void addReference(java.lang.String name, java.lang.Object value)
```

This method adds a reference to the project, given a name and value.

```
public java.util.Hashtable getReferences()
```

This method returns a hashtable of the Reference objects belonging to the project.

Class ProjectHelper

```
public class ProjectHelper
```

Description

ProjectHelper will configure a project (complete with targets and tasks) based on an XML buildfile.

Methods

```
public static void configureProject(Project project,
                                    java.io.File buildFile)
```

This method configures the project with the contents of the given XML file.

```
public static void configure(java.lang.Object target,
             org.xml.sax.AttributeList attrs, Project project)

public static void addText(java.lang.Object target, char[] buf,
                           int start, int end)
```

This method adds the contents of #PCDATA(buf) sections to an element from start to end.

```
public static void addText(java.lang.Object target,
                           java.lang.String text)
```

This method adds the contents of #PCDATA(target) sections to an element.

```
public static String replaceProperties(Project project,
                           String value, Hashtable keys)
```

This method replaces the property at ${NAME} with the given value.

Class RuntimeConfigurable

```
public class RuntimeConfigurable
```

Description

RuntimeConfigurable is a wrapper class that maintains the attributes of a task and configures it at runtime.

Constructor

```
public RuntimeConfigurable(java.lang.Object proxy)
```

This constructor initializes the element to wrap (proxy).

Methods

```
public void setAttributes(org.xml.sax.AttributeList attributes)
```

This is the setter method for the attributes for the wrapped element.

```
public org.xml.sax.AttributeList getAttributes()
```

This is the getter method for the attributes for the wrapped element.

```
public void addChild(RuntimeConfigurable child)
```

This method adds a child element to the wrapped element.

```
public void addText(java.lang.String data)
```

This method adds characters from #PCDATA(data) areas to the wrapped element.

```
public void addText(char[] buf,  int start, int end)
```

This method adds the contents of #PCDATA(buf) sections to an element.

```
public void maybeConfigure(Project p)
```

This method configures the wrapped element and all children within the given project space unless it has already been done.

Class Target

```
public class target
```

Inheritance Information

Extends: java.lang.Object

Description

This class implements a collection of work in Ant. A target lives within an Ant project and can contain its own targets and tasks.

Methods

```
public void setProject(Project project)
```

This is the setter method for the parent project.

```
public Project getProject()
```

This is the getter method for the parent project.

```
public void setDepends(java.lang.String depS)
```

This method sets the "depends" property for the target. For example:

```
<target depends="prepare" description="Compile the source tree" name="com-
pile">
```

sets the "depends" property for the compile target to the entity named Prepare within the project's scope.

```
public void setName(java.lang.String name)
```

This is the setter method for the "name" attribute.

```
public java.lang.String getName()
```

This is the getter method for the "name" attribute.

```
public void addTask(Task task)
```

This method adds the given task to the target's definition. For example:

```
<target name="prepare" depends="set-version">
        <mkdir dir="${build.dir}"/>
    </target>
```

adds a mkdir(type) task to the target named prepare.

```
public Task[] getTasks()
```

This is the getter method for the current set of tasks to be executed by this target.

```
public void addDependency(java.lang.String dependency)
```

This method adds a "dependency" attribute to the task.

```
public java.util.Enumeration getDependencies()
```

This method returns a collection of dependencies associated with the target.

```
public void setIf(java.lang.String property)
```

This is the setter method for the "If" property.

```
public void setUnless(java.lang.String property)
```

This is the setter method for the "Unless" property.

```
public void setDescription(java.lang.String description)
```

This is the setter method for the "Description" property.

```
public java.lang.String getDescription()
```

This is the getter method for the "Description" property.

```
public java.lang.String toString()
```

This method overrides method in String.

```
public void execute() throws BuildException
```

This is the key method when you're using this target. It will call execute() on all tasks within the target.

Class Task

```
public class Task
```

Inheritance Information

Extends: java.lang.Object

Description

You know that in Ant, a *task* is defined as a unit of work. A practical example of a task would be to delete a directory or a file, to check the latest version of a class out from a source control system, or to send an email message to your system administrator informing him that a build was successful or that it failed (along with the reasons why). All these tasks are part of the existing Ant framework, but as a developer you may need to create a new task customized to your (or your client's) specific processes and/or needs. For instance, you may want to set up a custom task to make an entry in a database or a spreadsheet, or you may want to restart system services (or restart the Unreal Tournament server that coexists in your production environment). To create a custom task, you create a class that directly or indirectly extends org.apache.tools.ant.Task.

The key method of a given Task object is the execute() method. When you're creating a new task, the execute() method will contain the framework for the job to be performed. When a task is executed, an object of the org.apache.ant.Task class is instantiated and configured and then executes to perform a specific function.

An oversimplified example implementation of a new custom task is listed here:

```
package org.apache.tools.ant.taskdefs;
import org.apache.tools.ant.*;
public class GreetJon extends Task {
    public void execute() throws BuildException{
        System.out.println("Hello Jon!");
    }
}
```

For each property created in a task, there should be public setter and getter methods. The properties built into the abstract class Task are as follows:

The only constructor for Task has no parameters, but for practical purposes it will probably be instantiated and initialized within a project using the createTask() method.

It is important to remember that a task usually exists within the scope of both a project and one or more of its child targets.

Methods

```
public Project getProject()
```

This is the getter method for the project to which this task belongs.

```
public void setOwningTarget(Target target)
```

This is the setter method for the owning target object of this task.

```
public Target getOwningTarget()
```

This is the getter method for the owning target object of this task.

```
ublic void setTaskName(java.lang.String name)
```

This is the setter method for the "name" property to use in logging messages.

```
public java.lang.String getTaskName()
```

This is the getter method for the "name" property to use in logging messages.

```
public void log(java.lang.String msg)
```

This method logs a message with the default (INFO) priority.

```
public void log(java.lang.String msg, int msgLevel)
```

This method logs a message with the given priority.

```
public void setDescription(java.lang.String desc)
```

This is the setter method for the description of the current action.

```
public java.lang.String getDescription()
```

This is the getter method for the description of the current action.

```
public void init()
```

This method is called by the project to let the task initialize properly.

```
public void execute()throws BuildException
```

This method is called by the project or target to execute the task.

```
public Location getLocation()
```

This method returns the file location where this task was defined.

```
public void setLocation(Location location)
```

This is the setter method for the file location where this task is defined.

```
public RuntimeConfigurable getRuntimeConfigurableWrapper()
```

This is the getter method for the wrapper class for runtime configuration.

```
public void maybeConfigure()
```

This method configures this task, unless it has already been done.

Class TaskAdapter

```
public class TaskAdapter
```

Inheritance Information

Extends: Task

Description

TaskAdapter uses introspection to adapt a bean (using the Bridge design pattern).

Methods

```
public void execute()
```

This method executes the adapted task.

```
public void setProxy(java.lang.Object o)
```

This is the setter method for the target object class.

```
public java.lang.Object getProxy()
```

This is the getter method for the target object class.

Class UnknownElement

```
public class UnknownElement
```

Description

UnknownElement is a class that wraps all information necessary to create a task that did not exist when Ant started.

Constructor

public **UnknownElement**(java.lang.String elementName)

Methods

```
public java.lang.String getTag()
```

This is the getter method for the corresponding XML tag.

```
public void maybeConfigure()
```

This method configures this task, unless its been done already.

```
public void execute()
```

This method executes when the real task has been configured for the first time.

```
public void addChild(UnknownElement child)
```

This method adds a child element.

```
protected void handleChildren(java.lang.Object parent,
RuntimeConfigurable parentWrapper)
```

This method executes children.

Class XmlLogger

```
public class XmlLogger
```

Inheritance Information

Extends: org.apache.tools.ant.XmlLogger

Implements: BuildListener, java.util.EventListener

Description

XmlLogger creates a file (log.xml) in the current directory with an XML description of what happened during a build.

Constructor

```
public XmlLogger()
```

This constructor initializes a new XmlLogger that logs build events to an XML file.

Methods

```
public void buildStarted(BuildEvent event)
```

This method executes before any targets are started.

```
public void buildFinished(BuildEvent event)
```

This method executes after the last target has finished, whether or not errors occurred.

```
public void targetStarted(BuildEvent event)
```

This method executes when a target is started.

```
public void targetFinished(BuildEvent event)
```

This method executes when a target has finished, whether or not errors occurred.

```
public void taskStarted(BuildEvent event)
```

This method executes when a task is started.

```
public void taskFinished(BuildEvent event)
```

This method executes when a task has finished, whether or not errors occurred.

```
public void messageLogged(BuildEvent event)
```

This method executes whenever a message is logged.

Putting it All Together

Now, to put all this information together, we will programmatically create a project, give it a single target and task, and call execute() on it. Using our task GreetJon from the description of the Task class, we will build a task that can be executed using its own Main() method.

The project file is as follows:

```
import org.apache.tools.ant.*;

public class ChapterAntProject extends org.apache.tools.ant.Project{

    public ChapterAntProject(){
        super.init();
    }

    public static void main(String[] args){
        try{
            /*
             Create the Project object and add the custom Tag
             */
            Project proj = new ChapterAntProject();
            proj.setName("jonsProject");
            GreetJon task = new GreetJon();
            proj.addTaskDefinition("jonsTask", task.getClass());
            /*
             Create the Target Object as a child
             of the project and add the Task to
             it
             */
            Target targ = new Target();
            targ.setName("jonsTarget");
            targ.addTask(task);
            proj.addTarget("jonsTarget",targ);
            proj.setDefaultTarget("jonsTarget");
            /*
             Execute the Target
             */
            proj.executeTarget("jonsTarget");
        }
        catch(Exception e){
            e.printStackTrace();
            throw new BuildException("An error occurred while building and
running your custom task",e);
```

```
        }
     }

  }
```

The task file is as follows:

```
import org.apache.tools.ant.*;
public class GreetJon extends Task {

 public GreetJon(){
        ;}

        public void execute() throws BuildException{
        System.out.println("Hello Zach!");
 }
 }
```

Running the project from a Java environment will produce output equivalent to the following Ant build.xml file:

```
<?xml version="1.0"?>

<project name="jonsProject" basedir = "." default = "jonsTarget">
    <target name="jonsTarget">
        <taskdef name="jonsTask" classname="GreetJon"/>
    </target>
</project>
```

This example is meant to be a simplified launching point from which you can build many custom tasks, projects, and targets to perform specific actions within the Ant framework.

JUnit API Reference

This chapter summarizes the JUnit API. Classes used by developers as part of their everyday testing are emphasized.

Package junit.framework

The junit.framework package contains all the classes developers need to begin writing JUnit tests. The TestCase class forms the center of the package, and developers subclass it to create automated unit tests. The rest of the classes in the package support TestCase: collecting its results, aggregating many instances into a test suite, and providing assertion facilities. The Test interface is another crucial package member—it defines a common contract for TestCases and TestSuites, as well as providing a hook into the framework for extensions to use.

Class Assert

```
public class Assert
```

Inheritance Information

Extends: Object

Direct known subclasses: TestCase, TestDecorator

Description

Assert comprises a set of static assert methods that can be used to fail tests. Because TestCase and TestDecorator extend Assert, Assert's methods can be used by their unqualified names in subclasses of these two classes.

If the condition tested by the assert method evaluates to false, it throws an AssertionFailedError. The framework treats this error as a test failure. Assertion methods are used in TestCases to set up the pass/fail conditions for the test method.

Every Assert method is overloaded to take an additional String parameter as its first argument. This message will be attached to the AssertionFailedError, should it be thrown. The following code sample illustrates ways to use Assert's methods to verify that the code under test has produced the correct results.

```
public void testOpenPortal(){
   Portal hadesPortal = dimensionalGateway.openPortal(new Plane("Hades"));

   /*verify that a portal object was returned*/
   assertNotNull("null portal returned", hadesPortal);

   /*verify the portal is open*/
   assertTrue(hadesPortal.isOpen());

   /*check that the portal has the correct name*/
   assertEquals("portal name check", "HadesPortal", hadesPortal.getName());
   /*try opening a portal to a plane that does not exist*/
   try{
      dimensionalGateway.openPortal(new Plane("xxxfooyyy"));
      fail("should have gotten a PlaneNotFoundException e");
   }
   catch(PlaneNotFoundException e){/*behavior is as expected*/}
}
```

Methods

```
assert(boolean condition) Deprecated
public static void assert(boolean condition)
```

Use assertTrue(boolean condition).

These are the most basic forms of assertions. If the boolean is not true, the assertion fails. The assert() and assert(String) methods were deprecated in favor of assertTrue() to avoid a conflict with the assert keyword in Java 1.4+.

```
assert(String message, boolean condition) Deprecated
public static void assert(String message, boolean condition)
```

Use assertTrue(String message, boolean condition).

```
assertTrue(boolean condition)
public static void assertTrue(boolean condition)
```

```
assertTrue(String message, boolean condition)
public static void assertTrue(String message, boolean condition)
```

```
assertEquals(String message, Object expected, Object actual)
public static void assertEquals(String message, Object expected,
      Object actual)
```

```
assertEquals(Object expected, Object actual
public static void assertEquals(Object expected, Object actual
```

```
assertEquals(String message, double expected, double actual, double delta)
public static void assertEquals(String message, double expected,
     double actual, double delta)
```

```
assertEquals(double expected, double actual, double delta
public static void assertEquals(double expected, double actual,
     double delta)
```

```
assertEquals(String message, float expected, float actual, float delta)
public static void assertEquals(String message, float expected,
     float actual, float delta)
```

```
assertEquals(float expected, float actual, float delta)
public static void assertEquals(float expected, float actual,
     float delta)
```

```
assertEquals(String message, long expected, long actual)
public static void assertEquals(String message, long expected,
     long actual)
```

```
assertEquals(long expected, long actual)
public static void assertEquals(long expected, long actual)
```

```
assertEquals(String message, boolean expected, boolean actual
public static void assertEquals(String message, boolean expected,
     boolean actual
```

```
assertEquals(boolean expected, boolean actual)
public static void assertEquals(boolean expected, boolean actual)
```

```
assertEquals(String message, byte expected, byte actual)
public static void assertEquals(String message, byte expected,
                                byte actual)
```

```
assertEquals(byte expected, byte actual)
public static void assertEquals(byte expected, byte actual)
```

```
assertEquals(String message, char expected, char actual)
public static void assertEquals(String message, char expected,
     char actual)
```

```
assertEquals(char expected, char actual)
public static void assertEquals(char expected, char actual)
```

```
assertEquals(String message, short expected, short actual)
public static void assertEquals(String message, short expected,
     short actual)
```

```
assertEquals(short expected, short actual)
public static void assertEquals(short expected, short actual)
```

```
assertEquals(String message, int expected, int actual)
public static void assertEquals(String message, int expected, int actual)

assertEquals(int expected, int actual)
public static void assertEquals(int expected, int actual)
```

These methods compare the first (nonmessage) argument to the second and fail if they are not equal. The test for equality is == for primitives and equals() for objects. Floating-point comparisons are made with respect to the delta argument (that is, if the difference between expected and actual is greater than the delta, the test fails).

> These comparisons require the delta because floating-point calculations can result in slight precision errors; these errors would cause a test that depended upon exact equality to fail even though the calculated result was as close to the desired result as floating point calculations could make it.

All the assertEquals methods automatically display the values of the expected and actual parameters as part of their failure message.

```
assertNotNull(Object object)
public static void assertNotNull(Object object)

assertNotNull(String message, Object object)
public static void assertNotNull(String message, Object object)

assertNull(Object object)
public static void assertNull(Object object)

assertNull(String message, Object object)
public static void assertNull(String message, Object object)
```

This method checks whether a given reference is null.

```
assertSame(String message, Object expected, Object actual)
public static void assertSame(String message, Object expected,
    Object actual)

assertSame(Object expected, Object actual)
public static void assertSame(Object expected, Object actual)
```

This method verifies that the expected and actual arguments are the same object. This method uses the == method of comparison, not the .equals() method**fail(String message)**.

```
public static void fail(String message)

fail()
public static void fail()
```

This method fails the test by throwing an AssertionFailedError. It's useful for asserting that a given point in code should not be reached, as with an exception that should have been thrown (see the example at the beginning of this section).

Interface Protectable

```
public inteface Protectable
```

Description

The JUnit framework and custom extensions use the Protectable interface to indicate code that requires JUnit-style exception handling. Developers can use an inner class to implement Protectable, defining its protect() method so that it calls relevant code (in the framework, calls to setUp(), the test method, and tearDown() are ultimately located within a protect() method). The Protectable can then be passed to a TestResult object, which will catch and log any exceptions resulting from the call to protect(). See TestResult.runProtected for details and an example. Everyday testing should not require the use of this interface.

Method

```
protect()
public void protect()
```

This method wraps a call to a method requiring protection. (Note: This method throws Throwable.)

Interface Test

```
public interface Test
```

Description

Part of the Composite design pattern, Test represents the common interface for single (TestCase), composite (TestSuite), and special (TestDecorator) tests. The shared interface allows all types of tests to be treated similarly by the framework.

Methods

```
countTestCases()
public int countTestCases()
```

This method counts the number of TestCases that will be run by this test (1 for TestCases, or the grand total of contained TestCases for suites).

```
run(TestResult result)
public void run(TestResult result)
```

This method runs this test and collects the results in the TestResult parameter.

Class TestCase

```
public abstract class TestCase
```

Inheritance Information

Extends: Assert

Implements: Test

Known subclasses: ExceptionTestCase

Description

TestCase is the central class of the JUnit framework. Subclasses of TestCase form the building blocks of automated test suites in JUnit. A TestCase subclass is usually designed to exercise the public interface of the class under test.

The standard template for a subclass is a String constructor, a setUp() method, a tearDown() method, and any number of (public) test methods named according to the form *test<name of method to be tested>()*. The setUp() method ensures that the test fixture is initialized, and the tearDown() method performs cleanup after a given test. When tests are run, each test method is run as part of a separate instance of the TestCase to which it belongs. The series of steps for test method execution is:

```
setUp()
<testMethod>
tearDown()
```

A *test fixture* is loosely defined as all the data and/or objects the test code needs in order to run properly. A TestCase for a sorting method might have a test fixture consisting of several unsorted arrays and a properly instantiated Sorter object.

Constructor

```
TestCase(String name)
public TestCase(String name)
```

TestCase() constructs an instance of the TestCase based on the name argument. TestCase follows the Pluggable Selector design pattern, in which the behavior of an object can modified externally. In the case of TestCase, this means each TestCase instance will run only *one* of its test methods when a caller invokes run(). Unless the behavior of runTest() is overridden, the name of the TestCase specifies which test method is executed.

Suppose a method testHeatUp() exercises heatUp() on a Weather object. To run this test method in the JUnit framework, we create a new TestCase with the following syntax:

```
TestCase testToRunSoon = new WeatherTest("testHeatUp");
```

When run() is called on testToRunSoon, TestCase uses reflection to find and execute testHeatUp(). Subclasses should provide a String constructor that calls TestCase(String) to maintain this behavior.

Initialization code should be located in the setUp() method rather than in the constructor, a method called by the constructor, or an instance initializer block. See setUp() for more information.

Methods

```
countTestCases()
public int countTestCases()
```

This method returns the number of TestCases—in other words, one.

```
createResult()
public TestResult createResult()
```

This method instantiates a new TestResult object.

```
getName()
public String getName()
```

This method returns the name of this TestCase instance. The name usually corresponds to the name of the method under test by this instance.

```
name() Deprecated
public String name()
```

Use getName().

```
run()
public TestResult run()
```

This is a convenience method that runs the test case and returns a new TestResult containing the results.

```
TestResult result = new WeatherTest("testHeatUp").run();
if (!result.wasSuccessful()){
    sendIrateEmailToClassAuthor();
}
run(TestResult result)
public void run(TestResult result)
```

This method runs the whole test, including setUp() and tearDown(), and collects the result in the TestResult argument. See the description of TestResult and Test for more information.

```
runBare()
public void runBare()
```

This method runs the TestCase, including setUp() and tearDown(). It provides no result-gathering functionality. If an exception is thrown during runBare(), the test has failed. This method is used mainly by the framework.

```
runTest()
public void runTest()
```

This method defines the testable behavior (as opposed to setup or result-gathering code) of this instance of the TestCase. The runTest() method is called as part of the run(TestResult) method. The default implementation uses reflection to run the method corresponding to the name of the TestCase.

Instead of using the default implementation, you can also override this method in an anonymous inner class to execute the desired test code. The following two methods of instantiating a WeatherTest that runs the testHeatUp() method are equivalent:

```
TestCase innerClassCase = new WeatherTest("I could use any name here"){
  public void runTest(){
    testHeatUp();
  }
};

TestCase defaultCase = new WeatherTest("testHeatUp");
```

The anonymous inner class method of specifying TestCase behavior is more type safe and is described in the JUnit documentation. However, it seems to be primarily an artifact from an earlier version of JUnit where the reflection-based implementation did not exist. For most purposes, the reflection implementation is simpler.

setName()
```
public void setName(String name)
```

This method sets the name of the TestCase instance in a manner identical to the String constructor.

setUp()
```
public void setUp()
```

Because setUp() is called by TestCase before the execution of test code, subclasses should override this method to set up the test fixture for test methods to run against. Each test method in the class is executed within a separate instance of the TestCase, so there is no benefit in putting shared setup code in a constructor or an initializer block instead (because these will be run as often as setUp()).

> In versions of JUnit previous to 3.7, exceptions generated in code that ran as part of TestCase construction yielded confusing stack traces—all the more reason to stick to setUp().

All the test methods in the following subclass would now have access to a catalog with two products in it when executed with run(TestResult):

```
public void setUp(){
  /*initialize an instance variable.*/
  testCatalog = new Catalog();
  testCatalog.addProduct(new Product("Original Koozie"));
  testCatalog.addProduct(new Product("Executive Chubber"));
}
```

suite()
```
public static Test suite()
```

The static suite() method is defined by convention in TestCase subclasses. It provides a convenient way of turning all the test methods in a TestCase into a single TestSuite. The suite() method can also be used by TestCases that define no test methods but instead serve as assemblers of other TestSuites. For TestCases with test code in them, suite() methods should probably follow this form:

```
public static Test suite(){
  //shortcut to add all test methods in the class
  return new TestSuite(YourTestCase.class);
}
```

Alternatively, suite() can add the different TestCases to the suite by hand. This technique is convenient when you need more granularity (maybe a test method executes so slowly that you remove it temporarily during development):

```
public static Test suite(){
  //more granular implementation, add each test by hand
  TestSuite suite = new TestSuite();
  suite.addTest(new YourTestCase("testFirstMethod"));
```

```
   //suite.addTest(new YourTestCase("testVerySlowMethod"));
   return suite;
}
```

TestCases that serve as assemblers of other tests should use the following form:

```
public static Test suite(){
   TestSuite suite = new TestSuite();
   suite.addTest(FirstClassInPackage.suite());
   suite.addTest(SecondClassInPackage.suite());
   //etc.
   return suite;
}
```

The last implementation shows why it is conventional to define a suite() method for each TestCase()—doing so makes it simpler for assembler TestCases to add all the tests in a package to their *own* suite() method.

tearDown()
```
public void tearDown()
```

This method tears down the test fixture. The tearDown() method is called by TestCase after the test method is finished. Generally, tearDown() should free shared resources such as database connections and perform cleanup. In addition, because a TestSuite may store instantiated and setup TestCases until the test run is complete, it is a good idea to dereference any memory-intensive instance variables:

```
public void tearDown(){
   databaseConnection.close();
   testFile.delete();
   giantArray = null;
}
```

toString()
```
public String toString()
```

This method returns a String representation in the form *<name of instance>(<name of class>)*.

Interface TestListener

```
public interface TestListener
```

Description

The TestListener interface is used by the TestRunners provided by the JUnit framework. Its methods inform the listener object that a test has started, an error or a failure has been encountered, or a test has ended. These notifications allow the TestRunners to build a dynamic view of this information. TestListeners are registered with a TestResult.

Methods

addError(Test test, Throwable t)
```
public void addError(Test test, Throwable t)
```

```
addFailure(Test test, AssertionFailedError t)
public void addFailure(Test test, AssertionFailedError t)

endTest(Test test)
public void endTest(Test test)

startTest(Test test)
public void startTest(Test test)
```

Class TestFailure

```
public class TestFailure
```

Inheritance Information

Extends: Object

Description

The TestFailure class mates a failed Test with the exception that caused it to fail. It provides a constructor and accessor methods for the Test and the exception. The toString() method returns a short description of the failure.

Constructor

```
TestFailure(Test failedTest, Throwable thrownException)
public TestFailure(Test failedTest, Throwable thrownException)
```

Methods

```
failedTest()
public Test failedTest()

thrownException()
public Throwable thrownException()

toString()
public String toString()
```

Class TestResult

```
public class TestResult
```

Inheritance Information

Extends: Object

Description

TestResult is an example of the Collecting Parameter design pattern. The results of an arbitrary number of tests can be collected by passing the same TestResult to each Test's run method.

In addition to aggregating results, TestResult lets you run TestCases and interpret thrown exceptions as test failures. JUnit recognizes two types of negative Test result: failures and errors. *Failures* are the result of assertions that proved untrue at runtime and are represented by AssertionFailedErrors. *Errors* are unanticipated exceptions thrown by the test code (such as ClassCastExceptions). TestResult wraps both types of exceptions in TestFailure objects but stores them differently. In addition to exposing the collections of TestFailures, TestResult also provides a wasSuccessful() method to determine whether all tests passed.

TestResult is used mostly by the JUnit framework, because the provided TestRunners encapsulate code that displays the results of a test run. TestRunners interact with the TestResult through the TestListener interface. TestListeners are registered with the TestResult, which calls the appropriate methods to notify the listener of test lifecycle events (start, end, failure, and error). Here is an example of how we might use TestResult without the framework:

```
TestResult result = new TestResult();
result.addListener(someCustomListener);

nightlyTestSuite.run(result);
if(!result.wasSuccessful()){
  Enumeration eFailures = result.failures();
  while(eFailures.hasMoreElements()){
    TestFailure failure =(TestFailure)eFailures.nextElement();
    System.out.println(failure.failedTest() + " failed with exception " +
                       failure.thrownException());
  }
  if(result.failureCount() + result.errorCount() > 10){
    printBigRedWarning();
  }
}
```

Constructor

```
TestResult()
public TestResult()
```

Methods

```
addError(Test test, Throwable t)
public void addError(Test test, Throwable t)

addFailure(Test test, AssertionFailedError t)
public void addFailure(Test test, AssertionFailedError t)
```

These methods each add an error or failure to the TestResult. The second parameter in each case represents the exception that caused the test to fail.

```
addListener(TestListener listener)
public void addListener(TestListener listener)
```

This method registers a TestListener with this TestResult.

```
endTest(Test test)
public void endTest(Test test)
```

This method informs the TestResult (and by extension, its registered listeners) that the specified test is complete.

```
errorCount()
public int errorCount()
```

This method returns the number of detected errors stored in this TestResult.

```
errors()
public Enumeration errors()
```

This method returns an Enumeration of the detected errors stored in this TestResult.

```
failureCount()
public int failureCount()
```

This method returns the number of detected failures stored in this TestResult.

```
failures()
public Enumeration failures()
```

This method returns an Enumeration of the detected failures stored in this TestResult.

```
removeListener(TestListener listener)
public void removeListener(TestListener listener)
```

This method unregisters the specified TestListener.

```
run(TestCase test)
protected void run(TestCase test)
```

This method runs the specified TestCase and adds any thrown exceptions to the lists of failures or errors as appropriate.

```
runCount()
public int runCount()
```

This method returns the total number of TestCases whose results are gathered in this TestResult.

```
runProtected(Test test, Protectable p)
public void runProtected(Test test, Protectable p)
```

This method runs the given Protectable under JUnit protection (all caught exceptions, except ThreadDeathException, are added to the error/failure list). The runProtected() method is used internally as part of standard TestCase execution, and it can be used by extensions that execute code in addition to the code directly under test. Any exceptional conditions in the Protectable's protect() method are logged in the TestResult and associated with the Test parameter:

```
//encapsulate database setup inside an anonymous Protectable
Protectable p = new Protectable(){
  public void protect(){
    insertTestDataIntoDB();
  }
};
result.runProtected(testToAssociateFailuresWith, p);
```

runTests() *Deprecated*
```
public int runTests()
```

Use runCount().

shouldStop()
```
public boolean shouldStop()
```

This method checks whether a series of tests being run with this TestResult should stop (usually meaning prematurely). Users of TestResult can signal a premature stop with the stop() method.

startTest(Test test)
```
public void startTest(Test test)
```

This method notifies the TestResult (and its listeners) that the given Test will be started.

stop()
```
public void stop()
```

This method signals that the series of tests being run with this TestResult run should stop rather than finishing.

testErrors() *Deprecated*
```
public int testErrors()
```

Use errorCount().

testFailures() *Deprecated*
```
public int testFailures()
```

Use failureCount().

wasSuccessful()
```
public boolean wasSuccessful()
```

This method returns true if all the Tests run with this TestResult were successful, or false otherwise.

Class TestSuite

```
public class TestSuite
```

Inheritance Information

Extends: Object

Implements: Test

Direct known subclass: ActiveTestSuite

Description

TestSuite represents a composite of Tests. TestSuite implements the Test interface, so TestSuites can contain other TestSuites. Suites are generally used to collect and run all the test methods in a TestCase or all the TestSuites in a package. By nesting TestSuites within TestSuites, you can test portions of a codebase at an arbitrary level of granularity.

TestSuite handles exceptional conditions during Test addition (no valid constructor for the TestCase, exceptions in the constructor, no test methods found in the class during automatic addition, and so on) by adding a new Test to the suite that will fail automatically with an appropriate warning message.

Constructors

```
TestSuite()
public TestSuite()

TestSuite(String name)
public TestSuite(String name)
```

This constructor constructs an empty TestSuite. New Tests can be added to the suite by calling the addTest(Test) method.

```
TestSuite(Class theClass)
```

This constructor constructs a TestSuite containing a TestCase for each test method in the Class argument. *Test methods* are defined as public methods in the class that take no arguments, declare a void return type, and begin with the word *test*:

```
TestSuite suite = new TestSuite(WeatherTest.class);
```

Methods

```
addTest(Test test)
public void addTest(Test test)
```

This method adds the specified test to the TestSuite. It's used to hand construct a TestSuite—usually for the purpose of adding other TestSuites to this suite:

```
/*add a single Test*/
theSuite.addTest(new PortalTest("testOpenPortal"));
/*suite() method returns the suite for that class*/
theSuite.addTest(WeatherTest.suite());

addTestSuite(Class testClass)
public void addTestSuite(Class testClass)
```

This method adds all the test methods in the specified class to the suite. It's equivalent to a call to:

```
addTest(new TestSuite(testClass));
```

countTestCases()
```
public void countTestCases()
```

This method counts the total number of TestCases in this suite (including TestCases within contained TestSuites).

getName()
```
public void getName()
```

This method returns the name of this TestSuite (as specified by the String constructor or setName()). TestSuites are not required to have a name.

run(TestResult result)
```
public void run(TestResult result)
```

This method runs all the Tests (including TestCases and other TestSuites) contained within the suite. The total results are gathered in the TestResult. The run() method is usually called by one of the framework's TestRunners.

runTest(Test test, TestResult result)
```
public void runTest(Test test, TestResult result)
```

This method runs the given Test with the given TestResult. It's equivalent to test.run(result) in the default implementation. Subclasses can override runTest() to customize how Tests are run by the suite.

setName(String name)
```
public void setName(String name)
```

This method sets the name of the TestSuite.

testAt(int index)
```
public Test testAt(int index)
```

This method returns the Test at the given index. Tests are stored internally in a list, so the index corresponds to the position in the list (the first Test added is index 0, the second is index 1, and so on). The testAt() method is rarely used in everyday testing.

testCount()
```
public int testCount()
```

This method returns the number of Tests immediately contained by this suite (not the grand total number of Tests).

tests()
```
public java.util.Enumeration tests()
```

This method returns the Tests immediately contained by this suite as an Enumeration.

```
toString()
public String toString()
```

This method returns a String representation of the TestSuite. In version 3.7, this is the name of the TestSuite.

Package junit.extensions

The junit.extensions package contains a few useful classes that add functionality to the basics contained within junit.framework. In addition to these, the package contains the TestDecorator class that serves a superclass for third-party extensions to the framework. See Chapter 14 for examples of how JUnitPerf uses the TestDecorator class to add functionality to existing JUnit TestCases.

Class ActiveTestSuite

```
public class ActiveTestSuite
```

Inheritance Information

Extends: TestSuite

Description

This is a subclass of TestSuite that runs each of the Tests in the suite in its own thread. The suite does not finish running until the last thread has terminated. ActiveTestSuite does not extend its multi-threaded nature to contained suites. In other words, if an ActiveTestSuite A, contains a normal TestSuite B, all of B's tests will execute within the single thread that A assigns to B (unless B specifies some other behavior).

To employ an ActiveTestSuite, simply instantiate it and use it as you would a normal TestSuite. Individual tests can be hand-added to the suite, or all of the test methods in a class can be added. The following code samples illustrate both approaches.

```
//Create an ActiveTestSuite by hand-adding several copies of the same //Test-
-perhaps to test performance in a multi-threaded environment:
TestSuite suite = new ActiveTestSuite();
suite.addTest(new YourTestCase("testFirstMethod"));
suite.addTest(new YourTestCase("testFirstMethod"));
suite.addTest(new YourTestCase("testFirstMethod"));

//Replace the standard suite() method so that it uses an ActiveTestSuite
public static Test suite(){
   //shortcut to add all test methods in the class
   return new ActiveTestSuite(YourTestCase.class);
}
```

Methods

```
run(TestResult result)
public void run(TestResult result)
```

This method runs each Test contained by the suite in its own thread.

```
runTest(Test test, TestResult result)
public void runTest(Test test, TestResult result)
```

This method spawns a new thread and runs the specified Test within it.

> Although TestResult synchronizes many of its methods to provide a measure of thread safety, calling runTest(Test, TestResult) on an ActiveTestSuite will result in a new, unsupervised thread. Unless you have a good reason to do so, it is probably not worth calling this method externally.

```
runFinished(Test test)
public void runFinished(Test test)
```

This method notifies the suite that a test thread is about to complete.

> The runFinished() method may be public by mistake. Calling this method externally could result in premature termination of the suite (before all Tests are run).

Class ExceptionTestCase

```
public class ExceptionTestCase
```

Inheritance Information

Extends: TestCase

Description

ExceptionTestCase is a subclass of TestCase that expects a specified exception when run and fails if one is not thrown. This class seems to be of dubious usefulness. If it were subclassed, all instances of the subclass would expect the exception specified in the constructor. As a result, it would be impossible to put test methods that did not throw the exception into such a subclass. If ExceptionTestCase is not subclassed, no convenient way exists to specify which method the TestCase instance should run as the code under test. Anonymous inner classes could solve this problem, but are hardly easier than the alternate syntax for checking an exception:

```
try{
  codeUnderTest();
  fail("expected an ExpectedException");
}
catch(ExpectedException e){/*ignore*/}
```

Constructor

```
ExceptionTestCase(String name, Class exception)
public ExceptionTestCase(String name, Class exception)
```

This constructor constructs the test with the specified name and class of the exception expected to be thrown when the test runs.

Method

```
runTest()
protected void runTest()
```

This method runs this test case. If an exception of the class specified in the constructor is *not* thrown, the test fails.

Class RepeatedTest

```
public class RepeatedTest
```

Inheritance Information

Extends: TestDecorator

Description

RepeatedTest is a simple TestDecorator that runs the decorated Test the number of times specified by the constructor. The constructor expects the interface Test (as do most TestDecorators) so that TestCases or TestSuites are all valid targets for repetition (other TestDecorators are also valid targets for repetition—see the code samples for JUnitPerf's use of RepeatedTest in Chapter 14) . The run(TestResult) method simply calls run(TestResult) on the decorated Test the specified number of times. Generally, this means that setUp() and tearDown() are called for each repetition on each contained TestCase. However, any fixture set up or dismantling that occurs *outside* of these methods (such as in the constructor of a TestCase) will not be executed multiple times because run() is called multiple times on *the same instance* of the Test.

Constructor

```
RepeatedTest(Test test, int repeat)
public RepeatedTest(Test test, int repeat)
```

This constructor specifies the Test to decorate and the number of repetitions.

Methods

```
countTestCases()
public int countTestCases()
```

As specified in the Test interface, this method counts the total number of TestCases contained in the Test. In the case of RepeatedTest, this count is arrived at by multiplying the number of repetitions by the result of a call to countTestCases() on the decorated test.

```
run(TestResult result)
public void run(TestResult result)
```

```
toString()
public String toString()
```

Class *TestDecorator*

```
public class TestDecorator
```

Inheritance Information

Extends: Assert

Implements: Test

Direct known subclasses: RepeatedTest, TestSetup

Description

TestDecorator is the preferred base class for extensions that decorate (add additional behavior to) Tests. TestDecorator implements Test, so it can be used to decorate suites or TestCases; in addition, decorators can be nested within other decorators. TestDecorator defines the basic structure of a decorator and provides a few convenience functions. Test developers extend TestDecorator and override the run(TestResult) method to provide custom Test decoration.

Constructor

```
TestDecorator(Test test)
public TestDecorator(Test test)
```

This constructor constructs a TestDecorator that wraps the specified Test. Subclasses should provide a constructor that calls this constructor.

Methods

```
basicRun(TestResult result)
public void basicRun(TestResult result)
```

Subclasses can call this method during their own run() method to run the wrapped test without any decoration. See the run() method for an example of use.

```
countTestCases()
public int countTestCases()
```

This method counts the total number of TestCases run by this Test. Subclasses should override this method if the decoration code affects how many TestCases are actually run.

```
getTest()
public Test getTest()
```

This method returns the contained Test that is decorated.

```
run(TestResult result)
public void run(TestResult result)
```

This method runs the contained Test in cooperation with the decoration code. This is the key place for subclasses to define such code:

```
public class RandomTest extends TestDecorator{
  public RandomTest(Test test){
    super(test);
  }

  public void run(TestResult result){
    if(Math.random() > .5){
      basicRun(result);
    }
  }
}
```

Although this decorator violates XP principles (why would you ever *not* run a test?), it shows how decorators can add functionality to a Test.

toString()
```
public String toString()
```

This method simply returns toString() on the enclosed Test in the base implementation. Subclasses should override it to provide additional description of the decoration.

Class TestSetup

```
public class TestSetup
```

Inheritance Information

Extends: TestDecorator

Description

TestSetup is a base class for decorators that wish to provide additional fixture setup and teardown. If TestSetup decorates a TestSuite, it's setUp() and tearDown() methods will be executed once for all the tests within the suite. Therefore, subclasses of TestSetup are an ideal place to put expensive set up code (such as the insertion of test data into a database) that does not need to be repeated for each individual test.

Uncaught exceptions resulting from setUp() or tearDown() code are caught and logged in the TestResult as associated with the TestSetup instance. The following subclass sets the specified system properties before the contained test runs:

```
public class PropertiesSetup extends TestSetup{
  java.util.Properties props;
  public PropertiesSetup(Test test, java.util.Properties props){
    super(test);
    this.props = props;
  }

  protected void setUp(){
    System.getProperties().putAll(props);
  }
```

```
    protected void tearDown(){
      for(Iterator i= props.keySet().iterator(); i.hasNext();){
          System.getProperties().remove(i.next());
      }
    }
}
```

Methods

```
run(TestResult result)
public void run(TestResult result)
```

This method runs setUp(), then the enclosed Test, and then tearDown().

```
setUp()
protected void setUp()
```

Subclasses should override this method to provide additional one-time fixture code surrounding the decorated Test.

```
tearDown()
protected void tearDown()
```

Subclasses should override this method to dismantle the fixture created by setUp() after the contained Test has run.

Cactus API Reference

This chapter covers the Cactus API, which extends and employs the JUnit API described in Chapters 13 and 31. The Cactus API includes a slew of classes that support the complicated task of getting test cases called *outside* the servlet container to run *inside* it. The classes that test developers use every day are grouped together under the org.apache.cactus package. This chapter accordingly focuses primarily on this package, with a smattering of classes from the other packages thrown in when coverage reveals an important detail about the operation of Cactus.

Package org.apache.cactus

The center of this package is AbstractTestCase, from which the three types of TestCases in Cactus derive. Developers will extend these subclasses (ServletTestCase, JspTestCase, and FilterTestCase) to create their own test cases. These TestCases use the WebRequest and WebResponse classes that represent the client-side request to and response from the servlet respectively. Both of these classes have a variety of convenience methods that make the construction and verification of a test easier. The rest of the classes in the package assist one of these classes or act as "framework machinery."

Class *AbstractTest Case*

```
public abstract class AbstractTestCase
```

Inheritance Information

Extends: junit.framework.TestCase

Implements: junit.framework.Test

Direct Known Subclasses: ServletTestCase, FilterTestCase

Description

AbstractTestCase is the base class from which Cactus server-side tests are derived. Cactus supports three concrete subclasses of AbstractTestCase: ServletTestCase, JspTestCase (which extends ServletTestCase), and FilterTestCase. You should extend these classes instead of AbstractTestCase directly. In general, the principles that apply to one type of TestCase apply to the others as well. The main difference between the types of TestCase from a developer's point of view is the implicit objects available within each.

The JUnit framework already expects that your test cases will define a number of methods with the general name pattern testXXX(). XXX usually corresponds to the name of the method under test. Cactus TestCases also expect the (optional) presence of methods with the signature beginXXX(WebRequest) and endXXX(WebResponse). These methods are called by AbstractTestCase in the following order:

❑   beginXXX(WebRequest) (client side; specific to testXXX())

❑   setUp() (server side; global to the test case)

❑   testXXX() (server side)

❑   tearDown() (server side; global to the test case)

❑   endXXX(WebResponse) (client side; specific to testXXX())

setUp(), testXXX(), and tearDown() are executed in a separate copy of the TestCase instantiated in the servlet container, so they do not share state with beginXXX() and endXXX(). The preferred means of communication between beginXXX()/endXXX() and the server-side methods are the "WebRequest" parameter of beginXXX() and the "WebResponse" parameter of endXXX(). See the method descriptions for further information about the use of these objects and their relationship to the setUp(), testXXX(), tearDown() triad.

The section on ServletTestCase contains an example of how to write Cactus TestCases in general—the section on Cookie contains another example.

Constructor

```
AbstractTestCase(String theName)
public AbstractTestCase(String theName)
```

This constructor constructs a new AbstractTestCase with the name of the method to be tested (testXXX). It has functionality similar to that of the public junit.framework.TestCase constructor of the same signature. Because other methods—beginXXX(), endXXX()—are associated with the test method through the shared XXX portion of the name, the only way for instances to specify the test method to be run is through the constructor. For this reason, subclasses should maintain a constructor of this form:

```
public SubclassOfServletTestCase(String name){
  super(name);
}
```

FieldsAlthough AbstractTestCase does not itself define any fields of interest to test developers, each of its subclasses specifies a number of instance variables that correspond to the objects implicitly available within the context of the server component the TestCase is designed to exercise (a servlet, JSP, or Filter in Cactus). The variables are initialized just before setUp() is called. Because the redirector handles their initialization, these fields will remain null if executed outside of the container. The following code (taken from a ServletTestCase) would throw a NullPointerException because it executes on the client:

```
public void endDoGet(WebResponse resp)throws Exception{
   /*session was not  initialized on the client!*/
   session.getAttribute("some attribute");
}
```

Methods

```
runBare()
public void runBare() throws Throwable
```

This method is overridden from junit.framework.TestCase to remove calls to setUp() and tearDown() (which are executed separately on the server side by the redirector servlet), leaving what amounts to a call to runTest().

```
runBareServerTest()
public void runBareServerTest() throws Throwable
```

This method is intended to be executed on the server side. It calls the test method specified by the constructor along with the setUp() and tearDown() methods in the following order:

```
setUp()
testXXX()
tearDown()
```

```
runServerTest()
protected void runServerTest() throws Throwable
```

This method runs the method corresponding to the name passed to the constructor. This method plays a similar part to the runTest() method in JUnit, except that it is intended to be executed on the server side.

```
runTest()
protected abstract void runTest() throws Throwable
```

This method is overridden by FilterTestCase, ServletTestCase, and JspTestCase. It serves as a starting point for the execution of the TestCase on the server side. Unlike in basic JUnit, the runTest() method is not meant to be overridden in anonymous inner classes.

Expected Methods

Although not technically defined by AbstractTestCase, the machinery of the class expects a number of methods defined with the following general signature patterns.

```
beginXXX(WebRequest request)
public void beginXXX(WebRequest request)
```

This method is executed on the client side before setUp().You can define this method to construct the client request that will eventually arrive at the code under test (see the section on WebRequest for more information). Cactus 1.1 defined a similar method that expected a ServletTestRequest as its parameter.

```
testXXX()
public void testXXX()
```

This method exercises your code. It's executed on the server by the redirector using reflection.

```
endXXX(WebResponse response)
public void endXXX(org.apache.cactus.WebResponse response)
```

or

```
public void endXXX(com.meterware.httpunit.WebResponse response)
```

AbstractTestCase executes this method on the client side after tearDown().It serves as the place to assert expected response values like cookies, headers, and the textual body of the response.

There are two possible signatures for an endXXX method in Cactus (either of which will be called after server-side execution by the framework). Cactus 1.1 defined a different end signature, expecting a java.net.HttpUrlConnection (this alternate signature remains in deprecated form). The first signature takes a Cactus WebResponse as its parameter, the second takes an HttpUnit WebResponse. These two objects differ mainly in their assertion capabilities. The Cactus version supports limited assertion functionality (such as String comparisons) while the HttpUnit version supports sophisticated analysis of a returned HTML document. See the sections on "WebResponse" in this chapter as well as in Chapter 33 for more details.

Class Cookie

```
public class Cookie
```

Inheritance Information

Extends: Object

Implements: Serializable

Description

Cookie represents a client view of an HTTP cookie. This class can be used to add cookies to an HTTP request (in the beginXXX() method of the TestCase) or to verify server-set cookies in an HTTP response (in the endXXX method).

In order for the Web server to accept a cookie sent in the request it must belong to that server's domain; in this case, the cookie domain must match the one specified for the redirector (as mapped in the cactus.properties file) or the domain of the host set with the setURL() method.

The listing below contains the code for a "Preferences" servlet that sends all of the request parameters back to the client as cookies (to be used in the future as user preferences. The servlet also prints the names and values of all the existing cookies to the response. The accompanying test demonstrates how to set up and verify cookies in Cactus.

```
package xptoolkit.cactus;
```

```
import javax.servlet.http.HttpServlet;
import javax.servlet.http.HttpServletRequest;
import javax.servlet.http.HttpServletResponse;
import javax.servlet.http.Cookie;
import java.util.*;
import java.io.PrintWriter;
import java.io.IOException;

public class PreferencesServlet extends HttpServlet{

  public void doGet(HttpServletRequest request,
                    HttpServletResponse response)throws IOException{

    Map cookieMap =  convertParametersToMap(request);
    addCookiesToResponse(response, cookieMap);

    Cookie[] cookies = request.getCookies();
    addCookiesToMap(cookies, cookieMap);

    PrintWriter writer = response.getWriter();
    printMap(writer, cookieMap);
  }

  public Map convertParametersToMap(HttpServletRequest request){
    Map map = new HashMap();
    Enumeration e = request.getParameterNames();
    while(e.hasMoreElements()){
      String name = (String)e.nextElement();
      String value = request.getParameter(name);
      map.put(name, value);
    }
        return map;
  }

  public void addCookiesToMap(Cookie[] cookies, Map map){
    for(int i =0; i < cookies.length; i++){
      map.put(cookies[i].getName(), cookies[i].getValue());
    }
  }

  public void addCookiesToResponse(HttpServletResponse response, Map map){
    Set mapEntries = map.entrySet();
    for(Iterator iter = mapEntries.iterator(); iter.hasNext();){
      Map.Entry entry = (Map.Entry)iter.next();
      Cookie cookie = new Cookie((String)entry.getKey(),
                                 (String)entry.getValue());
      cookie.setComment("Set by user through PreferencesServlet");
      response.addCookie(cookie);
    }
  }

  private void printMap(PrintWriter writer, Map map){
        Set mapEntries = map.entrySet();
```

```
    for(Iterator iter = mapEntries.iterator(); iter.hasNext();){
       Map.Entry entry = (Map.Entry)iter.next();
       String entryStr = entry.getKey() + "=" + entry.getValue();
       writer.println(entryStr);
    }
  }
}

package xptoolkit.cactus;

import javax.servlet.http.HttpServlet;
import javax.servlet.http.HttpServletRequest;
import javax.servlet.http.HttpServletResponse;
import java.util.*;
import java.io.PrintWriter;
import java.io.IOException;
import junit.framework.*;
import org.apache.cactus.*;

public class PreferencesServletTest extends ServletTestCase {
  PreferencesServlet servlet;

  /* Standard constructor, suite(), and so on, omitted */

  public void setUp() throws Exception{
    servlet = new PreferencesServlet();
    servlet.init(this.config);
  }

  public void beginDoGet(WebRequest request)throws Exception{
    request.addCookie("existingName1", "existingValue1");
    Cookie secondCookie = new Cookie("localhost", "existingName2",
                                     "existingValue2");
    request.addCookie(secondCookie);
    request.addParameter("newName1", "newValue1");
  }

  public void testDoGet()throws Exception {
    servlet.doGet(request, response);
  }

  public void endDoGet(WebResponse response){
    String[] lines = response.getTextAsArray();
    List responseList = Arrays.asList(lines);
    assertTrue(responseList.contains("existingName1=existingValue1"));
    assertTrue(responseList.contains("existingName2=existingValue2"));
    assertTrue(responseList.contains("newName1=newValue1"));
    Cookie cookie = response.getCookie("newName1");
    assertEquals("newValue1", cookie.getValue());
  }
}
```

Constructors

```
Cookie(String theDomain, String theName, String theValue)
public Cookie(String theDomain, String theName, String theValue)
```

This constructor creates a new Cookie with the specified name, value, and domain. See the Description section for information about the domain.

Methods

```
equals(Object theObject)
public boolean equals(Object theObject)
```

A Cookie is considered to equal another Cookie if they possess the same name, path, and domain.

```
getComment()
public String getComment()
```

This method returns the comment describing this cookie (if one was set).

```
getDomain()
public String getDomain()
```

This method returns the domain that this cookie belongs to.

```
getExpiryDate()
public Date getExpiryDate()
```

This method returns the Date on which this Cookie will expire.

```
getName()
public String getName()
```

```
getPath()
public String getPath()
```

This method returns the "path" of the cookie. This cookie should only be viewed by resources at URLs conforming to the path.

```
getValue()
public String getValue()
```

```
isExpired()
public boolean isExpired()
```

```
isSecure()
public boolean isSecure()
```

This method returns whether this cookie should only be sent over a secure connection.

```
isToBeDiscarded()
public boolean isToBeDiscarded()
```

This method returns true if the HTTP cookie should not persist any longer than the user's session.

```
setComment(String theComment)
public void setComment(String theComment)
```

This method sets the descriptive comment to go along with this cookie.

```
setDomain(String theDomain)
public void setDomain(String theDomain)
```

This method sets the domain that your cookie is to "come from." See the Description section for details on what are acceptable domain values in Cactus.

```
setExpiryDate(Date theExpiryDate)
public void setExpiryDate(Date theExpiryDate)
```

```
setName(String theName)
public void setName(String theName)
```

```
setPath(String thePath)
public void setPath(String thePath)
```

```
setSecure(boolean isSecure)
public void setSecure(boolean isSecure)
```

Indicates that this cookie should only be sent over a secure connection.

```
setValue(String theValue)
public void setValue(String theValue)
```

FilterTestCase

```
public class FilterTestCase
```

Inheritance Information

Extends: AbstractTestCase

Implements: junit.framework.Test

Description

FilterTestCase provides access to the implicit objects available in a Filter (defined in Servlets 2.3). See AbstractTestCase for more information about how to use Cactus TestCases in general.

Fields

FilterTestCase defines four instance variables that contain either the actual objects available to the redirector or thinly wrapped versions thereof. In all cases the objects available in FilterTestCase implement the same interfaces as those available in an actual Filter. These fields are available in the setUp(), testXXX(), and tearDown() methods. They will contain null if referenced from a beginXXX() or endXXX() method.

```
config
public FilterConfigWrapper config
```

This variable provides a way to mock up initialization parameters. See the section on FilterConfigWrapper (in the org.apache.cactus.server package) for more details.

```
filterChain
public FilterChain filterChain
```

This variable contains the actual FilterChain object available to the filter redirector. Developers, however, can substitute a different FilterChain object to isolate their unit Tests. Since the FilterChain interface contains a single method, it lends itself to quick test implementations that make assertions easier. The following example illustrates a testXXX and FilterChain implementation that verify that a given filter calls doFilter() as expected. The full example can be found in Chapter 18.

```
/*helper class*/
class RecordingChain implements FilterChain{
  boolean doFilterInvoked = false;
  public void doFilter(ServletRequest servletRequest,
                       ServletResponse servletResponse) {
    doFilterInvoked = true;
  }

  public boolean verify(){
    return doFilterInvoked;
  }
}

/* testXXX method that uses RecordingChain*/
public void testDoFilter() throws Exception{
  RecordingChain recordingChain = new RecordingChain();
  filter.doFilter(request, response, recordingChain);
  assertTrue(recordingChain.verify());
}

request
public HttpServletRequestWrapper request
```

This field contains the same wrapper class used in ServletTestRequest.

```
response
public HttpServletResponse response
```

Class JspTestCase

```
public class JspTestCase
```

Inheritance Information

Extends: ServletTestCase

Implements: junit.framework.Test

Description

JspTestCase provides access to JSP implicit objects (pageContext and out) as member variables in addition to the implicit objects of ServletTestCase (see the sections on ServletTestCase and AbstractTestCase for more information about how to use both these classes). The framework authors intended JspTestCase to be used primarily for the testing of custom tags, which are the main type of code that relies specifically on the context provided by a JSP.

The following might represent a testXXX() method in a subclass of JspTestCase:

```
public void testPrintPageContext (){
  CustomJspDebugger.printPageContext(this.out, this.pageContext);
}
```

Fields

These fields contain the pageContext and out objects available in the JspRedirector. The fields are available in the setUp(), testXXX(), and tearDown() methods. The fields will contain null if referenced from a beginXXX() or endXXX() method. The pageContext object is wrapped by Cactus so as to return the correctly wrapped versions of the implicit objects that are also available in ServletTestCase. See the Fields section of AbstractTestCase for details about how this type of instance variable operates in Cactus.

```
pageContext
public org.apache.cactus.server..PageContextWrapper pageContext

out
public javax.servlet.jsp.JspWriter out
```

Class ServiceDefinition

```
public class ServiceDefinition
```

Description

ServiceDefinition specifies manifest constants used in communication between client-side test code and the redirector (which TestCase to load, which method to call, and so on). It's used primarily by the framework.

Class ServiceEnumeration

```
public class ServiceEnumeration
```

Description

ServiceEnumeration defines a list of valid services that the redirector can perform (such as executing a test or getting the results). It's chiefly a framework class.

Class ServletTestCase

```
public class ServletTestCase
```

Inheritance Information

Extends: AbstractTestCase

Implements: junit.framework.Test

Direct Known Subclasses: JspTestCase

Description

ServletTestCase is a central class of the Cactus API for test developers. It extends JUnit's TestCase class and adds features to support the testing of methods that depend on objects made available in the servlet container. It's behavior serves as a model for the behavior of the other two redirector test cases available in Cactus.

The next listing demonstrates how to use ServletTestCase (and by extension, the other redirector test cases). The class under test is Insulter, which contains a static method demonize() that depends upon a servlet request and response. InsulterTest passes its request and response member variables to demonize() in its testDemonize() method. The other methods of the TestCase serve to set up and dismantle the test fixture, as well as to assert the results.

```java
package xptoolkit.cactus.reference;
import javax.servlet.http.HttpServletRequest;
import javax.servlet.http.HttpServletResponse;
import javax.servlet.http.HttpSession;

//Class under test
public class Insulter{
   public static void demonize(HttpServletRequest request,
                               HttpServletResponse response,
                               InsultGenerator generator) throws
                                          java.io.IOException{

      HttpSession sess = request.getSession();
      User user = (User)sess.getAttribute("USER_KEY");
      if(user == null){
        throw new IllegalStateException("no user in session");
      }

      String strengthStr = request.getParameter("INSULT_STRENGTH");
      int strength = Integer.parseInt(strengthStr);
      user.setSelfEsteem(user.getSelfEsteem()-strength);

      generator.setStrength(strength);
      generator.printInsult(response.getWriter());
   }

}


package xptoolkit.cactus.reference;
import org.apache.cactus.*;
import org.apache.cactus.util.*;
import javax.servlet.http.HttpServletRequest;
```

```
import java.net.HttpURLConnection;
import junit.framework.*;

public class InsulterTest extends ServletTestCase{
  private InsultGenerator generator;
  private User user;

  public InsulterTest(String name){
      super(name);
  }
  /*
   * Methods are placed in the order of execution.
   */

  /*client side*/
  public void beginDemonize(WebRequest request){
    request.addParameter("INSULT_STRENGTH", "5");
  }

  /*server side*/
  public void setUp(){
    /*instantiate the User and put it into the session*/
    user = new User("TestUserName");
    user.setSelfEsteem(10);
    this.session.setAttribute("USER_KEY", user);

    /*instantiate the InsultGenerator*/
    generator = new InsultGenerator("pederast");
  }

  /*server side*/
  public void testDemonize()throws Exception{
    /*call the method under test*/
    Insulter.demonize(this.request, this.response, this.generator);

    /*test that self esteem equals inital value minus insult strength*/
    assertEquals("self esteem correct", 5, user.getSelfEsteem());
  }

  /*server side*/
  public void tearDown(){
    generator = null;
  }

  /*client side*/
  public void endDemonize(WebResponse response) {

      //assertTrue(user.isCrying());--would throw a NullPointerException,
      //                             because user was never instantiated
      //                             on the client side.
```

```
        String clientResponse = response.getText();

        assertTrue("insult strength in response",
                    clientResponse.indexOf("5") > -1);

        assertTrue("insult in response",
                    clientResponse.indexOf("pederast") > -1);
    }

    public static TestSuite suite(){
        TestSuite suite = new TestSuite(InsulterTestCase.class);
        return suite;
    }

    public static void main(String[] args){
        junit.textui.TestRunner.run(suite());
    }
  }

}
```

Constructor

ServletTestCase(String theName)
public ServletTestCase(String theName)
Subclasses should maintain a String constructor that calls this constructor.
See the Constructors section on AbstractTestCase for details.

Fields

ServletTestCase specifies the instance variables request, response, session, and config, which are initialized to versions of implicit objects available in the redirector servlet. Details on the wrapper classes can be found in the org.apache.cactus.server section.

config
public ServletConfigWrapper config

request
public HttpServletRequestWrapper request

response
public HttpServletResponse response

session
public HttpSession session

> If the automaticSession property of the ServletTestRequest in beginXXX() is set
> to false, this value will not be initialized.

Class ServletTestRequest Deprecated

```
public class ServletTestRequest
```

Inheritance Information

Extends: Object (in 1.1) / WebRequest (in 1.2)

Description

This class was deprecated in Cactus 1.2 in favor of the class WebRequest. This section represents the public interface as of 1.1. In general, changes or deletions are few; the new WebRequest class has mainly added functionality.

Methods

addCookie(String theName, String theValue)
```
public void addCookie(String theName, String theValue)
```

addHeader(String theName, String theValue)
```
public void addHeader(String theName, String theValue)
```

addParameter(String theName, String theValue)
```
public void addParameter(String theName, String theValue)
```

getAutomaticSession()
```
public boolean getAutomaticSession()
```

getCookieNames()
```
public Enumeration getCookieNames()
```

getCookieValue(String theName)
```
public String getCookieValue(String theName)
```

getHeader(String theName)
```
public String getHeader(String theName)
```

getHeaderNames()
```
public Enumeration getHeaderNames()
```

getHeaderValues(String theName)
```
public String[] getHeaderValues(String theName)
```

getMethod()
```
public String getMethod()
```

getParameter(String theName)
```
public String getParameter(String theName)
```

getParameterNames()
```
public Enumeration getParameterNames()
```

getParameterValues(String theName)
```
public String[] getParameterValues(String theName)
```

```
getURL()
public ServletURL getURL()

setAutomaticSession(boolean isAutomaticSession)
public void setAutomaticSession(boolean isAutomaticSession)

setMethod(String theMethod)
public void setMethod(String theMethod)

public void setURL(...)
public void setURL(String theServerName, String theContextPath,
     String theServletPath, String thePathInfo, String theQueryString)
```

Class ServletURL

```
public class ServletURL
```

Inheritance Information

Extends: Object

Description

ServletURL simulates the URL of an HTTP request to a servlet. This class is employed by Cactus to yield values from URL-related function calls in HttpServletRequest that correspond to expected real-world values rather than those of the redirector servlet. The constructor takes five arguments, each of which represents a subsection of the simulated URL.

Constructor

```
public ServletURL(...)
public ServletURL(String theServerName,
                  String theContextPath,
                  String theServletPath,
                  String thePathInfo,
                  String theQueryString)
```

Constructs a simulated URL in this format:

```
"http://" + serverName [includes port] + contextPath + servletPath +
pathInfo + "?" + queryString
```

Each parameter will be available for retrieval from the TestCase's.request field using the appropriate method from HttpServletRequest. Only "theServerName" cannot be null. The middle three parameters follow the format

```
"/"+name
```

where *name* is the appropriate path (application context, servlet context, path to the resource). "theQueryString" emulates the query string of an HTTP request. In Cactus 1.2 and higher, the parameters in "theQueryString" are automatically added to the actual request, in addition to any set with addParameter(). As a result, the request may contain parameters not present in the query string.

Consult the servlet specification for more details on the parts of a servlet URL.

> In Cactus 1.1 and earlier, the query string parameter used will affect only the results of HttpServletResquest.getQueryString(); its value will have no effect on the request's parameters and vice versa.

Methods

```
getContextPath()
public String getContextPath()

getPathInfo()
public String getPathInfo()

getQueryString()
public String getQueryString()

getServerName()
public String getServerName()

getServletPath()
public String getServletPath()

getURL()
public java.net.URL getURL()
```

This method returns the java.net.URL corresponding to this ServletURL.

```
loadFromRequest(HttpServletRequest theRequest)
public static ServletURL loadFromRequest(HttpServletRequest theRequest)
```

This method instantiates a new ServletURL using parameters saved into the request by saveToRequest.

```
saveToRequest(WebRequest theRequest)
public void saveToRequest(WebRequest theRequest)
```

This method saves the state of this ServletURL to the request as a series of parameters.

Class WebRequest

```
public class WebRequest
```

Inheritance Information

Extends: Object

Description

WebRequest encapsulates all the HTTP request data that will be sent from the client-side TestCase to the server-side instance. The data will be available to the setUp(), testXXX(), and tearDown() methods through the TestCase's.request variable (which implements HttpServletRequest). WebRequest contains methods to set request parameters, headers, cookies, and the method of the request (POST or GET). It also lets you create simulated URL data and specify whether a session should automatically be created by the redirector servlet.

> **Some important restrictions exist on the domain of cookies sent to the redirector. See the section on the Cookie class for details.**

The following example illustrates how to add setUp information for a specific testXXX method to the request that will be sent to the server.

```
public void beginGoOnVisionQuest(WebRequest request){
   /* The URL being constructed is:
      http://nationalparks.org/organ-pipe-monument/long_walk.do
    */
   request.setURL("nationalparks.org",
                  "/organ-pipe-monument",
                  null,
                  "/long_walk.do",
                  null);

   /*multiple values for same key*/
   request.addParameter("SPIRIT_GUIDES", "Coyote");
   request.addParameter("SPIRIT_GUIDES", "Snake");

   request.addCookie("PREPARED", "true");

}
```

Methods

> **Most of the accessor methods are used by the framework during the translation of this class into an actual HTTP request. These methods work like the methods specified in HttpServletRequest with the same signatures.**

addCookie(Cookie theCookie)
public void addCookie(Cookie theCookie)

This method adds the org.apache.cactus.Cookie instance to the request. See the Cookie class for details on the cookie domains in Cactus.

addCookie(String theName, String theValue)
public void addCookie(String theName, String theValue)

This method adds a cookie consisting of the specified name/value pair to the HTTP request with "localhost" as the cookie domain. See the Cookie class for details on the cookie domains in Cactus.

addCookie(String theDomain, String theName, String theValue)
```
public void addCookie(String theDomain, String theName, String theValue)
```

This method adds a cookie with the specified name, value, and domain to the request. See the Cookie class for details on the cookie domains in Cactus.

addHeader(String theName, String theValue)
```
public void addHeader(String theName, String theValue)
```

This method adds a header consisting of the specified name/value pair to the request. Multiple headers with a given name can be added.

addParameter(String theName, String theValue)
```
public void addParameter(String theName, String theValue)
```

This method adds a request parameter consisting of the specified name/value pair. Multiple parameter values can be added under a given name (to support retrieval with HttpSevletRequest.getParameterValues(String) on the server side).

getAutomaticSession()
```
public boolean getAutomaticSession()
```

This method is the accessor for the automaticSession property. (See the session on setAutomaticSession for more details.)

getCookies()
```
public Vector getCookies()
```

getHeader(String theName)
```
public String getHeader(String theName)
```

getHeaderNames()
```
public Enumeration getHeaderNames()
```

getHeaderValues(String theName)
```
public String[] getHeaderValues(String theName)
```

getMethod()
```
public String getMethod()
```

getParameter(String theName)
```
public String getParameter(String theName)
```

getParameterNames()
```
public Enumeration getParameterNames()
```

getParameterValues(String theName)
```
public String[] getParameterValues(String theName)
```

getURL()
```
public ServletURL getURL()
```

This method returns the simulated URL of this request.

```
setAutomaticSession(boolean isAutomaticSession)
public void setAutomaticSession(boolean isAutomaticSession)
```

This method sets whether a session should be created automatically for this request. The default value is true. If it's set to false, the session variable in the server-side TestCase (if any) called with this request will be null.

```
setMethod(String theMethod)
public void setMethod(String theMethod)
```

This method sets the method of the HTTP request (GET/POST); the default is POST.

```
public void setURL(...)
public void setURL(String theServerName, String theContextPath,
        String theServletPath, String thePathInfo, String theQueryString)
```

This method sets the simulated URL of the HTTP request. It's used so that the URL associated with the TestCase on the server resembles an actual URL instead of the URL used to call the redirector servlet. setURL() essentially calls the ServletURL constructor with the same argument list. See the section on ServletURL for more details.

Class WebResponse

```
public class WebResponse
```

Inheritance Information

Extends: Object

Description

WebResponse represents a client-side view of the server's response to a specific request. TestCases interact with this object when the framework passes it into the automatically called endXXX() method. WebResponse supports simple assertions; for more complicated assertions, you should use the alternate endXXX() signature that that takes a com.meterware.httpunit.WebResponse.

See the section on the Cookie class for an example of how to use WebResponse in an endXXX() method.

Constructors

```
WebResponse(WebRequest theRequest, HttpURLConnection theConnection)
public WebResponse(WebRequest theRequest, HttpURLConnection theConnection)
```

This constructor builds a new WebResponse from the original WebRequest used to generate an HTTP request to the server and the HttpURLConnection containing the actual response.

Methods

```
getConnection()
public HttpURLConnection getConnection()
```

This method returns the HttpURLConnection that contains the server's raw response to the request made by the TestCase.

```
getCookie(String theName)
public Cookie getCookie(String theName)
```

This method returns the first Cookie in the response with the specified name (or null if no such Cookie was found).

```
getCookies()
public Cookie[] getCookies()
```

This method returns an array of all of the Cookies sent by the server in this response.

```
getInputStream()
public InputStream getInputStream()
```

This method returns a buffered input stream for reading data out of the underlying response.

```
getText()
public String getText()
```

This method returns the body of the server's response (no headers or Cookies) as a String.

```
getTextAsArray()
public String[] getTextAsArray()
```

This method returns an array of Strings, each corresponding to a single line of the server's response; the headers and cookies are omitted.

```
getWebRequest()
public WebRequest getWebRequest()
```

This method returns the original WebRequest that was configured in the beginXXX() method.

Class WebTestResult

```
public class WebTestResult
```

Inheritance Information

Extends: Object

Implements: Serializable

Description

WebTestResult stores the result of the TestCase's run on the server. The redirector sends a serialized version of this object back to the client after the test is complete so that the TestCase can provide failure information on the client if necessary.

Constructors

```
WebTestResult(Throwable theException)
public WebTestResult(Throwable theException)
```

This constructor constructs a WebTestResult with the specified Throwable as the reason for failure.

```
WebTestResult()
public WebTestResult()
```

This constructor constructs a WebTestResult that indicates success.

Methods

```
getExceptionClassName()
public String getExceptionClassName()

getExceptionMessage()
public String getExceptionMessage()

getExceptionStackTrace()
public String getExceptionStackTrace()

hasException()
public boolean hasException()
```

This method returns true if the WebTestResult contains an exception (that is, if the test failed).

Package org.apache.cactus.util

Both of the classes in the util package have been deprecated in Cactus 1.2. ClientCookie has been improved to become org.apache.cactus.Cookie and the functionality of AssertUtils has been rolled into WebResponse.

Class AssertUtils Deprecated

```
public class AssertUtils
```

Inheritance Information

Extends: Object

Description

The functionality of this class has been incorporated into WebResponse as of Cactus 1.2.

AssertUtils is a class of static utility functions that simplify the extraction of information from HttpUrlConnections. Such information can then be used in assertions:

```
/*this is the Cactus 1.1 endXXX() method signature.*/
public void endSomeTestMethod(java.net.HttpURLConnection conn) {

        /*cookie assertions*/
        Hashtable allCookies = AssertUtils.getCookies(conn);
```

```
        List chocolateChipCookies = (List)allCookies.get("C_CHIP");
        assertEquals("only one chocolate chip cookie set",
                        1, chocolateChipCookies.size());

        ClientCookie cookie = (ClientCookie)chocolateChipCookies.get(0);
        assertTrue(cookie.getMaxAge() < this.FRESHNESS_DATE);

        /*response assertions*/
        String allResponseText = AssertUtils.getResponseAsString(conn);
        assertTrue("contains descriptive text",
                        allResponseText.indexOf("Cookies 4 U") > -1);

        String[] allTextArray = AssertUtils.getResponseAsStringArray(conn);
        int last = allTextArray.length;
        assertTrue("html tag closed",
                        allTextArray[last].endsWith("</html>"));
    }
```

Methods

getCookies(HttpURLConnection theConnection)
```
public static Hashtable getCookies(HttpURLConnection theConnection)
```

This method returns a Hashtable containing cookie names as keys. The associated values are Lists (Vectors) of ClientCookie objects that can be inspected.

getResponseAsString(HttpURLConnection theConnection)
```
public static String getResponseAsString(HttpURLConnection
        theConnection) throws IOException
```

This method returns the output stream contained in the connection as a String.

getResponseAsStringArray(HttpURLConnection theConnection)
```
public static String[] getResponseAsStringArray(HttpURLConnection
        theConnection) throws IOException
```

This method returns the output stream contained in the connection as an array of Strings, where each String corresponds to a line in the output stream.

Class ClientCookie Deprecated

```
public class ClientCookie
```

Inheritance Information

Extends: Object

Description

The functionality of this class has been expanded and included in the Cookie class of Cactus.

ClientCookie is a simple class for storing the information about a cookie contained in a set-cookie header. It is usually instantiated by AssertUtils.getCookies(HttpUrlConnection connection).

Constructor

```
public ClientCookie(...)
public ClientCookie(String theName, String theValue, String theComment,
        String theDomain, long theMaxAge, String thePath,
        boolean isSecure, float theVersion)
```

Methods

The following methods are accessors for all the properties specified in the constructor; they correspond to the different parts of the set-cookie response header.

```
getComment()
public String getComment()

getDomain()
public String getDomain()

getMaxAge()
public long getMaxAge()

getName()
public String getName()

getPath()
public String getPath()

getValue()
public String getValue()

getVersion()
public float getVersion()

isSecure()
public boolean isSecure()
```

Package org.apache.cactus.server

This package contains several framework classes (such as the redirector servlet) that are not covered in this chapter because test developers do not interact with them directly. However, it also contains wrapper classes for several implicit servlet objects with additional or slightly changed behavior. These classes are covered briefly.

Class FilterConfigWrapper

```
public class FilterConfigWrapper
```

Inheritance Information

Extends: Object

Implements: FilterConfig

Description

Wraps the original FilterConfig passed by the container to the filter redirector. Like ServletConfigWrapper, FilterConfigWrapper returns a wrapped version of ServletContext from getServletContext and provides setter methods for the Filter name and init parameters.

Methods

The methods are as specified in FilterConfig along with the following:

```
getInitParameterNames()
public Enumeration getInitParameterNames()
```

This method returns an enumeration containing both the init parameter names specified in the web.xml as well as those specified by a call to setInitParameter(). The values set by setInitParameter() take precedence.

```
setFilterName(String theFilterName)
public void setFilterName(String theFilterName)
```

This method sets a simulated Filter name that will be returned by getFilterName().

```
setInitParameter(String theName, String theValue)
public void setInitParameter(String theName, String theValue)
```

This method sets an "init" parameter for this FilterConfig as if it had been specified in the web.xml file. Initialization parameters set with this method will "shadow" those actually specified in the web.xml file.

Class HttpServletRequestWrapper

```
public class HttpServletRequestWrapper
```

Inheritance Information

Extends: Object

Implements: javax.servlet.http.HttpServletRequest

Description

HttpServletRequestWrapper is a thin wrapper around the HttpServletRequest object passed to the redirector servlet by the container.

Constructor

```
HttpServletRequestWrapper(HttpServletRequest theRequest,
                          ServletURL theURL)
```

```
public HttpServletRequestWrapper(HttpServletRequest theRequest,
                                 ServletURL theURL)
```

This constructor constructs a wrapper around the given request with the simulated URL contained in the "ServletURL" parameter.

Methods

The methods are generally identical to those specified in HttpServletRequest, except that URL methods such as getQueryString() return the values specified by the ServletURL passed to the constructor rather than those of the actual URL used to invoke the redirector servlet (unless the "ServletURL" parameter was null).

Two other significant changes exist:

```
getOriginalRequest()
public HttpServletRequest getOriginalRequest()
This method returns the original request that arrived at the
redirector.getRequestDispatcher(String thePath)
public RequestDispatcher getRequestDispatcher(String thePath)
```

Returns a RequestDispatcherWrapper instead of a RequestDispatcher. See the section on RequestDispatcherWrapper for details.

Class PageContextWrapper

```
public class PageContextWrapper
```

Inheritance Information

Extends: AbstractPageContextWrapper (and thereby javax.servlet.jsp.PageContext.)

Description

Wraps a PageContext object so that the implicit objects it returns are the appropriate Cactus-wrapped version of those objects.

Class RequestDispatcherWrapper

```
public class RequestDispatcherWrapper
```

Inheritance Information

Extends: Object

Implements: javax.servlet.RequestDispatcher

Description

RequestDispatcherWrapper is a thin wrapper for a RequestDispatcher object. The wrapper's purpose is to ensure that forwards and includes are carried out with the original HttpServletRequest instead of the Cactus wrapper (which could cause problems). Any includes or forwards in the tested code will lose the URL simulation capacities of the Cactus request wrapper after the forward. (If A forwards to B, the request received by B will not be a wrapped Cactus request, but the original HttpServletRequest generated by the container.)

> **In Cactus 1.1 and earlier, this wrapper is returned from ServletContextWrapper.getRequestDispatcher(String) but not from HttpServletRequestWrapper.getRequestDispatcher(String). This inconsistency could yield unexpected results.**

Constructor

```
RequestDispatcherWrapper(RequestDispatcher theOriginalDispatcher)
public RequestDispatcherWrapper(RequestDispatcher
                                        theOriginalDispatcher)
```

Methods

The methods are as specified in RequestDispatcher, except that the include and forward methods will unwrap the "HttpServletRequest" parameter to use the underlying request.

Class ServletConfigWrapper

```
public class ServletConfigWrapper
```

Inheritance Information

Extends: Object

Implements: javax.servlet.ServletConfig

Description

ServletConfigWrapper wraps a ServletConfig object provided by the container to the redirector servlet. Because this object is the config for the redirector servlet, static initialization parameters expected by test code must be included in the web.xml file used by the redirector servlet or they must be set manually using the setInitParameter() method.

Constructor

```
ServletConfigWrapper(ServletConfig theOriginalConfig)
public ServletConfigWrapper(ServletConfig theOriginalConfig)
```

Methods

Methods are as specified in ServletConfig, except the following:

```
getInitParameterNames()
public Enumeration getInitParameterNames()
```

Will return an enumeration containing both the init parameter names specified in the web.xml as well as those specified by a call to setInitParameter. The values set by setInitParameter take precedence.

```
setInitParameter(String theName, String theValue)
public void setInitParameter(String theName, String theValue)
```

This method sets an "init" parameter for this ServletConfig as if it had been specified in the web.xml file. Initialization parameters set with this method will "shadow" those actually specified in the web.xml file.

```
setServletName(String theServletName)
public void setServletName(String theServletName)
```

This method sets the servlet's name (retrieved by the getName() method).

Class ServletContextWrapper

```
public class ServletContextWrapper
```

Inheritance Information

Extends: AbstractServletContextWrapper

Implements: javax.servlet.ServletContext

Description

ServletContextWrapper is a simple wrapper that delegates almost all its calls to the wrapped ServletContext. One notable exception is that all messages passed to the wrapper's log methods are stored in a Vector of Strings (as well as being passed to the original log method) which can be retrieved with getLogs(). Beyond that, theonly differences are that getServletContext and getRequestDispatcher return the Cactus wrapper objects, and it supports both getResourcePaths() for Servlet 2.2, and getResourcePaths(String) for Servlet 2.3.

Methods

```
getLogs()
public Vector getLogs()
```

This method returns a Vector of Strings containing each message that was logged with any of the ServletContext's log methods.

HttpUnit API Reference

HttpUnit abstracts elements of an HTTP "conversation" between a server and a client in a way that makes it possible to run JUnit assertions against the result. This chapter details the HttpUnit framework. HttpUnit is designed so that most of the classes that are not directly used by a test developer are hidden from immediate view (as package-level access classes, inner classes, and so on). We used the published Javadoc for HttpUnit as a guide to help us choose which classes to include in this chapter.

HttpUnit automatically parses the HTML contained in a server response into a Document Object Model (DOM) tree. This is one of the key features of the framework as it enables most of the methods that return data about the server response, such as getLinks(). In addition to relying on the DOM tree under the covers, HttpUnit exposes the DOM to allow direct inspection. By interacting directly with the DOM when necessary, TestCases can perform more sophisticated assertions than are available through HttpUnit's convenience methods , but at the price of additional development effort.

Chapter 16 gives a basic example of DOM manipulation with HttpUnit. If you are interested in reading more, see http://www.w3.org/DOM/ for general information and to download the DOM API in Java.

Package com.meterware.httpunit

This package contains all the classes that comprise the HttpUnit framework. The key classes in the framework are WebConversation (and its parent class WebClient), WebRequest, and WebResponse. A few classes represent elements of an HTML page (e.g., WebLink and WebTable), others sublcass one of the three central players (e.g., PostMethodWebRequest) to provide specific functionality, and a final few act in a supporting role (HttpUnitException, for instance.)

Class AuthorizationRequiredException

```
public class AuthorizationRequiredException extends RuntimeException
```

Inheritance Information

Extends: Object

Implements: Serializable

Description

AuthorizationRequiredException is thrown when the server returns a response that indicates the user must be authorized to view the resource. (See the section on WebClient for an example.)

Methods

```
getAuthenticationParameter(String parameterName)
public String getAuthenticationParameter(String parameterName)
```

This method returns the authentication value for the specified parameter. Under the Basic authentication scheme, there is only one parameter: "realm".

```
getAuthenticationScheme()
public String getAuthenticationScheme()
```

This method returns the authentication scheme used for this resource: Basic or Digest.

```
getMessage()
public String getMessage()
```

Class GetMethodWebRequest

```
public class GetMethodWebRequest
```

Inheritance Information

Extends: WebRequestDescription

GetMethodWebRequest is a WebRequest that uses the GET method (see the section on WebRequest for more details).

Constructors

```
GetMethodWebRequest(String urlString)
public GetMethodWebRequest(String urlString)

GetMethodWebRequest(URL urlBase, String urlString)
public GetMethodWebRequest(URL urlBase, String urlString)

GetMethodWebRequest(URL urlBase, String urlString, String target)
public GetMethodWebRequest(URL urlBase, String urlString, String target)
```

See the section on WebRequest for a description of these constructors.

Methods

```
getMethod()
public String getMethod()
```

This method returns the HTTP method of the request (in this case, GET).

```
getURLString()
protected String getURLString()
```

This method returns the full URL of the request, including all the parameters set with setParameter encoded in the query string.

Class HTMLSegment

```
public interface HTMLSegment
```

Inheritance Information

Known implementing classes: WebResponse, TableCellDescription

HTMLSegment defines the public interface for a chunk of parsed HTML. This interface specifies finder methods for elements of HTML represented in HttpUnit: forms, tables, and links. All the methods in this interface will throw org.xml.sax.SAXExceptions if errors occur when the underlying HTML is parsed.

Many of the examples in this chapter use functionality contained in this interface. See the sections on WebForm, WebLink, and WebTable to see its methods in use.

> Much of the functionality contained in WebResponse is described in this section.

Methods

```
getForms()
public WebForm[] getForms() throws SAXException;
```

This method returns an array corresponding to the forms found within the HTML segment, in the order in which they occur.

```
getFormWithID(String ID)
public WebForm getFormWithID(String ID) throws SAXException
```

This method gets the form with the specified "id" attribute.

```
getFormWithName(String name)
public WebForm getFormWithName(String name) throws SAXException
```

This method gets the form with the specified "name" attribute.

getLinks()
```
public WebLink[] getLinks() throws SAXException
```

This method returns an array corresponding to the links found within the HTML segment, in the order in which they appear.

getLinkWith(String text)
```
public WebLink getLinkWith(String text) throws SAXException
```

This method gets the first link with the specified user-clickable text in the underlying HTML.

getLinkWithImageText(String text)
```
public WebLink getLinkWithImageText(String text) throws SAXException
```

This method gets the first image link with the specified text as its "alt" attribute in the underlying HTML.

getTables()
```
public WebTable[] getTables() throws SAXException
```

This method returns an array corresponding to the top-level tables found within the HTML segment, in the order in which they appear.

getTableStartingWith(String text)
```
public WebTable getTableStartingWith(final String text) throws
                                                SAXException
```

This method returns the first table in the HTML segment that has the specified text as the entire contents of its first non-blank row and non-blank column (no partial matches are allowed).

> Both getTableStartingWith(final String text) and getTableStarting-WithPrefix(String text) will recurse into any nested tables in an attempt to match their search criteria.

getTableStartingWithPrefix(String text)
```
public WebTable getTableStartingWithPrefix(String text) throws
                                                SAXException
```

This method returns the first table in the HTML segment that has the specified text as the beginning of the contents of its first non-blank row and non-blank column (in other words, partial matches are allowed). See the following list for an example.

```
/*
Supposing that the response object was based on the following HTML:
<!--begin-->
<table>
  <tr>
    <td>
      Pizza Hut
    </td>
    <td>
```

```
            restaurant
        </td>
      </tr>
    </table>
    <table>
      <tr>
        <td>
          Pizza
        </td>
        <td>
            Food
        </td>
      </tr>
    </table>
    <!--end-->
    The following test would pass:
    */

    public void testTableMatching() throws Exception{
        /*will retrieve the second table because a full match is required*/
        WebTable foodTable = response.getTableStartingWith("Pizza");

        /*will retrieve the first table as the prefix matches*/
        WebTable restaurantTable = response.getTableStartingWithPrefix("Pizza");

        assertEquals("Food", foodTable.getCellAsText(0,1));
        assertEquals("restaurant", restaurantTable.getCellAsText(0,1));
    }
```

getTableWithSummary(String summary)
```
public WebTable getTableWithSummary(String summary) throws SAXException
```

This method returns the first table with the specified String as its "summary" attribute.

getTableWithID(final String ID)
```
public WebTable getTableWithID(final String ID) throws SAXException
```

This method returns the first table with the specified String as its "id" attribute.

Class HttpException

```
public class HttpException
```

Inheritance Information

Extends: RuntimeException

Direct known subclasses: HttpInternalErrorException, HttpNotFoundException

Description

HttpException is thrown when the Web server under test would return a status code corresponding to a client or server error (4xx or 5xx):

```
public void testIllegalPageAccess() throws Exception{
  WebConversation wc = new WebConversation();
  try{
    wc.getResponse("http://www.junit.org/thispagedoesnotexist.jsp");
  }
  catch (HttpException e){
    System.out.println(e);
    assertEquals(404, e.getResponseCode());
  }
}
```

Methods

getResponseCode()
```
public int getResponseCode()
```

This method returns the HTTP status code of the response that caused the exception.

getMessage()
```
public String getMessage()
```

This method returns a String containing the status code as well as the reason given (if any) for the error.

Class HttpInternalErrorException

```
public class HttpInternalErrorExceptionInheritance Information
```

Inheritance Information

Extends: HttpExceptionDescription

HttpInternalErrorException is thrown when a request results in a response with a status code of 5xx (server error). See the section on HttpException for details.

Class HttpNotFoundException

```
public class HttpNotFoundException
```

Inheritance Information

Extends: HttpException

Description

HttpNotFoundException is thrown when a request results in a response with a status code of 4xx (client error, generally a "not found" error). See the section on HttpException for details.

Class HttpUnitOptions

```
public abstract class HttpUnitOptions
```

Description

This class provides static setters and getters for a variety of properties that parameterize the behavior of HttpUnit. Because the options are stored in static member variables (and will thus affect all HttpUnit tests) , we advise you to take care in setting them. The preferred strategy is to use setUp() to set the parameter and tearDown() to reset it to its default value:

```
public void setUp(){
   HttpUnitOptions.setParserWarningsEnabled(true);
}

public void tearDown(){
   HttpUnitOptions.setParserWarningsEnabled(false);
}
```

For options that should be set for entire suites of tests, you can use junit.extensions.TestSetup to make the setting and resetting of the property apply to the suite as a whole.

Methods

This "Methods" section is presented a little differently than others because HttpUnitOptions essentially consists of a set of exposed properties. Therefore, we've grouped the setters and getters instead of presenting them in alphabetical order.

```
autoRefresh
public static boolean getAutoRefresh()
public static void setAutoRefresh(boolean autoRefresh)
```

Default = false. This option specifies whether the WebClient automatically follows page refresh requests (that is, immediately calls getResponse() on the refresh request if latestResponse.getRefreshRequest() does not return null). The default of false allows for the redirect page to be inspected before the next page appears.

Setting this property to true could result in an infinite loop if a page refreshes itself.

```
defaultCharacterSet
public static String getDefaultCharacterSet()
public static void setDefaultCharacterSet(String characterSet)
public static void resetDefaultCharacterSet()
```

Default = "iso-8859-1". This option specifies the character encoding that will be used for responses that do not specify encoding in their content-type header. resetDefaultCharacterSet() resets the default character set to iso-8859-1.

```
imagesTreatedAsAltText
public static boolean getImagesTreatedAsAltText()
public static void setImagesTreatedAsAltText(boolean asText)
```

Default = false. If this option is set to true, images will be treated as the value of their "alt" attribute for the purpose of searches (for example, WebResponse.getLinkWith(String)) and displays.

loggingHttpHeaders
```
public static boolean isLoggingHttpHeaders()
public static void setLoggingHttpHeaders(boolean enabled)
```

Default = false. If this option is set to true, both incoming and outgoing HTTP headers are logged to the System.out stream.

matchesIgnoreCase
```
public static boolean getMatchesIgnoreCase()
public static void setMatchesIgnoreCase( boolean ignoreCase )
```

Default = true (matches are case insensitive). This option controls whether methods such as WebResponse.getTableStartingWith() are case-sensitive in their attempts to match the arguments to the returned HTML.

parameterValuesValidated
```
public static boolean getParameterValuesValidated()
public static void setParameterValuesValidated(boolean validated)
```

Default = true. This option specifies whether the values that are set in a WebRequest are checked against the legal values that the underlying form (if any) would allow.

parserWarningsEnabled
```
public static boolean getParserWarningsEnabled()
public static void setParserWarningsEnabled(boolean enabled)
```

Default = false. If this option is set to true, JTidy (the HTML parser used by HttpUnit) will print warnings to the System.out stream when it encounters HTML that is not structured according to the specification. This option can be useful in debugging unexpected results from HttpUnit. (See the section on WebForm for more information.)

redirectDelay
```
public static int getRedirectDelay()
public static void setRedirectDelay(int delayInMilliseconds)
```

Default = 0 milliseconds. This option controls how long WebClient will wait before following a redirect. It may need to be set higher if the server will not be ready for the redirect request immediately after the redirect is sent (an uncommon occurrence).

Class HttpUnitUtils

```
public class HttpUnitUtils
```

Description

HttpUnitUtils is used internally by WebResponse; it provides a static method to parse a header for content type and encoding information. Content type can also be retrieved from WebResponse.getContentType():

```
public void testContentAndEncoding()throws Exception{
  WebConversation wc = new WebConversation();
```

```
        WebResponse response = wc.getResponse("http://www.objectmentor.com/");
        String header = response.getHeaderField("Content-type");
        String[] typeAndEncoding = HttpUnitUtils.parseContentTypeHeader(header);
        assertEquals("text/html",  typeAndEncoding[0]);
        /*don't expect encoding to be included*/
        assertNull(typeAndEncoding[1]);
    }
```

Method

```
parseContentTypeHeader(String header)
public static String[] parseContentTypeHeader(String header)
```

The returned array contains the content type and the character encoding contained in the header (in that order). If no character encoding information is included, the second entry will be null.

Class IllegalRequestParameterException

```
public abstract class IllegalRequestParameterException
```

Inheritance Information

Extends: RuntimeException

Direct known subclasses: IllegalFileParameterException, IllegalNonFileParameterException, IllegalParameterValueException, IllegalSubmitButtonException, IllegalUnnamedSubmitButtonException, MultipartFormRequiredException, NoSuchParameterException, SingleValuedParameterException

Description

IllegalRequestParameterException is thrown when code attempts to set a request parameter that could not be set in a Web browser. See the section on WebForm for a description of how to create a request associated with an HTML form.

Various inner exception classes extend IllegalRequestParameterException to provide more specific information about the exact violation of the form's potential parameters. Most of the exceptions are self-explanatory and include helpful information in their messages (see the "Inheritance Information" section for a list of these exceptions). Following is an example of using IllegalRequestParameterException:

```
public void testIllegalSetting() throws Exception {
    WebConversation wc = new WebConversation();
    WebResponse resp = wc.getResponse("http://www.flimflam.com/order");
    WebForm form = response.getFormWithName("product_choice");
    WebRequest submit = form.getRequest();
    submit.setParameter("product_id", "101");//ok
    try{
        submit.setParameter("shipping_method", "Ultra-quick");
        fail("Ultra-quick shipping only available to logged-in users.");
    }
    catch(IllegalRequestParameterException e){}
}
```

Class MessageBodyWebRequest

```
public abstract class MessageBodyWebRequest
```

Inheritance Information

Extends: WebRequest

Direct known subclasses: PostMethodWebRequest, PutMethodWebRequest

Description

This class is used internally to support the stream-handling needs of PostMethodWebRequest and PutMethodWebRequest.

Methods

```
MessageBody newMessageBody();
protected abstract MessageBody newMessageBody();

completeRequest(URLConnection connection)
protected void completeRequest(URLConnection connection)
```

Class PostMethodWebRequest

```
public abstract class PostMethodWebRequestInheritance Information
```

Inheritance Information

Extends: MessageBodyWebRequest

Description

PostMethodWebRequest represents a request using the POST method. Tests will usually interact with this object through its superclass WebRequest (see the section on that class for details).

Constructors

```
PostMethodWebRequest(String urlString)
public PostMethodWebRequest(String urlString)

PostMethodWebRequest(String urlString, InputStream source,
                     String contentType)
public PostMethodWebRequest(String urlString, InputStream source,
                           String contentType)
```

This constructor constructs a PostMethodWebRequest that uses the specified InputStream as the message body, overriding any parameters/files set by other means. The "contentType" parameter specifies the content type of the body, including any character set information.

```
PostMethodWebRequest(URL urlBase, String urlString, String target)
public PostMethodWebRequest(URL urlBase, String urlString, String target)
```

Methods

```
MessageBody newMessageBody();
protected MessageBody newMessageBody();
```

This method returns a MessageBody containing the stream specified by the constructor (if any), or an encoded representation of the parameters and files set so far on this request. newMessageBody() is used by the framework to select how the request will be written to the java.net.URLConnection.

```
String getMethod()
public String getMethod()
```

This method returns the method of this request (in this case, POST).

```
selectFile(String parameterName, File file)
public void selectFile( String parameterName, File file )

selectFile(String parameterName, File file, String contentType)
public void selectFile(String parameterName, File file,String contentType)
```

These methods specify a file to be included in the request. They will throw an IllegalRequestParameter if the "parameterName" does not correspond to an expected file parameter.

Class PutMethodWebRequest

```
public class PutMethodWebRequest
```

Inheritance Information

Extends: MessageBodyWebRequest

Description

PutMethodWebRequest represents a request using the PUT method.

> **Any parameters or files specified with selectFile() or setParameter() will be ignored. The content of the request is solely specified by the InputStream provided to the constructor.**

Constructor

```
PutMethodWebRequest(String url, InputStream source, String contentType)
public PutMethodWebRequest(String url, InputStream source,
                          String contentType)
```

This constructor constructs a request with the specified InputStream forming the body of the request (the request headers are the only other information that will be sent). The "contentType" parameter specifies the content type of the body, including any character set information.

Methods

```
String getMethod()
public String getMethod()
```

This method returns the method of this request (in this case, PUT).

```
MessageBody newMessageBody()
protected MessageBody newMessageBody()
```

This method returns a MessageBody based solely on the InputStream provided in the constructor.

Class SubmitButton

```
public class SubmitButtonInheritance
```

Information

Extends: Object

Description

SubmitButton represents a submit button in an HTML form. It's used with WebForm to create form submissions that simulate the user clicking a particular button. (See the section on WebForm for details and an example.)

Methods

```
getName()
public String getName()
```

This method returns the name of the button.

```
getValue()
public String getValue()
```

This method returns the value of the button.

```
isImageButton()
public boolean isImageButton()
```

This method returns true if the button is an image map.

Class TableCell

```
public class TableCell
```

Inheritance Information

Extends: ParsedHTML (package-access-level class)

Implements: HTMLSegment

Description

TableCell represents a cell in an HTML table. This class implements the HTMLSegment interface (see the section on that interface for more details), so test developers can interact with it through the methods (getLinks, getForms, getTables, and so on) defined there. In addition, TableCell provides a few methods specific to table cells (see the section on WebTable for an example).

Methods

asText()
```
public String asText()
```

This method returns the contents of the cell as a String.

getColSpan()
```
public int getColSpan()
```

This method returns the value of the "colspan" attribute of this cell in the underlying HTML document.

getDOM()
```
public org.w3c.dom.Node getDOM()
```

This method returns an org.w3c.dom.Node corresponding to the contents of this table cell represented as a DOM.

getRowSpan()
```
public int getRowSpan()
```

This method returns the value of the "rowspan" attribute of this cell in the underlying HTML document.

Class WebClient

```
public abstract class WebClient
```

Inheritance Information

Extends: ObjectDescription

WebClient emulates a Web browser for the purpose of maintaining context for a series of HTTP requests. It manages cookies, computes relative URLs, and presents a single object interface for sending requests to and retrieving responses from a server. Generally, every test method in an HttpUnit-based test case will need to access a WebClient.

WebClient is an abstract class with a single concrete subclass (WebConversation) within the HttpUnit framework; the closely related ServletUnit framework defines another one. As such, you will primarily use instances of WebConversation to access the functionality of WebClient.

The following example illustrates the basic use of WebClient/WebConversation:

```
public void testSiteAuthorization() throws Exception {
  WebConversation wc = new WebConversation();
  String siteUrl = "http://www.eDogFood.com/ordering.jsp";
  boolean caught = false;
  try{
    WebResponse resp = wc.getResponse(siteUrl);
  }
  catch(AuthorizationRequiredException e){
```

```
      System.out.println(e);
      caught = true;
   }
   assertTrue(caught);
   wc.setAuthorization("Jane Tester", "TestPassword123");
   WebResponse resp = wc.getResponse(siteUrl);
   assertEquals("Logged In - Welcome", resp.getTitle());
}
```

Methods

```
addCookie(String name, String value)
public void addCookie(String name, String value)
```

This method adds the specified name/value pair to the list of cookies to be sent with every request to the server. The server may also set such cookies:

```
public void testCookieLogonTransfer() throws Exception{
   WebConversation wc = new WebConversation();
   String siteUrl = "http://www.eDogFood.com/ordering.jsp";
   wc.setAuthorization("Jane Tester", "TestPassword123");
   WebResponse resp = wc.getResponse(siteUrl);

   String sessionIdKey = resp.getNewCookieNames()[0];
   String sessionIdValue = resp.getNewCookieValue(sessionKey);
   WebConversation newBrowser = new WebConversation();
   newBrowser.addCookie(sessionKey, sessionValue);
   newBrowser.getResponse(siteUrl);
   /*--would throw AuthorizationRequiredException if not logged in*/
}
```

```
getCookieHeaderField()
protected String getCookieHeaderField()
```

This method returns the value of the cookie header as a String. It appears to be used internally by WebClient, but it could be used externally for validation purposes.

```
getCookieNames()
public String[] getCookieNames()
```

```
getCookieValue(String name)
public String getCookieValue(String name)
```

These methods return the names and values of the active cookies that will be sent to the server with each request. (See addCookie() for an example.)

```
getFrameContents(String frameName)
public WebResponse getFrameContents(String frameName)
```

This method gets the contents of the frame with the specified name as a WebResponse. (See getFrameNames() for an example.)

```
getFrameNames()
public String[] getFrameNames()
```

This method returns a String[] containing the names of all the currently active frames in the virtual Web browser represented by the WebClient. The topmost frame can be retrieved with the keyword _top. As each request is made, the contents of the appropriate frame are replaced with the WebResponse resulting from the request. Assuming the String "fooFrame" is the target of the WebRequest request, resp and frame would refer to the same object after these lines were executed:

```
WebResponse resp = conversation.getResponse(request);
WebResponse frame = conversation.getFrameContents("fooFrame");
```

The next listing details how you can use frame interaction with HttpUnit. It may help to review the page the example is based on: http://java.sun.com/j2se/1.3/docs/api/index.html (the Javadoc for class URLConnection in java.net).

```
public void testFrameInteraction() throws Exception{
   /*Note: uses collections from java.util*/

   String site = "http://java.sun.com/j2se/1.3/docs/api/index.html";
   WebClient wc = new WebConversation();
   WebResponse response = wc.getResponse(site);

   /*assert that all of the expected frames exist*/
   String[] frameNames = wc.getFrameNames();
   List frameList = Arrays.asList(frameNames);
   assertTrue(frameList.contains("classFrame"));
   assertTrue(frameList.contains("packageListFrame"));
   assertTrue(frameList.contains("packageFrame"));
   assertTrue(frameList.contains("_top"));

   /*get the frame with the name 'packageFrame'*/
   response = wc.getFrameContents("packageFrame");

   /*follow a link which updates the classFrame
   *and assert that we end up in the correct place
   */
   WebLink link = response.getLinkWith("URLConnection");
   assertEquals("classFrame", link.getTarget());
   response = wc.getResponse(link.getRequest());
   String frameString = response.getText();
   assertTrue(frameString.indexOf("URLConnection") > -1);

   /*check that the frame that was updated was actually the classFrame */
   WebResponse frameContents = wc.getFrameContents("classFrame");
   assertSame(response, frameContents);
}


   protected java.util.Dictionary getHeaderFields()
```

This method returns a Dictionary containing all the active headers that will be sent to the server (including headers set by earlier responses and also those set by calls to setHeaderField).

```
getResponse(java.lang.String urlString)
public WebResponse getResponse(java.lang.String urlString)
                      throws java.net.MalformedURLException,
                             java.io.IOException,
                             org.xml.sax.SAXException
```

This method returns a WebResponse containing the result of a GET method request to the specified URL. It's essentially a convenience method for getResponse(new GetMethodWebRequest(urlString)) (see that method for details).

```
getResponse(WebRequest request)
public WebResponse getResponse(WebRequest request)
                      throws java.net.MalformedURLException,
                             java.io.IOException,
                             org.xml.sax.SAXException
```

One of the key methods in the HttpUnit API, getResponse() embodies a Web-browser request and server response. Functionally, it sends the specified WebRequest to the server using all the state information (cookies, headers, and so on) stored in the WebClient.

The list of exceptions is large but manageable. In most test methods, you'll want to declare that the test method throws Exception and allow JUnit to treat these occurrences as test failures. The java exceptions are simply passed on from classes in the java.net package (representing an illegal URL and IO problem during network connection respectively). The SAXException occurs when an error occurs while parsing the received page as XML.

```
getUserAgent()
public String getUserAgent()
```

This method gets the User-Agent header (the type of browser this WebClient is emulating) that is sent to the server.

```
newResponse(WebRequest request)
protected abstract WebResponse newResponse(WebRequest request)
                                  throws java.net.MalformedURLException,
                                         java.io.IOException
```

This method is used internally to talk to the server and create a new WebResponse from the results.

```
setAuthorization(String userName, String password)
public void setAuthorization(String userName, String password)
```

This method sets the Authorization header using the basic authorization scheme. (See the "Description" section of this class for an example.)

```
setHeaderField(String fieldName, String fieldValue)
public void setHeaderField(String fieldName, String fieldValue)
```

This method sets a header that will be sent to the server with every request. If a header is set to null, that header is removed from future requests:

```
conversation.setHeaderField("Cache-Control", "Cache-Control : no-cache");
```

setUserAgent(String userAgent)
```
public void setUserAgent(String userAgent)
```

This method sets the User-Agent header (used to emulate a type of browser).

updateClient(WebResponse response)
```
protected final void updateClient(WebResponse response)
                        throws java.net.MalformedURLException,
                               java.io.IOException,
                               org.xml.sax.SAXException
```

This method is used internally to update the state of the WebClient to reflect the results of the latest transaction.

Class WebConversation

```
public class WebConversation
```

Inheritance Information

Extends: WebClient

Description

WebConversation is the concrete implementation of WebClient; it provides no new external behavior. See the section on WebClient for details and examples.

Constructor

WebConversation()
```
public WebConversation()
```

Method

newResponse(WebRequest request)
```
protected WebResponse newResponse(WebRequest request)
                        throws java.net.MalformedURLException,
                               java.io.IOException
```

Class WebForm

```
public class WebForm
```

Inheritance Information

Extends: ObjectDescription

This class represents an HTML form present in a Web page. It provides a variety of shortcut methods that make examining the form and writing assertions against it easier. It also provides the facility to create a WebRequest that simulates the submission of this form. (See the section on WebRequest for more details.)

A listing we discussed earlier (in the section on WebRequest) contains an example of using WebForm and WebRequest to access a form, verify it, and simulate a user's submission to that form.

Methods

```
getCharacterSet()
public String getCharacterSet()
```

This method gets the character set encoding for this form. This information is contained in the Content-type header for the parent page.

```
getDOMSubtree()
public org.w3c.dom.Node getDOMSubtree()
```

This method returns a copy of the DOM Node representing this form in the underlying page.

```
getID()
public String getID()
```

This method gets the "id" attribute of this form from the underlying HTML.

```
getName()
public String getName()
```

This method gets the HTML form name.

```
getOptions(String name)
public String[] getOptions(String name)
```

This method gets an array of Strings corresponding to the displayed options for the specified parameter name.

```
getOptionValues(String name)
public String[] getOptionValues(String name)
```

This method gets an array of Strings corresponding to the option values for the specified parameter name.

```
getParameterNames()
public String[] getParameterNames()
```

This method returns the names of all of the input parameters in the form in order.

```
String getParameterValue(String name)
public String getParameterValue(String name)
```

This method gets the default value associated with the given input parameter, or the first default value if multiple values are possible.

```
getParameterValues(String name)
public String[] getParameterValues(String name)
```

This method gets an array corresponding to the default values of the given input parameter. (If the input parameter supports only one value, the array will contain a single element.)

```
getRequest()
public WebRequest getRequest()
```

This method gets a request that simulates a submission of this form using the default button (see getRequest(SubmitButton button) for more information).

```
getRequest(String submitButtonName, String submitButtonValue)
public WebRequest getRequest(String submitButtonName,
                             String submitButtonValue)
```

This method gets a request that simulates a submission of this form using a submit button with the specified name and value. It will throw an IllegalSubmitButtonException if no such button exists.

```
getRequest(String submitButtonName)
public WebRequest getRequest(String submitButtonName)
```

This method gets a request that simulates a submission of this form using a submit button with the specified name. It will throw an IllegalSubmitButtonException if no such button exists.

```
getRequest(SubmitButton button)
public WebRequest getRequest(SubmitButton button)
```

This method gets a request that simulates a submission of this form using the specified submit button. If the "button" argument is null, getRequest() will attempt to submit using the default button (either the unnamed form button or the only button available in the form).

```
getRequest(SubmitButton button, int x, int y)
public WebRequest getRequest(SubmitButton button, int x, int y)
```

This method acts like getRequest(SubmitButton button) except it also sets the submit position on the button to the specified coordinates. This method will have an effect only if the button is an image button.

```
getSubmitButton(String name)
public SubmitButton getSubmitButton(String name)
```

This method gets the submit button for this form with the specified name (or null if there is no such button).

```
getSubmitButton(String name, String value)
public SubmitButton getSubmitButton(String name, String value)
```

This method gets the submit button for this form with the specified name and value (or null if there is no such button).

```
getSubmitButtons()
public SubmitButton[] getSubmitButtons()
```

This method gets an array of all the buttons declared in this form.

```
getTarget()
public String getTarget()
```

This method returns the "target" attribute of the underlying HTML form, or the parent page's target if no such attribute exists.

```
isFileParameter(String name)
public boolean isFileParameter(String name)
```

This method returns true if the named input parameter is of type "file", or false if not.

```
isMultiValuedParameter(String name)
public boolean isMultiValuedParameter(String name)
```

This method returns true if the named input parameter accepts multiple values, or false if not.

```
isSubmitAsMime()
public boolean isSubmitAsMime()
```

This method returns true if the form should be submitted with MIME encoding (URLEncoding is the default setting).

```
isTextParameter(String name)
public boolean isTextParameter(String name)
```

This method returns true if the named input parameter accepts raw text, false if not.

Class WebLink

```
public class WebLink
```

Inheritance Information

Extends: ObjectDescription

This class represents a link in an HTML page. You can retrieve the text of the link, the URL it points to, its target, or its DOM structure. WebLink also provides a method to get a WebRequest version of the link that can be fed back into a WebConversation/WebClient.

The following example gets all the links on a page and follows each one. If no exceptions are thrown, the link is assumed to be good:

```
public void testAllLinks() throws Exception {
  WebConversation wc = new WebConversation();
  WebResponse response = wc.getResponse("http://www.objectmentor.com/");
```

```
        WebLink[] links = response.getLinks();
        for(int i =0; i < links.length; i++){
          WebResponse resp = wc.getResponse(links[i].getRequest());
          System.out.println(i+ " followed link " +
                links[i].getRequest().getURL());
                  /*no exceptions, page is OK!*/
        }
      }
```

Methods

asText()
```
public String asText()
```

This method returns the user-clickable text corresponding to this link.

getDOMSubtree()
```
public org.w3c.dom.Node getDOMSubtree()
```

This method returns a copy of the DOM Node representing this form in the underlying page.

getRequest()
```
public WebRequest getRequest()
```

This method gets a new WebRequest equivalent to a user click on the link.

getTarget()
```
public String getTarget()
```

This method gets the target frame for this link.

getURLString()
```
public String getURLString()
```

This method returns the "href" attribute of the underlying HTML tag.

Class WebRequest

```
public abstract class WebRequest
```

Inheritance Information

Extends: Object

Direct known subclasses: GetMethodWebRequest, MessageBodyWebRequest

Description

WebRequest represents a generic HTTP request to a Web server. This class is one of the most frequently used in the HttpUnit framework. Several other classes declare methods that return WebRequests representing specific types of requests (such as form submissions and link-clicks). WebRequests can also be constructed from a String representing a URL. In all cases, you can set request parameters and inspect various properties of the request before sending it to the server through a WebClient.

If you use a WebForm to create a WebRequest (and the parameterValuesValidated property of HttpUnitOptions is set to true), then the WebForm will restrict the possible values a given parameter can be set to. The following code snippet would not work unless jojoForm contained a parameter named "mojo" that accepted "zombo" as an input value:

```
WebForm jojoForm = response.getFormWithName("jojoForm");
WebRequest request = jojoForm.getRequest();
request.setParameter("mojo", "zombo");
```

As a result, some of the methods exposed as public in this class will always throw exceptions in certain subclasses (selectFile will never work in a GetMethodWebRequest, which cannot be based on a form).

The listing below gives an example of using WebRequest and WebForm to simulate a user's form submission.

```
//<form name="dogInfo" enctype="multipart/form-data"  method="post">
//Name of Your Dog:<INPUT type="text" NAME="name" VALUE="Rover">
//<BR>
//Type Of Dog Food:
//<SELECT NAME="dogFood" multiple>
//<OPTION VALUE="1">1. Kibbles & Bits</OPTION>
//<OPTION VALUE="2">2. Feisty Brand</OPTION>
//<OPTION VALUE="3" SELECTED>3. Chelmore Dog Crunch</OPTION>
//</SELECT>
//<BR>
//Tell us some activities your dog likes:<SELECT NAME="activities">
//<OPTION VALUE="frisbee">frisbee</OPTION>
//<OPTION VALUE="walks">walks</OPTION>
//<OPTION VALUE="dogGolf">Dog Golf!</OPTION>
//</select>
//<BR>
//Upload a Cute Dog Picture!:<input type="file" name="dogPicture"/>
//<p>
//<input type="submit" value="Bark!"/>
//<input type="submit" value="Woof!"/>
//
//</form>
public void testFormSubmission() throws Exception{
  WebConversation wc = new WebConversation();
  WebResponse response = wc.getResponse("http://www.eDogFood.com");
  WebForm form = response.getFormWithName("dogInfo");
  /*check important parameters*/
  assertTrue(form.isFileParameter("dogPicture"));

  String[] activities = form.getParameterValues("activities");
  assertEquals("frisbee", activities[0]);
  /*Note: only gets the *selected* parameter values.*/

  assertTrue(form.isMultiValuedParameter("dogFood"));
  submitForm(form);
```

```
    }

    private void submitForm(WebForm form) throws Exception{
      /*could also use the shortcut methods to get a request*/
      SubmitButton button = form.getSubmitButton("submit", "Bark!");
      WebRequest request  = form.getRequest(button);

      /*would throw an IllegalRequestParameterException-- activity is not in
      the list of acceptable values.*/
      //request.setParameter("activities", "canineBowling");

      request.selectFile("dogPicture", new java.io.File("C:\\edgar.jpg"));
      request.setParameter("dogFood", new String[]{"1","3"});

      /*Test submission without the Dog's name:*/
      request.removeParameter("name");

      WebResponse response = conversation.getResponse(request);
      /*do assertions on the response*/
    }
```

```
    WebRequest(String urlString)
    protected WebRequest(String urlString)
```

This constructor constructs a new WebRequest to point to the specified URL (represented as a String).

```
    WebRequest(URL urlBase, String urlString)
    protected WebRequest(URL urlBase, String urlString)
```

This constructor constructs a WebRequest by concatenating the base URL with the relative urlString.

```
    WebRequest(URL urlBase, String urlString, String target)
    protected WebRequest(URL urlBase, String urlString, String target)
```

This constructor is the same as WebRequest(URL urlBase, String urlString), except it also specifies the target frame of the request.

```
    WebRequest(URL urlBase, String urlString, String target,
              WebForm sourceForm, SubmitButton button)
    protected WebRequest(URL urlBase, String urlString, String target,
                    WebForm sourceForm, SubmitButton button)

    WebRequest(WebRequest baseRequest, String urlString, String target) protected
    WebRequest (WebRequest baseRequest, String urlString,
                      String target) throws MalformedURLException
```

These two protected constructors are used internally by the framework to build requests out of forms and other requests.

Methods

```
completeRequestURLConnection connection)
protected void completeRequest(URLConnection connection)
                                        throws IOException
```

This method is meant to be overridden to provide the actual machinery for sending the request to the server using different methods (POST, GET, PUT, and so on).

```
getCharacterSet()
protected final String getCharacterSet()
getMethod()
public abstract String getMethod()
```

This method returns the method of the HTTP request (POST, GET, PUT, and so on).

```
getParameter(String name)
public String getParameter(String name)
```

This method returns the value of the named parameter in the request, or null if one has not been set.

```
getParameterNames()
public java.util.Enumeration getParameterNames()
```

This method returns an Enumeration containing the names of all the parameters set in the request so far (either using the methods of WebRequest or specified as defaults in the form on which this request is based).

```
getParameterString()
protected final String getParameterString()
```

See getQueryString().

```
getParameterValues(String name)
public String[] getParameterValues(String name)
```

This method returns all the values set so far for the named parameter as a String array.

```
getQueryString()
public String getQueryString()
```

This method returns the query string for this request. It will work even if the request would not generate a visible query string in real life. The number of characters in the query string is limited only by the capacity of the java String.

```
getTarget()
public String getTarget()
```

This method returns the target frame for this request.

```
getURL()
public java.net.URL getURL() throws MalformedURLException
```

This method returns a new URL corresponding to the URL that will be used to submit this request.

```
getURLBase()
protected final URL getURLBase()

getURLString()
protected String getURLString()

hasNoParameters()
protected final boolean hasNoParameters()

isFileParameter(String name)
protected boolean isFileParameter(String name)

isMimeEncoded()
protected final boolean isMimeEncoded()
```

These methods are all used internally by WebRequest and its subclasses.

```
removeParameter(String name)
public void removeParameter(String name)
```

This method removes a previously set parameter from the request.

```
selectFile(String parameterName, File file)
public void selectFile(String parameterName, File file)

selectFile(String parameterName, File file, String contentType)
public void selectFile(String parameterName, File file,
                       String contentType)
```

These methods select a file for upload if the form this WebRequest is based on supports the named parameter as a file upload parameter.

```
setParameter(String name, String value)
public void setParameter(String name, String value)

setParameter(String name, String[] values)
public void setParameter(String name, String[] values)
```

These methods set the named parameter either to the single value or the String array, depending on which method is called. If the underlying form (if any) would not allow such a value to be set, an IllegalRequestParameterException will be thrown.

```
toString()
public String toString()
```

This method returns the method type and URL string for this request.

Class WebResponse

```
public abstract class WebResponse
```

Inheritance Information

Extends: Object

Implements: HTMLSegment

Description

WebResponse represents the response from the Web server to a request. It is one of the core abstractions of the HttpUnit framework. This class provides a variety of methods that expose properties of the underlying response for inspection. Users of the class can get a DOM tree representing the HTML document, get newly set cookie names and values, inspect header fields, and so on. A variety of examples of WebResponse use appear throughout this chapter. Because WebResponse is abstract, WebResponse objects that appear in HttpUnit tests will likely be of type HttpWebResponse (a package-level access class).

> **WebResponse implements the HTML segment interface. For the sake of brevity, methods belonging to that interface are defined and described there. WebResponse also declares several methods as protected. Because WebResponse is not meant to be subclassed as part of ordinary development, these methods are listed but not described.**

Constructor

```
WebResponse(String target, URL url)
protected WebResponse(String target, URL url)
```

Methods

```
defineRawInputStream(InputStream inputStream)
protected final void defineRawInputStream(InputStream inputStream)
```

```
getCharacterSet()
public String getCharacterSet()
```

This method returns the charset portion (if any) of the HTTP Content-type header for this response.

```
getContentType()
public String getContentType()
```

This method returns the content type portion (as distinct from the character set portion) of the HTTP Content type header for this response.

```
getDOM()
public org.w3c.dom.Document getDOM() throws org.xml.SAXException
```

This method attempts to return the DOM tree associated with this response. If the response is determined to be HTML, a special HTML-savvy parser (JTidy) will be used. If not, a regular SAX parser will be used on the response text. If errors are encountered during parsing (for instance, if the response contains neither HTML nor XML), a SAXException will be thrown.

```
getFrameNames()
public String[] getFrameNames() throws SAXException
```

This method returns an array containing the names of all the frames contained in this page. You can retrieve the contents of individual frames by these names from the WebClient (see that section for details).

getHeaderField(String fieldName)
```
public String getHeaderField(String fieldName)
```

This method gets the contents of the header field specified by the given name:

```java
public void testContentLength() throws Exception{
   WebConversation conversation = new WebConversation();
   WebResponse response = conversation.getResponse("http://www.junit.org");
   assertEquals("6575", response.getHeaderField("CONTENT-LENGTH"));
}
```

getInputStream()
```
public InputStream getInputStream()
```

This method returns the textual contents of this response as an input stream.

getNewCookieNames()
```
public String[] getNewCookieNames()
```

This method returns all the cookie names defined as part of this response. (See the section on WebClient.addCookie for an example of this method in action.)

getNewCookieValue(String name)
```
public String getNewCookieValue(String name)
```

This method returns the value associated with the given new cookie name (see getNewCookieNames()).

getRefreshDelay()
```
public int getRefreshDelay()
```

This method returns the delay specified by the refresh metatag contained in the header (or 0 if none is found). This delay corresponds the waiting period before a standard browser would follow the refresh request.

getRefreshRequest()
```
public WebRequest getRefreshRequest()
```

This method gets the WebRequest embodying the refresh URL contained in the refresh metatag in the header (or null if none exists).

getResponseCode()
```
public abstract int getResponseCode()
```

This method returns the HTTP response code for this request.

getTarget()
```
public String getTarget()
```

This method gets the frame in which the WebResponse resides (the default frame for any WebRequests originating from this response).

getTitle()
```
public String getTitle() throws SAXException
```

This method returns the title element of the underlying HTML page.

getText()
```
public String getText() throws IOException
```

This method returns a String representation of the underlying HTML page (roughly equivalent to calling "view source" in a traditional browser). This method is preferred over toString() for the retrieval of page contents.

getURL()
```
public java.net.URL getURL()
```

This method returns the URL of the request that generated this response.

isHTML()
```
public boolean isHTML()
```

This method returns true if the content type for the underlying page is specified as "text/html".

loadResponseText()
```
protected void loadResponseText() throws IOException
```

newResponse(URLConnection connection)
```
public static WebResponse newResponse(URLConnection connection)
                                            throws IOException
```

readRefreshRequest(String contentTypeHeader)
```
protected final void readRefreshRequest(String contentTypeHeader)
```

setContentTypeHeaderString value)
```
protected void setContentTypeHeaderString value)
```

toString()
```
public String toString()
```

In the default implementation, this method returns the response text. In HttpWebResponse (the only concrete subclass in the HttpUnit API), it returns only the response headers.

Class WebTable

```
public class WebTable
```

Inheritance Information

Extends: ObjectDescription

WebTable represents an HTML table. It provides methods to get various attributes of a table (row count, column count, id, and summary) and methods to get single table cells (as TableCells or as text), and also lets you convert the entire table into a arraybased representation.

Methods

asText()
public String[][] asText()

This method returns the entire table as a two-dimensional String array. The first dimension contains the rows, and the second dimension contains the cells.

getCell(int row, int column) *Deprecated*
public String getCell(int row, int column)

Use getCellAsText(int row, int column).

getCellAsText(int row, int column)
public String getCellAsText(int row, int column)

This method returns the contents of the cell in the given position as text. The row and column numbers are zero based, and this method will throw an IndexOutOfBoundsException if the parameters are not within the table's range.

getColumnCount()
public int getColumnCount()

getID()
public String getID()

getRowCount()
public int getRowCount()

getSummary()
public String getSummary()

getTableCell(int row, int column)
public TableCell getTableCell(int row, int column)

This method returns the contents of the cell in the given position as a TableCell. The row and column numbers are zero based, and this method will throw an IndexOutOfBoundsException if the parameters are not within the table's range.

purgeEmptyCells()
public void purgeEmptyCells()

This method removes from this table all rows and columns in that do not contain anything.

JUnitPerf API Reference

JUnitPerf is a small set of test decorators and related classes that extend the JUnit API. In order to use JUnitPerf, you will need to be familiar with the functionality and use of basic JUnit tests as well as junit.extensions.TestDecorator.

Package com.clarkware.junitperf

This package contains all of the classes that make up JUnitPerf. The key classes in this package are LoadTest and TimedTest (as well as TimedTest's associated Timer interface). ConstantTimer and RandomTimer provide implementations of the Timer interface. The remaining classes are used mainly by the framework.

Class ConstantTimer

```
public class ConstantTimer
```

Inheritance Information

Extends: Object

Implements: Timer

Description

ConstantTimer is a Timer that always returns a constant delay. (See the sections on Timer and LoadTest for more information.)

Constructor

```
ConstantTimer(long delay)
public ConstantTimer(long delay)
```

This constructor constructs a Timer with the specified delay in milliseconds.

Method

```
getDelay()
public long getDelay()
```

This method returns the delay specified by the constructor.

Class LoadTest

```
public class LoadTest
```

Inheritance Information

Extends: Object

Implements: junit.framework.Test

Description

LoadTest runs a Test with a specified number of concurrent users and/or a specified number of iterations for each user. Each Test is run in a separate thread, and LoadTest waits until all these threads have completed before ending the test. To create a Test with 20 simulated users, you would use the following code:

```
Test targetTest = new ServerTest("testProcessPage");
LoadTest loadTest = new LoadTest(targetTest, 20);
```

To create a LoadTest that simulates users who run a test multiple times, first wrap the test in a junit.framework.RepeatedTest and decorate it, or use the convenience constructor provided by LoadTest to do the same thing (see the listing below and the "Constructors" section for examples).

You can combine LoadTests with Timers to provide ramping behavior. Adding a Timer instance provides a delay between the addition of each new user to the pool of active users. The timer's getDelay() method specifies the amount of time between additions.

> **The Timer specifies the delay between the addition of users, not the delay between successive runs of the same decorated Test, which is controlled by a Timer-unaware junit.extensions.RepeatedTest. However, it would be trivial to extend RepeatedTest to add Timer functionality to it. See the listing below for an example.**

You can combine LoadTest with a TimedTest to provide performance criteria for the load test. Either a TimedTest can be used to decorate the LoadTest (to ensure that execution of the whole test does not exceed a certain period of time) or the LoadTest can decorate a TimedTest (so that no individual Test exceeds the specified time, even when the system is under load).

LoadTest lets users specify the atomicity of the test under decoration. There are two modes: atomic and non-atomic. A LoadTest that does not enforce atomicity waits only for the threads simulating users to terminate before terminating itself--the Test is assumed to police its own threads. If atomicity is enforced, the LoadTest waits on all threads spawned by the decorated Test. In addition, an uncaught exception thrown during atomic LoadTest execution will interrupt all the threads spawned by the test.

This code demonstrates the use of LoadTest with other test decorators to create complex performance expectations:

```
import junit.framework.*;
import junit.extensions.RepeatedTest;
import com.clarkware.junitperf.*;
import test.com.company.ServerTest;

public class ServerLoadTest{

  public static Test suite(){

    /*create a basic JUnit test*/
    Test basicTest = new ServerTest("testProcessPage");

    /*
      Wrap basicTest in a TimedTest--a page load should
      never exceed 5 seconds.
     */
    Test timedTest = new TimedTest(basicTest, 5000L);

    /*
      Wrap timedTest in a RepeatedTimerTest (defined below) to simulate
      multiple page hits with time between repeat page views.
     */

     /*average 3.5 s. between views, with a variation of 2.5 s.*/
     Timer timer = new RandomTimer(3500L, 2.50);
     /*25 page views per user*/
     Test repeatedTest = new RepeatedTimerTest(timedTest, 25, timer);

     /*
       Now make the repeated page viewing part of a load test: 10
       concurrent users, added at constant 5s intervals.
      */
     timer = new ConstantTimer(5000);
     Test loadTest = new LoadTest(repeatedTest, 10, timer);

      /*
        Finally set a maximum time out for the load test with another
        TimedTest: time should not exceed 350 s.
       */
```

```
          Test loadTestWithTimeOut = new TimedTest(loadTest, 350000);

          return loadTestWithTimeOut;
     }//end suite()

       public static void main(String[] args){
           junit.textui.TestRunner.run(suite());
       }
}


/**
 * Adds a delay specified by a Timer between iterations of
 * the test.
 */
class RepeatedTimerTest extends RepeatedTest{
  Timer timer;
  private int repeats;
  public RepeatedTimerTest(Test test, int repeats, Timer timer){
    super(test, repeats);
    this.repeats = repeats;
    this.timer = timer;
  }

  public void run(TestResult result) {

    for (int i= 0; i < repeats; i++) {

       /*verifies that the test should continue*/
       if (result.shouldStop()){
         break;
       }

       /*wait for delay given by timer*/
       try {
         Thread.sleep(timer.getDelay());
       }
       catch(InterruptedException ignored) {
       }

       /* run the Test*/
       basicRun(result);

    }
  }

}//class
```

Constructors

```
LoadTest(Test test, int users)
public LoadTest(Test test, int users)
```

This constructor decorates the specified Test as a LoadTest with the specified number of concurrent users and a user-addition delay of zero milliseconds (all threads start at once).

```
LoadTest(Test test, int users, int iterations)
public LoadTest(Test test, int users, int iterations)
```

This constructor decorates the specified Test as a LoadTest with the specified number of concurrent users, the number of iterations per user (that is, the number of times the Test is repeated), and a user-addition delay of zero milliseconds (all threads start at once).

```
LoadTest(Test test, int users, int iterations, Timer timer)
public LoadTest(Test test, int users, int iterations, Timer timer)
```

This constructor decorates the specified Test as a LoadTest with the specified number of concurrent users, the number of iterations per user, and a user-addition delay drawn from the Timer argument.

```
LoadTest(Test test, int users, Timer timer)
public LoadTest(Test test, int users, Timer timer)
```

This constructor decorates the specified Test as a LoadTest with the specified number of concurrent users and a user-addition delay drawn from the Timer argument.

Methods

```
countTestCases()
public int countTestCases()
```

This method returns the total number of TestCases run by this LoadTest (essentially decoratedTest.countTestCases() multiplied by the number of users).

```
run()
public int countTestCases()

setEnforceTestAtomicity(boolean isAtomic)
public void setEnforceTestAtomicity(boolean isAtomic)
```

This method sets the enforcement policy of the LoadTest with respect to test atomicity. The policy should be set to true when the completion of threads spawned by the decorated Test is essential to the completion of the Test but the decorated Test does not wait on its own spawned threads.

Class RandomTimer

```
public class RandomTimer
```

Inheritance Information

Extends: Object

Implements: Timer

Description

RandomTimer is a Timer (see the sections on Timer and LoadTest) that returns random delays based on the average delay and variation specified in the constructor.

Constructor

```
RandomTimer(long delay, double variation)
public RandomTimer(long delay, double variation)
```

Both the base delay and the potential variation are in milliseconds (despite the difference in types). getDelay() will return a number between delay and delay + variation. (In other words, the variation will never be negative.)

Method

```
getDelay()
public long getDelay()
```

Class ThreadBarrier

```
public class ThreadBarrier
```

Inheritance Information

Extends: Object

Description

ThreadBarrier waits for a constructor-defined number of threads to complete execution and reports on whether the number has been reached. LoadTest uses it in non-atomic mode to keep track of the status of the threads used for test-running.

Constructor

```
ThreadBarrier(int numDispatched)
public ThreadBarrier(int numDispatched)
```

This constructor constructs a ThreadBarrier with the given number of threads to wait for.

Methods

```
onCompletion(Thread t)
public synchronized void onCompletion(Thread t)
```

This method is called when the "Thread" argument has finished execution.

```
isReached()
public boolean isReached()
```

This method returns true if the thread barrier has been reached--that is, if the number of Threads specified in the constructor equals the number of times onCompletion() has been called.

> If onCompletion() is called *more* times than the number of threads waited for, the isReached() method will return false. Because the ThreadBarrier class is intended for internal use, this result should not present a problem for test developers.

Class ThreadedTest

```
public class ThreadedTest
```

Inheritance Information

Extends: Object

Implements: junit.framework.Test

Description

ThreadedTest is a decorator that runs a Test in a separate thread. LoadTest uses this class internally to manage the creation of multiple users running a Test simultaneously.

Constructors

```
ThreadedTest(Test test)
public ThreadedTest(Test test)
```

This constructor creates a Test that will run in its own thread. The new thread belongs to the current thread group.

```
ThreadedTest(Test test, ThreadGroup group, ThreadBarrier barrier)
public ThreadedTest(Test test)
```

This constructor creates a Test that will run in its own thread. The new thread belongs to the specified thread group and will register its completion with the ThreadBarrier.

Methods

```
countTestCases()
public int countTestCases()

run(TestResult result)
public void run(TestResult result)

toString()
public String toString()
```

Class ThreadedTestGroup

```
public class ThreadedTestGroup
```

Inheritance Information

Extends: ThreadGroup

Description

ThreadedTestGroup is a subclass of ThreadGroup used by the framework for exception handling while using ThreadedTests. Uncaught exceptions in a ThreadedTestGroup are added as failures or errors to the TestResult passed into setTestResult() . This class is used by LoadTest to keep track of and manage threads that simulate users.

Constructor

```
ThreadedTestGroup(Test test)
public ThreadedTestGroup(Test test)
```

This constructor constructs a new ThreadGroup associated with the given Test (the association is maintained so that accurate failures will result from testing).

Method

```
setTestResult(TestResult result)
public void setTestResult(TestResult result)
```

This method sets the TestResult object that failures should be registered with.

```
uncaughtException(Thread t, Throwable e)
public void uncaughtException(Thread t, Throwable e)
```

This method is overridden from ThreadGroup to catch uncaught, non-ThreadDeath throwables and record them as test failures. It interrupts all the threads in the group if such a throwable is caught.

Class TimedTest

```
public class TimedTest
```

Inheritance Information

Extends: junit.framework.extensions.TestDecorator

Implements: junit.framework.Test

Description

TimedTest is a TestDecorator that fails the decorated Test if the specified time limit is exceeded. You could use this class on individual TestCases for fine-grained results, or on TestSuites/TestDecorators (such as RepeatedTests or LoadTests) for aggregate results. (See the section on LoadTest for information about how to combine the two decorators.)

> The time a JUnit test takes to run includes the time consumed by the setUp() and tearDown() methods as well as the running of the actual test. Users of TimedTest should factor the effect of setUp() and tearDown() into their specified performance criteria.

You can construct two types of TimedTests. The first waits until the Test has completed and then checks the elapsed time against the specified maximum. The second fails immediately if the elapsed time exceeds the maximum.

This second kind of TimedTest carries a few caveats; you should weigh these drawbacks against the advantages of faster test runs, should the maximum time be exceeded. First, TimedTest spawns a thread to run the decorated test that is not externally terminated, even if the time runs out. Second, because of implementation details, a slim chance exists that a TimedTest using this method will not fail even if the maximum time has been exceeded. The likelihood of this occurrence increases as the number of threads running as peers of the thread that called run() on the TimedTest increases. Because of this possibility, it is bad idea to wrap a TimedTest using the second method in a LoadTest (where the number of threads running as peers of the TimedTest can be high).

Constructors

```
TimedTest(Test test, long maxElapsedTime)
public TimedTest(Test test, long maxElapsedTime)
```

This constructor decorates the specified Test with the given time in milliseconds. The TimedTest will wait for the completion of the test and then measure the elapsed time against the specified maximum. If the elapsed time exceeds the maximum, the test will fail. TimedTests that fail in this manner include the information on the expected versus actual time in their failure messages. The following code creates a new ServerTest instance that executes the testProcessPage method, and then decorates it so it will fail (after the fact) if the test takes longer than half a second to complete:

```
long maximumTime = 500;
Test targetTest = new ServerTest("testProcessPage");
TimedTest test = new TimedTest(targetTest, maximumTime);
```

```
TimedTest(Test test, long maxElapsedTime, boolean waitForCompletion)
public TimedTest(Test test, long maxElapsedTime, boolean
                                        waitForCompletion)
```

This constructor decorates the specified Test with the given time in milliseconds. Depending on the value of waitForCompletion, the TimedTest will either wait for the completion of the test and then measure the elapsed time against the specified maximum (true, see the previous constructor) or fail the test immediately if the specified time is exceeded (false).

This TimedTest will fail after 2.5 seconds if the ServerTest has not finished its execution by that point:

```
long maximumTime = 2500;
Test targetTest = new ServerTest("testPotentially30SecondMethod");
TimedTest test = new TimedTest(targetTest, 2500, false);
```

Methods

```
countTestCases()
public int countTestCases()
```

See junit.framework.TestDecorator.

```
outOfTime()
public boolean outOfTime()
```

This method returns whether the TimedTest exceeded the specified maximum time. This method is intended to be called after run() as a reporting tool.

```
run(junit.framework.TestResult result)
public void run(junit.framework.TestResult result)
```

This method runs the test in one of the two ways specified by the constructor.

```
runUntilTestCompletion(junit.framework.TestResult result)
protected void runUntilTestCompletion(TestResult result)

runUntilTimeExpires(junit.framework.TestResult result)
protected void runUntilTimeExpires(final junit.framework.TestResult result)
```

These methods provide the two types of timed execution. They're used internally.

```
toString()
public String toString()
```

This method informs you whether the test is waiting or non-waiting, but it does not give information about the maximum time specified for this TimedTest instance.

Interface Timer

```
public interface Timer
```

Description

This interface defines a timer that can be used with LoadTest to regulate the addition of new users to the LoadTest This interface can be implemented by developers who wish to customize the simulation of user loads.

Method

```
getDelay()
public long getDelay()
```

This method returns a number of milliseconds representing the delay between two events regulated by this Timer.

Example Applications Used in This Book

This chapter describes the sample applications used in this book. It is important that you understand the purpose and structure of these applications because we build, test, and deploy them throughout Part II of the book.

Writing example applications requires a delicate balance. If the applications are too simple, it is difficult to see how you would apply the concepts being taught to real-life projects. If the applications are too robust and full-featured, it can be difficult to follow the concepts being presented because the application's complexity gets in the way. We've tried to solve this problem by including two types of example applications in this book: simple applications and case studies.

Simple applications are used throughout the book to demonstrate a specific technique. These "applications" are very brief—sometimes only a few lines of code—so as not to get in the way of showing you how to use the underlying tools or how to deploy a component.

The case studies are stripped-down versions of a real application. They are long enough to be realistic and indicative of common Web applications, but they are not full-featured, stand-alone applications. The case studies are frameworks for demonstrating complex techniques with the automated testing and integration tools.

None of the case studies or simple examples do much in the way of exception-handling, in an effort to keep the code straightforward and easy to follow. If this were a book on style or object-oriented design, we would have written the samples much differently.

Where To Get the Example Applications

You can download the complete code listings and updated build instructions for all the applications in this book at www.wrox.com.

Simple Example: Model 2 Hello World

The Model 2 Hello World example is a simple application used to demonstrate Ant and some of the basic concepts of the other tools. You can download the complete code for this example at www.wrox.com. Model 2 Hello World involves building, deploying, and testing an applet, a servlet, a few JavaServer Pages (JSPs), an application, several Java classes, and two Enterprise JavaBeans (EJBs).

The applet is delivered to a browser using the plugin tag from a JSP. Then, the applet talks to a servlet. The servlet communicates with the EJB server, which maps a JavaBean into the session and redirects to a second JSP. The second JSP makes a call on the JavaBean, which calls an enterprise bean, which is a session bean. The session bean in turn calls an entity bean. Here is a graphical representation:

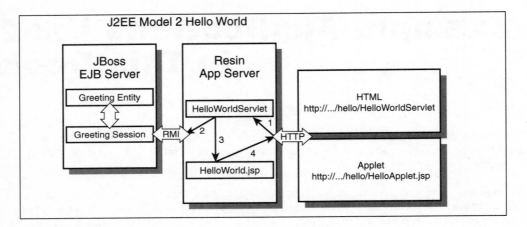

All of these components must be packaged and configured so they can speak to one another. In this example, we create a JAR file, an EJB JAR file, a WAR file, and an EAR file, each with the appropriate manifest and deployment descriptors using Ant.

Case Study Example: The Pet Store

The case study application is an online pet store. In this example, we have a catalog system stored in a database that is accessed by a Web application. This example can display the catalog to customers and also has a small content-management system that enables the owner of the pet store to enter catalog information (for example, new pets and new categories of pets). You can download the complete code from www.wrox.com.

The case study application is a more complex—but more realistic—example for demonstrating how open source tools are used in a real production environment. Even so, this example is by no means a complete pet store like the J2EE Blueprint Pet Store. Sun's purpose for building the J2EE Blueprint Pet Store is to show good design and coding techniques for building an e-commerce application with J2EE. Conversely, our pet store case study is built to demonstrate good techniques for testing, building, and deploying a J2EE application with open source tools.

We'll work through several iterations of the pet store. The baseline version has no connection pooling and no EJBs. This iteration is a simple, small example. It has several JSPs, a few classes that use JDBC, and some tables in a database. We discuss the details of the baseline version in subsequent sections of this chapter.

The second iteration of the case study changes the content management piece of the system to a container managed persistence (CMP) entity bean, which implements the backend product management. This approach allows online product entry (add, delete, and edit). This iteration demonstrates how to incorporate enterprise bean deployment into your Web application and how to ensure that the unit testing of the category systems still works after the addition of the CMP entity bean support.

The third iteration of the case study uses an EJB stateless session bean to add pooling of connections and prepared statements. We use this iteration to demonstrate the use of JUnitPerf and show the time savings from pooling prepared statements when the site is hit by many users (the original, non-pooled version would most likely be a bottleneck under heavy traffic).

The fourth iteration of the case study creates a Catalog TagLib. We use Cactus to test this TagLib. This is an excellent example to show how to operate and run Cactus tests and how to integrate them in the build/deploy process.

> **Database**
>
> **The example applications in this book use MS SQL Server, primarily because it is what a large number of developers use. Realizing the irony of writing a book about open source tools, yet using a closed source database, we ported several of the example applications to HSQL (a very fast, light-weight, open source database written in Java). These example applications are available on the book's Web site at: www.wrox.com.**

The fifth iteration of the case study refactors the JSPs using the Apache Struts project. Then, it uses HttpUnit to test that the application still works. The HttpUnit test is run against the baseline and the new version to show that the new version works like the old.

The sixth and final iteration of the case study refactors the Web application to use Extensible Style Language Transformation (XSLT) instead of JSP to do the catalog view. It then compares the throughput of the two approaches using JMeter.

Baseline Version of the Pet Store

This section is an overview of the baseline version of the pet store case study, its components, the associated Ant files, and the JUnit tests (details of working with Ant files and JUnit tests are covered in Chapters 4 through 13). All other iterations of the case study in this book are based on this baseline version, so it is important that you see it laid out in one place.

In the next sections we describe the classes used, the public interface, the implementation for the baseline version, the Web interface, and the Ant buildfile structure used to build the case study. Later, we highlight an Ant buildfile that is used to create sample data for our testing. Finally, we cover some of the JUnit tests that are executed by the test. Note that a complete listing of the baseline case study appears at the end of this appendix; we don't cover the full application line by line because the focus is on the buildfiles, not the Java code.

Model Classes (Public Interface)

The online store system for the baseline consists of a navigation system. The CategorySystem class is the façade class that is mapped into the session of the Web application. Through the CategorySystem, the Web applications can access the model data (Category, Product, and Category instances) for listing views and detail views (see the following code listing and illustration). The model is the public interface to the catalog system.

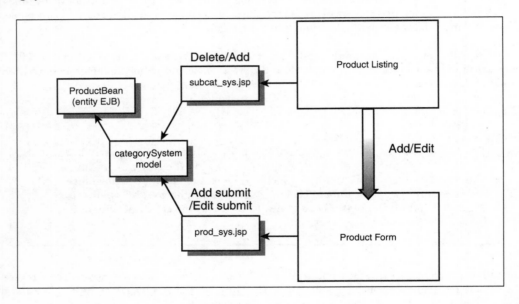

```java
package xptoolkit.petstore.model;

public class CategorySystem {
    private Category currentCategory;
    private Subcategory currentSubcategory;
    private Product currentProduct;

    public CategorySystem() throws Exception {
        currentCategory = Category.getCategory();
        currentCategory.setId(777);
    }

    public Category getCurrentCategory() {
        return currentCategory;
    }

    public Subcategory getCurrentSubcategory() {
        return currentSubcategory;
    }
}
```

```
    public Product getCurrentProduct() {
        return currentProduct;
    }

    public Subcategory getSubcategory(int id) throws Exception {
        currentSubcategory = currentCategory.getSubcategory(id);
        return currentSubcategory;
    }

    public Product getProduct(int id) throws Exception {
        currentProduct = currentSubcategory.getProduct(id);
        return currentProduct;
    }
}
```

dbmodel Classes (Implementation)

The catalog system model only defines the public interface into our catalog system. The actual implementation is in the dbmodel package. The baseline version of the case study uses old-school JDBC with no connection pooling. In a later implementation we use EJB to provide the connection and prepared statement pooling for this application. Fortunately, we will not have to change many of our tests and JSPs, because the public interface to the system will still be the model. The implementation is hidden behind the public interface to the system. See the following figure for the dbmodel class diagram. You can find the complete dbmodel code at the end of this appendix.

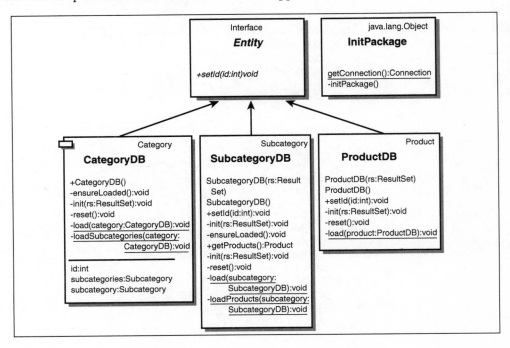

Database Schema

The dbmodel classes read data from a database. Again, our example endeavors to be simple, and the database schema certainly reflects this approach (see the following figure and listing). The SQL Data definition language (DDL) for the schema in the following figure is very simple.

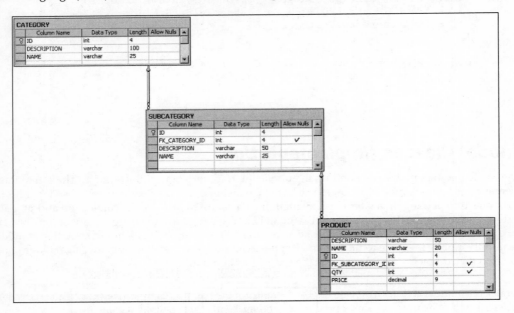

```
CREATE TABLE CATEGORY (
    ID int PRIMARY KEY,
    DESCRIPTION varchar (100) NOT NULL ,
    NAME varchar (25)  NOT NULL
)

CREATE TABLE SUBCATEGORY (
    ID int PRIMARY KEY,
    FK_CATEGORY_ID int REFERENCES CATEGORY(ID),
    DESCRIPTION varchar (50) NOT NULL ,
    NAME varchar (25)  NOT NULL
)

CREATE TABLE PRODUCT (
    ID int IDENTITY (1, 1) PRIMARY KEY,
    DESCRIPTION varchar (50) NOT NULL ,
    NAME varchar (20)  NOT NULL ,
    FK_SUBCATEGORY_ID int REFERENCES SUBCATEGORY(ID),
    QTY int DEFAULT (5),
    PRICE DECIMAL(10,2) NOT NULL,
```

Web Interface

The main Web page for the case study has a side navigation that contains the subcategories. The product listing for the subcategory is in the middle of the page:

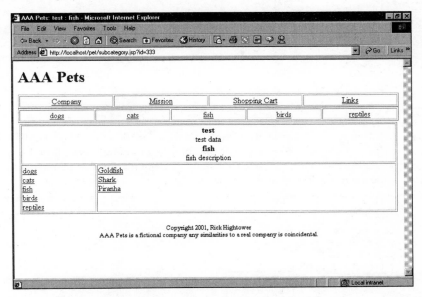

The category name and description appear in the center of the page, along with the subcategory name and description. When you click on a product, a product detail page opens:

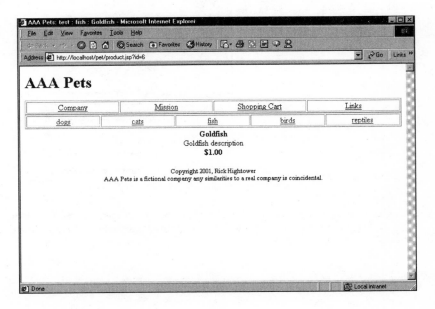

The Web interface has seven JSP pages, as follows:

- ❏ index.jsp
- ❏ category.jsp
- ❏ subcategory.jsp
- ❏ product.jsp
- ❏ category_sys.jsp
- ❏ header.jsp
- ❏ footer.jsp

The names of the JSP pages are somewhat indicative of their functionality. The product.jsp page displays product details. The subcategory.jsp page shows the subcategory details as well as the product listing for that subcategory (see the following figure for a visual representation of the JSP page structure). The code for all the JSPs appears in the listings at the end of this chapter.

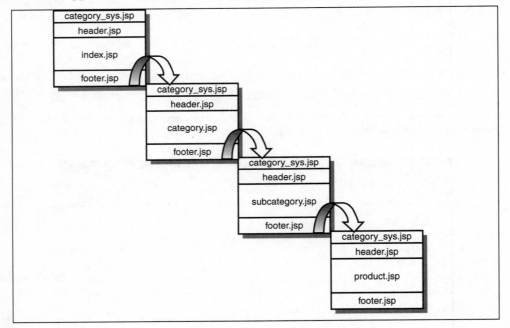

The JSPs use the CategorySystem to display the object model of the application. Each page includes header.jsp, which in turn includes category_sys.jsp, which uses jsp:useBean to map in a CategorySystem instance as follows:

```
<%@page import="xptoolkit.petstore.model.*" %>
<jsp:useBean id="categorySystem" class="CategorySystem" scope="session"/>
```

All the JSPs use the categorySystem to create and get objects. For example, here is a partial listing of the Product.jsp page:

```
    . . .
    Category category = categorySystem.getCurrentCategory();
    Subcategory subcategory = categorySystem.getCurrentSubcategory();

    String productId = request.getParameter("id");
    Product product = subcategory
.getProduct( Integer.parseInt(productId) );
    . . .
    <b><%= product.getName() %></b>
        <br>
    <%= product.getDescription() %>
```

The baseline version of the application just reads data out of the database. Later versions of the application will edit, add, and delete products using an extended categorySystem.

Build System

This section jumps the gun a bit. We explain how the build system is structured, but we have not yet covered Ant and JUnit. The idea is to give you a glimpse of things to come. Please read this section with the realization that the material covered in this section is explained in detail later.

The case study baseline uses five buildfiles:

❑ main

❑ model

❑ webapplication

❑ test

❑ setupDB

The *main* buildfile is located in the root directory of the baseline version (see figure below). The main buildfile orchestrates the execution and deployment of the other buildfiles.

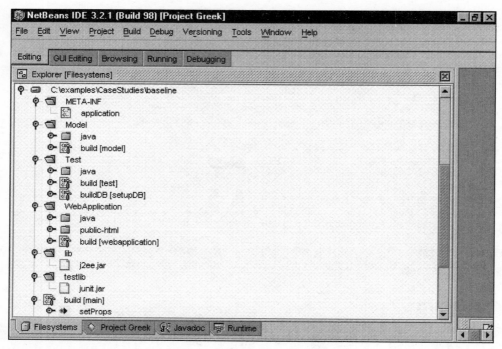

The *model* buildfile builds and packages the model and dbmodel classes. The end result of the model buildfile is a JAR file (petmodel.jar) that is stored in the lib directory of the output:

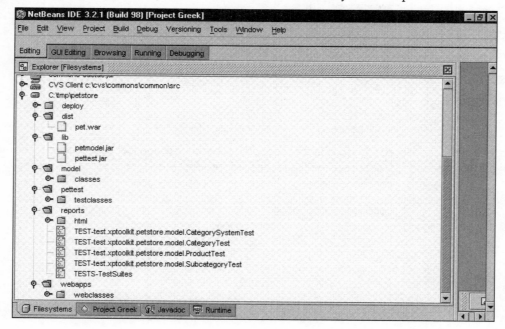

The *webapplication* buildfile compiles and builds the Web application. The end result of the webapplication buildfile is a WAR file (pet.war) that can be deployed to any J2EE compliant servlet/JSP engine such as WebLogic, Resin, Tomcat, or Orion.

The *test* buildfile packages and builds the test classes (JUnit) and runs the tests. The test results are stored in XML files in the reports directory. Then, the test buildfile transforms the XML into an HTML report (see the next two figures, which show the test results in a browser).

The *setupDB* buildfile sets up the database schema and populates the database with sample data that is used for testing. This will be covered in detail in the next section.

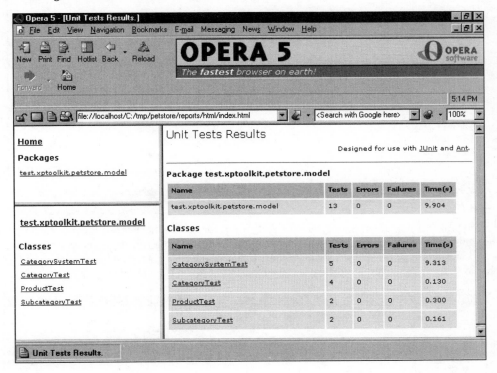

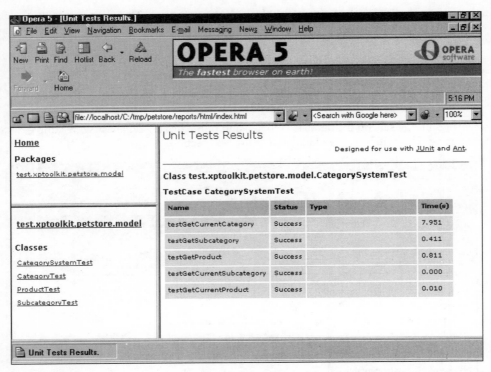

The main buildfile has seven targets (see figure below). *Targets* are like actions that are executed. We'll explain the concept of a target in depth in Chapter 5, "Building Java Applications with Ant." We'll explore the nuances of target names in Chapters 5, 6, and others. By the end of those chapters, you will be able to determine what a buildfile does just by looking at the target names.

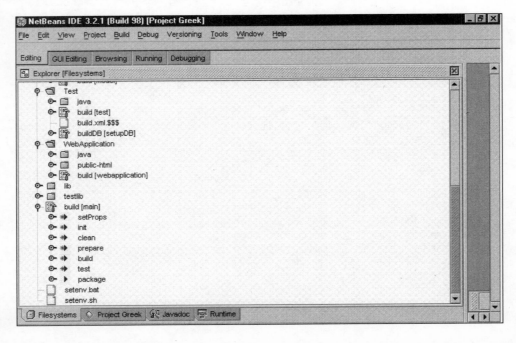

The main buildfile orchestrates the execution of other targets in the other buildfiles. For example, the main buildfile target test does the following:

```
<target name="test" depends="clean,build"
        description="build the model and application modules.">
    <ant dir="./Test" target="cleanTest">
        <property name="outdir" value="${outdir}" />
        <property name="setProps" value="true" />
    </ant>
</target>
```

This code invokes the cleanTest target on the test buildfile. It also causes the clean and build file targets to be executed for main, which in turn call the clean and build targets on the model and webapplication buildfiles. For example, here is the clean target of main that calls the clean target of model and webapplication as follows:

```
<target name="clean" depends="init"
        description="clean up the output directories.">
    <ant dir="./Model" target="clean">
        <property name="outdir" value="${outdir}" />
        <property name="setProps" value="true" />

    </ant>


    <ant dir="./WebApplication" target="clean">
        <property name="outdir" value="${outdir}" />
        <property name="setProps" value="true" />
        <property name="ejb" value="true" />
    </ant>

    <delete dir="${outdir}" />

</target>
```

Setting Up the Database with Test Data: A Small Taste Of Ant

Testing applications with database access can be tricky. One of the problems is that you need data in the database to test the application. It's a classic chicken-or-egg problem: What do you do first? Another problem with databases is realizing that the DDL for the schema is source code and should be managed in the Concurrent Versioning System (CVS) or equivalent. In this example, to solve the problem of needing data to test our model objects, we created an Ant script that can populate the database (see the listing below). Although we haven't covered Ant yet, we included the listing here because it shows the structure of the database for the sample application.

The fundamental problem with testing code that interacts with a database is that you cannot test database access layer code unless you have data. The data must be repeatable so that the test cases have a point of reference. The populateTables target solves the problem by populating the database with sample data that we can test for later in the unit tests.

You should also have a development and/or test database so that you can set the database back to a testable state. The code in the following listing helps you put the database into a testable state. You could connect the populateTables target to the Ant test buildfile as a dependency. We will cover this topic further in the Chapter 13 when we discuss database access layer unit testing.

```xml
<?xml version="1.0"?>

<project name="setupDB" basedir="." default="build">

    <property name="driver" value="sun.jdbc.odbc.JdbcOdbcDriver" />
    <property name="url" value="jdbc:odbc:petstore" />
    <property name="user" value="" />
    <property name="password" value="" />

    <target name="createTables">
        <sql    driver="${driver}" url="${url}"
                userid="${user}" password="${password}" >

            CREATE TABLE CATEGORY (
                ID int PRIMARY KEY,
                DESCRIPTION varchar (100) NOT NULL ,
                NAME varchar (25)  NOT NULL
            )

            CREATE TABLE SUBCATEGORY (
                ID int PRIMARY KEY,
                FK_CATEGORY_ID int REFERENCES CATEGORY(ID),
                DESCRIPTION varchar (50) NOT NULL ,
                NAME varchar (25)  NOT NULL
            )

            CREATE TABLE PRODUCT (
                DESCRIPTION varchar (50) NOT NULL ,
                NAME varchar (20)  NOT NULL ,
                ID int IDENTITY (1, 1) PRIMARY KEY,
                FK_SUBCATEGORY_ID int REFERENCES SUBCATEGORY(ID),
                QTY int DEFAULT (5),
                PRICE DECIMAL(10,2) not null,
            )
        </sql>
    </target>

    <target name="dropTables">
        <sql    driver="${driver}" url="${url}"
                userid="${user}" password="${password}" >

            DROP TABLE PRODUCT
            DROP TABLE SUBCATEGORY
            DROP TABLE CATEGORY

        </sql>
    </target>

    <target name="populateTables">
```

```
<sql     driver="${driver}" url="${url}"
         userid="${user}" password="${password}" >

insert into category (description, name, id)
         values ('test data', 'test',777)

insert into subcategory (name, description, fk_category_ID, id)
         values ('dogs', 'dogs description', 777, 111)
insert into subcategory (name, description, fk_category_ID, id)
         values ('cats', 'cats description', 777, 222)
insert into subcategory (name, description, fk_category_ID, id)
         values ('fish', 'fish description', 777, 333)
insert into subcategory (name, description, fk_category_ID, id)
         values ('birds', 'birds description', 777, 444)
insert into subcategory (name, description, fk_category_ID, id)
         values ('reptiles', 'reptiles description', 777, 555)

insert into Product (description, name, price, fk_subcategory_id)
         values('Poodle description','Poodle',1,111)
insert into Product (description, name, price, fk_subcategory_id)
         values('Scottie description','Scottie',1,111)
insert into Product (description, name, price, fk_subcategory_id)
         values('Schnauzer description','Schnauzer',1,111)
insert into Product (description, name, price, fk_subcategory_id)
         values('Calico description','Calico',1,222)
insert into Product (description, name, price, fk_subcategory_id)
         values('Jaguar description','Jaguar',1,222)
insert into Product (description, name, price, fk_subcategory_id)
         values('Siamese description','Siamese',1,222)
insert into Product (description, name, price, fk_subcategory_id)
         values('Goldfish description','Goldfish',1,333)
insert into Product (description, name, price, fk_subcategory_id)
         values('Shark description','Shark',1,333)
insert into Product (description, name, price, fk_subcategory_id)
         values('Piranha description','Piranha',1,333)
insert into Product (description, name, price, fk_subcategory_id)
         values('Parakeet description','Parakeet',1,444)
insert into Product (description, name, price, fk_subcategory_id)
         values('Canary description','Canary',1,444)
insert into Product (description, name, price, fk_subcategory_id)
         values('Wren description','Wren',1,444)
insert into Product (description, name, price, fk_subcategory_id)
         values('Iguana description','Iguana',1,555)
insert into Product (description, name, price, fk_subcategory_id)
         values('Boa description','Boa',1,555)
insert into Product (description, name, price, fk_subcategory_id)
         values('Python description','Python',1,555)
insert into Product (description, name, price, fk_subcategory_id)
         values('African Tree Frog description','African Tree
Frog',1,555)

    </sql>
  </target>
```

```
<target name="build" depends="createTables,populateTables" />


</project>
```

This code listing uses the Ant SQL task to create the tables, populate the tables, and (later) drop the tables. In order to use the SQL task, we need to pass it the JDBC URL, user name, and password. Because we will do this three times, we define some properties to hold these values:

```
<property name="driver" value="sun.jdbc.odbc.JdbcOdbcDriver" />
<property name="url" value="jdbc:odbc:petstore" />
<property name="user" value="" />
<property name="password" value="" />
```

Each time we call the SQL task, we pass it these values. Here is the SQL task used in BuildDB:

```
<target name="createTables">
    <sql    driver="${driver}" url="${url}"
            userid="${user}" password="${password}" >
```

The first thing we do with the SQL task is create the database tables. There are only three tables, so creating them is easy:

```
    <sql    driver="${driver}" url="${url}"
            userid="${user}" password="${password}" >

    CREATE TABLE CATEGORY (
        ID int PRIMARY KEY,
        DESCRIPTION varchar (100) NOT NULL ,
        NAME varchar (25)  NOT NULL
    )

    CREATE TABLE SUBCATEGORY (
        ID int PRIMARY KEY,
        FK_CATEGORY_ID int REFERENCES CATEGORY(ID),
        DESCRIPTION varchar (50) NOT NULL ,
        NAME varchar (25)  NOT NULL
    )

    CREATE TABLE PRODUCT (
        ID int IDENTITY (1, 1) PRIMARY KEY
        DESCRIPTION varchar (50) NOT NULL ,
        NAME varchar (20)  NOT NULL ,
        FK_SUBCATEGORY_ID int REFERENCES SUBCATEGORY(ID),
        QTY int DEFAULT (5),
        PRICE DECIMAL(10,2) not null,
    )
    </sql>
```

> **IDENTITY**
>
> One problem with this example is that it uses the IDENTITY keyword to define the primary key ID of the product. The IDENTITY keyword is removed in the second iteration of our application. If you are using a database that does not support the IDENTITY keyword (such as Access or Oracle), then you will have to change this line of code to something equivalent for your RDBMS system.

After we create the tables, we need to populate them with some sample data. The tables model a hierarchal data structure, so we have to insert category rows, then subcategory rows, and then products.

First we insert the parent category.

```
insert into category (description, name, id)
             values ('test data', 'test',777)
```

Then we insert the subcategory and associate it with the parent category:

```
insert into subcategory (name, description, fk_category_ID, id)
             values ('dogs', 'dogs description', 777, 111)
    . . .
```

Finally, we add products to the subcategory:

```
insert into Product (description, name, price, fk_subcategory_id)
             values('Poodle description','Poodle',1,111)
insert into Product (description, name, price, fk_subcategory_id)
             values('Scottie description','Scottie',1,111)
insert into Product (description, name, price, fk_subcategory_id)
             values('Schnauzer description','Schnauzer',1,111)
    . . .
```

Sometimes we need to make additions to the tables, and we want to incorporate the additions into the build. Thus, it is very convenient to delete the tables and the test data. We add the target dropTables, defined as follows:

```
<target name="dropTables">
    <sql    driver="${driver}" url="${url}"
            userid="${user}" password="${password}" >

        DROP TABLE PRODUCT
        DROP TABLE SUBCATEGORY
        DROP TABLE CATEGORY

    </sql>
</target>
```

Notice from the DDL in the createTables target that there are primary key constraints; thus the tables must be dropped in the order specified here.

Complete Listings

The complete code for the pet store case study can be downloaded from www.wrox.com.

Model Package Complete Listings

The model is the business interface for the system. It is the façade covering the rest of the systems. Most of the tests can be run against the model classes.

```java
package xptoolkit.petstore.model;

public class CategorySystem {
    private Category currentCategory;
    private Subcategory currentSubcategory;
    private Product currentProduct;

    public CategorySystem() throws Exception {
        currentCategory = Category.getCategory();
        currentCategory.setId(777);
    }

    public Category getCurrentCategory() {
        return currentCategory;
    }

    public Subcategory getCurrentSubcategory() {
        return currentSubcategory;
    }

    public Product getCurrentProduct() {
        return currentProduct;
    }

    public Subcategory getSubcategory(int id) throws Exception {
        currentSubcategory = currentCategory.getSubcategory(id);
        return currentSubcategory;
    }

    public Product getProduct(int id) throws Exception {
        currentProduct = currentSubcategory.getProduct(id);
        return currentProduct;
    }
}


package xptoolkit.petstore.model;

import java.util.*;

public abstract class Category extends CatalogItem {

    protected Subcategory[] subcategories;
```

```java
    public static Category getCategory() throws ClassNotFoundException,
                                                InstantiationException,
                                                IllegalAccessException {

        String className =
            System.getProperty("xptoolkit.petstore.category.class",
                               "xptoolkit.petstore.dbmodel.CategoryDB");

        Class categoryClass = Class.forName(className);

        return (Category)categoryClass.newInstance();
    }

    public Subcategory[] getSubcategories() throws Exception {
        return subcategories;
    }

    public abstract Subcategory getSubcategory(int id) throws Exception;

    public String toString() {
        return "Category [ " +
            super.toString() +
            "]";
    }
}



package xptoolkit.petstore.model;

public abstract class CatalogItem {

    protected int id;
    protected String name;
    protected String description;

    public int getId() {
        return id;
    }

    public void setId(int id) throws Exception {
        this.id = id;
    }

    public String getName() {
        return name;
    }

    public void setName(String name) {
        this.name = name;
    }

    public String getDescription() {
        return description;
```

```java
    }

    public void setDescription(String description) {
        this.description = description;
    }

    public String toString() {
        return "" + id + ", " + name + ", " + description;
    }
}



package xptoolkit.petstore.model;

public abstract class Subcategory extends CatalogItem {

    protected int fkCategoryId;

    protected Product[] products;

    public int getFkCategoryId() throws Exception {
        return fkCategoryId;
    }

    public void setFkCategoryId(int fkCategoryId) {
        this.fkCategoryId = fkCategoryId;;
    }

    public Product[] getProducts() throws Exception {
        return products;
    }

    public abstract Product getProduct(int id) throws Exception;

    public String toString() {
        return "Subcategory [ " +
            super.toString() + ", " +
            fkCategoryId +
            "]";
    }
}



package xptoolkit.petstore.model;

public abstract class Product extends CatalogItem {

    protected int price;
    protected int qty;
    protected int fkSubcategoryId;

    public int getPrice() {
        return price;
    }
```

```
    public void setPrice(int price) {
        this.price = price;
    }

    public int getQty() {
        return qty;
    }

    public void setQty(int qty) {
        this.qty = qty;
    }

    public int getFkSubcategoryId() {
        return fkSubcategoryId;
    }

    public void setFkSubcategoryId(int fkSubcategoryId) {
        this.fkSubcategoryId = fkSubcategoryId;
    }

    public String toString() {
        return "Product [ " +
            super.toString() + ", " +
            price + ", " +
            qty + ", " +
            fkSubcategoryId +
            "]";
    }
}
```

dbmodel Package Complete Listings

The dbmodel package is the implementation of the model. It uses JDBC to get rows out of the database and converts them to Java objects that can be manipulated by the JSPs.

```
package xptoolkit.petstore.dbmodel;

import xptoolkit.petstore.model.Category;
import xptoolkit.petstore.model.Subcategory;
import xptoolkit.petstore.model.Product;
import java.sql.*;
import java.util.ArrayList;
import java.util.HashMap;
import java.util.Map;

public class CategoryDB extends Category implements Entity {

    public static final String COLUMNS = "ID, NAME, DESCRIPTION";

    private static Connection connCategory;
    private static Connection connSubcategory;
    private static PreparedStatement prepLoadCategory;
```

```java
    private static PreparedStatement prepLoadSubcategories;

    boolean loaded = false;

    static
    {
        try {
            String load = "select " + COLUMNS
                + " from CATEGORY where ID = ? ";
            connCategory = InitPackage.getConnection();
            prepLoadCategory = connCategory.prepareStatement(load);

            load = "select " + SubcategoryDB.COLUMNS
                + " from SUBCATEGORY where FK_CATEGORY_ID = ?";
            connSubcategory = InitPackage.getConnection();
            prepLoadSubcategories =
                        connSubcategory.prepareStatement(load);
        }
        catch (java.lang.Exception e) {
            System.err.println(
                "Unable to load prepared statements for CategoryDB.");
        }
    }

    public CategoryDB() {
        id = -1;
    }

    public void setId(int id) throws Exception {
        this.id = id;
        subcategories = null;
        load(this);
    }

    private void ensureLoaded() throws Exception {
        if (!loaded)
            load(this);

        if (subcategories == null)
            loadSubcategories(this);
    }

    public Subcategory[] getSubcategories() throws Exception {
        ensureLoaded();
        return subcategories;
    }

    public Subcategory getSubcategory(int id) throws Exception {
        ensureLoaded();
        if (subcategories != null) {
            for (int x = 0; x < subcategories.length; x++) {
                if (subcategories[x].getId() == id)
                    return subcategories[x];
            }
```

```
    }

    return null;
}

private void init(ResultSet rs) throws SQLException {
    id = rs.getInt(ID);
    name = rs.getString(NAME);
    description = rs.getString(DESCRIPTION);
}

private void reset() {
    name = null;
    description = null;
}

private static synchronized void load(CategoryDB category)
    throws SQLException {

    ResultSet resultSet = null;
    try {
        prepLoadCategory.setInt(1, category.getId());
        resultSet = prepLoadCategory.executeQuery();
        if ( resultSet.next() ) {
            category.init(resultSet);
            category.loaded = true;
        }
        else {
            category.reset();
            category.loaded = false;
        }
    }
    finally {
        if (resultSet != null)
            resultSet.close();
    }
}

 private static synchronized void
    loadSubcategories(CategoryDB category) throws SQLException {

    ArrayList list = new ArrayList();
    ResultSet results = null;

    try {
        prepLoadSubcategories.setInt(1, category.getId());
        results = prepLoadSubcategories.executeQuery();
        while( results.next() ) {
            SubcategoryDB subcategory = new SubcategoryDB(results);
            Integer key = new Integer(subcategory.getId());
            list.add(subcategory);
        }
    }
    finally{
```

```
                if(results!=null)results.close();
        }

        category.subcategories = new SubcategoryDB[list.size()];
        category.subcategories = (Subcategory[])
                        list.toArray(category.subcategories);
    }
}


package xptoolkit.petstore.dbmodel;

import java.sql.*;
import java.util.*;
import xptoolkit.petstore.model.*;

public class SubcategoryDB extends Subcategory implements Entity {

    public static final String COLUMNS =
        "ID, NAME, DESCRIPTION, FK_CATEGORY_ID";

    private static final String FK_CATEGORY_ID = "FK_CATEGORY_ID";

    private static Connection connSubcategory;
    private static Connection connProducts;
    private static PreparedStatement prepLoadSubcategory;
    private static PreparedStatement prepLoadProducts;

    boolean loaded = false;
    Product[] products = null;

    static {
        try {
            String load = "select " + COLUMNS
                + " from SUBCATEGORY where ID = ?";
            connSubcategory = InitPackage.getConnection();
            prepLoadSubcategory = connSubcategory.prepareStatement(load);

            load = "select " + ProductDB.COLUMNS
                + " from PRODUCT where FK_SUBCATEGORY_ID = ?";
            connProducts = InitPackage.getConnection();
            prepLoadProducts = connProducts.prepareStatement(load);
        }
        catch (java.lang.Exception e){
            System.err.println(
                "Unable to load prepared statements for SubcategoryDB.");
            e.printStackTrace();
        }
    }

    SubcategoryDB(ResultSet rs) throws SQLException {
        init(rs);
    }
```

```
SubcategoryDB() {
    id = -1;
}

public void setId(int id) throws Exception{
    this.id = id;
    load(this);
}

private void ensureLoaded() throws Exception {
    if (!loaded)
        load(this);

    if (products == null)
        loadProducts(this);
}

public Product[] getProducts() throws Exception {
    ensureLoaded();
    return products;
}

public Product getProduct(int id) throws Exception {
    ensureLoaded();
    if (products != null) {
        for (int x = 0; x < products.length; x++) {
            if (products[x].getId() == id)
                return products[x];
        }
    }

    return null;
}

private void init(ResultSet rs) throws SQLException {
    this.id = rs.getInt(ID);
    this.name = rs.getString(NAME).trim();
    this.description = rs.getString(DESCRIPTION).trim();
    this.fkCategoryId = rs.getInt(FK_CATEGORY_ID);
}

private void reset() {
    this.name = null;
    this.description = null;
    this.fkCategoryId = -1;
}

private static synchronized void load(SubcategoryDB subcategory)
    throws SQLException {

    ResultSet resultSet = null;
    try {
        prepLoadSubcategory.setInt(1, subcategory.getId());
        resultSet = prepLoadSubcategory.executeQuery();
```

```
            if ( resultSet.next() ) {
                subcategory.init(resultSet);
                subcategory.loaded = true;
            }
            else {
                subcategory.reset();
                subcategory.loaded = false;
            }
        }
        finally {
            if (resultSet != null)
                resultSet.close();
        }
    }

    private static synchronized void loadProducts(
                                    SubcategoryDB subcategory)
        throws SQLException {

        ArrayList list = new ArrayList();
        ResultSet resultSet = null;

        try {
            prepLoadProducts.setInt(1, subcategory.getId());
            resultSet = prepLoadProducts.executeQuery();
            while( resultSet.next() ) {
                ProductDB product = new ProductDB(resultSet);
                Integer key = new Integer(product.getId());
                list.add(product);
            }
        }
        finally {
            if (resultSet != null) resultSet.close();
        }

        subcategory.products = new Product[list.size()];
        subcategory.products =
                    (Product[])list.toArray(subcategory.products);
    }
}


package xptoolkit.petstore.dbmodel;

import java.sql.*;

public interface Entity {

    public static final String ID = "ID";
    public static final String NAME = "NAME";
    public static final String DESCRIPTION = "DESCRIPTION";

    public void setId(int id) throws Exception;
}
```

```
package xptoolkit.petstore.dbmodel;

import java.sql.*;

public class InitPackage extends java.lang.Object {

    private static String url;

    static {
        url = System.getProperty("petstore.jdbc.url",
                                 "jdbc:odbc:petstore");
        try {
            String driver =
                System.getProperty("petstore.jdbc.driver",
                                   "sun.jdbc.odbc.JdbcOdbcDriver");
            Class.forName(driver);

        }
        catch (Exception e){
            System.err.println("unable to load driver");
        }
    }

    static Connection getConnection() throws SQLException {
        return DriverManager.getConnection(url);
    }

    private InitPackage() {}
}
```

Test Package Complete Listings

The test package tests each class in the model class; these classes are really implemented in the dbmodel. The concepts in these classes will be covered in detail in Chapter 13.

```
package test.xptoolkit.petstore.model;
import xptoolkit.petstore.model.CategorySystem;

import junit.framework.*;

public class CategorySystemTest extends TestCase {
    CategorySystem system;

    public CategorySystemTest(java.lang.String testName) {
        super(testName);
    }

    public static void main(java.lang.String[] args) {
        junit.textui.TestRunner.run(suite());
    }

    public static Test suite() {
        TestSuite suite = new TestSuite(CategorySystemTest.class);
```

```
            return suite;
    }

    protected void setUp()throws Exception {
        system = new CategorySystem();
    }


    /** Test of getCurrentCategory method, of class
        xptoolkit.petstore.model.CategorySystem. */
    public void testGetCurrentCategory() throws Exception{
        assertNotNull(system.getCurrentCategory());
    }

    /** Test of getSubcategory method, of class
        xptoolkit.petstore.model.CategorySystem. */
    public void testGetSubcategory() throws Exception{
        assertNotNull(system.getSubcategory(111));
    }

    /** Test of getProduct method, of class
        xptoolkit.petstore.model.CategorySystem. */
    public void testGetProduct() throws Exception {
        testGetSubcategory();
        assertNotNull(system.getProduct(1));
    }

        /** Test of getCurrentSubcategory method, of class
            xptoolkit.petstore.model.CategorySystem. */
    public void testGetCurrentSubcategory() throws Exception{
        testGetSubcategory();
        assertNotNull(system.getCurrentSubcategory());
    }

    /** Test of getCurrentProduct method, of class
        xptoolkit.petstore.model.CategorySystem. */
    public void testGetCurrentProduct() throws Exception{
        testGetSubcategory();
        testGetProduct();
        assertNotNull(system.getCurrentProduct());
    }


}



package test.xptoolkit.petstore.model;

import java.util.*;
import junit.framework.*;

import xptoolkit.petstore.model.Category;
import xptoolkit.petstore.model.Subcategory;
```

```java
public class CategoryTest extends TestCase {

    Category category; //object under test

    public CategoryTest(java.lang.String testName) {
        super(testName);
    }

    public static void main(java.lang.String[] args) {
        junit.textui.TestRunner.run(suite());
    }

    public static Test suite() {
        TestSuite suite = new TestSuite(CategoryTest.class);

        return suite;
    }


    public void setUp()throws Exception{
        category = Category.getCategory();
        category.setId(777);
    }
    /** Test of getCategory method, of class
        xptoolkit.petstore.model.Category. */
    public void testGetCategory() throws Exception{
        System.out.println("testGetCategory");
        Category category = Category.getCategory();
        category.setId(777);
        this.assertNotNull("category", category);

    }

    /** Test of getSubcategories method, of class
        xptoolkit.petstore.model.Category. */
    public void testGetSubcategories() throws Exception {
        Subcategory [] categories = category.getSubcategories();
        assertNotNull("categories", categories);
        for (int index=0; index < categories.length; index++){
            assertNotNull("subcategory", categories[index]);
        }
    }

        /** Test of getSubcategory method, of class
            xptoolkit.petstore.model.Category. */
    public void testGetSubcategory() throws Exception {
        Subcategory [] categories = category.getSubcategories();
        assertNotNull("categories", categories);
        for (int index=0; index < categories.length; index++){
            Subcategory subcat=categories[index];
            int id = subcat.getId();
            assertNotNull("subcategory", category.getSubcategory(id));
```

```
            }
        }


    public void testGetters() throws Exception {
        assertNotNull("name", category.getName());
        assertNotNull("description", category.getDescription());

    }

}




package test.xptoolkit.petstore.model;
import junit.framework.*;
import xptoolkit.petstore.model.*;


public class SubcategoryTest extends TestCase {
    CategorySystem system;
    Subcategory category;

    protected void setUp()throws Exception{
        system = new CategorySystem();
        category = system.getCurrentCategory().getSubcategory(111);
    }


    public SubcategoryTest(java.lang.String testName) {
        super(testName);
    }

    public static void main(java.lang.String[] args) {
        junit.textui.TestRunner.run(suite());
    }

    public static Test suite() {
        TestSuite suite = new TestSuite(SubcategoryTest.class);

        return suite;
    }

    /** Test of getFkCategoryId method, of class
        xptoolkit.petstore.model.Subcategory. */
    public void testGetters() {
        assertNotNull("name", category.getName());
        assertNotNull("description", category.getDescription());
    }


    /** Test of getProducts method, of class
        xptoolkit.petstore.model.Subcategory. */
    public void testGetProducts() throws Exception{
```

```
        String [] testDataExpected = new String []
                      {"Poodle", "Scottie", "Schnauzer"};

        Product products [] = category.getProducts();
        for (int index = 0; index < products.length; index++){
            Product product = products[index];
            assertEquals("check Name", testDataExpected[index],
product.getName());
        }

    }


}


package test.xptoolkit.petstore.model;
import xptoolkit.petstore.model.*;
import junit.framework.*;

public class ProductTest extends TestCase {

    CategorySystem system;
    Product product;

    protected void setUp()throws Exception{
        system = new CategorySystem();
        system.getSubcategory(111);
        product = system.getProduct(1);
    }


    public ProductTest(java.lang.String testName) {
        super(testName);
    }

    public static void main(java.lang.String[] args) {
        junit.textui.TestRunner.run(suite());
    }

    public static Test suite() {
        TestSuite suite = new TestSuite(ProductTest.class);

        return suite;
    }

    /** Test of getPrice method
        of class xptoolkit.petstore.model.Product. */
    public void testSetters() {
        product.setName("Boo");
        product.setDescription("Designer");
        product.setPrice(5);
        product.setQty(5);
    }
```

```
    /** Test of getPrice method
        of class xptoolkit.petstore.model.Product. */
    public void testGetters() {
        this.assertEquals("name", product.getName(), "Poodle");
        this.assertEquals("description",
                          product.getDescription(),
                          "Poodle description");
        testSetters();
        this.assertEquals("name", product.getName(), "Boo");
        this.assertEquals("description",
                          product.getDescription(),
                          "Designer");

    }

}



package xptoolkit.petstore.dbmodel;

import java.sql.*;
import junit.framework.*;

public class InitPackageTest extends TestCase {

    public InitPackageTest(java.lang.String testName) {
        super(testName);
    }

    public static void main(java.lang.String[] args) {
        junit.textui.TestRunner.run(suite());
    }

    public static Test suite() {
        TestSuite suite = new TestSuite(InitPackageTest.class);

        return suite;
    }

    /** Test of getConnection method, of class
        xptoolkit.petstore.dbmodel.InitPackage. */
    public void testGetConnection() throws SQLException{
        System.out.println("testGetConnection");
        Connection connection=InitPackage.getConnection();
        assertNotNull("connection", connection);

    }

}
```

JSPs and Web.xml Complete Listings

The JSPs don't have a corresponding test like the model. They will be added after we cover the HttpUnit in Chapter 16.

```jsp
<%@ include file="category_sys.jsp" %>

<html>
    <head>
        <title>
            AAA Pets: <%= request.getParameter("title")%>
        </title>
</head>

<body>
    <h1>AAA Pets</h1>

    <table border="1" width="100%">
        <tr>
            <td width="20%" align="center">
                <a href="index.jsp">Company</a>
            </td>
            <td width="20%" align="center">
                <a href="under_construction.html">Mission</a>
            </td>
            <td width="20%" align="center">
                <a href="under_construction.html">Shopping Cart</a>
            </td>
            <td width="20%" align="center">
                <a href="under_construction.html">Links</a>
            </td>

    </table>

    <table border="1" width="100%">
        <tr>
        <%
            Category category = categorySystem.getCurrentCategory();
            Subcategory [] subcategories = category.getSubcategories();
            for (int index=0; index < subcategories.length; index++){
                Subcategory subcategory = subcategories[index];
        %>
            <td width="20%" align="center">
                <a href="subcategory.jsp?id=<%=subcategory.getId()%>">
                    <%=subcategory.getName()%>
                </a>
                <br />
            </td>
        <%}%>
    </table>

    <table width="100%">
```

```
            <tr>
                <td width="100%" align="left">
                </td>
            </tr>
        </table>

        <p align="center">
            <font size="-1">
                Copyright 2004, Rick Hightower<br>
                AAA Pets is a fictional company any similarities to a real
company is coincidental.
            </font>
        </p>

        </body>
</html>
```

```
<%@page import="xptoolkit.petstore.model.*" %>
<jsp:useBean id="categorySystem" class="CategorySystem" scope="session"/>
```

```
<jsp:include page="header.jsp" flush="true">
        <jsp:param name="title" value="Welcome"/>
</jsp:include>

    <div align="center">
        <b>Welcome to AAA Pets</b>
    </div>

<jsp:include page="footer.jsp" flush="true" />
```

```
<jsp:include page="header.jsp" flush="true">
        <jsp:param name="title" value="Welcome"/>
</jsp:include>

    <div align="center">
        <b>Sorry, I could not find that page.</b>
    </div>

<jsp:include page="footer.jsp" flush="true" />
```

```
<%@ include file="category_sys.jsp" %>
<%
    String categoryId = request.getParameter("id");
    Category category = categorySystem.getCurrentCategory();
```

```
        category.setId( Integer.parseInt(categoryId) );
%>

<jsp:include page="header.jsp" flush="true">
      <jsp:param name="title" value="<%= category.getName() %>"/>
</jsp:include>

    <table border="1" width="100%">
        <tr>
            <td width="100%" colspan="2" align="center">
                <b>
                    <%= category.getName() %>
                </b>
                <br>
                <%= category.getDescription() %>
            </td>
        </tr>
        <tr>
            <td width="20%">

<%
    Subcategory[] subcategories = category.getSubcategories();
    for (int index = 0; index < subcategories.length; index++) {
        Subcategory subcategory = subcategories[index];
%>
<a href="subcategory.jsp?id=<%=subcategory.getId()%>">
<%=subcategory.getName()%></a>
        <br>
<%
    }
%>

            </td>
            <td> </td>
        </tr>
    </table>

<jsp:include page="footer.jsp" flush="true" />



<%@ include file="category_sys.jsp" %>
<%
    Category category = categorySystem.getCurrentCategory();
    Subcategory[] subcategories = category.getSubcategories();
    String subcategoryId = request.getParameter("id");
    int id = Integer.parseInt(subcategoryId);
    Subcategory subcategory = categorySystem.getSubcategory(id);

    String title = category.getName() + " : " + subcategory.getName();
%>

<jsp:include page="header.jsp" flush="true">
      <jsp:param name="title" value="<%= title %>"/>
```

```
        </jsp:include>

            <table border="1" width="100%">
                <tr>
                    <td width="100%" colspan="2" align="center">
                        <b>
                            <%= category.getName() %>
                        </b>
                        <br>
                        <%= category.getDescription() %>
                        <br>
                        <b>
                            <%= subcategory.getName() %>
                        </b>
                        <br>
                        <%= subcategory.getDescription() %>
                    </td>
                </tr>
                <tr>
                    <td width="20%" valign="top">

<%
    for (int index = 0; index < subcategories.length; index++) {
        Subcategory subcat = subcategories[index];
%>
<a href="subcategory.jsp?id=<%=subcat.getId()%>">
<%=subcat.getName()%></a>
        <br>
<%
    }
%>
            </td>
            <td valign="top">
<%
    Product[] products = subcategory.getProducts();
    for (int pindex = 0; pindex < products.length; pindex++) {
        Product product = products[pindex];
%>
        <a href="product.jsp?id=<%= product.getId()%>" target="_blank"><%=
product.getName() %></a>
        <br>
<%
    }
%>
            </td>
        </tr>
    </table>

<jsp:include page="footer.jsp" flush="true" />



<%@ page import="java.text.NumberFormat,java.util.Locale" %>
<%@ include file="category_sys.jsp" %>
<%
    Category category = categorySystem.getCurrentCategory();
```

```
          Subcategory subcategory = categorySystem.getCurrentSubcategory();

          String productId = request.getParameter("id");
          Product product = subcategory.getProduct( Integer.parseInt(productId) );

     String title = category.getName() +
                         " : " + subcategory.getName() +
                         " : " + product.getName();
     %>

     <jsp:include page="header.jsp" flush="true">
          <jsp:param name="title" value="<%= title %>"/>
     </jsp:include>


     <%
          Locale locale = request.getLocale();
          NumberFormat format = NumberFormat.getCurrencyInstance(locale);
          String price = format.format(product.getPrice());
     %>

          <div align="center">
              <b><%= product.getName() %></b>
              <br>

              <%= product.getDescription() %>
              <br>

              <STRONG><%= price %></STRONG>
              <br>
          </div>

     <jsp:include page="footer.jsp" flush="true" />



     <?xml version="1.0" encoding="ISO-8859-1"?>

     <!DOCTYPE web-app
        PUBLIC "-//Sun Microsystems, Inc.//DTD Web Application 2.2//EN"
        "http://java.sun.com/j2ee/dtds/web-app_2_2.dtd">

     <web-app>

         <error-page>
             <error-code>404</error-code>
             <location>/notfound.jsp</location>
         </error-page>

        <!-- The Usual Welcome File List -->
        <welcome-file-list>
          <welcome-file>index.jsp</welcome-file>
        </welcome-file-list>

        <servlet-mapping url-pattern='/servlet/*' servlet-name='invoker'/>

     </web-app>
```

Conclusion

This book uses two types of examples: simple examples and case studies. The simple examples demonstrate how to use the tools; they teach you the mechanics of using the tools. The case studies are more involved samples that demonstrate how the tools fit in the larger context of deploying, testing, and refactoring the application.

This appendix also highlights the structure of the pet store case study by showing you the structure of the classes, JSP files, and buildfiles.

Index